The Book of Daniel

George Wesley Buchanan

Wipf and Stock Publishers
Eugene, Oregon

Wipf and Stock Publishers
199 West 8th Avenue, Suite 3
Eugene, Oregon 97401

The Book of Daniel
By Buchanan, George Wesley
Copyright©1999 Buchanan, George Wesley
ISBN: 1-59244-021-5
Publication Date: April, 2005
Previous edition by Mellen Biblical Press, The Mellen Biblical Commentary Old Testament Series, Volume 25.

Library of Congress Cataloging-in-Publication Data to previous Mellen edition

Buchanan, George Wesley.
    The book of Daniel / George Wesley Buchanan
    p.   cm. -- (The Mellen biblical commentary. Old Testament series ; v. 25)
    Includes bibliographical references and index.
    ISBN 0-7734-2470-9
    1. Bible.   O.T.   Daniel Commentaries   I. Title   II. Series.
BS1555.3B83
224'.5077--dc21
                                                        99-27735
                                                           CIP

TO MY BROTHER

RUSSELL HOWARD BUCHANAN

TABLE OF CONTENTS

INTRODUCTION 1
   THE PURPOSE OF THE INTRODUCTION 1
      Midrash. 1
      Cyclical time. 3
   THE HISTORICAL PERIOD INVOLVED 5
      The time period. 5
      Typology. 7
   RULES OF RHETORIC 8
   KIND OF LITERATURE 8
   LITERARY FORMS 9
      Inclusion. 9
      Chiasms. 10
   RELEVANT DETAILS 11
      The Tetragrammaton. 11
      Political Points. 12

CHAPTER ONE 16
   HEBREW TEXT 16
   TECHNICAL DETAILS 17
   ENGLISH TEXT 17
   COMMENTARY 18
      The reign of Jehoiakim. 18
      Nebuchadnezzar came to Jerusalem. 18
      The Lord gave Jehoiakim into his hand. .. 20
      Some of the vessels of the house of God. .. 20
      The land of Shinar. 21
   TEXT 21
   COMMENTARY 21
      His chief eunuch. 21
      Some of the children to Israel. 22
      Without blemish. 23

TEXT	23
COMMENTARY	24
He should teach them.	24
Literature and the Chaldean language.	24
The king's food and wine.	25
Three years.	25
There were among them.	25
The chief eunuch gave them [different] names.	26
TEXT	26
COMMENTARY	27
Daniel.	27
Daniel ... would not defile himself.	27
The king's food and wine	25
Give us some vegetables.	29
I am afraid.	30
Test, if you will, your servants for ten days.	30
TEXT	30
COMMENTARY	31
Their appearances seemed ... healthier	31
God gave these four youths knowledge	31
At the end of the period	31
They stood before the king	32
Daniel was [there] until the first year of king Cyrus.	32
CHAPTER TWO	**34**
HEBREW AND ARAMAIC TEXT	34
ENGLISH TEXT	36
TECHNICAL DETAILS	37
COMMENTARY	40
During the second year.	40
Nebuchadnezzar had dreams.	41
He could not sleep.	42
Ordered [someone] to call the magicians.	42
The Chaldeans spoke to the king in Aramaic.	43
King, live for ages!	43
Tell the dream to your servants.	43
TEXT	44
COMMENTARY	44
The word from me is publicly known.	44
You will be cut into pieces.	44
You are trying to gain time.	45
TEXT	45
COMMENTARY	46
Answered before the king.	46
No one on earth.	46

Except the gods whose living is not with flesh. 46
The matter which the king asks is difficult. 46
TEXT 46
COMMENTARY 47
The king became furious. 47
The chief executioner. 47
Hananiah, Mishael, and Azariah. 48
He would show the interpretation. 48
Receive mercy from the God of heaven. 48
Concerning this mystery. 49
TEXT 49
COMMENTARY 50
He blessed the God of heaven. 50
From the [current] age to the age [to come]. 51
He changes the times and the seasons. 51
He removes kings, and he establishes kings. 51
He gives wisdom to the wise. 52
He reveals the deep things and mysteries. 52
God of my fathers. 52
TEXT 53
COMMENTARY 54
Destroy the wisemen of Babylon. 54
Hurried and brought Daniel before the king. 54
A man who is a Jew. 54
Makes known to King Nebuchadnezzar. 54
The last days. 54
Davidic-Solomonic rule. 56
TEXT 57
COMMENTARY 57
Thoughts went out to you. 57
That which will take place. 57
More wisdom than any other living being. 59
You may know the thoughts of your mind. 60
TEXT 60
COMMENTARY 60
You were watching. Now look! 60
Its appearance was frightening. 61
This statue. 61
Its legs were of iron. 61
Partly iron and partly clay. 61
Became a huge mountain. 61
Is told before the king. 62

TEXT	63
COMMENTARY	63
You, O King, are the king of kings.	63
God of heaven has given the kingdom.	64
You are the head of gold.	64
TECHNICAL DETAILS	65
COMMENTARY	66
After you will raise another kingdom.	66
Will rule over all the land.	70
A fourth kingdom, strong as iron.	72
It will break and shatter all of these.	73
TEXT	73
COMMENTARY	74
The feet and toes.	74
Part of them potter's clay and part of them iron.	75
TEXT	75
COMMENTARY	75
A kingdom that will be for the ages.	75
Its kingdom will not be left to another people.	76
It will bring an end to all of these kingdoms.	76
What will happen after this.	77
The dream is sure.	77
TEXT	79
COMMENTARY	79
Worshiped Daniel.	79
Revealer of mysteries.	80
Administration of the country.	80
The gate of the king.	81
CHAPTER THREE	**82**
ARAMAIC TEXT	82
INTRODUCTION	83
ENGLISH TEXT	84
COMMENTARY	84
During the eighteenth year.	84
From India to Ethiopia.	84
The dedication.	85
Statue which Nebuchadnezzar set up.	85
In the Dura Valley.	85
The king sent [someone] to gather.	86
All peoples, nations, and ... languages.	86
Every kind of music.	86
Fell down and worshiped the golden statue.	87

TEXT 87
COMMENTARY 88
    Chaldean men came forward. 88
    Said malicious things about. 88
    If you are prepared... 88
    Thrown into the flaming, fiery furnace 88
    Is there a god that will deliver you? 89
TEXT 89
COMMENTARY 90
    We have no need. 90
    Look! There is a God. 90
    He will save us. 90
    From your hand. 91
    But even if not. 91
    We will not worship your god. 91
    The expression on his face changed. 91
    Fell into the flaming, fiery furnace. 91
    Coats, trousers, turbans. 91
    The flame of the fire killed these men. 91
TEXT 92
COMMENTARY 92
    Answered and said. 92
    But I see four men released. 92
    The fourth is like a Son of God. 93
    The midst of the fire. 93
    Most High God. 94
TEXT 94
COMMENTARY 95
    Who sent his angel. 95
    They did not worship or bow down. 95
    Who says anything against the God of Shadrach,
        Meshach, and Abednego. 96
TEXT 96
TECHNICAL DETAILS 97
COMMENTARY 97
    To all peoples, nations, and ... languages. 97
    God has performed with me. 97
    A kingdom of the age. 97
SUMMARY 98
THE PRAYER OF AZARIAH AND HYMN
    OF THE JEWISH CAPTIVES 98
    COMMENTARY 101
CHAPTER FOUR 103
    ARAMAIC TEXT 103
    TECHNICAL DETAILS 104

TEXT	109
COMMENTARY	110
I, Nebuchadnezzar.	110
Nebuchadnezzar was comfortable.	110
Generation and generation.	111
The magicians, enchanters, sorcerers, ... came.	111
Belteshazzar, named after my gods.	111
In whom was the spirit of the holy gods.	112
Told the dream before.	112
TEXT	112
COMMENTARY	112
Belteshazzar, great magician.	112
The spirit of the holy gods is in you.	112
TEXT	113
COMMENTARY	113
A tree in the midst of the land.	113
Its height touched heaven.	114
TEXT	115
COMMENTARY	115
Underneath it was sheltering beasts.	115
The visions of my head.	115
TEXT	115
TECHNICAL DETAILS	116
COMMENTARY	116
A watcher, a holy one from heaven.	116
Leave the stump from its roots.	116
An iron and brass band.	117
The dew of heaven.	117
His lot will be with the beasts.	117
The mind of a beast will be given to it.	117
Seven times will pass over it.	117
A decree of the watchers.	118
The Most High rules the kingdom of human beings.	118
Gives it to whomever he will.	118
He appoints over it the humblest of people.	118
All the wisemen of my kingdom.	118
The spirit of the holy gods.	119
TEXT	119
COMMENTARY	119
Daniel ... was puzzled.	119
Do not let the dream ... trouble you.	120
May the visions of your dream be for your enemies.	120
Whose height reached heaven.	120
The one who has become great and strong.	120
OG Your mind has been supercilious.	120

TEXT	120
TECHNICAL DETAILS	121
COMMENTARY	122
They will drive you.	122
Seven times.	122
You know the sovereignty is from Heaven.	122
TEXT	123
COMMENTARY	124
Redeem your sins.	124
Walking on the [roof of the] palace.	124
Is not this great Babylon?	125
Which I have built.	126
The glory of my majesty.	126
The kingdom has been taken from you.	126
I lifted up my eyes to heaven.	126
What are you doing?	126
I was confirmed over my kingdom.	126
TECHNICAL DETAILS	127
COMMENTARY	128
At the end of [the previously determined] days.	128
My time of redemption came.	129
The troops of heaven and the residents of the land.	129
His rule is the rule of the age.	129
Those who walk in pride he is able to humble.	129
THE SEPTUAGINTAL ENDING	130
TEXTUAL DETAILS	131
CHAPTER FIVE	**132**
ARAMAIC TEXT	132
ENGLISH TEXT	133
TECHNICAL DETAILS	134
COMMENTARY	134
King Belshazzar.	134
Made a huge feast.	134
He drank wine before the thousand.	135
Bring the vessels of gold and silver.	135
They praised the gods of gold.	136
TEXT	136
COMMENTARY	136
Suddenly the fingers of a man reached out.	136
The king saw the hollow of the hand that wrote.	136
His loins were loosened.	136
The enchanters, the Chaldeans, and the counselors.	137
Anyone who reads the writing.	137
All the king's wisemen came.	137

TEXT	137
COMMENTARY	138
Because of the words of the king.	138
The queen entered the drinking house.	138
Do not let your mind be alarmed.	138
There is a man.	138
TEXT	139
COMMENTARY	139
Daniel was brought before the king.	139
I have heard about you.	139
My father, the king, brought from Judah.	140
But they were not able.	140
The spirit of the gods is in you.	140
You are able.	141
A gold chain around your neck.	141
TEXT	141
COMMENTARY	141
Let your gifts be for yourself.	141
Nebuchadnezzar, your father.	141
He was driven from among human beings.	141
TEXT	142
COMMENTARY	142
Now you, his son, Belshazzar.	142
Have not humbled your mind.	142
TEXT	143
COMMENTARY	144
God in whose hand is your breath.	144
Muh-náy, muh-náy, tuh-káyl, oo-fár-seen.	144
God has measured your kingdom and concluded it.	144
Weighed in the scales.	145
Medes and the Persians.	145
A gold chain around his neck.	145
Belshazzar, the king of the Chaldeans, was killed.	145
TECHNICAL DETAILS	146
CHAPTER SIX	**147**
ARAMAIC TEXT	147
TECHNICAL DETAILS	148
ENGLISH TEXT	149
COMMENTARY	149
Darius the Mede.	149
120 governors.	152
So the king would not suffer loss.	153
TEXT	153
TECHNICAL DETAILS	153

COMMENTARY 153
    Trying to find out a complaint against Daniel. 153
    In the law of his god. 153
TEXT 154
COMMENTARY 154
    Offers prayer. 154
    Except you, O king. 154
    The den of lions. 154
    Law of the Medes and the Persians. 154
TEXT 154
COMMENTARY 155
    When Daniel found ... the document had been signed. 155
    In his roof chamber windows that opened
        towards Jerusalem. 155
    Three times that very day. 155
    Found Daniel praying. 155
TEXT 156
COMMENTARY 156
    Have you not signed a prohibition? 156
    Anyone who prays. 156
    Daniel, ... among the exiles of the Jews. 156
TEXT 156
COMMENTARY 156
    He tried to save him. 156
    Law of the Medes and the Persians. 157
    Be informed, O king. 157
    The den of lions. 157
    The stone was brought ... at the mouth of the den. . 157
TEXT 158
COMMENTARY 158
    Sleep fled from him. 158
    He went hurriedly to the den of lions. 158
    Servant of the God of life. 159
    King, live for ages. 159
    I was found virtuous before him. 160
    God sent his angel. 160
    The men were brought before him. 160
    They, their children, and their wives. 160
TEXT 161
COMMENTARY 162
    The God of Daniel. 162
    His kingdom will not be destroyed. 162
    His rule is until the end. 162

CHAPTER SEVEN **163**
ARAMAIC TEXT 163
INTRODUCTION 164
ENGLISH TEXT 165
COMMENTARY 166
Belshazzar, king of Babylon. 166
Daniel dreamed a vision. 166
He wrote down the dream. 166
The beginning of his words. 166
I was seeing visions. 166
The four winds of heaven. 167
Forcing [the waves] of the ... Sea. 167
Four huge beasts came up from the sea. 167
TEXT 168
COMMENTARY 169
Like a lion with wings of an eagle. 169
A human mind was given to it. 170
Like a bear. 170
Rise up and eat lots of flesh. 170
Like a leopard. 171
TEXT 171
COMMENTARY 172
Terrible, frightening, and very strong. 172
It had ten horns. 172
Another horn, a small one. 173
Eyes of a human being. 173
A mouth speaking extensively. 173
He made war with the saints. 173
Thrones were set up. 175
The Ancient of Days sat down. 176
TEXT 176
TECHNICAL DETAILS 177
COMMENTARY 178
His clothes were white as snow. 178
His throne was surrounded with fire. 178
A million [assistants] served him. 178
A hundred million stood up ... before him. 179
The court sat. 179
The books [of the contenders] were opened. 180
The many words which the horn was speaking. 180
The beast was killed. 180
The rest of the beasts' kingdoms. 182

TEXT	184
COMMENTARY	185
I kept on observing in the visions.	185
With the clouds of heaven.	185
Came one like a Son of man.	187
To the Ancient of Days.	206
To him was given.	206
Ruling authority of an age.	213
His kingdom would not be destroyed.	213
TEXT	214
COMMENTARY	214
I Daniel.	214
My breath.	214
The visions in my head alarmed me.	214
One of those standing there.	215
TEXT	215
COMMENTARY	215
Are four kings.	215
Rising up from the ground.	216
The saints of the Most High will receive the kingdom.	216
TEXT	217
TECHNICAL DETAILS	217
COMMENTARY	217
I wanted [to know] the truth.	217
Different from all the rest.	218
The ten horns which were on its head.	218
The horn which had eyes and a mouth.	218
Made war with the saints.	218
TEXT	219
COMMENTARY	219
Then the time arrived.	219
Another king will arise after them.	220
He will exhaust the saints of the Most High.	221
He will try to change the calendar and the religion.	221
They will be given into his hand.	221
The court will sit in judgment.	223
His authority will be removed.	224
The greatest kingdom under all the heavens.	224
To the saints of the Most High.	224
All ruling authorities will serve and obey it.	226
Here is where the word ends.	227
DANIEL 7 AND ANCIENT COURT SESSIONS	227
Introduction.	227
Antiochus on Trial.	228

xv

    The Participants. 229
    Divine Symbols. 230
  JUDGMENT DAY AND JEWISH FEASTS 231
  CONCLUSIONS TO DANIEL SEVEN 233
CHAPTER EIGHT **235**
 HEBREW TEXT 235
 ENGLISH TEXT 236
 TECHNICAL DETAILS 237
 COMMENTARY 237
    The kingdom of King Belshazzar. 237
    A vision appeared to me. 237
    I Daniel. 237
    I was in Susa the capital ... of Elam. 237
    Alongside the River of Ulai. 238
    A ram. 238
    The larger one came up last. 238
    Westward, northward, and southward. 238
 TEXT 238
 COMMENTARY 239
    A goat came from the West. 239
    A conspicuous horn between his eyes. 240
    He threw him to the ground and trampled him. . . 240
    The large horn was broken. 240
    From one of them went out a small horn. 241
    To the south, to the east, and
      to the glorious land 242
    It grew until it reached the troops of Heaven. . . . 242
    It trampled some of them. 244
    The military general. 244
    The place of his temple was thrown down. 245
    An army was directed
      against the continual offering 245
    He acted and was successful. 246
 TEXT 246
 COMMENTARY 247
    How long is the vision? 247
    He said to me. 247
    The sanctuary will be vindicated. 248
    The vision is for the time of the end. 248
    Something like the appearance of a man. 250
    I fell on my face. 250
 TEXT 251
 COMMENTARY 251
    The ram which you saw with two horns. 251
    The male goat was the king of the Greeks. 252

At the end of their kingdoms.	252
A king of a defiant countenance.	253
Not by his own power.	253
He will be frightfully destructive.	253
Including the people of the saints.	253
Deceit will in his hand prosper.	253
Take a stand against the leading military general.	253
He will be broken.	254
TEXT	254
COMMENTARY	254
The vision of the evening and the morning.	254
Seal up the vision, for it belongs to many days.	254
The work of the king.	254
CHAPTER NINE	**255**
HEBREW TEXT	255
INTRODUCTION	256
ENGLISH TEXT	256
COMMENTARY	257
The first year of Darius.	257
I, Daniel, was studying in the books.	258
TEXT	259
COMMENTARY	260
Fasting, sack cloth, and ashes.	260
Prayed to Yehowah.	260
PRAYERS OF SOLOMON AND DANIEL	262
TECHNICAL DETAILS	264
THE PRAYER OF HEZEKIAH	265
TEXT	265
COMMENTARY	266
God, great and terrible.	266
Extend your ears.	266
TEXT	266
COMMENTARY	266
Open your eyes.	266
Look at our desolations.	266
All the lands.	267
TEXT	267
COMMENTARY	268
O Lord, great and terrible.	268
Who keeps treaty.	268
Who love him.	269
We have sinned.	269
We have committed iniquity.	269
We have behaved wickedly.	269
Turned away from your commandments.	270

TEXT	270
COMMENTARY	271
The prophets who spoke in your name.	271
Our kings, our generals, and our fathers.	271
All the people of the land.	272
Yours is righteousness.	272
Ours is the shame.	272
Both near and far.	272
In all the lands where you have pushed them.	272
TEXT	273
COMMENTARY	273
To the Lord our God belongs mercy and forgiveness.	273
We have not listened to the voice of Yehowah.	273
TEXT	274
COMMENTARY	275
All Israel.	275
Poured out upon us.	276
The curse and the oath which is written in the Torah.	276
Watched over evil.	276
As of this day.	277
TEXT	277
COMMENTARY	278
Please turn away your anger.	278
Make your face shine.	278
TEXT	278
COMMENTARY	279
Open your eyes.	279
Listen.	280
O Lord, forgive.	280
Over your city and over your people.	281
TEXT	281
COMMENTARY	281
The man Gabriel.	281
The word went out.	281
TEXT	282
COMMENTARY	282
Seventy weeks are determined.	282
Your people and over your holy city.	284
To complete [the punishment required] for transgression.	284
Seal the sins.	286
Atone the iniquity.	287
Introduce ages of righteousness.	288

xviii

            Seal the vision and the prophet. 289
            Anoint the holy of holies. 289
    TEXT 290
    TECHNICAL DETAILS 291
    COMMENTARY 291
            From the going out of the word. 291
            Seven weeks. 292
            Until the anointed leader. 292
            For 62 weeks it will again be rebuilt. 293
            With streets and suburbs. 293
            In difficult times. 293
            The Messiah will be cut off. 293
            And have no [help]. 293
            The people of the leader. 294
            Will destroy the city and the temple. 294
            Its end will be with a flood. 294
            Until the end of the war. 294
            Desolations are predestined. 294
            He will enforce a treaty on the many for a week. . . 295
            For half a week. 295
            On the wing ... an abomination of desolations. . . . 297
            The decreed end. 298

CHAPTER TEN **299**
    HEBREW TEXT 299
    ENGLISH TEXT 300
    COMMENTARY 300
            In the third year of Cyrus, king of Persia. 300
            The war was extensive. 300
    TEXT 301
    COMMENTARY 302
            I Daniel. 302
            I was in mourning for three weeks. 302
            Beside the great river which is the Tigris. 302
            A man dressed in linen. 303
            The sound of his voice. 303
            The men who were with me. 303
    TEXT 303
    COMMENTARY 303
            I saw this great vision. 303
            My face to the ground. 303
    TEXT 304
    COMMENTARY 304
            Do not be afraid. 304
            Stand on your feet. 305
            Humble yourself before God. 305

TEXT	305
COMMENTARY	305
General of the Persian kingdom.	305
What will happen to your people.	306
Michael, one of the first generals.	306
I remained there with the Persian kings.	306
TEXT	306
COMMENTARY	307
Something like a human being.	307
Touched my lips.	308
My Lord, in the vision.	308
Touched me and made me strong.	308
TEXT	309
COMMENTARY	309
I will fight the Persian general.	309
The Greek general.	309
The Book of Truth.	309
CHAPTER ELEVEN	**310**
HEBREW TEXT	310
TEXT	311
TECHNICAL DETAILS	311
COMMENTARY	312
Darius the Mede.	312
Media and the Succession of Empires.	313
TEXT	314
COMMENTARY	314
The truth.	314
Three more kings will arise in Persia.	314
As he becomes strong.	314
He will stir up ... against the Greek kingdom.	315
TEXT	315
COMMENTARY	315
A mighty king will arise.	315
Will be broken into the four winds.	316
But not to his posterity.	316
Not according to his dominion.	317
TEXT	317
COMMENTARY	317
THE PTOLEMY FAMILY TREE	317
TEXT	318
COMMENTARY	318
After some years they will make an agreement.	318
The daughter of the King of the South.	318
She will not retain the strength of her arm.	318
A branch from her roots will arise in his place.	319

He...enter the fortress of the king of the North. ... 319
He will bring into captivity to Egypt. 319
He will stay away. 320
TEXT 321
COMMENTARY 321
    He will return to his own land. 321
    His sons will ... gather many troops. 321
    Spread out and pass over. 321
    As far as his fortress. 322
    He will make tens of thousands fall. 322
    But he will not become strong. 322
    Return and raise a still bigger mob. 322
    After a few years. 323
TEXT 323
TECHNICAL DETAILS 323
COMMENTARY 324
    Many will rise up against the king of the South. .. 324
    The sons of the violent ones of your people. 324
    Capture the fortified city. 325
    The forces of the South will not stand. 325
    He will stand on the glorious land. 325
    Everything will be in his hand. 325
    He will give him the daughter. 325
    The daughter of women. 325
    To destroy it. 326
    But it will not stand, and it will not be his. 326
TEXT 326
COMMENTARY 326
    Put an end to his insolence. 326
    He will turn his face to the islands. 327
    Will not be found. 327
TEXT 328
THE SELUCID FAMILY TREE 328
COMMENTARY 328
    One will arise in his place. 328
    The glory of his kingdom. 329
    In a few days he will be broken. 329
    A despised person will arise in his place. 329
    Will not be given to him. 329
    He will come quietly and seize the kingdom. 330
    The troops will be utterly swept before him. 330
    Also the leader of the treaty. 330

TEXT	331
COMMENTARY	331
With a small nation.	331
With the richest men of the region.	332
That which his fathers had never done.	333
But up to a time.	334
He will stir up his power.	334
TEXT	335
COMMENTARY	335
These two kings.	335
At an appointed time.	336
TEXT	336
COMMENTARY	337
An appointed time.	337
The latter [experience] will not be like the first.	337
The ships of the Kittim.	337
Will come against him.	340
He will be emotionally crushed and turned back.	341
TEXT	341
COMMENTARY	341
He will become furious against the holy treaty.	341
Those who abandoned the holy treaty.	343
TEXT	346
COMMENTARY	348
Powerful ones.	348
Plundered the temple.	348
They will turn away the continual offering.	349
Those who break the treaty.	349
The people who knows its God.	350
Those who instruct the people ...	352
They will stumble.	353
For a time.	354
They will receive a little help.	354
Many will join them with deceptions.	359
The appointed time.	359
TEXT	360
COMMENTARY	360
The king will do whatever he wants.	360
Until the wrath is completed.	361
Will not acknowledge the gods.	361
The one beloved of women.	361
He will glorify the god of fortresses.	362
He will increase in glory.	362
He will divide the land for a price.	362

TEXT	362
TECHNICAL DETAILS	363
Antiochus the Great.	364
Royal failure.	364
Relevance to dates.	365
COMMENTARY	367
At the time of the end.	367
With cavalry, chariots, and many boats.	367
Come to the glorious land.	368
Edom, Moab, and most of the Ammonites.	368
The land of Egypt will not be able to escape.	368
He will leave with great fury.	368
He will plant his palatial tents.	368
Between the sea and the glorious holy mountain.	368
He will come to his end.	368

CHAPTER TWELVE **371**

HEBREW TEXT	371
TECHNICAL DETAILS	371
ENGLISH TEXT	373
COMMENTARY	373
At that time arose.	373
Michael the great general.	374
It was a time of such oppression.	374
As has never been.	374
Your people will escape.	374
TEXT	375
TECHNICAL DETAILS	376
COMMENTARY	376
Many who sleep in the dust of the ground.	376
To the embarrassment ... of the age.	379
Those who provide knowledge.	381
Like the luminary of heaven.	382
Those who justify the many.	382
TEXT	384
TECHNICAL DETAILS	385
COMMENTARY	385
The time of the end.	385
Many will wander.	385
Knowledge will increase.	385
TEXT	386
COMMENTARY	386
I Daniel.	386
Two were standing.	386
The shore of the river.	387
Who was above the river.	387

	How long [will it be] until the end?	387
	These fantastic things.	387
	Swore by the life of the age [to come].	388
	A time, two times, and half a time.	388
	The one who breaks the power of the holy people.	389
TEXT		390
COMMENTARY		390
	I heard, but I did not understand.	390
	The words are closed and sealed.	390
	The time of the end.	391
	Many will be purified, whitened, and tested.	391
	The wicked ones will act wickedly.	391
	None of the wicked ones will understand.	392
	But the teachers will understand.	392
	The provision of the abomination of desolations.	392
	1,290 days.	392
	Blessed are those who wait.	392
	1,335 days.	393
	You will rest and stand in your portion.	393
TECHNICAL DETAILS		394
	Dan 11:17-12:13 and Sir 36:1-17.	394
	The last verse of Daniel and the scrolls.	395
TEXT		395
COMMENTARY		395
CONCLUSIONS		**396**
INTRODUCTION		396
	The significance of Daniel.	396
	Prophetic deductions.	396
	Purpose of the study.	397
	Myth and history.	398
	Texts.	399
STORIES OF REDEMPTION		400
	Introduction	400
	The Success of Daniel	400
	The King's Statue	401
	Daniel's drama in stone.	401
	Scholarly Interpretations.	401
	Mythic confusion.	403
	The Fiery Furnace	403
	Trees and Kingdoms	404
	Writing on the Wall	405
	The Lions' Den	405
	The Heavenly Court	406
	Daniel's dream.	406
	The plaintiff's mythical title.	406

Jubilee justice.	408
The Day of Atonement.	409
Daniel Seven and the Date of Composition	410
The Horns	414
The function of horns.	414
Temple plundered.	415
Antiochus stopped.	415
Daniel's Exegesis	416
The kingdoms of the South and of the North	417
The battles rage.	417
The little help.	418
ANTIOCHUS III AND THE SECOND ENDING	420
Problems.	420
Confusion of Kings.	420
He will come to his end.	422
SUMMARY	423
THE TEXT OF DANIEL ELEVEN	423
SITUATION	426
Time periods.	429
Beginning and end.	430
AUTHORSHIP	430
THE ORIGINAL READERS OR HEARERS	432
Hasmoneans and the Hasidim.	432
Persecution and patriotism.	434
Merits and militarism.	434
THE STRUCTURE OF THE DOCUMENT	435
Unity problems.	435
Medieval insights.	436
Biblical anthologies.	437
Damiel as redemption literature.	438
Committee and composition.	440
DANIEL AND THE CANON	440
FROM DRAMA TO PROPHECY	442
Faith and Nationalism after Daniel	444
The Kingdom without End	445
THE SECTS OF JUDAISM	450
Internal divisions.	450
The Nazorean Sect.	450
Jews and Christians in the diaspora.	451
War torn land.	451
Jewish and Christian Conflicts.	452
The new Beth-horon.	453
Daniel as prophecy.	453

THE ETHICS OF CONQUEST THEOLOGY 454
        Activist ethics. 454
        Passive ethics. 455
        A non-Palestinian illustration. 456

APPENDIX I. SUZANNA **458**
APPENDIX II. BEL AND THE DRAGON **471**

PREFACE

My academic interest in the Book of Daniel began with the Dead Sea Scrolls. When I was studying all of the available scrolls to learn the eschatology reflected I found that the expression, usually translated "at the end of days" (*buh-ah-khah-reét hah-yah-meém*, באחרית הימים; or *buh-ah-khah-reét yoh-máh-yah* באחרית יומיא, did not mean what I had always thought. Scholars had normally taken this to be a reference to the end of time, of the world, or of the cosmos, but in the Dead Sea Scrolls it obviously meant something less extensive. It meant simply "in the future," "after this," or at the end of some particular time period, such as the end of the exile or of the "debtor enslavement," before the rest of the Sabbath year or Jubilee release. When I examined all of the references to this expression in the FT and its Greek translation in the NT I learned that the expression never looked forward to the end of time or of the cosmos. The meaning was consistent in the Dead Sea Scrolls and in the Bible. This was especially clear in the Book of Daniel where the expression was used in parallel with another expression that means "after this" (*ah-khah-ráy deh-náh*, אחרי דנה) (Dan 2:28-29).[1] That insight that I learned in 1956 stimulated my interest in the Book of Daniel that has never waned.

What is the real meaning of the Book of Daniel? I wondered. Popular evangelists have been warning Christians that the world is coming to an end very soon.[2] They proved this from the Book of Daniel. The problem was that the end they promised that would come within a prescribed time never came. They always had to revise their schedule and determine that there would be another slightly later date at which time the end would

---

[1] See further Buchanan, "Eschatology and the `End of Days,'" *Journal of Near Eastern Studies* 20 (1961):188-93.

[2] One of the popular evangelists is Hal Lindsey, *The 1980's: Countdown to Armageddon* (U.S. and Canada: Bantam Books, 1981) and H. Lindsey with C. C. Carlson (Grand Rapids: Zondervan Publishing House, 1971). After the Six-Day War (1967) he thought we were living in the last week (1967-74). That period has passed, but he still thinks we are the last generation before the end. Jewish Zionists were just as certain as Lindsey after the Six-Day War that we were living in the last days. One was C. Shvilly, *The Book of Calculations of the Redemption* (Jerusalem, c1964) with updating additions in 1969 [in Hebrew]. He predicted the third world war which he thought would be an atomic war that would begin during the 3 ½ year period after 1970 and would continue until 1990. He was killed in the Golan Heights during the Yom Kippur War, probably believing he was fighting in the war that would bring about Israel's complete redemption. See further Buchanan, *New Testament Eschatology: Historical and Cultural Background* (Lewiston: Mellen Biblical Press, c1993), pp. 241-45.

come, but it did not. Not only evangelists had trouble with adaptations of the dates in Daniel, but so did the scholars. They visualized history breaking off and becoming chaos or some undefined age to come. Some thought time would circle up into eternity. Instead of reading Daniel historically, they transferred the concept into mysticism, philosophy, or psychology. Instead of a historical end they thought of the ends mentioned in Daniel as ends in terms of meaning or conviction.[3]

Both evangelists and scholars were troubled by the fact that the Book of Daniel was accepted in the Jewish and Christian canons. Therefore it must have religious significance. It was written as if it were historical, dealing in terms of years and days, but some scholars "existentialized" temporal ends to mean ends in terms of quality or commitment. It did not matter what it once meant. The question is, "What does it mean to the modern reader?" This succeeded in avoiding the problem of the book. The Book of Daniel referred to specific time periods—days, weeks, and years. The days mentioned have been gone for hundreds of years. Daniel has been accepted as if it were prophecy, but the prophesied time periods ended years ago. How then can this book be understood? What can be its relevance for today? Why was it accepted into the canon?

Suppose we were to stop reading this book as if it were an ink blot test into which we were free to infuse all sorts of external feelings and disciplines, what then would be its meaning? That is what I set out to discover. It meant I had to learn as much as possible about the period of history from which this book originated. What was the geography, languages, customs, politics, rules of rhetoric, and religious attitudes involved?

After I had spent 40 years acquiring the background necessary to understand this problematic book, I discovered that it is not at all as complex as evangelists and scholars have thought. No knowledge of western philosophy, psychology, astrology, or numerology is necessary to grasp its meaning. Once readers realize that the Book of Daniel was not originally written as a prophecy intended to be fulfilled anytime after the second century BIA, the book begins to make sense. The various chapters, if read as dramas, rather than tracts for hard times, are readily understood in terms of festivity and celebration, as it was originally intended.

The work that was necessary to acquire the background needed for this study was both very difficult and wonderfully enjoyable. I spent the summer of 1957 in Nablus, Jordan, taking part in an archaeological excavation with the aid of a Bollingen grant. While I was there, I regularly visited Arabs in their nearby tents, learning their customs and language.[4] An Association of Theological Schools grant permitted me to discover the northern boundaries of the Promised Land during the summer of 1966, when I lived in a station wagon and traveled widely between Turkey and Egypt.[5] During that time I visited often with Syrians and Labenese, learning not only topography and geography of the land, but also customs of the Near East. This was increased during the summer of 1973.

Indispensable to my academic development were three years spent in Cincinnati with the financial aid of Horowitz and Sheuer interfaith fellowships to study Semitic languages and literature at Hebrew Union College-Jewish Institute of Religion and

---

[3] For a survey of scholarly opinions relevant to eschatology and the Book of Daniel see Buchanan, "Introduction," R. H. Charles, *Eschatology* (Reprinting, New York: Schocken Books, c1963), pp. i-xxx.
[4] I also had dissentery all summer long from eating with Bedouin and drinking water from goatskin bags.
[5] The account of this discovery is reported in Buchanan, *The Consequences of the Covenant* (Leiden : E. J. Brill, 1970), pp. 91-109

classical Greek at the graduate school of the University of Cincinnati. This was further strengthened by a year of study at Jerusalem with the aid of a Hebrew Union College Biblical and Archaeological School fellowship during 1966-67. I spent the summer of 1972 in linguistic studies in Jerusalem, and the year 1973-74, also in Jerusalem, translating theological, apocalyptic, and poetic documents composed from the time of Bar Cochba until the end of the Crusades.[6] That was when I learned the real nature of the class of literature to which the Book of Daniel belongs. It is called "Redemption Literature."

Thanks to an Association of Theological Schools grant and the Claremont-Society of Biblical Literature Fellowship, I was able to spend the entire year, 1980-81, at the Institute for Antiquity and Christianity, writing and using the computer and library facilities there to increase my facility with classical Greek and ancient rhetoric. All of this is necessary to understand the background for the Book of Daniel.

Most people who have seen me in any academic setting have also become acquainted with my wife, Harlene. She has traveled with me and lived with me in many interesting, primitive, and educational situations, while always encouraging me in various kinds of research that I thought were important. She proofreads all of my books and articles, improving my literary style, grammar, and format. She is able to recognize typographical errors in English, German, Hebrew, and Greek. All of my writings are better because of her contribution. All of that in addition to being a wonderful wife!

My good friend, former student, and member of my advisory group at the seminary is Rev. Tom Gregory. He has taught me almost all that I know about computer hardware and software. It is because of his capable tutoring that I am able to produce a volume such as this with a computer. The Rev. Allen Mueller, librarian, and Ms. Howartine L. Farrell Duncan, reference librarian, at Wesley Theological Seminary, by their capable and friendly assistance, have been very helpful to me. I am also grateful to my esteemed colleague Dr. David C. Hopkins, editor of *Near Eastern Archaeology* and professor of Archaeology and Biblical Interpretation at Wesley Theological Seminary. He directed and procured all of the maps in this volume as well as the colored picture of Beth-horon, taken from the air by Dr. Richard Cleave, ROHR PRODUCTIONS, LTD. My good neighbor and friend, Ms. Norma Creel, on the basis of a photograph provided by the British Museum sketched the picture of Asshur on page 186. It is used with permission and appreciation to both. The Hebrew and Aramaic pages are copied from Linguist's Software. I am grateful to all of these people for their kind assistance.

My brother, Russell Howard Buchanan, was the seventh of eight boys in a family of ten children. Our mother said the seventh son would be blessed. This was not because he was born into riches. On the contrary, He was born at a time of severe economic hardship, but he was blessed in other ways. He has learned to find happiness and meaning in all sorts of situations. He has been very rich and very poor, but he is always the same secure person with consistent values. He has become a very successful businessman, but that is only a secondary virtue. His primary blessedness comes from being a wonderful husband, father, and grandfather. The many people who know Russell have recognized him as a capable counselor, a kind friend, and a devoted churchman. I am proud to claim him as my brother and dedicate this book to him.

---

[6] The collection of these translations is found in Buchanan, *Jewish Messianic Movements from AD 70 to AD1300* Eugene: Oregon: Wipf and Stock Publishers, 2003).

ABBREVIATIONS

AJSL	American Journal of Semitic Languages and Literatures
ArO	Anciennes Orientales
AUSS	Andrews University Seminary Studies
AusBR	Australian Biblical Review
bBer	Babylonian Talmud, Berakoth
BRShen	Babylonian Talmud, Rosh HaShenah
Bib	Biblica
BAR	Biblical Archaeology Review
BR	Biblical Research
BASOR	Bulletin of the American School of Oriental Research
CJT	Canadian Journal of Theology
CBQ	Catholic Biblical Quarterly
CIP	Classical Philology
DS	Dominican Studies
DSD	Dead Sea Discoveries
ETL	Ephemerides Theologicae Lovaniense
EQ	Evangelical Quarterly
ExAud	EX Auditu
ExodR	Exodus Rabba
ET	Expository Times
GTJ	Grace Theological Journal
HTR	Harvard Theologicla Review
HE	History of the Church, Eusebius
HAR	Hebrew Annual Review
HUCA	Hebrew Union Collage Annual
HBT	Horizons in Biblical Theology
ISBE	International Standard Biblical Encyclopedia
Int	Interpretation
IDB	Interpreter's Dictionary of the Bible
Ant	Josephus, Antiquities
JSOT	Journal for the Study of the Old Testament
JBL	Journal of Biblical Literature
JETS	Journal of the Evangelical Theological Society
JJS	Journal of Jewish Studies
JNES	Journal of Near Eastern Studies
JTS	Journal of Theological Studies
Mek, Amalek	Mekilta, Amalek
mAboth	Mishnah, Aboth
NTS	New Testament Studies
NovT	Novum Testamentum

OS	Oudtestamentische Studien
PrepEvang	Preparation for the Gospel, Eusebius
QC	The Qumran Chronicle
RB	Revue Biblique
REJ	Revue Etude Juives
RevQ	Revue de Qumran
RHR	Revue d'Histoire des Religions
Sem	Semitica
SE	Studian Evangelica
ST	Studia Theologica
TRu	Theologische Rundschau
TSK	Theologische Studien und Kritiken
TJT	Toronto Journal of Theology
TB	Tyndale Bulletin
VT	Vetus Testamentum
WTJ	Westminster Theological Journal
ZATW	Zeitschrift fuer die Alttestamentliche Wissenschaft
ZNTW	Zeitschrift fuer die Neutestamentliche Wissenschaft

INTRODUCTION

THE PURPOSE OF THE INTRODUCTION

The purpose of this introduction is to prepare the reader for the commentary that follows. It does not include conclusions reached as a result of the research, such as 1) basic message, 2) date and place of authorship, 3) identification of author or authors, and 4) original readers or hearers. Those are reserved for the end of the study, when readers have enough facts at their disposal to judge the conclusions. It is not assumed that all readers will reach the same conclusions as the author, but they will rely on basically the same facts. The commentary is designed to provide the necessary facts for judgment. The introduction is brief and will include only the necessary concepts for understanding the commentary--definitions, a basic map, and a survey of the historical period involved.

Midrash. Midrash is a literature about a literature. It is a literary form whereby the author elaborates and interprets an earlier literary text. Years ago midrash was thought to have occurred only in rabbinic literature. Later scholars recognized that the New Testament (NT) also contained some of the same literary phenomena. It has been only during the last 40 years that midrash has been discovered in the First Testament (FT).[1] The midrashic method of exegesis, which has been employed by the authors of the Book of Daniel, was basic to Jewish, Samaritan, and Christian understanding of the significance of scripture to the legal and ethical conduct of life. Those who practice this method of interpretation treat the scripture in the same way modern lawyers build arguments on the basis of the constitution and earlier judicial precedents in which laws were applied to current situations.

There were basically three kinds of midrash that were used in the scripture: 1) homiletic midrash, 2) running midrash, and 3) narrative midrash. Authors of various parts of the Book of Daniel have used two of these forms.

---

[1] Buchanan, "Midrashim Pre-Tannaïtes," *RB* 72 (1965):227-39.

Homiletic midrash is employed whenever an author builds a sermon, using basically one text, even though he or she might use many other texts as illustrations in the formation of a sermon. Rabbinic examples of this are Pesikta Rabbati and Pisikta de Rav Kahana. In the NT this is evident in the Book of Hebrews, where Ps 110 is the basic text for Heb 1-12. In the FT the ten commandments of Deut 5 provide the text for the commentary of Deut 6:1-11:25. Prov 2-7 is a homily based on Deut 6:4-9//11:18-22 in which the preacher emphasized three points that he took from his text: 1) lying down, 2) rising up, 3) walking in the way. Today it is current practice to call the text used as the basis for the narrative the "intertext." This means that Ps 110 is the intertext for Heb 1-12; Deut 6:4-9//11:18-22 is the intertext for Prov 2-7; and the ten commandments form the intertext for Deut 6:1-11:25. Deut 6:1-11:25, Prov 2-7, and Heb 1-12 are all homilies.

Running midrash occurs when an author sets out to comment on every passage of a certain book or part of a book. In Rabbinic literature Mekilta is a running commentary on the early chapters of Exodus. Sifrá is a running commentary or midrash on the entire book of Leviticus. Sifré is a running commentary on parts of Numbers and Deuteronomy. Midrash Rabbah is a set of commentaries on the five books of the Torah and five of the writings of the FT (Lamentations, Esther, Song of Songs, Ruth, and Ecclesiastes).

These commentators wrote in much the same way that a musical composer might, using many repetitious themes throughout the composition, weaving them in and out. As one melody fades into the background, another theme is raised to prominence so as to vary and blend while moving from score to score. Authors of running midrashim use texts the same way, effectively repeating arguments and thoughts while commenting on continuing texts. Some texts are expounded in detail, whereas the same argument might be summarized in relationship to another text.[2] Running midrashim do not occur in the Book of Daniel, but they are currently composed by all modern authors of commentaries.

Narrative midrash is evident in many places in rabbinic literature, the FT, and the NT. Authors of narrative midrash weave words from an intertext in ways that the untrained reader would not recognize, but the one familiar with scripture would see it and understand the context to which it belonged originally. Then the reader would realize that there was more meaning intended than the exact words seem to say. This is the way the author of Dan 2 applied words taken from Gen 41 to remind the learned reader of Joseph in Egypt. Words have been taken from the priestly benediction (Num 6:24-26) and applied to many of the Psalms (Pss 4:1, 6; 13:1, 3; 29:11; 31:16, 21-23; 41:2, 4, 10-13; 67:1, 6-7; 80:3, 7, 19; 118:26-27; 119:29, 132, 135). The benediction was also used by the author of Dan 9:17 and many other books. It was obviously a very popular benediction. Narrative midrash appears throughout the Book of Daniel and will be evident as intertexts are pointed out in the parallel columns together with the text of Daniel.

In addition to scripture, biblical authors also used other authoritative books in their composition, which are no longer preserved. For example,

---

[2] Buchanan, *To the Hebrews* (Garden City: Doubleday & Co., 1972), pp. xix-xxii defines midrash in similar ways.

describing boundaries the author of Numbers quoted **The Book of the Wars of Yehowah** (Num 21:14). Dan 11-12 evidently comes from the author's primary source called **The Book of Truth**. Near the end of Dan 10 are these words

> .. Look! the Greek general will come, but I will tell you what is written in **The Book of Truth.**

Then near the beginning of Dan 11, are these words,
> Now I will tell you **the truth** (Dan 11:2).

That which follows is a lengthy account of the conflicts that took place between the Syrians and the Egyptians on the Promised Land after the Greeks took possession of Syria.

Cyclical time. Basic to Jewish concepts is the belief that time moves in cycles that reflect and imitate one another. Just as seasons and feasts take place in a consistent order, so also do days of the week, months of the year, Sabbath years, and Jubilee years. There was no notion that the world or the cosmos would come to an end. It would simply re-cycle. The scripture says:

> All the days of the land, seedtime and harvest, cold and heat, summer and winter, day and night. They will never cease (Gen 8:21-22).

> A generation comes and a generation goes, but the land exists for the age (Eccles 1:4).

> What has been is what will be
> and what has been done is what will be done (Eccles 1:9).

According to 1Enoch:

> Observe the earth and consider its works . . .that nothing at all changes (*1Enoch* 2.2).

The temporal ends that occurred in relationship to time were all ends of cycles. The end of one cycle marked also the beginning of another. At the end of one week, another week began. The same was true of seasons, months, and ages. The conviction that this was the way events took place in time provided the Jews with a distinct advantage over others. By studying cycles they could discern the predestined order of events and make plans accordingly.

Second Isaiah ridiculed the idols of the gentiles that could not tell of the things that had already happened. They also could not foretell the future the way Jews could (Isa 41:21-24). This was possible because Jews had at their disposal the scripture, which was God's word. Jews had access to God's word through which they could learn what had happened to the nation in the past. They also knew about cycles of time by which they could predict the future.

This meant that the God of the Jews was superior to the gods of the gentiles. For example, from the scripture Jews could learn about the captivity of Egypt in the past. Because of this they were not completely surprised by the exile into Babylon. It was a new captivity and provided a pivot by which Jews could determine their position in the predestined cycles of time. This enabled them to predict events in the Babylonian captivity that were still to come. Since they had the scripture, they could pinpoint an event in one cycle and identify it with another similar event in an earlier or later cycle. This enabled them to prophesy the future in the same way and with about the same success as almanacs predict the weather a year in advance. Since the Israelites came through the wilderness from Egypt to the Promised Land, the prophet presumed that the Jews would have to come through the wilderness to return to the Promised Land (Isa 35).

It was Dan 9 that told the Jews that the Hasmonean Rebellion lasted 3½ years, even though Josephus said it lasted only three years. Once Daniel was accepted as scripture, later Jews thought any future war with a dominating country would also last 3½ years before it was concluded in victory. After the war with the Romans lasted nearly 3½ years (66-70 IA), prophets expected God's intervention at any time to destroy the Romans and redeem the Jews. Although that war did not conclude as Jews expected, they did not lose faith. The rebellion of Bar Cochba also lasted 3½ years before the Romans defeated the Jewish rebels.

After the conclusion of the Bar Cochba rebellion, there were three examples of a 3½ year war between Jews and their imperial enemies:

1) the Hasmonean Revolt,
2) the Jewish-Roman war of 66-70 IA,
3) the Bar Cochba revolt of 132-135 IA

On that basis a twentieth century scholar deduced that the war between Nebuchadnezzar and the Jews which was completed in 586 BIA must also have lasted 3½ years. She also reasoned that the destruction of the first temple (586 BIA), the destruction of the second temple (70 IA), and the defeat of Bar Cochba at Beitar (135 IA) all must have occurred on the ninth of Ab.[3] She further held that the second temple was reconstructed exactly (*buh-dee-yoók*, בדיוק) 70 years after its destruction.[4] Josephus concluded that the temple was destroyed the second time (70 IA) on exactly the day and month as the first destruction in 586 BIA. This proved to Josephus the scientific accuracy of the cycles of time (*khráwnohn peh-ree-áw-dois*, χρόνων περιόδοις) (*War* 6.250). Jews were so completely convinced of the exactness of cycles that they forced dates to fit the cycles, just to prove their dogma.

Jewish faith in cyclical time was so strong that Jews fought zealously for 3½ years before admitting defeat. Later Jews continued to interpret earlier history

---

[3] L. E. Zusman, *Jerusalem: Your City* (Jerusalem: Khakhmah Publishing, 1989), p. 73. In Hebrew
לאה אסתר זוסמן. ולירושלים עירך (הוצאת חכמה, ירושלים).
[4] Zusman, *Jerusalem*, p. 141.

on the basis that this portion of all cycles was 3½ years in length. The Book of Daniel was composed with these assumptions. The following chart shows the Jewish concept of time in relationship to the Egyptian cycle, which began with Joseph in Egypt and ended with the destruction of the temple in 586 BIA.

THE HISTORICAL PERIOD INVOLVED

The time period. The Book of Daniel consists of a group of narratives that dramatize the period from the beginning of the Babylonian exile to the celebration of Hanukkah, marking the end of the Babylonian captivity and the beginning of Jewish freedom. This was understood as the end of the captivity era and the beginning of the era of liberty. It was also the completion of a cycle that began with the original construction of Solomon's temple. Some of the relevant events and dates of the Babylonian era are these:

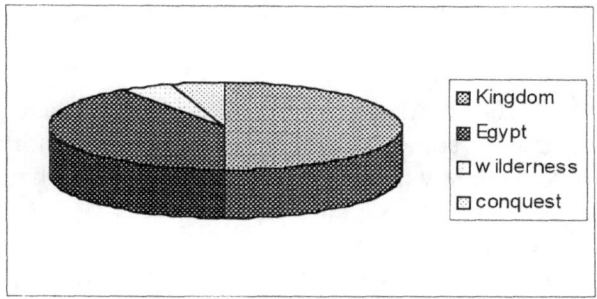

The cycle began with the exile in Egypt where Israelites spent 400-430 years. This was followed by the 40 years spent in the wilderness and an additional 40 years spent in the conquest of Canaan. The kingdom began with David and Solomon who built the temple about 1,000 BIA. This kingdom lasted until 586 BIA when Jews were taken captive into Babylon. The next cycle began in Babylon about 586 BIA. Jews understood that this was to begin as an antitype of the captivity in Egypt. This concluded the Egyptian cycle and began a new cycle. The Book of Daniel began telling of events that took place in the second cycle, but it told second cycle events in relationship to the Egyptian cycle as a background. Some of the historical events included in the second cycle are these:

605 BIA. The Battle of Carchemish when Nebuchadnezzar defeated the Egyptians and extended his influence westward. After the battle he traveled to Jerusalem, met with King Jehoiakim and set down the terms by which he would allow Jehoiakim to continue to rule from Jerusalem.

597 BIA. Jehoiakim led a rebellion against Babylonian rule in Judah. Nebuchadnezzar sent enough troops to quell the rebellion, remove Jehoiakim from the throne, and replace him with his brother Jehoiakin. Nebuchadnezzar at that time imprisoned a few of the governmental leaders and took them back with him to Babylon.

586 BIA. Nebuchadnezzar entered Jerusalem with many troops, burned the temple, plundered the city, confiscated the wealth and vessels of the temple, and took approximately 10,000 Jewish leaders captive back to Babylon. This included all of the professional people, large business magnates, physicians, rabbis, government leaders, and all of the people skilled in crafts.

539 BIA. Cyrus of Persia overpowered Babylon during a feast without a war. This was accomplished with some effective intelligence cooperation from people inside the city. This happened at a time when thousands of Jews formed a large, powerful minority group in Babylon.

171 BIA. The Hellenistic Syrian king, Antiochus IV Epiphanes, made a treaty with the Jewish leaders in Jerusalem.

168 BIA. The treaty made was broken, and guerrilla war was declared against Syria.

January or February, 164 BIA. After three years of constant guerrilla warfare, Judas the Maccabee won some important battles at Beth-horon. Antiochus IV Epiphanes died in Persia a few months either before or after that battle.

December, 164 BIA. After several months of preparation, preparing liturgy, program, and cleansing the temple (1Macc 4:36-58), Jews celebrated their third Hanukkah. The first was celebrated when Solomon was king; the second when Nehemiah was governor of Judah. This celebration lasted eight days and was an important factor in the composition of the Book of Daniel.

May, 142 BIA. Under the leadership of Simon, the oldest of the Hasmonean brothers, Judah was given full independence. This involved permission to have an army, removal of the Syrian garrison from Jerusalem, and discontinuance of all taxes to Syria. This prompted an eight-day celebration and the establishment of a new calendar, beginning with that date.

63 BIA. The Roman general, Pompey, was admitted into Jerusalem to take part in a civil war. Roman soldiers killed many Jewish citizens, and Pompey entered the temple and defiled it. He took no vessels or wealth, and he ordered the priests to cleanse the temple again, but everyone knew that Jewish liberty was vanishing.

55 BIA. The Roman general, Crassus, entered Jerusalem and robbed the temple of all of its wealth.

6/7 IA. Romans removed the ethnarch, Archelaus, and established their own governor, Quirinius, and local procurators. They also instituted a general taxation of the Jews to raise money for Rome. At that time there was a Jewish rebellion led by Judas of Galilee (*War* 2.117-118) in which the Jews tried to recover their lost freedom. Uprisings continued during feasts at Jerusalem until the Jews declared an all-out war against Rome in 66 IA.

Typology. Cycles of time constituted only one extension of the belief in typology. Typology is the conviction that objects, persons, and institutions exist and take place in relationship to other objects, events, persons, and institutions that correspond to one another. Things on earth, for example, when thought of in relationship to heavenly things, typologically, are held to be antitypes of prior and corresponding heavenly prototypes or archetypes which were patterns by which the things on earth were created. For example, the temple at Jerusalem was believed to be the antitype of a heavenly temple in a heavenly Jerusalem. When typology is applied within the limits of earthly things, the pattern normally followed is that the earlier event or object and is called the "type." The later event or object is held to be the "antitype," and it is believed to be patterned after the earlier type.

Typology is not the same as allegory. The antitype was not designed to give a hidden meaning to the type or to change the meaning originally intended. Instead the type was recognized as an earlier event, person, object or institution that corresponded to some later event, person, object, or institution in some imitative way. For example the captivity in Egypt was an earlier type for a later captivity in Babylon, which was noted as an antitype. The exodus from Egypt was a type for the later antitype of a return from Babylon to the Promised land, the antitype. The later Messiah was expected as an antitype for the earlier Moses or David. Pilate thought Jesus was an antitype for the earlier John the Baptist. Some people thought Jesus was the new Jeremiah or one of the prophets. That means they thought he was an antitype of John. The new law that was given as the Sermon on the Mount was understood as the antitype of the law that had been given earlier by Moses on Mount Sinai. The wise Daniel of Babylon that interpreted dreams was an antitype of the earlier wise Joseph of Egypt, who had also interpreted dreams.

Cyclical time patterns fit in with typological logic just as neatly as bolts fit into nuts. The exodus from Egypt belonged to a cycle that was earlier than the cycle to which the exodus from Babylon belonged. The Babylonian Daniel fit into the Babylonian cycle at the same position that the Egyptian Joseph held in the Egyptian cycle. In true cyclical imitation, the Jews from Babylon were expected to go through the wilderness before they could reach the Promised Land (Isa 35). The new Hanukkah that was celebrated in 164 BIA was patterned after the Hanukkah celebrated by the Israelites under the leadership of Solomon about 1,000 BIA. Neither typology nor cyclical time included an end of the cosmos or of time as part of its pattern. Both were basic to an understanding of the Book of Daniel, because they were accepted as realities by the authors of Daniel.

Dan 1 will begin by calling the readers' attention to the comparison between the experience of Daniel and the earlier experience of Joseph of Egypt. It will be especially evident in the author's use of the Genesis story in the composition of Dan 2. At the same time the midrashic method of composition will be obvious.

RULES OF RHETORIC

The rabbis defined authors who wrote both the FT and the NT also practiced rules of rhetoric that --

1. there is nothing in the world that is not in the scripture. This does not mean that all the ontological phenomena of the world—the trees, sky, people, animals, birds, etc. are in the scripture. This is a legal, rhetorical claim. It means that in court, neither the plaintiff nor the defendant was allowed to base an argument on any source that was not scriptural. Only laws of scripture might be used. So far as legalists were concerned there was nothing else but the scripture.
2. there is no before and after in scripture. This means a contestant was allowed to use scripture that was written later to prove the meaning of a text written earlier, or *vice versa*.
3. all prophecy was prophesied only for the days of the Messiah. This rule allowed commentators to use any of the scripture texts to apply to the contemporary situation. Jeremiah or Isaiah, for example, spoke to their own age, but any later interpreter as prophecy for a later situation could use their messages. The author of 1Pet, for example, said it was revealed to the prophets **that they were serving not themselves but you** (1Pet 1:12). Jesus reportedly said, **All the prophets and the law prophesied until John** (Matt 11:13). By this he meant that John and his contemporaries were living in the days of the Messiah when these prophecies would be fulfilled.

KIND OF LITERATURE

You may have been told that apocalyptic literature is disengaged from the world in a way that is not true of the earlier prophetic literature. It is instead a literature of desperation. Hanson said,

> When separated from the realism, the vision leads to a retreat into the world of ecstasy and dreams and to an abdication of the social responsibility of translating the vision of the divine order into the realm of everyday earthly concerns.[5]

If that were true then the Book of Daniel could not be considered apocalyptic. To be sure there are dreams and dramas in the Book of Daniel, but they are not irrelevant, unreal, or dramas of desperation. These dramas surround the restoration of the Promised Land, and therefore belong to a class of literature better labeled "Redemption Literature."[6]

---

[5] P.D. Hanson, *The Dawn of Apocalyptic* (Minneapolis: Fortress Press, c1986), p. 30.
[6] The following two paragraphs were taken almost entirely from Buchanan, *The Book of Revelation: Its Introduction and Prophecy* (Lewiston: The Edwin Mellen Press, c1993), pp. 33-34.

The entire genre, apocalypse, may be a misnomer. It gets its origin from one word in Rev 1:1, but Mazzaferri insisted that the Book of Revelation is not an apocalypse:

> The title, apocalyptic, certainly derives from Rev, but this is irrelevant. *Apokáloopsis,* Ἀποκάλυψις is not a technical term in John's day, although he employs it prophetically. In terms of actual generic definition, Rev cannot be equated with apocalyptic in form.[7]

Betz was correct in saying that apocalyptic literature has never been satisfactorily defined.[8] Rowley went too far in saying, "That apocalyptic is the child of prophecy, yet diverse from prophecy, can hardly be disputed."[9] Hill held that Revelation was more like Hebrew Scripture prophecy than like apocalypses--assuming, of course, that some of the literature that is like the Book of Revelation are apocalypses, even though they never use the term "revelation" in their texts.[10] Knibb argued that Daniel was more of a scribe and a wiseman than a prophet.[11]

All of the so-called apocalyptic literature documents might better be called "Redemption Literature." This is similar to the designation Ibn Shemuel gave to his collection of medieval Jewish literature of this nature. He called it *midresháy ge'uláh,* מדרשי גאולה "Midrashim on the subject of Redemption" or "Redemption Midrashim."[12] A midrash is a literature about a literature. The literature in Ibn Shemuel's volume deals with the redemption or restoration of the Promised Land. This literature is composed of interpretations of biblical literature. Daniel, Zechariah, Jeremiah, Ezekiel, and many other biblical and inter-testamental books, belong to the same category. Redemption literature began with the Assyrian exile of the North Israelites and was further developed with the Babylonian exile of the Jews of Judah. The Book of Daniel was centered on the restoration of the Promised Land. It was dramatically composed, but it was not written in desperation.

LITERARY FORMS

Inclusion. An inclusion (Latin *inclusio* [*een-kloó-see-oh*]) is a literary form that brings the reader at the end of a literary unit back to the beginning to tell him or

---

[7] F. D. Mazzaferri, *The Genre of the Book of Revelation from a Source-critical Perspective* (New York: DeGruyter Press, 1998), p. 258
[8] H. D. Betz, "Zum Problem des religionsgeschichtlichen Verstännisses der Apokalyptik," *ZTK* 63 (1966):592.
[9] H. H. Rowley, *The Relevance of Apocalyptic* (London: Lutterworth Press, 1947; New York, 1963), p. 15.
[10] D. Hill, "Prophecy and Prophets in the Revelation of St. John," *NTS* 18 (1971/72): 401-405.
[11] M. A. Knibb, "Are You Indeed Wiser than Daniel?" *The Book of Daniel in the Light of New Findings* (Leuven: University Press, 1993), pp. 399-411.
[12] Ibn Shemuel, *Midreshe Ge'ulah* (Jerusalem: 1968) exists only in Hebrew. The documents he collected plus many more have been translated into English and published with notes as Buchanan, *Revelation and Redemption: Jewish Documents of Deliverance from the Fall of Jerusalem to the Death of Nahmanides* (Dillsboro: c1978; sold by Mercer U Press).

her that the message is complete. Sometimes the inclusion frames a very small unit, such as the treasury of merits teaching in Matt 6:19-20:

> "Do not lay up for yourselves . . .
> but lay up for yourselves treasures . . ."

A larger unit is Matt 7:16-20, which begins and ends with the words—
"from your fruits you shall know them."
In between is a short discussion on the relationship of plants to the fruits they produce. Whatever the content of the section between the beginning and the ending statements is, it takes the central position much like meat or cheese in a sandwich. The beginning and conclusion act as bread on the outside of the sandwich. The author of Hebrews used inclusions very effectively, binding them together with connecting sentences. For example, Heb 1:1-3 is an inclusion completed by the connecting sentence, Heb 1:4 which relates the first inclusion to a second inclusion (Heb 1:5, 13), which has Heb 1:14 as a concluding sentence.[13] A homily (Deut 6:4-11:19) is enclosed by the exhortation at both ends to teach these laws to children while sitting in the house, while walking in the way, while lying down at night, and while rising in the morning. The Book of Daniel also has several inclusions. For example Dan 7 begins with the words,

> [7:1]During the first year of [the reign of] Belshazzar, king of Babylon, Daniel dreamed a vision, and [there were] visions in his head [as he lay] on his bed. Then he wrote down the dream. At the beginning of the words, he said, . . .

That chapter concludes as follows:

> [28]Here is where the word ends. As for me, Daniel, my thoughts alarmed me very much. My appearance changed, and I kept the words in my mind.

Chiasms. Chiasm (Latin, *chiasmus* [*khee-áz-muss*]) is derived from the Greek *khee-ád-zayne* (χιάζειν), to mark with a *khee* (X) which looks like the Latin X. The literary form, chiasm, is one which includes at least two units, whether they are words, lines, ideas, or paragraphs. Each of these units must have at least two parts, so that four parts are required to form the four points of a *khee*. Like the inclusion, these form a sandwich-like expression, but in a much more precise way than the inclusion requires. Arranging the words of the first unit in one sequence and those of the second in reverse order, to form an arrangement such as this forms the *khee*:

---

[13] See B. C. Butler, *The Originality of St. Matthew* (Cambridge: Cambridge U. Press, 1951), p. 150; F. C. Fenton, "Inclusion and Chiasmus in Matthew," *SE* (1959):174-79; and Buchanan, *The Gospel of Matthew* (Lewiston: The Edwin Mellen Press, c1996) I, pp. 41-42.

```
        A           B
             X
        B           A
```

An example of this is Matt 19:30:

```
    Many  first ones        will be last
                    X
    and the last             first.
```

The chiasm in Matt 19:30 is repeated in 20:16, thus forming an inclusion with a chiasm at both ends (see also Matt 10:28; 12:49-50). In addition to words, phrases are sometimes put together chiastically, as in Matt 7:6:

```
A. Do not give to the dogs what is holy,         Dogs           hogs
B. and do not throw their pearls before hogs              X
B lest they [the hogs] trample them underfoot,   hogs           dogs
A and they [the dogs] turn to bite you.
```

A euphonic chiasm is in Heb 4:16:

```
So that we might receive      mercy      hee-nah lah-boh-mehn    él-eh-aws
           X                                          X
and grace              we might find.    Kai kháh-reen    hee-yoó-roh-mehn.¹⁴
```

There are also chiasms in the Book of Daniel, as Goldingay observed in Dan 6:

```
A. Daniel's success.
   B. Darius signed an injunction and Daniel took his stand.
      C. Daniel's colleagues planned his death.
         D. Darius hoped for Daniel's deliverance.
                        X
         D' Darius witnessed Daniel's deliverance.
      C' Daniel's colleagues met their deaths.
   B'. Darius signed a decree and took his stand.
A' Daniel's success.¹⁵
```

RELEVANT DETAILS

The Tetragrammaton. For many years scholars have mistakenly assumed that the Tetragrammaton was to be correctly pronounced *Yáh-weh*, treating the central vowel as if it were a consonant. This error has recently been corrected. Among the scrolls was found a fragment of a Greek translation of a passage in Leviticus that

---

¹⁴ These examples are taken from Buchanan, *Matthew* I, pp. 41-43.
¹⁵ J. E. Goldingay, *Daniel* (Dallas: Word Books, c1989), p. 124.

transliterated the Tetragrammaton into Greek. This was unique, because in other OG texts the Tetragrammaton was either translated as "the Lord" (*ho keé-ree-aws*, ὁ κύριος) or it was retained in Hebrew, untranslated. In this fragment, however, the word was transliterated as *Yah-oh* (ΙΑΩ) (*4QOG* Lev). This means that the central vowel *oh* was pronounced. This was not a coincidence, as can be discerned by the spelling of proper names that employed the Tetragrammaton. Some such names are Jehoshaphat (*Yah-hóh-shah-faht*), "Yaho has judged," Jonathan (*Yah-hóh-nah-thahn*), "Yaho has given," Jochanan (*Yah-hóh-khah-nan*), "Yaho has been gracious," Elijah (*Eh-lee-Yáh-hoo*), "My God is Yahu," Zechariah (*Zeh-kahr-Yáh-hoo*), "Yahu has remembered." Throughout the FT the spelling is consistent. The central vowel is never treated as if it were a consonant. Originally there was probably a final *ah* pronounced in the name.

Among the scrolls, words that end in a consonant often have a final *ah*. For example, words like *lah-héhm* (להם) "to them," and *lah-khéhm* (לכם) "to you" (pl.) are spelled in the scrolls *lah-hehm-áh* (להמה) and *lah-khehm-áh* (לכמה). In Arabic the vowel is pronounced, but the consonant is omitted. So the Masoretic *hoo* (הוא), "he," which in the scrolls is spelled and pronounced *hoó-ah* (הואה) is spelled *hoo* (הוא) in Arabic, but pronounced *hoó-ah*. In antiquity, the Masoretic text (MT) Hebrew was probably pronounced like modern Arabic. In which case a word like *Yah-hoo* or *Yah-hoh* would probably have been spelled יהוא (as in 2Kings 10:18) or יהו and pronounced *Yah-hoo-áh* or *Yah-hoh-áh*. This is consistent with the church fathers and the Aramaic papyri. The name could be either *Yah-hoh-wah* or *Yeh-hoh-wah*. There are arguments for both. Based on this data the divine name will be spelled arbitrarily *Yehowah* in this commentary.[16] Others may choose to use *Yah-hoh-wah* or *Yah-hoo-wah*. It is important to have the central vowel recognized.

Political Points. For centuries Christians and Jews have practiced the fine art of insulting. Jews have insulted other Jews, and Christians have insulted other Christians. Jews have also insulted Christians, and Christians have insulted Jews. It is called "defamation," and both groups have done it. There is no benefit to be gained in counting sins to show who has been the most insulting. At this stage in the game the best thing to do is to see how we can reduce the insults. Some efforts will be made in this commentary to achieve that goal. We will be most successful if instead of trying to prevent others from defaming us, we stop defaming others.

Christians have called the canonical books written before the NT the "Old Testament," implying that it has been transcended and made out of date. This was not done facetiously without scriptural basis. Jeremiah, on the basis of Deut 24:1, said that God had divorced his people, and sent them out of his house. This implied that he had also given them a divorce document (Jer 3:8), thus fulfilling the two requirements for divorce: 1) writ of divorce and 2) sending the bride from

---

[16] Taken from Buchanan, *Matthew* I, pp. 49-50. See further Buchanan, "Some Unfinished Business with the Dead Sea Scrolls," *RevQ* 49-52 (1988) *Mémorial Jean Carmignac*, ed. García Martínez et E. Peuch (Paris, 1988), pp. 413-20. For the use of Yehowah rather than Yahowah see the Ph.D. thesis of Dr. Gérard Gertoux, יהוה *in Fame Only?: A Historical Record of the Divine Name* (Institut Catholique de Paris). The first syllable remains uncertain.

the groom's house (*mGittin* 1-9).[17] On the basis of Jeremiah, then, Christians believed there was no contract between God and his people until Jesus formed a new contract.[18] The initial contract was old and invalid (Heb 8:6-13; 10:16; 12:24).

Second Isaiah, however, disagreed with Jeremiah. He said even though God sent his people away from his temple (house), he did not give them a writ of divorce (*get*, גט). Therefore the divorce was not complete, and the initial contract is still valid (Isa 50:1). On this basis, Jews argue that there was no need for a new contract, and the initial contract is not old. Therefore they refuse to call the books related to the contract "the Old Testament." Instead they call it "the Hebrew Scripture" or the *Tanak*.

Christians and Jews can disagree on the contracts, but as literature, none of the scripture is out of date, neither for Jews nor Christians. There is a problem, however with calling these books the "Hebrew Scripture." For some this confuses them with only the books written in Hebrew; i.e., the Masoretic text (MT). Others also call the books that have been translated into Greek as "The Christian Bible," because Christians have preserved them, and that translation includes some books not included in the Masoretic text. The canonical books that were composed before the New Testament (NT) are not antiquated—neither the Greek nor the Hebrew canons. This will become especially obvious in this series of commentaries where the pre-NT canonical texts that were used by authors of the NT will be given special consideration.

Here the pre-NT canonical books will not be called the "Old Testament," "Christian Testament," or the "Hebrew Scripture." Instead the collection will be referred to as "The First Testament," (FT) and it will include all of the books of the Roman Catholic canon. This will reduce the offense Jews have experienced in having their scripture considered out of date. It will also avoid staging a conflict between the Greek translations and the MT. It will not characterize these books as Jewish books as over against Greek Christian books. The text of the FT canon comes in Hebrew *and in Greek*. The Greek version is called the "Septuagint" (OG) whereas the Hebrew text is called the "Masoretic text" (MT).

With the victories of Constantine, Christians believed that this was a confirmation that the new contract God made with Jesus was valid, and that this was the beginning of a new era. They began a new calendar, just as Jews had done during the days of Simon, the Hasmonean, and during the revolt of Bar Cochba. Christians called the beginning of this era *anno domine* (AD).

Jews have also been offended by the Christian reference to the calendar as BC (before Christ) and AD. Since Jesus is not their Lord, they do not participate in this offense. Instead they refer to this calendar as BCE and CE—before the common era and the common era. This designation is just as offensive to Christians as BC and AD is to Jews. That which is called "common" by Jews means that which is pagan, profane, idolatrous, gentile. Lev 10:10 commanded Israelites to discriminate between that which was holy (*kah-dóhsh*, קדש) and that

---

[17] See further Buchanan, *Biblical and Theological Insights from Ancient and Modern Civil Law* (Lewiston: The Edwin Mellen Press, *c*1992), pp.74-82.

[18] See further Buchanan, *Matthew* II, pp. 964-82.

which was common (*khohl*, חול) (Ezek 22:26). Ezekiel accused the priests of his day of not making these distinctions. He ordered the priests to observe them (Ezek 44:23).

Peter reportedly refused to eat anything that was common (*koi-nón*, κοινόν) or unclean. Following Levitical commandments the author of Rev 21:27 said the new Jerusalem would be holy, not containing anything that was common (*koi-nón*, κοινόν). Distinctions between that which is holy and that which is common have been retained for thousands of years. For instance, one of the prayers Jews recite at the conclusion of each Sabbath is:

> Blessed are you, Lord our God, king of the age, who discriminates between the holy (*kah-dóhsh*, קדש) and the common (*khól*, חול), between light and darkness, between Israel and the peoples [of the nations], between the Sabbath and the six working days. Blessed are you, Lord, who discriminates between the holy and the common.[19]

This means that the age Christians call the Christian era, Jews call the profane era. The term "holy" is reserved for Jerusalem, Palestine, the Jewish priests, the Jewish festivals, Jewish Sabbaths, and the Jewish people.

Shifting the designation from one insult to the other does nothing to reduce hostility. Christians originally called this the Christian era as a confession of faith. Jews called it common, because it was not under the control of Jews. The Hasmonean age was holy in distinction from the common era when Antiochus Epiphanes was ruling Palestine. It seems unnecessary for these offenses to continue. On the one hand Christians do not rule the world and should give up all aspirations to that effect. We might be willing to call the period marked by the calendar "the International Age." Jews, on the other hand, might also give up any goals they might have for acquiring a holy age and be willing to stop calling Christians "common."

First Testament will include the books of the apocrypha. Language references will call the Hebrew text the Masoretic text (MT) and the Greek text the Septuagint (OG). Changing names from "Christian age" (AD and BC) or "common era" (CE and BCE) to "International Age" (IA and BIA) or changing titles like "Old Testament," "Hebrew Scripture," or "Christian Testament" to "First Testament" (FT) will not change any facts of history or literary data, but it might make a small change in the way Christians and Jews treat one another and think of one another.[20]

Conquest theology for both Christians and Jews should be relegated to history. We need another calendar designation. Since the era and the literature belong to all of us—or none of us—we need some neutral, inoffensive names. If the ones suggested here are not suitable, someone should suggest better ones. The

---

[19] The Hebrew text of this prayer is found in S. Singer (ed.), *The Authorized Daily Prayer Book of the United Hebrew Congregations of the British Empire* (London: Eyre and Spottiswoodes, 1900), pp. 216-17.

[20] This is not the first generation to have problems about calendar. See *mGit* 8.5.

only reason "age" is preferred to "era" is that the abbreviation IE might also be confused for *id est*. The abbreviations for historical periods and scriptural texts suggested here will be used in this commentary on an experimental basis.[21]

---

[21] Taken from Buchanan, *Matthew* I, pp. 47-49.

CHAPTER ONE

HEBREW TEXT

1:1 בִּשְׁנַ֣ת שָׁל֔וֹשׁ לְמַלְכ֖וּת יְהוֹיָקִ֣ים מֶֽלֶךְ־יְהוּדָ֑ה בָּ֣א נְבוּכַדְנֶאצַּ֧ר מֶֽלֶךְ־בָּבֶ֛ל יְרוּשָׁלַ֖͏ִם וַיָּ֥צַר עָלֶֽיהָ׃ 2 וַיִּתֵּן֩ אֲדֹנָ֨י בְּיָד֜וֹ אֶת־יְהוֹיָקִ֣ים מֶֽלֶךְ־יְהוּדָ֗ה וּמִקְצָת֙ כְּלֵ֣י בֵית־הָֽאֱלֹהִ֔ים וַיְבִיאֵ֥ם אֶֽרֶץ־שִׁנְעָ֖ר בֵּ֣ית אֱלֹהָ֑יו וְאֶת־הַכֵּלִ֣ים הֵבִ֔יא בֵּ֖ית אוֹצַ֥ר אֱלֹהָֽיו׃ 3 וַיֹּ֣אמֶר הַמֶּ֔לֶךְ לְאַשְׁפְּנַ֖ז רַ֣ב סָרִיסָ֑יו לְהָבִ֞יא מִבְּנֵ֧י יִשְׂרָאֵ֛ל וּמִזֶּ֥רַע הַמְּלוּכָ֖ה וּמִן־הַֽפַּרְתְּמִֽים׃ 4 יְלָדִ֣ים אֲשֶׁ֣ר אֵֽין־בָּהֶ֣ם [כָּל־]מְאוּם֩ [מאום] וְטוֹבֵ֨י מַרְאֶ֜ה וּמַשְׂכִּילִ֣ים בְּכָל־חָכְמָ֗ה וְיֹ֤דְעֵי דַ֙עַת֙ וּמְבִינֵ֣י מַדָּ֔ע וַאֲשֶׁר֙ כֹּ֣חַ בָּהֶ֔ם לַעֲמֹ֖ד בְּהֵיכַ֣ל הַמֶּ֑לֶךְ וּֽלְלַמְּדָ֥ם סֵ֖פֶר וּלְשׁ֥וֹן כַּשְׂדִּֽים׃ 5 וַיְמַן֩ לָהֶ֨ם הַמֶּ֜לֶךְ דְּבַר־י֣וֹם בְּיוֹמ֗וֹ מִפַּת־בַּ֤ג הַמֶּ֙לֶךְ֙ וּמִיֵּ֣ין מִשְׁתָּ֔יו וּֽלְגַדְּלָ֖ם שָׁנִ֣ים שָׁל֑וֹשׁ וּמִ֨קְצָתָ֔ם יַֽעַמְד֖וּ לִפְנֵ֥י הַמֶּֽלֶךְ׃ 6 וַיְהִ֥י בָהֶ֖ם מִבְּנֵ֣י יְהוּדָ֑ה דָּנִיֵּ֣אל חֲנַנְיָ֔ה מִֽישָׁאֵ֖ל וַעֲזַרְיָֽה׃ 7 וַיָּ֧שֶׂם לָהֶ֛ם שַׂ֥ר הַסָּרִיסִ֖ים שֵׁמ֑וֹת וַיָּ֨שֶׂם לְדָֽנִיֵּ֜אל בֵּ֣לְטְשַׁאצַּ֗ר וְלַֽחֲנַנְיָה֙ שַׁדְרַ֔ךְ וּלְמִֽישָׁאֵ֣ל מֵישַׁ֔ךְ וְלַעֲזַרְיָ֖ה עֲבֵ֥ד נְגֽוֹ׃ 8 וַיָּ֤שֶׂם דָּנִיֵּאל֙ עַל־לִבּ֔וֹ אֲשֶׁ֧ר לֹֽא־יִתְגָּאַ֛ל בְּפַתְבַּ֥ג הַמֶּ֖לֶךְ וּבְיֵ֣ין מִשְׁתָּ֑יו וַיְבַקֵּשׁ֙ מִשַּׂ֣ר הַסָּרִיסִ֔ים אֲשֶׁ֖ר לֹ֥א יִתְגָּאָֽל׃ 9 וַיִּתֵּ֤ן הָֽאֱלֹהִים֙ אֶת־דָּ֣נִיֵּ֔אל לְחֶ֖סֶד וּֽלְרַחֲמִ֑ים לִפְנֵ֖י שַׂ֥ר הַסָּרִיסִֽים׃ 10 וַיֹּ֜אמֶר שַׂ֤ר הַסָּרִיסִים֙ לְדָ֣נִיֵּ֔אל יָרֵ֤א אֲנִי֙ אֶת־אֲדֹנִ֣י הַמֶּ֔לֶךְ אֲשֶׁ֣ר מִנָּ֔ה אֶת־מַאֲכַלְכֶ֖ם וְאֶת־מִשְׁתֵּיכֶ֑ם אֲשֶׁ֡ר לָמָּה֩ יִרְאֶ֨ה אֶת־פְּנֵיכֶ֜ם זֹֽעֲפִ֗ים מִן־הַיְלָדִים֙ אֲשֶׁ֣ר כְּגִֽילְכֶ֔ם וְחִיַּבְתֶּ֥ם אֶת־רֹאשִׁ֖י לַמֶּֽלֶךְ׃ 11 וַיֹּ֥אמֶר דָּנִיֵּ֖אל אֶל־הַמֶּלְצַ֑ר אֲשֶׁ֤ר מִנָּה֙ שַׂ֣ר הַסָּֽרִיסִ֔ים עַל־דָּנִיֵּ֣אל חֲנַנְיָ֔ה מִֽישָׁאֵ֖ל וַעֲזַרְיָֽה׃ 12 נַס־נָ֥א אֶת־עֲבָדֶ֖יךָ יָמִ֣ים עֲשָׂרָ֑ה וְיִתְּנוּ־לָ֜נוּ מִן־הַזֵּרֹעִ֛ים וְנֹאכְלָ֖ה וּמַ֥יִם וְנִשְׁתֶּֽה׃ 13 וְיֵרָא֤וּ לְפָנֶ֙יךָ֙ מַרְאֵ֔ינוּ וּמַרְאֵה֙ הַיְלָדִ֔ים הָאֹ֣כְלִ֔ים אֵ֖ת פַּתְבַּ֣ג הַמֶּ֑לֶךְ וְכַאֲשֶׁ֣ר תִּרְאֵ֔ה עֲשֵׂ֖ה עִם־עֲבָדֶֽיךָ׃ 14 וַיִּשְׁמַ֥ע לָהֶ֖ם לַדָּבָ֣ר הַזֶּ֑ה וַיְנַסֵּ֖ם יָמִ֥ים עֲשָׂרָֽה׃ 15 וּמִקְצָת֙ יָמִ֣ים עֲשָׂרָ֔ה נִרְאָ֤ה מַרְאֵיהֶם֙ ט֔וֹב וּבְרִיאֵ֖י בָּשָׂ֑ר מִן־כָּל־הַיְלָדִ֔ים הָאֹ֣כְלִ֔ים אֵ֖ת פַּתְבַּ֥ג הַמֶּֽלֶךְ׃ 16 וַיְהִ֣י הַמֶּלְצַ֗ר נֹשֵׂא֙ אֶת־פַּתְבָּגָ֔ם וְיֵ֖ין מִשְׁתֵּיהֶ֑ם וְנֹתֵ֥ן לָהֶ֖ם זֵרְעֹנִֽים׃ 17 וְהַיְלָדִ֤ים הָאֵ֙לֶּה֙ אַרְבַּעְתָּ֔ם נָתַ֨ן לָהֶ֧ם הָֽאֱלֹהִ֛ים מַדָּ֥ע וְהַשְׂכֵּ֖ל בְּכָל־סֵ֣פֶר וְחָכְמָ֑ה וְדָנִיֵּ֣אל הֵבִ֔ין בְּכָל־חָז֖וֹן וַחֲלֹמֽוֹת׃ 18 וּלְמִקְצָת֙ הַיָּמִ֔ים אֲשֶׁר־אָמַ֥ר הַמֶּ֖לֶךְ לַהֲבִיאָ֑ם וַיְבִיאֵם֙ שַׂ֣ר הַסָּרִיסִ֔ים לִפְנֵ֖י נְבֻכַדְנֶצַּֽר׃ 19 וַיְדַבֵּ֣ר אִתָּם֮ הַמֶּלֶךְ֒ וְלֹ֤א נִמְצָא֙ מִכֻּלָּ֔ם כְּדָנִיֵּ֣אל חֲנַנְיָ֔ה מִֽישָׁאֵ֖ל וַעֲזַרְיָ֑ה וַיַּעַמְד֖וּ לִפְנֵ֥י הַמֶּֽלֶךְ׃ 20 וְכֹ֗ל דְּבַר֙ חָכְמַ֣ת בִּינָ֔ה אֲשֶׁר־בִּקֵּ֥שׁ מֵהֶ֖ם הַמֶּ֑לֶךְ וַֽיִּמְצָאֵ֞ם עֶ֤שֶׂר יָדוֹת֙ עַ֚ל כָּל־הַֽחַרְטֻמִּ֣ים הָֽאַשָּׁפִ֔ים אֲשֶׁ֖ר בְּכָל־מַלְכוּתֽוֹ׃ 21 וַֽיְהִי֙ דָּֽנִיֵּ֔אל עַד־שְׁנַ֥ת אַחַ֖ת לְכ֥וֹרֶשׁ הַמֶּֽלֶךְ׃

Jer 46:2; 2Kgs 24:11

2Chron 36:5-7

Isa 39:7

2Kgs 25:30//Jer 52:34

1Kgs 8:50

TECHNICAL DETAILS

The drama of Daniel is exciting from beginning to end. This collection of miraculous success stories dramatized the life of the Jews in the Middle East after the deportation of Jews from Jerusalem to Babylon. These hero stories were written for the entertainment of religious Jews after the major crises were over. The dramas were well told and nicely organized. For example, Goldingay has correctly observed the following chiastic outline in Dan 1:

Panels	Verses	
1A		*tension* Babylonians defeat Israel
2A	3-7	Young men are taken for training
3(i)A	8	Daniel wants to avoid defilement
3(ii)A	9-14	and takes on a test
3(ii)B	15	*resolution* Daniel is triumphant in the test
3(i)B	16	and avoids defilement
2B	17-20	Young men are triumphant in the training
1B	21	Daniel outlasts the Babylonians[1]

A similar chiastic organization is evident among the chapters 2-7.

This is the beginning of the stories people enjoy reading and hearing over and over again.

ENGLISH TEXT

Daniel	First Testament Intertexts
	Jer 46:2 **Concerning the army of Pharaoh Neco that was alongside the Euphrates River at Carchemish that Nebuchadnezzar, king of Babylon**
1:1 **During the third year of the reign of Jehoiakim, king of Judah,**	defeated, **during the** fourth **year of Jehoiakim**, son of Josiah, **king of Judah**.
Nebuchadnezzar, king of Babylon came to Jerusalem, **and besieged it.**	2Kgs 24:11 **Nebuchadnezzar, king of Babylon, came** against the city, **and** his servants **besieged it** (also Jer 39:1).
²**The Lord gave Jehoiakim king of Judah,**	2Chron 36:5 **Jehoiakim** was 25 years old when he became **king.**
	2Chron 36:6 **Nebuchadnezzar, king of Babylon, came** up against him. He bound him with brass [cuffs], **and**

---

[1] J. E. Goldingay, *Daniel* (Dallas: Word Books, c1989), p. 8.

and some of the vessels of the house of God, into his hand, and he brought them to the land of Shinar, to the house of his god, and he brought the vessels [to] the treasury of his god. made him walk to Babylon, ⁷and some of the vessels of the house of Yehowah Nebuchadnezzar brought to Babylon, and he put them in his palace in Babylon.

^{Jer 20:4} All **Judah I will give into** the **hand** of **the king of Babylon.**

COMMENTARY

The reign of Jehoiakim. **Jehoiakim** was the throne name for Eliakim. Pharaoh Neco renamed Eliakim **Jehoiakim** when he made him king after the death of his father, Josiah (2Kgs 23:34). The name "Eliakim" means "God upholds or makes stand." **Jehoiakim** means "Yehowah upholds or makes stand." The only difference is that Pharaoh made the name of the deity more specific. This seems odd but may suggest that Pharaoh Neco was himself a worshiper of Yehowah and that perhaps the name "Yehowah" was the name of a deity that the Israelites learned from the Egyptians during their exile in Egypt.[2] The other, more likely, possibility is that Pharaoh gave this name to him in derision.

Jehoiakim lived during a tense time. His father had initiated reforms that Jeremiah approved, but, because of his nationalistic activity, the Egyptians killed Josiah at Megiddo and laid a heavy tax on Judah. Pharaoh appointed **Jehoiakim** king because **Jehoiakim** was not in sympathy with his father's reforms, and he was willing to be subservient to Egypt. Consequently he was also in conflict with Jeremiah (Jer 22:13-19, 25; 36). His rule began at 609 BIA. Babylonians drove the Egyptians out of Syria at the Battle of Carchemish (Jer 46:2, 605 BIA), in the first year of Nebuchadnezzar's reign. **Jehoiakim** led a rebellion against the Babylonians (602 BIA). **Jehoiakim** may have been killed in battle when Nebuchadnezzar organized Ammonites, Moabites, and Syrians to attack Judah and put down **Jehoiakim's** rebellion (d. 601 BIA). Babylonians did not invade Judah until 597 BIA.

Nebuchadnezzar came to Jerusalem. This could be rendered "went" **to Jerusalem**, rather than **came**. It is translated **came** here, because it seems more likely that the author of Dan 1 was writing from Palestine than that he wrote while residing in Babylon. The choice of translation depends upon the date and location of the composition.

After his death his brother, Jehoiakin, became king. That was the time when **Nebuchadnezzar** besieged **Jerusalem**. Jehoiakin, then, surrendered to

---

[2] Based on biblical poetry, proper Hebrew names, a fragment of the OG among the scrolls found near the Dead Sea, and Greek transliterations in the works of the church fathers it is certain that the central vowel *oh* or *oo* was not omitted in antiquity when the Tetragrammaton was still pronounced. See further Buchanan, "Some Unfinished Business with the Dead Sea Scrolls," *RevQ* 49-52 13 (1988):411-20. The name was pronounced "Yeh-hoh-wáh" or "Yeh-hoo-wáh," not "Yáh-veh" or "Yáh-way."

Nebuchadnezzar and was taken to Babylon together with his family, servants, and palace officials. This happened during the eighth year of Nebuchadnezzar's reign (597 BIA, 2Kgs 24:11-12).[3]

Dan 1:1 reported the invasion of Judah as if it happened during Jehoiakim's third year as king (606 BIA), which would have been before **Nebuchadnezzar** became king. Jeremiah said that the Battle of Carchemish was fought during Jehoiakim's fourth year (605 BIA), but that was not the year that **Nebuchadnezzar** attacked Jerusalem and took treasures and prisoners. How did the author of Dan 1 become so confused? Part of the problem is intertextual.

The Kings historian reported three times that **Nebuchadnezzar came to Jerusalem**. The first time was when Jehoiakim was king, and it may have been in the year 605 BIA just after he had conquered Carchemish. At that time, he only visited with Jehoiakim, telling him the terms under which Jehoiakim might rule, but **Nebuchadnezzar** did not make any military moves at that time to take any prisoners or treasures back to Babylon. Jehoiakim was pro-Egyptian, and he did not like being subject to Babylon. Jehoiakim acted as **Nebuchadnezzar's** servant for three years, and then he rebelled, and much blood was shed around **Jerusalem** before Jehoiakim died from unreported causes (2Kgs 24:1-7). Jehoiakim was succeeded by Jehoiakin, and it was early in his reign, rather than Jehoiakim's, that Nebuchadnezzar returned to Jerusalem, this time with troops, during **Nebuchadnezzar's** eighth year as king of Babylon (597 BIA). This was the time that **Nebuchadnezzar** took Jehoiakin, his family, palace nobility, treasures, and vessels from the temple.[4]

The Chronicler treated the second trip of **Nebuchadnezzar** to **Jerusalem** as if that which happened to Jehoiakin had all happened eight years earlier to Jehoiakim (2Chron 36:5-7). The third time **Nebuchadnezzar came to Jerusalem**, he overthrew Judah, burned the temple, plundered the treasury, and took 10,000 upper class leaders and crafts people in exile to Babylon (586 BIA). These are all reported in the Kings account (2Kgs 24-25).

The author of Dan 1 chose to follow Chronicles rather than Kings. He may have done this uncritically, or he may not have known the account in Kings as some scholars have suggested. Collins followed Montgomery in concluding that the author was not exact in his calculations and that this is not intended as history but as legend.[5] This is true, but there may have been apologetic reasons for ignoring Kings and accepting the account given by the Chronicler that other scholars have overlooked.

The author of Dan 1 wanted the events he related to be associated with the earliest date possible. This would have been when Jehoiakim was king rather than Jehoiakin, and it would have implied that **Nebuchadnezzar** captured Judah at the same time he defeated the Egyptians at the Battle of Carchemish. The author of Dan 1 was mistaken in some of his initial assumptions, but, whether these

---

[3] The date given by Jeremiah and Kings is confirmed by the Babylonian Chronicle See *BASOR* 143 (1956):28-33; *BA* 19 (1956):50-60.

[4] There are different ways to interpret the data of Dan 1:1-2. For a careful study see M. K. Mercer, "Daniel 1:1 and Jehoiakim's Three Years of Servitude," *AUSS* 27 (1989):179-92.

[5] J. J. Collins, *A Commentary on the Book of Daniel* (Minneapolis: Fortress Press, 1993), p. 133.

mistakes were made accidentally or deliberately, these assumptions were followed in other places in the Book of Daniel. In order to understand the logic of the author, therefore, we will treat the narrative as if **Nebuchadnezzar** had attacked Jerusalem in the year 605 BIA and had taken Jehoiakim, his family, and palace officials prisoners into Babylon at that time. The author wanted the reader to think that 605 BIA was the time Daniel, Hananiah, Mishael, and Azariah were all imported into Babylon. All three of these had priestly names (Ezra 7:1; 8:2; Neh 8:4; 10:2, 6, 23).The reasons for this dating will become evident when dates are studied in Dan 2.

The Lord gave Jeohiakim into his hand. The Book of Daniel began with the mention of two kings: 1) **Nebuchadnezzar, king of Babylon** and 2) **Jehoiakim, king of Judah**. It was evident to all that Nebuchadnezzar was the greater king. It was Nebuchadnezzar who came to Jerusalem, plundered it and took temple vessels to Babylon. This proved to the Babylonians that their god Marduk was greater than the Jews' God. Babylon was the great city that the god, Marduk, created.[6] Nebuchadnezzar plundered Jerusalem, the city of the Jewish God. This should have marked the end of the Jewish religion, as well as their nation. When Jews were defeated so was their God, in the estimation of the Babylonians. Jews, however, believed differently. They thought it was not Nebuchadnezzar or Marduk but the God of Israel who had driven the Jews into the hand of Nebuchadnezzar.

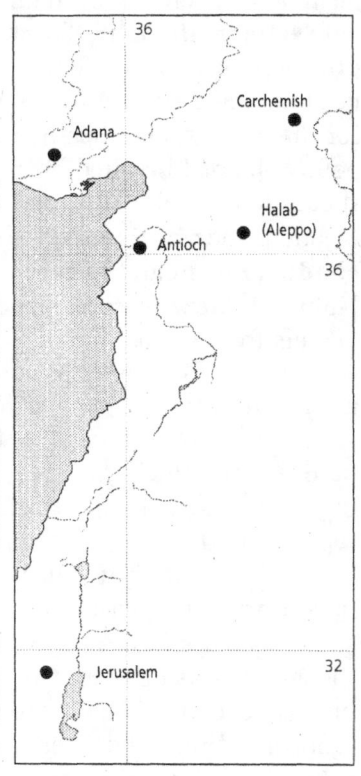

Some of the vessels of the house of God. Temples in most countries of antiquity were not only places of worship. They were national fortresses and also national treasuries. Kings wanted to plunder them to obtain their contents. Temples often had vessels that were used in worship that were made of gold, silver, and were sometimes decorated with precious jewels. Jerusalem was no exception. The Babylonians took these back to their own country--not to smelt for their cash value but to decorate their own temples. They were trophies from war that were treated as museum pieces.[7] The removal of these **vessels** from the Jerusalem temple is reported in 2Chron 36:7, 10, 18 and Jer 52:17-23. **Vessels** are mentioned here in

---

[6] E. A. Speiser (tr.), "The Creation Epic," *Ancient Near Eastern Texts* ed. J. B. Pritchard (Princeton: Princeton U. Press, 1969), p. 68.

[7] The vessels taken from the temple were returned later with the exiles (Ezra 1:7-11).

the introduction to prepare the reader for Dan 5 where **the vessels** receive more attention. **The house of** his **god** and "the treasury of his god" were both the same building.

The land of Shinar. This was an ancient name for an area that initially included Babylon, Erech, and Akkad (Gen 10:10). It is the place where the Tower of Babel was reportedly built (Gen 11:2). A certain king named Amraphel, an enemy of Abram, was from **Shinar** (Gen 14:1, 9). Isaiah prophesied that the Lord would rescue a remnant of his exiled people from **Shinar** (Isa 11:11). Babylon was often identified with **the land of Shinar**. Instead of **Shinar**, the OG has "Babylon." As late as the sixth century Babylon was still called **the land of Shinar**, the place where wickedness was stationed (Zech 5:8-11). (Jer 25:9-11, 18-26; 46:25-26; 2Kgs 24:7).

TEXT

Daniel	First Testament Intertexts
³The king told Ashpenaz, his chief **eunuch**, to bring **some of** the children of Israel—some of the royal children, and some of the nobility--⁴youths who are without blemish, attractive, and learned in all academic disciplines, well educated and informed, and capable of standing **in the palace of the king.**	Isa 39:7 **Some of** your **sons**, who will go out from you, whom you will father, they will take, and they will become **eunuchs** **in the palace of the king** of Babylon

COMMENTARY

His chief eunuch. The chief eunuch was called "Ashpenaz," a Persian name, which means "innkeeper." It could either be a proper name or it could refer to the **chief eunuch's** office. Some of the OG texts took it to be a proper name and translated that into *"Ah-vee-éhz-ree"* (Αβιεζερ = אביעזר. 2Sam 23:27 or אבי העזרי. Judges 8:32) which is a good Hebrew name, meaning "My father has helped" or "my father is a helper." It was transliterated into Greek from some Hebrew text. Most kings in antiquity had **eunuchs** as their most trusted servants. There were no national social security systems in antiquity to provide for people in their old age. Children were commanded to honor their parents by providing them food, housing, and clean clothing in their old age. **Eunuchs**, however, were men who were deprived of children, so they had no posterity to care for them in their old age. Therefore they depended on the favor of the king for their security, and would not dare to disobey him (Herodotus 2.92).

They could also be entrusted with the care of the queens and the kings' harems without anxiety that they would be sexually involved with any of them. Queen Jezebel, for example, had a staff of **eunuchs** (2Kgs 9:32-33). Isaiah warned Hezekiah that his own sons would be taken into bondage to Babylon where they would be made **eunuchs** for the king of Babylon (2Kgs 20:18). Josephus held that some Jewish captives were made eunuchs (*Ant* 10.186), but he may have made that judgment on the basis of Isaiah's prophecy. Some rabbis thought the three friends of Daniel were all **eunuchs** (*bSan* 93b; *Pirke de REliezer* on Isa 39:7; 56:4-5).

King Jeconiah of Judah had his staff of eunuchs (Jer 29:2; 34:19). King Zedekiah did also, one of whom was the general of his armed forces. Nebuchadnezzar took all of these captive (Jer 52:25). If Joseph of Egypt had been made a **eunuch** when he was sold as a slave to Potiphar, Potiphar's wife would not have tried to lure him into sexual activity (Gen 39:6-20). Nehemiah, who was the cupbearer for King Artaxerxes of Persia (Neh 2:1) was probably a eunuch. When his life was in danger, some suggested that he go to the temple for security. He responded, **What man such as I would go into the temple and live** (Neh 6:11). The reason "such a man" as Nehemiah would not enter the temple may have been that **eunuchs** were blemished people who were forbidden by law to come near to the altar (Lev 21:17-20; also Lev 22:24).

Some of the children of Israel. **Israel** is here used generally to include all twelve tribes. Actually only people from Judah were involved. Isaiah had prophesied earlier that the Babylonians would come and plunder Judah. When that happened they would take everything that was in King Hezekiah's house as booty, and they would carry it off to Babylon. They would also take **some of** the king's own sons captive into Babylon where they would become eunuchs and serve in the palace of the king.

The author of Dan 1 took the words of the prophecy and gave them a different turn. The eunuch in the king's palace was Ashpenaz, someone from Persia or Babylon rather than Jewish princes. As Isaiah said, the king of Babylon would take children of Israel, nobles, and princes, captive, but **the children of Israel** who would come to Babylon would not come as servants but as scholars to live in the palace of the king as special guests. Those who stood in attendance of some important person were usually people who offered counsel. They were not household servants. They were people of status (Deut 1:38; 1Kgs 10:8; 12:8).

The children of Israel may be an expression meaning nothing more definite than that they were **Israelites**, or, more accurately, Jews. Most scholars, however, take the word *yeh-lah-déem* (ילדים) to mean "young men." The probable basis for that is that they were young enough to be trained, and Daniel remained in the king's court until Cyrus conquered Babylon (539 BIA). They were included in the introduction so that the readers would recognize them as they appeared in other chapters, especially Dan 3.

During his first invasion of Judah, according to Daniel, Nebuchadnezzar took Jehoiakim and some Jews as captives back to Babylon. There is a mistaken textual support for the capture of Jehoiakim and the confiscation of the temple vessels (2Chron 36:6-7), but there is no other report of other Jews having been taken to Babylon as exiles. During Nebuchadnezzar's first visit to Jerusalem, following his victory at Carchemish, in 605 BIA he took no captives or treasures.

The capture of the king, other Jews, and temple treasures happened only on the second arrival in 598 BIA. The Chronicler made a mistake, so Daniel did, also.

It was after his third invasion (586 BIA) that Nebuchadnezzar took thousands of the Jews to Babylon as exiles, but not all of them. Those he took were the upper class Jews--the nobles, princes, professional people, big business magnates, and skilled crafts people. Those he left were the unskilled lower class Jews. This division of Judah into the rich Jews of Babylon and the poor people of Judah built up a segregationist attitude on the part of the Babylonian Jews that has had a strong influence in later history. When the Babylonian Jews returned to Palestine they did not consider the local people to be long-separated brothers. Instead, they treated them condescendingly and called them the "people of the land," (*ah-máy hah áh-retz*, עמי הארץ) as distinct from themselves who were the "redeemed." They took over the leadership of the country, forced the local Jews to give up their foreign wives and **children**, and in other ways developed an apartheid system between themselves and the local residents.

Without blemish. The implication may be that the young men reported in Dan 1 were qualified for the Jewish priesthood (Lev 22:18-25). That would mean that they were free from any physical deformity and were ritually undefiled. To be that pure they could not have been eunuchs, but since they had been palace servants, rather than temple servants, the likelihood that they were all eunuchs is rather good. The freedom from blemish was probably not as ritualistic as priests would have required. The qualification was made by Nebuchadnezzar and not by the Jewish ritualists. The young men were some of the most competent men in Judah, but they may not have satisfied the priestly requirements designed for those who offer sacrifice in the temple.

S. Paul compared the selection, instruction, and care of servant women taken in captivity in the account of the Mari tablets to the report in Dan 1 of the selection of Jewish youths to serve in the court of the king. The servant women chosen from those who had been brought as booty from captured nations would be selected for their ability, health, and beauty. They had to be free from any disfiguration from the hair of their head to the soles of their feet. They should be talented in weaving, and they should be given further instructions in Mari. Their diet should be controlled to keep them healthy and attractive. The manager in charge of their instruction and well being was responsible to the king.[8] The rules given in the Mari tablets were very similar to those applied to Daniel and his colleagues, according to the report in Dan 1.

TEXT

Daniel	First Testament Intertexts
He should teach them literature and the Chaldean language. ⁵**The king** would	2 Kgs 25:30 // Jer 52:34 For his allotment, he was given

---

[8] S. Paul, "From Mari to Daniel: Instruction for the Reception of Female Servants into the Royal Court," *Eretz-Israel* 24 (1993):161-62 [in Hebrew].

assign for them **a daily allotment, everyday, from the king's** food and wine. He should develop them for three years, and at their completion they should stand before the king. ⁶There were among them, from the Jewish youths, Daniel, Hananiah, Mishael, and Azariah. ⁷The chief eunuch gave them [different] names. He named Daniel Belteshazzar; Hananiah [he named] Shadrach; Mishael [was named] Meshach; and [he named Azariah] Abednego.

a daily allotment from the king, continually **everyday** all the days of his life.

COMMENTARY

He should teach them. Some scholars have argued among themselves about the subject matter of this education. Some said they studied law; others said that would not be so, because the king would not need people to become proficient in law. This assumes that Nebuchadnezzar would have been training them for his own use there in Babylon, but that is not the most likely reason for the education.

This was the earliest forerunner of the English Rhodes scholarships and the American Fulbright scholarships. They were designed to select the most promising leaders of their former enemies and train them in Babylonian science, literature, language, and politics. This was done primarily to reduce foreign hostility. The originators of this program believed that this would develop a pro-Babylonian attitude in all of the Jews of Babylon.

These potential leaders, if left in Jerusalem and not redirected, might lead revolts. Babylonians were probably as successful at this as Rhodes and Fulbright scholarships have been in developing pro-Anglicanism and pro-Americanism among foreign leaders. The exclusivism of Ezra and Nehemiah had been influenced by the religion of Ahura Mazda. Second Isaiah and the Babylonian Talmud were both products of Babylon, and Babylon continued to be the academic center for later Judaism. Ben Sira said that Jewish youths were eager to to become schooled in various sorts of wisdom, so that they might be employed to work with prominent people and be seen with leaders (*Sir* 39:1-4).

According to Daniel, these new recruits all stayed in Babylon, and did not return to Judah immediately after their education. That, however, was to fulfill the Jewish authors' needs for training doctrine rather than Babylon's need for sending leaders back into the distant parts of the empire to propagate Babylonian culture and politics.

Literature and the Chaldean language. Hartman thought the term **Chaldean** here referred to fortune telling or astrology skills rather than learning Akkadian literature and the **language** spoken in Babylon.⁹ He was possibly correct, because the word **Chaldean** was applied both to the people and customs related to the Babylonian area and to a class of priests who also supposedly were trained in the ability to interpret dreams. **Chaldeans** lived in a special quarter of Babylon and were known as native philosophers. Originally **the Chaldeans** had come from a region called Kaldu, southeast of Babylon on the Persian Gulf (Strabo 16.1 #6). Daniel and his friends did, in fact, become trained in arcane skills. It would seem unlikely, however, that people would have been brought to Babylon at national expense to the government just so that they could learn to become priests and astrologers. This was more likely a politically motivated program than one geared to improving psychological or fortune telling skills in foreign youth. Such a program would require all of the students to learn the language spoken in Babylon.

The king's food and wine. The word rendered **the king's food** is *paht bahg* (פת בג), a morsel of **food** or booty. A *paht léh-khem* (פת לחם) is a morsel of bread (Prov 17:1). It was food that the youths were given, and it was given free of charge, like booty. Although the Hebrew meaning of this word makes sense, it is probably derived from the Persian *patibaga*, which means a portion or ration of **food**.¹⁰ This was not ordinary **food.** They were given the best gourmet **food** of Babylon. Three years of this favored treatment was designed to make them realize that they had never had it so good in Palestine. The king assumed that this would enable them to give up their former provincial points of view, their language, ideas about economics, politics, and religion, and embrace the points of view accepted in Babylon. After Jehoiakim's brother, Jehoiakin, was taken captive into Babylon, the Babylonian king had his prison clothes removed, and he was liberated to eat at the king's table every day (2Kgs 25:27-29).

Three years. Three years was a standard length of time allowed for Persian religious training.¹¹

There were among them. Jews were not the only foreigners brought to Babylon. Nebuchadnezzar had expanded his empire extensively, and he needed to form a unity of this large country that had formerly consisted of several small countries with different languages, religions, and political orientations. To do this he would have to train people from all of these different countries to think and speak like Babylonians. He might then allow these Babylonian converts to return to their own countries where their leadership skills might be employed to spread Babylonianism in the local provinces. If they did not return, at least they would be safe in Babylon, where they could not use their leadership skills to lead rebellions against Babylon.

---

⁹ L. F. Hartman and A. A. DiLella, *The Book of Daniel* (Garden City: Doubleday & Co. 1978), p. 129.
¹⁰ So Hartman, *Daniel*, p. 130
¹¹ Prescribed in the Avesta. *Sacred Books of the East* (2d edition; 4.311 ff.). So J. A. Montgomery, *A Critical and Exegetical Commentary on the Book of Daniel* (New York: Charles Scribner's Sons, 1927), p. 122.

The chief eunuch gave them [different] names. This entire scholarship program was intended as a conversion process. It would begin by giving all of the youths Babylonian names. All the rest was expected to follow. They would speak Babylonian, eat Babylonian food, think Babylonian, and worship Babylonian gods. Changing names had a legal significance. After God made a contract with Abram his **name** was changed to Abraham (Gen 17:1-8). After Jacob wrestled with the angel at Peniel the angel gave Jacob a new **name**, Israel (Gen 32:22-28). Pharaoh gave the Jewish king, Eliakim, the name "Jehoiakim" (2Kgs 23:34). When people moved to other countries and became citizens of new countries, they were said to be legally "born again," and they were given new names.[12] When people were taken captive in war they were often made to wear special clothing and change their names to indicate their change of identity. They died legally to their old identity and were born again as different people.[13] This was what was expected to happen to the Jewish young men who had been taken to Babylon.

Daniel, like the other Jews, was given a Babylonian name, Belteshazzar, formed from the god "Bel." It meant "Protect the king's life." Although this was to be Daniel's new **name**, it was mentioned only eight times in the Book of Daniel, whereas the **name**, "Daniel," occurs 70 times. Since Daniel was the Jewish hero, it was necessary to identify him by his Jewish **name**. Azariah was called Abednego, "a slave of the god nego." Hananiah was named "Shadrach" or "Shining." Mischael was called "Meschach,"--"Mithra." Although these Jews accepted their new Babylonian **names** they did not assimilate and become emotional Babylonians. They continued to hold to their Jewish **names** among themselves. That tradition continues until today. Many Jews have two **names**. One is a popular **name** and the other is a traditional Jewish **name**. For example, a Jew who is popularly called "Maurice," among his Jewish friends and family would be called "*Mohshay*," (מושה), Hebrew for Moses. Many Jews who moved from various countries in the world to Israel to become Israeli citizens were renamed when they settled in Israel.

TEXT

Daniel	First Testament Intertexts
[8]Daniel made up his mind that he **would not defile himself** with the king's **food** and wine, so he requested the chief eunuch that he not **be defiled**,	Ezek 4:14 Then I said, "Lord Yehowah, Look! I **have not defiled myself** from my youth." 1Macc 1:63 They accepted death rather than **be defiled** by food.

---

[12] Buchanan, *Biblical and Theological Insights from Ancient and Modern Civil Law* (Lewiston: The Edwin Mellen Press, c1992), pp. 13-15.
[13] O. Patterson, *Slavery and Social Death* (Cambridge: Harvard U. Press, 1982).

⁹and God **gave** Daniel contractual support and **mercy before** the chief eunuch. ^(1Kgs 8:50) **Give** them **mercy before** their captors.

¹⁰The chief eunuch said to Daniel, "I am afraid of my master, the king, who has provided your food and beverage, for why should he see your faces appear more sorrowful than the youths of your age, and [why should you] jeopardize my head to the king?"¹¹ Then Daniel said to the manager whom the chief eunuch set over Daniel, Hananiah, Mishael, and Azariah, ¹² "Test, if you will, your servants for ten days, ¹³and give us some vegetables and let us eat, and let us drink water. Then our appearances will be seen before you and [also] the appearances of the youths who eat the food of the king, and just as you see act with your servants."

COMMENTARY

Daniel. **Daniel** is a *persona* in this play. He did not exist as a real person who really had the experiences attributed to him in this book. The name was taken from a heroic figure known in earlier history. Ezekiel referred to Daniel, Noah, and Job as well-known wisemen (Ezek 14:14; 28:3). There was a later **Daniel**, the son of the priest Ithamar, who went to Babylon in exile (Ezra 8:2). Throughout the Book of **Daniel**, **Daniel** appears as a hero who was famous for his wisdom. The name **Daniel** was chosen for this character in the drama, because he was characterized as a man who was famous for his wisdom. He was like the earlier hero mentioned by Ezekiel.

Many scholars have called Dan 1-6 "court tales." Müller said the dramas of **Daniel** were like the novel of Esther, the stories of Joseph, son of Tobias, Suzanna, Elijah and Elisha, and the martyr legends of early Christianity. He also described the wishful character of **Daniel** as a feelingless person who had no anxiety, hate, or sympathy.[14] Although many scholars have thought of **Daniel** as a book with two kinds of literature, Dan 1-6, and Dan 7-12, Müller noted that the dramas themselves also were eschatological. The eschatological theme began as early as Dan 2. The Drama character of the literature is also present throughout the document. The first drama is played out in Dan 1.

Daniel made up his mind that he would not defile himself.[15] The text does not say what food the king served that was **defiling** or why some food was objectionable. Since pork was part of the Babylonian army's ration, it was probably served also at the palace. Dan 1 was written for a Jewish audience, so the author assumed that everyone knew the problems. Grains and vegetables were not objectionable,

---

[14] H. P. Mueller, "Märchen, legende und Enderwartung," *VT* 26 (1976):339-42.
[15] D. L. Smith-Christopher, *The Book of Daniel* (Nashville: Abingdon Press, c1996), p. 40, apparently confused two Hebrew words. He said, ". . . stating that he would be 'polluted' (גאל, *gah-áhl*) by them. This powerful term is highly suggestive for the exilic and post-exilic experience." The Hebrew word *gah-áhl* can mean either "pollute" or "redeem," depending on the context. It is the word *gah-láh* (גלה) that means "go into exile" and also "reveal," depending on the context.

according to the Torah. Neither were certain kinds of meat, provided that they were properly slaughtered and sacrificed. In antiquity not only Jews and Israelites sacrificed their meat, offering portions of it to their deity. All religions did the same. That means that all meat that was not slaughtered in the name of Yehowah was probably sacrificed in the name of some pagan deity. It was the priests' responsibility to teach the people about the proper and improper foods (Lev 10:10; 11:47; Ezek 44:23). There was also another factor. Eating in the Near East is a symbol of hospitality and acceptance of one another's beliefs and trust. Accepting hospitality places an extensive responsibility on the host and was not either offered or accepted carelessly (Matt 10:6-15).[16]

Hosea warned the North Israelites that Ephraim would return to Egypt and in Assyria they would eat impure food. This would happen because they would be taken away from the land of Yehowah into Egypt and Assyria (Hos 9:3). Hosea assumed that when they left the Promised Land that they would give up their dietary laws and eat the food of the gentiles, which would not be *kah-sháyr* (כשר).[17]. When Evil-merodach became king of Babylon, he released Jehoiakin, former king of Judah, from prison and allowed him to eat at the table of the king all the rest of the days of his life. There is no report indicating that Jehoiakin had any objections to his royal fare at the king's table (2Kgs 25:27-30). That is not true of the hero of the Daniel stories.

For **Daniel**, this was the beginning of the conflict between Judaism and Babylonianism, and **Daniel** chose to draw the line at the outset. **Daniel** was here introduced as the principal hero of the Book of **Daniel**. He was a doctrinal character designed by the author of **Daniel** to teach Jews how they should behave in foreign lands. The first step was to maintain a friendly attitude toward the citizens of the land while holding fast to their convictions and not surrendering any of their Jewish principles. Once this was clear, then the rest of the details would naturally follow. They would not concede Nebuchadnezzar's main goal. They would not become assimilated into the Babylonian way of life. They had left Jerusalem, the city of their God, and had been brought to Babylon, the city of the god, Marduk. They were expected to give up the worship of their God and become worshipers of Marduk. This they refused to do.

The villain in this conflict was Nebuchadnezzar. **Daniel** was the hero. **Daniel** matched off against Nebuchadnezzar as a David-Goliath match. At this point in the game, **Daniel** had decided to take a stand.

There were many other people in antiquity who were named **Daniel** (Ezek 14:14-20; 28:3; 1Chron 3:1; Ezra 8:2; Neh 10:6). These were real people, but the name in the Book of **Daniel** was applied to a character in a play--not to a historical figure.[18]

---

[16] See further Buchanan, *The Consequences of the Covenant* (Leiden: E. J. Brill, 1970), pp. 194-218 and D. Soesilo, "Why Did Daniel Reject the King's Delicacies? (Daniel 1:8),"*The Bible Translator* 45 (1994):441-45.

[17] See *Tob* 1:10-11; *Jub* 22.16.

[18] S. R. Driver, *An Introduction to the Literature of the Old Testament* (Cleveland: World Publishing Co, 1956), pp. 510-511, had no doubt that the Daniel reported in this book was a real historical person. C. F. Keil, *Biblical Commentary on the Book of Daniel* (Grand Rapids: William B. Eerdmans, n.d.), tr. M. G. Easton, p. 32, assumed that the Book of Daniel was written early

The king's food and wine. The first challenge Daniel made seemed like a rather harmless one. He had already, publicly, accepted the Babylonian name, while holding on to his Jewish name, but he refused to eat any food that was not *kah-sháyr* (כשר).[19] At this early stage in confrontation, he did not demand that the **king** serve him meat that had been sold at a Jewish meat market. He would eat at the **king**'s table, as the **king** demanded, and he did not demand that any special food be brought to him and his friends that had been cooked in special dishes. Jews were expected to observe careful dietary laws (*Tob* 1:10-11; *4Macc* 5.3, 14; *Judith* 12:1-2). Instead of calling attention to the conflict involved he dealt in generalities that would protect his specific restrictions. His first request was to the chief eunuch who was in charge of the entire program, and that person refused Daniel's request, since he would be put in jeopardy with the **king** if anything went wrong. Daniel, however, did not give up easily. He next tried a subordinate manager, the one the chief eunuch appointed to be responsible for the Jewish youths. It was the lower officer who consented to the test Daniel proposed. He probably did not find out that the chief eunuch had already rejected Daniel's proposal.

Give us some vegetables. Although the Jews were refugees and guests who were honored to be given the gourmet food of the King, Daniel had the audacity to ask that they give them something different. The word here rendered **vegetables** is *zay-roh-éem* (זרעים), which literally means "seeds." This refers to things eaten that are not flesh, eggs, or milk. It would limit the diet to food raised as crops to be eaten, such as grain products, like bread, cereal, and other baked goods and food cooked, such as beans and other garden produce. It is here translated **vegetables**, because that is a general term for food that is not meat. At a table where both meat and **vegetables** were served, Daniel and his friends would avoid all meats. In that way they would not eat meat offered to idols or meat from fish without scales and fins and animals that did not chew the cud and have cloven hooves. The king's food was all given to the students, free of charge, but Daniel was determined to forfeit none of his nationalistic principles. During the reign of Antiochus, Judas the Maccabee, while living in the wilderness with his troops, provided for them only wild vegetation so that they would not become defiled (2Macc 5:27).

The Jewish youths were permitted by their dietary laws to eat the **vegetables** served to everyone else. If, however they did not abstain from the meat, dairy products, and the king's wine, which would have been offered as a libation offering to a pagan deity, they would have broken Jewish prohibitions.

---

enough so that it was used by the authors of Nehemiah, Ezra, and Zechariah. It is much more likely that the authors of Daniel used these works as sources for this document.

[19] Pronounced *kóh-sher* by Eastern-European Jews. For the Nabonidus Cyrus Chronicle see R. P. Doughtery, *Nabonidus and Belshazzar* (Yale Oriental Series): Barton, *Archaeology and the Bible* (c 20 p Pinches, PSBA 1916, 27ff). Josephus, *Contra Apionem* 1:20; Berossus in Eusebius, *PrepEv.* 1.20; Poetry: Dan 9:2-20 ff; 3:33 (4:3): f:31 ff, 34-35, 6:27-28. Jerome in Porphyry; Saadia Gaon, *Commentary on Daniel*, see Malter, *Saadia Gaon* (1921, p. 325). On the four medals of Hesiod, *Works and Days*, 106 ff (cf. Ovid, Metam., 1.89 ff). Re: Dan 4, Eusebius, *PrepEv.* 9.41.6. J. M. Wills, *A Jew in the Court of a Foreign King* (Minneapolis: Fortress Press, c1990), pp. 35, 79-91. Borosus—*Ant* 10.11,1.

Nebuchadnezzar was playing a subtle game of converting these foreign students to Babylonianism in a step by step program. It began with a name change and continued with Babylonian food. It was an honor to be permitted to eat at the table of the king, and it was considered a royal offense to refuse such an invitation as that. Daniel and his friends were placed in a situation often confronted by Jews who mingle with non-Jews in society.

Daniel reacted just as subtly as the king. He declined only part of the food. He was all set to receive all of the benefits of the king's hospitality that were available free of charge, but he was determined to forfeit none of his national and religious principles.

I am afraid. The chief eunuch had good reason to be **afraid** of his master, the king. Anyone who disobeyed the king might face the death penalty. He could even be tortured to death. The king had designed the program to be followed precisely. The king himself would have known that students who insisted on following their own national customs would not become converted to Babylonianism. The chief eunuch had been misled into thinking the only reason the king had for providing this special food was to be sure that the young men had good health. Jews insisting on the right to follow their own dietary rules were like Scots insisting on wearing their respective tartans, the Irish wearing the green, or the Palestinians waving their own flags during the Intifada. Daniel knew better than to deal with the king on this matter. This was something to be settled on a middle-management level where deception was more nearly possible.

Test, if you will, your servants for ten days. Following the anxiety of the chief eunuch that the only problem was a matter of health, Daniel suggested that a **test** be made **for ten days** to see if that diet caused any health problem. The results would be **tested** only by the young men's appearances. It was a very superficial **test**, and it was the one Daniel suggested rather than the one the chief eunuch might have preferred. Its purpose was to divert attention from the real issue and keep the discussion of loyalty out of the range of the king. All decisions were made on the level of lower management. No one raised the important question of **testing** the young men's loyalty to Babylon or their willingness to accept the Babylonian way of life. This **ten days** expression was a popular intertext for later authors (*Jub* 19.8; *T12Pat, mAboth* 5.4; Rev 2:10).

TEXT

[14]He listened to this argument and tested them for ten days. [15]At the end of ten days their appearances seemed better and their flesh healthier than all the [other] youths who were eating the king's food, [16]so the manager removed their food and the wine from their beverage and gave them vegetables. [17]God gave these four youths knowledge, skills in all academic disciplines, and wisdom, and Daniel became learned in all visions and dreams. [18]At the end of the period which the king designated to bring them, the chief eunuch brought them before Nebuchadnezzar. [19]The king spoke with them, and there was not found in any of

them [scholarship] like [that shown by] Daniel, Hananiah, Mishael, and Azariah, and they stood before the king. [20][In response to] every item of scholarly understanding which the king asked them, they were found ten times better than all of the magicians, men, and enchanters in his entire kingdom. [21]Daniel was [there] until the first year of King Cyrus.

COMMENTARY

Their appearances seemed better and their flesh healthier. This means that the Jewish youths passed the test that was not important. It proved only that people can live very healthily without meat, dairy products, or wine. In recent years westerners have learned that avoidance of meat, dairy products, and alcoholic beverages not only allows human beings to survive, but those who avoid these items of food have fewer heart attacks and do not face the many problems that alcohol causes. The test that was most important was not mentioned. It was the permission given to the Jewish students to maintain their religious practices in Babylon without assimilating into the foreign gentile customs. Of course, it was not the chief eunuch who realized this, but only Daniel and his friends.

The success of this adventure was the fulfillment of Solomon's prayer that when the Israelites are punished by being taken captive into a foreign land that God would give them mercy at the hands of their captors. Ostensibly it was the chief eunuch who had shown mercy to Daniel and his friends, but religiously, it was a sign that God was with his people in a foreign land. According to Daniel, God not only gave them mercy as Solomon's prayer requested. He also gave them contractual support (*khéh-sehd*, חסד). This was important, because Jews believed that when they had been driven out of God's house and off the land, that meant that they had been divorced from God (Deut 24:1), and that God had annulled that treaty. Hypothetically all of these experiences Daniel had with the chief eunuch happened about 605 BIA before the temple had been destroyed (586 BIA). This would mean that Daniel and his friends were still under treaty with God.

God gave these four youths knowledge. The Babylonian king was prepared to **give these four youths** gourmet food and excellent academic training. They refused the gourmet food and asked to be given only vegetables. They concluded that it was **God**, rather than the king, who **gave** them **knowledge** just as it was **God** who **gave** them support from Ashpenaz, and it was **God** who **gave** them into the hand of Nebuchadnezzar in the first place. The king was not given credit either for his military skills and power, the kindness of his officer, or for his own generosity (see further Isa 47).

At the end of the period. This was the three-year **period** that was originally established. It was time for the second test. The first one was of their health; the second test was about their wisdom. Their Jewish names, Daniel, Hananiah, Mishael, and Azariah, were used to remind the readers that they had not given up these names or their Jewish identity, even though the youths had been given Babylonian names.

They stood before the king. It was an honor to be permitted to **stand before a king. Before** a **king** most people prostrated themselves at his feet. If the **king** asked the person to arise and stand, that was a favorable reception. The Proverbial counselor advised students not to put themselves forward so as to **stand before a king** or **before** famous people. Rather they should wait until they were told to come up and **stand** in the presence of noble leaders (Prov 25:6-7). **The king** was the highest judge in the land. He had authority to hurt or favor people as he chose. If a defendant was prostrate before him, and the **king** asked him to **stand**, that was good news. It meant the defendant was about to receive a favorable verdict.[20]

In the case of Daniel and his friends, they were invited to **stand before the king**. They **stood before the king** for examination, or they **stood before the king** as his personal attendants. It is certain that they were examined whether or not they became the personal attendants of **the king** as a result of their success. Of course, the hero and his friends would not have failed any test of intellect. They not only passed the course with flying colors. They excelled all of the students gathered, and they even showed themselves to be ten times as competent as the wisemen and the magicians of Babylon. Chapter 1 of Daniel successfully demonstrated the way Jews might enter a country at the bottom of the social ladder and quickly climb to the top. This experience also showed that the God of the Jews had not been defeated. He could be trusted to deliver his people from danger, and he was in control of history.

Daniel was [there] until the first year of King Cyrus. The Book of **Daniel** begins in chapter one, at the beginning of the exile anticipating the end of the exile when **Cyrus** allowed the Jews to return to the Promised Land. This means **Daniel** remained in the king's court in Babylon until after Nebuchadnezzar died (562 BIA). **Cyrus** conquered Babylon in 539 BIA. The author of this chapter implied that **Daniel** and his three Jewish friends were taken into Babylon at the first time Nebuchadnezzar entered Jerusalem in 605 BIA, although most of the exiles were brought to Babylon in the second invasion (586 BIA). There would have been 66 years between 605 and 539 BIA or 47 years between 586 and 539 BIA In either case **Daniel** would not have been as old as Methuselah, but he would have been an old man by the time **Cyrus** liberated the Jews from Babylon. The text does not say whether Daniel returned to the Promised Land with Ezra and Nehemiah or not.

The author of Dan 1 probably wrote this chapter after all the rest of the Book had been organized. The final editor knew he had stories that included events that were reported to have happened under the rule of Nebuchadnezzar (Dan 2:1; 3:1; 4:1), Nabonidus and Belshazzar (Dan 5:1; 7:1; 8:1), Darius (Dan 6:1; 9:1), and **Cyrus** (Dan 6:29; 10:1). Because these were all centered on **Daniel**, the author reasoned that **Daniel** had to have lived long enough to make all of these stories reasonable.

The symbolic significance of this is that **Daniel** was in competition with Nebuchadnezzar. During that time 1) Nebuchadnezzar did not succeed in

---

[20] Buchanan, *Insights,* pp. 57-58.

assimilating **Daniel** into Babylonian customs, philosophy, or religion. 2) **Daniel** outlasted Nebuchadnezzar, having remained in Babylon 25 years after Nebuchadnezzar's death (562 BIA). 3) Daniel came to Babylon as a captive at the very beginning of the Babylonian exile, and he survived to return to Palestine when **Cyrus** released the Jews in 538 BIA. Daniel and his friends had followed Jeremiah's advice to settle down in Babylon and support the welfare of that city, because they would find welfare in its welfare (Jer 29:7). There is no suggestion that **Daniel** or his friends returned with Ezra or Nehemiah, because the author de-emphasized the sixth century redemption and return to Palestine. The next chapter turns the clock back to **Daniel's** earlier experiences with Nebuchadnezzar.

In this drama **Daniel** and his three friends represented the 10,000 Jews who lived as a strong upper-class minority in Babylon. Nebuchadnezzar, in turn, represented the Babylonian government with all of its national power. The drama reflected the way Jews in Babylon managed the situation. When Nebuchadnezzar brought all of these Jews to Babylon and kept them together, he invited a strong security threat to the nation. When Tiglath-Pileser took the upper class Israelites from North Israel, he avoided that kind of threat by selling the Israelites as slaves and scattering them in other foreign lands. The North Israelites never were able to unify again. The Jews in Babylon, on the other hand, were all organized there in the city of Babylon available to negotiate with **Cyrus** to take over Babylon.

Most scholars and casual readers of the Book of Daniel have been aware of the theme of reversals that appears over and over again in this document.[21] This is evident in Dan 1. At the outset Jews are taken captive to Babylon. That normally proved to people in that area that Marduk, the Babylonian deity, was more powerful than Yehowah, the Jewish God. Marduk had aided Babylonia in conquering Jerusalem and taking the best of its population captive. At the end of the story, the Jews were given high positions in the government and were shown to be superior to the Babylonians in every way. This also proved that it was Yehowah and not Marduk who controlled human affairs. Steps within the chapter were correspondingly reversals. For example, the youths who were expected to become weak, unattractive, and unintelligent because of their diet instead appeared more attractive, healthier, and ten times more intelligent than any of the wisemen of Babylon.

This chapter was designed to set the stage of the drama in which Nebuchadnezzar was the arch villain, and Daniel was the nationalistic hero. The chapter concluded before this last sentence was added, in all probability. Some later editor added this sentence to tell the reader what became of Daniel and to prepare the reader to meet **Daniel** again in the next chapter.

---

[21] For example see Z. Stefanovic, "Daniel, A Book of Significant Reversals," *AUSS* 30 (1992):139-50.

CHAPTER TWO

HEBREW AND ARAMAIC TEXT

2:1 וּבִשְׁנַת שְׁתַּיִם לְמַלְכוּת נְבֻכַדְנֶצַּר חָלַם
נְבֻכַדְנֶצַּר חֲלֹמוֹת וַתִּתְפָּעֶם רוּחוֹ וּשְׁנָתוֹ נִהְיְתָה עָלָיו: 2 וַיֹּאמֶר
הַמֶּלֶךְ לִקְרֹא לַחַרְטֻמִּים וְלָאַשָּׁפִים וְלַמְכַשְּׁפִים וְלַכַּשְׂדִּים לְהַגִּיד   Gen 41:1, 8
לַמֶּלֶךְ חֲלֹמֹתָיו וַיָּבֹאוּ וַיַּעַמְדוּ לִפְנֵי הַמֶּלֶךְ: 3 וַיֹּאמֶר לָהֶם הַמֶּלֶךְ
חֲלוֹם חָלָמְתִּי וַתִּפָּעֶם רוּחִי לָדַעַת אֶת־הַחֲלוֹם: 4 וַיְדַבְּרוּ הַכַּשְׂדִּים
לַמֶּלֶךְ אֲרָמִית מַלְכָּא לְעָלְמִין חֱיִי אֱמַר חֶלְמָא לְעַבְדָיִךְ [לְעַבְדָךְ]   Ps 77:5
וּפִשְׁרָא נְחַוֵּא: 5 עָנֵה מַלְכָּא וְאָמַר לְכַשְׂדָּיֵא [לְכַשְׂדָּאֵי] מִלְּתָא מִנִּי אַזְדָּא   1Kgs 1:31; Neh 2:3
                                                                                                Gen 41:8
הֵן לָא תְהוֹדְעוּנַּנִי חֶלְמָא וּפִשְׁרֵהּ הַדָּמִין תִּתְעַבְדוּן וּבָתֵּיכוֹן נְוָלִי
יִתְּשָׂמוּן: 6 וְהֵן חֶלְמָא וּפִשְׁרֵהּ תְּהַחֲוֹן מַתְּנָן וּנְבִזְבָּה וִיקָר שַׂגִּיא
תְּקַבְּלוּן מִן־קֳדָמָי לָהֵן חֶלְמָא וּפִשְׁרֵהּ הַחֲוֻנִי: 7 עֲנוֹ תִנְיָנוּת וְאָמְרִין
מַלְכָּא חֶלְמָא יֵאמַר לְעַבְדוֹהִי וּפִשְׁרָה נְהַחֲוֵה: 8 עָנֵה מַלְכָּא וְאָמַר
מִן־יַצִּיב יָדַע אֲנָה דִּי עִדָּנָא אַנְתּוּן זָבְנִין כָּל־קֳבֵל דִּי חֲזֵיתוֹן דִּי
אַזְדָּא מִנִּי מִלְּתָא: 9 דִּי הֵן־חֶלְמָא לָא תְהוֹדְעֻנַּנִי חֲדָה־הִיא דָתְכוֹן וּמִלָּה
כִדְבָה וּשְׁחִיתָה הַזְמִנְתּוּן [הִזְדְּמִנְתּוּן] לְמֵאמַר קָדָמַי עַד דִּי עִדָּנָא יִשְׁתַּנֵּא   Gen 41:8
לָהֵן חֶלְמָא אֱמַרוּ לִי וְאִנְדַּע דִּי פִשְׁרֵהּ תְּהַחֲוֻנַּנִי: 10 עֲנוֹ כַשְׂדָּיֵא [כַשְׂדָּאֵי]
קֳדָם־מַלְכָּא וְאָמְרִין לָא־אִיתַי אֱנָשׁ עַל־יַבֶּשְׁתָּא דִּי מִלַּת מַלְכָּא   1Kgs 8:27
יוּכַל לְהַחֲוָיָה כָּל־קֳבֵל דִּי כָּל־מֶלֶךְ רַב וְשַׁלִּיט מִלָּה כִדְנָה לָא   Gen 41:10
שְׁאֵל לְכָל־חַרְטֹם וְאָשַׁף וְכַשְׂדָּי: 11 וּמִלְּתָא דִי־מַלְכָּה שָׁאֵל יַקִּירָה
וְאָחֳרָן לָא אִיתַי דִּי יְחַוִּנַּהּ קֳדָם מַלְכָּא לָהֵן אֱלָהִין דִּי מְדָרְהוֹן   Gen 41:12
עִם־בִּשְׂרָא לָא אִיתוֹהִי: 12 כָּל־קֳבֵל דְּנָה מַלְכָּא בְּנַס וּקְצַף שַׂגִּיא
וַאֲמַר לְהוֹבָדָה לְכֹל חַכִּימֵי בָבֶל: 13 וְדָתָא נֶפְקַת וְחַכִּימַיָּא   Gen 41:13
מִתְקַטְּלִין וּבְעוֹ דָנִיֵּאל וְחַבְרוֹהִי לְהִתְקְטָלָה: פ 14 בֵּאדַיִן
דָּנִיֵּאל הֲתִיב עֵטָא וּטְעֵם לְאַרְיוֹךְ רַב־טַבָּחַיָּא דִּי מַלְכָּא דִּי נְפַק   Gen 24:3; Ezra 1:4
                                                                                                Amos 3:7
לְקַטָּלָה לְחַכִּימֵי בָבֶל: 15 עָנֵה וְאָמַר לְאַרְיוֹךְ שַׁלִּיטָא דִּי־מַלְכָּא   Gen 41:25
עַל־מָה דָתָא מְהַחְצְפָה מִן־קֳדָם מַלְכָּא אֱדַיִן מִלְּתָא הוֹדַע אַרְיוֹךְ
לְדָנִיֵּאל: 16 וְדָנִיֵּאל עַל וּבְעָה מִן־מַלְכָּא דִּי זְמָן יִנְתֵּן־לֵהּ וּפִשְׁרָא   Ps 41:14; 90:2
לְהַחֲוָיָה לְמַלְכָּא: פ 17 אֱדַיִן דָּנִיֵּאל לְבַיְתֵהּ אֲזַל וְלַחֲנַנְיָה   Neh 9:5; Job 12:23
מִישָׁאֵל וַעֲזַרְיָה חַבְרוֹהִי מִלְּתָא הוֹדַע: 18 וְרַחֲמִין לְמִבְעֵא מִן־קֳדָם
אֱלָהּ שְׁמַיָּא עַל־רָזָה דְּנָה דִּי לָא יְהֹבְדוּן דָּנִיֵּאל וְחַבְרוֹהִי עִם־שְׁאָר   Job 12:22; Ps 36:10
                                                                                                Ps 139:12; Amos 5:8
חַכִּימֵי בָבֶל: 19 אֱדַיִן לְדָנִיֵּאל בְּחֶזְוָא דִי־לֵילְיָא רָזָה גֲלִי אֱ רָזָה דָּנִיֵּאל   1Chron 29:20
דָּנִיֵּאל בָּרִךְ לֶאֱלָהּ שְׁמַיָּא: 20 עָנֵה דָנִיֵּאל וְאָמַר   Job 12:16
לֶהֱוֵא שְׁמֵהּ דִּי־אֱלָהָא מְבָרַךְ מִן־עָלְמָא וְעַד־עָלְמָא
דִּי חָכְמְתָא וּגְבוּרְתָא דִּי לֵהּ־הִיא: Gen 41:14

21 וְהוּא מְהַשְׁנֵא עִדָּנַיָּא וְזִמְנַיָּא מְהַעְדֵּה מַלְכִין וּמְהָקֵים מַלְכִין יָהֵב חָכְמְתָא לְחַכִּימִין וּמַנְדְּעָא לְיָדְעֵי בִינָה: Gen 41:12
22 הוּא גָּלֵא עַמִּיקָתָא וּמְסַתְּרָתָא יָדַע מָה בַחֲשׁוֹכָא וּנְהִירָא [וּנְהוֹרָא] עִמֵּהּ שְׁרֵא: Gen 41:25, 28
23 לָךְ ׀ אֱלָהּ אֲבָהָתִי מְהוֹדֵא וּמְשַׁבַּח אֲנָה דִּי חָכְמְתָא וּגְבוּרְתָא יְהַבְתְּ לִי Isa 2:2
וּכְעַן הוֹדַעְתַּנִי דִּי־בְעֵינָא מִנָּךְ דִּי־מִלַּת מַלְכָּא הוֹדַעְתֶּנָא:
24 כָּל־קֳבֵל דְּנָה דָּנִיֵּאל עַל עַל־אַרְיוֹךְ דִּי מַנִּי מַלְכָּא לְהוֹבָדָה לְחַכִּימֵי בָבֶל אֲזַל ׀ וְכֵן אֲמַר־לֵהּ לְחַכִּימֵי בָבֶל אַל־תְּהוֹבֵד הַעֵלְנִי קֳדָם מַלְכָּא וּפִשְׁרָא לְמַלְכָּא אֲחַוֵּא: ס 25 אֱדַיִן אַרְיוֹךְ בְּהִתְבְּהָלָה הַנְעֵל לְדָנִיֵּאל קֳדָם מַלְכָּא וְכֵן אֲמַר־לֵהּ דִּי־הַשְׁכַּחַת גְּבַר מִן־בְּנֵי גָלוּתָא דִּי יְהוּד דִּי פִשְׁרָא לְמַלְכָּא יְהוֹדַע: 26 עָנֵה מַלְכָּא וְאָמַר לְדָנִיֵּאל דִּי שְׁמֵהּ בֵּלְטְשַׁאצַּר הַאִיתָיִךְ [הַאִיתָךְ] כָּהֵל לְהוֹדָעֻתַנִי חֶלְמָא דִי־חֲזֵית וּפִשְׁרֵהּ: 27 עָנֵה דָנִיֵּאל קֳדָם מַלְכָּא וְאָמַר רָזָה דִּי־ Isa 11:9
מַלְכָּא שָׁאֵל לָא חַכִּימִין אָשְׁפִין חַרְטֻמִּין גָּזְרִין יָכְלִין לְהַחֲוָיָה Jer 27:4
לְמַלְכָּא: 28 בְּרַם אִיתַי אֱלָהּ בִּשְׁמַיָּא גָּלֵא רָזִין וְהוֹדַע לְמַלְכָּא Jer 27:6; 28:14
נְבוּכַדְנֶצַּר מָה דִּי לֶהֱוֵא בְּאַחֲרִית יוֹמַיָּא חֶלְמָךְ וְחֶזְוֵי רֵאשָׁךְ עַל־
מִשְׁכְּבָךְ דְּנָה הוּא: פ 29 אַנְתָּה [אַנְתְּ] מַלְכָּא רַעְיוֹנָךְ עַל־מִשְׁכְּבָךְ
סְלִקוּ מָה דִּי לֶהֱוֵא אַחֲרֵי דְנָה וְגָלֵא רָזַיָּא הוֹדְעָךְ מָה־דִי לֶהֱוֵא:
30 וַאֲנָה לָא בְחָכְמָה דִּי־אִיתַי בִּי מִן־כָּל־חַיַּיָּא רָזָא דְנָה גֱּלִי לִי לָהֵן
עַל־דִּבְרַת דִּי פִשְׁרָא לְמַלְכָּא יְהוֹדְעוּן וְרַעְיוֹנֵי לִבְבָךְ תִּנְדַּע:
31 אַנְתָּה [אַנְתְּ] מַלְכָּא חָזֵה הֲוַיְתָ וַאֲלוּ צְלֵם חַד שַׂגִּיא צַלְמָא דִּכֵּן רַב Jer 31:27
וְזִיוֵהּ יַתִּיר קָאֵם לְקָבְלָךְ וְרֵוֵהּ דְּחִיל: 32 הוּא צַלְמָא רֵאשֵׁהּ דִּי־
דְהַב טָב חֲדוֹהִי וּדְרָעוֹהִי דִּי כְסַף מְעוֹהִי וְיַרְכָתֵהּ דִּי נְחָשׁ: 33 שָׁקוֹהִי
דִּי פַרְזֶל רַגְלוֹהִי מִנְּהוֹן [מִנְּהֵין] דִּי פַרְזֶל וּמִנְּהוֹן [וּמִנְּהֵין] דִּי חֲסַף: 34 חָזֵה
הֲוַיְתָ עַד דִּי הִתְגְּזֶרֶת אֶבֶן דִּי־לָא בִידַיִן וּמְחָת לְצַלְמָא עַל־רַגְלוֹהִי דִּי
פַרְזְלָא וְחַסְפָּא וְהַדֵּקֶת הִמּוֹן: 35 בֵּאדַיִן דָּקוּ כַחֲדָה פַּרְזְלָא חַסְפָּא
נְחָשָׁא כַּסְפָּא וְדַהֲבָא וַהֲווֹ כְּעוּר מִן־אִדְּרֵי־קַיִט וּנְשָׂא הִמּוֹן רוּחָא
וְכָל־אֲתַר לָא־הִשְׁתְּכַח לְהוֹן וְאַבְנָא ׀ דִּי־מְחָת לְצַלְמָא הֲוָת לְטוּר Isa 49:23
רַב וּמְלָת כָּל־אַרְעָא: 36 דְּנָה חֶלְמָא וּפִשְׁרֵהּ נֵאמַר קֳדָם־מַלְכָּא: Gen 41:32; Deut 10:17
37 אַנְתָּה [אַנְתְּ] מַלְכָּא מֶלֶךְ מַלְכַיָּא דִּי אֱלָהּ שְׁמַיָּא מַלְכוּתָא חִסְנָא וְתָקְפָּא
וִיקָרָא יְהַב־לָךְ: 38 וּבְכָל־דִּי דָיְרִין [דָאֲרִין] בְּנֵי־אֲנָשָׁא חֵיוַת בָּרָא וְעוֹף־ Gen 41:33-34
שְׁמַיָּא יְהַב בִּידָךְ וְהַשְׁלְטָךְ בְּכָלְּהוֹן אַנְתָּה־הוּא [אַנְתְּ־הוּא] רֵאשָׁה דִּי דַהֲבָא: Gen 41:41
39 וּבָתְרָךְ תְּקוּם מַלְכוּ אָחֳרִי אֲרַעָא מִנָּךְ וּמַלְכוּ תְלִיתָיָא [תְלִיתָאָה] אָחֳרִי
דִּי נְחָשָׁא דִּי תִשְׁלַט בְּכָל־אַרְעָא: 40 וּמַלְכוּ רְבִיעָיָה [רְבִיעָאָה] תֶּהֱוֵא
תַקִּיפָה כְּפַרְזְלָא כָּל־קֳבֵל דִּי פַרְזְלָא מְהַדֵּק וְחָשֵׁל כֹּלָּא וּכְפַרְזְלָא דִּי־
מְרָעַע כָּל־אִלֵּין תַּדִּק וְתֵרֹעַ: 41 וְדִי־חֲזַיְתָה רַגְלַיָּא וְאֶצְבְּעָתָא מִנְּהוֹן
[מִנְּהֵין] חֲסַף דִּי־פֶחָר וּמִנְּהוֹן [וּמִנְּהֵין] פַּרְזֶל מַלְכוּ פְלִיגָה תֶּהֱוֵה וּמִן־נִצְבְּתָא
דִי פַרְזְלָא לֶהֱוֵא־בַהּ כָּל־קֳבֵל דִּי חֲזַיְתָה פַּרְזְלָא מְעָרַב בַּחֲסַף טִינָא:
42 וְאֶצְבְּעָת רַגְלַיָּא מִנְּהוֹן [מִנְּהֵין] פַּרְזֶל וּמִנְּהוֹן [וּמִנְּהֵין] חֲסַף מִן־קְצָת
מַלְכוּתָא תֶּהֱוֵה תַקִּיפָה וּמִנַּהּ תֶּהֱוֵה תְבִירָה: 43 דִּי [וְדִי] חֲזַיְתָ פַּרְזְלָא
מְעָרַב בַּחֲסַף טִינָא מִתְעָרְבִין לֶהֱוֹן בִּזְרַע אֲנָשָׁא וְלָא־לֶהֱוֹן דָּבְקִין
דְּנָה עִם־דְּנָה הֵא־כְדִי פַרְזְלָא לָא מִתְעָרַב עִם־חַסְפָּא: 44 וּבְיוֹמֵיהוֹן
דִּי מַלְכַיָּא אִנּוּן יְקִים אֱלָהּ שְׁמַיָּא מַלְכוּ דִּי לְעָלְמִין לָא תִתְחַבַּל
וּמַלְכוּתָהּ לְעַם אָחֳרָן לָא תִשְׁתְּבִק תַּדִּק וְתָסֵיף כָּל־אִלֵּין מַלְכְוָתָא
וְהִיא תְּקוּם לְעָלְמַיָּא: 45 כָּל־קֳבֵל דִּי־חֲזַיְתָ דִּי מִטּוּרָא אִתְגְּזֶרֶת אֶבֶן
דִּי־לָא בִידַיִן וְהַדֵּקֶת פַּרְזְלָא נְחָשָׁא חַסְפָּא כַּסְפָּא וְדַהֲבָא אֱלָהּ
רַב הוֹדַע לְמַלְכָּא מָה דִּי לֶהֱוֵא אַחֲרֵי דְנָה וְיַצִּיב חֶלְמָא וּמְהֵימַן
פִּשְׁרֵהּ: פ 46 בֵּאדַיִן מַלְכָּא נְבוּכַדְנֶצַּר נְפַל עַל־אַנְפּוֹהִי
וּלְדָנִיֵּאל סְגִד וּמִנְחָה וְנִיחֹחִין אֲמַר לְנַסָּכָה לֵהּ: 47 עָנֵה מַלְכָּא
לְדָנִיֵּאל וְאָמַר מִן־קְשֹׁט דִּי אֱלָהֲכוֹן הוּא אֱלָהּ אֱלָהִין וּמָרֵא מַלְכִין

וְגָלֵה רָזִין דִּי יָכְלָתְ לְמִגְלֵא רָזָה דְנָה: 48 אֱדַיִן מַלְכָּא לְדָנִיֵּאל רַבִּי וּמַתְּנָן רַבְרְבָן שַׂגִּיאָן יְהַב־לֵהּ וְהַשְׁלְטֵהּ עַל כָּל־מְדִינַת בָּבֶל וְרַב־סִגְנִין עַל כָּל־חַכִּימֵי בָבֶל: 49 וְדָנִיֵּאל בְּעָא מִן־מַלְכָּא וּמַנִּי עַל עֲבִידְתָּא דִּי מְדִינַת בָּבֶל לְשַׁדְרַךְ מֵישַׁךְ וַעֲבֵד נְגוֹ וְדָנִיֵּאל בִּתְרַע מַלְכָּא: פ

ENGLISH TEXT

Daniel	First Testament Intertexts

$^{2:1}$During **the second year** of Nebuchadnezzar's kingdom, **Nebuchadnezzar had dreams**;

$^{Gen\ 41:1}$At the end of **two years** Pharaoh had a dream... ^{8}In the morning

his spirit was troubled; and he could not sleep.

his spirit was troubled, and he

^{2}The king **ordered [someone] to call the magicians**, enchanters, sorcerers, and the Chaldeans to disclose his dreams to the king. They came and stood before the king. ^{3}"**I dreamed a dream, and my spirit is troubled** to learn the dream."

asked and called every **magician** in Egypt and all the wise men.

^{4}The Chaldeans **spoke to** the king **in Aramaic**:

$^{Isa\ 36:11}$Please **speak to** your servants **in Aramaic**.

$^{1Kings\ 1:31}$Then Bath Sheba bowed her head to the ground and worshiped the king and said,
"**May** my Lord, David the **king, live for the age!**"

"**King, live for ages!**

$^{Neh\ 2:3}$I said, "**May the king live for the age!** Why should not my face be sad when the city of the graves of my fathers lies in ruins and its gates are consumed with fire?"

Tell the dream to your servants and we will show the interpretation."

$^{Gen\ 41:8}$Pharaoh **told them his dream**,

$^{Ps\ 77:5}$You have seized control of my eyes; I am **troubled**, and I cannot speak.

TECHNICAL DETAILS

Joseph of Egypt set the pattern for Dan 2. Dan 2 is a midrash based on early scripture. In reading Dan 2 the reader will think of the story of Joseph of Egypt in his relationship with the pharaoh, especially as an interpreter of the pharaoh's dreams. This was a normal text for an exegete. Joseph began life in Egypt as a slave. He soon became the highest officer in Egypt, subject only to the pharaoh. Joseph's family moved to Egypt and became very prosperous at first. Later they were in conflict with the government and spent many years enduring treatment that they considered slavery.

Israelites remembered Egypt and described it in terms of captivity and exile. Jews thought of Babylon as an antitype of Egypt. The cycle of time had turned around so that Jews were in the same position in the cycle as the Israelites had been when they were in Egypt. Since there was an Israelite in Egypt who rescued the Israelites by his wisdom, there must have been some character in Babylon who played the same role. This is the way Jews thought time progressed. It moved in cycles.[1] That which had happened before would happen again. Therefore it was reasonable to deduce from one cycle the unknown events of another cycle. The new Joseph in Babylon was called "Daniel." There probably never was a historical person in Babylon who functioned as this Daniel did, because this Daniel originated in the mind of the exegete who composed this midrash on Gen 41.

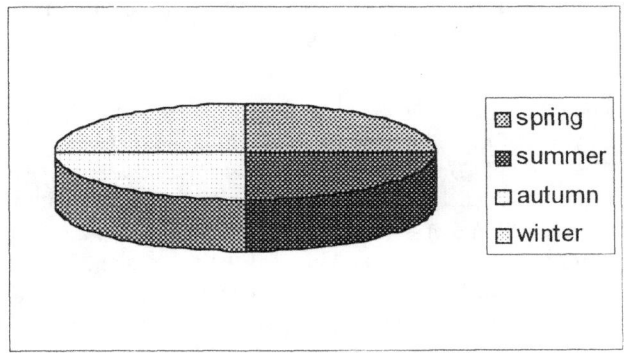

In order to understand the logic of the author of this chapter it is necessary to realize that the author, like most people of his day and location, thought in terms of cycles and typology. It was normal for ancients to think of time as moving in cycles, rather than in a horizontal line, as many modern theologians

---

[1] R. E. Murphy, "History, Eschatology, and the Old Testament," *Continuum* 7 (1969/70):593, said, "The cyclic concept of history involved in the Old Testament actualization of the saving events of the past is not only biblical, but presently viable, in the light of historic Israelite and Christian practice." See also M. Eliade, *Cosmos and History*, tr. W. R. Trask (New York: Harper, 1959), and Buchanan, *Jesus the King and his Kingdom* (Macon: Mercer U. Press, c1984), pp. 253-83.

affirm without evidence.² Ancient Greeks, Jews, and most other ancient peoples knew days followed nights in regular sequence. Furthermore weeks and months began and ended systematically, one after another. Time never ended; it just cycled. They knew that night followed every day, and they could plan for it. In the same way they knew that seasons recurred, year after year, in predictable fashion--spring, summer, autumn, and winter. They always fit into a circle.

They presumed that ages did the same. Therefore they studied earlier periods of history to learn when ages began and ended. When Jews came to Babylon as captives, they related their experience to that which had happened before in Egypt. Since they knew what had happened in the Egyptian age, they expected the same events to occur again in the Babylonian age. Even though they were treated very well in Babylon, they described this experience as if it were the same kind of slavery they read about in Egypt. Therefore they called it "captivity," even though they were allowed to amass wealth, hold positions in the government, and own houses. They called it a bad experience and wanted it to come to an end. The end which they anticipated while they were in Babylon was the end of the exile, just as it had happened in Egypt.

They thought there would be another return to the Promised Land, at the predestined time. The Jews would again go through the wilderness, where miracles would be performed just as there had been before (Isa 35). On the basis of a known past, they attempted to prophesy the future. Since in Egypt, there had been a Hebrew who associated with the king, who had been able to interpret dreams, there must have been one in Babylon, as well. The Babylonian age was the antitype of the Egyptian age, which was the corresponding earlier type. Therefore there had to be a Daniel, just as there had been a Joseph. This is a brief survey of the concepts on which the Book of Daniel was written. Placed in a horizontal time line, the times involved are these:

---

[222] For example, O. Cullmann, *Christ and Time*, tr. F. V. Filson (Philadelphia: Westminster Press, 1950), pp. 52, 61-63, was only one of many biblical scholars who thought Jewish time was linear. For a list of others see G. W. Trompf, *The Ideas of Historical Recurrence in Western Thought* (Berkeley: University of California Press, 1979), pp. 117-18. Cullmann agreed with most scholars that the words for age, *oh-láhm* (עולם) and *aye-ohn* (αἰών), were both names that referred to units of time, but he also agreed with most scholars in thinking that the expression, "into the age" (*aystáwn aye-ôh-nah*, εἰς τὸν αἰῶνα) meant "eternity." Cullmann held, however, that "eternity" meant "endless time" rather than the trans-temporal Greek ideal of eternity. He was partly right. He concentrated on the temporal aspect of this term which means "age." *Oh-láhm* almost never means anything spacial, such as "world." He was mistaken in thinking that time ever spiraled up into eternity in ancient Jewish or Greek thought. Greeks thought that time cycled both in heaven and on earth and that the way time cycled on earth is a reflection of the way it cycles in heaven. S. B. Frost, "Eschatology and Myth," *VT* 2 (1952):70, 76, said nothing follows the eschaton, and that the term "eschatological" should be reserved for the expectation of the end of history. J. Muilenburg, "The Biblical View of Time," *HTR* 54 (1961):234, thought time was linear but not straight.

Ancients learned from the seasons the way time cycled. Summer was always followed by autumn, which was followed by winter, then spring, and back to summer again. It did not go on and on, *ad infinitim*. Because this was so, Jews planned feasts to coincide with seasons, and they expected them to recur every year. The days of the week followed in a sequence of seven, after which the first day of the week appeared again. In the same way there were cycles of Sabbath years and Jubilee years.

ca. 1400 BIA Joseph-------------------------ca. 1,000 BIA Temple
ca. 605 BIA Daniel---------------------------ca. 164 BIA Hanukkah

1400   minus 1,000 = 400
605   minus   164 = 441

The lengths of these periods are close enough to be thought provoking. Since the dates for Joseph are only approximate, they might be reconstructed and estimated favorably. For instance, why not conjecture that his era in Egypt began at 1,441 BIA? The reason is another text. In Gen 15:13, it said that Jews would be in Egypt for 400 years. Religious dogmaticians have little trouble making adjustments to make the text fit the circumstances. Although restrained by the text of Gen 15:13, it is by such reasoning that the author of Dan 2 had the Babylonian exile begin at 605 BIA rather than 586 BIA. He might also have followed Exod 12:41 rather than Gen 15:13. That would allow for a 430 year period in Egypt. Bultmann was mistaken in thinking that the idea of two aeons replaced the concept of cyclical periods.[3] Like other ancients Jews believed time moved in cycles, but they also believed every cycle was divided into two aeons or ages. One of these was controlled by the gentiles, and the other was one in which Jews were independent in their own land. Placed in cycles, the time periods would look like this:

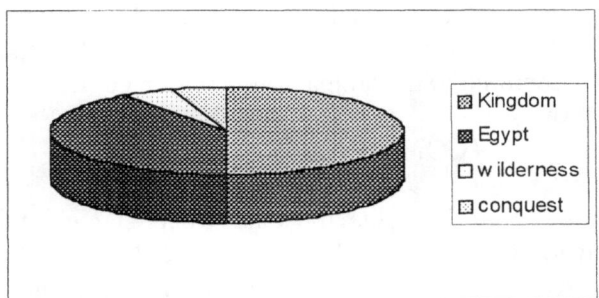

The point between the conquest and the kingdom is about 1,000 BIA. That is the time when Solomon dedicated the temple. The point at the end of the kingdom is 586 BIA when the Davidic-Solomonic kingdom was ended and the Babylonian Captivity began. The new cycle, that followed the Egyptian cycle, was expected to imitate the Egyptian cycle in important details. The difference was that it began later, just as summer came later in the year than spring. Instead of beginning at the beginning of the Israelite experience in Egypt, it started at the beginning of the Jewish experience in Babylon. This began with Daniel in Babylon at 605 BIA. At the bottom of the circle, the point between the kingdom and the exile is 586 BIA. This was the judgment day when the Davidic-Solomonic kingdom came to an end and the Babylonian Captivity began. At that time the temple was destroyed. The point at the end of the war is 164 BIA. That marks the restoration of the temple and

---

[3] R. Bultmann, *The Presence of Eternity* (New York: Harper and Brothers, 1957), p. 29.

the beginning of the Hasmonean kingdom. That is the typological equivalent of the dedication of Solomon's temple in the Egyptian cycle. The treaty with Antiochus IV began about 171 BIA. The war began about 3½ years later (ca. 168 BIA).

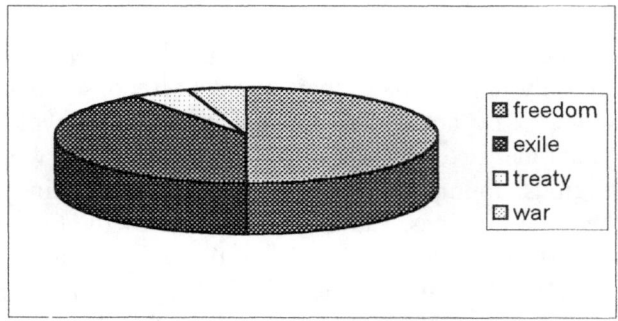

The war lasted about 3½ years before the rededication of the temple at Hanukkah. From a typological point of view the two 3½ year periods are the equivalent of the two 40-year periods in the Egyptian cycle, described as the wilderness and the conquest of Canaan. The author of Dan 2 dealt with extensive periods generally, but he provided very little to show what happened in Jewish or Samaritan history from the time of Ezra and Nehemiah until the Hasmonean Revolt. The author further deduced more than he reported facts. Joseph had prophesied the events of Egyptian economy for 14 years. Daniel, on the other hand, "prophesied" events that would happen 441 years later, according to the drama as it is presented in Dan 2.

COMMENTARY

During the second year[4]. Dan 1:1 gave the date when Daniel and his friends supposedly were taken to Babylon from Jerusalem. Dan 2:1 gave the date when Nebuchadnezzar supposedly had a dream. Both dates were designed to meet the needs of the dramas involved rather than the historical facts. According to Dan 1:1, Nebuchadnezzar invaded Jerusalem during the third **year** of Jehoiakim's reign. That would have been 606 or 605 BIA. At that time Daniel was taken prisoner to Babylon. There he was trained for three **years** before he passed all of his tests and became recognized as a competent scholar. This would be at least as late as 602 BIA. Nebuchadnezzar, however, did not become king until 605 BIA, which means he invaded Judah either before he became king or during his first **year**. During his **second year** (604-603 BIA), Daniel was already reported as a prominent leader in Babylon, before his three **years** of training were completed. These dates do not cohere, and this suggests that Dan 1 and Dan 2 originated separately and were not made to fit one another perfectly, but both chapters presume that Daniel was taken to Babylon in the year 605 BIA.

---

[4] Josephus (*Ant* 10.10, 3) said that the second year mentioned here was after the sack of Egypt.

This 11-verse passage (Dan 2:1-11) is a midrash based on an eight verse passage from Genesis (Gen 41:1-8). The new king was Nebuchadnezzar rather than Pharaoh. The midrash began, like the text in Genesis with reference to **two years**. There was not a scribal error here where the ten dropped out. It was not intended to read "twelve **years**," as some have suggested, because there was no number twelve in Gen 41. The author of Daniel gave the number two here to give the reader the clue to his intertext. Because this date was taken completely from Genesis, it is clear that it had no direct historical value.

Nebuchadnezzar had dreams; his spirit was troubled. The word for **troubled** is *hit-pah-áym* (התפעם). It means being struck or tossed. **His spirit** was being attacked and disturbed. These words applied to Nebuchadnezzar are the very words associated with Pharaoh. The only change was the name of the monarchs. The author of Dan 2 reasoned that Nebuchadnezzar must have **had dreams**, and **his spirit** must have been **troubled** because that was true of Pharaoh. Daniel's report was more complicated. Nebuchadnezzar **had** more **dreams** than one, and he was not able to remember them. Therefore the Daniel exegete did not give a corresponding passage to parallel Pharaoh's **dream**. He moved immediately to the action of the king following the **dream**. Ancients had magic ways of dealing with **dreams**.

> If a man has had a dream and cannot [remember it] he shall wash his hands with soap in his bed before he sets his foot on the floor then he shall recite (this) conjuration three times and he will be lucky.[5]

Another way to protect himself from a forgotten **dream** was to cut a piece from the right side of his garment and stand in front of a lamp. Then he should say a certain prayer to the god Nusku, asking that if **the dream** was good that the dreamer might benefit from it, but if, it was something evil, he prayed that it might be removed from him, just as the cloth was removed from his garment. He could also emphasize the distance of the removal by taking one reed from a bundle, reminding the deity that the reed could no longer be replaced into the bundle in the place where it was.[6]

Rabbis said that if you **had a dream** and could not remember it you should stand before the priests. Then the priests should spread out their hands, and the dreamer should say,

> Master of the age, I am yours and my dreams are yours. I have had a dream, and I do not know what it is . . . If they are good, hold them and strengthen them, like the dreams of Joseph. If, however, they require healing heal them as the waters of Marah at the hands of Moses our master and as Miriam [was healed] of her leprosy, and as Hezekiah from his illness, and as the waters of Jericho [were sweetened] at the hands of Elisha, and as the curses of

---

[5] A. L. Oppenheim, *The Interpretation of Dreams in the Ancient Near East* (Philadelphia: The American Philosophical Society, 1956), p. 300.

[6] Oppenheim, *Dreams*, p. 298.

wicked Balaam were changed into blessing, thus change all of my dreams to good things for me (bBer 55b).

If a man had a bad dream he could avoid its evil consequence by saying, before he set his foot on the floor in the morning: "The dream I have had is good, good, verily good before Sin and Shamash!" In this way he makes a good *egirrû* for himself and evil of his dream will not happen.[7]

Since the narrative of Dan 2 was based on scripture, the author did not think of himself as a fiction writer. Based on the accepted rules of Jewish rhetoric, that which happened in Egypt must have happened in Babylon.

He could not sleep. Following the OG **sleep left him** (*kai haw héep-naws ow-toó eh-géh-neh-tah ahp ow-tóo*, καὶ ὁ ὕπνος αὐτοῦ ἐγένετο ἀπ' αὐτοῦ.)

Ordered [someone] to call the magicians. The word rendered **magicians** *(khar-too-méem,* חרטמים*)* meant "writers," originally. This put them in a class of scribes. In the Genesis account, the pharaoh ordered **the magicians** and all the wisemen **to be called**. The author of this chapter of Daniel interpreted **magicians** to be a general heading under which are classified **the magicians**, the enchanters, sorcerers, and the Chaldeans. This list constituted **all the wisemen,** mentioned in Gen 41. The enchanters (*ah-shah-phéem,* אשפים) were "purifiers," probably those who were able to perform the liturgies necessary to remove ritual defilement. The word translated "sorcerers" here are the *meh-kásh-uh-féem* (מכשפים). They are probably the same group of people referred to in Deuteronomy by the same name (Deut 18:10; Jer 27:9; Mal 3:5).

In all cases they were forbidden existence among the Israelites and were assured of negative divine judgment. Israelites were probably warned against them, because they were foreign and might lead Israelites away from their tradition. These three groups would have been the professional wisemen of Babylon. The Danielic exegete thought this was what the Genesis author had in mind when he said **all the wisemen**. **Magicians** were priests both in Egypt and in Babylon (Herodotus 1.132, 139). Chaldeans in Babylon were also priests (Herodotus 1.181-83).

The wisemen both of Egypt and Babylon were professional people who claimed to be able to interpret dreams. Both **magicians** and Chaldeans were priests. Perhaps the members of these professions were similar to the modern psychologists, psychiatrists, and psychoanalysts. Some of these were probably members of professions like those who reportedly came to Bethlehem from the East to see Jesus after he had been born (Matt 2:1). Many ancients believed that dreams were media through which God spoke to human beings. Therefore it was important to remember dreams and to be able to interpret them. Some rabbis also professed to interpret dreams. Others argued that dreams were only emotional reactions to daily activities. Daniel, Hananiah, Mishael, and Azariah were among

---

[7] Oppenheim, *Dreams*, p. 300.

the wisemen of Babylon, and Daniel was especially distinguished as being able to interpret dreams and visions.

The Chaldeans spoke to the king in Aramaic. At one time the term **Chaldeans** referred to people from a region in the East near Babylon. Later they were known as scholarly priests (Herodotus 1.171; Diodorus Siculus 1.4). They were some of the wisemen in Babylon. According to Strabo they lived in a special quarter of the city of Babylon (Strabo 15.1, 6).

This is an exceptional example of a literary expression. Normally people honored kings **in Aramaic** by **speaking** "before them" rather than **to** them as here (Dan 1:4). These were the last words written in Hebrew in the entire Book of Daniel until Dan 8, when Hebrew was begun again. Dan 2-7 that followed consists of a literary unit formed by a chiasm. That unit was composed in **Aramaic**. Scholars have conjectured that the entire book was originally written in either **Aramaic**[8] or Hebrew, but no one can know for sure. The only fragments of Daniel that were found among the Dead Sea Scrolls were written in the same language as the Masoretic Text (MT), with the Hebrew portions in Hebrew and the **Aramaic** portions in **Aramaic**. One fragment consists of part of Dan 2:2-6. Dan 2:2-3 is in Hebrew, and Dan 2:4-6 is in **Aramaic**. Dan 3:22-28 is also in **Aramaic** (*1QDan* 71-72). Dan 8:20-21 (*6Q* 1); Dan 10:8-16 (*6Q*2-5); and 11:33-36 (*6Q* 6-7), however, although very fragmentary, are clearly in Hebrew. The word **Aramaic** seems to be a later gloss. It does not occur in *1Qdan^a*. It was probably added originally in the margin of the text to alert the reader that from this point on, the narrative would be in **Aramaic** rather than Hebrew.[9] **Aramaic** was a language spoken in Babylon (Xenophon, *Cyrop* 7.5) and probably in most of the Near East. Scholars formerly thought that **Aramaic** was the only language spoken in Palestine, but the number of Hebrew documents found among the Dead Sea Scrolls has changed that assumption.

King, live for ages! An **age** was a unit of time, usually determined by the events that occur in it. For example, there was the **age** of the Egyptian exile, the **age** of the wilderness, the **age** of the conquest, etc. Sometimes ages were defined by rulers, such as the **age** of David or of David and Solomon. The rule of Nebuchadnezzar might be called the **age** of Nebuchadnezzar, but the greeting hoped that he would live for many **ages**. This was a greeting of deference often used to address kings.

Tell the dream to your servants. Since the pharaoh **told** his **dream** both **to** the wisemen of Egypt and **to** Joseph, this was part of the text on which the exegete chose to comment. He chose, however, to make the task more difficult than the pharaoh had done. This would demonstrate that Daniel was even wiser than Joseph of Egypt.

---

[8] R. H. Charles, *A Critical and Exegetical Commentary on the Book of Daniel* (Oxford: Clarendon Press, 1929), pp. xxxvii-l, argued strongly for an Aramaic original.

[9] There are also small fragments; some of which include the name Daniel, but they are too fragmentary to shed light on the Book of Daniel itself. See J. J. Collins, "Pseudo-Daniel Revisited," *RevQ* 17 (1995):111-35.

The professional interpreters of dreams who gathered around the pharaoh of Egypt had been told the pharaoh's **dream**, but they had not been able to interpret it. The Babylonian **dream** scholars were not even told what **the dream** was. Nonetheless, they were required to tell the king what **the dream** was that he could not remember and also tell him what it meant. They objected. This was more than any interpreter of **dreams** was expected to do. If the king would just tell them the dream, as Pharaoh had done, they were confident that they could interpret it.

TEXT

⁵The king answered and said, "The word from me is publicly known. If you do not disclose to me the dream and its interpretation you will be cut into pieces and your houses will be made a dunghill. ⁶If, however, you show the dream and its interpretation, you will receive gifts, presents, and great honor from me. Therefore, show me the dream and its interpretation." ⁷They answered a second time, "King, tell the dream to your servants, and we will show you its interpretation." ⁸The king answered and said, "I know for sure that you are trying to gain time, because you see that the word from me is publicly known ⁹that if you do not disclose to me the dream there is but one sentence for you. You have agreed to speak deceptive and destructive words before me until the times change. Therefore, tell me the dream, and I will know that you can show me its interpretation."

COMMENTARY

The word from me is publicly known. This means it cannot be withdrawn. It has been announced; people know it. This probably means that the town crier had already announced it through the streets of the city. There is nothing equivocal about it. No one needs to ask any more questions about it. It is like the laws of the Medes and the Persians that cannot be changed. No amount of pleading or negotiating will modify the declaration. According to Bevan, the word translated **publicly known** comes from the Persian and means "certain" or "sure."[10]

You will be cut into pieces. This is the impulsive way many ancient monarchs behaved. There was no superior power that could limit the damage they might do to citizens. It is only necessary to read Sutonian's *The Lives of the Caesars* to find examples of kings as inhumane as Nebuchadnezzar is presented. When David became king of Israel he had seven of Saul's sons killed. Herod had even his own family members killed. When the Median king, Astyges, learned that one of his most trusted servants, Harpagus, had disobeyed him, he invited Harpagus to a banquet, where all other guests were served lamb. Unknown to Harpagus, Astyges had had Harpagus' son killed and cooked as if it were lamb. After all had dined, Astyges asked Harpagus if he had enjoyed his meal. When he said he had, Astyges had the servants bring the rest of the parts of his child to the table—all cooked just as

---

[10] A. A. Bevan, *A Short Commentary on the Book of Daniel* (Cambridge: University Press, 1892), p. 68.

that which he had eaten. Harpagus had no choice but to respond to the king in a complimentary way (*Herodotus* 1.119).

In the author's judgment, Nebuchadnezzar was crueler and less reasonable than Pharaoh was, and the author had stronger negative feelings against Nebuchadnezzar than against Pharaoh. The period he was covering in his exegesis dealt primarily with the Babylonian exile. For him the Egyptian exile was only an intertext. He concentrated, however, on the cruelty of the Babylonian king. Just as Daniel was the hero of this drama, so Nebuchadnezzar was the arch villain. Coxon asked rhetorically,

> What is it, for example, that makes *Paradise Lost* a riveting read over against *Paradise Regained*? Imagine the tedium of reading "Snow White" without the witch, or "Little Red Riding Hood" without the wolf, "Cinderella" without the malignant sisters, and "Robin Hood" without the Sheriff of Nottingham! Wouldn't the architectural splendour of the creation story be asymmetrical without the snake? And in the case of the court tales, do not the activities of Daniel and his colleagues hold our interest because of the negative charge transmitted by the King of Babylon? The stories would be lacklustre without him.[11]

According to the text, Pharaoh offered rewards; whereas Nebuchadnezzar also threatened with fatal punishments. Since this document is more doctrine than history, it is not possible to learn from the Book of Daniel alone how cruel Nebuchadnezzar actually was in comparison to Pharaoh. Since Nebuchadnezzar was the king that took the Jews into Babylon as prisoners, he was chosen as the villain for most of the dramas in the Book of Daniel. But even in the Book of Daniel this villain appears, not only cruel, but also generous and fair. Sometimes it was his advisors who were the real villains with Nebuchadnezzar emerging as the just king. He even showed respect for the God of the Jews.

You are trying to gain time. The king recognized that the wisemen were stalling. They were **trying to** distract the king into a lengthy discussion in the hope that he might later soften his mood and his action.

TEXT

Daniel	First Testament Intertexts
[10]The Chaldeans answered before the king and said, "**No one** on earth **is able to interpret** the word of the king, for no great king or ruler has asked such a question as this of any magician, enchanter, or Chaldean. [11]The matter which	Gen 41:8 But there was **none of them** who **was able to interpret** for Pharaoh.

---

[11] P. Coxon, "Nebuchadnezzar's Hermeneutical Dilemma," *JSOT* 66 (1995):87.

the king asks is difficult, and **there is no one else who can interpret** it before the king except **the gods** whose **living** is not with flesh."   ¹Kgs 8:27 Will **God** truly **live** on the land?

COMMENTARY

Answered before the king. In proper etiquette, ordinary citizens did not speak "to" a king. They spoke **before** him, but there are a few places in Daniel where an address was made "to" a king (Dan 2:4). The situation which the speech suggests is that anyone who spoke to a king came **before** him while he was seated on the throne.

No one on earth. This claim was more extensive than Gen 41 noted. The Joseph story noted only that none of the wisemen in Egypt could interpret the dream. The Babylonian wisemen, however, objected because the king asked more than any king in the world had a right to expect of wisemen. The irony was that the assignment which seemed impossible to the wisemen of Babylon was possible for Daniel.

Except the gods whose living is not with flesh. This text was based on the question in Genesis, "Will God **live** on the land?" The author of Daniel, however, did not present this as a question. Gods did not **live** in human **flesh**; this was a fact. The author used this firm statement, however, to introduce the discussion that would follow in relationship to Daniel.

The matter which the king asks is difficult. It was a hard question. The implication is that it was too hard. Kings should not expect this much of professional advisers.

TEXT

Daniel	First Testament Intertexts
	Gen 41:9 The chief butler spoke to Pharaoh, saying, "I remember my sin today."
¹²Then **the king became** angry and very **furious** and he ordered all of the wisemen of Babylon to be destroyed. ¹³The decree went out, and the wisemen were being killed, and they looked for Daniel and his friends so that they could be killed. ¹⁴Then Daniel responded courteously with counsel to Arioch, **chief executioner** of the king, who had gone out to kill the wisemen of	¹⁰ **Pharaoh became furious** with his servants, and he put me and the chief baker under guard in the house of the chief executioner. ¹¹He and I both had dreams the same night, each one according to the interpretation. ¹²There is with us a young Hebrew slave belonging to the **chief executioner**. We told him and he interpreted for us our dreams, he

Babylon. ¹⁵He answered and said to Arioch, "Why is the decree from before the king so severe?" Then Arioch made known the matter to Daniel. ¹⁶Then Daniel went up and requested of the king that he be given an appointment with him and he would show the **interpretation** to the king. ¹⁷Then Daniel went to his house, and the matter became known to Hananiah, Mishael, and Azariah, his friends, ¹⁸so that they might request mercy from **before the God of Heaven**

concerning this **mystery**, so that Daniel and his friends might not be destroyed with the rest of the wisemen of Babylon. ¹⁹Then [the solution to]

the mystery was **revealed to** Daniel in a vision to Daniel in the night.

interpreted each according to his dream.

¹³ and just as he **interpreted** for us it happened."

Neh 1:4 I fasted and prayed **before the God of Heaven.**

Gen 24:3 I will make you swear by **the God of Heaven** and of the land.

Amos 3:7 The Lord Yehowah does not do any thing unless he **reveals his secret to** his servants, the prophets.

COMMENTARY

The king became furious. The Danielic exegete was still following the intertext of Gen 41. Since Pharaoh was reported to have **become furious**, it was necessary for Nebuchadnezzar also to have **become furious**. The Danielic exegete then explained in detail the reason for **the king's fury** and the results of his anger. This was done homiletically. The pharaoh's **fury** did not follow with fatal punishments destined for the wisemen, but Nebuchadnezzar's **fury** resulted in threats. The author assumed that this was the kind of action one might expect from a **king's fury**.

The chief executioner. Some scholars object to this translation, arguing that it should be rendered "chief cook," "butcher," or "body guard." The officer who was given this name may have had some other responsibilities, such as managing the prison. The author of Dan 2, however, understood the office to be that of carrying out capital punishment, and his exegesis shows that this officer was the one who would be responsible for carrying out the king's orders of executing the wisemen.

The chief executioner in Genesis was the person who happened to be in charge of the prison where Joseph was held. His vocation had nothing to do with the king's anger. It was just an incidental fact that was reported in the Joseph story. Since, however, there was a **chief executioner** involved in Gen 41, the Danielic homiletician had to weave this character into his story. This was done by explaining the extent of Nebuchadnezzar's fury. He made up this portion of his story on the basis of two words, "fury" and **chief executioner**. The king decreed that all of the incompetent wisemen would be destroyed. This required **a chief executioner**. Pharaoh's anger was not directed to the wisemen. He had become angry in response to an earlier situation that had no bearing on the wisemen of Egypt.

Hananiah, Mishael, and Azariah. These were the Hebrew names of Daniel's friends, and Daniel himself was not called Belteshazzar. This mention was not just an editorial note to introduce Dan 3. It was traditional for Jews to pray in groups, preferably in groups of ten undefiled males (a *minyon*) who had completed their Bar Mitzwah. Two or three were enough to make a valid testimony in court (Matt 18:19-20; *mAboth* 3.2). Rabbis said that the acceptable time for the Lord to answer prayer was when the community prays (*bBer* 8a).[12] When Daniel needed God's help he called on the Jews that were near.

He would show the interpretation to the king. Here Daniel was introduced as the **interpreter** of dreams. He was mentioned earlier for his skill in **interpreting** dreams and visions (Dan 1:17). The emphasis here was on **interpretation** of dreams, but the real source of the message was the scripture that the author himself had read. This was the word of God that was revealed to the author of Daniel when he read Genesis 41. The author of Daniel was busy **interpreting** earlier scriptural texts by which he might know what happened in the later cycle. Here in Dan 2 this would be illustrated. Daniel then played the role of a new Joseph. Just as Joseph had accurately **interpreted** dreams in the home of the chief executioner, so here Daniel claimed before the chief executioner that he could interpret the king's dreams.

Daniel's method of interpreting dreams was not different from that of the other wisemen. If one of the other advisers had interpreted the dream, that wiseman would have attributed his insight to some deity. When Hammurabi needed a code of laws he employed the best jurists in the country, but after the code was formed it was attributed to the goddess, Shamash, and the pillar which held the code showed a picture of Shamash handing the laws to Hammurabi. It was interpreted as a revelation from Shamash. Babylonians also believed that the deity communicated messages to special people in dreams. The special people would have been kings, wisemen, scribes, prophets, and priests.[13] Some of these would have been the ones expected to be able to interpret dreams and omens as messages from the deity.

Receive mercy before the God of heaven. The wisemen of Babylon had said that God did not dwell in human flesh, but if they could have told Nebuchadnezzar his dream they would have accepted the insight as a direct message from the deity. It was the deity who had given Nebuchadnezzar the dream. Therefore only the deity could reveal it again. Since the king could not remember it, there could be no human solution to the problem. In the Genesis intertext, Joseph recognized that it was not he who revealed mysteries and dreams. It was God. True to his text, the Danielic

---

[12] See further Buchanan, *The Gospel of Matthew* (Lewiston: The Edwin Mellen Press, c1996), pp. 740-41.

[13] See further J. N. Lawson, "'The God Who Reveals Secrets': The Mesopotamian Background to Daniel 2:47," *JSOT* 74 (1997):61-76.

exegete pictured Daniel requesting revelation from God. This homiletician not only mentioned that Daniel offered a prayer to God for wisdom and revelation, he also included the prayer that Daniel must have prayed. This prayer was also based on earlier appropriate intertexts.

Concerning this mystery. The word here rendered **mystery** might also be translated "riddle" or "secret." The riddle or secret was the problem that confronted the king. What was his dream, and what did it mean? The Aramaic word *rahz* or *rah-zah* (רז, רזא) occurs only in Daniel (Dan 2:18, 19; 4:6) in the entire FT. It occurs, however, in the Dead Sea Scrolls. Lawson said it is part of Persian thought-form.

> I would submit that it is because Nebuchadnezzar comes from a cultural tradition in which secrets are regularly revealed by divinity to humanity. It is a tradition with which the Jewish exiles became familiar during the time in Babylonia and which finds expression in a postexilic apocalyptic work.[14]

TEXT

Then Daniel blessed the God of Heaven. [20]He answered and said,

Daniel	First Testament Intertexts
May the name of God be blessed / from the [current] age until the age [to come], /	[Ps 41:14] **Blessed be** Yehowah, **God of** Israel **from the [current] age until the age [to come]**
	[Ps 113:2] **May the name of Yehowah be blessed from now until the age [to come].**
	[Neh 9:5] **From the [current] age until the age [to come], may your glorious name be blessed** and **exalted above blessing and praise.**
	[Ps 90:2] **From the [current] age to age [to come] you are God.**
because **wisdom and power are his.** / [21]**He changes** the times and the seasons; / he removes kings and he establishes kings. / He gives **wisdom** to the wise /	[Job 12:13] **With him are wisdom and power**; / to him belong counsel and

---

[14] Lawson, "Secrets," p. 62.

and knowledge to those who have **understanding.** /

understanding.

^(Job 12:23) He makes the nations great and destroys them; / he enlarges the nations and leads them away.

^(Gen 41:25) Joseph said to Pharaoh, "The dream of Pharaoh is one: that which God is doing, **he has revealed** to Pharaoh."

^(Isa 45:7) I form **light** and create **darkness.**

²²**He reveals the deep things** and mysteries. / He knows what is in **darkness**, / and **light** dwells with him. / ²³I give **thanks and praise** to you,

^(Job 12:22) **He reveals the deep things** from **darkness** / he brings out **light** from deep darkness.

^(Ps 36:10) With you is the source of **light**, and in your **light** we see **light**.

^(Ps 139:12) **Darkness** is not **dark** with you, and **darkness** is as **light**.

^(Amos 5:8) **He changes** deep **darkness** into morning, and day he **darkens** into night.

^(1Chron 29:20) All the congregation **blessed** Yehowah, **God of** their **fathers** and they bowed down and worshiped both Yehowah and the king.

God of my **fathers**, / because you have given me **wisdom and strength**. / You have informed me of that which I have requested of you. You have made known to us the matter of the king.

^(Job 12:16) With him are **strength and wisdom**.

COMMENTARY

He blessed the God of heaven. This is a beautiful, poetic, midrashic, prayer, based primarily on intertexts from Psalms, Amos, Nehemiah, and Job. The expression **God of heaven** occurs 13 times in those books. The sacred name of **God**, Yehowah, seldom occurs in the Book of Daniel, and when it does it is most frequent in prayers that are dependent on intertexts that use the name Yehowah. Terms like **the God of heaven**, "**God of** my fathers," **God**, and "the Lord" are substitutes. The poem that follows is not just a later foreign intrusion. It is an integral part of Dan 2. It provides an important function in the development of the narrative.[15]

From the [current] age to the age [to come]. This expression is rendered "forever and ever" in the RSV and most English and American translations and commentaries,[16] but this misses the eschatological dimension of the expression. Jews and early Christians believed that there were two **ages** that were successive halves of a cycle. They were chronologically related. The evil **age** was a period of captivity, when parties to the contract were forced to live away from the Promised Land and under the rule of a foreign government. For Joseph, this was Egypt; for Daniel, it was Babylon. **The age to come** was in the future. That was **the age** when the Promised Land would be restored under the rule of Israel's own king. **The age to come** came when the Hasmoneans overthrew the Syrian Greeks in the second century BIA.

He changes the times and the seasons. This means that God is in charge of the world. As Amos had noticed years before, God **changes** day into night and then night into day again. He moves the seasons in cycles. Spring is always followed by summer; summer is followed by autumn; autumn is followed by winter; and after winter, spring returns to its position in the cycle. This is reliable. It always happens the same way every year, but it does not happen all by itself. **God** is the one who makes the **changes**, and members of the contract community had feasts of celebration to go with each **change** of **times and seasons**. God not only **changed** the days and the seasons; he **changed** ages from the age of the gentiles to the age of the Israelites and back again. These were sometimes called the age of darkness and the age of light. Gentiles were correspondingly called children of darkness and Jews were called children of light. According to the earliest Dead Sea Scroll document discovered, the members of the sect represented should walk before him perfectly. To do this they were required to keep all things revealed for the appointed seasons, to love all the sons of light, each one according to his lot in the council of God, and to hate all the sons of darkness, each one according to his guilt (*1QS* 1.8-10).

He removes kings, and he establishes kings. This was an important belief of the author. He believed that God changed the ages and the **kings** just as he changed night into day. Jews could be forced into evil ages and evil nations under foreign **kings**, like Pharaoh and **King** Nebuchadnezzar, but God could remove these **kings** from their positions. It was on this basis that Paul said, **There is no authority except from God** (Rom 13:1). Because of this Christians were encouraged to **fear God** and **honor the king** (1Pet 2:17). Since God appointed the **kings** those who

---

[15] See further G. T. M. Prinsloo, "Two Poems in a Sea of Prose: The Content and Context of Daniel 2.20-23 and 6.27-28" *JSOT* 93 (1993):93-100.

[16] For example, C. F. Keil, *Biblical Commentary on the Book of Daniel* tr. M. B. Easton (Grand Rapids: William B. Eerdmans and Co., c1976), p. 98.

feared God would also honor God's agents, the **kings**. God could change the ages from the current evil age to the prosperous age to come when Jews would all live under their own vines and their own fig trees, in their own Promised Land, and with their own **king**. In another chapter Daniel argued that **the Most High rules the human kingdom and gives it to whomever he will** (Dan 4:32). During the ages in which Joseph and Daniel reportedly lived, God had given the kingdom to Pharaoh and **King** Nebuchadnezzar, but when he chose he might also give the kingdom back to Jews in Palestine, just as he had done during the days of David and Solomon. By the time this author was writing, this had already happened again, and the Jews were probably getting ready to celebrate their faith at Hanukkah.

He gives wisdom to the wise. Solutions to dreams were not hopeless, just because God did not dwell in human flesh. God communicated with human beings and selectively **gave wisdom to the wise**. Babylonians would agree about this. It was the question of which deity did the selection and whom he selected. Babylon's **wisdom** and knowledge split it into parts, according to Second Isaiah (Isa 47:10). It was to Joseph and Daniel, as well as Daniel's friends, who had studied academic subjects in Babylon, that **wisdom** and understanding was **given**. They observed the dietary laws prescribed in the Torah, so God rewarded them with good health, beauty, and **wisdom**. The author of Dan 2 was confident that Daniel's friends would prosper if they observed the rules of the scripture, because Exod 23:23-33 **gave** the conditions of the treaty Jews had made. This scripture told what would happen to Israelites if, on the one hand, they should imitate the idolaters and, on the other hand, if they should keep these laws faithfully. Those who observed the law would be blessed, and those who followed the ways of the pagans would be cursed.

He reveals the deep things and mysteries. These were the hidden things that most people wondered about but few people knew. These insights came to individuals in visions and dreams that required interpretation. Although visions and dreams had deep and hidden meanings, God **revealed** their meaning to faithful and competent scholars, such as Joseph and Daniel. The chosen people had an advantage over all others. They had the scriptures, and they believed that everything that was in the world was in the scriptures. The **things revealed** to the sectarians who walked perfectly were the scriptural rules related to the appointed seasons (*1QS* 1.8-9). Every **mystery** could be solved by the careful exegesis of texts. That is why the author of Dan 2 read Genesis to learn about the problems of Babylon. The dreams and their interpretation in Daniel were literary patterns that permitted the author to tell his story, but the author himself received this word of God by reading the scriptures.

God of my fathers. This is a favorite expression of the Chronicler. It occurs 25 times in those documents.

TEXT

Daniel

²⁴Then Daniel went to Arioch whom the king had appointed to destroy the wisemen of Babylon. He went and said this to him, "Do not destroy the wisemen of Babylon. **Take me up before the king**, and I will show the king the **interpretation**." ²⁵**Then**
Arioch **hurried**
and
brought Daniel **before the king**, and this is what he said to him, "I have found **from among** the exiles a man who is **a Jew** who can

make known the **interpretation** to the king." ²⁶The king answered and said to Daniel, whose name was Belteshazzar, "Have you the ability to show me the **dream** that I have seen and its **interpretation**?" ²⁷Daniel answered before the king and said, "The mystery which the king has asked, none of the wisemen, enchanters, magicians, or astrologers was able to interpret to the king, ²⁸but there is a **God** in heaven who reveals mysteries and **makes known**
to King Nebuchadnezzar

what **will happen at the**
last days [of the current age]. Your dream and the visions of your head on your bed are as follows:

First Testament Intertexts

Gen 41:14 **Then** Pharaoh sent and called Joseph, and they **hurried** him from the pit. Then he shaved, changed garments, **and came to Pharaoh.**

¹²There **with us was**
a young **Hebrew** slave belonging to the chief executioner. We told him, and he **interpreted** for us

our **dreams**.

²⁵**God**
has made known
to Pharaoh
that which he is doing.
²⁸This is the matter which I told to Pharaoh **which God is doing he has shown to Pharaoh.**

Isa 2:2 //Micah 4:1 **It will happen at the last days** [of the current era] the mountain of the house of
Yehowah will be established as the highest of the mountains.

COMMENTARY

Destroy the wisemen of Babylon. At the death of a certain crown prince of Persia, Smerdis, a magician named Gaumata, pretended to be the king. A maiden who was a member of the pseudo-king's harem risked her life to expose him. Her name was Phaedyma. When the Persians learned that this person who pretended to be the king was really a magician and not a legitimate king, they killed every magician they could find and were only prevented by nightfall from killing every magician in Persia. Persians still celebrated this occasion every year during the time when Herodotus lived. It was called the slaughter of the magi. Atkins is probably correct in suggesting that the story of Esther is a Jewish revision of this story.[17] Jews still celebrate Purim every year. The author of Dan 2 was probably familiar with the story behind the Persian celebration.

Hurried and brought Daniel before the king. Still depending on the intertext from Genesis to guide his narrative the exegete had Arioch **bring Daniel** in haste to **the king**, just as Pharaoh sent and had Joseph **hurriedly brought** before him. In both cases the royal leaders were eager to have their dreams interpreted. For **Daniel** the need for haste was much more urgent, because if this failed all of the wisemen in Babylon, including **Daniel** and his friends would be killed. Joseph was not in any such crisis as that. He lived in the pit, because he was the chief executioner's slave, and this was his place of employment.

A man who is a Jew. Both of these stories were tendentious. Neither Joseph nor Daniel was an ordinary person. Joseph was a Hebrew and Daniel **was a Jew**. These were both central characters in national hero stories. The irony of both situations is that these two kings were humbled to the position that they had to consult prisoners and captives for advice.

Makes known to King Nebuchadnezzar. Ancients believed that dreams were some of the ways in which the deity communicated with human beings, so it was urgent to learn the message the deity wanted the dreamer to know. It was neither Joseph's skill nor Daniel's insight that was at work here. Following the Joseph story, Daniel argued that it was God who **made** these dreams and interpretations **known to the king**. That which was implied, of course, was that both wisemen had special influence with God. They understood how God revealed his messages, and their God controlled dreams. Without Joseph and Daniel these dreams would have been mysteries.

The last days. This is an Aramaic idiom, *buh-ah-khah-reét yoh-máh-yah* (באחרית יומיא), which literally, means at **the last of days**. When scholars say this is "a typical eschatological term,"[18] they are not saying anything very definitive. Anything that deals with the **last** or end of anything is eschatological. It is an eschatological expression to say, "Friday is the end of the working week." The

---

[17] So R. I. Atkins, "The Origins of the Esther Tale," *BR* 13 (Feb. 1997):8-9.
[18] L. F. Hartman and A. A. DiLella, *The Book of Daniel* (Garden City: Doubleday & Co, 1978), p. 140.

Aramaic expression used here has often been misconstrued to mean **the last days** of the world or **the last days** of the cosmos or of time, but the context rebels against that.[19] Montgomery correctly followed Driver in holding that this expression is relative, not absolute, and its meaning is determined by its context.[20] Frerichs was ridiculing the dispensationalists when he said,

> All those time charts of the dispensationalists have proved wrong, but we can confidently expect them to reappear near the end of this century, because for them we are coming to the end of the sixth millennium (or world age) since creation in 4000 B.C.[21]

The question is, "What does this eschatological expression mean?" "What is the end involved?" It means the same as the expression, *ah-kha-ráy deh-náh* (אחרי דנה), **after this**, which is parallel to it in the next verse.[22] The end involved was not the end of the world or the climax of history, but the end that would follow when the dream was fulfilled.[23] This was based on Isa 2:2 which reported at **the last days** that the mountain of the house of Yehowah would become the highest of the mountains and gentiles would stream to it for instruction in Zion.

Both Joseph and Daniel lived at the beginning of the days of their respective exiles. It was Joseph who was the first Israelite to enter Egypt. He had been taken to Egypt as a slave, and he later brought all of his family to Egypt to rescue them from famine. The end of days of his prophecy would have been 14 years. He did not prophesy events that would take place at the end of the exile in Egypt, which would have been either 400 (Gen 15:13) or 430 (Exod 12:41) years. If Joseph had prophesied for a time that was comparable to the period of the

---

[19] T. H. Gaster (tr.), *The Dead Sea Scriptures in English Translation* (Garden City: Doubleday, 1956), and B. D. Eerdmans, *The Religion of Israel* (Leiden: Brill, 1947), pp. 322-23, hold that the idiom means "in the future." G. B. Caird, "Les eschatologies du Noveau Testament," *RHR* 49 (1969): 217-27, said that he thought four fifths of what is called "eschatology" in the Bible has nothing to do with eschatology as such and should be classified with metaphor, parable, typology, and allegory. S. B. Frost, "Eschatology and Myth," *VT* 2 (1952):70, however, said, "The *eschaton* is the goal of the time process, that after which nothing further can occur: it is the climax of teleological history." R. H. Charles, *Religious Development between the Old and the New Testaments* (London: Williams and Northgate, c1914), p. 17, said, "Eschatology is strictly the doctrine of the last things." N. A. Dahl, "Eschatologie und Geschichte im Licht der Qumran Texte," *Zeit und Geschichte*, ed. E. Denkler (Tübingen: Mohr, 1964), pp. 3-19, noted that the Qumran texts follow the hopes of Israel in their eschatological thought and recognized similar trends in the NT. This is different from the interpretations of Schweitzer and Bultmann. Dahl said the whole basis of eschatology should be reexamined.

[20] J. A. Montgomery, *A Critical and Exegetical Commentary on Daniel* (New York: Charles Scribner's Sons, 1927), p. 162.

[21] W. W. Frerichs, "How Many Weeks until the End?," *Word and World* 15 (1995):167.

[22] *Contra* Keil, *Daniel*, p. 101.

[23] See further Buchanan, "Eschatology and the 'End of Days,'" *JNES* 20 (1961):188-93 and *New Testament Eschatology: Historical and Cultural Background* (Lewiston: The Edwin Mellen Press, 1993). Contra D. S. Russell, *Daniel* (Philadelphia: Westminster, c1981), p. 47, and others. Y. Kaufman, *The Religion of Israel from its Beginnings to the Babylonian Exile*, tr. and abridged M. Greenberg (Chicago:University of Chicago Press, c1960), p. 241, said, "Possession of the land is the religious eschatological motif of Israelite religion. It is the ultimate goal of the people."

Babylonian exile, he would have foreseen the time that began when Joseph went to Egypt and continued until the Israelites were returned to Palestine under the Davidic-Solomonic rule.

Davidic-Solomonic rule. The time that elapsed until David and Solomon would have involved even more than the 400 years after Joseph first went to Egypt, because there was still the period in the wilderness and the conquest of Canaan before the exile age came to an end. The end involved in that eschatology was the establishment of the Davidic-Solomonic kingdom. The total length of time from Joseph's entrance into Egypt to the establishment of the kingdom would have been approximately the same as the 490 years that Daniel prophesied for the Babylonian exile. That is probably the way the author of Daniel understood it.

The end of the Babylonian age would arrive when the Jews were able to return to the Promised Land liberated from foreign rule. That would be the time when Mount Zion would become the highest of the mountains (Isa 2:2). Daniel anticipated the end of those **days**, but, like Joseph, he lived at the beginning, according to the author of Daniel. Daniel hypothetically lived at the beginning of the Babylonian exile and prophesied its end, about 441 years later (605 minus 164 = 441). The author of Dan 2 may have been satisfied to have the prophecy fulfilled at the end of nine Jubilees, but in this he differed from the author of Dan 9 who reported it as 490 years (Dan 9:24). In terms of Jubilees, 441 constitutes nine Jubilees, if the fiftieth year is not counted ($49 \times 9 = 441$). Since the fiftieth years were not counted to total the 490 years of Daniel's prophecy, that is apparently the method used. That is not quite the ten Jubilees the author of Daniel claimed, but the author was evidently thinking in those terms. This was the apologetic reason the author of Dan 1 began his narrative according to the report of the Chronicler rather than the report in the Kings account.

The author evidently forced things to reach the desired sabbatical eschatological formula. The precise dogma was more important than precise mathematics. The drama began with an exile at 605 BIA that did not take place until 597 BIA, when the Judean king taken to Babylon was Jehoiakin rather than Jehoiakim. If the author had made an effort to be historically and mathematically correct the result would not have come out to a perfect nine Jubilees, which the author of Dan 9 called ten Jubilees. For some doctrinal reason the number ten seemed to have been more important than nine. Daniel and his friends were tested for ten days, and they were later ten times more intelligent than any of the wisemen of Babylon. The authors of the various dramas in the Book of Daniel apparently studied carefully the similarity of the time periods of the two exiles when they prepared these Dramas of Daniel.[24] They were similar enough to be thought provoking, so they distorted historical facts enough to satisfy sabbatical doctrine. The editor who brought all of these Daniel chapters together did not try to make the calculations of Dan 2 agree with Dan 9.

---

[24] As early as the third century.

TEXT

²⁹Thoughts went out to you, O King, [as you lay] on your bed of what would happen after this, and the one who reveals mysteries has made known to you that which will take place. ³⁰[As for me], I do not have any more wisdom than any other living being. This mystery has been revealed to me, therefore, so that the interpretation might be known to the king, and that you might know the thoughts of your mind.

COMMENTARY

Thoughts went out to you. The idea was that the king did not think of these dreams by himself. It was God who sent him the dreams. That is why it was very important that he learn what the messages were.

That which will take place. **That which will take place** is that which will happen **after this** or **at the last of days**. It refers to the future of the time presumably under discussion, not the end of the world. The king needed to know that which would happen in the future so that he might plan for it the way Pharaoh in Egypt planned for the future of prosperity and famine as Joseph forecast, for the next 14 years--not for the end of the world. That was a period of time that was important to the pharaoh's administration. Daniel's prophecy was for a longer time, because it was not intended for Nebuchadnezzar's benefit but for the benefit of the original readers. The original readers did not live at a time that was many millennia in the future, after the world had come to the end or after time had ceased to be, as many modern eschatologists assume. That would have been useless to them. Speaking, with "tongue-in-cheek," of Christians who still expect the prophecies of Daniel to be fulfilled, Frerichs said,

> The predictive element in prophecy is of the greatest consequence since many events foretold by Daniel have already happened or soon will. In 1948, God's time clock, which apparently stopped when Jerusalem fell to the Romans was restarted by the beginning of the state of Israel, and the 70ᵗʰ week of Daniel 9 will soon unfold.[25]

Three of the popular Christian eschatologists are H. Lindsey, who had three small paperback books on the best seller list at the same time,[26] W. White,[27] and Pat Robinson, who was a candidate for the president of the United States.[28]

Lindsey thought the prophets predicted events that happened centuries after the prophecy. For instance, some prophecies of Isaiah and Micah were fulfilled in the time of Jesus, but some were never fulfilled. These will be fulfilled

---

[25] Frerichs, "How Many Weeks?" p. 170.
[26] H. Lindsey, *The Late Great Planet Earth* (Grand Rapids: Zondervan, c1970), *The Countdown to Armageddon* (New York: Bantam, c1980), and *The Rapture: Truth or Consequences* (New York: Bantam, 1983).
[27] W. White, *Arming for Armageddon* (Milford: Mott Media, c1983).
[28] C. M. Fishbein, "Pony up for Front Row Seats to see Good vs. Evil Battle," *The Spotlight* (300 Independence Ave, SE, Washington, D.C., 20003: July 13, 1987):15.

in our own time, according to Lindsey. The clue for this is that the last week of years of Daniel's prophecy could not begin until Israel became a state.[29] This puts eschatologists on guard to match events of our day to the prophecies. Russia could be the country that Ezekiel called Magog (Ezek 39:6). The Arab-Israel war is the fulfillment of Dan 11:40 and Zech 12:2-3. People's Republic of China constituted the Oriental forces prophesied by Rev 16:12. The fourth beast is Rome, and contemporary Rome includes the entire European Common Market.

White said that the ten nations of the Common Market represent the ten toes of Dan 2:41-45.[30] The dictator who will lead this group of nations might be King Juan Carlos of Spain, who could qualify as the Antichrist.[31] Before the anticipated tribulation, White expected that all born again Christians would be taken up to heaven in the rapture. Then the sinners who are left will be killed in a war with Russia. Both Jewish and Christian eschatologists expect to see Russian corpses scattered all over the Golan Heights.[32] In that war 5/6 of the Soviet army is destined to be destroyed in the Golan Heights. White may have had to up-date his prophecies to take account of the break-up of the Soviet Union and the extension of the Common Market.

Robertson was sure that the last seven years of Dan 9 would have begun with Israel's seizure of the temple area in Jerusalem in 1967. He said,

> I guarantee you by the fall of 1982, that there is going to be a judgment on the world . . . This whole thing [Armageddon/nuclear war] is now in place. It can happen any time . . . But by fall [1982] undoubtedly something like this will happen, which will fulfill Ezekiel. The United States is in that Ezekiel passage, and . . . we are standing by [for Armageddon].[33]

Two of the modern Jewish eschatologists are Shiloh and Shvilly.

Shiloh claimed his prophecy had a 99,999999999...% chance of being correct. Shiloh argued that 1973 would be the year the Messiah would come, and Israel would expand its borders to include all of the land from the Nile to the Euphrates. All Jews would return to the Promised Land, and all the world would be transformed to the kingdom of the messianic king and the revelation of the Kingdom of Heaven.[34] The last war would accomplish the following: "1) punishment of the gentiles, 2) the deliverance of Israel and its redemption, and 3) the Kingdom of Heaven and the rule of peace and righteousness."[35] He observed,

---

[29] Lindsey, *Great Planet*, pp. 14-41.
[30] White, *Arming*, pp. 152-53.
[31] White, *Arming*, pp. 154-55.
[32] White, *Arming*, pp. 140-41, 144.
[33] For these and other examples and analyses of modern Christian eschatologists see Buchanan, *New Testament Eschatology: Historical and Cultural Background* (Lewiston: Mellen Biblical Press, c1993), pp.232-53.
[34] S. Shiloh, *The War of the Russians in Israel: The Year 1973* [Hebrew] (Jerusalem: Shiloh: 2nd, December, 1973), pp. 8, 10, 17.
[35] Shiloh, *War*, p. 27.

> The boundaries of the land will have to be expanded so as to absorb all the people (Jews) who will return to the land. The government in the land will also have to be changed (as noted above in Ezekiel). Now we also stand before the end of the "treaty with the many" (the gentiles) who desolated our temple (further on in Daniel). The Kingdom of Heaven which will be revealed at the end of the war will bring peace, righteousness, and eternal goodness in Israel and in the world.[36]

Shvilly organized a calendar of events related to the formation of the state of Israel (1948). "The end of days" (three and a half years) took place from 1964-1967. He related the great historical events from 1967-69. He then predicted the coming atomic war, the attack of the land, the war of Gog and Magog in Jewish Jerusalem, the kingdom of the righteous Messiah, construction of the temple, and the completion of all the rest of the steps involved in the redemption (1970-90).[37] Shvilly was killed in battle in the Golan Heights during the Yom Kippur War, probably thinking that this was the third world war, the one that would fulfill the prophecies of Daniel and Ezekiel.

All of these zealous Jews and Christians have misunderstood the intention of the Book of Daniel. Dan 2 did not predict the current events of the twentieth or twenty-first centuries. Daniel's "prediction" was for more than 400 years, but not 2,000. The time when all of this dream would be fulfilled was 164 BIA. The reason Daniel could "predict" a time this far in advance was that the author wrote all of this after the dream had already been fulfilled, and the original readers already knew about it. The history between 605 and 164 BIA had already happened.[38] According to the author of this chapter, there were four pagan countries involved in subjecting Judah during this time. These ruling forces all lost their power over Palestine, the Battles of Beth-horon and Beth-zur had been won, and the Jews were preparing to celebrate all of this at Hanukkah, so the author of the dream story had some historical data by which to compose the dream. Since the history of the period all turned out happily for the Jews, the Book of Daniel is very optimistic for the Jews but very pessimistic for the gentiles.

More wisdom than any other living being. This was the humble claim the author pictured Daniel as portraying before the king. Of course, the reader is led to believe that this is not so, but the important confession is that it was not Daniel's **wisdom** that counted. It was his religion. He had the right scripture, and he worshiped the right God. Since Nebuchadnezzar had left all of the ignorant, uneducated, unskilled Jews in Palestine, the upper class, well-educated Jews in Babylonia stood out among

---

[36] Shiloh, *War*, p. 27. See also p. 30.
[37] C. Shvilly, *The Book of Calculations of the Redemption* [Hebrew] (Jerusalem c1964 with additions in 1969).
[38] There are extant some Akkadian prophecies that, like these dramas in Daniel, were written after the events had taken place as if they had been foretold. So H. Ringgren, "Akkadian Apocalypses," Helholm (ed.), *Apocalypticism in the Mediterranean World and the Near East* (Tübingen: Mohr, 1983), p.379-86.

the all-class society of Babylon. That made it possible for them to justify their claim to superiority in wisdom that was characterized by Daniel. Had Nebuchadnezzar taken to Babylon the lower classes of Jews rather than the upper classes, their comparison with other Babylonians would have been different.

You may know the thoughts of your mind. It was assumed that God had put **thoughts** in Nebuchadnezzar's **mind** during his dreams. Nebuchadnezzar, however, had forgotten his dreams, so he needed to have some wiseman tell him what his own ideas were and what they meant. He was desperate to learn that which the deity wanted him to know. Daniel had come to his rescue during this crisis. This, of course, put Daniel in a superior position. It meant that the king was prepared to accept whatever Daniel told him, so Daniel could exploit this opportunity if he so chose. The hero, Daniel, was brought to Babylon as a captive. Nebuchadnezzar, the arch villain, was the powerful, pagan king. By this point in the story, however, the villain reached such confusion that he did not **know the thoughts of** his own **mind**. But of course the hero not only **knew** his own **thoughts**; he also **knew** the king's thoughts. Instead of being subject to a pagan king, the pagan king was subject to Daniel. This is one of the characteristic reversals of the Book of Daniel.

TEXT

[31]King, you were watching. Now look! A statue--this powerful statue was huge, and it was very bright. It stood before you, and its appearance was frightening. [32][As for] this statue--its head was of fine gold; its chest and its arms were of silver; its midsection and thighs were of bronze; [33]its legs were of iron; and its feet were partly iron and partly clay. [34]You kept watching until a stone was cut without [the use of] hands and it struck the feet of iron and clay and shattered them. [35]Then the iron, clay, bronze, silver, and gold were all broken into pieces at once, and they became as chaff on a summer threshing floor. The wind took them up so that no trace of them could be found.

Daniel	First Testament Intertexts
The stone which smashed the statue became a huge mountain **and filled all the land.** [36]That was the dream, and its interpretation is told before the king.	[Isa 11:9]**The land will be filled** with the knowledge of Yehowah as waters cover the sea.

COMMENTARY

You were watching. Now look! This was a typical way to introduce a vision, especially in Zechariah (Zech 1:8). Another similar expression is **I lifted up my eyes. Now look!** (Zech 2:1; 5:1; 6:1.)

Its appearance was frightening. This should have come as no surprise to the king. When he woke up from his dream, he had forgotten the dream, but his mind was troubled. He knew that he had had a bad dream. Daniel spelled out its fearful content in detail. The king did not dispute the accuracy of Daniel's claim. Since the king had already forgotten his dream, he had no way of knowing whether Daniel's report was correct or not. If Daniel had created a dream out of his own imagination, how could he lose? The worst that could happen was that the king would deny that this was his dream. In that case things would have been just as they were before Daniel appeared before the king. If the king accepted Daniel's story, Daniel and his friends were destined to survive and prosper.

This statue. **The statue**, which the king saw in his dream, was **frightening**, because it was the statue of a pagan deity, and pagan deities were mostly monstrous. The statue was constructed of four different kinds of material.[39] The most precious was used for the head, and the least precious for the feet. No part of the statue was spared. It was completely destroyed; its metals were ground to dust; and the wind blew the dust away. This was the result of the dream, but the question still to be answered was, "What does all of this mean?" Daniel did not leave the king in suspense.

Its legs were of iron. This was to reflect the kind of weapons Alexander the Great used in his military attacks.

Partly iron and partly clay. **Clay**, when wet, is a substance that can be formed and shaped into many kinds of objects. After it has been baked in a pottery kiln, however, it becomes very brittle and cannot be mixed at all--with iron or almost anything else. This is the picture given here. All attempts to mix **the iron and** pottery into some kind of unified substance were destined to fail.[40]

Became a huge mountain. This is **the mountain** of the Lord's house to which all the gentiles would come streaming to receive instruction in Mount Zion at the last days of the current era. This was to be the center of all the earth. (Isa 2:2-4). Whenever possible Montgomery avoided anything nationalistic or militaristic in his interpretation of Daniel. He preferred the word "sovereignty" to "kingdom," but he had to admit that the **mountain** that fills the whole earth or the whole land was not a spiritual kingdom.[41] Neither were the kingdoms the rock destroyed. Furthermore, the

---

[39] Hesiod, *The Works and Days*, 1.109-201, visualized the gods creating the races of human beings. The first was gold, the second, silver, the third, brass, and the fourth was iron. With each successive race came further disintegration of moral character. With the race of iron came war.

[40] See J. L. Kelso, "The Ceramic Vocabulary of the Old Testament," *BASOR Supplementary Studies*, nos. 5-6 (1948):7.

[41] Montgomery, *Daniel*, p. 178. I. Frölich *Time and Times and Half a Time* (Sheffield: Sheffield Academic Press, c1956), pp. 31-33, argued that Dan 2 originally reported the collapse of the Babylonian empire. She said the four parts refer not to kings or empires but to rules of four Babylonian kings and that Cyrus of Persia was the rock that broke the statue. Then a later editor revised it to apply to four empires (p 35). The author of Dan 2 may have had sources at his disposal, but it is not possible to conjecture what they were or how many.

rock crushed the entire statue. It was a final destruction. Not a speck of the statue was left. Burkitt said,

> The stone cut without hands does not merely claim the right to exist: it is the conscious rival of the Imperial Statue. In other words, Judaism is to the author of Daniel a cosmic world-religion, and that not merely by detached and occasional glimpses, but consciously and at all time.[42]

Heaton said Daniel simplified the conflict between Israel and the nations by posing the Kingdom of God against the kingdoms of the world.[43] The kingdoms of the world in those days included the nations from Egypt and Spain in the West to India in the East. To the people in Babylon, Egypt was the other end of the world.[44] Jews were not thinking in cosmic terms. Dan 2 was written after the outcome of the conflict between the statue and the stone was known. The Battle of Beth-horon had been fought. The stone survived, and the nations were defeated. This was a *fait accompli*; there was no prediction of something that would happen in the future, 2,000 years later. Rabbis interpreted the stone that destroyed the pagan kingdoms to be the kingdom of the Messiah (*Tanhuma* 31.4, 34; *PirkeEliezer* chapter 2; *bBer* 70b; *NumR* 13).

Collins held that the rock must be interpreted quite differently from the drama of the one like a Son of man in Dan 7.[45] There may be some difference, but it is not very much. The rock might symbolize all of the victorious Israel, rather than the Son of man who liberated Israel from the nations represented by the statue, but that does not remove the Son of man from national leadership. Collins correctly claims, however, that the ten toes of the statue have the same significance as the ten horns of Dan 7. These are the Seleucid kings.[46] It follows, then that the rock that crushed the toes is the same character that defeated the little horn in the heavenly court scene. In both cases God interceded. He made the rock crush the statue, and he made the judgment in the heavenly court case.[47]

Is told before the king. Most scholars render this Hebrew verb as qal imperfect (*nay-mahr*, נאמר), "we will tell" or "we will say." This has the support of the OG and Theodotion, and both may be correct, but since the subject is Daniel, it seems odd to have him refer to himself in the plural, but maybe he did. With a slight vowel change, without changing any consonants, the verb can be cast in the niphal (passive voice). This would be pronounced *neh-eh-máhr* (נאמר) and mean "it is said" or **it is told**. In the passive voice it might mean **God tells the king**.

---

[42] F. C. Burkitt, *Jewish and Christian Apocalypses* (London: British Academy, 1914), p. 6-7.
[43] E. W. Heaton, *The Book of Daniel* (London: SCM Press, 1956), p. 85.
[44] E. J. Bickerman, *From Ezra to the last of the Maccabees* (New York: Schocken Books, 1970, c1962), p. 9.
[45] J. Collins, *A Commentary on the Book of Daniel* (Minneapolis: Fortress Press, 1993), p. 34.
[46] Collins, *Daniel*, p.36.
[47] I. Frölich, "Daniel 2 and Deutero-Isaiah," *The Book of Daniel in the Light of New Findings*, ed. A. S. Van der Woude (Leuven: Peeters, 1993), pp. 266-70, thought the oracle was first used in relationship to Cyrus as the rock.

TEXT

Daniel	First Testament Intertexts

^{37} You, O King, are the **king of** kings to whom **the God of** heaven

has given the kingdom, power, might, and glory. ^{38}Every place where human beings, **beasts of the field, and birds of the heaven** livel he **has given**

into your **hand**, and your governing authority is over all of them.

$^{Jer\ 27:4}$ Thus has said Yehowah of armies, **the God of** Israel, . . .

$^{Jer\ 27:6}$ I **have given** all these lands **into the hand** of Nebuchadnezzar, **king of** Babylon, my servant. Even the beasts of the field I have given him to serve him (also Jer 28:14).

$^{Ps\ 8:7-8}$ You have put all things under his feet—all sheep and cattle, also the **beasts of the fields, the birds of the heaven, and** the fish of the sea

You are the head of gold. ^{39}After you will arise another kingdom that is inferior to you. Then there will be a third kingdom of bronze that will rule over all the land. ^{40}There will be a fourth kingdom, strong as iron, and just as iron breaks and crushes everything, and as iron, which shatters, it will break and shatter all of these.

COMMENTARY

You, O King, are the king of kings. This title was used of Nebuchadnezzar (Ezek 26:7) and normally of Persian **kings** (Ezra 7:12). Flattering addresses to a king were not intended to be statistically correct. It was diplomatically necessary. Nevertheless, Babylon was a great capital of a great country. Bevan praised it as follows:

> There was no other area of cultivation in Western Asia so wide and productive as Babylonia; there were no other cities so large and populous as those on the banks of the two rivers; no centres of industry to compare with those great hives of labour; no wisdom like the wisdom of the Chaldaeans; no king so exalted as the "King of kings." The influence of Babylon radiated as far as the Mediterranean on the west and India on the east.[48]

Media was also a great country that existed alongside of Babylon. Media once included both Assyria and Persia. Media did not follow Babylon in succession of empires. The soldiers of Astyges deserted to Cyrus (549 BIA). Cyrus took Babylon in 539 BIA. The superlative address given means that Nebuchadnezzar was the greatest of all kings and that other kings were subordinate. He had

---

[48] E. R. Bevan, *The House of Seleucus* (New York: Barnes & Noble, 1966) I, p. 239.

conquered other countries and added them to his empire. One of the kingdoms that he conquered was Judah, and he severely limited King Jehoiakim's powers. At that time Nebuchadnezzar was the king of King Jehoiakim and other such subordinate rulers.

God of heaven[49] *has given the kingdom.* Daniel did not **give** Nebuchadnezzar any credit for his expansionistic achievements. Rather, he followed Joseph in Egypt in believing that **God** was in charge of government and that he could **give kingdoms** to anyone he chose.

You are the head of gold. At the time this chapter reflects, Nebuchadnezzar ruled all of the territory from the Euphrates to Ethiopia (*Ant* 10.221-28). This is where the demythology begins. This whole dream was a mythologization of history. A lot of the demythologization that has gone on in recent NT scholarship has been inventive and misleading, because scholars have tried to demythologize that which had never been myth. This is a mistake; it is distracting and not helpful. It is no more possible to demythologize literature which is not myth than it is to pluck feathers off a fish. In Daniel it is obvious that we are dealing with myth, because the author took time to demythologize it.

Myth is not fiction or foolishness. The ancient myth was drama, one of the primary means of communicating feeling, doctrine, or thought. Meaning that could not be adequately expressed in prose was sometimes written in poetry or communicated through music, sculpture, or painting. When all of these failed, the play, the drama, the myth, was the successful medium. Shakespeare's Hamlet said, "The play's the thing wherein I'll catch the conscience of the king" (*Hamlet*, Act 2, sc 2, line 622).

History consists of events that take place in time and geographical location. Historians narrate these in relationship to countries, cities, forests, bodies of water, deserts, and fields. They also relate them in chronological sequence. If a historian were compared to a photographer, then the mythologist, by analogy, would be an artist. An artist does not attempt to make his or her painting or sculpture exactly like the person, object, or scene that has captured his or her attention. The artist tries to communicate a message through the painting that shows what the artist sees. The camera can provide a technically accurate image of that which the artist paints, but it cannot show the artist's message or interpretation. This is sometimes more obvious in cartoons than in oil paintings. The cartoonist deliberately distorts the character to communicate the point he or she has in mind.

The mythologist does the same with history. The mythologist describes events of history in a dramatic, sometimes religious or political, way. Taking all of the history for granted, he or she sets out to tell what all of this means--what is the message of this accumulation of historical facts? What meaning does it convey to the one who examines this history from a certain point of view, namely the mythologist's? This is done by taking the history out of normal, factual,

---

[49] Baal Shamayim, "the Lord of Heaven," was identified with Olympian Zeus. Chronos, Jupiter, and other gods were thought to live in heaven above the clouds of Mount Olympus. For example see Hesiod, *The Works and Days*, 1.201-250. Jews later gave this title to their own God, Yehowah.

historical form and distorting its objective perspective to suit the mythologist's desired emphasis, providing a religious, apologetic, dramatic literary mold. In other words, he or she interprets or mythologizes history just as an artist paints his or her own perspectives into a painting. When it is done, the author assumes that his or her intended readers know the history and can therefore grasp the meaning that has been dramatized. Even later historians, who are adequately acquainted with the history, have little trouble demythologizing much of the narrative and recognizing the history slightly disguised in the myth in the Book of Daniel.

A modern example of this kind of drama is "The Music Man." The Music man was a rogue, looking for a female victim. He told his friend the kind of girl he wanted, "To no Diana will I fall prey . . . I hope; I pray, that Hester will get just one more A. A sadder but wiser girl's the girl for me. A sadder but wiser girl for me." The author of these lines assumed the audience knew that Diana was the goddess of chastity and that Hester was the character in *The Scarlet Letter* who was forced to wear the letter A on all of her dresses and blouses to testify to all that she was an adulteress. Daniel used scripture in the same way through allusions and quotations.

One of the canonical documents that is best known for its mythologization of history is the Book of Daniel. This is the easiest document of the Bible to decode, because the author interrupted the myth from time to time to explain to the reader precisely what the myth meant in simple terms. In other cases the mythologist thought the myth was so simple and obvious that the reader could easily deduce it. Many scholars have recognized the mythical character of Daniel 2-6. Some have argued that Dan 1 was written as an introduction to the chapters that follow. It provides a suitable setting, and it uses many of the terms and concepts that are found in other chapters.[50] Wills classified all of these myths as court legends and compared them to legends circulating around Cyrus, Croesus, and others.[51] The next step here will be to see how well all of this mythology was composed.

TECHNICAL DETAILS

In Dan 2 the myth was staged in the form of a dream, but the author did not leave the reader to his or her own imagination to deduce the code. He took time to interpret the drama. The myth begins, as does the Book of Daniel, with the stage set at the historical date and geographical location of the beginning of the Babylonian captivity. The author has given several clues to that point.

1) First, he began the book reporting Nebuchadnezzar's conquest of Jerusalem under the reign of Jehoiakim, during 605 BIA, as if that had been the very beginning of the exile to Babylon. It actually happened later, but the author needed it to have happened as early as he reported it. At that time, the author claimed, Nebuchadnezzar plundered the treasuries of Jerusalem. This was later followed by the complete removal of Jewish leaders to Babylon.

---

[50] L. M. Wills, *The Jew in the Court of the Foreign King* (Minneapolis: Fortress Press, c1990), pp. 79-81.
[51] Wills, *Jew in the Court*, pp. 61-70.

2) Second, he chose as his main character, Daniel, an antitype of Joseph, who was a wiseman at the very beginning of the Egyptian captivity. The exile to Egypt began with Joseph taken into slavery to Egypt. This was followed by the complete removal of the family of Jacob to Egypt. Daniel and his friends were cast as the first Jews to come to Babylon in 605 BIA. Later, in 586, all the professional and upper class Jews followed Daniel and were exiled to Babylon. This meant the author understood that Daniel lived at the very same point in the cycle of time as Joseph lived in the earlier cycle of time.

3) The myth was Nebuchadnezzar's dream. Nebuchadnezzar was the king who initiated the Babylonian Captivity.

4) The myth, which the author of Daniel composed, mythologized the historical period that began with Nebuchadnezzar's rule. He was the "head of gold" in the mythologized historical report. This means he was the king at the beginning of the historical account that was mythologized.

COMMENTARY

After you will arise another kingdom. The author did not say that this was the **kingdom** of silver, but he said there was a second **kingdom** of silver, and he quickly moved on to the third **kingdom**. There was also a third **kingdom** that was the kingdom of bronze, so the implication is that there was a **kingdom** in between the gold **kingdom** and the bronze **kingdom** that matched the head and a chest and arms of silver in the statue. This apparently refers to Media.

Media was adjacent to Babylon. The first Median king was Deioces (709 - 656 BIA). Media was under Scythian rule from 634 to 606 BIA. Except for these 28 years the Medians ruled all of Asia, except Babylon, for 128 years (687-449 BIA). Medians were ruling at the time of the Babylonian captivity (586 BIA).[52] Before the invasion of Cyrus, Media controlled all of Persia and even Nineveh. Media ruled the territory that had belonged to Assyria at the time of the North Israelite captivity. Media never gained control of Babylon, and it did not succeed Babylon in ruling the Near East. The author of Dan 2 probably knew all of this, and he deliberately told the situation related to Media in an inexact and rather blurred way.

The author was not maliciously distorting facts when he placed Media as a successor to Babylon. He knew his scripture, and since there was nothing in the world that was not in the scripture, he was free, according to the rules of rhetoric of his day, to treat prophecy as if it had been fulfilled. Isaiah, for instance, said that God was stirring up Media to crush Babylon, leaving that city like Sodom and Gomorrah, never again to be inhabited (Isa 13:17-22). He envisioned Media laying seige to Babylon so that Babylon would fall (Isa 21:2, 9). Jeremiah followed suit. He foresaw Babylon taken when a nation from the north would come against it. The country north of Babylon was Media (Jer 50:2, 8-10, 39-42;

---

[52] Josephus correctly noted that 586 BIA was the 18th year of Nebuchadnezzar's reign (Apion 1.21).

51:11). God would be the one who would stir up the Medes to destroy Babylon for the damage Babylon did to the Lord's temple.

Since both Isaiah and Jeremiah were true prophets, their predictions must have happened. Therefore Media must have taken Babylon, following this logic. On the basis of these two prophetic authorities the argument given could hold up in court. Media was a strong country and a constant threat to Babylon. The queen Nicotris of Babylon fortified both the river and the city as a defense against the Medes, and her efforts were effective. Media never did conquer Babylonia.

Cyaxares was king of Media at the same time Nebuchadnezzar was king of Babylon. One of his daughters married Nebuchadnezzar. Cyaxares' granddaughter, Mandane, was a Mede and the mother of Cyrus of Persia.[53] Cyrus first conquered Media, and he later conquered Babylon. Neither victory required an excessive amount of warfare. Cyrus' agents persuaded the Median soldiers to join Cyrus and give up their country to him. He also had agents inside Babylon who arranged for his admission into the city without a war.

Tobit mistakenly reported that Nebuchadnezzar was king of Media when Media took Assyria captive (*Tob*14:14). The author of Judith thought Nebuchadnezzar was king of Assyria (*Judith* 1:1, 4; 2:19; 3:1, 8; 4:1.[54] No matter what the situation, Jews seemed to name Nebuchadnezzar as the chief villain of myths, even though he did not fit all of the times or localities.

The author of Dan 2 was confused about this second kingdom. It did not really fit into the succession of empires. Media did not conquer Babylon, and it did not succeed Babylon, although there were interrelationships among the Persians, the Babylonians, and the Medians. Cyrus was of Median descent, and the first country Cyrus annexed was Media. Prior to Cyrus' conquest, Persia was a small country south of Media, and at one time, it was part of Media. Persia increased both in size and in prominence when Cyrus became its ruler.

Cyrus was king of Persia at the time he conquered Babylon. This is usually considered a Persian conquest rather than a Median conquest. The Median kingdom was neither smaller than nor inferior to the Babylonian kingdom. Because the same territory that was once Assyria later was either Media or Persia, Herodotus sometimes called the inhabitants "Assyrians" and at other times "Medes," even though they were parts of Persia at the time. In the Behistan Inscription, made by Darius I to acknowledge his achievements (522-486 BIA) Darius referred to Media as an existing territory, and he called his army the army of the Medes and the Persians, indicating that Media did not lose its identity when it became part of Persia. Since Media accepted Cyrus as its leader without being taken militarily, the relationship between Persia and Media continued to be favorable, even after the capital of Persia changed to Babylon.[55]

In the time of Cyrus, nearly all of Media went over to Cyrus without a battle, but there continued to be a small country near the Caspian Sea that remained

---

[53] See further A. R. Millard, "Medes; Media," *ISBE* III, pp. 297-99.
[54] The author of *Judith* spelled the name of the king of Assyria *Neh-boo-khah-daw-naw-sawr*, (Nebouxodonosor), but he apparently had the same king in mind.
[55] A. Cowley (ed.), "The Behistan Inscription,"1.12; 2.22-26, *Aramaic Papyri of the Fifth Century B.C.* (Osnabrueck: Otto Zeller, 1967), pp. 258.

independent, and was still called Media. It was adjacent to Armenia and a country with which Mark Anthony had to reckon when he tried to conquer the Parthians (36 IA, Dio, 49.25-44). Rome was never able to acquire this country within Roman borders, but this was not the large empire that was listed in this succession list.

Media found its way into Daniel's succession of empires because of an earlier tradition. Josephus noted this obvious conflict between known history and Daniel's dogmatic reconstruction. He solved it by picturing Cyrus and Darius the Mede together conquering Babylon (*Ant* 10.232).

The author of this chapter was not the first to think of the Near East in terms of successive kingdoms. Before the time of Alexander the Great Greeks knew of the succession of the nations as Assyria, Media, and Persia (Herodotus 1.95, 130). After Alexander's victory over Persia at the Battle of Gaugamela (331 BIA) it was not difficult to add Macedonia or Greece as the fourth. Following Swain,[56] Flusser argued that the theory of four kingdoms originated in Persia, and was found in the Avesta itself. The succession is reflected in the Fourth Sibyl as Assyria, Media, Persia, Macedonia (*SibOr* 4.49-95).[57]

In the second century BIA, after the fall of Carthage, Polybius compared the fall of that great city to the fall of other great empires—Assyria, Media, and Persia (Polybius 38.22)—all of which **had risen** and fallen in succession by the time Carthage fell. Grecian Syria was still to fall. That would happen, not under the leadership of Jewish generals and kings, but under the leadership of the Roman general, Pompey. Swain quoted the following passage from Amilius Sura, which was written between 189 and 171 BIA.

> The Assyrians were the first of all races to hold power, then the Medes, after them the Persians, and then the Macedonians (Vellius, *Paterculus* 1.6.6).[58]

This was written before the Book of Daniel, and it shows that the theory of a succession of empires in the Middle East was not the invention of any of the Danielic authors. They obtained the notion from surrounding sources. It further suggests that this idea came from the general area surrounding the Tigris-Euphrates Valley, probably from Persia. There is no mention of Egypt, Carthage, or Rome. When Sura mentioned "all races," he meant all of the races in this area. He had no concept of the entire globe. Sura's philosophy of four empires was also thought by later Romans to be followed by a fifth, and that would be Rome.

Later Roman writers held that the fifth empire would be greater than any of the four preceding nations. Appian (95-165 IA) listed Assyria, Media, and Persia as those countries that preceded Alexander the Great, but none of these empires was as great as Rome. The Medes and Persians held only the Gulf of Pamphylia, the island of Cyprus, a few small islands in the Mediterranean Sea, and the Persian Gulf. By

---

[56] J. W. Swain, "The Theory of the Four Monarchies Opposition History under the Roman Empire," *Classical Philology* 35 (1940):7, 9.

[57] D. Flusser, "The Four Empires in the Fourth Sibyl and in the Book of Daniel," *Israel Oriental Studies* 2 (1972):148-75.

[58] Swain, "Four Monarchies," p. 2.

the middle of the second century IA, however, Rome ruled all the land from the Western (Atlantic) Ocean to the Indian Ocean, including Egypt and Ethiopia. (Appian, *Roman History*, preface 9). The notion that there were four succeeding empires was developed before the time of the Maccabees,[59] and continued to be accepted by countries other than Judah. Arrian said,

> For it was already fated that the rule of Asia should be taken from Persia [and given] to the Macedonians, just as the Medes had been captured by the Persians, and before it went to the Medes, the Assyrians [ruled Asia] (Arrian, *Anabasis*[60] 2.7).

The author of the fourth Sibyl was correct. The succession followed in exactly the order he reported. 1) Assyria was the first great country in the Near East. 2) Media conquered Assyria and became the second great empire; 3) Cyrus of Persia annexed Media and conquered Egypt, Asia Minor, and Babylon so that Persia became the third great country. 4) Alexander the Great overcame Persia and became the fourth vast empire. The Sibyl knew that. Jews may have been the first to think of themselves as the projected fifth in the line of succession, but Romans soon thought of themselves as the true fifth empire, but revised the succession to fit their own doctrine and needs. The authors of Daniel were not Samaritans, but Jews. The assignment given to each of the authors of dramas in Daniel covered the period of the Jewish captivity, which began in Babylon.

It was the North Israelites that were taken into captivity to Nineveh by Tiglath-Pileser. The Jews were not sorry about this invasion. In fact it was they who invited Tiglath-Pileser to plunder North Israel. In their judgment the Assyrian captivity was not very important to the Jewish program. That was past history. For them the exile began with Nebuchadnezzar and Babylon rather than Tiglath-Pilesar and Assyria.[61] Therefore they reorganized the succession. Instead of beginning with Assyria and ending with Rome, the Danielic succession was designed to begin with Babylon and end with Judah, even though the normal succession did not follow logically by simply replacing Assyria with Babylonia. When Babylon is placed first, Media does not really fit into the succession pattern.

The author of Dan 2 evidently knew of the correct succession, but for his drama, things began with Babylon rather than Assyria, so he dropped Assyria and added Babylon to his series. Against this concept of successions, Daniel relayed

---

[59] Swain, "Four Monarchies," p. 5. G. Widengren, "Les Quatre ages du monde," *Apocalyptique Iranienne et Dualisme Qumranânien* (Paris: Adrien Maisonneuve, 1995), pp. 23-62, has given several examples of lists of four or seven ages of the world in Persian, Indian, and Greco-Roman literature.
[60] Arrian, *Anabasis Alexandri* (Cambridge: Harvard U. Press, 1956) in 2 vols.
[61] There is no literary evidence to support this guess. The idea, however, that the four-nations concept which began with Assyria and ended with the restoration of the Promised Land would have been attractive for the North Israelites is thought-provoking. The North Israelites were really taken away by the Assyrians and might have anticipated their own restoration to follow the fourth kingdom. The author of Daniel might then have adapted the North Israelite hypothesis to Judah after the Battle of Beth-horon. This is a conjecture that may never have been a fact.

the dream in terms of historical periods. In a time-line the divisions would have looked like this:

605 BIA--Gold____Silver_____Bronze____Iron_____Rock--164 BIA

Placed in a cycle, they would look like this:

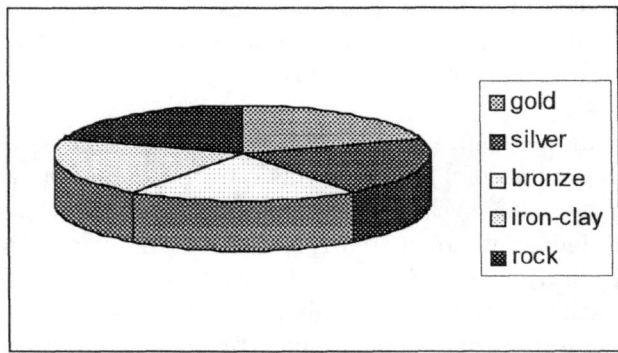

After Daniel had been transformed into a prophecy and was interpreted, the four successive nations were listed as: 1) Babylon, 2) Media-Persia, 3) Greece, and 4) Rome. After the development of Islam, Jews and Christians listed the countries as: 1) Persia, 2) Rome, 3) Greece, and 4) Islam.

Will rule over all the land. This was the third kingdom of bronze, evidently Persia. Cyrus' invasion of Babylon was no surprise to the Jews of Babylon. Before the event, Second Isaiah prophesied that Jerusalem would be reinhabited and that the cities of Judah would be rebuilt. This would happen because Cyrus would be the one who would make all of this happen (Isa 44:26-28). God would make Cyrus succeed by opening doors before him and seeing that gates were not closed (Isa 45:1). Cyrus took Babylon on a feast day when most Babylonians were drunk. Herodotus said this conquest happened without any military battle. The *Nabonidus Chronicle* confirmed the report that Babylon had been taken without a battle.[62]

Xenophon's account of the war was more extensive, telling how Cyrus first took all of the cities and fortresses from Sardis to Babylon before he entered Babylon.[63] Wherever possible, Cyrus obtained intelligence by finding some disgruntled person in the enemy's camp to describe the situation there, so he could attack most effectively, or who would infuence the inhabitants of the camp to surrender to Cyrus. When Xenophon described the Persian invasion of Babylon he did not say that it was bloodless, but it involved killing only as few people as possible to obtain control (*Cyrop* 6.1-7.16). He said that as Cyrus approached Babylon a deserter came out and told Cyrus the plans of the Babylonians.

---

[62] James B. Pritchard (ed.), *Ancient Near Eastern Texts* (Princeton: Princeton University Press, 1969), p. 306.

[63] Xenophon was himself a good general and knew the techniques of war. His style was conversational, so that many of his details may have been those he conjectured would have been suitable things said on the various occasions.

Herodotus did not know how Cyrus learned of the earlier work of Queen Nicotris of Babylon. Jews and Christians, however, who are familiar with Second Isaiah's certainty of the results of Cyrus' conquest, might reasonably suspect that Jews in Babylon were as deeply involved in Cyrus' movement as Christians were later in relationship to Constantine. Nebuchadnezzar had taken 10,000 upper class Jews into Babylon. Seven thousand of these were the administrators, business magnates, professors, physicians, and lawyers. Another 1,000 were skilled craftsmen. The last 2,000 were probably military leaders, but the text does not say so. Nebuchadnezzar left only the very poorest in the land (2Kgs 24:14-17).[64] Those that he took to Babylon constituted a large and influential group with which to deal. Here was a concentration of the most intelligent Jewish leaders in the world. It formed the first of the upper class ghettos. Babylonian Jews were able to accomplish for Cyrus that which they promised, and they were not likely to relax comfortably in Babylon. Jews and Christians do not have a history of passively waiting, without involvement, to see how international affairs will progress.

Queen Nicotris was preparing Babylon's defense against the Medes when she fortified the Euphrates River and Babylon. She created a lake north of Babylon by diverting the Euphrates River into it. While the riverbed south of the lake was dry she had the banks lined with bricks to prevent an invasion, and she had a movable bridge prepared so that one side of Babylon could cross the river to the other side. Then she had the river returned to the newly lined riverbed so that it ran deeply through the middle of Babylon. When Cyrus learned of this he rediverted the river into the same lakebed, so that his troops could have entrance into Babylon. This all happened during a feast when Babylonians were drinking and dancing.

The skillful invasion of Cyrus required planned intelligence work. Before these events occurred Second Isaiah anticipated Jewish release in the near future. It happened in 539 BIA, 47 years after the Jewish exile began in 586 BIA. That is why Second Isaiah could easily interpret this whole movement in terms of Jubilee release and redemption. To be sure, Cyrus was the Lord's anointed (Isa 45:1), but God himself was the redeemer (Isa 43:14; 44:6, 22, 23; 47:4; 48:17, 20; 49:7; 50:2; 52:9; 54:5, 8; 59:20; 60:16; 62:12; 63:16).

By the time Cyrus had invaded Babylon, there was a large, powerful, upper class minority of Jews in Babylon. One of them (Nehemiah) later became cup bearer for the king (Neh 2:1-20). They were deeply enough involved in politics and business to be able to gain an audience with Cyrus of Persia and initiate negotiations. They also had enough communication skills to influence others to oppose Nabonidus and favor Cyrus. They were the ones who knew Cyrus was going to make the invasion. He had already negotiated an agreement with the Jews to return them to Judah and rebuild the nation after he conquered Babylon (Isa 45:1-3;

---

[64] Jeremiah reports a different number. According to him there were three times when Nebuchadnezzar took captives to Babylon: 1) 3,023, 2) 832, 3) 745. This totals 4,600 (Jer 52:28-30). He may have counted only the fathers of families, rather than the entire group.

Herodotus 1.189-91).[65] There had probably been several communications between Cyrus and the Babylonian Jews before this. When Cyrus completed this skillful plot he **ruled over all the land**, just as Daniel reported. Babylon was so well prepared to accept Cyrus as its king that Cyrus entered the city in royal procession; people spread green branches before him; and peace was imposed on the city.[66]

Anyone reading Daniel at this point who knows Jewish history would expect the author to tell how Jews fared with Cyrus after all of their expectations. Did Cyrus then allow them to return to Palestine as they wished? Were the prophecies of Second Isaiah fulfilled? Was Cyrus really the anointed of the Lord? This history is no secret. It is reported in Ezra, Nehemiah, Haggai, and Zechariah, but there is only a very slight reference to this redemption in the entire Book of Daniel (Dan 9:25).

Cyrus was a benevolent despot. He ruled like a monarch, but he had a generous regard for the many diverse people in his empire. One of the reasons that he was able to persuade peoples of other nations to transfer their allegiance to him was that people had heard of the nature of his government, and they liked it. He not only allowed people to practice their own religions, he supported the worship of the gods of his subjects. He stopped the Babylonian practice of humiliating and deporting subject people of his empire (Ezra 1:1-8). This generosity was applied also to Jews. Cyrus took prompt action to see that the temple was rebuilt and the walls were repaired (Ezra 1:2-4). This was not just a move to be kind; Cyrus needed a secure defense to protect his western border.

There was really deliverance for the Jews. Cyrus promptly allowed them to return. They rebuilt the walls of Jerusalem (Neh 4:10-23, 27) and the temple. Daniel did not report that, because it would have distracted from his thesis that Daniel's prophecy during the time of Nebuchadnezzar was not fulfilled until the rededication of the temple in 164 BIA. Instead of reporting the earlier return from Babylon, the author immediately directed his attention to the fourth kingdom.

A fourth kingdom, strong as iron. The Greek kingdom that crushed the Persians in the Near East was strong.[67] Alexander the Great was the general that led the Greek forces east. He conquered the territory from Macedonia into India, taking the entire Fertile Crescent by the time he was 33 years of age (d. 323 BIA). Egypt, Assyria, Media, Babylon, Palestine, Arabia, Asia Minor, and Syria were all parts of the Persian kingdom before Alexander moved east. When he took Persia this expanded his kingdom many times its earlier size.

---

[65] No one knows precisely where or when Herodotus was born or died. His approximate dates are 484 BIA to 424 BIA. Babylon was captured in 539 BIA.

[66] A. Leo Oppenheimer (tr.), "Babylonian and Assyrian Historical Texts," *Ancient Near Eastern Texts*, p. 306.

[67] Except for Porphyry, Ephraem Syrus, and Polychronius all of the early Jewish and Christian historians and religious leaders identified the fourth kingdom with Rome. These four correctly held that the fourth kingdom in Daniel was Greece. So G. Pfandl, "Interpretations of the Kingdom of God in Daniel 2:44," *AUSS* 34 (1995):249-68. All of these wrote after the Hasmonean rule had been crushed by Rome. They could no longer think of the Hasmonean Kingdom as God's Kingdom still to come. Christians and Jews have continued to update the fourth kingdom to their current situations. This is a very old midrashic and typological tradition, but it is not good historical analysis.

After Alexander's death his empire was divided among his generals. These fought among themselves until the number was reduced to four: Antigonus, Ptolemy, Seleucus, and Lysimachus. Ptolemy started with Egypt, but quickly added Libya and Palestine to his territory. Seleucus had the area around Babylon. Soon Antigonus took most of Asia Minor and Syria, but the other three kings, Seleucus, Callandrus, and Lysimachus fought with Antigonus, killed him, and divided his country among them. This war and treaty gave Syria and Palestine to Seleucus, and Asia Minor to Lysimachus. Then Seleucus overpowered Lysimachus and took most of the lowland cities of Asia Minor and Thrace. He moved his capital to Antioch in Syria. In 199 BIA, at the famous battle of Panias, Antiochus III, a descendant of Seleucus, drove the Egyptians out of Palestine and added Palestine to his empire.

This fourth kingdom, that which began with Alexander and continued through the Seleucid dynasty, was the one that conquered all of the previous kingdoms. Egypt and Syria were two of the parts of the fourth kingdom. One of these was the "iron" and the other was the "clay" at the feet of the statue. Geographically Palestine was between these two great kingdoms, and wars between them were often fought on Palestine's soil. There were several attempts at peace. Treaties were signed, and kings' daughters were given as bonds to confirm the seriousness of the treaties (Herodotus 1.74), but marriages did not guarantee peace between the countries. Judah vacillated between Egypt and Syria as the great super power that it would back, and sometimes some Jews supported Egypt while others supported Syria. Judah often bargained for terms with both of these countries and received as many concessions and as much money from each as possible.

It will break and shatter all of these. **All of these** evidently means **all** of the previous kingdoms that ruled before him. This is the iron kingdom crushing the gold, silver, and bronze kingdoms. The OG added "**all** the land will be shaken" (OGDan 2:40), an apt description of Alexander's movement. A parallel expression appears in relationship to the giant rock: **It will break and bring to an end all of these kingdoms** (Dan 2:44), meaning all four of the previous kingdoms.

TEXT

[41]The feet and toes which you saw, part of them of potter's clay and part of them of iron, will be a divided kingdom. Some of the firmness of iron will be in it, just as you saw iron mixed with clay. [42]The toes of the feet, part of them iron and part of them pottery, [means] part of the kingdom will be strong and part will be brittle.

Daniel	First Testament Intertexts
⁴³The iron mixed with clay which you saw will be mixed **with human seed**, but they will not hold together, one with the other, just as iron will not mix with clay.	ᴶᵉʳ ³¹:²⁷ Look! The days are coming, said Yehowah, when I will sow the house of Israel and the house of Judah **with human seed** and animal seed.

COMMENTARY

The feet and toes. The iron legs probably constituted the Greek kingdom of Alexander the Great, and **feet and toes** were the two surviving Greek kingdoms that were constantly at war over Palestine, Egypt and Syria. Both Ptolemy and Seleucus wanted to rule the entire kingdom of Alexander, but this unification would have been possible only if one completely overpowered the other and took control of the entire area. There could be no lasting treaty, because both had selfish motives for every action. **The feet and toes** were also Egypt and Syria at the time of an international marriage. This is what is involved in the expression, **They will be mixed with human seed** (MT Dan 2:43).

Both the dynasties of the Ptolemies of Egypt and of the Seleucids of Syria were successors to Alexander, but they were as different as iron and pottery. They were both Greeks, and they both ruled parts of Alexander's empire, and they both promoted Hellenization. Hellenization began in Palestine very early. When Alexander reached Palestine, Hellenization was already in place. Egypt had been strongly influenced by the Greeks, and Greek mercenaries had been stationed in Palestine when Egypt ruled the country. Greek merchants traveled throughout Asia Minor, Egypt, Palestine, and Syria, so Greek objects are still found in Palestine by archaeologists. Philistine merchants also brought to Palestine Greek pottery, coins, and figurines. Palestine was so thoroughly Hellenized that the principle currency of Palestine in the fifth century BIA was Athenian.[68] Bickerman said,

> The Jewish territory was practically in the midst of Hellenic cities: Ascalon, Akko (Ptolemais), Joppa (Jaffa), Appollonia and others on the coast; Samaria, Scythopolis (Rabath Amana) beyond the river Jordan; and Marisa in the south.[69]

Although it is next to impossible to identify which Seleucids were the ten "horns" that were ten kings (Dan 7:7, 24), the [ten] toes of the statue may have been intended to make the same identification.[70]

---

[68] Bickerman, *From Ezra*, pp. 17-18
[69] Bickerman, *From Ezra*, p.58.
[70] So also Hartman, *Daniel*, p. 149.

Part of them potter's clay and part of them iron. One of these substances represented the Seleucids and the other part the Ptolemies. The two families made several treaties, but they never lasted, so there were frequent wars between them.

TEXT

"⁴⁴During the days of these kings, the God of heaven will raise up a kingdom which will be for ages, and will not be overthrown. Its kingdom will not be left to another people. It will break and bring an end to all of these kingdoms, and it will endure for ages. ⁴⁵Just as you saw that a rock was cut from the mountain without the use of [human] hands and shattered iron, bronze, clay, silver, and gold, a great God has made known to the king what will happen after this. The dream is certain and its interpretation is reliable."

COMMENTARY

A kingdom that will be for the ages. Discussing the Zionistic attitude reflected in the Book of Daniel, Sheriffs correctly said, "No place is given to foreign nations in the covenant. At best foreign nations simply pass from the scene before the kingdom of God arrives."[71] The previous **kingdoms** identified in relationship to the mythical statue were not just any **kingdoms** of the world. They were the **kingdoms** that ruled Palestine after Nebuchadnezzar plundered Jerusalem, destroyed the temple, and took the leading citizens captive to Babylon. This was all told from a Jewish, rather than a North Israelite, point of view, because the author was Jewish.

The statue mythologized the historical period from the time of Jehoiakim and Jehoiakin until the time of the Hasmonean Revolt. After more than three years of guerrilla warfare, Judas the Maccabee won an important military victory over the Syrian Greeks at Beth-horon followed by another at Beth-zur. After these victories, Syrian troops retreated north like dogs with their tails between their legs, and Jewish troops returned to Jerusalem, had the temple cleansed, and Jews celebrated the first Hanukkah (164 BIA).[72] This was the turning point in the war that lasted until, under the leadership of Judas' older brother Simon, the Greeks were forced to acknowledge Jewish independence and remove all foreign taxes (142 BIA). This was the time that Jewish independence was restored to the condition it had before Nebuchadnezzar entered Jerusalem, confiscated the money from the temple and palace treasuries, and took King Jehoiakin prisoner.[73]

---

[71] D. C. T. Sheriffs, "'A Tale of Two Cities'—Nationalism in Zion and Babylon," *Tyndale Bulletin* 39 (1988):42. See further Sheriffs' lengthy discussion showing all the nationalism that appears in the Book of Daniel. He said, "The theme of the book of Daniel is the kingdom of God, brought to a sharp focus by chapter 7 in which the human-like figure receives the kingdom" (p. 41).

[72] Although Solomon dedicated the first temple (1Kgs 8) at approximately 1000 BIA, Jews celebrate Hanukkah on the basis of the restoration of the temple during the time of Judas the Maccabee.

[73] Actually, we have no other report that Jehoiakim was ever taken into captivity to Babylon. The author seems to have confused Jehoiakim with his son, Jehoiakin, who was taken into captivity to Babylon (2Kgs 24:15). This may have been done intentionally to fit in perfectly with the author's

The **kingdom** that followed the fourth **kingdom** in ruling the Promised Land was the Hasmonean **kingdom**. This was not a foreign **kingdom**. It was the **kingdom** God had promised his chosen people. Once it was restored to Jewish hands, Jews were convinced that they would never give it up again. It would last **for ages**. An **age** was a chronological term. Each of the earlier **kingdoms** had ruled for one **age** in succession. There was a Babylonian **age**, a Median **age**, a Persian **age**, and a Greek **age**. The **kingdom** that followed would not be limited by any such time constraints. It would endure **for** many **ages.**

Its kingdom will not be left to another people. This means this **kingdom** does belong to a **people**, namely the **people** of Israel. Heaton said,

> He clearly implies that the victory of God will mean also the triumph of Israel, to whose hands his kingly Rule will be delegated (cf. 7.13, 18, 27).[74]

This also implies that the **kingdom** involved is the nation of Israel with its capital city at Jerusalem. This entire chapter deals with the relationship of nations, one of which was Israel. Keil also said,

> As it is evident that a stone, in order to its rolling without the movement of the human hand, must be set free from a mountain, so in the express mention of the mountain there can be only a reference to Mount Zion, where the God of heaven has founded His kingdom.[75]

It will bring an end to all of these kingdoms. Just as the "little horn" would be broken without any human hand (Dan 8:25), so here the "rock" **brought an end to all of these kingdoms**. When it fell on the feet of the statue and crushed them, the rest of the statue was destined to tumble. This was the result of the Hasmonean **kingdom** that God raised up, in the author's judgment. The other **kingdoms** in the Near East did not cease to be. Rome, Egypt, Syria, and Carthage still existed. That which came **to an end** was the political control and taxation that they had over Palestine. This **kingdom** that was destined to endure for many ages was mythicized in the dream as a rock that was cut without the work of human hands. It was God's own design; it fell out from the mountain and crushed the Babylonians, Medians, Persians, and Greeks, destroying all of this foreign power that had ruled Palestine. Actually the Hasmoneans fought only the Syrian Greeks, but other **kingdoms** had fallen like dominoes. According to the author's analysis the Medians and Persians crushed the Babylonians, and the Greeks subdued the Persians. All that was left to destroy was the Greek kingdom of iron. Klausner said,

---

number system. He needed that date 605 to begin his program so that he would have 441 years before 164. 441 constitutes 9 Jubilee years of 49. Jehoiakin came along too late for that.

[74] Heaton, *Daniel*, p. 133.

[75] C. Keil, *Biblical Commentary on the Book of Daniel* (Grand Rapids: Eerdmans Publishing Co., c1976), p. 110.

> The Hasmoneans were influenced by a strong faith that the hour had come for the "kingdom of Heaven," that is the kingdom of the God of heaven, to be revealed to the world and for the kingdom of Greece to fall. They established, after severe struggles, a Jewish kingdom, which, to be sure, did not spread over the whole world and did not destroy all of the kingdoms of the Gentiles, but did achieve independence.[76]

Klausner thought that the **Kingdom** of God did not come with the Hasmoneans, but the reason it did not was not that the Kingdom of God was a non-earthly **kingdom**. The problem was that it did not succeed in replacing all of the gentile nations and finally ruling the world. If they had done that, the Hasmoneans would have ruled the **Kingdom** of God.

What will happen after this. The **this** about which the dream was designed to describe was the time after the rule of Nebuchadnezzar and until the time of Judas the Maccabee. The end of this period was also called the last days (*buh-ah-kha-reét yoh-máh-yah*, באחרית יומיא) (Dan 2:28). It made no reference to the end of time, the cosmos, or history. That which followed the Greeks and was "**after**" them was the Hasmonean kingdom, the fulfillment of the prophecy of Isa 2:2.

Hartman argued that Dan 2 had to have been completed no later than the beginning of the second century BIA, because, he said,

> There is nothing in the chapter to suggest that the author knew anything of the troubles that Antiochus IV Epiphanes brought on the Jews[77]

Hartman overlooked the fact that the author's main theme was optimistic. He spoke after he was convinced that God had already changed the times and seasons, removing and establishing kings (Dan 2:21). He knew what had happened at the last days (Dan 2:28). He knew how wicked the fourth kingdom had been, but he also knew that it was no longer a threat to Judah, because it had been displaced and was succeeded by a kingdom that God would raise up (Dan 2:44-45). The troubles that Antiochus IV Epiphanes brought on the Jews were over. The scope of the myth was a long period, from 605 to 164 BIA. The author omitted many things that occurred during that period, including the return of the Jews to Palestine under the leadership of Ezra and Nehemiah. That does not mean the author wrote before Ezra and Nehemiah. The victorious tone of the chapter was based on the fact that the rock had already crushed all four of these parts of a pagan statue and left them as dust for the wind to blow away.

The dream is sure. The reason that the interpretation of **the dream** was so precise and accurate is that it was really a mythization of the history that had already

---

[76] J. Klausner, *The Messianic Idea in Israel*, tr. W. F. Stinespring (New York: Macmillan, 1955), p. 235.
[77] Hartman, *Daniel*, p. 143.

taken place by the time the author wrote. Prophecies made by the eighth century prophets (Isaiah, Micah, Amos, and Hosea) were all general. They all foresaw the fall of North Israel. Prophecies of Jeremiah and Ezekiel prophesied the fall of Judah into the hands of the Babylonians, but they made no attempt to predict schedules and order of events for more than a 400-year period. Josephus called Daniel a prophet and considered him to be unique among the prophets, because he prophesied the future precisely. Furthermore he was optimistic; he prophesied good things rather than calamity (*Ant* 10.267-68). Josephus also noted that the temple had been defiled exactly three years before the time when it was cleansed and rededicated (*Ant* 12.320). Keil tried to fit Daniel among the prophets of distant generalities, while assuring his readers that the prophecy was true. The word *yaht-seév* (יציב) means "firm, sure," said Keil,

> but at the same time the word assures the readers of the book the certainty of the fulfillment, *since it lay far remote* [Italics added], and the visible course of things in the present and in the proximate future gave no indication or only a very faint prospect of the fulfillment.[78]

The dream, which **was sure**, was not just "a very faint prospect of the fulfilment." It had already been partially fulfilled. The four empires were followed-- first by the Battles of Beth-horon and Beth-zur, and then Hanukkah was immediate. The confidence of Daniel's fulfillment was sure, and its fulfillment was not in the far remote future.

The difference between Daniel and the other prophets is that the author of this **dream** myth was really not a prophet, but a biblical exegete and mythologist of history that had already occurred. He created Dan 2, following the story of Joseph in Egypt (Gen 41). He then related the history of Joseph to the events that had happened in his own day and the period of history between the beginning of the Babylonian captivity in 605 BIA and the cleansing of the temple in 164 BIA.[79]

The author mythologized the history of Palestine from 605 to 164 BIA the same way Hawthorne mythologized the situation in America at the time of the early pilgrims when he wrote *The Scarlet Letter*. It is also the same way Victor Hugo wrote *Les Miserables*, mythologizing the conditions in France during the French Revolution; and following the same methodology that Charles Dickens used when he wrote *A Tale of Two Cities*. These authors were not simply writing pure fiction. They were trying, through drama, to expose the social and political situations of their particular geographical territory at the time when their myths were cast. Each author had a teaching to communicate. The same was true of the author of Dan 2.

---

[78] Keil, *Daniel*, p. 112.
[79] The notion that Daniel was written during the second century BIA is not of recent origin. Jerome reported (prologue to *In Danielem Prophetam* PL25, col 491) that Porphyry (233-304 IA) said that the Book of Daniel was not written by Daniel but by someone in the second century BIA who lived during the days of Antiochus Epiphanes. Porphyry was a pagan and anti-Christian, but evidently a rather good historian (*HE* 6.19, 2-4)

TEXT

Daniel	First Testament Intertexts

⁴⁶Then King Nebuchadnezzar fell

on **his face** and
worshiped Daniel and commanded incense to be offered to him. ⁴⁷Then the king answered Daniel and said, "Truly

^{Isa 49:23} Kings will be your providers; their supply ships will support you. With **their faces** to the ground they will **worship** you; they will lick the dust of your feet.

^{Isa 44:14} They will pass over to you and become yours; they will walk after you in chains. They will pass over to you and **worship** you. They will pray, "Surely **God** is with you, and there is no other except **God**. ¹⁵Therefore you are a god who hides himself, **the God of** Israel, a savior."

your God
is the God of gods / and the Lord of kings / and a revealer of mysteries, / because you have been able / to reveal this mystery."

^{Deut 10:17} Yehowah is **your God. He is God of gods and Lord of** lords.

^{Gen 41:32} The matter is established by **God**, and **God** will hurry and do it.

⁴⁸Then **the king gave** Daniel honor and many great gifts and **governing authority over all the country of Babylon** and
administrator over all the wisemen of Babylon. ⁴⁹Daniel requested of the king that he might **appoint** Shadrach, Meshach, and Abednego **over the administration of the country of** Babylon, while Daniel [became judge of the court] at the gate of the king.

^{Gen 41:33-34} Joseph said, "Now let Pharaoh look for a man who is prudent and wise and set him **over the land of** Egypt, and let Pharaoh act **to appoint administrators over the land**."

^{Gen 41:41} Look! I have set you **over** all **the land of** Egypt.

COMMENTARY

Worshiped Daniel. It was normal for citizens to **worship** monarchs in the Orient. This was sometimes done also in Rome.⁸⁰ Alexander the Great accepted this Persian practice, and it was also practiced in relationship to some of the later Seleucids, but it was not a normal Hellenistic practice. Bath Sheba worshiped King David (1Kgs

---

⁸⁰ For example, when the embassy from Egypt came to Rome pleading for help to save the nation from Antiochus Epiphanes, they came unwashed, unshaven, with olive branches in their hands. They came before the Senate and prostrated themselves to the ground (*Liv* xliv.19).

1:31). Those who worshiped usually bowed in deference to someone in a higher position. It was unusual indeed for a king to **worship** a citizen and offer incense to be poured over him. This was one of the great reversals repeated several times in the Book of Daniel. It was to show that **Daniel** was honored more highly even than Joseph. It reminds the reader of the treatment Mordecai had received from the Persian king (Esth 6:3-13). It also appears as a fulfillment of the promise given by Second Isaiah that gentiles would bow down and worship Jews. Many scholars have been rather surprised and shocked that **Daniel**, a Jew, would allow anyone, even a foreigner to **worship** him, but Bevan said,

> We need not stop to inquire whether a strict monotheist would suffer himself to be thus worshipped, for the whole description is ideal-- Neb. At the feet of Dan. represents the Gentile power humbled before Israel (*cf.* Is. 49:23; 60:14).[81]

This was also the idea behind the report that Alexander the Great bowed down before the Jewish high priest (*Ant* 11.331). That is true, but it is not even necessary to resort to that argument to justify the practice. The Israelites bowed down and worshiped both David and God at the same time (1Chron 29:20), and David did not object. Israelites were willing for people to worship them; they refused to worship others. This may have been partially a matter of status.

Revealer of mysteries. The expectation that God would reveal mysteries was not a belief that was unique to Jews. In the time of Nebuchadnezzar it was customary for Babylonians to assume that all wisdom, including the civilizing arts and sciences, came from the gods. This is evident from Akkadian documents.[82]

Even though Daniel was honored above the status of a human king, the king recognized that it was Daniel's God who made all of this happen. Daniel did not have to tell him this. Babylonians believed that anytime insight was obtained it was because some deity provided it. Since it was Daniel who gained the knowledge, it must have been his god who provided the interpretation. The expression "God of gods" is a superlative idiom meaning that he is the greatest of all gods, and he is Lord of kings, meaning that all kings are subject to him.[83]

Administration of the country. Joseph asked the Pharaoh to appoint administrators to manage the food program Joseph recommended. Daniel asked the king to set his friends over the administration of the country—ancient practices of nepotism.

---

[81] So Montgomery, *Daniel*, p. 181; Bevan, *Short Commentary*.
[82] Lawson, "'Reveals Secrets,'" pp. 61-76.
[83] For a different interpretation see H. L. Ginsberg, "'King of Kings' and 'lord of kingdoms,'" *AJSL* 57 (1940):71-74.

The gate of the king. At least from the time of Ruth and Boaz people have gathered at the gates of the city to obtain justice (Ruth 4:1; 2Sam 15:1-4; Esth 3:2). This is the place where the king also held court.

CHAPTER THREE

ARAMAIC TEXT

3:1 נְבוּכַדְנֶצַּר מַלְכָּא עֲבַד צְלֵם דִּי־דְהַב רוּמֵהּ אַמִּין שִׁתִּין
פְּתָיֵהּ אַמִּין שֵׁת אֲקִימֵהּ בְּבִקְעַת דּוּרָא בִּמְדִינַת בָּבֶל: 2 וּנְבוּכַדְנֶצַּר
מַלְכָּא שְׁלַח לְמִכְנַשׁ ׀ לַאֲחַשְׁדַּרְפְּנַיָּא סִגְנַיָּא וּפַחֲוָתָא אֲדַרְגָּזְרַיָּא
גְדָבְרַיָּא דְּתָבְרַיָּא תִּפְתָּיֵא וְכֹל שִׁלְטֹנֵי מְדִינָתָא לְמֵתֵא לַחֲנֻכַּת צַלְמָא
דִּי הֲקֵים נְבוּכַדְנֶצַּר מַלְכָּא: 3 בֵּאדַיִן מִתְכַּנְּשִׁין אֲחַשְׁדַּרְפְּנַיָּא סִגְנַיָּא
וּפַחֲוָתָא אֲדַרְגָּזְרַיָּא גְדָבְרַיָּא דְּתָבְרַיָּא תִּפְתָּיֵא וְכֹל שִׁלְטֹנֵי מְדִינָתָא
לַחֲנֻכַּת צַלְמָא דִּי הֲקֵים נְבוּכַדְנֶצַּר מַלְכָּא וְקָאֲמִין [וְקָיְמִין] לָקֳבֵל צַלְמָא
דִּי הֲקֵים נְבוּכַדְנֶצַּר: 4 וְכָרוֹזָא קָרֵא בְחָיִל לְכוֹן אָמְרִין עַמְמַיָּא
אֻמַּיָּא וְלִשָּׁנַיָּא: 5 בְּעִדָּנָא דִּי־תִשְׁמְעוּן קָל קַרְנָא מַשְׁרוֹקִיתָא
קַיתָרוֹס [קַתְרוֹס] סַבְּכָא פְּסַנְתֵּרִין סוּמְפֹּנְיָה וְכֹל זְנֵי זְמָרָא תִּפְּלוּן וְתִסְגְּדוּן
לְצֶלֶם דַּהֲבָא דִּי הֲקֵים נְבוּכַדְנֶצַּר מַלְכָּא: 6 וּמַן־דִּי־לָא יִפֵּל
וְיִסְגֻּד בַּהּ־שַׁעֲתָא יִתְרְמֵא לְגוֹא־אַתּוּן נוּרָא יָקִדְתָּא:
7 כָּל־קֳבֵל דְּנָה בֵּהּ־זִמְנָא כְּדִי שָׁמְעִין כָּל־עַמְמַיָּא קָל קַרְנָא
מַשְׁרוֹקִיתָא קַיתָרֹס [קַתְרֹס] שַׂבְּכָא פְּסַנְטֵרִין וְכֹל זְנֵי זְמָרָא נָפְלִין כָּל־
עַמְמַיָּא אֻמַּיָּא וְלִשָּׁנַיָּא סָגְדִין לְצֶלֶם דַּהֲבָא דִּי הֲקֵים נְבוּכַדְנֶצַּר מַלְכָּא:
8 כָּל־קֳבֵל דְּנָה בֵּהּ־זִמְנָא קְרִבוּ גֻּבְרִין כַּשְׂדָּאִין וַאֲכַלוּ
קַרְצֵיהוֹן דִּי יְהוּדָיֵא: 9 עֲנוֹ וְאָמְרִין לִנְבוּכַדְנֶצַּר מַלְכָּא מַלְכָּא
לְעָלְמִין חֱיִי: 10 אַנְתָּה [אַנְתְּ] מַלְכָּא שָׂמְתָּ טְעֵם דִּי כָל־אֱנָשׁ דִּי־יִשְׁמַע קָל
קַרְנָא מַשְׁרוֹקִיתָא קַיתָרֹס [קַתְרֹס] שַׂבְּכָא פְּסַנְתֵּרִין [וְסוּפֹּנְיָה] וְסוּמְפֹּנְיָה וְכֹל
זְנֵי זְמָרָא יִפֵּל וְיִסְגֻּד לְצֶלֶם דַּהֲבָא: 11 וּמַן־דִּי־לָא יִפֵּל וְיִסְגֻּד יִתְרְמֵא
לְגוֹא־אַתּוּן נוּרָא יָקִדְתָּא: 12 אִיתַי גֻּבְרִין יְהוּדָאיִן דִּי־מַנִּיתָ יָתְהוֹן עַל־
עֲבִידַת מְדִינַת בָּבֶל שַׁדְרַךְ מֵישַׁךְ וַעֲבֵד נְגוֹ גֻּבְרַיָּא אִלֵּךְ לָא־שָׂמוּ
עֲלָךְ [עֲלָיךְ] מַלְכָּא טְעֵם לֵאלָהָיִךְ [לֵאלָהָךְ] לָא פָלְחִין וּלְצֶלֶם דַּהֲבָא דִּי
הֲקֵימְתָּ לָא סָגְדִין: ס 13 בֵּאדַיִן נְבוּכַדְנֶצַּר בִּרְגַז וַחֲמָה אֲמַר לְהַיְתָיָה
לְשַׁדְרַךְ מֵישַׁךְ וַעֲבֵד נְגוֹ בֵּאדַיִן גֻּבְרַיָּא אִלֵּךְ הֵיתָיוּ קֳדָם מַלְכָּא:
14 עָנֵה נְבֻכַדְנֶצַּר וְאָמַר לְהוֹן הַצְדָּא שַׁדְרַךְ מֵישַׁךְ וַעֲבֵד נְגוֹ לֵאלָהַי
לָא אִיתֵיכוֹן פָּלְחִין וּלְצֶלֶם דַּהֲבָא דִּי הֲקֵימֶת לָא סָגְדִין: 15 כְּעַן הֵן
אִיתֵיכוֹן עֲתִידִין דִּי בְעִדָּנָא דִּי־תִשְׁמְעוּן קָל קַרְנָא מַשְׁרוֹקִיתָא
קַיתָרֹס [קַתְרֹס] שַׂבְּכָא פְּסַנְתֵּרִין וְסוּמְפֹּנְיָה וְכֹל ׀ זְנֵי זְמָרָא תִּפְּלוּן וְתִסְגְּדוּן
לְצַלְמָא דִי־עַבְדֵת וְהֵן לָא תִסְגְּדוּן בַּהּ־שַׁעֲתָה תִתְרְמוֹן לְגוֹא־אַתּוּן
נוּרָא יָקִדְתָּא וּמַן־הוּא אֱלָהּ דִּי יְשֵׁיזְבִנְכוֹן מִן־יְדָי: 16 עֲנוֹ שַׁדְרַךְ
מֵישַׁךְ וַעֲבֵד נְגוֹ וְאָמְרִין לְמַלְכָּא נְבוּכַדְנֶצַּר לָא־חַשְׁחִין אֲנַחְנָה
עַל־דְּנָה פִּתְגָם לַהֲתָבוּתָךְ: 17 הֵן **אִיתַי אֱלָהַנָא** דִּי־**אֲנַחְנָא** פָלְחִין
יָכִל **לְשֵׁיזָבוּתַנָא** מִן־**אַתּוּן נוּרָא** יָקִדְתָּא וּמִן־יְדָךְ מַלְכָּא יְשֵׁיזִב:
18 וְהֵן לָא יְדִיעַ לֶהֱוֵא־לָךְ מַלְכָּא דִּי לֵאלָהָיךְ לָא־אִיתַינָא [אִיתַנָא] פָלְחִין

Isa 36:18; 37:12

Ps 107:2

וּלְצֶלֶם דַּהֲבָא דִּי הֲקֵימֶת לָא נִסְגֻּד: ס 19 בֵּאדַיִן נְבוּכַדְנֶצַּר הִתְמְלִי חֱמָא וּצְלֵם אַנְפּוֹהִי אֶשְׁתַּנּוֹ [אֶשְׁתַּנִּי] עַל־שַׁדְרַךְ מֵישַׁךְ וַעֲבֵד נְגוֹ עָנֵה וְאָמַר לְמֵזֵא לְאַתּוּנָא חַד־שִׁבְעָה עַל דִּי חֲזֵה לְמֵזְיֵהּ: 20 וּלְגֻבְרִין גִּבָּרֵי־חַיִל דִּי בְחַיְלֵהּ אֲמַר לְכַפָּתָה לְשַׁדְרַךְ מֵישַׁךְ וַעֲבֵד נְגוֹ לְמִרְמֵא לְאַתּוּן נוּרָא יָקִדְתָּא: 21 בֵּאדַיִן גֻּבְרַיָּא אִלֵּךְ כְּפִתוּ בְּסַרְבָּלֵיהוֹן פַּטְּשֵׁיהוֹן [פַּטִּישֵׁיהוֹן] וְכַרְבְּלָתְהוֹן וּלְבֻשֵׁיהוֹן וּרְמִיו לְגוֹא־אַתּוּן נוּרָא יָקִדְתָּא: 22 כָּל־קֳבֵל דְּנָה מִן־דִּי מִלַּת מַלְכָּא מַחְצְפָה וְאַתּוּנָא אֵזֵה יַתִּירָא גֻּבְרַיָּא אִלֵּךְ דִּי הַסִּקוּ לְשַׁדְרַךְ מֵישַׁךְ וַעֲבֵד נְגוֹ קַטִּל הִמּוֹן שְׁבִיבָא דִּי נוּרָא: 23 וְגֻבְרַיָּא אִלֵּךְ תְּלָתֵּהוֹן שַׁדְרַךְ מֵישַׁךְ וַעֲבֵד נְגוֹ נְפַלוּ לְגוֹא־אַתּוּן־נוּרָא יָקִדְתָּא מְכַפְּתִין: פ 24 אֱדַיִן נְבוּכַדְנֶצַּר מַלְכָּא תְּוַהּ וְקָם בְּהִתְבְּהָלָה עָנֵה וְאָמַר לְהַדָּבְרוֹהִי הֲלָא גֻבְרִין תְּלָתָא רְמֵינָא לְגוֹא־נוּרָא מְכַפְּתִין עָנַיִן וְאָמְרִין לְמַלְכָּא יַצִּיבָא מַלְכָּא: 25 עָנֵה וְאָמַר הָא־אֲנָה חָזֵה גֻּבְרִין אַרְבְּעָה שְׁרַיִן מַהְלְכִין בְּגוֹא־נוּרָא וַחֲבָל לָא־אִיתַי בְּהוֹן וְרֵוֵהּ דִּי רְבִיעָיָא [רְבִיעָאָה] דָּמֵה לְבַר־אֱלָהִין: ס 26 בֵּאדַיִן קְרֵב נְבוּכַדְנֶצַּר לִתְרַע אַתּוּן נוּרָא יָקִדְתָּא עָנֵה וְאָמַר שַׁדְרַךְ מֵישַׁךְ וַעֲבֵד־נְגוֹ עַבְדוֹהִי דִּי־אֱלָהָא עִלָּיָא [עִלָּאָה] פֻּקוּ וֶאֱתוֹ בֵּאדַיִן נָפְקִין שַׁדְרַךְ מֵישַׁךְ וַעֲבֵד נְגוֹ מִן־גּוֹא נוּרָא: 27 וּמִתְכַּנְּשִׁין אֲחַשְׁדַּרְפְּנַיָּא סִגְנַיָּא וּפַחֲוָתָא וְהַדָּבְרֵי מַלְכָּא חָזַיִן לְגֻבְרַיָּא אִלֵּךְ דִּי לָא־שְׁלֵט נוּרָא בְּגֶשְׁמְהוֹן וּשְׂעַר רֵאשְׁהוֹן לָא הִתְחָרַךְ וְסַרְבָּלֵיהוֹן לָא שְׁנוֹ וְרֵיחַ נוּר לָא עֲדָת בְּהוֹן: 28 עָנֵה נְבוּכַדְנֶצַּר וְאָמַר בְּרִיךְ אֱלָהֲהוֹן דִּי־שַׁדְרַךְ מֵישַׁךְ וַעֲבֵד נְגוֹ דִּי־שְׁלַח מַלְאֲכֵהּ וְשֵׁיזִב לְעַבְדוֹהִי דִּי הִתְרְחִצוּ עֲלוֹהִי וּמִלַּת מַלְכָּא שַׁנִּיו וִיהַבוּ גֶשְׁמְהוֹן [גֶשְׁמֵיהוֹן] דִּי לָא־יִפְלְחוּן וְלָא־יִסְגְּדוּן לְכָל־אֱלָהּ לָהֵן לֵאלָהֲהוֹן: 29 וּמִנִּי שִׂים טְעֵם דִּי כָל־עַם אֻמָּה וְלִשָּׁן דִּי־יֵאמַר שֵׁלָה [שָׁלוּ] עַל אֱלָהֲהוֹן דִּי־שַׁדְרַךְ מֵישַׁךְ וַעֲבֵד נְגוֹא הַדָּמִין יִתְעֲבֵד וּבַיְתֵהּ נְוָלִי יִשְׁתַּוֵּה כָּל־קֳבֵל דִּי לָא אִיתַי אֱלָה אָחֳרָן דִּי־יִכֻּל לְהַצָּלָה כִּדְנָה: 30 בֵּאדַיִן מַלְכָּא הַצְלַח לְשַׁדְרַךְ מֵישַׁךְ וַעֲבֵד נְגוֹ בִּמְדִינַת בָּבֶל: פ 31 נְבוּכַדְנֶצַּר מַלְכָּא לְכָל־עַמְמַיָּא אֻמַּיָּא וְלִשָּׁנַיָּא דִּי־דָאֲרִין [דָיְרִין] בְּכָל־אַרְעָא שְׁלָמְכוֹן יִשְׂגֵּא: 32 אָתַיָּא וְתִמְהַיָּא דִּי עֲבַד עִמִּי אֱלָהָא עִלָּיָא [עִלָּאָה] שְׁפַר קָדָמַי לְהַחֲוָיָה: 33 אָתוֹהִי כְּמָה רַבְרְבִין וְתִמְהוֹהִי כְּמָה תַקִּיפִין מַלְכוּתֵהּ מַלְכוּת עָלַם וְשָׁלְטָנֵהּ עִם־דָּר וְדָר:

Isa 43:2

Exod 14:24

Isa 43:2
Exod 14:24

Isa 43:2

2Chron 32:21-22
Exod 14:19; 20:2-5
Exod 34:14; Ps 95:6

Exod 34:14

Ps 145:5, 13

INTRODUCTION

The Masoretic Text (MT) is not trustworthy, according to Charles. His first reason for this judgment is that the MT did not begin as other chapters. It is not consistent with "our author's method." This argument is based on the belief that one author wrote all of Daniel. On that basis, Charles deduced the author's style, method, and vocabulary. Then he assumed that every variation from Charles' conjectured style was a scribal or translator's mistake or a later intrusion. Since there are many variations, not only in vocabulary, style, and method, but also in languages, it is more reasonable to assume that there were more authors than one in this undertaking. This means that different units reflect different authors rather than revisions and intrusions.

Charles also thought that the author should have mentioned that on the same date at which the statue was constructed, Nebuchadnezzar also plundered Jerusalem and destroyed the temple (Jer 32:1; 52:29; *Apion* 1.21).[1] Ancient writers did not always write that which modern scholars think they should have written. Nor did they always write in the style and organization that scholars think would be best, using always the words modern scholars would prefer. The original authors rather than later scribes might sometimes have made mistakes. Taken alone, Dan 3 forms a literary unit and needs no interference with the vocabulary. The following chapter will ignore some of Charles' corrections, following basically the MT.

ENGLISH TEXT

[OG: [3:1]During the eighteenth year of Nebuchadnezzar's conquest of cities and countries, and all of those who live in the land from India to Ethiopia, he . . .] [MT: [3:1]King Nebuchadnezzar] made a statue of gold, which was 90 feet tall and nine feet wide. He set it up in the Dura Valley in the city of Babylon. [2]Then the king sent to gather the satraps, administrators, governors, judges, treasurers, counselors, sheriffs, and all local rulers to come to the dedication of the statue which King Nebuchadnezzar set up. [3]Then the satraps, administrators, governors, judges, treasurers, counselors, sheriffs, and all local rulers congregated at the dedication of the statue which King Nebuchadnezzar set up, and they stood before the statue which Nebuchadnezzar set up. [4]The crier called aloud, saying, "Peoples, nations, and [those who speak various foreign] languages, [5]whenever you hear the sound of the ram's horn, pipe, lyre, trigon,[2] harp, bagpipe,[3] and every kind of music you must fall down and worship the golden statue which King Nebuchadnezzar set up. [6]Anyone who does not fall down and worship, at that moment will be thrown into a flaming, fiery furnace. [7]Therefore, at the time when all the peoples heard the sound of the rams horn, pipe, lyre, trigon, harp, and every kind of music, all the peoples, nations, and [those who speak various foreign] languages fell down and worshiped the golden statue which King Nebuchadnezzar erected.

COMMENTARY

During the eighteenth year. Counting from 605 or 604 BIA this would be 587 or 586 BIA, the very year that the temple was burned. This date is not given in the Hebrew text. It might have been a later editorial, interpretative addition, calling attention to the fact that Nebuchadnezzar constructed this pagan statue the same year he plundered the temple in Jerusalem.[4]

All those who live in the land from India to Ethiopia. The words eh-peé tays gáys (ἐπὶ τῆς γῆς) (OG Dan 3:1) can mean either "on the earth" or "on the land." Most of the times in biblical literature it means "on the land," and means "on the Promised

---

[1] R. H. Charles, *A Critical and Exegetical Commentary on the Book of Daniel* (Oxford: Clarendon Press, 1929), pp. 56-57.
[2] A triangular instrument with four strings.
[3] The *soom-phoh-neé-ah* was some kind of a wind instrument, like a saxophone, clarinet, bassoon, or bagpipe.
[4] So A. LaCocque, *The Book of Daniel* (Atlanta: John Knox Press, 1979), p. 56.

Land." Here, however, the meaning includes all of the land of the Babylonian Empire. If it should be rendered "on the earth" then the earth was understood to be circumscribed by these east-west dimensions. This addition to Dan 3 is reported only in the old Greek text. The same translator was consistent in further describing Nebuchadnezzar as "king of kings and lords of the whole universe" (*táys oi-koo-méh-nays* (τῆς οἰκουμένης) (OG Dan 3:2) The universe was an expression in NT times that applied to the Roman Empire. Here it clearly belongs to the Babylonian Empire. In this parallel relationship the term "land" has the same meaning as "universe." It described the entire country of Babylon.

The dedication. The term used for dedication here (*khah-noo-káht*, חנכת) is the same word Jews used for the rededication of the temple at Hanukkah in 164 BIA. The term was also used for the dedication of Solomon's temple (1Kgs 8:63; 2Chron7:5) and for its rededication under Ezra (Ezra 6:16). Jews who had been willing to die for the dedication of their own temple were also willing to die rather than participate in a pagan dedication.

Statue which Nebuchadnezzar set up. It was rather usual for kings to have statues of themselves set up in important places. Antiochus III, for example, had a statue of himself set up in the temple of Athena in Coronea, Greece (Livy 36.20, 2-3), and the Roman emperor Gaius attempted to have a statue of himself erected in the temple at Jerusalem (*War* 2.184-203). Herodotus said in his day there was a large golden statue of Zeus in Babylon that was 18 feet tall (Herodotus 1.83). Diodorus Siculus 2.9 said there were three golden images on the top of the Belus temple, dedicated to Zeus, Hera, and Rhea. The Statue of Zeus was 60 feet tall. People were often expected to worship statues of emperors, but they were also expected to worship monstrous statues of deities. Driver thought the statue discussed in Dan 3 would have been a statue of Nebuchadnezzar,[5] but that would have been a strangely proportioned statue. This statue was about 90 feet tall and 9 feet wide. If it had been a statue of a person it would have been a rather thin one. Proportionately, a person six feet tall would have to be only 7.2 inches across the shoulders. The text does not say what kind of statue it was. It could have been a pillar with a statue of a king on the top. Prophets ridiculed such idols as this (Isa 40:19; 41:7; Jer 10:3-5).

In the Dura Valley. Oppert may have found the Dura Valley. There is a Dura river that runs into the Euphrates about six miles south of Babylon. There are tels in the vicinity and the base of a statue 14 meters square, and six meters high that may be the base for the statue reported by Daniel.[6] This is not the only possibility for the location of Dura Valley. Another suggestion made by Cook may be correct in holding that the word "Dura" in Akkadian means "wall." Therefore there is some likelihood that the word is a loan word into Aramaic. That would mean that passage should be translated "the plain of the wall" and refer to the plain before the great wall of Babylon built by Nebuchadnezzar and described by Herodotus (Herodotus

---

[5] S. R. Driver, *The Book of Daniel* (Cambridge: University Press, 1912), pp. 35-36.

[6] Oppert, *Expedition Scientifique en Mesopotamie* I, pp. 238ff.

1.178-82).⁷ Shea thinks rather that it was the open plain between the inner and outer walls of Babylon.⁸

The king sent [someone] to gather. The people commanded to come to this dedication did not include the scholars, like Daniel and his friends. Those invited included all of the national leaders, from the local sheriffs to the satraps of provinces. The exact function of each of these officers is not known. Their names are mostly Persian rather than Akkadian. This may reflect a later composition, but Persia and Babylon were close enough geographically to have shared some verbal terms. None of the titles is Greek. Why did Nebuchadnezzar fail to include the scholars? Or, put differently, why did the author of this document not include Daniel among the leaders invited to the dedication?

All peoples, nations, and [those who speak foreign] languages. Babylon was a large empire in those days. Nebuchadnezzar had conquered all of the countries between the Tigris-Euphrates Valley and the Mediterranean Sea, including Judah and Israel. People in these countries spoke Hebrew, Aramaic, Greek, Arabic, and other Near Eastern languages. These had earlier been independent nations that spoke their own languages. Nebuchadnezzar was a king of kings, because the kings of all of these countries were subordinate to him.

Every kind of music. Most of the instruments listed here are loan words from the Greek:⁹ The lyre (*kaith-uh-ros*, קיתרוס = *kee-thár-ahs* (κιθάρας);¹⁰ trigon (*sab-úh-kah*, סבכא) = *sahm-boó-kays* (σαμβύκης); harp (*psahn-tay-reén*, פסנתרין) = *psahl-tay-reé-os* (ψαλτηρίου); bagpipe (*soom-phoh-neh-yáh*, סומפניה) = *soom-phoh-neé-ahs* (συμφωνίας).¹¹ These Greek words suggest to the reader that this pericope was composed at a date later than the time of Nebuchadnezzar. They indicate a date sometime after the conquest of Alexander the Great in the fourth century BIA. The instrument, *soom-phoh-nee-ah*, for instance is not found in other Greek literature until the beginning of the second century BIA. If this had been written during the sixth century BIA then the list would be composed of instruments known in Babylonian (Akkadian) rather than Greek. Although written in Aramaic, the words were those that would have been known by Greek speaking people.

Hartman has noted several words in this chapter which are also loan words from Persian,¹² but that does not mean that this narrative was written during the Persian rule. Alexander the Great initially set out to spread Greek culture, but the Hellenism he propagated was a mixture of Persian and Greek. Greek culture was centered on the *polis*, the city-state, but the city-state was too small for a large

---

⁷ E. M. Cook, "In the Plain of the Wall," *JBL* 108 (1989):115-16.
⁸ From personal conversation.
⁹ For a technical description of the instruments see P. Grelot, "L'orchestre de Daniel iii 5, 7, 10, 15," *VT* 29 (1979):23-38.
¹⁰ It is from this Greek word that we get the American word "guitar."
¹¹ From this word we get the term "symphony." This may have been some kind of accompanying instrument.
¹² L. F. Hartman and A. A. DiLella, *The Book of Daniel* (Garden City: Doubleday & Co., Inc., 1978), pp. 156-58.

empire. Hellenistic peoples finally had to accept the monarchy. This was true both in Asia and in Europe.[13]

Waldbaum has argued from the archaeological viewpoint that the Greek influence was not reflected in the East except along the Mediterranean shore from the 10th to the 4th centuries BIA.[14] He held that there would not have been Greek influences as far east as Babylon in the 6th century BIA.

Alexander imitated Cyrus when he conquered Persia and afterward was influenced by Persian philosophy and governing policies. Greek influence had been propagated widely before Alexander and had already been confused with other cultures. Even the language became infiltrated with Persian loan words. Although this drama was told as if Nebuchadnezzar were the king, and this were a historical account, the language betrays a later date. Nebuchadnezzar played the role of the arch villain in this play. Just as Shakespeare wrote plays of earlier English kings, so this myth was applied to a king who lived earlier than the author.

Fell down and worshiped the golden statue. That is to say that they prostrated themselves with their faces to the ground. This was normal court etiquette. Those who came into the presence of the king were expected to prostrate themselves before him, just as citizens in U.S.A. normally rise when the judge enters the court room, and refer to him or her as "your honor." We salute the flag and stand for the national anthem. The text does not say what the image represented. It was too narrow to have been a statue of Nebuchadnezzar. It was probably something that was identified with the nation so that this action would have shown respect and allegiance to the current administration. Most citizens in antiquity would have felt no guilt in doing this, any more than citizens have problems with saluting the flag.

TEXT

[8]Consequently, at that time certain Chaldeans came forward and said malicius things about the Jews. [9]They answered and said to Nebuchadnezzar, the king, "King, live for ages! [10]You, king, have issued a command that everyone who hears the sound of the trumpet, pipe, lyre, trigon, harp, bagpipe, and every kind of music must fall down and worship the golden statue. [11]Anyone who does not fall down and worship will be thrown into the flaming, fiery furnace. [12]There are men who are Jews whom you have appointed over the management of the province of Babylon--Shadrach, Meshach, and Abednego. These men have not obeyed[15] your royal command; they do not worship your god; and the golden statue which you erected they do not worship." Then Nebuchadnezzar in heated anger ordered that Shadrach, Meshach, and Abednego be brought. [13]Then these men appeared before the king. [14]Nebuchadnezzar answered and said, "Is it true, Shadrach, Meshach, and Abednego, that you do not worship my god, and you do not worship the golden statue that I erected? [15]Now, if you are prepared, at the time when you hear the

---

[13] So also E. R. Bevan, *The House of Seleucus* (New York: Barnes & Noble, Inc., c1902, 1966) I, p. 17.
[14] J. Waldbaum, "Greeks *in* the East or Greeks *and* the East?" *BASOR* 305 (1997):1-17.
[15] Following Theodotion.

sound of the ram's horn, pipe, lyre, trigon, harp, bagpipe, and every kind of music, [and] you fall down and worship the statue which I made [you will not be punished],

Daniel	First Testament Intertexts
But if you do not worship, at that instant you will be thrown into the flaming, fiery furnace. Is there a **god** that **will deliver** you **from** my **hands**?"	Isa 36:18 Has any **god** of the nations **delivered** his land **from the hand** of the king of Assyria? (see also 37:12).

COMMENTARY

Chaldean men came forward. This is a predictable pattern. The Chaldeans were local citizens. They were also priests and professional counselors. The Jews were foreigners. They had entered Babylon as captives; they obtained the best education available in Babylon, free of charge; they quickly gained the chief positions in the government. It was certain that the local citizens would have been jealous and watched attentively for an opportunity to injure them in some way, if not get rid of them altogether. They probably studied the Jewish practices to find something that would irritate the king. They may have been the ones who suggested the statue and the conditions to the king in the first place.

Said malicious things about. Literally, "ate the pieces of." Generally it means to slander or accuse falsely.

If you are prepared. . . . [and] you fall down and worship the statue which I made [you will not be punished]. This sentence does not include the conclusion, which has been put in brackets, because it is obvious. This is not a unique construction. When Moses pleaded with God in behalf of the Israelites, he said, **Now, if you will forgive their sin** [don't punish them but accept them as your people] (Exod 32:32).
    The king was prepared to give the group a second chance. He first asked them if the accusation was true. If it was, it might have been an oversight or a misunderstanding. If that were so, they could conform at the next time the music was sounded, and they would escape unharmed.
    Keil assumed that this entire account is historical and that these words are the very words of Nebuchadnezzar.[16]

Thrown into the flaming, fiery furnace. Ancient furnaces were usually made to look like half a globe with the flat surface on the ground. They had thick walls of clay. Bakers built fires inside the furnaces to heat the furnace itself. When the walls became hot enough, they put the loaves of bread into the furnace itself, closed the entrance, and allowed the heat from the walls to bake the bread. The furnace reported here must have been huge, with a door at the bottom, and a hole at the top

---

[16] C. Keil, *Biblical Commentary on the Book of Daniel* tr. M. G. Easton (Grand Rapids: Eerdmans Publishing Co., c1976), pp. 134-35.

for the smoke to escape. It was from that hole at the top that fuel was provided, and it was from that hole that the victims were to be thrown.

This seems like cruel and inhuman treatment in Western countries today, but in antiquity kings were very resourceful in torturing those who irritated them. Jeremiah reported that the king of Babylon roasted Zedekiah and Ahab in the fire (Jer 29:22). When Judah learned that his daughter-in-law was pregnant, without being married, he ordered her to be burned (Gen 38:24). Antiochus Eupator ordered Menelaus to be dragged through burning coals until his body became ashes (2Macc 13:4-7). Death punishment by burning was prescribed for punishing a priest's daughter who had become a prostitute (Lev 21:9) and also for a man who married both a mother and her daughter (Lev 20:14). The fiery furnace was just one more method of torturous execution.

Is there a god that will deliver you? This is a rhetorical question. It means that there is no god who can deliver them. This is the question that set the stage for the next event in the narrative. The author here has deliberately quoted from a passage in Isaiah to remind the reader of the time Rabshakeh came to Jerusalem with thousands of Assyrian soldiers. He jeered at Hezekiah, reminding him of the great successes the Assyrian king had demonstrated in conquering other countries. He asked if any of the gods of those nations delivered their lands from the king of Assyria (Isa 36:19-20; 37:11-12. 2Kgs 18:33-35; 19:12-13). The answer, of course, was, "No." Nevertheless, Hezekiah prayed, and the next morning 185,000 Assyrian soldiers lay dead outside the walls of Jerusalem. The fiery furnace experience was intended to become a repeat performance, and the three Jewish believers acted with the same confidence as Hezekiah.

TEXT

Daniel	First Testament Intertexts
	Deut 4:20 Yehowah has taken you and brought you out from an iron **furnace**, from Egypt.
¹⁶Shadrach, Meshach, and Abednego answered King Nebuchadnezzar and said, "We have no need to answer you on this matter. ¹⁷Look! There is a **God** whom we worship. He is able **to save** us from the flaming, **fiery furnace**,	Ps 107:2 Let **the redeemed** of **Yehowah** say, / "We went through **fire** and through water, but you brought us out to a spacious place."
and he will **save** [us] from your **hand**, O King, ¹⁸but [even] if not, let it be known to you that we will not worship your god, nor worship the golden statue that you have erected."	[It is Yehowah] who **has saved** you **from** the **hand** of the oppressor. Isa 43:3 For I am **Yehowah**, your **God**, / the holy One of Israel, your **Savior.**

¹⁹Then Nebuchadnezzar was filled with anger, and the expression on his face changed against Shadrach, Meshach, and Abednego. He ordered that the furnace be heated seven times more than it was normal to heat it, ²⁰and he ordered the officers of his army to overpower Shadrach, Meshach, and Abednego and to throw them into the flaming, fiery furnace. ²¹Then they overpowered these men in their coats, trousers, turbans, and [other] clothing and hurled them into the flaming, fiery furnace.[17] ²²Because the order of the king was urgent, and the furnace was very hot, the flame of the fire killed these men who carried Shadrach, Meshach, and Abednego, ²³and, being thrown down, these three men--Shadrach, Meshach, and Abednego--fell into the flaming, fiery furnace.

COMMENTARY

We have no need. This may be a legal answer meaning that there was no court requirement that they answer the king. They might have been exempted on the basis of an early example of the American fifth amendment to the constitution. When Jesus was on trial he refused to answer the interrogation (Matt 26:64) that might have incriminated him.

Look! There is a God. This comes as an answer to the question, "**Is there a god** that will deliver you (Dan 3:15)?" This clause has given nearly every commentator trouble in translating. It could be rendered, "If **there is a God** whom we worship he is able to save us from the flaming, fiery furnace, and he will save us from your hand, O King." Then the next verse continues, "But if not . . ." The word rendered "Look!" is the same word that can be translated "if" (*hayn*, הן)." Any way this is rendered it confuses confidence with insecurity. On the one hand there might be a God who could save us or there might not. Or, there is the confidence that there is such a God, but on the other hand there might not be. The "ifs" disturb many exegetes. Most commentators are not happy with their own translations. Basically it says that God is here being put to the test. The Jews who face the king are willing to take the risk. They are not sure that God will save them, but in any case, they will not submit to the demands of the king. The author of this chapter was asking the reader to feel the courage and insecurity of Hezekiah when Rabshakeh had jeered him.

He will save us. The men thought that God was able to save them, because that was what the scripture said. God had delivered Israelites before in situations such as that faced by Hezekiah; therefore he was able to do it again. If he could save them from water it followed that he could also save them from fire. They had only to trust. The same outspoken courage reflected here appears without question or doubt in the story of the mother whose seven sons died for their faith. She was presented as if she were speaking to Antiochus personally.

---

[17] Some render this "tunics." It probably comes from some Persian word, but its meaning can only be discerned from its context. See A. A. Bevan, *A Short Commentary on the Book of Daniel* (Cambridge: University Press, 1892), p. 84.

> You wretch! On the one hand, you may release us from our present life, but after we have died for the sake of his laws, the king of the cosmos will raise us up to live for the age [to come] (2Macc 7:9).

From your hand. Not only could God save his people from fire and water. He could save them from any oppressor. That is what the Psalmist said. This meant that God could save them from the hand of the king.

But even if not. This was an affirmation of loyalty. Death to them was better than apostasy, but it implies that the defendants were not completely sure of God's action. Coxon has shown the extent early translators and interpreters have gone to avoid the implications of this verse.[18]

We will not worship your god. This seems like an arrogant statement to address to the king of a nation to which these men had been brought as captives. The king paid to have them nourished, trained, and given all the other provisions they needed. They first began by rejecting the king's gourmet food. Then they refused the king's religion. The king trained them as he did so that they might become converted to Babylonian culture, language, and religion. Then the young men said they would concede nothing of that which he asked in response for his generosity. It is not surprising that he became angry.

The expression on his face changed. Of course his expression changed. He had been insulted. These men from Judah were not only disrespectful; they were offensive. Here they were in the king's court, and they observed none of the normal court etiquette that they had been taught. Up to that point the king was being kind to these men. He was giving them every reasonable doubt. He was trying to coax them into fulfilling the national law. Then they rejected rather impudently all of his offers. As expected, his facial expression changed from cheerfulness to fury.

Fell into the flaming, fiery furnace. The prospects for survival did not seem very good for these captives. This method of execution had been used successfully before at normal temperatures, but this time the furnace was heated seven times normal heat. The men were forcibly picked up bodily and dropped into the hole in the furnace above the flame. There seemed no escape.

Coats, trousers, turbans. These items of clothing may not be exactly translated. It is not certain what clothes Babylonians wore at that time. Whatever it was, these Jews were completely dressed and were thrown into the fire wearing all of their clothes.

The flame of the fire killed these men. The men involved were those who stayed outside of the furnace. They had only to get close enough to the door to drop the young men into the furnace. A furnace that hot would sizzle those who were thrown inside.

---

[18] P. W. Coxon, "Daniel III 17: A Linguistic and Theological Problem," *VT* 26 (1976):400-409.

TEXT

Daniel

²⁴Then King Nebuchadnezzar was surprised and rose up in haste. He answered and said to his leaders, "Were there not three men thrown bound into the midst of **the fire**?" They answered and said, "You are right, King." ²⁵He answered and said, "But I see four men released, **walking in the midst of the fire**, and they **have no injury**, and the appearance of the fourth is like a son of God." ²⁶Then Nebuchadnezzar approached the door **of** the flaming, **fiery** furnace. He answered and said, "Shadrach, Meshach, and Abednego, servants of the Most High God, come out and come here!" Then Shadrach, Meshach, and Abednego came out from **the midst of the fire**. ²⁷When the satraps, administrators, governors, and leaders of the king gathered together they saw these men whose bodies **the fire did not** rule; the hair of their heads had not been singed; their coats had **not been injured**; and **the** smell of **fire** did not come over them.

First Testament Intertexts

Isa 43:2 When you pass through the water I will be with you, / in the rivers, they will not drown you.

When you **walk in the midst of the fire** you **will not be injured**.

Exod 14:24 Then Yehowah appeared to the camp of the Egyptians in a pillar **of fire** and cloud, and he disturbed the camp of the Egyptians.

Ps 66:12 We came through **fire** and through water. You brought us out to a place of abundance.

Isa 43:2 When you **walk in the midst of the fire** you **will not be injured.**

The **fire will not** burn you, ³for I am Yehowah, your God, / the holy One of Israel, your Savior.

COMMENTARY

Answered and said. This is a typical Semitic expression. It does not mean that Nebuchadnezzar was answering anyone's question. In fact he was asking a question. Instead of saying, simply, "He said," Semites normally reported that "he answered and said," even if he initiated the conversation.

But I see four men released. Of course, he was surprised. How did the fourth man get there? That was a surprise to the king, of course, but not to the Jews who remembered that there was an angel who rescued Hezekiah in his crisis (Isa 37:36). The next surprise for the king was, "Why were they not burned to ashes by this time?" Why were they walking around in the midst of the fire and not fried into charcoal? Neither was this a surprise to faithful Jews who remembered Isaiah's promise that believers might walk through fire without being hurt (Isa 43:2).

Without special asbestos suits with oxygen tanks, Westerners of the twentieth century would not only be surprised to learn that such a thing as this had happened. They would not believe it if they were told, but that is because they would miss the methodology upon which this narrative was based. The author was not reporting history; he was preparing a sermonic narrative based on an earlier text and some well-accepted rules of Jewish rhetoric. So far as legal argument was concerned, 1) there is nothing in the world that is not in the scripture, and 2) all prophecy is to be fulfilled in the days of the Messiah. The author thought he was living in those days. The Messiah was expected to come during Israel's crises, overthrow all of Israel's enemies, and rule the Promised Land from Jerusalem. 3) It took two or three witnesses to prove a case in court. The author of this myth was confident that what he said was true, because he found the words in the scripture, 1) **The angel of the Lord went forth and killed 185,000 in the camp of the Assyrians** (Isa 37:36); 2) **If you walk in the midst of the fire, you will not be burned** (Isa 43:2). He also knew of examples where the Israelites walked through bodies of water without being drowned. Therefore Isaiah's prophecy must have been fulfilled. All the author had to do was report it.

The fourth is like a Son of God. How would the king know that? Where would he learn what a Son of God looked like? Of course this is really a moot question when dealing in drama. Kings were called sons of God, but so were Israelites and divine beings (Gen 6:2; 1Kgs 22:19; Job 1:6). Kings could be recognized by their crowns and royal garments, but how could Israelites be distinguished from other human beings? How would the king know what a divine being looked like? In this same context, however, the being that delivered the three men was called an angel (*mah-lah-káh,* מלאכה). Furthermore this being did not function as any other human being would maneuver in the midst of a fire, so the king who called the being a Son of God and also an angel thought it was a divine being.

The midst of the fire. Both the Psalmist and Isaiah knew the story of the exodus from Egypt, when Israelites went through the water of the sea without being drowned. They also accompanied Joshua in crossing the river Jordan without injury. On this basis he assured his readers that they also could count on God's willingness to save them again if they came to a body of water that threatened them. He also encouraged them further by promising that the same kind of deliverance would be provided if they were threatened with fire. He learned this from the same text. The Exodus text spoke of a pillar of fire, so Isaiah used both the water and the fire for his exegesis. He concluded that Israelites could walk right through the midst of the fire without being injured, just as the Israelites had earlier walked through the sea at the border of Egypt without being drowned, and they were accompanied by the pillar of fire. The Psalmist said that the Israelites had come through both water and fire when they escaped from Egypt.

The author of Dan 3 knew the events of the exodus from Egypt and the entrance into the Promised Land. He also knew the prophecy of Isaiah and the testimony of the Psalmist. This provided him with two or three witnesses. Since at least two witnesses were required to prove a case in court, he knew he had all the evidence it took to compose this narrative. He had only to fill in the details.

The author had to compose a narrative, however, that made sense against known history. Otherwise his hero story would have been ridiculed rather than canonized. This narrative could not have been written during the time of Nebuchadnezzar when Jews were still lamenting their captivity. From the words of the text alone it is evident from the mention of Greek musical instruments rather than Babylonian musical instruments that the narrative was composed later than Nebuchadnezzar. Greek terms would not have been familiar before the Greek kingdom had become well established. The narrative of Dan 3 is a victory narrative that would not have had much purpose if there had not already been a period in history that Jews knew which had been victorious. By the time the author wrote, the Jews had been through their "fiery furnace" in terms of the Maccabean Revolt in which many Jews were tortured and others were killed.

The author was able to compose this victory drama of Daniel and his friends, because there had already been some national crisis that threatened the faith of Jews in a foreign land, but there also had to have been a successful outcome to have made the story convincing. The story was based on a "fiery furnace" period and a deliverance from such an experience, because that is what the author mythologized. It had to have been written after there had been an exodus from Egypt and a later deliverance of some kind. The author of Dan 2 compared the success of Daniel of Babylon to the success of Joseph of Egypt. Similarly the author of Dan 3 compared the deliverance of Shadrach, Meshach, and Abednego to that of the exodus from Egypt and the entrance of the Israelites into the Promised Land. The author of Dan 3 also used as an additional intertext the deliverance of Hezekiah from the Assyrians. He was comparing later deliverances to earlier ones.

Most High God. Melchizedek offered a blessing for Abram and also for **God Most High** (Gen 14:20). One of the Dead Sea Scrolls called a Jewish king "Son of the **Most High**" (*4Q246*).[19] Jesus was called "the prophet of the **Most High**" (Luke 1:76). The term is used frequently in intertestamental literature.

TEXT

Daniel	First Testament Intertexts
[28]Nebuchadnezzar answered and said, "Blessed be the **God** of Shadrach, Meshach, and Abednego **who sent his angel and saved** his servants who believed in him and transgressed the word of the king. They gave their bodies and	[2Chron 32:21] **Yehowah sent an angel, who** destroyed all the mighty warriors . . . [22]**and Yehowah saved** Hezekiah.

---

[19] See further Buchanan, "*4Q246* and the Political Titles of Jesus," *QC* 4 (1994):77-87.

did not worship or

bow down before any
god except their
God. ²⁹Now I will make a decree that every people, nation, and [person who speaks a foreign] language, who says anything against the God of Shadrach, Meshach, and Abednego, will be cut in pieces and his house will be made a dunghill, because no **other god** is able to save as this one." ³⁰ Then the king promoted Shadrach, Meshach, and Abednego in the Babylonian government.

Exod 14:19 Then the **angel of God** traveled and walked before the camp of the Israelites and he walked after them, and the pillar of cloud went before them, and it stood after them.

Exod 20:2 I am Yehowah, your **God**, who brought you out of the land of Egypt, from the house of bondage. ³You shall have no other gods before me. . .
⁵**you shall not worship** them or serve them, because I, Yehowah, your **God**, am a zealous **God.**

Exod 34:14 You **shall not worship any other god** because Yehowah's name is Zealous. He is a zealous **God**.

Ps 95:6 Come, let us **worship and bow down**; let us kneel **before** Yehowah our maker, because he is our **God.**

COMMENTARY

Who sent his angel. An **angel** is a messenger. This **angel** was an **angel** sent from God and was the interpretation given to the "son of God," mentioned earlier (Dan 3:25). Since God was understood to live in heaven, it was further assumed that any action God would take on earth would have to be through the agency of messengers. There was an **angel** at the sea when the Israelites crossed. The **angel** went before the Israelites and removed the water of the sea for them so that they might walk through the sea uninjured. Then it turned and went behind them to put the water back so that the Egyptians could not cross. When Nebuchadnezzar saw that Shadrach, Meshach, and Abednego had been saved he realized some god must have sent an **angel** to deal with the situation, just as Yehowah had sent an **angel** to kill the Assyrian soldiers that threatened Hezekiah. The author introduced the **angel** for his narrative, because there was an **angel** in his text that reported the deliverance at the sea and the deliverance from the Assyrians.

They did not worship or bow down. The narrator knew the actors did not worship, because he created them to be perfectly law-abiding Jews. They obeyed the commandment that was given first at the mountain (Exod 20), and given again after the incident with the golden calf (Exod 34).

Who says anything against the God of Shadrach, Meshach, and Abednego. The Jews, according to the author of Daniel, were able to obtain special privileges under the authority of a pagan king—privileges not even the pagan citizens were given. Not only were all other people of the country not allowed to injure Jews, but they also were not allowed to say anything uncomplimentary about Jewish religion. Non-Jewish citizens of the empire who defamed Jews in this way would not just be fined or scolded. They would be killed; their bodies would be cut into pieces; and their houses would be confiscated and bulldozed. Although the author did not use any special words from the Book of Esther, the theme is so similar that it either reflects knowledge of that book or else both Daniel and Esther reflect a strong theme in early Jewish tradition. At the beginning of Dan 3 the king made a decree that everyone must worship the statue. The story closes with a decree from the king that everyone must respect the worshipers of the God of the Jews. This is another one of the great reversals in the Book of Daniel.

King Ahasuerus, at Esther's request, gave Jews of his empire the privilege of avenging their enemies. After which, the Jews stabbed all of their enemies with the sword; they killed and destroyed [them]; and they did with their enemies whatever they wished (Esth 9:5).

> They killed the ten sons of Haman, 500 enemies in the city of Susa,
> and 75,000 enemies in the rest of the provinces (Esth 9:6, 10, 16).

Then the Jews in Persia were placed in special positions of authority in the government. This is the same theme narrated in Daniel. Shadrach, Meshach, and Abednego were promoted (Dan 3:30); Mordecai was given a position, like Joseph of Egypt, next to the king in authority (Esth 10:3), just as had also been true of Daniel (Dan 2:48). There probably is no historical value to the events described either in Esther or Dan 3. Both are drama and not actual facts. The only thing that is historical in both narratives is the way Jews felt about their enemies and their wishful thinking.

TEXT

$^{MT\ 3:31;\ OG\ 4:1}$King Nebuchadnezzar to all the peoples, nations, and [people who speak foreign] languages who live in all the land, "May your peace be increased!" $^{MT\ 3:32;\ OG\ 4:2}$The signs and miracles which God has performed with me I wish to announce.

Daniel	First Testament Intertexts
3:33; OG 4:3 How great are his signs! / How **mighty** are his **miracles**! /	Ps 145:5 I will speak of your miraculous deeds; / your **mighty miracles** they will tell; / I will write of your **great** deeds.
His **kingdom is a kingdom of the age**, /and his **government** with **generation and generation**.	Ps 145:13 Your **kingdom is a kingdom of** all **ages**, / **and** your **government** of every **generation and generation**.

TECHNICAL DETAILS

The author of Dan 3 concluded his manuscript with a poem, just as the author of Dan 7 did. Ministers today still often conclude sermons with appropriate poems to summarize the main points of the sermon.

This little poem was placed at the conclusion of chapter 3 in the Aramaic text, but at the beginning of chapter 4 in the OG. The author of either chapter did not originally compose it, but it fits into the manuscript as a conclusion of Dan 3 better than as an introduction to Dan 4. The poem itself was composed by appropriating select verses from Ps 145. The introduction to the poem attributed it to Nebuchadnezzar as a confession, just as the introduction of the poem concluding Dan 7.

COMMENTARY

To all peoples, nations, and [people who speak foreign] languages. The Babylonian Empire in Nebuchadnezzar's time reached from the Tigris-Euphrates Valley to Egypt. There were many small countries swallowed up in this empire that continued to be indigenous to the locality. They continued to speak their own language.

God has performed with me. The preposition here is important. The signs and miracles described in Dan 3 were not performed *for* Nebuchadnezzar. They were performed for Shadrach, Meshach, and Abednego, but they were performed in Nebuchadnezzar's kingdom. Therefore they took place *with* him. Keil correctly noted that the Nebuchadnezzar character in Daniel does not cohere with the active life of Antiochus Epiphanes.[20] In the dramas of Daniel, Nebuchadnezzar was shown in a favorable light by the Jewish authors. He always took the side of the Jews and treated them respectfully. It was his officers who tried to get Daniel and his friends killed, and that was against the will of Nebuchadnezzar. Nebuchadnezzar punished the officers and rewarded Daniel and his friends. Antiochus IV, on the other hand, was generally cruel in his treatment of the Jews.

A kingdom of the age. An **age** is an unspecified length of time. It lasts during a certain king's rule, a dynasty, or the endurance of a kingdom. For example there was

---

[20] Keil, *Daniel*, p. 116. It does not follow, however, that the stories of Daniel and his friends were all historically true, as Keil supposed.

the age of David (Amos 9:11) and the Egyptian age which ended with the Exodus (*NeoTarg*Exod 12.41-42).

When conditions change, ages change. An age is not the world or the cosmos. It is a period of time, like a month, year, Sabbath of years, or Jubilee of years. At the end of one age, another age begins. The **kingdom of the age** discussed here is the Jewish **kingdom** that followed the Greek **kingdom**. It lasted for several generations, from 142 BIA to 6 IA, nearly 150 years. This was **the kingdom** that was mythologized as the stone that crushed the statue (Dan 2:44). It was destined to last for several generations, but not forever.

SUMMARY

Dan 3 was not a historical account. It is a midrash, primarily based on texts related to the exodus from Egypt. It was created as an antitype of that event. It also echoed the crisis and victory theme of the Book of Esther and Hezekiah. Shadrach, Meshach, and Abednego were the new Israelites who walked in the fire without being burned, just as Isaiah promised, and just as the Israelites walked through the water at the sea without being drowned. The angel that protected the Israelites at the sea and Hezekiah at the walls of Jerusalem also protected these Jews in the furnace. In relationship to Esther Shadrach, Meshach, and Abednego were the new Mordecai, and Nebuchadnezzar was the new Ahasuerus. Both Ahasuerus and Nebuchadnezzar functioned as the new Pharaoh. This narrative was a myth, antityping through the medium of theater the themes of earlier victory reports. This narrative does not include the character of Daniel, and was probably originally composed as a separate document. The same is true of the poetic addition that follows.

The Prayer of Azariah and Hymn of the Jewish Captives

OG Addition. ^{3:24}They walked **in the midst of the flame**, singing a hymn to God and blessing the Lord. ²⁵When he had stood up Azariah prayed thus. Having opened his mouth **in the midst of the fire**, he said:

²⁶Blessed are you, Lord,
    God of our fathers,
and praised and glorified
    may your name be
        for the age [to come],
²⁷because you are righteous
    over all the things
        you have done to us.
All of your works are true;
    your ways are straight;
        and your judgments are
            fair.

²⁸You have made righteous judgments
    in everything that you have
        brought against us,
and against Jerusalem your holy city of
    our fathers.
Therefore in truth and justice
    you have done all these things
        because of our sins.
²⁹We have sinned and broken laws
    in everything, turning away from you.
We have committed all kinds of sin,
    and we have not obeyed
        the commandments of your law.

³⁰We have neither kept [your law]
    nor performed as you have
        commanded us,
in order that it may be well with us.
³¹Now, everything which you have
    brought against us,
and everything which you have
    done to us,
        you have done in
            righteous judgment.
³²You have handed us over to
    our lawless, apostate,
        and hateful enemies,
³³and now there is no basis for us
    to open our mouths.
Shame and disgrace has
    come upon your servants
    who worship you.
³⁴For the sake of your name,
    do not hand us over finally,
        and do not invalidate
        your treaty.
³⁵Do not remove your mercy from us
because of Abraham, your beloved,
    Isaac, your servant,
        and Israel your saint.
³⁶As you have spoken to them saying,
Your seed shall be multiplied
    as the stars of heaven, and
        as the sand along the shore
            of the sea (Gen 22:17),
³⁷because, Master, we have been
    depreciated more than any nation,
and we are humiliated in all the earth,
    today, because of our sins.
³⁸At this time we have no ruler,
    prophet, or leader,
no **whole burnt offering, sacrifice,**
    presentation, or incense,
no place to offer first fruits before you
    to find mercy,
³⁹but with a **broken** heart and (OG Ps 50:17)
    a humbled **spirit** we offer,
as with whole burnt offerings of rams
    and **bulls** and as **ten thousands**
        of fat lambs (Micah 6:6-7).
⁴⁰Thus, let our **sacrifice be to you**,
    today, and be reconciled after
        you (OGPs 140:2),
⁴¹Now we follow you with a whole
    heart;
we fear you; and we seek your face.
    Do not put us to shame,
⁴²but act with us according to your
    kindness and
according to the **multitude**
    of your **mercies**
        (Isa 55:8).
⁴³Deliver us according to your
    miraculous deeds.
⁴⁴Let all those who have shown evil
    to your servants be avenged,
and let them be ashamed of every power;
    and let their strength be crushed.
⁴⁵Let them know that you alone
    are the Lord God,
        glorified by the entire
        world.

⁴⁶Now the servants of the king who threw them in did not stop kindling the furnace when they threw the three in at once for the furnace. The furnace was kindled seven times its normal heat, and when they threw them in, the ones who threw them in, on the one hand, were above them, and, on the other hand, those who from below were underneath them, feeding the flames with wicks [soaked in] naphtha, and all kinds of kindling wood. ⁴⁷The flame poured out above the furnace 49 cubits, ⁴⁸and it spread out and burned those of the Chaldeans who were found around the furnace, ⁴⁹but an angel of the Lord came down at the same time to be together with Azariah in the furnace and extinguish the flame of the fire from the furnace, ⁵⁰and he made the center of the furnace like a dewy breeze blowing

through, and the fire did not touch them at all; it did not hurt, and it did not injure them. ⁵¹Then the three took up the hymn as of one voice and glorified and praised and exalted God in the furnace, saying,
⁵²Blessed are you, Lord, God of our fathers,
> and praised and exalted
>> for the age [to come].

Blessed be your glorious name,
> which is holy, praised, and
>> exalted to every age.

⁵³Blessed are you in the temple
> of your holy glory,

praised and exalted above all
> for the age

⁵⁴Blessed be the throne of your kingdom. Praised and exalted above all for the age.
⁵⁵Blessed are you who sees the depths
> while **seated on the cherubim**
>> (1Sam 4:4; 2Sam 6:2; Ps 8:2; 99:1),

and praised and glorified
> for the age.

⁵⁶Blessed are you in the foundation
> of heaven,

and praised and glorified
> for the age.

⁵⁷Bless the Lord, all you creatures
> of the Lord.

Praise and exalt him for the age.
⁵⁸Bless the Lord, you angels
> of the Lord.

Praise and exalt him for the age.
⁵⁹Bless the Lord, you heavens!
Praise and exalt him for the age
⁶⁰Bless the Lord, all you water
> above the heaven.

Praise and exalt him for the age
⁶¹ Bless, all you powers of the Lord
Praise and exalt him for the age.
⁶²Bless the Lord, you sun and moon.
Praise and exalt him for the age.
⁶³Bless the Lord, all you stars of heaven.
Praise and exalt him for the age.
⁶⁴Bless the Lord, all of you—
> rain, storm, and dew.

Praise and exalt him for the age.
⁶⁵Bless the Lord, all you winds.
Praise and exalt him for the age.
⁶⁶Bless the Lord, you fire and heat.
Praise and exalt him for the age.
⁶⁷Bless the Lord, frost and cold.
Praise and exalt him for the age.
⁶⁸Bless the Lord, dew and snow.
Praise and exalt him for the age.
⁶⁹Bless the Lord, frost and cold.
Praise and exalt him for the age.
⁷⁰Bless the Lord, frost and snow.
Praise and exalt him for the age.
⁷¹Bless the Lord, night and day.
Praise and exalt him for the age.
⁷²Bless the Lord, light and darkness.
Praise and exalt him for the age.
⁷³Bless the Lord, lightning and clouds.
Praise and exalt him for the age.
⁷⁴Bless the Lord, the land.
Praise and exalt him for the age.
⁷⁵Bless the Lord, mountains and hills.
Praise and exalt him for the age
⁷⁶Bless the Lord, everything born.
Praise and exalt him for the age.
⁷⁷Bless the Lord, springs.
Praise and exalt him for the age.
⁷⁸Bless the Lord, seas and rivers.
Praise and exalt him for the age.
⁷⁹Bless the Lord, you whales and
> all living things in the water.

Praise and exalt him for the age.
⁸⁰Bless the Lord, all the birds of heaven.
Praise and exalt him for the age.
⁸¹Bless the Lord, all you four-footed
> creatures and beasts of the land

Praise and exalt him for the age.
⁸²Bless the Lord, you sons of men.
Praise and exalt him for the age.
⁸³Bless the Lord, you Israelites.
Praise and exalt him for the age.

⁸⁴Bless the Lord, you priests.
Praise and exalt him for the age.
⁸⁵Bless the Lord, you servants.
Praise and exalt him for the age.
⁸⁶Bless the Lord, you spirits and
    souls of the righteous.
Praise and exalt him for the age.
⁸⁷Bless the Lord, you pious
    and humble of heart.
Praise and exalt him for the age
⁸⁸Bless the Lord, Hananiah, Azariah,
    and Mishael.
Praise and exalt him for the age,
Praise and exalt him for the age,
because he has rescued us from Hades
    and saved us from the hand of
        death.
He has rescued us from the burning
    flame,
    and delivered us from the fire.
⁸⁹Make your confession to the Lord,
    because he is useful. His mercy
        is for the age.
⁹⁰Bless the God of gods, all you
    worshipers.
Praise and confess, because his mercy
    is for the ages of ages.

⁹¹It happened while the king was standing and listening to their hymn singing, he saw them alive. Then King Nebuchadnezzar was surprised, and he went up in a hurry and said to his friends, "Look! I see four men, unbound, walking around in the fire, and there has been no destruction in them, and the appearance of the fourth is like an angel of God."

COMMENTARY

This OG passage consists of two poems with a prose introduction, conclusion, and explanatory passage to relate the two poems to the story of the three Jews in the fiery furnace.

The first poem seems to have been written before the Battle of Beth-horon. The poet reminded God of his promises, which the Jews had not yet received. The poet was sure that God was justified in punishing and torturing the Jews as he had, but he reminded God that this was severe. Jews were left without a temple for sacrifice, without prophets, kings, or leaders of any kind. The nation had become a disgrace. The peoples of the nations that surround Palestine shamed the Jews. The poet pleaded for vengeance, deliverance, and reconciliation, which they obviously did not have at the time. The vengeance Jews received at the Battles of Beth-horon and Beth-zur had not yet come. This poem reflects the plight of the Jews in Palestine during the Maccabean Rebellion.

If the twelve chapters of the Book of Daniel had reflected this mood, scholars would be justified in picturing the first listeners to these dramas as people who "hoped against hope that God would make it all right in the end," as Burkitt suggested.[21] That, however, is not the case. The dramas of Daniel indicate the kind of mood that is expressed in the following poem.

The second poem was one of gratitude and blessings. It is an exhortation poem, addressed to the congregation in behalf of God (Ps 95; 100, 145, 148, 150). It was composed at a time when there was a temple and a throne of God's

---

[21] F. C. Burkitt, *Jewish and Christian Apocalypses* (London: British Academy, 1914), p. 16.

kingdom (Dan 3:53-54). This motivated the poet to list the many things in the world for which Jews might be thankful. Over and over again he praised God and exalted him "for the age" that had come. This means the old age of Syrian rule was over; the new age had arrived. The "end of days" had reached its conclusion. God had rescued his people from Hades, saved them from the hand of death. The vengeance, mercy, deliverance, and reconciliation for which the first poem pleaded had taken place, so this poet had only to offer the appropriate gratitude for the new age that had begun. Jews had received God's mercy which they were prepared to confess and for which they would praise and exalt God for ages of ages (Dan 3:88-90). This would have been a beautiful litany to have been used as a responsive reading during the first Hanukkah or the celebration of the removal of the Syrian taxation and the introduction of a new age with a new calendar.

CHAPTER FOUR

ARAMAIC TEXT

4:1 אֲנָה נְבוּכַדְנֶצַּר שְׁלֵה הֲוֵית בְּבֵיתִי וְרַעְנַן בְּהֵיכְלִי: 2 **חֵלֶם**	Exod 41:1
חֲזֵית וִידַחֲלִנַּנִי וְהַרְהֹרִין עַל־מִשְׁכְּבִי וְחֶזְוֵי רֵאשִׁי יְבַהֲלֻנַּנִי:	
3 וּמִנִּי שִׂים טְעֵם לְהַנְעָלָה קָדָמַי **לְכֹל חַכִּימֵי** בָבֶל דִּי־פְשַׁר חֶלְמָא	Exod 41:8
יְהוֹדְעֻנַּנִי: 4 בֵּאדַיִן עָלְלִין [עָלִּין] חַרְטֻמַּיָּא אָשְׁפַיָּא כַּשְׂדָּיֵא [כַּשְׂדָּאֵי] וְגָזְרַיָּא	Exod 41:8
וְחֶלְמָא אָמַר אֲנָה קָדָמֵיהוֹן וּפִשְׁרֵהּ לָא־מְהוֹדְעִין לִי: 5 וְעַד אָחֳרֵין **עַל**	Exod 41:38
קָדָמַי **דָּנִיֵּאל** דִּי־שְׁמֵהּ בֵּלְטְשַׁאצַּר כְּשֻׁם אֱלָהִי וְדִי רוּחַ־**אֱלָהִין**	Exod 41:17
קַדִּישִׁין **בֵּהּ** וְחֶלְמָא קָדָמוֹהִי **אַמְרֵת:** 6 בֵּלְטְשַׁאצַּר רַב חַרְטֻמַּיָּא	Ezek 28:3
דִּי ׀ אֲנָה יִדְעֵת דִּי רוּחַ אֱלָהִין קַדִּישִׁין בָּךְ וְכָל־**רָז לָא־אָנֵס לָךְ**	
חֶזְוֵי חֶלְמִי דִי־חֲזֵית וּפִשְׁרֵהּ אֱמַר: 7 וְחֶזְוֵי רֵאשִׁי עַל־מִשְׁכְּבִי	
חָזֵה הֲוֵית	
וַאֲלוּ אִילָן בְּגוֹא אַרְעָא וְרוּמֵהּ שַׂגִּיא:	Ezek 31:3
8 רְבָה אִילָנָא וּתְקִף וְרוּמֵהּ יִמְטֵא לִשְׁמַיָּא	Gen 11:4
וַחֲזוֹתֵהּ לְסוֹף **כָּל־אַרְעָא:**	
9 עָפְיֵהּ שַׁפִּיר וְאִנְבֵּהּ שַׂגִּיא וּמָזוֹן לְכֹלָּא־בֵהּ	Ezek 31:6
תְּחֹתוֹהִי תַּטְלֵל ׀ חֵיוַת בָּרָא וּבְעַנְפוֹהִי יְדֻרוּן [יְדוּרָן] **צִפֲּרֵי שְׁמַיָּא**	Gen 11:5
וּמִנֵּהּ יִתְּזִין כָּל־בִּשְׂרָא:	
10 חָזֵה הֲוֵית בְּחֶזְוֵי רֵאשִׁי עַל־מִשְׁכְּבִי **וַאֲלוּ** עִיר וְקַדִּישׁ **מִן־שְׁמַיָּא**	Isa 11:1
נָחִת: 11 קָרֵא בְחַיִל וְכֵן אָמַר	
גֹּדּוּ אִילָנָא וְקַצִּצוּ **עַנְפוֹהִי** אַתַּרוּ עָפְיֵהּ וּבַדַּרוּ אִנְבֵּהּ	
תְּנֻד **חֵיוְתָא** מִן־תַּחְתּוֹהִי **וְצִפֲּרַיָּא מִן־עַנְפוֹהִי:**	
12 בְּרַם **עִקַּר שָׁרְשׁוֹהִי** בְּאַרְעָא שְׁבֻקוּ	
וּבֶאֱסוּר דִּי־פַרְזֶל וּנְחָשׁ בְּדִתְאָא דִּי בָרָא	
וּבְטַל שְׁמַיָּא יִצְטַבַּע וְעִם־חֵיוְתָא חֲלָקֵהּ בַּעֲשַׂב אַרְעָא:	
13 לִבְבֵהּ מִן־אֲנוֹשָׁא [אֲנָשָׁא] יְשַׁנּוֹן וּלְבַב חֵיוָה יִתְיְהִב לֵהּ	
וְשִׁבְעָה עִדָּנִין יַחְלְפוּן עֲלוֹהִי:	
14 בִּגְזֵרַת עִירִין פִּתְגָמָא וּמֵאמַר קַדִּישִׁין שְׁאֵלְתָא עַד־דִּבְרַת	
דִּי יִנְדְּעוּן חַיַּיָּא דִּי־שַׁלִּיט עִלָּיָא [עִלָּאָה] בְּמַלְכוּת אֱנוֹשָׁא [אֲנָשָׁא] וּלְמַן־	
דִּי יִצְבֵּא יִתְּנִנַּהּ וּשְׁפַל אֲנָשִׁים יְקִים עֲלַיַּהּ [עֲלַהּ]: 15 דְּנָה חֶלְמָא חֲזֵית	
אֲנָה מַלְכָּא נְבוּכַדְנֶצַּר וְאַנְתָּה [וְאַנְתְּ] בֵּלְטְשַׁאצַּר פִּשְׁרֵא אֱמַר ׀ כָּל־קֳבֵל	
דִּי ׀ כָּל־חַכִּימֵי מַלְכוּתִי לָא־יָכְלִין פִּשְׁרָא לְהוֹדָעֻתַנִי וְאַנְתָּה [וְאַנְתְּ] כָּהֵל	
דִּי רוּחַ־אֱלָהִין קַדִּישִׁין בָּךְ: 16 אֱדַיִן דָּנִיֵּאל דִּי־שְׁמֵהּ	
בֵּלְטְשַׁאצַּר אֶשְׁתּוֹמַם כְּשָׁעָה חֲדָה וְרַעְיֹנֹהִי יְבַהֲלֻנֵּהּ עָנֵה מַלְכָּא	
וְאָמַר בֵּלְטְשַׁאצַּר חֶלְמָא וּפִשְׁרֵא אַל־יְבַהֲלָךְ עָנֵה בֵלְטְשַׁאצַּר	

וְאָמַר מָרַאי [מָרִי] חֶלְמָא לְשָׂנְאָיךְ [לְשָׂנְאָךְ]
וּפִשְׁרֵהּ לְעָרַיךְ [לְעָרָךְ]: 17 אִילָנָא דִּי חֲזַיְתָ
דִּי רְבָה וּתְקִף וְרוּמֵהּ יִמְטֵא לִשְׁמַיָּא וַחֲזוֹתֵהּ לְכָל־אַרְעָא: 18 וְעָפְיֵהּ
שַׁפִּיר וְאִנְבֵּהּ שַׂגִּיא וּמָזוֹן לְכֹלָּא־בֵהּ תְּחֹתוֹהִי תְּדוּר חֵיוַת בָּרָא
וּבְעַנְפוֹהִי יִשְׁכְּנָן צִפֲּרֵי שְׁמַיָּא: 19 אַנְתְּה [אַנְתְּ־]הוּא מַלְכָּא דִּי רְבַיְתָ
וּתְקֵפְתְּ וּרְבוּתָךְ רְבָת וּמְטָת לִשְׁמַיָּא וְשָׁלְטָנָךְ לְסוֹף אַרְעָא:
20 וְדִי חֲזָה מַלְכָּא עִיר וְקַדִּישׁ נָחִת ׀ מִן־שְׁמַיָּא וְאָמַר גֹּדּוּ אִילָנָא
וְחַבְּלוּהִי בְּרַם עִקַּר שָׁרְשׁוֹהִי בְּאַרְעָא שְׁבֻקוּ וּבֶאֱסוּר דִּי־פַרְזֶל
וּנְחָשׁ בְּדִתְאָא דִּי בָרָא וּבְטַל שְׁמַיָּא יִצְטַבַּע וְעִם־חֵיוַת בָּרָא חֲלָקֵהּ
עַד דִּי־שִׁבְעָה עִדָּנִין יַחְלְפוּן עֲלוֹהִי: 21 דְּנָה פִשְׁרָא מַלְכָּא וּגְזֵרַת
עִלָּיָא [עֶלְיוֹנָא] הִיא דִּי מְטָת עַל־מַרְאי [מָרִי] מַלְכָּא: 22 וְלָךְ טָרְדִין מִן־
אֲנָשָׁא וְעִם־חֵיוַת בָּרָא לֶהֱוֵה מְדֹרָךְ וְעִשְׂבָּא כְתוֹרִין ׀ לָךְ יְטַעֲמוּן וּמִטַּל
שְׁמַיָּא לָךְ מְצַבְּעִין וְשִׁבְעָה עִדָּנִין יַחְלְפוּן עֲלָיךְ [עֲלָךְ] עַד דִּי־תִנְדַּע דִּי־
שַׁלִּיט עִלָּיָא [עִלָּאָה] בְּמַלְכוּת אֲנָשָׁא וּלְמַן־דִּי יִצְבֵּא יִתְּנִנַּהּ: 23 וְדִי אֲמַרוּ
לְמִשְׁבַּק עִקַּר שָׁרְשׁוֹהִי דִּי אִילָנָא מַלְכוּתָךְ לָךְ קַיָּמָה מִן־דִּי תִנְדַּע
דִּי שַׁלִּטִן שְׁמַיָּא:
24 לָהֵן מַלְכָּא מִלְכִּי יִשְׁפַּר עֲלָיךְ [עֲלָךְ] וַחֲטָיָךְ [וַחֲטָאָךְ] בְּצִדְקָה
פְרֻק וַעֲוָיָתָךְ בְּמִחַן עֲנָיִן הֵן תֶּהֱוֵה אַרְכָה לִשְׁלֵוְתָךְ: 25 כֹּלָּא מְּטָא
עַל־נְבוּכַדְנֶצַּר מַלְכָּא: פ 26 לִקְצָת יַרְחִין תְּרֵי־עֲשַׂר עַל־
הֵיכַל מַלְכוּתָא דִּי בָבֶל מְהַלֵּךְ הֲוָה: 27 עָנֵה מַלְכָּא וְאָמַר הֲלָא
דָא־הִיא בָּבֶל רַבְּתָא דִּי־אֲנָה בֱנַיְתַהּ לְבֵית מַלְכוּ בִּתְקָף חִסְנִי
וְלִיקָר הַדְרִי: 28 עוֹד מִלְּתָא בְּפֻם מַלְכָּא קָל מִן־שְׁמַיָּא נְפַל לָךְ
אָמְרִין נְבוּכַדְנֶצַּר מַלְכָּא מַלְכוּתָה עֲדָת מִנָּךְ: 29 וּמִן־אֲנָשָׁא לָךְ
טָרְדִין וְעִם־חֵיוַת בָּרָא מְדֹרָךְ עִשְׂבָּא כְתוֹרִין לָךְ יְטַעֲמוּן וְשִׁבְעָה
עִדָּנִין יַחְלְפוּן עֲלָיךְ [עֲלָךְ] עַד דִּי־תִנְדַּע דִּי־שַׁלִּיט עִלָּיָא [עִלָּאָה] בְּמַלְכוּת
אֲנָשָׁא וּלְמַן־דִּי יִצְבֵּא יִתְּנִנַּהּ: 30 בַּהּ־שַׁעֲתָא מִלְּתָא סָפַת עַל־נְבוּכַדְנֶצַּר
וּמִן־אֲנָשָׁא טְרִיד וְעִשְׂבָּא כְתוֹרִין יֵאכֻל וּמִטַּל שְׁמַיָּא גִּשְׁמֵהּ יִצְטַבַּע   Ps 145:13
עַד דִּי שַׂעְרֵהּ כְּנִשְׁרִין רְבָה וְטִפְרוֹהִי כְצִפְּרִין: 31 וְלִקְצָת
יוֹמַיָּה אֲנָה נְבוּכַדְנֶצַּר עַיְנַי ׀ לִשְׁמַיָּא נִטְלֵת וּמַנְדְּעִי עֲלַי יְתוּב   Isa 46:17
וּלְעִלָּיָא [וּלְעִלָּאָה] בָּרְכֵת וּלְחַי עָלְמָא שַׁבְּחֵת וְהַדְּרֵת
דִּי שָׁלְטָנֵהּ שָׁלְטָן עָלַם וּמַלְכוּתֵהּ עִם־דָּר וְדָר: Ps 45:9; Sir 36:8
32 וְכָל־דָּאֲרֵי [דָּיְרֵי] אַרְעָא כְּלָה חֲשִׁיבִין וּכְמִצְבְּיֵהּ עָבֵד בְּחֵיל שְׁמַיָּא
וְדָאֲרֵי [וְדָיְרֵי] אַרְעָא
וְלָא אִיתַי דִּי־יְמַחֵא בִידֵהּ וְיֵאמַר לֵהּ מָה עֲבַדְתְּ:
33 בַּהּ־זִמְנָא מַנְדְּעִי ׀ יְתוּב עֲלַי וְלִיקַר מַלְכוּתִי הַדְרִי וְזִוִי יְתוּב
עֲלַי וְלִי הַדָּבְרַי וְרַבְרְבָנַי יְבַעוֹן וְעַל־מַלְכוּתִי הָתְקְנַת וּרְבוּ
יַתִּירָה הוּסְפַת לִי: 34 כְּעַן אֲנָה נְבוּכַדְנֶצַּר מְשַׁבַּח וּמְרוֹמֵם וּמְהַדַּר
לְמֶלֶךְ שְׁמַיָּא דִּי כָל־מַעֲבָדוֹהִי קְשֹׁט וְאֹרְחָתֵהּ דִּין וְדִי מַהְלְכִין
בְּגֵוָה יָכִל לְהַשְׁפָּלָה: פ

TECHNICAL DETAILS

R. H. Charles was a competent apocalyptic scholar, but he was mistaken when he concluded that both the Book of Daniel and the Book of Revelation were products of one individual author each and that both were written carelessly or badly revised.

In dealing with the Book of Daniel Charles said that one person whose work has been badly preserved wrote it. Charles has attempted to correct it and discover the one true text from which all of the variants departed. When he came to chapter four he observed that there were many differences between the OG and the MT, and concluded, "Both cannot be right. There is of course the possibility that the order of both texts is wrong."[1]

The book of Daniel, however, is not as badly preserved or as poorly composed as Charles thought. There are three insights that Charles failed to recognize that explain the variances and give Daniel more credit for good style than has previously been recognized. 1) One of these is the midrashic content which requires a different style. 2) A second is the use of inclusion and chiasm, and 3) a third is the recognition that this is not a unit but a collection of essays.

Lenglet was the first to see the chiastic structure of Dan 2-7. The chapters are organized as follows:

Dan 2: Prophecy of the nations   Dan 7 Prophecy of the Nations
   Dan 3 Fiery furnace   Dan 6 Lions' den
      Dan 4 Nebuchadnezzar's   Dan 5 Belshazzar's downfall
      insanity.[2]

Inspired by Lenglet, Shea studied Dan 4 for inner signs of inclusions and chiasms and recognized a pattern he designed as this:

Dan 4:1 *Prologue*   Dan 4:34-38 *Epilogue*
Post-fulfillment   Post-fulfillment
Proclamation   Restoration
Poem 1   Poem 2

  Dan 4:4-7 Dream Reception   Dan 4:28-33 Dream Fulfillment

    Dan 4:8-9 Dialogue 1   Dan 4:27 Dialogue 3
    King to Daniel   Daniel to King

      Dan 4:10-17   Dan 4:20-26
      Dream Recital   Dream Interpretation

        Dan 4:18-19a   Dan 4:19b
        King to Daniel   Daniel to King

          Dialogue 2.[3]

---

[1] R. H. Charles, *A Critical and Exegetical Commentary on the Book of Daniel* (Oxford: Clarendon Press, 1929), p.79.
[2] A. Lenglet, "La Structure literretaire de Daniel 2-7," *Bib* 53 (1972):169-90.
[3] W. H. Shea, "Further Literary Structures in Daniel 2-7: An Analysis of Daniel 4, " *AUSS* 23 (1985):202.

Within this chiasm Shea also pointed to another beautiful pattern in the epilogue of Dan 4:

Dan 4:34a) I Nebuchadnezzar
    lifted my eyes to heaven
  b) my reason returned to me
  c) I blessed the Most High and
    praised and honored him who lives for the age

  Dan 4:34d-35 POEM

36a) my reason returned to me
  b) my kingdom was re-established
37a) I Nebuchadnezzar
  b) praise and extol and honor
  c) the King of heaven
  d) His ways are just, he humbles the proud.

The balance between these two parts of the epilogue is obvious and well structured. Shea has also pointed out the verbal balance between the narrative of the dream and the corresponding narrative of the interpretation.[4] The literary style of Dan 4 is not nearly as carelessly composed as it has sometimes been thought. The apparent lack of unity of the entire Book of Daniel is appreciated more when recognized as an anthology of essays, and the literary style of the essays is observed.

    When the Book of Daniel is compared with several other similar documents, with which Charles was familiar, it seems more than should be expected that the Book of Daniel alone should be distinguished as the book that was written by only one author. Books like 1Enoch, The Book of Revelation,[5] 2Baruch, and 4Ezra are anthologies that include several different documents each. The individual units in each document vary in style and message. In two of these anthologies, namely 2Baruch and 4Ezra, parallel sources are evident. That does not mean that there was one author who alone composed both documents. Rather there were two final editors who organized the two documents using some of the same sources.

    In all four of these examples, there are some units that are in poetry and others in prose. The divisions within each collection are not difficult to detect. All the units of each collection are related in subject material to form a generally unified message. Most scholars do not suppose that one author composed all of the various units within each document. Charles might not have reached his erroneous conclusion if he had had access to some medieval documents that were not well known in his day.

    In addition to the documents Charles made available to English and American scholars there are two major anthologies that were collected during the Crusades. One of these anthologies is called "The Book of Zerubbabel" and the other

---

[4] Shea, "Literary Structures," pp. 193-202.
[5] For the organization and structure of the Book of Revelation see Buchanan, *The Book of Revelation: its Introduction and Prophecy* (Lewiston: The Edwin Mellen Press, c1994).

collection is different enough to have four different names: "The Prayer of Rabbi Shimon ben Yohai," "The Secrets of Rabbi Shimon ben Yohai," "The Mysteries of Rabbi Shimon ben Yohai," and "The Future Events." These documents are as similar and as different as 4Ezra and 2Baruch.

The Book of Zerubbabel, for instance is preserved in four different texts: "Pirke Hecalot Rabbati," "Wertheimer's text," "Jellinek's text," and "Bodleian Library text." It would be foolish to try to determine from these different versions the original text from which the other documents deviated, because they were not formed that way. Sometimes Jellinek's text parallels more or less with the Bodleian text, and sometimes it does not. Sometimes Wertheimer's text parallels, more or less, with the Bodleian Library text when Jellinek's does not. Sometimes each of these texts has units that other texts do not have. These various versions have been preserved in different ways, and the various editors have felt free to modify them, as it seemed appropriate to them. Not only do these various versions preserve many of the same documents, but some of the units they preserve are also contained in the anthologies associated with Rabbi Shimon ben Yohai.

The various collections related to Rabbi Shimon ben Yohai are very similar to the anthology of the Book of Zerubbabel. Parts of them are parallel to parts of other collections, and parts are unique.

It is apparent that there were many documents circulating during this period of history, and that different editors made different collections of the same kind of units. All of these documents belong to a classification called "Redemption Literature," because they are all centered around the subject of the redemption of Israel, and the redemption of Israel meant the restoration of the Promised Land and the Davidic kingdom. Some units within these collections may have been composed centuries earlier, but they were edited, revised, updated, and directed to the historical period approximately a millennium after the fall of Jerusalem (70 IA). At that time both Jews and Christians were competing with each other, politically and militarily, to gain control of the Promised Land, then held by the Muslims. Both interpreted the signs of the times in terms of typology, fulfillment of scripture, events in current history, and cycles of time, in ways very similar to those applied to the Book of Daniel.[6]

Not only are many of the same units contained in different medieval Jewish anthologies, but also they are available to be read independently, so that it is certain that they were separately composed. There is no one editor who composed any of these entire collections who can be identified as "our author," the way Charles tried to do with the books of Daniel and Revelation. Anyone who reads these medieval Jewish documents and sees them in relationship to the period of history they interpret and then reads the Book of Daniel can quickly see the similarity. The canonical books of Daniel and Revelation are superior in style, content, and organization to any of these later collections, but they belong to the same class of literature and were composed for the same reason. They are properly called "Redemption Literature."

---

[6] These documents are translated and interpreted in Buchanan, *Revelation and Redemption: Jewish Documents of Deliverance from the Fall of Jerusalem to the Death of Nahmanides* (Dillsboro: Western North Carolina Press, c1978; sold by Mercer U. Press).

Among the insights gained from reading the Jewish medieval literature is the realization that there is no one single way in which all ancient scholars had to compose literature. They did not fit everything into any certain groove that can be determined a millennium later. Just because a twentieth century scholar is able to remove awkward expressions and smooth out organizational imperfections does not prove that the final result is the earliest form of the document. One story can be preserved in this literature in many different versions, copied, paraphrased, and restructured by many authors over a long period of time. Such a story was obviously well known, and it is difficult or impossible to discern its true origin and respective modifications.

Once this becomes generally evident, it effects the way scholars examine Dan 4. It means scholars do not need to try to deduce the single author of Dan 4 and assume the author was the same as the author of other chapters. The OG and the MT may have developed independently using most of the same sources, but also some different ones. The OG is not just a translation of the MT or vice versa. It is not necessary to try to determine whether the Hebrew or the Aramaic is the original language for the Book of Daniel. Different units were probably composed originally in different languages, and the final editor did not bother to translate them. The original readers or hearers probably were able to understand both Hebrew and Aramaic. Many of them could also read and understand Greek. We cannot be sure at this point. It is better just to take the text as it is and try to understand it.

The story in Dan 4 is a three-act play. 1) The first act (Dan 4:1-24) reports the king's dream and Daniel's interpretation. 2) The second act (Dan 4:25-30) is the story of the king's illness, and 3) the final act (Dan 4:31-34) reports the king's restoration to health and prosperity. Like the previous chapters, this narrative is apologetic. It is designed to make the most powerful of the gentiles look stupid and be forced to recognize the superiority of Judaism. The historical value of the narrative in itself is questionable, but that which is obvious is the point of view of the author.

Religious people sometimes exaggerate to express their feelings. Some of this is done for apologetic reasons, and some hyperbole is expressed for entertainment and humor. For example, Jeremiah accused Judah of playing the harlot, committing adultery with stones and trees (Jer 3:9). He was not talking about an individual person, but a government, a nation. This is not a precisely accurate description of the nation's "sexual" behavior. Jeremiah was speaking of Judah's religious association with pagan cults, finding fault with Judah's ecumenicity. The legal basis for his accusation was that Jews had made a marriage treaty with Yehowah to worship no other deities. When they worshiped foreign gods, Jeremiah said they were unfaithful to Yehowah, and they were therefore adulterers. When they bowed down to images of stone or wood that was committing adultery with stones and trees. His criticism reflects more of Jeremiah's feelings about the situation than sexual factuality.

The Jews of Hasmonean times who accepted Hellenistic practices and customs were accused of "making themselves uncircumcised" (1Macc 1:15). Pharisees accused Jews that mingled with gentiles in business and society of being harlots, even though they were males (Matt 21:31; 15:30). Dan 4 may be an example of similar exaggeration. It is drama rather than history.

TEXT

Daniel

^{OG 4:1}I, Nebuchadnezzar, the king, to all the peoples, tribes, and [all those who speak foreign] languages who dwell in all the land, may your peace be increased!
²The **signs and miracles**, which the Most High God did with me, it seemed good before me to announce to you ³as being great and mighty. His

kingdom is a kingdom of the age, and his authority is **for generation and generation**.

(In the text that follows, the first number is the MT and the second is the Theodotion (Th) from 1-9 and Old Greek (OG) from 10 on. Thus 2/5 means MT 4:2 and Th 4:5).

^{MT 4:3/Th4:4}I, Nebuchadnezzar, was comfortable in my house, thriving in my palace.

^{2/5Th}**I had a dream**, and it frightened me. The thoughts on my bed, and the visions of my head startled me. ^{3/6Th}Then I issued a decree that **all the wisemen** of Babylon should be brought before me who should make known to me the interpretation of the dream. ^{4/7Th}Then the magicians, enchanters, sorcerers, and the Chaldeans came, and
I told my dream before them, but they **could not** make known its meaning to me. ^{5/8Th}[The problem was left unsolved] until later

First Testament Intertexts

^{Deut 6:22} Yehowah provided great and terrible **signs and miracles** in Egypt.

^{Exod 7:3} I will multiply **signs and miracles** in the land of Egypt.

^{Ps 145:13} Your **kingdom is a kingdom of** all **ages** and your government, **from** every **generation to generation.**

^{Gen 41:1} At the end of two years Pharaoh **had a dream**. . . ⁸In the morning his spirit was troubled, and he asked and called every magician in Egypt and **all the wisemen**.

Pharaoh **told them his dream, but** there was **none of them** who **was able** to interpret for Pharaoh. ¹⁴Pharaoh sent and called Joseph, and he hurriedly came

Daniel **came before** me. [Daniel was the one] whose name was Belteshazzar, named after my gods, **in whom was the spirit of the** holy **gods**. I **told** my dream **before** him.	from the dungeon. He shaved, changed his clothes, **and came to** Pharaoh. ³⁸**Can** such a person as this be found **in whom is the spirit of the gods**? ¹⁷Then Pharaoh **said to** Joseph . . .

COMMENTARY

I Nebuchadnezzar. This chapter begins as if **Nebuchadnezzar** were either making an official statement under oath or were writing a general epistle. Royal epistles were known in antiquity, even in the scripture (Ezra and Esther).

Reid told of a practice in Zambia, where spirit possession is called "Bansanga possession." After one seer died, another medium might deny his or her own independent spirit but instead prophesy in the name of the dead seer. When he or she did this the formula for announcing it was "**I am Monze**." Reid suggested that the same understanding should be applied to the expression "**I Daniel**" (Dan 10:2).[7] The same principle might be considered here. The author of Dan 4 might not have been trying to imply that **Nebuchadnezzar** actually had this dream himself, but that it was attributed to him by some later king who had some of the same ideas as **Nebuchadnezzar** had. If so, then he would have thought that he was himself possessed of **Nebuchadnezzar's** spirit. Reid correctly suggested that this was not literary forgery.[8]

Koch compared the Qumran oracle of Nabonidus (*4QOrNab*), the inscription discovered at Harran, and Dan 4. All three texts began with the formula: "I Nabonidus" (Harran), "I Nabonay," (*4QOrNab*), or "**I Nebuchadnezzar**" (Dan 4:1) and paralleled one another in structure and message in an interesting way. It seems likely that *4QOrNab* is dependent upon the Harran text. All three texts tell of Nabonidus (**Nebuchadnezzar**) leaving Babylon for Teima. The Harran text, however, held that he was there 10 years, rather than 7.[9]

Nebuchadnezzar was comfortable. Like the narratives of Dan 1, 2, and 3, this story begins with **Nebuchadnezzar** as one of the chief characters. This beginning is just as formal as if the storyteller had said, "Once upon a time . . ." The reason for relating the story to **Nebuchadnezzar** is that he was the monarch of Babylon who took the Jews captive into Babylon. That made him the arch villain of the story. Because they believed that time moved in cycles, Jews thought that the exile from the Promised Land in Babylon was an antitype of the exile in Egypt, away from the Promised Land. Therefore whatever had happened in Egypt was a pattern for what had to have happened in Babylon. At the beginning of the Egyptian exile there was a

---

[7] S. B. Reid, *Enoch and Daniel* (Berkeley: BIBAL Press, c1989), p. 113.
[8] It is the author here who attributed all of this to Nebuchadnezzar, and it describes more of the feeling of the author toward Nebuchadnezzar than the actual words of Nebuchadnezzar.
[9] K. Koch, "Gottes Herrschaft über das Reich des Menschen: Daniel 4 im Licht neuer Funde," *The Book of Daniel in the Light of New Findings*, ed. A. S. Van der Woude (Leuven: University Press, 1993), pp. 90-92.

pharaoh in Egypt who had dreams; there was an Israelite, named Joseph, who interpreted them and became famous. At the beginning of the Babylonian cycle there had to have been another monarch who had dreams, and another "Joseph" who interpreted them and became famous. This story differs from Dan 2 and 3 in that **Nebuchadnezzar** here is reported to have been confessing his experience, himself. The motivation and doctrine of Dan 2, 3, and 4, however, are all the same.

The story attributed to **Nebuchadnezzar** was originally applied to Nabonidus. **Nebuchadnezzar** was the first king of Babylon to take the Jews into captivity. Nabonidus was the last to rule Babylon before Cyrus of Persia conquered it. The Cyrus Cylinder says,

> (17) Without fighting or battle, he [Cyrus] secured his entrance into Babylon. His city Babylon he spared distress. Nabu-na'id, the king, who did not fear him, he delivered into his hand.[10]

Generation and generation. The meaning of this expression can be taken from the previous line, both from Daniel and from the Psalm intertext. It is God's kingdom that will last for continuing **generations**. It is the kingdom of the age or the kingdom of ages. This is a temporal connotation in which one age follows the one previous, and one **generation** follows the previous **generation**, just as day follows night and as one day, week, or month follows the previous day, week, or month. It does not mean "eternal" or "forever," although these later terms also have a temporal meaning. The author of Dan 4 changed the "ages" of Ps 145 to "age." This probably means that he expected the age of the rock that followed the destruction of the statue (Dan 2) or the age of the Son of man that followed the empires of the beasts (Dan 7) to be long enough to equal many normal ages.

The magicians, enchanters, sorcerers, and the Chaldeans came. These were the same professional priests and psychologists that appeared in Dan 2 and 3. **Chaldeans** (Herodotus 1.132) and **magicians** were both priests. They were just as incompetent as the wisemen and **magicians** of Pharaoh and the same skilled Babylonians in Dan 2 and 3. These were apparently standard lines used by Jewish storytellers. In this case, however, **Nebuchadnezzar** was not reported to have been angry, as Pharaoh had been (Gen 41:10), and he did not threaten to kill them all as he had according to Dan 2:5-13. Just as in the case with the pharaoh, **Nebuchadnezzar** here was willing to tell his dream before he asked for its interpretation as he did in Dan 2.

Belteshazzar, named after my gods. The intention of this statement is to suggest that the deity **named** "Bel" was part of **Belshazzsar**'s name. Actually the name had some other origin, but the author of this chapter apparently did not know that. The author seems to have confused the name "Belshazzar," which means "Bel, protect the king!" with **Belteshazzar**. Since the king knew Daniel as well as he seems to have, it is strange that he would not have called Daniel in the first place. The reason,

---

[10] Charles, *Daniel*, p. cxxiv.

of course, is for dramatic effect. The author wanted to show that all of the wisemen of Babylon had failed before Daniel appeared on the stage.

In whom was the spirit of the holy gods. The verbal similarity of this expression and its intertext in Gen 41 shows how the author of this chapter developed a homily out of Gen 41. The author may have deduced that **the spirit of the holy gods** was in Belteshazzar, because the name "Bel" was in his name. The significance, however, probably means more than that. It probably means that the person to whom this expression was accredited was a legal agent who could speak for the deity. When Saul and David were anointed to become monarchs they both received **the spirit**. Various ones of the judges were reported to have received **the spirit** when they assumed their roles as national leaders. Jesus received **the spirit** when he was baptized, and afterwards he was recognized as one who spoke with authority and not as the scribes. He was also called "messiah," "king," "Son of God," and other royal titles that went with reception of **the spirit.**

Told the dream before. Here the king told his dream *before* the wisemen and Daniel. The reference of a statement before someone, rather than to someone, is done almost always before a king or other superior ranking person. The king would be expected to have told his dream *to* them.

TEXT

Daniel	First Testament Intertexts
6/9"Belteshazzar, great magician, I know that the spirit of the holy gods is in you, and **no mystery** is troublesome to **you**. [Here is] the vision of my dream which I saw. Now tell me its interpretation. 7/OG 10Th The visions of my head on my bed that I saw [were these]:	Ezek 28:3 Look! You are wiser than Daniel. They can hold **no mystery** from **you**.

COMMENTARY

Belteshazzar great magician. This is the name reportedly given to Daniel when he joined the academic fellows (Dan 1:7). The other three fellows also had Babylonian names. Many Jews today have two names, one is public and the other a religious name. **Magicians** in antiquity were official priests, offering prescribed sacrifices (Xenophon, *Cyrop* 7.35 *et alia*). Like other priests, however, they also seem to have played approximately the same role in antiquity as psychologists, psychiatrists, and psychoanalysts do today.

The spirit of the holy gods is in you. Frequently **the spirit** was used as a legal term. It might mean that Belteshazzar was authorized and licensed as a magician in Babylon. That which was "**in** him" was in him legally. Since Babylonians were polytheists those who were licensed to do something legally had to be authorized by all of the Babylonian gods. This would have included Bel, Nebo, and Marduk.

Charles noted that in earlier chapters Daniel was wiser than all of the wisemen in Babylon, and he was one of the most important leaders of the nation. The king knew how intelligent and capable he was. He was at the king's right hand.

> The relative positions of Daniel and the wisemen during Nebuchadnezzar's reign were settled once and for all in chap. 2.[11]

Why then, asked Charles, did the king not consult Daniel first of all, rather than call all the incompetent wisemen of the nation first? This is a good question if credence is given to Charles' assumption that one person wrote the whole Book of Daniel. Without that assumption, it is obvious that chapter four was written by a different author from the authors of earlier chapters. Since the author of Dan 4 had not read the earlier chapters, he did not assume all of the items reported in those chapters.

TEXT

Daniel	First Testament Intertexts
Look! A tree in the midst of the land. / **It was very tall.** / [7]The tree grew and became strong. /	[Ezek 31:3]**Look!** I will compare you to a cedar of Lebanon. Its branches were beautiful, a forest shade. **It was very tall.**
Its height touched **heaven**, / and it was visible to **all the land**. / [8/12]Its leaves were beautiful, / and its fruit was abundant. / It had food for all. /	[Gen 11:4]They said, "Let us build for ourselves a city and a tower, and **its** head in **heaven**, and we will make for ourselves a name, lest we be scattered over the face of **all the land**."

COMMENTARY

A tree in the midst of the land. The **tree** in this parable was Nabonidus, and the parable was patterned after a parable told by Ezekiel. Ezekiel's **tree** was compared to the Pharaoh of Egypt. The parable of Daniel's **tree** was applied to Nabonidus, because, although he was king of Babylon for many years, he left Babylon under the leadership of his son, while he moved west to administer the western part of his empire. During that time he rebuilt the temple to the god Sin in Harran. He became ill when he was in Anti-Lebanon. He made his headquarters on the oasis of Teima in Arabia.[12] There is no evidence for his having lost his mind. He may have gone to Teima for his health. According to one text he went there to extend his empire. He

---

[11] Charles, *Daniel*, p. 81.
[12] A. L. Oppenheim, "Nabonidus," *IDB* III, pp. 493-95.

took troops with him, captured the city of Teima, and fortified it. He stayed in Teima for nearly 10 years, but he returned just before Cyrus conquered Babylon. When he left Babylon, he was like a tall **tree**; when he returned he was only a stump, by comparison. We do not have an objective analysis of Nabonidus in this chapter. A Jew wrote the story, and the Jews at the time of Nabonidus were supporting the invasion of Cyrus, while defaming Babylon and Nabonidus.

Christians and Jews have both been propagandists with strong feelings. When they have hostile feelings against one another they sometimes use their religious holidays as occasions to vent these feelings. While reviewing past events in their history, they describe these events in ways that stir up negative feelings and actions against local enemies. At Easter, for example, sometimes local, twentieth century Jews are identified with the Jews who killed Jesus 2,000 years ago. Jews, in turn, while reading the Book of Esther out loud in the synagogue sometimes do it in such a way as to motivate Jews to want to treat contemporary Christians and Muslims they know the way Esther's and Mordecai's contemporary Jews dealt with Haman and other gentiles in Persia.

Sometimes these feasts result in actual violence in which innocent people are injured or even killed. In a similar way this story is geared to defame Nabonidus as a crazy man with no more brains than a beast, and it was told as if it were about an earlier generation when Nebuchadnezzar was king, but local Jews would have understood all the allusions and implications. The details of this story are so close to the events related to Nabonidus that they suggest that it was written either near the end of his rule or later. It included the report of his return from Teima to Babylon as a stump. There are some historically verifiable points in this narrative, but the purpose of the narrative is obvious. Historians should not accept propaganda and insult as if it were objective historical fact. [13]

Its height touched heaven. Neither Nabonidus nor Nebuchadnezzar was the only national leader to be compared to trees. Xerxes had a dream in which he visioned himself wearing a crown composed of a shoot from an olive tree, and its branches covered the entire earth (*Herodotus* 7.19). Like the figure in Dan 4, Xerxes' tree was part of a dream. It was Pharaoh of Egypt that was compared to the giant cedar tree (Ezek 31) whose top was among the clouds. Ezekiel's parable was one to which the author of Dan 4 alluded.

Ostensibly the tree was identified with Nebuchadnezzar, but the description fits Nabonidus very well, and Nebuchadnezzar, not at all. Why was this story of Nabonidus told as if it were about Nebuchadnezzar? Before answering that question we will compare the tree to Nabonidus.

---

[13] Nabonidus probably was not the recluse that Daniel has painted him, but he apparently had a special interest in religious reform. This may have caused the Jewish irritation that is reflected in Dan 4.

TEXT

Daniel	First Testament Intertexts
Underneath it was sheltering **the** wild **beasts, / and in its branches the birds of the heaven** were living, / and all flesh were obtaining food from it. ⁹/¹³I continued watching the visions of my head on my bed.	^{Ezek 31:6} **In its branches** all **the birds of the heaven** made nests, and **under its branches** all **the beasts** gave birth.

COMMENTARY

Underneath it was sheltering the beasts. The king of the huge empire of Babylon had extensive authority and responsibility. All the people of the land depended on him for provision and protection. The "tree" was arrogant and Babylonian. It was like the tower of Babylon. It was intended to be greater than all the towers on earth.

The visions of my head. All of this was part of the vision which was to be continued.

TEXT

Daniel	First Testament Intertexts
Now look! A watcher, / a holy one from **heaven descended.** / ¹¹/¹⁴He cried aloud, and this is what he said,	^{Gen 11:5} Yehowah **descended** to see the city and the tower which the human beings had built
"**Cut down** the **tree**, and cut off	^{Job 14:7} There is hope for a tree. If it is **cut down** it will sprout again.
its **branches**, / strip off its leaves, and scatter its fruit. / Let **the beasts** flee from under it, / and **the birds, from its branches**. ¹²/¹⁵But leave the **stump from its**	^{Ezek 31:6} From **its branches** all **the beasts** gave birth.
roots in the land, / [tied] with an iron and brass band in the grass of the field. / With the dew of heaven it will be moistened. /	^{Isa 11:1} There will be a **stump from the branch** of Jesse; / a **branch** will grow out **from its roots**.

>   Its lot will be with the beasts in the grass of the land.
> ^{13/16}Its mind will be changed from a human mind,
>   and the mind of a beast will be given to it.
>   Seven times will pass over it.
> ^{14/17}The decree of the watchers is a demand,
>   and the word of the holy ones is a judicial sentence,
>   until it is known of the living that the Most High
>   rules the kingdom of human beings.
>   He gives it to whomever he will
>   and appoints over it the humblest of people."

TECHNICAL DETAILS

These verses constitute the king's confession, and the entire dream is cast in poetry. This means that the poem is central and integral to the entire chapter. The first verses are shown in parallel relationship with certain FT texts to demonstrate their midrashic character. The second half of the poem is free from midrash.

COMMENTARY

A watcher, a holy one from heaven. The Lord was expected to function very much like a king. He had a council of advisors (1Kgs 22:19; Ps 89:7; Jer 23:18), a group of security guards, and ambassadors to communicate with people in distant places. The ambassadors were also called angels. An angel is simply a messenger of some kind. It might be almost any human being on earth and be sent to almost any other human being. It might simply deliver a letter or a package, or it might also be an apostle with authority to act and speak in behalf of the one who sent it.

This angel was a watcher or a wakeful one. It was probably either one, who stayed awake night and day, always prepared to carry out missions, or it constantly guarded the throne. Another possibility is that it was the Lord's espionage agent. As a watcher, he was assigned to investigate and spy out certain situations and report back to the Lord. He also brought messages to certain people in their visions and dreams.

This angel was a special one that came from heaven. Therefore the principal who sent it would have been God. "A holy one" (*káh-deesh*, קדיש) was just another name for an angel (*mah-lahk*, מלאך) from God (Job 5:1; 15:15; Ps 89:6, 8). One of the types of angels was the watcher (*eer*, עיר). The angel of Yehowah who came down from heaven was probably intended to remind the reader of the time Yehowah came down from heaven to see what the Babylonians were doing. Then Yehowah punished the Babylonians, because they were trying to reach heaven (Gen 11:1-9). When this angel came down from heaven it was part of a dream to a Babylonian king that promised punishment for him.

Leave the stump from its roots. The stump was Nabonidus, the last king of Babylon. He may have been killed during or after the Persian invasion. He returned from his investigation and leadership in Arab countries in the western part of his empire. He arrived at Babylon just before Cyrus of Persia invaded Babylon. The demise of Nabonidus reminded the author of the fall of the Davidic dynasty, which left a stump from its roots (Isa 11:1).

An iron and brass band. Koch saw the importance of the art drawn in Khorsabad of a sacred tree made with golden leaves and metal bands around the trunk. At the tree's top is a sun disk with wings and an art form of Assurbanipal II within the disk.[14] The disk was a sign of the deity surrounding the king. Mendenhall has shown that the winged sun disk indicated the manifestation, glory, power, and dignity of gods like Horus, Re, Zeus, Ahura Mazda and Baal Shamem.[15] It often provided a frame for the king himself, as has been done here, to show that the king functioned with the authority of the deity. For Hebrews the clouds or the angel was the sign of God's presence, such as the Son of man appearing before the Ancient of Days in a cloud (Dan 7:13). The symbol of the sun disk is also evident in the Song of Deborah, **But your friends be like the sun [disk] rising in its power** (Judges 5:31).[16]

The dew of heaven. In the Near East there is a heavy dew almost every night, because the days are hot and the nights are cold. The night temperature condenses the moisture from the air. Because of this moisture, crops may continue to grow during the summer and birds and beasts that eat the wet grass obtain fluid their bodies need.

His lot will be with the beasts. This means he lived in a rural area. When Judas fled to the wilderness to lead a guerrilla movement against the Syrians, he and his followers were reported to have lived on herbs for food the way animals do (2Macc 5:27).

The mind of a beast will be given to it. It was bad enough to be forced to associate with **beasts**, but this report was that the person involved actually achieved a **mind** like a **beast**. Applying the characteristics of beasts to human beings is not unique for legends. Many of Aesop's Fables are designed to do this. Furthermore there were in antiquity stories of human beings that became at least partially beasts. These were known in ancient Akkadian literature as well as in Greek literature. The point of these stories was to show that the person involved had about the same characteristics when he or she was a beast as when he or she was a human being.[17] Job says God **turns away the mind of chiefs of the people of the land; he makes them wander in confusion without a path** (Job 12:23).

Seven times will pass over it. Seven years will pass. The word *ee-dah-neén* (עדנין) means "times." In Daniel these times are the same as years. The *ee-dah-neén* (Dan

---

[14] Koch, "Neuer Funde," pp. 104-106.
[15] E. Mendenhall, *The Tenth Generation* (Baltimore: John Hopkins Press, c1973), pp. 210-11.
[16] See further, Buchanan, *Biblical and Theological Insights from Ancient and Modern Civil Law* (Lewiston: The Edwin Mellen Press, 1995), pp. 105-106.
[17] See further Pierre Grelot, "Nabuchodonosor Changé en Bête," *VT* 44 (1994):10-17.

7:25) are also called *moh-ah-deén* (Dan 12:7) where 3½ times has the same meaning as "half a week of years" (Dan 9:27).

A decree of the watchers. This is a general statement that is not confined to the special angel who made this **decree**. This sentence deals with plural subjects. In all cases, **decrees** from **watchers** (*eer-eén*, עירין) are final. They are not debatable or negotiable. **A decree** of God's agents is the same as **a decree** from God himself. The **decree** here has the same effect as **a decree from the Most High** (Dan 4:21). It was assumed that there was a counsel in heaven that functioned in consultation with God (Job 1:6, 12; 2:1, 6; Ps 89:6, 8; Jer 23:18).[18] On the basis of Dan 4:17, Rabbi Johanan said that God did nothing without consulting the family above (*bSan* 38b; 94a). His family above was his heavenly court or his assembly of angels. A **watcher** was one category of angels. Some of God's angels were legal agents who had authority, whereas others merely carried out orders. The ones who were legal agents made **decrees**. God would have approved the commands they gave. Such **decrees** would have had the same authority as if God gave them.

So far as the king was concerned, he was receiving an irreversible, irrevocable sentence. God had already judged his case, and the angel simply delivered his verdict. It was this verdict that came to the king in a dream, and it was Daniel who was assigned to interpret it. This is similar to the decree Nabonidus supposedly received before he said that no deity or human being had the power to avert the Fates (Eusebius, *PraepEvang* 9.4).

The Most High rules the kingdom of human beings. When Yehowah descended from heaven and saw what the Babylonians were trying to do, he confused their tongues so that they could not continue their tower (Gen 11:1-9). He let them know in this way that he was in control over all earthly kingdoms. This was a message King Nabonidus had to learn from Daniel.

Gives it to whomever he will. This means that there is no higher judge to rule against him.[19]

He appoints over it the humblest of people. The people the author had in mind, of course, were the Jews. They had come to Babylon as captives from a foreign country only about 30 miles long and 30 miles wide. In Babylon, one of their group, Nehemiah, soon became cup-bearer to the Persian king. They may have had still further designs by the time this document was written.

All the wisemen of my kingdom. This is a theme that is often repeated. It had its origin in the Joseph stories of Genesis. When pagan wisemen failed, a Jew could be moved from slavery to becoming the chief counselor to the monarch.

---

[18] See further S. B. Parker, "The beginning of the Reign of God—Psalm 82 as Myth and Liturgy," *RB* 102-104 (1995):532-59.
[19] See A. Hurvitz, "The History of a Legal Formula," *VT* 32 (1982):257-77.

The spirit of the holy gods. Daniel was believed to be able to interpret dreams because of this qualification. He had whatever training and authorization was required to have obtained this ability. To be consistent with the thought of the message, it was the spirit of the pagan gods that was in him. The king was a pagan, and he thought it was **the spirit of the gods** he worshiped that were in Daniel. Daniel was in Babylon, not Judah, and the Babylonian government--not Jewish legislation, acknowledged his authority. The king thought Daniel was a legal agent of the deity. Therefore he would have special insight into the thoughts and actions of the deity.

TEXT

15/18"This is the dream which I, King Nebuchadnezzar, saw. Now you, Belteshazzar, tell the interpretation, even though all the wisemen of my kingdom were not able to disclose the interpretation to me. 15/19You, however, are able, because the spirit of the holy gods is in you." 16/19Then Daniel, whose name is Belteshazzar, was puzzled for a while. His thoughts troubled him. The king answered and said, "Belteshazzar, do not let the dream and its interpretation trouble you." Belteshazzar said, "My Lord, may the visions of your dream be for your enemies, and its interpretation, for your adversaries. 17/20The tree which you saw that grew up and became strong, whose height reached heaven and was visible to all the land, 18/21whose leaves were beautiful and whose fruit was abundant and in which was food for all--under it dwelled the beasts of the field, and in its branches lived the birds of the heaven.

19/22"You, O King, are the one who has become great and strong. Your greatness has grown and reaches heaven, and your sovereignty is to the end of the land. 20/23And when the king saw a watcher, even a holy one come down from heaven and said, 'Cut down the tree and destroy it, but the stump of its roots leave in the land, but tied with a band of bronze and iron in the grass of the field. Let it be moistened with the dew of heaven and its portion be with the beasts of the field until seven times pass over it.'"

COMMENTARY

Daniel . . . was puzzled. Up to this time, the main character was Nebuchadnezzar. Readers were expected to identify with him. The purpose of the change of voice at this point was to prevent the reader from identifying too closely with this one character. That is because the story is not only told by Nebuchadnezzar. It is also about Nebuchadnezzar. The reader no longer learns the story from the point of view of a Babylonian king but of a wise Jew. That makes the author's slant more direct.[20]

Daniel was evidently puzzled—not primarily about the meaning of the dream. He was troubled about the problem of disclosing its meaning to the king, safely. He needed the assurance that the king offered. The king was much kinder and more patient with Daniel than he was shown to have been in relationship with the wisemen of Babylon in Dan 2. Instead of threatening him with death if he failed, the

---

[20] T. Meadowcroft, "Point of View in Storytelling: An Experiment in Narrative Criticism in Daniel 4:1," *Didaskolia* 8 (1997):30-34.

king reassured Daniel that he was confident that Daniel knew the right answer, and the king was prepared to accept it, whatever it was. The expression "for an instant" (*réh-gah eh-kháhd*, רגע אחד) in Hebrew is rendered in the Targum as "for an hour" (*shah-áh khah-dáh*, שעה חדא). It was probably not understood as exactly a 60 minute hour. Here it is roughly rendered "a while."

Do not let the dream and its interpretation trouble you. Daniel needed the king's assurance that he would not be punished for telling **the dream**. Kings sometimes killed the messengers who brought them bad news. For example, David killed the messenger that told him of Saul's death (2Sam 1:14), even though David was glad to have Saul dead. This was the politically correct thing to do, just as David's mourning was (2Sam 1:17-27).

May the visions of your dream be for your enemies. This is a way of breaking the bad news. Daniel knew what the **dream** meant. Since it was a decree of the holy watchers it could not be revoked. His wish was that the king's enemies would also have misfortune as bad as this.

Whose height reached heaven. The OG adds **and whose top touches the clouds** (OG 4:22).

The one who has become great and strong. The status and power of the king was magnificent. Everything in his land depended on him for food and sustenance. The king knew all of this; it was the rest of the dream that was the nightmare.

OG Your mind has been supercilious. An OG addition is included here telling the king that he had not only become arrogant, but he had done evil works. The most notable thing was the destruction of the temple of the God of life and his sin against the holy people (OG Dan 4:22). This was the reason for the adverse judgment of God against him. That is why the heavenly messenger said to chop down the tree.

TEXT

Daniel	Babylonian Legend
21/25"This is the interpretation, O King. It is the decree of the Most High that has come upon my Lord, the king. 22/26 They will drive you from human beings to be dwelling with the beasts of the field. They will make you eat grass like cattle. You will be moistened from the dew of heaven, and seven times will pass over you before you learn that the sovereignty of the Most High is with the kingdom of human beings, and he will give it to	I, Nebuchadnezzar, announce to you beforehand the coming misfortune, which Bel, my ancestor and the Queen Beltis are alike powerless to persuade the Fates to avert. A Persian mule [i.e., Cyrus] will come, having your own deities as his allies, and will bring slavery. He who will help him in this undertaking will be Medes, the boast of Assyria. Would that, before my citizens were betrayed, some Charybdis or sea

whomever he will. ²³/²⁷When they commanded to leave the stump of its roots of the tree, [this means] that your kingdom will survive for you from the time that you know that sovereignty is of Heaven

might receive him, and utterly extinguish him! Or else that, betaking himself elsewhere, he might be driven through the desert, where is no city nor track of man, where wild beasts have their pasture and birds do roam, and that among rocks and ravines he might wander alone! (Eusebius, *PraepEvang* 9.4).

TECHNICAL DETAILS

The narrative reported in Dan 4 was probably adapted from a legend told about Nebuchadnezzar as if he had himself received a message from the deity. Like Dan 9, it begins with the words, "I Nebuchadnezzar." He announced that the message was from his ancestor, "Bel," another name for Marduk. It was a decree that could not be changed or averted. He was foretold that a Persian mule (Cyrus) would come into Babylon, having Babylonian deities as his allies. Medes and Babylonians would help this mule in his project. Nebuchadnezzar hoped that before all of this happened that this mule would be driven through the desert, where only birds and wild beasts were his company. Otherwise he would be alone. (Eusebius, *PraepEvang* 9.4). Driver agreed with Bevan in following Shrader,[21] who said,

> It is therefore probable that some Babylonian legend on the subject of Nebuchadnezzar had, perhaps in a very distorted form, reached the ears of the author of Daniel, who adapted the story in order to make it a vehicle of religious instruction.[22]

The author of Dan 4 applied the curses that Nebuchadnezzar wanted to fall on the Persian "mule" (Cyrus) to Nebuchadnezzar himself. Then he directed a few facts about Nabonidus into the legend, so as to make it currently useful as anti-Nabonidus propaganda. The author of the Babylonian legend was anti-Cyrus. The author of Dan 4 reorganized it to be pro-Cyrus and anti-Babylonian. Neither narrative is objective history.

There are important similarities between the account in Daniel and that in the Babylonian legend: 1) In both a divine voice is heard; 2) Both take place with the king on the roof; 3) Doom is pronounced in both. 4) Nebuchadnezzar was the king in both cases,[23] even though in Daniel the account seems to be directed to Nabonidus. The Babylonian legend was supposedly told by Megasthenes (ca. 300

---

[21] Shrader, "Nebuchadnezzar's Madness," *Jahrbücher für Protest. Theol.* (1881):618 ff.
[22] S. R. Driver, *The Book of Daniel* (Cambridge: University Press, 1912), p. 60.
[23] Here it is Cyrus who was called a mule, but this was also a name given to Nebuchadnezzar, because the name Nabu-kudana-usur is really scurrilous etymology, meaning "Nabu, protect the mule." The real name was Nebuchadrezzar (Nabu-kudurra-usur), "Nabu protect the crownprince." The offense of being called a mule is that female mules cannot reproduce. See further W. W. Hallo, "Scurrilous Etymologies," *Pomegranates and Golden Bells* ed. D. P. Wright, D. N. Freedman, and A. Hurvitz. (Winona Lake: Wisenbrauns, c1995), p. 772.

BIA) who lived many years after either Nebuchadnezzar (604-561 BIA) or Nabonidus (555-539 BIA). The Babylonian legend presumes a familiarity about the invasion of Cyrus into Babylon.

COMMENTARY

They will drive you. **They** here is a euphemism for God. It was not people but God who determined the affairs of human beings, and it would be God who would deal adversely with Nebuchadnezzar. This is a pejorative analysis of Nabonidus' decision to spend several years away from Babylon, living in the western part of his empire, among the Arabs. The Jew who wrote this account was probably not giving an objective analysis of the events. Jews, Israelites, and Hebrews have been in conflict with Arabs ever since Ishmael and Isaac. Anti-Arab feelings are reflected in the narratives that picture the older brother, Ishmael, displaced by the younger brother, Isaac; the older brother, Esau, outwitted by the younger brother, Jacob; and the parables of Jesus whereby the older brother (the Pharisee) is displaced by the younger brother (the tax collector). It is also evident in historical reports of activities during the Hasmonean period, and it is still true today.

When this anti-Arab author described Nabonidus' activity as being crazy and eating grass like cattle, this may have been just a hyperbolic way of saying he was living away from civilized Babylonians among the "uncivilized" Arabs in rural Arabia. Hostile descriptions of enemies about one another should not be taken for accurate analyses. The attitude of Jews toward Nabonidus is reflected in the probability that they were instrumental in getting him displaced and assisting Cyrus of Persia in conquering Babylonia.[24] According to the Babylonian texts, Nabonidus first established an image of a new deity, Nanna, in Babylon. This made many citizens of Babylon angry. Then he angered them further by building a temple for it. After that, for political reasons, he entrusted the rule of the kingdom of Babylon to his eldest son. Then he took the military troops of Akkad with him and headed west to enlarge the kingdom in that direction. He conquered Teima and made his residence there. He built up and fortified the city there.[25]

Seven times. This evidently means "**seven** years," because "a time, two times, and half a time" in Daniel means 42 months or three and a half years.

You know the sovereignty is from Heaven. This is the earliest biblical reference to God by the name **Heaven**. The evangelistic message Daniel had for the king was that in his current condition, his mind was deranged and he would continue to be crazy until he embraced the Jewish religion.

---

[24] According to Xenophon, *Cyrop* 7.28-30, it was two of Cyrus' leaders, Gobryas and Gadatas, who had personal grudges against Nabonidus, who actually killed Nabonidus.

[25] A. L. Oppenheim (tr.), "Babylonian and Assyrian Historical Texts," *Ancient Near Eastern Texts* ed. J. B. Pritchard (Princeton: Princeton U. Press, 1969), p. 313.

TEXT

²⁴/²⁸Therefore, O King, let my advice be favorable to you, [which] is to redeem your sins with righteousness and blot out your iniquities [by caring for] the poor. Maybe your tranquillity will be lengthened." ²⁵/ All of this came upon King Nebuchadnezzar.
    ²⁶/²⁹At the end of twelve months he was walking on the [roof of the] palace of the kingdom of Babylon. ²⁷/³⁰The king answered and said, "Is not this great Babylon which I have built into a royal house by my great power and for the glory of my majesty?" ²⁸/³¹While the word was still in the mouth of the king.

Daniel	First Testament Intertexts
A voice fell from heaven,	Isa 40:6 **A voice** saying, "Cry!"

"To you it is spoken, King Nebuchadnezzar, the kingdom has been taken from you. ²⁹/³²You will be driven from human beings, dwelling with beasts of the field. They will make you eat grass like cattle, and seven years will pass over you until you find out that the Most High rules the kingdoms of human beings, and he gives it to whomever he will." ³⁰/³³Instantly the word was fulfilled on Nebuchadnezzar. He was driven from human beings; he was fed grass like cattle; his body was wet from the dew of heaven; his hair grew long as eagles' [feathers], and his nails like birds' [claws]. ³¹/³³"At the end of [the previously determined] days, I, Nebuchadnezzar, lifted up my eyes to heaven, and my senses returned to me.

Daniel	First Testament Intertexts
I blessed the Most High, / and **I praised and honored the One who lives for the age,** / for **his rule is the rule of** the age, / **and his kingdom is with generation and generation**. /	Ps 145:13 **For your kingdom is the kingdom of** all **ages, and his rule is with** every **generation and generation**.
³²/³⁴**All the** residents of the land are valued **as nothing**. / He does as he wishes with the troops of heaven / and the residents on the land. / There is no one who can hinder his **hand** / or **say,** **'What are you doing?'**	Isa 40:17 **All the** nations are **as nothing** against him; they will be considered to him **as nothing.** Sir 36:8 Who can **say** to you, **"What are you doing?"** Ps 45:9 Does the clay say to its maker, **"What are you doing?"** or "Your product has no **hands**?"

^{33/35}At that time my senses returned to me,
> and the glory of my kingdom,
>> my honor and majesty returned to me;
my counselors and my officers looked for me,
> and I was confirmed over my kingdom,
>> and even more greatness was added to me.
^{34/36}Thus I, Nebuchadnezzar, praise, exalt, and honor the King of Heaven,
> because all of his works are true,
>> and his paths, just.
Those who walk in pride he is able to humble."

COMMENTARY

Redeem your sins. Except for sins that required a death penalty or excommunication, sins were corrected in court by paying for the offenses in terms of goods or currency. A civil offense was an offense both against some other member of the community and against God or the nation. The local community and the nation called attention to some of these crimes, and citizens were given opportunities to restore their status by paying their fines to the state and becoming reconciled to the people they had injured.

The Aramaic word *puh-roók*, (פרק) means either "**redeem**" or "**stop!**" "**break off.**" The best translation here is **redeem**, because it is not enough to stop sinning. The Day of Atonement requires the sinner to pay for previous sins and iniquities. This is done by bringing adequate gifts to the altar on the Day of Atonement, after first compensating all of the people whom the sinner has injured. When Jacob wanted to be **redeemed** from all of his sins, he first sent to Esau numerous gifts to pay for his crimes against Esau. Then he returned to Esau both Esau's blessing and his birthright. This meant that he allowed Esau to go back and claim his property and status unimpeded at Hebron, in the south, while Jacob bought for himself property around Shechem in the north.

In this way he redeemed his sins so far as Esau was concerned. He still had to bring the proper gifts to the temple on the Day of Atonement (Gen 33). When Zacchaeus wanted to be approved as one of Jesus' followers, he said, **Look! Lord, the half my goods I give to the poor; and if I have defrauded anyone of anything I will restore it fourfold** (Luke 19:5-8). This was to **redeem** his sins, and it is what Nebuchadnezzar was advised to do. Faithfulness and loyalty was believed to make atonement for sin (Prov 16:6).

No list of sins was given, but there probably were many things about any Babylonian king that Jews would not have liked. The emphasis here is not his arrogance. The possibility that Jews may have been instrumental in bringing about the fall of Nabonidus' kingdom and his own death suggests that Jews had negative feelings against him.

He was walking on the [roof of the] palace of the kingdom of Babylon. This means that **he was walking on the roof of his palace**. In the Near East, particularly in cities, houses are made with cement **roofs** on which people walk just as they would

walk on a floor. King David **was walking on the roof of his palace** when he was attracted to Bath Sheba, who was bathing on her **roof** (2Sam 11:2). In the legend of Nebuchadnezzar, announcing a divine message from Bel to his people about the Persian mule (Cyrus) that would conquer Babylon, he did this from **the roof** of his palace (Eusebius, *PraepEvang.* 9.4). This is one of the details the author of Dan 4 seems to have taken from that legend. According to the OG Nebuchadnezzar was **walking on** the walls of the city and through the towers made into the walls (OG 4:29). From this position, as from **the of his palace**, the king could view and admire the city.

Boys Flying Kites on Roofs of Buildings in Jerusalem

Is not this great Babylon? At the time Nebuchadnezzar was king, **Babylon** was one of the **greatest** and most cultured cities of the civilized world. It was the capital city of a nation that extended from the Tigris-Euphrates valley to Egypt. At the time of Nabopolassar Assyria was forced by military conflicts to liberate Babylon from taxation and rule. According to the cylinder of Nabopolassar Babylon had

> an elevated nest which comes level with the heavens, a strong shield closing the mouth of the enemy land, the very wide courtyard of Agog, the broad precinct of the Annuli, a stairway to the heavens, staircase to the underworld, station-place of Lugal-girra and Meslamta-ea, open-air shrine of Isshtar the great queen (*Babylon* 2, Col. 2.11-17).[26]

Babylon was believed to have been the residence of Marduk, the place where he established his kingship. It was the home of the great gods. It was called the sanctuary, and the city of the king of the gods, [27]because it contained the famous

---

[26] D. C. T. Sheriffs, "'A Tale of Two Cities'—Nationalism in Zion and Babylon," *Tyndale Bulletin* 39 (1988):21.
[27] Sheriffs, "A Tale," p. 35.

Ziggurat.[28] Like Jerusalem Babylon was thought by its citizens to have been a holy city. Kings of **Babylon** ruled all the lands between the seas to the north and the seas to the south, and they collected taxes from all nations under **Babylonian** dominion.[29]

Which I have built. Babylon existed long before Nebuchadnezzar became king. Nebuchadnezzar rebuilt Babylon extensively, but he did not build it originally.[30]

The glory of my majesty. According to Deuteronomy the Israelites should not allow a foreigner to act as king over them (Deut 17:15), and the king that rules them should not let his mind be lifted up above his brothers (Deut 17:20). The author seems to have applied this rule for Israelite kings to the foreign king Belshazzar. The king of Tyre became proud and considered himself to be god who sat in the council of the gods. Kings, like David, were assumed to belong to the council of God when they ruled (Acts 13:36). Ezekiel reminded the king of Tyre that he was still human and not so wise as Daniel was (Ezek 28:2-3).

Isaiah accused the king of Babylon of becoming arrogant, because, as king, he should belong to the council of gods and would make himself like the Most High. He even presumed that his throne would be exalted to heaven. Isaiah reminded him that he was still a human being who would die and be brought down to Sheol like other human beings (Isa 14:12-15). Kings and judges were accepted as legal agents of the deity. As legal agents of the deity they were the deities incarnate, which is a very exalted position, but it did not mean that they were principals. They sometimes became arrogant and acted as if they were gods rather than human beings who were only agents. Prophets reminded them that they were human and would die like other human beings (Ps 82:1, 6). According to Dan 2, Belshazzar became arrogant like the king of Tyre or the king of Babylon to which Isaiah referred. He also dramatized the Jewish belief that the king was not as wise as Daniel was (Ezek 28:3).

The kingdom has been taken from you. This may refer to the time King Nabonidus left Babylon for a long stay in the West.

I lifted up my eyes to heaven. This is another way to say that he turned to God in prayer.

What are you doing? This question probably had its origin in Ps 45:9. Ben Sira then used it as an intertext, and Dan 4 took it from one or both of these earlier sources.

I was confirmed over my kingdom. According to Dan 4 this happened only after Nebuchadnezzar recognized his subordinate political position. God was the king of kings and not Nebuchadnezzar. It was God's kingdom that would endure for one generation after the other in the age to come.

---

[28] Sheriffs, "A Tale," p. 23.
[29] Sheriffs, "A Tale," pp. 32-33.
[30] G. F. Hasel, "The Book of Daniel: Evidences Relating to Persons and Chronology," *AUSS* 19 (1981):37-38.

TECHNICAL DETAILS

In addition to the poetic dream, as in Dan 2, Dan 3 concluded with a poetic confesssion of the king. This story follows the dream theme that is characteristic of Dan 2-3. The narrative reflects a legend about Nebuchadnezzar, the Babylonian king who first conquered Palestine and took the competent Jews into Babylon (605-562 BIA), but still more Nabonidus, the last Babylonian king to rule Babylon (555-539 BIA). For several years, Nabonidus gave authority to his son, Belshazzar, to rule the eastern part of the country and command the army, while he traveled in the West among Arab cities. During a short part of this time he was ill, but there is no other record that accused him of being mentally deranged during that time. Nor was he driven from his kingdom.

Nabonidus has probably not been fairly represented. Keil followed the research of Oppert and Dunker and agreed that Nabonidus was an effective king who completed the fortifications of Babylon on both sides of the river and restored the tower and pyramid. He also had a temple to the goddess Belit and the god Sin.[31] He evidently chose to pay attention to the western regions of his kingdom. This might have been a good decision, and he might have spent his time there very constructively. Frequently kings left their governments to the responsibility of their sons while dealing with other matters. For example, Antiochus III left his government at Antioch to his son, Seleucus, for several years while he conducted wars of expansion in Asia Minor. According to the Babylonian texts, Nabonidus conquered Teima in the far west, built up the city, and fortified it to extend his nation's borders.[32]

Jews evidently gave a pejorative interpretation to his absence from Babylon for their own political and doctrinal purposes. It was during Nabonidus' reign that Cyrus of Persia captured Babylon without a battle.[33] Jews had evidently had an underground movement going on against Nabonidus long before the city was taken. There is a legend that Nebuchadnezzar announced to the Babylonians that a Persian mule would come and enslave the Babylonians. The mule would have as its allies Babylonian deities (Eusebius, *PraepEvang* 9.41, 6). The "mule" was Cyrus, and this reflects the fall of Babylon with the aid of people within the city of Babylon itself.

Xenophon described the capture in detail. He said the city was taken during a feast when many of the citizens were drunk. Cyrus had only to kill a few guards and the king, but he had no military resistance. Shortly after the event, Cyrus met with Babylonian friends he had within the city, who gave him intelligence information he needed to help him with the campaign. Second Isaiah anticipated the event by announcing the forthcoming return of the Jews from Babylon to Judah with the support of the Messiah, Cyrus of Persia. It seems likely that these friends who sabotaged Babylon for Cyrus included local Jews. It was one of Cyrus' policies to use as little military force as possible. If he was able to undermine the enemy from within and find those inside the enemy forces who would betray their own country in order to support Cyrus, he used these to overthrow the country he wanted to rule.

---

[31] C. F. Keil, *The Book of Daniel*, tr. G. Easton (Grand Rapids: Eerdmans Publishing Co., c1976), p. 173.
[32] Oppenheim, "Babylonian Texts," p. 313.
[33] A. L. Oppenheim, "Nabonidus," *IDB* III, pp. 493-95.

The Jews in Babylon and Cyrus of Persia had some similar goals. The Jews wanted to recover Judah and return. Cyrus needed some military strength in Judah to support his western border. It was normal for these two to find ways to support one another.

Nabonidus was displaced with Nebuchadnezzar as the pagan king whom Daniel outwitted, just as was true of the previous chapters. The author may have taken that name from the Babylonian legend, just as he took several of the ideas from there. Daniel may have been given the name "Belteshazzar" to identify him with the son of Nabonidus who managed the country during the absence of King Nabonidus. These are guesses based on sketchy information about Nabonidus and his activities when he was out of the country. This narrative was composed as doctrine rather than history, but the author may have had some historical material about Nabonidus that he used midrashically and tendentially in much the same way biblical texts were used in Dan 1-3. It was dependent upon the activities of Nabonidus, whose rule over Babylon began seven years after the death of Nebuchadnezzar.

The following map shows the entire Babylonian empire. Belshazzar ruled the area near the Euphrates River, and Nabonidus gave special attention to the western part, which would have included Arabia, Asia Minor, and Palestine, the most extensive part of the empire.

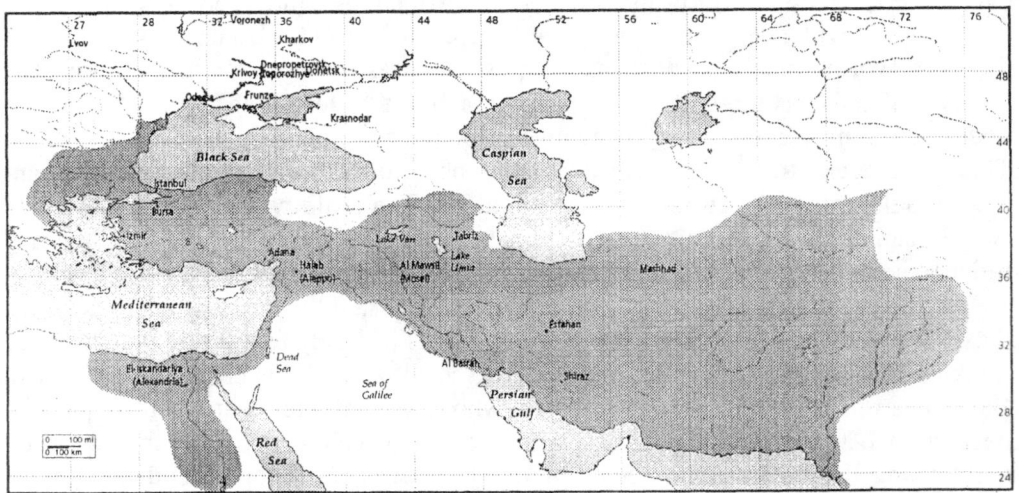

COMMENTARY

At the end of [the previously determined] days. The expression *kuh-tzáht yoh-máh-yah* (קצת יומיא), is sometimes taken to be a technical expression referring **to the end of** the world, time, or history. Here it obviously means **the end of** the seven-year period Nebuchadnezzar was predestined to live away from civilization.

My time of redemption came. This is a homiletic expansion. This exegete explained the details of redemption more extensively than the MT did. Deuteronomic law was here applied to Nabonidus. It was only to be applied by Israelites and Jews to Israelites and Jews. The fellow citizen who borrowed money was not required to pay interest, but if he could not pay he would have to work at half wages for the creditor until the debt was paid. If, however, the Sabbath year came around before the debt was paid, the creditor would have to release the debtor from his debt. This rule also applies to the Hebrew slave who has been purchased. After he has worked for six years, he must be set free on the seventh (Deut 15:1-12). The seventh year is the year of release, **the time of redemption**. For Nabonidus, his punishment was required for the full seven years. Only at the end of the seventh year was he released, but that was done according to sabbath year release, after the fines for his sins had been paid in full to the God of heaven.

The troops of heaven and the residents on the land. The author was not the first to recognize that God had such authority as this. Abraham made his old servant take an oath by "the God **of heaven and the** God of the earth (or land)" (Gen 24:3).

His rule is the rule of the age. **The age** involved is the age when the Promised Land was under **the rule of** Israel's king and the land was free from foreign rule. This was the time when God was considered to be king. As the true king God was recognized as the principal. All kings were only agents. The term **age** does not mean "forever." Neither does it mean "world" in almost all cases. This is a temporal term that is limited by the political situation. The author hoped that it would last for several generations (*dóhr wuh-dóhr*, דר ודר).

Those who walk in pride he is able to humble. The message that God not only is able but that he does exalt the humble is a well-known biblical doctrine. The Song of Hannah (1Sam 2:1-10) became the intertext of the Magnificat (Luke 1:47-55). The Psalmist praised the Lord who was seated on high and raised the poor from the dust and the ash heap and placed them on thrones with princes (Ps 113:5-9). The humble who were exalted in these cases were Jewish and North Israelite kings. The Song of Hannah was obviously composed initially as a birth narrative for King Saul, and the Magnificat was for the mother of Jesus. The Psalmist spoke generally about Jewish leaders who sat with princes. Exaltation was national exaltation. This was comparable to the exaltation of Nabonidus or Nebuchadnezzar.

The image here was first attracted to the king's walking in pride on the roof of his palace. It applies to foreign kings. The doctrine of this chapter is that those who walk humbly would be exalted. From an insider's point of view, Daniel behaved humbly in this situation, and, following Ezekiel, Daniel was wiser than the king was (Ezek 28:3). Like Joseph, he entered the palace of the king as a foreigner and was exalted to become the king's favorite counselor. He did not become king, but his exaltation took place in a political dimension.

THE SEPTUAGINTAL ENDING

^{OG33a}I Nebuchadnezzar, king of Babylon, was bound for seven years. They fed me hay like a cow, and I ate the grass of the earth. After seven years, I gave my soul to prayer, and I compensated for my sins also before the face of the Lord God of heaven and I prayed concerning my ignorance of the great God of gods of heaven. ^{33b}My hair became as eagle's wings and my nails as lion's [claws]. My flesh and my mind were changed. I walked naked with the beasts of the land. I saw a dream, and my thoughts seized me, and during the time of sleep took me and a deep sleep fell upon me. ³⁴At the end of seven years, my time of redemption came. My sins and my ignorant deeds were paid in full before the God of heaven. I had been bound because of my ignorance of the great God of gods of heaven. Now look! An angel from heaven called me, saying, "Nebuchadnezzar, serve the holy God of heaven, and give glory to the Most High. The government of your nation is given back to you." ³⁶At that time my kingdom was restored to me, and my glory was given back to me. ³⁷I confess the Most High, and I praise the creator of heaven and earth, the sea, the rivers and all that is in them. I confess and I praise, "He is the God of gods and the Lord of lords and King of kings, because he performs signs and miracles. He changes the times and the seasons, taking away the kingdom from kings and setting up others in their places. ^{37a}From now on I will serve him. From fear of him trembling had taken [control] of me, so I praise all of his saints. For the gods of the gentiles do not have in themselves ability to turn the kingdom of kings to another king and both to kill and create life and to perform great and fearful signs and miracles and change superior things, just as the God of heaven did with me. He changed very great things over me. All the days of my kingdom I will offer sacrifices to the Most High as a pleasing odor to the Lord, and before him I, my people, my nation, the countries that are under my authority, will do that which is pleasing before him. Whoever has said anything against the God of Heaven and whoever has been caught saying anything—these I will condemn to death."

^{37b} King Nebuchadnezzar wrote a circular epistle to the nations, regions, and languages of all people in every place who live in all the regions for generation after generation: "Praise the Lord God of heaven. Glorify him and bring him a sacrifice and an offering. I, the king of kings, confess and glorify him, because this is what he did to me. In the same day he seated me on my throne, and I acquired my authority and my kingdom among my people, and my greatness was returned to me."

^{37c}King Nebuchadnezzar to all nations, all regions, and all who live in them: "May peace be multiplied to you in every time. Now I will show you the deeds, which the great God has done with me. It has seemed [good] to me to demonstrate to you and to your scholars that God exists and his miracles are great. His kingdom is a kingdom for the age [to come], and his authority is for generation after generation."

He sent epistles concerning all the things that had happened to him in his kingdom to all the nations that were in his kingdom.

TEXTUAL DETAILS

The OG version of Dan 4 is much longer than the MT, but it adds little to the historical data. The extension is mostly confessional doctrine. Both at the beginning and at the end of the OG document there is an emphasis on signs and miracles that are not mentioned in the MT. The final editor of the MT version may have had the OG version at his disposal and chosen to abbreviate it, or the editor of the OG version may have had the MT in his possession and had chosen to add to it. Editors can either abbreviate or expand, as they wish. There is no dogma to force editors to function in only one way. Sometimes it is possible to tell in parallel documents which way the documents developed. That happens when one document has an entire poem (as in Matt 10), and the other one has only one verse of the same poem (as in Mark 13) or when one document has a chrea (as in Matt 15) which another document (Mark 7) has expanded into a homily. Sometimes midrashic development is obvious, as in the use of Gen 41 in Dan 1 and 2, but when that is not the case it is not wise to make dogmatic conclusions.

Even this long OG version probably was itself abbreviated. At the conclusion there are three apparent introductions to the king's confession. Only one of the three (37b) includes the confession. The other two (37c) may have been parts of longer confessions that were omitted. This suggests, as does the appendix of Dan 11:40-45, that the final editor of Daniel had some duplicate sources at his disposal.

CHAPTER FIVE

ARAMAIC TEXT

5:1 בֵּלְשַׁאצַּר מַלְכָּא עֲבַד לְחֶם רַב לְרַבְרְבָנוֹהִי אֲלַף וְלָקֳבֵל
אַלְפָּא חַמְרָא שָׁתֵה: 2 בֵּלְשַׁאצַּר אֲמַר ׀ בִּטְעֵם חַמְרָא לְהַיְתָיָה
לְמָאנֵי דַּהֲבָא וְכַסְפָּא דִּי הַנְפֵּק נְבוּכַדְנֶצַּר אֲבוּהִי מִן־הֵיכְלָא דִּי
בִירוּשְׁלֶם וְיִשְׁתּוֹן בְּהוֹן מַלְכָּא וְרַבְרְבָנוֹהִי שֵׁגְלָתֵהּ וּלְחֵנָתֵהּ: 3 בֵּאדַיִן
הַיְתִיו מָאנֵי דַהֲבָא דִּי הַנְפִּקוּ מִן־הֵיכְלָא דִּי־בֵית אֱלָהָא דִּי
בִירוּשְׁלֶם וְאִשְׁתִּיו בְּהוֹן מַלְכָּא וְרַבְרְבָנוֹהִי שֵׁגְלָתֵהּ וּלְחֵנָתֵהּ: 4 אִשְׁתִּיו
חַמְרָא וְשַׁבַּחוּ לֵאלָהֵי דַּהֲבָא וְכַסְפָּא נְחָשָׁא פַרְזְלָא אָעָא וְאַבְנָא:
5 בַּהּ־שַׁעֲתָה [נְפַקָה] נְפַקוּ אֶצְבְּעָן דִּי יַד־אֱנָשׁ וְכָתְבָן לָקֳבֵל נֶבְרַשְׁתָּא עַל־
גִּירָא דִּי־כְתַל הֵיכְלָא דִּי מַלְכָּא וּמַלְכָּא חָזֵה פַּס יְדָה דִּי כָתְבָה:
6 אֱדַיִן מַלְכָּא זִיוֹהִי שְׁנוֹהִי וְרַעְיֹנֹהִי יְבַהֲלוּנֵּהּ וְקִטְרֵי חַרְצֵהּ מִשְׁתָּרַיִן
וְאַרְכֻבָּתֵהּ דָּא לְדָא נָקְשָׁן: 7 קָרֵא מַלְכָּא בְּחַיִל לְהֶעָלָה לְאָשְׁפַיָּא
כַּשְׂדָּיֵא [כַּשְׂדָּאֵי] וְגָזְרַיָּא עָנֵה מַלְכָּא וְאָמַר ׀ לְחַכִּימֵי בָבֶל דִּי כָל־אֱנָשׁ דִּי־
יִקְרֵה כְּתָבָה דְנָה וּפִשְׁרֵהּ יְחַוִּנַּנִי אַרְגְּוָנָא יִלְבַּשׁ וְהַמּוֹנְכָא [וְהַמְנִיכָא] דִי־דַהֲבָא
עַל־צַוְּארֵהּ וְתַלְתִּי בְמַלְכוּתָא יִשְׁלַט: 8 אֱדַיִן עָלְלִין [עָלִּין] כֹּל
חַכִּימֵי מַלְכָּא וְלָא־כָהֲלִין כְּתָבָא לְמִקְרֵא וּפִשְׁרָא [וּפִשְׁרֵהּ] לְהוֹדָעָה
לְמַלְכָּא: 9 אֱדַיִן מַלְכָּא בֵלְשַׁאצַּר שַׂגִּיא מִתְבָּהַל וְזִיוֹהִי שָׁנַיִן עֲלוֹהִי
וְרַבְרְבָנוֹהִי מִשְׁתַּבְּשִׁין: 10 מַלְכְּתָא לָקֳבֵל מִלֵּי מַלְכָּא וְרַבְרְבָנוֹהִי
לְבֵית מִשְׁתְּיָא עֲלַלַת [עַלַּת] עֲנָת מַלְכְּתָא וַאֲמֶרֶת מַלְכָּא לְעָלְמִין חֱיִי
אַל־יְבַהֲלוּךְ רַעְיוֹנָךְ וְזִיוָיךְ אַל־יִשְׁתַּנּוֹ: 11 אִיתַי גְּבַר בְּמַלְכוּתָךְ   Gen 41:8; Gen 41:12a
דִּי רוּחַ אֱלָהִין קַדִּישִׁין בֵּהּ וּבְיוֹמֵי אֲבוּךְ נַהִירוּ וְשָׂכְלְתָנוּ וְחָכְמָה   Gen 41:38
כְּחָכְמַת־אֱלָהִין הִשְׁתְּכַחַת בֵּהּ וּמַלְכָּא נְבֻכַדְנֶצַּר אֲבוּךְ רַב חַרְטֻמִּין
אָשְׁפִין כַּשְׂדָּאִין גָּזְרִין הֲקִימֵהּ אֲבוּךְ מַלְכָּא: 12 כָּל־קֳבֵל דִּי רוּחַ ׀
יַתִּירָה וּמַנְדַּע וְשָׂכְלְתָנוּ מְפַשַּׁר חֶלְמִין וַאֲחַוָיַת אֲחִידָן וּמְשָׁרֵא   Gen 41:12b; Judges 14:14
קִטְרִין הִשְׁתְּכַחַת בֵּהּ בְּדָנִיֵּאל דִּי־מַלְכָּא שָׂם־שְׁמֵהּ בֵּלְטְשַׁאצַּר
כְּעַן דָּנִיֵּאל יִתְקְרֵי וּפִשְׁרָה יְהַחֲוֵה: פ 13 בֵּאדַיִן דָּנִיֵּאל הֻעַל   Gen 41:14-15
קֳדָם מַלְכָּא עָנֵה מַלְכָּא וְאָמַר לְדָנִיֵּאל [אַנְתָּה] אַנְתְּ־הוּא דָנִיֵּאל דִּי־מִן־   Gen 41:38-39
בְּנֵי גָלוּתָא דִּי יְהוּד דִּי הַיְתִי מַלְכָּא אַבִי מִן־יְהוּד: 14 וְשִׁמְעֵת עֲלַיִךְ [עֲלָךְ]
דִּי רוּחַ אֱלָהִין בָּךְ וְנַהִירוּ וְשָׂכְלְתָנוּ וְחָכְמָה יַתִּירָה הִשְׁתְּכַחַת בָּךְ:
15 וּכְעַן הֻעַלּוּ קָדָמַי חַכִּימַיָּא אָשְׁפַיָּא דִּי־כְתָבָה דְנָה יִקְרוֹן וּפִשְׁרֵהּ
לְהוֹדָעֻתַנִי וְלָא־כָהֲלִין פְּשַׁר־מִלְּתָא לְהַחֲוָיָה: 16 וַאֲנָה שִׁמְעֵת עֲלַיִךְ [עֲלָךְ]   Gen 42:42
דִּי־תוּכַל [תִיכּוּל] פִּשְׁרִין לְמִפְשַׁר וְקִטְרִין לְמִשְׁרֵא כְּעַן הֵן תּוּכַל [תִּכוּל] כְּתָבָא
לְמִקְרֵא וּפִשְׁרֵהּ לְהוֹדָעֻתַנִי אַרְגְּוָנָא תִלְבַּשׁ וְהַמּוֹנְכָא [וְהַמְנִיכָא] דִי־דַהֲבָא
עַל־צַוְּארָךְ וְתַלְתָּא בְמַלְכוּתָא תִּשְׁלַט: פ 17 בֵּאדַיִן עָנֵה דָנִיֵּאל

וַאֲמַר קֳדָם מַלְכָּא מַתְּנָתָךְ לָךְ לֶהֱוְיָן תְּבִזְבְּיָתָךְ לְאָחֳרָן הַב בְּרַם כְּתָבָא אֶקְרֵא לְמַלְכָּא וּפִשְׁרָא אֲהוֹדְעִנֵּהּ: 18 אַנְתָּה [אַנְתְּ] מַלְכָּא אֱלָהָא עִלָּיָא [עִלָּאָה] מַלְכוּתָא וּרְבוּתָא וִיקָרָא וְהַדְרָה יְהַב לִנְבֻכַדְנֶצַּר אֲבוּךְ: 19 וּמִן־רְבוּתָא דִּי יְהַב־לֵהּ כֹּל עַמְמַיָּא אֻמַּיָּא וְלִשָּׁנַיָּא הֲווֹ זָאֲעִין [זָיְעִין] וְדָחֲלִין מִן־קֳדָמוֹהִי דִּי־הֲוָה צָבֵא הֲוָא קָטֵל וְדִי־הֲוָה צָבֵא הֲוָה מַחֵא וְדִי־הֲוָה צָבֵא הֲוָה מָרִים וְדִי־הֲוָה צָבֵא הֲוָה מַשְׁפִּיל: 20 וּכְדִי רִם לִבְבֵהּ וְרוּחֵהּ תִּקְפַת לַהֲזָדָה הָנְחַת מִן־כָּרְסֵא מַלְכוּתֵהּ וִיקָרָה הֶעְדִּיו מִנֵּהּ: 21 וּמִן־בְּנֵי אֲנָשָׁא טְרִיד וְלִבְבֵהּ ׀ עִם־חֵיוְתָא שַׁוִּי [שַׁוִּיו] וְעִם־עֲרָדַיָּא מְדוֹרֵהּ עִשְׂבָּא כְתוֹרִין יְטַעֲמוּנֵּהּ וּמִטַּל שְׁמַיָּא גִּשְׁמֵהּ יִצְטַבַּע עַד דִּי־יְדַע דִּי־שַׁלִּיט אֱלָהָא עִלָּיָא [עִלָּאָה] בְּמַלְכוּת אֲנָשָׁא וּלְמַן־דִּי יִצְבֵּה יְהָקֵים עֲלַיהּ [עֲלַהּ]: 22 וְאַנְתָּה [וְאַנְתְּ] בְּרֵהּ בֵּלְשַׁאצַּר לָא הַשְׁפֵּלְתְּ לִבְבָךְ כָּל־קֳבֵל דִּי כָל־דְּנָה יְדַעְתָּ: 23 וְעַל מָרֵא־שְׁמַיָּא ׀ הִתְרוֹמַמְתָּ וּלְמָאנַיָּא דִי־בַיְתֵהּ הַיְתִיו קדמיך [קָדָמָךְ] ואנתה [וְאַנְתְּ] ורברבניך [וְרַבְרְבָנָךְ] שֵׁגְלָתָךְ וּלְחֵנָתָךְ חַמְרָא שָׁתַיִן בְּהוֹן וְלֵֽאלָהֵ֣י **כַסְפָּֽא־וְ֠דַהֲבָא נְחָשָׁ֨א פַרְזְלָ֜א אָעָ֣א וְאַבְנָ֗א** דִּ֣י לָֽא־חָזַ֧יִן וְלָא־שָׁמְעִ֣ין וְלָ֣א יָדְעִין֮ שַׁבַּ֣חְתָּ וְלֵֽאלָהָ֞א דִּֽי־נִשְׁמְתָ֥ךְ בִּידֵ֛הּ וְכָל־אֹרְחָתָ֥ךְ לֵ֖הּ לָ֥א הַדַּֽרְתָּ: 24 בֵּאדַ֙יִן֙ מִן־קֳדָמ֔וֹהִי שְׁלִ֖יחַ פַּסָּ֣א דִֽי־יְדָ֑א וּכְתָבָ֥א דְנָ֖ה רְשִֽׁים: 25 וּדְנָ֥ה כְתָבָ֖א דִּ֣י רְשִׁ֑ים מְנֵ֥א מְנֵ֖א תְּקֵ֥ל וּפַרְסִֽין: 26 דְּנָ֖ה פְּשַֽׁר־מִלְּתָ֑א מְנֵ֕א מְנָֽה־אֱלָהָ֥א מַלְכוּתָ֖ךְ וְהַשְׁלְמַֽהּ: 27 תְּקֵ֑ל תְּקִ֥ילְתָּה בְמֹֽאזַנְיָ֖א וְהִשְׁתְּכַ֥חַתְּ חַסִּֽיר: 28 פְּרֵ֑ס פְּרִ֙יסַת֙ מַלְכוּתָ֔ךְ וִיהִיבַ֖ת לְמָדַ֥י וּפָרָֽס: 29 בֵּאדַ֣יִן ׀ אֲמַ֣ר בֵּלְשַׁאצַּ֗ר וְהַלְבִּ֤שׁוּ לְדָֽנִיֵּאל֙ אַרְגְּוָנָ֔א והמונכא [וְהַֽמְנִיכָ֤א] דִֽי־דַהֲבָ֖א עַֽל־צַוְּארֵ֑הּ וְהַכְרִ֣זֽוּ עֲל֔וֹהִי דִּֽי־לֶהֱוֵ֥א שַׁלִּ֛יט תַּלְתָּ֖א בְּמַלְכוּתָֽא: 30 בֵּ֚הּ בְּלֵ֣ילְיָ֔א קְטִ֕יל בֵּלְאשַׁצַּ֖ר מַלְכָּ֥א כשדיא [כַשְׂדָּאָֽה]: פ

Deut 4:28; Ps 115:4
Gen 41:32; Job 12:10
Job 33:4

Gen 42:42
Esth 8:15

ENGLISH TEXT

⁵:¹King Belshazzar made a huge feast for a thousand of his national officials, and he drank wine before the thousand. ²While tasting the wine Belshazzar told [his servants] to bring the vessels of gold and silver which his father, Nebuchadnezzar had brought from the temple of Jerusalem and the king, his national officials, his wives, and his concubines would drink with them. ³Then the vessels of gold which had been brought from the palace of the temple which is in Jerusalem were brought, and the king, his national officials, his wives, and his concubines drank with them.

Daniel	First Testament Intertexts
⁴They drank wine and praised the **gods of gold, silver**, bronze, iron, **wood, and stone**.	Deut 4:28 You will serve there **gods** made with human hands of **wood and stone** that cannot see, hear, eat, or smell.
	Isa 46:6 They pour out **gold** from their purse, and they weigh out **silver** with a scale. They hire a smith and he makes it into a **god**.

TECHNICAL DETAILS

Biblical authors often play on words in ways that are effective. For example, When Amiziah, the priest of Bethel, told Amos, **Go! Flee to the land of Judah, . . . never again** *prophesy* **in Bethel.** Amos replied, **The Lord said to me,** *Go! Prophesy* **to the people of Israel** (Amos 7:12, 15). When a potential disciple said to Jesus, *Permit* **me first to** *go away* **and** *bury* **my father,** Jesus said, *Permit* **the dead** *to bury* **their own dead, but you, after you have** *gone away*, **announce the kingdom of God** (Luke 9:59-60). When some of the scribes and Pharisees asked Jesus for *a sign*, he said, **An evil and adulterous generation looks for** *a sign*, **but** *a sign* **shall not be given except** *the sign* **of Jonah the prophet** (Matt 12:38-39). These are examples in which the same word is used with a different message. The authors of Dan 5 and 6 have used the same kinds of word plays effectively in describing the relationship between Daniel and the king.

COMMENTARY

King Belshazzar. **Belshazzar** was the son of Nabonidus and not the son of Nebuchadnezzar I or II. The only son of Nebuchadnezzar was Evil-merodach who was put to death. There were four kings who followed Nebuchadnezzar, none of whom was named **Belshazzar**. The story, however, continues and is consistent with the characters in Dan 4. The story is written as if **Belshazzar** were the son of Nebuchadnezzar I, who had captured Palestine in 586 BIA and taken the Jewish leaders captive into Babylon. **Belshazzar** had never been king of Babylon. The *Nabonidus Chronicle* always refers to **Belshazzar** as the son of the king—not as king. Nevertheless, he ruled Babylon under appointment by his father, Nabonidus, for about ten years while his father was in the West, living among the Arabs. Nabonidus returned to Babylon just before Cyrus entered the city to annex it to the Persian empire. In the Cyrus Cylinder it says,

> (17) Without fighting or battle, he secured his entrance into Babylon. His city Babylon he spared distress. Nabu-na'id, the king, who did not fear him, he delivered into his hand.[1]

Made a huge feast. This chapter begins like the Book of Esther with a king having **a huge feast** with the leaders of his country. Orientals were famous for their lavish banquets (Isa 21:5; Jer 51:39). According to all the reports of the fall of Babylon, it took place when the leaders of the city were either drunk or asleep during a festival. This does not mean that the **feast** reported in Dan 4 has any historical validity but that the author had a solid base in customs to use a banquet as the situation around which to compose his drama. He wanted his readers to think that Cyrus was

---

[1] Quotation taken from R. H. Charles, *A Critical and Exegetical Commentary on the Book of Daniel* (Oxford: Clarendon Press, 1929), p. cxxiv.

successful in his invasion because Belshazzar had defiled the temple vessels from Jerusalem. This was God's punishment to Belshazzar.

He drank wine before the thousand. As in the banquet Esther prepared for the king, it was while they **were drinking wine** that the king asked Esther what would be the petition she would ask following his promise to fulfill it. It was as **he was drinking wine** that Belshazzar asked for the temple vessels to be brought for use at the banquet. These were not the only kings for whom **wine** became a problem.

Bring the vessels of gold and silver. One of the wordplays here is on the word *go* (active) or "bring" (causative) (*nah-fak* or *hahn-fayk*, נפק. הנפק). The king ordered servants to **bring the vessels of gold and silver** that **had been brought** from Jerusalem, and they **brought** them (Dan 5:1-3). Then the fingers of a hand *went* or "reached out" and wrote on the wall (Dan 5:5). The next word play was on *temple*. The vessels were first mentioned as those that Nebuchadnezzar **brought** from the *temple* (Dan 5:2) and then described more fully as those that **had been taken** from the *temple*, which was the house of God (Dan 5:3). These were t*emple* vessels that were used in religious feasts in Jerusalem. They were believed to be holy, and it was considered profane to have used them anywhere else for anything else than the purpose for which they were made. *Temple* **vessels were taken** for more than their cash value. They were trophies displayed to show victory over other nations. For many years the gods and **vessels** of Egypt were held by the Seleucids. It was a great victory for the Egyptian Ptolemy when he was able to recover these **vessels** and **return** them to Egypt. In the Arch of Titus in Rome is carved a replica of the procession made in Rome after the Roman victory over the Jews in 70 IA. Among the items **carried** in the procession were the candelabra and **vessels**. It was an embarrassment to any country to have their *temple* **vessels** confiscated. Jews were still further embarrassed when their holy **vessels** were used for ordinary festivities-- even worse when the festivities were common or idolatrous. Nebuchadnezzar only **took the vessels** back with him to Babylon. When Antiochus Epiphanes plundered the *temple he took* all of the valuable **vessels**, furniture and money to pay for his war expenses.

Equipment from the Temple in Jerusalem Taken by Romans in 70 IA

Photography by Ralph Tobias

They praised the gods of gold. This means that they worshiped **gods** that were made **of gold**, silver, and other materials. Not only did they defile the vessels by drinking from them at a drinking party, but they also offended Jews by engaging in pagan worship at the same time.

Nabonidus wanted the protection of as many **gods** as possible to protect the city of Babylon. He went throughout Babylon and gathered **gods** from all the major cities and brought them to the capital city. The people in the outlying cities were not happy about this. One of the first things Cyrus did after he had taken control of Babylon was to return **the gods** to the cities from which they were taken.[2]

TEXT

[5]Suddenly the fingers of a man reached out and wrote on the plaster of the wall of the king's palace, opposite the lamp, and the king saw the hollow of the hand that wrote. [6]Then the king's complexion changed; his thoughts frightened him; his loins were loosened; and his knees knocked against each other. [7]The king called loudly for the enchanters, the Chaldeans, and the counselors to come. The king answered and said to the wisemen of Babylon, "Anyone who reads this writing and shows me its interpretation will be dressed in purple with a gold chain on his neck and will be a third ruler in the kingdom." [8]Then all of the king's wisemen came, but none was able to decipher the writing and disclose its interpretation to the king. [9]Then King Belshazzar became very much alarmed; his countenance changed over him; and his chief officers were puzzled.

COMMENTARY

Suddenly the fingers of a man reached out. The hand **suddenly** appeared without the rest of an arm of a person and began writing a strange message that no one could understand. It seemed to everyone like a bad dream. The **suddenness** as well as the strangeness of the apparition seemed ghostly. The king was frightened and trembled all over.

The king saw the hollow of the hand that wrote. **The king** must have been in an odd position in relationship to **the** mysterious hand. Usually the palm of **the hand** is facing the object on which it is writing. Here that would be the plaster of the wall. Those away from the wall would see only the back of **the hand**. The most likely situation would be that the king was reclining on a mat next to the wall and **the hand** appeared above him.

His loins were loosened. Wolters has interpreted this to mean that Belshazzar's bowels were loosened, and he soiled his pants.[3] This accompanied his knocking

---

[2] A. L. Oppenheim (tr.), "Babylonian and Assyrian Historical Texts," *Ancient Near Eastern Texts* ed. J. B. Pritchard, (Princeton: Princeton University Press, 1969), p. 306.
[3] A. Wolters, "Untying the King's Knots: Physiology and Wordplay in Daniel 5," *JBL* 110 (1991):117-22.

knees and his mental terror. These were normal bodily and expression changes that indicate great fear.[4]

The enchanters, the Chaldeans, and the counselors. This is not the whole list of professional leaders that were called in the other chapters. The OG adds "magicians" to the list.

Anyone who reads the writing. It was not a problem of being able to **read** and **write**. All of the professional leaders of Babylon could do that. The question was, "What does it mean?" The reward would be the right to be dressed in royal purple robes, like Mordecai (Esth 8:15), and to wear a golden chain, like Joseph (Gen 41:42). Golden chains were given to special people by more kings than just those of Egypt. This was also a Persian custom (Xenophon, *Anabasis* 1.5, 8; 8.29). The competent person would also hold a high official position, known as the "third." This may have meant that he would be third in power after 1) Nabonidus and 2) Belshazzar, as Shea suggested.[5]

Instead of threatening these leaders with death if they were unable to **read** and interpret the message as Nebuchadnezzar did, Belshazzar used the reward technique, but the result was the same. Only Daniel was able to solve the problem.

All the king's wisemen came. There is some inconsistency here. The **king** had already addressed the **wisemen**, so they must have been there. It was after he had addressed them that they **came.** This suggests to many that some later scribe made some illogical improvements on the text. The problem is not that there is a logical problem here. The problem is that we do not know who caused the confusion. The original author may have been repetitious. If not, then why would any later scribe have thought it was necessary?

TEXT

Daniel	First Testament Intertexts
¹⁰Because of the words of the king and his chief officers, the queen entered the drinking house. The queen answered and said, "May the king live for ages. Do not let **your mind be alarmed**, and do not let your countenance change.	Gen 41:8 In the morning **his spirit was alarmed**.
¹¹**There is a man** in your kingdom	Gen 41:12a **There is** with us **a young man** who is a Hebrew, a slave of the chief executioner.
	Gen 41:38 Can we find such a man as this **in**

---

[4] See S. M. Paul, "Decoding a 'Joint' Expression in Daniel 5:6, 16," *JNES* 22 (1993):121-27, for other similar descriptions of fear in ancient literature.
[5] W. H. Shea, "Belteshazzar Meets Belshazzar," *AUSS* 26 (1988):70-71.

in whom is the spirit of the holy gods. In the days of your father light, insight, and wisdom like the wisdom of the gods were found in him, and King Nebuchadnezzar, your father, chief of the magicians, enchanters, and Chaldean counselors, your father the king exalted him, ¹²because an excellent **spirit**, knowledge, and insight **to interpret dreams**,

whom is the spirit of the gods?

Gen 41:12b **We told him [our dreams] and he interpreted our dreams for us. He interpreted each man according to his dream.**

Judges 14:14 **They were not able to explain the riddle**

explain riddles, and solve problems were found in him, namely in Daniel, whom the king named Belteshazzar, so **let Daniel be called**, and he will show its **interpretation."**

Gen 41:14 Pharaoh sent and **called** Joseph.

COMMENTARY

Because of the words of the king and his chief officers. This may mean that they sent for the queen and asked her to come to offer advice.

The queen entered the drinking house. The theme of a **queen entering** and becoming involved in the events of a drinking party is similar to that of **Queen** Esther (Esth 5:1-5) and also echoed in the report of Herodia before Herod, ordering the death of John the Baptist. It was not normal for a queen to enter a king's banquet without an invitation (Plutarch, *Symp* 1.1 and Macrobius 7.1. Herodotus 5.18, disagreed). **Queen** Esther **entered** with fear and trembling. Montgomery followed Josephus in suggesting that **the queen** mentioned here was probably **the queen** mother,[6] because she talked to Belshazzar as a mother to her son, rather than a wife to her husband or a consort to **a king**, advising him of his father's methods. According to the OG, she was invited to enter the banquet hall (OG Dan 5:9).

Do not let your mind be alarmed. This is obviously an intertext for John 14:1. It is itself based on the intertext of Gen 41:8.

There is a man. This **man** happens to be Daniel rather than Joseph, but like Joseph he was one in whom was **the spirit of the gods**. This was a quality that allowed both Daniel and Joseph to interpret dreams.

---

[6] J. A. Montgomery, *A Critical and Exegetical Commentary on the Book of Daniel* (New York: Charles Scribner's Sons, 1927), p. 257. According to the Annalistic Tablet ii.13 (KB. iii.2, p. 131; R.P. v.160), this queen mother died eight years earlier. *Keilinschriftliche Bibliothek*, Schrader, 1889-1900. So Charles, *Daniel*, p. 128.

TEXT

Daniel	First Testament Intertexts
¹³Then Daniel **was brought before the king, and the king** answered and **said to** Daniel, "Are you Daniel, one of the Jewish exiles whom my father, the king, brought from Judah? ¹⁴**I have heard about you, that**	ᴳᵉⁿ ⁴¹:¹⁴ Then he [Joseph] **came to Pharaoh,** ¹⁵**and Pharaoh said to** Joseph, "I have dreamed a dream, and no one can interpret it, but **I have heard**, saying **that you** hear a dream and can **interpret** it."
the spirit of the gods is in you and that light, insight, and	ᴳᵉⁿ ⁴¹:³⁸ Can there be found a man such as this whom **the spirit of the gods is in him?** ³⁹Pharaoh said to Joseph, "Since God has made all of this known to you, there is no one so prudent and
excellent **wisdom is in you**. ¹⁵Now the wisemen and enchanters, were brought before me to read this writing and inform me of its **interpretation**, but they were not able to show me the **interpretation** of the word. ¹⁶**I heard about you that you** are able to make **interpretations** and to solve problems, so if you are able to read the writing and to make known to me its **interpretation**, you will **wear** purple **clothing**; **a golden chain around** your **neck**; and be a third ruler in the kingdom."	**wise as you**." ᴳᵉⁿ ⁴¹:⁴² Then Pharaoh removed his signet ring from his hand and put it on Joseph's hand. He made him **wear** silk **clothing**, and put **a gold chain around** his **neck**.

COMMENTARY

Daniel was brought before the king. Like other **Daniel** stories, this one is based on the Joseph story in Genesis. Just as Joseph **was brought** before Pharaoh, so **Daniel was brought before the king.**

I have heard about you. These words were taken directly from the Joseph story, where Pharaoh told Joseph that **he had heard about** him, and the things he **heard** were that, like Joseph, Daniel would be able to solve the problem that had come before Belshazzar. If the Book of Daniel had been composed by one author there might have been some continuity among the chapters. Already in Dan 1 Daniel was recognized as the chief of all the wisemen of Babylon. Why did the king and his counsellors wait to the last minute to introduce him to the king? If the king had not known about Daniel until the queen told him about him, where did the king get the information about Daniel that the queen did not mention? If Daniel had been written as a continuous story, readers would have known that Daniel was the chief of the wisemen. When the wisemen were called, he should have been one of that group. Dan 5, however, was a separate drama, and the dramatist knew how to create a crisis and keep readers and listeners in suspense. He saved Daniel until all the rest of the wisemen had failed. This dramatized the importance of this hero.

My father, the king, brought from Judah. Belshazzar was the son of Nabonidus, not Nebuchadnezzar. It was Nebuchadnezzar and not Nabonidus who **brought** exiles to Babylon **from Judah**. There is a historical mistake here, but Dan 4 was not the only one to make it. Charles has astutely pointed out the problem.[7] Herodotus called Nabonidus "Labynetus," and said he was the son of Nebuchadnezzar (Herodotus 1.188). Baruch concurred (*1Bar* 1.11). In his *Contra Apion* 1.20, Josephus quoted from Berosus that Nebuchadnezzar was succeeded by his son, Evil-merodach, who was murdered by Neriglissar, who was succeeded by his son, Laborosoardochus. Laborosoardochus was killed by conspirators, one of whom was Nabonidus who ruled for 17 years. Although he knew that, Josephus also reported that Belshazzar was the grandson of Nebuchadnezzar (*Ant* 10.237). To make the data still more confusing, Josephus also said Nabonidus was Belshazzar (*Ant* 10.231).

But they were not able. All of the skilled professional wisemen of Babylon showed their incompetence before Belshazzar just as they had in Egypt before the pharaoh, so the king reported that phenomenon to Daniel, just as Pharaoh had to Joseph. Following a suggestion by LaCocque, Brewer argued that the text was written in cuneiform. That is the reason the wisemen of Babylon could not read it. They should not have had a problem with unpointed Aramaic. That was their native language. They also should have known cuneiform, but cuneiform depends on context for interpretation of most of its letters. There was no context for the strange saying written on the wall.

Cuneiform consists of a series of perpendicular and horizontal strokes. One perpendicular stroke can mean either 1 or 60, depending on its context, and a cross sign means "one half." When there is no context, the interpreter is required to rely on subjectivity and inventiveness. Brewer conjectured that the cuneiform looked like lll +, and he said Daniel rendered it 60 and 60 and 30. The following interpretation has to depend on Daniel's subjective desire. Then he translated these numerals into Aramaic, "mina, mina, shekel and a half."[8] Then he transferred these nouns into the adjectives that he needed to render the decree he wanted to give the king. Neither the king nor any of the wisemen could have proved him to be mistaken. Since this is a drama and not a historical report it is not very important to learn that which the wisemen of Babylon could not do. It is only important to notice that the stage is set to show Daniel's superiority and the Babylonian inferiority.

The spirit of the gods is in you. This is not just a general expression. This was the very idiom that Pharaoh used in his conversation with Joseph.

---

[7] Charles, *Daniel*, pp 108-111.
[8] D. I. Brewer, "Mene Mene Teqel Uparsin: Daniel 5:25 in Cuneiform," *TB* 42 (1991):310-16.

You are able. Pharaoh told Joseph that he had heard that Joseph was **able** to interpret dreams. Here Belshazzar told Daniel that he had heard that Daniel could solve problems such as the one that confronted the king.

A gold chain around your neck. Like Pharaoh the king was willing to dress Daniel in royal garments with a **gold chain around** his **neck**. This is a commentary based on Gen 41.

TEXT

[17] Then Daniel answered and said before the king, "Let your gifts be for yourself, and give your rewards to someone else. Nevertheless, I will read the writing to the king and tell you its interpretation. [18] [It is about] you, O King. The Most High God gave the kingdom, power, honor, and glory to Nebuchadnezzar, your father. [19] Some of the power which God gave him required all peoples, nations, and [people who spoke foreign] languages to tremble and become afraid of him. Whomever he chose he could kill and whomever he chose he could allow to live. Whomever he wished he could exalt, and whomever he wished he could humble. [20] When his mind became exalted and his spirit strong, he became proud, and he was taken from his throne, and his kingdom and glory were removed from him. [21] He was driven from among human beings, and his mind was equal to that of the beasts. He lived among wild donkeys, and he had vegetation to eat like cattle. His body was wet from the dew of heaven until he learned that the Most High rules human kingdoms and he established over it whomever he will.

COMMENTARY

Let your gifts be for yourself. This was political courtesy. Of course, Daniel accepted the **gifts** when they were offered. Josephus said Daniel refused the **gifts** holding that wisdom and divine things could not be bought with money or **gifts** (*Ant* 10.241).

Nebuchadnezzar, your father. **Nebuchadnezzar** was not Belshazzar's **father**. His **father** was Nabonidus. The author probably had some typological reason for confusing the two. In all of these stories reported in Dan 1-5, the villain is **Nebuchadnezzar** and the hero is Daniel. It was **Nebuchadnezzar** who destroyed Jerusalem, burned the temple, and took Jews captive into Babylon. Therefore, he was the one who was characterized as a demon. These stories were composed for their doctrinal, propagandistic value rather than their historical accuracy. They should be classified as historical fiction, belonging to the same class as *Les Miserables, The Scarlet Letter, A Tale of Two Cities*, and the Acts of the Apostles.

He was driven from among human beings. This is a repetition of the report in Dan 4, given here again in detail. Semites were not disturbed by repetition. Nabonidus **was** probably not **driven from among human beings**. He spent time in the western part of the empire. That may have been partially because of his health. He took his troops with him and engaged in normal royal expansion activity. He was not described fairly by the author of this chapter. We do not know all the facts; but it is certain that we have here a prejudicial account written by Nabonidus' enemies. Because he left the big city of Babylon, Jews from Babylon, who did not like the Arabs, who did not like Babylonian rulers, and who did like Cyrus referred to Nabonidus' campaign in depreciative terms. His existence among Arabs was not like eating grass like cattle.

TEXT

Daniel	First Testament Intertexts
²²Now you, his son, Belshazzar, have not humbled your **mind**, even though you knew all of this. ²³You **have exalted** yourself above **the Lord** of heaven, and the vessels of his temple were brought before you, and you, your chief officers, your wives, and your concubines drank wine with them,	Deut 8:14 **Your mind becomes exalted** and you forget Yehowah your God who brought you out of Egypt. Ezek 31:10-11 Therefore because its [the tree's] height **became exalted**, and it put its top among the clouds and its **mind** became proud of its height I will put it in the hand of the mighty one of the gentiles.
and you praised **the gods of gold, silver**, bronze, iron, **wood, and stone**, **that cannot see nor hear** nor understand.	Deut 4:28 And there you will serve **the gods of wood and stone** the work of human hands that do not see, hear, **eat, nor smell**. Ps 115:4 Their idols are **silver and gold**, the work of human hands.

COMMENTARY

Now you, his son, Belshazzar. **Belshazzar** was not Nebuchadnezzar's **son**, but Nabonidus' **son**.

Have not humbled your mind. This provided the author of this narrative an opportunity to scold the pagans from a condescending point of view, listing his offenses as if he were a judge pronouncing a sentence. He took full advantage of the opportunity.

TEXT

Daniel	First Testament Intertexts
But God	Gen 41:32 The word from **God** is true, and he will hurry to perform it.
	Job 12:10 The **hand** of Yehowah has done this;
in whose hand is your breath and to whom belongs all of your ways you have not honored." ²⁴Then from before him was sent the palm of a hand and this writing was written down. ²⁵*Muh-náy muh-náy tuh-káyl oo-fár-seen* (מנא מנא תקל ופרסין). ²⁶ This is the interpretation of the word. *Muh-náy muh-náy* [means] "God has measured your kingdom and concluded it." ²⁷*Tuh-káyl* [means] "You have been weighed in the scales, and you have been found to be deficient." ²⁸*Puh-ráys*" [means] "your kingdom has been broken asunder, and will be given to the Medes and the Persians."	**in whose hand is the breath** of all life, and the spirit of all human flesh. Job 33:4 The spirit of **God** has made me, and the **breath** of Shadai has given me life.
Then ²⁹Belshazzar ordered and	Gen 41:42 Pharaoh took his signet ring from his hand and placed it on Joseph's hand.
they **clothed** Daniel **in purple and** [put] **a gold chain around his neck**, and they announced about him that he would become the third power in the kingdom.	Gen 42:42 He **clothed** him **in** silk garments, **and he put a gold chain around his neck**. Gen 42:43 He set him over all the land of Egypt. Esth 8:15 Mordecai left the presence of the king **in** royal robes of blue and white, with a large golden crown and a robe of fine linen and **purple**.
³⁰That **night** Belshazzar, the king of the Chaldeans, **was killed**.	Job 34:20 In an instant they **die**; in the middle of the **night** people are shaken and they pass by; **the mighty** are removed by no human hand.

143

COMMENTARY

God in whose hand is your breath. Following Job, Daniel here warns the king that it is not he who is in charge, but God. In this regard he also followed Joseph in his conversation with Pharaoh. The king's breath is in the hand of God, and it was God who made a hand write on the wall of the king's palace.

Muh-náy muh-náy tuh-káyl oo-fár-seen (מנא מנא תקל ופרסין). Except for MT and Peshitta all texts have only one *muh-nay*, making only three words on the wall. Clermont-Ganneau suggested more than a century ago that these words really list three weights: 1) a mena, 2) a shekel, and 3) half a mena.[9] Weights were used with a scale in which an object to be weighed was put on one side and the standard weights were put on the other side. *Muh-nay* can mean "weigh," "measure" or "appraise." *Tuh-kahl* can mean "weigh" or "pay." "*Far-seen*" can mean either "divide," "extend," or "assess."[10] In the current context it does not mean that Babylon will be divided and give half to the Persians and half to the Medes. The term "Medes and Persians" was often used in antiquity to refer to the citizens of one country, the one ruled by Cyrus. It means Babylon was broken up by an invasion, and ruled by the invader.

The problem was not with the obvious meaning of the words. The king and all of the members of his party probably knew that. The question was, "What is the hidden meaning?" "How can you get a message from these three words?" Josephus listed these three words as *mah-náy* (μάνη, *theh-kéhl* (θεκέλ), and *fah-réhs* (φαρές). Modern scholars have offered solutions for this puzzle. Farehs, for example could refer to Persians. The interpretations, however, that are important for this study are the ones Daniel supposedly gave to the king.

God has measured your kingdom and concluded it. Daniel interpreted the hidden message by changing two of the nouns into verbs. *Mena* was taken to mean "numbered"; *tekel* would mean **measured;** and *farsin* would refer to the Persians. While Belshazzar was ruling Babylon, Jews were negotiating with Cyrus of Persia for Babylon's fall. The conquest of Babylon by Cyrus would enable Jews to return to Palestine under Persian approval and with Persian financial support. Second Isaiah knew about this before it happened. The author of this narrative probably wrote after the event of Nabonidus' death and Persian successful conquest. That which was weighed or judged was the kingdom of Nabonidus. The price that was paid to bring about justice was Babylon. In this judgment or weighing, Belshazzar's kingdom which was placed in one side of the scale did not weigh enough to survive. Job 34:16-30 warns the kings and nobles of the tenuousness of their positions. God shatters them without investigation; he upsets them during the night; in a moment they die. Job concluded, "The godless man should not rule" (Job 34:30).

---

[9] Clermont-Ganneau, *JA* Juillet-Aout (1886):36-37.
[10] See further A. Wolters, "The Riddle of the Scales in Daniel 5," *HUCA* 62 (1991):155-77.

Weighed in the scales. This is another way of saying the previous clause. Measuring the kingdom was the same as **weighing in the scales**. The "scales" involved were the scales of justice that balanced good deeds against crimes.

Medes and the Persians. The foreign king that overthrew Babylon was Cyrus of **Persia.** His country was sometimes called the kingdom of **the Medes and the Persians** (Esth 1:18-19), because Cyrus had united these two countries into one. The mother of Cyrus was a **Mede**, and Cyrus obtained the rule of **Media** when Harpagus, an officer in the army of King Astyges of **Media**, called upon Cyrus to take the kingdom away from Astyges. Cyrus did that with a great deal of cooperation from the **Median** army. **Media** became a part of **Persia,** but the two countries had the same laws and many of the same customs.

A gold chain around his neck. Daniel ostensibly said he did not want any reward, but the author saw to it that he was honored in precisely the same way that Joseph of Egypt was. He was royally clothed; he received **a gold chain to wear around his neck**; and it was publicly announced that he was exalted to a top governmental position (Gen 41:42). Purple robes constituted the distinctive royal garb which was a sign of high political rank in many countries (Esth 8:15; Xenophon, *Anabasis* 1.5, 8; 1Macc 10:20).

Bleek had believed that Dan 5 was really a summary of historical events that took place over a long period of time rather than one night as the drama appears. Keil, however, disagreed with Bleek, holding that in crises, such as a fire, many things can happen in a very short period of time. [11] The relationship of Daniel to the Babylonian king in Dan 5 is quite different from the relationship orthodox Jews, such as Mattathias, had with Antiochus IV.

Belshazzar, the king of the Chaldeans, was killed. Cyrus conquered the city of Babylon without a battle, because the Babylonians were celebrating a festival, and most of them were drunk. That event may have provided the inspiration for the drama of Dan 5. Although told as if they were events that happened in history, all of these chapters are dramas that only use history as a background for the message the authors intended to communicate. The first readers or hearers of this drama already knew about the entry of Cyrus into Babylon, together with the festival. This was very important to the Jews, because it meant that the Jews would be allowed to leave Babylon and return to the Promised Land. The drama of Dan 5 was composed to climax with that invasion as a direct punishment for the misuse of the temple vessels from Jerusalem. It meant that God acted directly to carry out that which Daniel said would happen. Although this drama does not mention the conquest of Babylon by the Persians, that suggestion is implied.

Belshazzar was never king of Babylon, and Nebuchadnezzar was not his father. The author may have called him king to match his position with that of Pharaoh

---

[11] C. F. Keil, *Biblical Commentary on the Book of Daniel,* tr. M. G. Easton (Grand Rapids: William B. Eerdmans Publishing Co., c1976), p. 37.

in the Joseph stories. Both he and Nabonidus, may have been **killed** in the invasion or shortly after.[12]

TECHNICAL DETAILS

Although Dan 5 is quite repetitious, Shea has noted that it was not carelessly composed. It was not as well designed as Dan 4, but it was organized chiastically.

Dan 5:1-4 Banquet	Dan 5:22-23 Interpretation of banquet
Dan 5:5 Handwriting on wall	Dan 5:24-28 Interpretation of handwriting
Dan 5:6-8a Offer of honors for interpretation	Dan 5:29 Bestowal of honors for interpretation
Queen's Speech Dan 5:9-12a Nebuchadnezzar, Daniel, gift of interpretation	*Daniel's Speech* Dan 5:13-21 Nebuchadnezzar's dream interpreted by Daniel
Literary Joint 1 Dan 5:12b-13a Daniel called; Daniel comes	*Literary Joint 2* Dan 5:16b-17 Daniel's speech; king requests; Daniel complies

Belshazzar's Speech
Dan 5:13b-16a: Nebuchadnezzar, Daniel, and the gift of interpretation.[13]

Dan 6 is another drama in which the gentiles that had taken the Jews into captivity were punished, and the Jews were rewarded. Also it was the Jew, Daniel, who was brought in as a captive that became the one on whom the ruler of Babylon had to depend for wisdom. This is the kind of success story that would receive standing ovations when read at the first Hanukkah.

---

[12] For a popular, valid account of Belshazzar see A. Millard, "Daniel and Belshazzar in History," *Biblical Archaelogical Review* 11 (1985):72-78.

[13] W. H. Shea, "Further Literary Structures in Daniel 2-7 an Analysis of Daniel 5, and the broader Relationships within Chapters 2-7," *AUSS* 23 (1985):290.

CHAPTER SIX

ARAMAIC TEXT

6:1 וְדָרְיָ֙וֶשׁ֙ מָֽדָיָ֔א [מָדָאָ֔ה] קַבֵּ֖ל מַלְכוּתָ֑א כְּבַ֥ר שְׁנִ֖ין שִׁתִּ֥ין וְתַרְתֵּֽין׃
2 שְׁפַר֙ קֳדָ֣ם דָּרְיָ֔וֶשׁ וַהֲקִים֙ עַל־מַלְכוּתָ֔א לַאֲחַשְׁדַּרְפְּנַיָּ֖א מְאָ֣ה וְעֶשְׂרִ֑ין דִּ֥י לֶהֱוֹ֖ן בְּכָל־מַלְכוּתָֽא׃ 3 וְעֵ֣לָּא מִנְּה֗וֹן סָרְכִ֤ין תְּלָתָא֙ דִּ֤י דָנִיֵּאל֙ חַֽד־מִנְּה֔וֹן דִּֽי־לֶהֱוֹ֞ן אֲחַשְׁדַּרְפְּנַיָּ֣א אִלֵּ֗ין יָהֲבִ֤ין לְהוֹן֙ טַעְמָ֔א וּמַלְכָּ֖א לָֽא־לֶהֱוֵ֥א נָזִֽק׃ 4 אֱדַ֙יִן֙ דָּנִיֵּ֣אל דְּנָ֔ה הֲוָ֣א מִתְנַצַּ֔ח עַל־סָרְכַיָּ֖א וַאֲחַשְׁדַּרְפְּנַיָּ֑א כָּל־קֳבֵ֗ל דִּ֣י ר֤וּחַ יַתִּירָא֙ בֵּ֔הּ וּמַלְכָּ֣א עֲשִׁ֔ית לַהֲקָמוּתֵ֖הּ עַל־כָּל־מַלְכוּתָֽא׃ 5 אֱדַ֙יִן֙ סָֽרְכַיָּ֣א וַאֲחַשְׁדַּרְפְּנַיָּ֔א הֲו֛וֹ בָעַ֥יִן עִלָּ֖ה לְהַשְׁכָּחָ֣ה לְדָנִיֵּ֑אל מִצַּ֖ד מַלְכוּתָ֑א וְכָל־עִלָּ֨ה וּשְׁחִיתָ֜ה לָֽא־יָכְלִ֣ין לְהַשְׁכָּחָ֗ה כָּל־קֳבֵל֙ דִּֽי־מְהֵימַ֣ן ה֔וּא וְכָל־שָׁלוּ֙ וּשְׁחִיתָ֔ה לָ֥א הִשְׁתְּכַ֖חַת עֲלֽוֹהִי׃ 6 אֱ֠דַיִן גֻּבְרַיָּ֤א אִלֵּךְ֙ אָֽמְרִ֔ין דִּ֣י לָ֧א נְהַשְׁכַּ֛ח לְדָנִיֵּ֥אל דְּנָ֖ה כָּל־עִלָּ֑א לָהֵ֕ן הַשְׁכַּ֥חְנָֽה עֲל֖וֹהִי בְּדָ֥ת אֱלָהֵֽהּ׃ ס 7 אֱ֠דַיִן סָרְכַיָּ֤א וַאֲחַשְׁדַּרְפְּנַיָּא֙ אִלֵּ֔ן הַרְגִּ֖שׁוּ עַל־מַלְכָּ֑א וְכֵ֣ן אָמְרִ֣ין לֵ֗הּ דָּרְיָ֥וֶשׁ מַלְכָּ֖א לְעָלְמִ֥ין חֱיִֽי׃ 8 אִתְיָעַ֜טוּ כֹּ֣ל ׀ סָרְכֵ֣י מַלְכוּתָ֗א סִגְנַיָּ֤א וַאֲחַשְׁדַּרְפְּנַיָּא֙ הַדָּֽבְרַיָּ֣א וּפַחֲוָתָ֔א לְקַיָּמָ֤ה קְיָם֙ מַלְכָּ֔א וּלְתַקָּפָ֖ה אֱסָ֑ר דִּ֣י כָל־דִּֽי־יִבְעֵ֣ה בָ֠עוּ מִן־כָּל־אֱלָ֨הּ וֶֽאֱנָ֜שׁ עַד־יוֹמִ֣ין תְּלָתִ֗ין לָהֵן֙ מִנָּ֣ךְ מַלְכָּ֔א יִתְרְמֵ֕א לְג֖וֹב אַרְיָוָתָֽא׃ 9 כְּעַ֣ן מַלְכָּ֔א תְּקִ֥ים אֱסָרָ֖א וְתִרְשֻׁ֣ם כְּתָבָ֑א דִּ֣י לָ֧א לְהַשְׁנָיָ֛ה כְּדָת־מָדַ֥י וּפָרַ֖ס דִּי־לָ֥א תֶעְדֵּֽא׃ 10 כָּל־קֳבֵ֣ל דְּנָ֔ה מַלְכָּ֖א דָּרְיָ֑וֶשׁ רְשַׁ֥ם כְּתָבָ֖א וֶאֱסָרָֽא׃ 11 וְ֠דָנִיֵּאל כְּדִ֨י יְדַ֜ע דִּֽי־רְשִׁ֧ים כְּתָבָ֣א עַ֗ל לְבַיְתֵהּ֮ וְכַוִּ֣ין פְּתִיחָ֣ן לֵהּ֮ בְּעִלִּיתֵהּ֒ נֶ֣גֶד יְרֽוּשְׁלֶ֒ם וְזִמְנִין֩ תְּלָתָ֨ה בְיוֹמָ֜א ה֣וּא ׀ בָּרֵ֣ךְ עַל־בִּרְכ֗וֹהִי וּמְצַלֵּ֤א וּמוֹדֵא֙ קֳדָ֣ם אֱלָהֵ֔הּ כָּל־קֳבֵל֙ דִּֽי־הֲוָ֣א עָבֵ֔ד מִן־קַדְמַ֖ת דְּנָֽה׃ ס 12 אֱדַ֣יִן גֻּבְרַיָּ֤א אִלֵּךְ֙ הַרְגִּ֔שׁוּ וְהַשְׁכַּ֖חוּ לְדָנִיֵּ֑אל בָּעֵ֥א וּמִתְחַנַּ֖ן קֳדָ֥ם אֱלָהֵֽהּ׃ 13 בֵּ֠אדַיִן קְרִ֨יבוּ וְאָמְרִ֥ין קֳדָם־מַלְכָּ֖א עַל־אֱסָ֣ר מַלְכָּ֑א הֲלָ֧א אֱסָ֣ר רְשַׁ֗מְתָּ דִּ֣י כָל־אֱנָ֡שׁ דִּֽי־יִבְעֵה֩ מִן־כָּל־אֱלָ֨הּ וֶֽאֱנָ֜שׁ עַד־יוֹמִ֣ין תְּלָתִ֗ין לָהֵן֙ מִנָּ֣ךְ מַלְכָּ֔א יִתְרְמֵ֕א לְג֖וֹב אַרְיָוָתָ֑א עָנֵ֨ה מַלְכָּ֜א וְאָמַ֗ר יַצִּיבָ֧א מִלְּתָ֛א כְּדָת־מָדַ֥י וּפָרַ֖ס דִּי־לָ֥א תֶעְדֵּֽא׃ 14 בֵּ֠אדַיִן עֲנ֣וֹ וְאָמְרִ֣ין קֳדָ֣ם מַלְכָּ֗א דִּ֣י דָנִיֵּ֡אל דִּי֩ מִן־בְּנֵ֨י גָלוּתָ֜א דִּ֣י יְה֗וּד לָא־שָׂ֨ם עֲלָ֤ךְ [עֲלָיךְ] מַלְכָּא֙ טְעֵ֔ם וְעַל־אֱסָרָ֖א דִּ֣י רְשַׁ֑מְתָּ וְזִמְנִ֤ין תְּלָתָה֙ בְּיוֹמָ֔א בָּעֵ֖א בָּעוּתֵֽהּ׃ 15 אֱדַ֣יִן מַלְכָּ֗א כְּדִ֤י מִלְּתָא֙ שְׁמַ֔ע שַׂגִּ֥יא בְּאֵ֖שׁ עֲל֑וֹהִי וְעַ֧ל דָּנִיֵּ֛אל שָׂ֥ם בָּ֖ל לְשֵׁיזָבוּתֵ֑הּ וְעַד֙ מֶֽעָלֵ֣י שִׁמְשָׁ֔א הֲוָ֥א מִשְׁתַּדַּ֖ר לְהַצָּלוּתֵֽהּ׃ 16 בֵּאדַ֙יִן֙ גֻּבְרַיָּ֣א אִלֵּ֔ךְ הַרְגִּ֖שׁוּ עַל־מַלְכָּ֑א וְאָמְרִ֣ין לְמַלְכָּ֗א דַּ֤ע מַלְכָּא֙ דִּֽי־דָ֣ת לְמָדַ֣י וּפָרַ֔ס דִּֽי־כָל־אֱסָ֥ר וּקְיָ֛ם דִּֽי־מַלְכָּ֥א יְהָקֵ֖ים לָ֥א לְהַשְׁנָיָֽה׃ 17 בֵּאדַ֙יִן֙ מַלְכָּ֣א אֲמַ֔ר וְהַיְתִיו֙ לְדָ֣נִיֵּ֔אל וּרְמ֕וֹ לְגֻבָּ֖א דִּ֣י אַרְיָוָתָ֑א עָנֵ֤ה מַלְכָּא֙ וְאָמַ֣ר לְדָנִיֵּ֔אל אֱלָהָ֗ךְ דִּ֣י אַנְתָּה [אַנְתְּ] פָּֽלַֽח־לֵ֛הּ בִּתְדִירָ֖א ה֥וּא יְשֵׁיזְבִנָּֽךְ׃ 18 וְהֵיתָ֙יִת֙ אֶ֣בֶן חֲדָ֔ה וְשֻׂמַ֖ת עַל־פֻּ֥ם גֻּבָּ֑א

1Kgs 8:44

1Kgs 8:45

וְחָתְמָה מַלְכָּא בְּעִזְקְתֵהּ וּבְעִזְקָת רַבְרְבָנ֑וֹהִי דִּי לָא־תִשְׁנֵא צְבוּ
בְּדָנִיֵּאל: 19 אֱדַיִן אֲזַל מַלְכָּא לְהֵיכְלֵהּ וּבָת טְוָת וְדַחֲוָן לָא־
הַנְעֵל קָדָמ֑וֹהִי וְשִׁנְתֵּהּ נַדַּת עֲלֽוֹהִי: 20 בֵּאדַ֙יִן֙ מַלְכָּא בִּשְׁפַּרְפָּרָא
יְקוּם בְּנָגְהָא וּבְהִתְבְּהָלָה לְגֻבָּא דִֽי־אַרְיָוָתָא אֲזַל: 21 וּכְמִקְרְבֵהּ
לְגֻבָּא לְדָנִיֵּאל בְּקָל עֲצִיב זְעִק עָנֵה מַלְכָּא וְאָמַר לְדָנִיֵּאל דָּנִיֵּאל
עֲבֵד אֱלָהָא חַיָּא אֱלָהָךְ דִּי אַנְתָּה [אַ֣נְתְּ] פָּֽלַח־לֵהּ בִּתְדִירָא הַיְכֵל
לְשֵׁיזָבוּתָךְ מִן־אַרְיָוָתָֽא: 22 אֱדַיִן דָּנִיֵּאל עִם־מַלְכָּא מַלִּל מַלְכָּא
לְעָלְמִין חֱיִֽי: 23 אֱלָהִי שְׁלַח מַלְאֲכֵהּ וּֽסֲגַר פֻּם אַרְיָוָתָא וְלָא חַבְּלוּנִי
כָּל־קֳבֵל דִּי קָֽדָמ֙וֹהִי֙ זָכוּ הִשְׁתְּכַ֣חַת לִי וְאַף קָדָמָיךְ [קָֽדָמָךְ֙] מַלְכָּא חֲבוּלָה
לָא עַבְדֵֽת: 24 בֵּאדַ֨יִן מַלְכָּא שַׂגִּיא טְאֵב עֲל֑וֹהִי וּלְדָנִיֵּאל אֲמַר
לְהַנְסָקָה מִן־גֻּבָּא וְהֻסַּק דָּנִיֵּאל מִן־גֻּבָּא וְכָל־חֲבָל לָא־הִשְׁתְּכַח
בֵּהּ דִּי הֵימִן בֵּאלָהֵֽהּ: 25 וַאֲמַר מַלְכָּא וְהַיְתִ֜יו גֻּבְרַיָּא אִלֵּךְ דִּי־
אֲכַ֣לוּ קַרְצ֙וֹהִי֙ דִּֽי־דָֽנִיֵּאל וּלְגֹ֤ב אַרְיָוָתָא֙ רְמ֔וֹ אִנּ֖וּן בְּנֵיה֣וֹן וּנְשֵׁיה֑וֹן
וְלָֽא־מְטוֹ לְאַרְעִית גֻּבָּא עַד דִּֽי־שְׁלִטוּ בְהוֹן אַרְיָוָתָא וְכָל־גַּרְמֵיה֥וֹן
הַדִּֽקוּ: 26 בֵּאדַיִן דָּרְיָוֶשׁ מַלְכָּא כְּתַב לְכָֽל־עַֽמְמַיָּא אֻמַּיָּ֜א
וְלִשָּׁנַיָּא דִּֽי־דָאֲרִין [דָּיְרִין] בְּכָל־אַרְעָא שְׁלָמְכוֹן יִשְׂגֵּֽא: 27 מִן־קֳדָמַי שִׂים
טְעֵם דִּי ׀ בְּכָל־שָׁלְטָן מַלְכוּתִ֗י לֶהֱוֹ֤ן זָאֲעִין [זָֽיְעִין֙] וְדָ֣חֲלִ֔ין מִן־קֳדָם אֱלָהֵהּ
דִּֽי־דָנִיֵּאל

דִּי־הוּא ׀ **אֱלָהָא חַיָּא** וְקַיָּם **לְעָלְמִין**   2Kgs 19:4; Isa 45:17b
וּמַלְכוּתֵהּ דִּי־לָא תִתְחַבַּל **וְשָׁלְטָנֵהּ** עַד־סוֹפָֽא: 1Chron 28:7; Ps 145:13
28 **מְשֵׁיזִב** וּמַצִּל וְעָבֵד **אָתִין וְתִמְהִין בִּשְׁמַיָּא וּבְאַרְעָא**   Isa 45:17a; Deut 4:34
דִּי שֵׁיזִיב לְדָנִיֵּאל מִן־יַד אַרְיָוָתָֽא: 29 וְדָנִיֵּאל דְּנָה   Deut 3:24
הַצְלַח בְּמַלְכוּת דָּרְיָוֶשׁ וּבְמַלְכוּת כּוֹרֶשׁ פַּרְסָיָא [פָּרְסָאָֽה]: פ

TECHNICAL DETAILS

Readers who have also read chapter 3 will notice some thematic similarities. This is part of the apparent chaism forming a unity of Dan 2-7:

3:12"There are men who are Jews whom you have appointed over the management of the province of Babylon-- Shadrach, Meshach, and Abednego. These men have not obeyed your royal command; they do not worship your god; and the golden statue which you erected they do not worship." Then Nebuchadnezzar in heated anger ordered that Shadrach, Meshach, and Abednego to be brought.

3:25"He answered and said, "But I see four men released, walking in the midst of the fire, and they have no injury, and the appearance of the fourth is like a son of God."

6:14"Then they answered and said before the king, "Daniel, who was from among the exiles of the Jews, has paid no attention to you, O King, or to the prohibition which you signed, but offers his prayer three times a day."

6:24"Then the king was very much pleased, and he commanded that Daniel be brought out from the den. Daniel was brought out from the den, and no injury was found in him, because he trusted in his God.

³:²⁸Nebuchadnezzar answered and said, "Blessed be the God of Shadrach, Meshach, and Abednego who sent his angel and saved his servants who believed in him and transgressed the word of the king. They gave their bodies and did not worship or bow down before any god except their God."

⁶:²³God has sent his angel and closed the mouths of the lions, and they have not hurt me, because I was found virtuous before him. I also committed no injury before you, O king.

Collins has listed five ways in which Dan 3 and 6 are similar to other narratives, such as those devoted to Joseph of Egypt, Esther and Mordecai, and Ahikar. 1) The heroes were found in a state of prosperity; 2) they experienced danger, 3) were condemned to prison, 4) were released, and 5) were restored. Some were even promoted.[1]

Goldingay has observed that Dan 6 was organized as an inclusion, chiastically.

A. Daniel's success
   B. Darius signed an injunction and Daniel took his stand.
      C. Daniel's colleagues planned his death.
         D. Darius hoped for Daniel's deliverance.
           X
         D.' Darius witnessed Daniel's deliverance.
      C'. Daniel's colleagues met their deaths.
   B'. Darius signed a decree and took his stand.
A'. Daniel's success.[2]

ENGLISH TEXT

⁶:¹Darius the Mede received the kingdom when he was about 62 years of age. ²Darius chose to appoint 120 governors who would be in his entire kingdom. ³Over them were three presidents, of whom Daniel was one of those to whom these governors gave account, so that the king would not suffer loss. ⁴Then this Daniel was made supervisor over all the presidents and governors, because of the superior spirit that was in him, and the king was preparing to set him over the entire kingdom.

COMMENTARY

Darius the Mede. **Darius the Mede** is reported only here in all extant literature. According to Daniel, he ruled Babylon after the time of Nebuchadnezzar and before the conquest of Cyrus of Persia. Who was **Darius the Mede**? Shea thought he might have been the well-known Guburu, who was Cyrus' commander-in-chief of the

---

[1] J. J. Collins, *A Commentary on the Book of Daniel* (Minneapolis: Fortress Press, c1993), pp. 45-46.
[2] J. E. Goldingay, *Daniel* (Dallas: Word Books, c1989), p. 124.

military forces when the Persians captured Babylon.³ San Nicolo believed that the individual was Cambyses.⁴ Wiseman and Colless claimed that **Darius the Mede** was reported as having done exactly the same things Cyrus was reported as having done. Cyrus of Persia was born from a mother who was a Mede, and Darius was born a Mede (Dan 9:1). Therefore *Darius the Mede* was none other than Cyrus of Persia himself.⁵ After analyzing all of these scholarly positions, Grabbe concluded,

> Our knowledge of Persian history may be skimpy on the whole, but it seems sufficient to say that there is no room for a king named Darius the Mede or a governor named Daniel the Jew early in Cyrus' reign, contrary to the picture of Daniel 6.⁶

There is no historical report other than this that Media, unattached to Persia, ever ruled Babylon, but other Danielic narratives picture Daniel as one who officiated **when Darius the Mede** governed the territory east of the Mediterranean Sea and before the conquest of Cyrus.

How did it come about that the author of Dan 6 invented this character? At first glance it looks as if the author was a fiction writer, pure and simple, but there is some literary and logical basis for his composition. The author knew of the widely held successors of the Middle East. They came in this order: 1) Assyria, 2) Media, 3) Persia, and 4) Greece. This would have been an ideal order for the North Israelites who had gone as exiles into Assyria. North Israelites might logically have deduced that they would become number 5.

The Jews in Babylon, however, were more successful than the North Israelites in gaining opportunities to return to the Promised Land. They were concentrated in Babylon and not scattered into many countries. Therefore they had the opportunity to organize and form a pressure group with extensive influence. The North Israelites might have had an eschatological interpretation of the time between their eighth century captivity and their expected return after the Greeks, but they could not bring it to fruition. We can only guess about this. There is no historical evidence for such a theology. There are many expressions in medieval Jewish literature of the belief that Samaria was destined to run interference militarily to remove Judah's enemy before Judah moved in to inherit the land. Rabbis may have traced their typology of the restoration of the land to the Jews from Babylon. They certainly held Saul as the earliest type, preparing the government for a Davidic rule.⁷

---

[3] W. H. Shea, "Darius the Mede: An Update," *AUSS* 20 (1982):229-47.

[4] M. San Nicolo, *Beitrage zu einer Prosopographie neubabylonischer Beamten der Zivil-und Tempel/verwaltung,* SPAW, Phil-hist Abteilung 2.2: (Munich:Bayerische Akademie der Wissenschaften, 1941), pp. 54-57.

[5] D. Wiseman, "Some Historical Problems in the Book of Daniel," *Notes on Some Problems in the Book of Daniel* (London: Tyndale, 1965), pp. 9-16, and B. E. Colless, "Cyrus the Persian as Darius the Mede in the Book of Daniel,"*JSOT* 56 (1992):113-26.

[6] L. L. Grabbe, "Another Look at the Gestalt of 'Darius the Mede,'" *CBQ* 50 (1988):213.

[7] Buchanan, *Revelation and Redemption: Jewish Documents of Deliverance from the Fall of Jerusalem to the Death of Nahmanides* (Dillsboro: Western North Carolina Press, c1978; sold by Mercer U. Press).

That which we have is an eschatology that was designed for Judah. By substituting Babylon for Assyria Jews could present a logical argument that would interpret their theology from the Babylonian captivity until the cleansing of the temple. The order would be 1) Babylon, 2) Media, 3) Persia, and 4) Greece. The problem was that Media never ruled this area after Babylon. It was not Media who conquered Babylon, but Persia. This meant the author had to deduce a Media that had conquered Babylon and which was, in turn, overpowered by Persia. Charles was the one who explained how this might be justified.[8]

During the time of Isaiah and Jeremiah Media was a serious threat to Babylon. It was because of this threat that Queen Nicotris lined the riverbed with bricks as a defense against Media. Knowing these facts Isaiah decreed an oracle against Babylon (Isa 13:1). He promised that the Lord would stir up **the Medes** against Babylon. **The Medes** would invade Babylon and kill everyone—not only the young men, but also all the children of Babylon, and Babylon would become like Sodom and Gomorrah. It would never be inhabited again. It would become a deserted place for wild beasts (Isa 13:17-22). Media and Elam would come up against Babylon and Babylon would fall (Isa 22:2-9). This was wishful thinking on the part of Isaiah, and Jeremiah concurred with Isaiah. He said the Lord would stir up a spirit of a destroyer against Babylon (Jer 51:1). The Lord would avenge Babylon, and Babylon would fall. Its end would come, because the Lord would stir up the kings of **the Medes** to avenge Babylon for destroying God's temple in Jerusalem (Jer 51:8-14, 28). Ezekiel said that the prophecies of these two prophets would be fulfilled by "Gog," an unknown country in the North (Ezek 38:17).

Actually none of these prophecies came true, but since they have been canonized as the word of the Lord spoken by two of the Lord's legal agents, they are legally true. No one was legally permitted to bring into court any outside evidence, such as proof that Media never destroyed Babylon. This often happens in court. People who have committed crimes are judged "not guilty," because the evidence that would prove that they committed the crimes was not admitted into court for various reasons. The necessary evidence may have been obtained by illegal means, or some such reason. Following the rule that "if it is not in the scripture, it is not in the world," the author of Dan 6 has rhetorical proof that Media destroyed Babylon. Therefore he had only to fill in the details, such as introducing the mythical **Darius the Mede**, but the author also had literary basis for introducing **Darius** into the picture.

Darius the Mede became the mythical king who fulfilled the prophecies of Isaiah, Jeremiah, and Ezekiel, filling the gap between Babylon and Persia. The order of succession, then, was 1) Babylon, 2) Media, 3) Persia, and 4) Greece. The readers of Daniel wanted this system to be established, so they accepted the conclusion. It is never hard to persuade those who are already convinced.[9]

---

[8] R. H. Charles, *A Critical and Exegetical Commentary on the Book of Daniel* (Oxford: Clarendon Press, 1929), pp. 141-42.

[9] To learn more about court logic, see Buchanan, *Biblical and Theological Insights from Ancient and Modern Civil Law* (Lewiston:The Edwin Mellen Press, c1992). Colless, "Cyrus the Persian," pp. 113-26, thought Jews gave Cyrus the name "Darius the Mede," to show that the prophecies of Jeremiah and Isaiah had been fulfilled.

Another rule of Jewish rhetoric is that all prophecy was prophesied only for the days of the Messiah. After the victories of Beth-horon and Beth-zur, many probably held Judas the Maccabee, unofficially, as the new Messiah, just as twentieth century Jews called the prime minister Menahem Begin, "Menahem the king" (*méhn-ah-khem hah-méh-lehk*, מנחם המלך). Judas' older brother, Simon, at least was later called the **prince of the people of Israel** (*ah-sáhr-ahm-áyl*, ασαραμελ= שר עם אל) (1Macc 14:27). Jews celebrated Hanukkah in the belief that the messianic age had already begun. Therefore prophecies of Isaiah, Jeremiah, and Ezekiel must have been fulfilled.

Charles also offered an explanation that justified the use of the name **Darius** as the conqueror of Babylon. There was a Persian, Darius Hystaspes, who ruled Persia 17 years after Cyrus conquered Babylon. He was reported in an Aramaic inscription to have twice reduced Babylon.[10] This knowledge provided the author with a king, a conquest, and Babylon. These are all the data the author of Dan 6 needed to construct his narrative. All the author had to do was to claim that this **Darius** was a **Mede** who ruled Media many years before Cyrus. Dan 6 may originally been composed in relationship to the Persian king, **Darius** I. In that case the narrative would make sense. The final editor who put all of the chapters together may have added **the Mede** to the narrative so that this chapter would cohere with other chapters that presumed the succession of nations to be 1) Babylon, 2) Media, 3) Persia, and 4) Greece.

All of the logic and argument used to justify the use of the adjective **the Mede** is legally true but historically false. **Darius the Mede** never existed, and **the Medes** were not the ones who conquered Babylon. Bevan correctly said,

> Nothing can be more unfortunate than the attempts of apologists to make these things appear probable.[11]

120 governors. The mythical **Darius the Mede** supposedly divided the kingdom into 120 geographical units. It was not a Mede, but the Persian, Darius Hystaspis (522-485 BIA), who first divided Persia into units (satrapies), and that was into 20 units rather than 120 (Herodotus 3.89-90). The division was made for efficiency in administration and taxation. Since the author or later editor converted the Persian, Darius Hystaspis, into Darius, the Mede, and transfered him from a later period of history into an earlier one, he could just as well increase the number of units in the then non-existent Median kingdom from 20 to 120. The relationship, however, between Darius I and the division of the empire into separate units was accurate.

If it had not been necessary to keep the role of Media between Babylon and Persia, this entire chapter would have made sense with the notion that the king involved was Darius I (521-486 BIA), one of the later kings of Persia. If the story stood alone, with no need to make it cohere to Dan 2, 7, and 8 that might once have been the case. The adjective "the Mede" does not occur in Dan 6:2 of the OG, but it

---

[10] Charles, *Daniel*, pp.143-44; A. Cowley, *Aramaic Papyri of the Fifth Century B.C.* (Osnabrück: Otto Zeller, 1967), pp. 248-59.

[11] A. A. Bevan, *A Short Commentary on the Book of Daniel* (Cambridge: University Press, 1892), p. 108.

belongs to an extra verse in chapter 5. Both of these instances make good sense as editorial additions.

So the king would not suffer loss. Apparently all of these officials were appointed to see that the taxes were all collected. There was a hierarchy of supervision to check on the tax collectors to see that they all reported accurately.

TEXT

⁵Then the governors and presidents were trying to find a complaint against Daniel effecting the kingdom, but they were not able to find any complaint or fault, because he was trustworthy, and there was no error or fault to be found in him. ⁶Then these men said, "In this Daniel we shall not find any fault unless ⁷we find it in the law of his god."

TECHNICAL DETALS

Following Arnold there is a play on words in Dan 6, just as there was in Dan 5. The words that are appropriated are "seeking" (bah-áh, בעה) and "finding" (shah-khákh, שכח). The other leaders were seeking to find a complaint against Daniel, but they were unable to find any, because no fault was found in him. They said to one another "We will not find any complaint against Daniel unless we find it in relation to the law of his God" (Dan 6:5-6).[12] The term for seeking was also used for "prayer" or "petition," but it is obvious that the author has used these terms with literary skill for special repetitive emphasis.

COMMENTARY

Trying to find a complaint against Daniel. **Trying** is better American than **searching** or "looking," but one of these other terms would better express the Aramaic term used. It is not difficult to understand why these leaders would resent Daniel. He was placed in a position superior to any of theirs, and he was just at the point of getting another promotion. They all had to report and give an accounting of their leadership to him--and he was not even a native citizen. He had entered Babylon as a captive, taken from a country Babylon had defeated in war. He was the Kissinger or Albright of his day. Charles thought it was preposterous for the king to have signed into law such an extensive rule without consulting his chief assistant, Daniel,[13] but this author was writing drama rather than history.

In the law of his god. In all administrative and political activities Daniel reportedly had fulfilled his office in an exemplary fashion. No local citizen could accuse him of being either inefficient or dishonorable. His Achilles heel was his unique religion. When he assimilated into Babylonian society and politics he held on to the religion of his fathers. To this extent he was not a true Babylonian.

---

[12] B. T. Arnold, "Wordplay and Narrative Technique in Daniel 5 and 6," *JBL* 112 (1993):483.

[13] Charles, *Daniel*, p. 146.

TEXT

Then these governors and presidents united to come to the king, and this is what they said to him, "King Darius, live for ages! ⁸All the presidents of the kingdom, the governors, managers, leaders, and prefects have agreed that the king should establish a statute and make binding a prohibition that anyone who offers prayer to any god or man for 30 days, except to you, O King, will be thrown into the den of lions. ⁹Now, O King, establish the prohibition and sign the document which cannot be changed, according to the law of the Medes and the Persians, which cannot be revoked."

COMMENTARY

Offers prayer. This is another way of saying "makes a **search**," using the same word for "**search**" that is used frequently in this chapter.

Except you, O King. In political propositions, the originators seldom reveal the true motive of the designed action. There are good reasons for doing something, and there are the real reasons. Politicians usually present the good reasons rather than the real ones. Here the good reasons were the increased loyalty and devotion to the king. The real reason was the trap set to get Daniel out of the way of those who proposed the action.

The den of lions. It was not unusual for kings to have dens of lions at their disposal. These were kept for athletic events held before theaters. Slaves and prisoners were made to fight lions.

Law of the Medes and the Persians. The **laws** of the two nations were probably very similar. They were geographically proximate, and some of **the Persian** kings were of **Median** ancestry. At one time, before the rule of Cyrus, all of Media and **Persia** were parts of **Media**.

TEXT

Daniel 6	First Testament Intertexts
	[1Kings 8:44] If your people goes out to war against its enemy in the way where you will send them,
¹⁰Therefore Darius signed the document and the prohibition. ¹¹When Daniel discovered that the document had been signed, he went **to** his **house**. He had in his roof chamber windows that opened **toward Jerusalem**. Three times that very day he bent his knees, bowed, and gave thanks	and they **pray to Yehowah** toward **the city** which you have chosen and **to the house** which I have constructed in your name. ⁴⁵Then you,

before his God, just as he had done before this. ¹²Then these men kept watch and found Daniel **praying** and making **supplication before his God**. Heaven, will hear their

prayer and their

supplication and conduct their legal case.

COMMENTARY

When Daniel found out that the document had been signed. This means that **Daniel** did not break the king's command out of ignorance. He realized the risks involved and chose to continue his religious duties anyway.

In his roof chamber windows that opened toward Jerusalem. In Solomon's prayer, the directions were given for the prayer of the people. When they were away from the temple, they should always offer their prayers in the direction of the temple. When they were away from **Jerusalem** they should face **Jerusalem** when they prayed. Those who had been taken captive into a distant land of their enemies, from there should turn their faces toward Jerusalem and offer their prayers (1Kings 8:38, 48-50; Ps 55:18), asking God (Heaven) to hear their prayers and be compassionate toward them. Rabbis said that a Jew should not pray in a house that did not have windows facing **Jerusalem** (*bBer* 34b).[14] To be sure that they were facing in the direction of **Jerusalem**, people studied maps to learn the exact direction. Then they sometimes made the mark of the cross (X) on the inner wall of the house that was nearest to **Jerusalem**. After that, they could pray before the cross in order to fulfill the commandments of the scripture. Many houses had a separate room on the roof with latticed windows where they might enjoy the evening breeze. These chambers were installed so that some of the windows faced **Jerusalem** for prayer. The upper room where Jesus met with his apostles for the Last Supper may have been in one of these roof rooms. In one such room Daniel regularly prayed before a window, facing **Jerusalem**.

Three times that very day. The word **very** reflects the Aramaic *hoo* (הוא), understood as an emphatic adjective rather than a personal pronoun. **Three times** was one of the Jewish and later Christian schedules of prayers (Ps 55:17). The authorities are not consistent. Sometimes it is reported as twice a day (1Chron 23:30). Muslims traditionally pray five times a day. The emphasis here is that he did not put off his practice one single day because of the threat.

Found Daniel praying. The words **found** (*hahsh-kah-khoó*, השכחו), and **praying** (*bah-áye*, בעה) are the two words on which the author of Dan 6 played throughout the chapter. The words "searching" and "finding" are balancing terms. The word rendered **praying** could be translated **searching**, or "making a request." It is a synonym for the following word **and making supplication** (*oo-meet-khah-nayn*, ומתחנן).

---

[14] Contra Goldingay, *Daniel*, p. 131, who said Jews did not have such special places for prayer.

TEXT

¹³Then they approached the king and spoke about the prohibition, "O King, have you not signed a prohibition that any man who prays to any god or man for 30 days, except to you, O King, will be thrown into the den of lions?" The king answered and said, "The word is true according to the law of the Medes and Persians, which cannot be changed." ¹⁴Then they answered and said before the king, "Daniel, who was from among the exiles of the Jews, has paid no attention to you, O King, or to the prohibition which you signed, but offers his prayer three times a day."

COMMENTARY

Have you not signed a prohibition? This was the moment for which these leaders were waiting. They had set the trap to catch Daniel, and now he had been caught. All they had to do then was to report the incident to the king. At this point their glee could hardly be disguised.

Anyone who prays. This is another use of the word usually rendered **search** (*yeevaye*, יבעא).

Daniel, who was from among the exiles of the Jews. They did not mention that he held the highest post in the government. That which was important was to remind the king that Daniel was only a foreign exile. He was the one who ignored the prohibition of the king.

TEXT

¹⁵When the king heard the message he was very badly distressed. He set his mind to deliver Daniel, and he tried to save him until the sun went down. ¹⁶Then these men came together to the king, and said to the king, "Be informed, O king, that the law of the Medes and Persians that any prohibition and statute which the king establishes cannot be changed." ¹⁷Then the king commanded and Daniel was brought and thrown into the den of lions. The king answered and said to Daniel, "May the god whom you worship continually save you." ¹⁸Then a stone was brought and placed at the mouth of the den, and the king sealed it with his signet ring and with the signet ring of his chief officers so that no intention might be changed concerning Daniel.

COMMENTARY

He tried to save him. The king was fond of Daniel. That is the reason he appointed him to the highest post in the land. When Daniel was caught in a legal snare, so was the king. He tried to find some legal loophole by which he could get around the prohibition he had signed.

Law of the Medes and the Persians. **The Medes** ruled **the Persians** for many years before the conquest of Cyrus. During that time, **the Persians** lived by the **laws of the Medes**. After Cyrus conquered **Media, the Persians** ruled **the Medes**. By that time the two countries probably had the same basic **laws**. After all, both countries ruled the same land at different times. The author of Daniel presumed that the king involved was not authorized to override such laws as these. Herodotus, however, said that the king of **Persia** could do whatever he pleased (Herodotus 3.31). Although this story was written as if it was during the hypothetical rule **of the Medes and** before **the Persians**, there was no reference to **the Medes and the Persians** until after **the Persians** ruled all of what was once **Media** and **Persia**. This points out the anachronistic problems of this chapter.

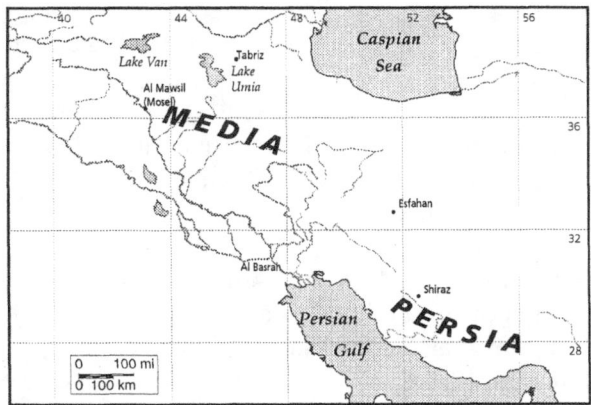

Be informed, O king. The pressure was on. The leaders were there to remind the king that there was no way he could get out of this. The law was clear and explicit. Daniel had broken it, so he would have to suffer the assigned punishment. They were not going to let the king ignore this situation and have it overlooked and by-passed by default.

The den of lions. An earlier Psalmist cried to the Lord in his distress, because his enemies had set traps to catch him. They put pits in his paths. He lay in the midst **of lions** with sharp teeth. He called to God to be merciful and rescue him (Ps 57:3-6).

The stone was brought and placed at the mouth of the den. **The den** was some kind of pit, possibly made by discovering a cave that was naturally created by water dissolving the limestone in the mountain. Local people often made cisterns out of these by sealing up the opening and making another opening at the top from which to draw water and also as a place to which to direct the streams when rain fell to fill up the cistern. **Dens** for lions might have been made by sealing the opening of caves with doors or gates rather than brick and stone. A more likely possibility in the non-mountainous valley where Babylon was located is an oven made of brick, like other buildings in Babylon. The oven had to be in or close to Babylon so that the king could go out easily to see the situation there.

The stone was placed at the mouth of the oven so that neither Daniel nor any of the lions might escape. Clay was then filled into the space between the rock and the wall, and the king's seal was pressed into the clay. In this way any movement of the rock would break the seal and show that someone had interfered with the action. This was the last act taken to seal the fate of Daniel.

TEXT

[19] Then the king went away to his palace, and spent the night fasting; his concubines were not brought before him; and sleep fled from him. [20] Then at dawn he arose in the morning and went hurriedly to the den of lions. [21] When he approached the den where Daniel was, he cried out in a loud voice. The king answered and said to Daniel,

Daniel	First Testament Intertext
"Daniel, **servant of the God of life**, has your God whom you serve continually been able to save you from the lions?"	Isa 44:26 Who upholds the word of **his servant**, and the counsel of his messengers he fulfills.

[22] Then Daniel spoke to the king, "May the king live for ages! [23] God has sent his angel and closed the mouths of the lions, and they have not hurt me, because I was found virtuous before him. I also committed no injury before you, O king." [24] Then the king was very much pleased, and he commanded that Daniel be brought out from the den. Daniel was brought out from the den, and no injury was found in him, because he trusted in his God.
    [25] The king ordered, and the men were brought to him who slandered Daniel, and they threw them to the den of lions, they, their children, and their wives, and they did not reach the ground of the den before the lions overpowered them and broke all of their bones into pieces.

COMMENTARY

Sleep fled from him. This is a personification expression. It personifies **sleep** by picturing it as a human being that could escape by running away. It means the king had not been able to **sleep** all night. He reportedly fasted and refrained from any diversion. The word rendered "concubines" is used only here in the Bible. It may mean "dancing girls" or "concubines." Since it was during the night that all of this took place, it seems more reasonable that he would normally be brought concubines rather than dancing girls.

He went hurriedly to the den of lions. Normally one might expect that a king would use messengers to obtain information like this. He could easily have asked someone of his servants what had happened in **the den of lions** the night before, but this king was so deeply concerned for Daniel that he went personally to check on the situation.

Servant of the God of life. Daniel was called the **Servant of the God of life**. His three companions were called **Servants of the Most High** (Dan 2:26). Bevan was the first to notice that Isa 52 and 53 were intertexts for Daniel.[15] He was followed by Ginsberg,[16] and many others, such as Gammie, have recognized the importance of this insight. Bevan and Ginsberg have concentrated on this influence in Dan 12, but Gammie has noted that the servant passages from Isaiah were used also in other chapters. This should not surprise anyone. Second Isaiah pronounced the good news that the exiles would be allowed to return to Judah and rebuild its cities. Daniel was announcing the good news that the exile had come to an end, and the temple would be cleansed and restored. Second Isaiah was a normal intertext for Daniel.

Just as the **servant of the Lord** had been marred (Isa 52:14), so the council of Darius tried to blemish Daniel's character (Dan 6:5). Just as the spirit rested upon the Lord's **servant** (Isa 42:1), so the spirit also rested upon Daniel (Dan 4:5-6, 15). Just as God made the **servant** wise (Isa 52:13), so God also granted Daniel wisdom (Dan 1:17).[17]

The expression **God of life** was not used frequently in the FT. When the king of Assyria sent Rabshakeh to confront Hezekiah, he was said to have come to mock **the God of life** (2Kings 19:4, 16; Isa 37:17). The Psalmist offered praise to **the God of life** (Ps 84:2). The Israelites were afraid of **the God of life**, believing that they alone of all people had heard the voice **of the God of life** and still lived (Deut 5:26). Jeremiah said Yehowah of armies was the true God, **the God of life**, the king of the age (Jer 10:10; 23:36). Hosea spoke of the Israelites as being "sons **of the God of life**" (MT Hos 2:1). Metaphorically the word **life** was used to describe existence within the treaty community. **The God of life** was **the God** who made a treaty with his chosen people. Here the expression was probably used to distinguish **the God** Daniel worshiped from the gods of the Medes and the Persians. When the king addressed Daniel's **God** as **the God of life**, it may imply that the king had himself become a believer. This was a theme that recurred in several places in the Book of Daniel. In Dan 1 Daniel and his friends were put into a program whereby they were conditioned to give up their Jewish beliefs and become true Babylonians. The end result was that the king himself was converted to Judaism. This is the kind of drama Jews would enjoy reading and hearing. There was a power struggle in which the great power of the greatest king of the world was subdued by the religious power of one of its captives. This is another David-Goliath theme, one of the many instances in the Book of Daniel where a great reversal took place.

King, live for ages. The first time this expression appears on the lips of Daniel is here. The goal of the Book of Daniel was not to honor foreign kings. The honor was usually directed to Daniel and his friends. An **age** was a temporal concept that was bordered by rather normal limits. An **age** could refer to the term of a king's office, a Jubilee, the period of a certain nation's rule, or some similar time. By this greeting Daniel told the king he wished that he would live for more time than many kings ruled.

---

[15] A. A. Bevan, *Short Commentary*, p. 202.
[16] H. L. Ginsberg, "The Oldest Interpretation of the Suffering Servant," *VT* 3 (1953):402-403.
[17] So also J. G. Gammie, "On the Intention and Sources of Daniel I-VI," *VT* 31 (1981):289-90.

I was found virtuous before him. The word **found** is one of the "search and **find**" words used by the author of Dan 6 for repeated emphasis. It is the basic teaching intended for the readers of this narrative. If Jews in foreign lands would keep all of their traditional laws in the face of difficult situations, and trust God, God would protect and reward them. This was the promise of the scripture (Exod 23:23-33).

God sent his angel. The Psalmist promised that the **angel** of the Lord would encamp around those who feared him and deliver them (Ps 34:7). The Aramaic word *mahláhk* (מלאך), like the Greek word *áhn-geh-laws* (ἄγγελος). means "messenger." Messengers were very important in antiquity when there were very few means of communication. No kingdom, shipping industry, or major business could operate without messengers by which a principal might communicate with others at a distance. Since God lived in heaven it was assumed that he managed all of his business on earth by means of messengers. Through messengers God closed the mouths of the lions. The lions did not injure Daniel because God had acted in his behalf. Lest anyone should say that the lions had been fed and were not hungry, Josephus held that the lions were fed amply before the conspirators were thrown into the lions' den, but they were suddenly devoured, anyway (*Ant* 10.260-62).

This experience was a trial by ordeal. In such a situation a person was thrown into some kind of danger and judged by whether or not he or she survived. The prescribed method of testing a woman's faithfulness to her husband, for example, was to make her drink a bitter solution, containing tentative curses. If she aborted, she was judged to be guilty. If she carried the fetus to birth, she was believed to be innocent (Num 5:11-31). Daniel's ordeal proved his innocence.

The men were brought before him. First Daniel **was brought** (*hah-yuh-teev*, היתיו) to be thrown to the lions. Then the stone **was brought** to cover the mouth of the den. Finally the men who plotted against Daniel **were brought** to endure the same punishment they designed for Daniel.

They, their children, and their wives. This is the final pay-off. These very men, all of whom were important government leaders and citizens of Babylon, who tried to have Daniel, the foreign exile, killed, were not only killed, but their entire families were destroyed with them. This was an enforcement of the Deuteronomic rule that the court should apply to the false witness the same punishment he wanted the defendant to receive (Deut 19:16-19). Keil said pagan kings often condemned **wives and children** to death with the law breakers, but he thought Jews did not do this because it was forbidden by the scripture (Deut 24:16).[18] He overlooked another reference that reported such an action as this actually having happened. When Achan was found to have broken some of the holy war rules, he, his **children** and all of his possessions were stoned and burned in fire (Josh 7:24-25). The Jewish king, Alexander Janneus had 800 of his political Jewish opponents crucified while their wives and children were killed before their eyes. The king was reclining and drinking wine with his concubines while he watched the event (*War* 1.97).

---

[18] C. F. Keil, *Biblical Commentary on the Book of Daniel,* tr. M. G. Easton (Grand Rapids: William B. Eerdmans Publishing Co., c1976), p. 218.

Ancients gave little attention to individuals. Status came in relationship to the group to which individuals belonged. Death was considered only a removal of the body, because all the rest was left to heirs—reputation, status, possessions, authority, etc. Life continued through the community. Real death left no heirs. This was the case with Achan, the opponents of Alexander Janneus, Haman, and the Persian leaders. The slaughter in Dan 6 was one of the great reversals in the Book of Daniel. Those who planned for Daniel's death achieved only their own.

The story was designed to show what happens to those who become enemies with God's chosen people. All of this was carried out by the orders of a foreign king in relationship to his own leading citizens. As in the Book of Esther, this gives the enemies of Israel an occasion to tremble, but for the chosen people, an opportunity to rejoice. All of their enemies get killed. The teaching here is that it pays to become friends of kings in foreign countries. If you do, you can become more powerful than any of the native citizens. This not only happened to Daniel, but also to Joseph of Egypt, Moses, Esther, Judith, and Nehemiah. This tradition was carried over into Christianity when its members became closely aligned with Constantine.

TEXT

^{26}Then King Darius wrote to all the peoples, nations, and [those who spoke foreign] languages who dwell in all the land, "May your peace be increased. ^{27}A decree was set before me that in all the power of my kingdom there should be trembling and fearing before the God of Daniel, because

Daniel	First Testament Intertexts
he is **the God of life**, /	$^{2Kings\ 19:4,\ 16}$ Which he has sent to mock **the God of life**.
and he continues **for ages**. /	$^{Isa\ 45:17b}$ They will not be ashamed or insulted **for ages**.
His kingdom will not be destroyed, /	$^{1Chron\ 28:7}$ I **will** establish **his kingdom for the age**.
and his rule is until the end. /	$^{Ps\ 145:13}$ **Your kingdom is a kingdom of** all **ages, and your rule** in every single generation.
^{28}He **delivers** and **saves**; /	$^{Isa\ 45:17a}$ Israel **will be saved** by Yehowah, a **deliverance of the ages**.
he performs **signs and miracles** /	$^{Deut\ 4:34}$ Has any god tried to go and take a nation . . . by **signs and miracles**, by war, and an outstretched arm.

in heaven and on the land.	Deut 3:24 Who is the god **in heaven or on the land** who performs such deeds or mighty works as you?

[He is the one] who saved Daniel from the lions." [29]This Daniel prospered in the kingdom of Darius and in the kingdom of Cyrus the Persian.

COMMENTARY

The God of Daniel. The typical way for a Jewish drama to end is for the pagans to be converted to Judaism, Wacholder said,

> A glance at the variety of Graeco-Jewish forgeries reveals that they have one common characteristic—pagans praising Jews or aspects of Judaism. The Jewish attributions to Homer, Hesiod, Linus, or Euripides, the Letter of Aristeas, the Judaeo-Spartan correspondence, and the suspected documents preserved by Josephus have this common denominator.[19]

The story began with a group conspiring to have Daniel killed because he worshiped a foreign deity. It ended with the group all killed and all citizens ordered to worship and tremble before Daniel's God—a complete reversal. The poem had been written before and was used by the author of Dan 6 to composed this document. He worked it into his composition so that it fit nicely. This is also true of the poems in Dan 2:20-23, 3:33, and 4:31-34--all of which are concluding confessions of the king.[20]

His kingdom will not be destroyed. God's **kingdom** was believed to be coterminous with Israel's **kingdom**. When Solomon sat on his throne in Jerusalem, he was ruling the **kingdom** of Yehowah (2Chron 28:5) and was held to be God's son (1Chron 28:6). This was the rock that crushed the gentile statue made of four different kinds of metals (Dan 2:44). That **kingdom** was destined to follow the fourth beast and also the rock that would crush the four metals of the pagan statue and rule continuously.

His rule is until the end. Since the Hasmonean rule had already begun with the victories of Beth-horon and possibly Beth-zur, the author was probably thinking of the Maccabean age which would not end for a long time, in his opinion. It actually ended with the beginning of Herod's rule.

---

[19] B. Z. Wacholder, "The Letter from Judah Maccabee to Aristobulus: Is 2 Maccabees 1:10b-2:18 Authentic?" *Hebrew Union College Annual* 49 (1978):128
[20] So also G. T. M. Prinsloo, "Two Poems in a Sea of Prose: The Content and Context of Daniel 2:20-23 and 6:27-28," *JSOT* 93 (1993):93-100.

CHAPTER SEVEN

ARAMAIC TEXT

7:1 בִּשְׁנַת חֲדָה לְבֵלְאשַׁצַּר מֶלֶךְ בָּבֶל דָּנִיֵּאל **חֵלֶם חֲזָה** וְחֶזְוֵי
רֵאשֵׁהּ עַל־מִשְׁכְּבֵהּ בֵּאדַיִן חֶלְמָא כְתַב רֵאשׁ מִלִּין אֲמַר: 2 עָנֵה
דָנִיֵּאל וְאָמַר **חָזֵה הֲוֵית בְּחֶזְוִי** עִם־לֵילְיָא וַאֲרוּ אַרְבַּע רוּחֵי שְׁמַיָּא Ezek 1:1
מְגִיחָן לְיַמָּא רַבָּא: 3 **וְאַרְבַּע חֵיוָן** רַבְרְבָן סָלְקָן מִן־**יַמָּא שָׁנְיָן** דָּא Ezek 1:5; Jer 52:17
מִן־דָּא: 4 קַדְמָיְתָא **כְאַרְיֵה** וְגַפִּין דִּי־נְשַׁר לַהּ חָזֵה הֲוֵית עַד דִּי־
מְרִיטוּ גַפַּיהּ וּנְטִילַת מִן־אַרְעָא וְעַל־רַגְלַיִן **כֶּאֱנָשׁ** הֳקִימַת וּלְבַב Ezek 1:7
אֱנָשׁ יְהִיב לַהּ: 5 וַאֲרוּ **חֵיוָה** אָחֳרִי תִנְיָנָה דָּמְיָה לְדֹב וְלִשְׂטַר־חַד
הֳקִמַת וּתְלָת עִלְעִין בְּפֻמַּהּ בֵּין שִׁנַּיהּ [שִׁנַּהּ] וְכֵן אָמְרִין לַהּ קוּמִי אֲכֻלִי Ezek 1:6-7
בְּשַׂר שַׂגִּיא: 6 בָּאתַר דְּנָה חָזֵה הֲוֵית וַאֲרוּ אָחֳרִי כִּנְמַר וְלַהּ גַּפִּין
אַרְבַּע דִּי־עוֹף עַל־**גַּבַּיַהּ** [גַּבַּהּ] **וְאַרְבְּעָה** רֵאשִׁין לְחֵיוְתָא וְשָׁלְטָן יְהִיב Ezek 1;1, 5
לַהּ: 7 בָּאתַר דְּנָה **חָזֵה הֲוֵית בְּחֶזְוֵי** לֵילְיָא וַאֲרוּ חֵיוָה **רְבִיעָיָה** [רְבִיעָאָה]
דְּחִילָה וְאֵימְתָנִי וְתַקִּיפָא יַתִּירָא וְשִׁנַּיִן דִּי־פַרְזֶל לַהּ רַבְרְבָן אָכְלָה
וּמַדֱּקָה וּשְׁאָרָא **בְּרַגְלַיַהּ** [בְּרַגְלַהּ] רָפְסָה וְהִיא מְשַׁנְּיָה מִן־כָּל־חֵיוָתָא דִּי
קָדָמַיהּ וְקַרְנַיִן עֲשַׂר לַהּ: 8 מִשְׂתַּכַּל הֲוֵית בְּקַרְנַיָּא וַאֲלוּ קֶרֶן אָחֳרִי
זְעֵירָה סִלְקָת בֵּינֵיהוֹן [בֵּינֵיהֵן] וּתְלָת מִן־קַרְנַיָּא קַדְמָיָתָא אֶתְעֲקַרוּ [אֶתְעֲקַרָה]
מִן־קֳדָמַיהּ [קֳדָמַהּ] וַאֲלוּ עַיְנִין כְּעַיְנֵי **אֲנָשָׁא** בְּקַרְנָא־דָא וּפֻם מְמַלִּל 1Kgs 22;19
רַבְרְבָן: 9 **חָזֵה הֲוֵית** Ps 55:20; Isa 6:1
עַד דִּי כָרְסָוָן רְמִיו וְעַתִּיק יוֹמִין יְתִב
לְבוּשֵׁהּ ׀ כִּתְלַג חִוָּר וּשְׂעַר רֵאשֵׁהּ כַּעֲמַר נְקֵא Ps 97:2
כָּרְסְיֵהּ שְׁבִיבִין דִּי־**נוּר** גַּלְגִּלּוֹהִי **נוּר דָּלִק**: Ps 97:3
10 נְהַר דִּי־**נוּר** נָגֵד וְנָפֵק מִן־קֳדָמוֹהִי Deut 4:24; 1Kgs 20:19
אֶלֶף אַלְפַיִם [אַלְפִין] יְשַׁמְּשׁוּנֵּהּ וְרִבּוֹ רַבְבָן [וְרִבְבָן] קָדָמוֹהִי יְקוּמוּן Ps 50:3
דִּינָא יְתִב וְסִפְרִין פְּתִיחוּ:
11 **חָזֵה הֲוֵית** בֵּאדַיִן מִן־קָל מִלַּיָּא רַבְרְבָתָא דִּי קַרְנָא מְמַלֱּלָה Ezek 1:4
חָזֵה הֲוֵית עַד דִּי קְטִילַת חֵיוְתָא וְהוּבַד גִּשְׁמַהּ וִיהִיבַת לִיקֵדַת
אֶשָּׁא: 12 וּשְׁאָר חֵיוָתָא הֶעְדִּיו שָׁלְטָנְהוֹן וְאַרְכָה בְחַיִּין יְהִיבַת לְהוֹן Ezek 1:4; Isa 6:4; 19:1
עַד־זְמָן וְעִדָּן: 13 חָזֵה הֲוֵית בְּחֶזְוֵי לֵילְיָא Ezek 1:5, 26; Isa 6:1
וַאֲרוּ **עִם־עֲנָנֵי שְׁמַיָּא כְּבַר אֱנָשׁ אָתֵה הֲוָה**
וְעַד־**עַתִּיק יוֹמַיָּא** מְטָה וּקְדָמוֹהִי הַקְרְבוּהִי:
14 וְלֵהּ יְהִיב שָׁלְטָן וִיקָר וּמַלְכוּ
וְכֹל עַמְמַיָּא אֻמַּיָּא וְלִשָּׁנַיָּא לֵהּ יִפְלְחוּן Gen 41:8
שָׁלְטָנֵהּ שָׁלְטָן עָלַם דִּי־לָא יֶעְדֵּה
וּמַלְכוּתֵהּ דִּי־לָא תִתְחַבַּל: פ

15 אֶתְכְּרִיַּת רוּחִי אֲנָה דָנִיֵּאל בְּגוֹא נִדְנֶה וְחֶזְוֵי רֵאשִׁי יְבַהֲלֻנַּנִי׃
16 קִרְבֵת עַל־חַד מִן־קָאֲמַיָּא וְיַצִּיבָא אֶבְעֵא־מִנֵּהּ עַל־כָּל־דְּנָה
וַאֲמַר־לִי וּפְשַׁר מִלַּיָּא יְהוֹדְעִנַּנִי׃ 17 אִלֵּין חֵיוָתָא רַבְרְבָתָא דִּי אִנִּין
אַרְבַּע אַרְבְּעָה מַלְכִין יְקוּמוּן מִן־אַרְעָא׃ 18 וִיקַבְּלוּן מַלְכוּתָא
קַדִּישֵׁי עֶלְיוֹנִין וְיַחְסְנוּן מַלְכוּתָא עַד־עָלְמָא וְעַד עָלַם עָלְמַיָּא׃
19 אֱדַיִן צְבִית לְיַצָּבָא עַל־חֵיוְתָא רְבִיעָיְתָא דִּי־הֲוָת שָׁנְיָה מִן־
כָּלְּהֵין [כָּלְּהֵן] דְּחִילָה יַתִּירָה שִׁנַּיהּ [שִׁנַּהּ] דִּי־פַרְזֶל וְטִפְרַיהּ דִּי־נְחָשׁ אָכְלָה
מַדֲּקָה וּשְׁאָרָא בְּרַגְלַיהּ רָפְסָה׃ 20 וְעַל־קַרְנַיָּא עֲשַׂר דִּי בְרֵאשַׁהּ
וְאָחֳרִי דִּי סִלְקַת וּנְפַלוּ [וּנְפַלָה] מִן־קֳדָמַיהּ [קֳדָמַהּ] תְּלָת וְקַרְנָא דִכֵּן וְעַיְנִין
לַהּ וּפֻם מְמַלִּל רַבְרְבָן וְחֶזְוַהּ רַב מִן־חַבְרָתַהּ׃ 21 חָזֵה הֲוֵית וְקַרְנָא
דִכֵּן עָבְדָה קְרָב עִם־קַדִּישִׁין וְיָכְלָה לְהוֹן׃ 22 עַד דִּי־אֲתָה עַתִּיק
יוֹמַיָּא וְדִינָא יְהִב לְקַדִּישֵׁי עֶלְיוֹנִין וְזִמְנָא מְטָה וּמַלְכוּתָא הֶחֱסִנוּ
קַדִּישִׁין׃
23 כֵּן אֲמַר חֵיוְתָא רְבִיעָיְתָא
מַלְכוּ רְבִיעָיָא [רְבִיעָאָה] תֶּהֱוֵא בְאַרְעָא דִּי תִשְׁנֵא מִן־כָּל־מַלְכְוָתָא
וְתֵאכֻל כָּל־אַרְעָא וּתְדוּשִׁנַּהּ וְתַדְּקִנַּהּ׃
24 וְקַרְנַיָּא עֲשַׂר
מִנַּהּ מַלְכוּתָה עַשְׂרָה מַלְכִין יְקֻמוּן וְאָחֳרָן יְקוּם אַחֲרֵיהוֹן
וְהוּא יִשְׁנֵא מִן־קַדְמָיֵא וּתְלָתָה מַלְכִין יְהַשְׁפִּל׃
25 וּמִלִּין לְצַד עִלָּיָא [עִלָּאָה] יְמַלִּל וּלְקַדִּישֵׁי עֶלְיוֹנִין יְבַלֵּא
וְיִסְבַּר לְהַשְׁנָיָה זִמְנִין וְדָת
וְיִתְיַהֲבוּן בִּידֵהּ עַד־עִדָּן וְעִדָּנִין וּפְלַג עִדָּן׃
26 וְדִינָא יִתִּב וְשָׁלְטָנֵהּ יְהַעְדּוֹן לְהַשְׁמָדָה וּלְהוֹבָדָה עַד־סוֹפָא׃
27 וּמַלְכוּתָה וְשָׁלְטָנָא וּרְבוּתָא דִּי מַלְכְוָת תְּחוֹת כָּל־שְׁמַיָּא
יְהִיבַת לְעַם קַדִּישֵׁי עֶלְיוֹנִין
מַלְכוּתֵהּ מַלְכוּת עָלַם וְכֹל שָׁלְטָנַיָּא לֵהּ יִפְלְחוּן וְיִשְׁתַּמְּעוּן׃
28 עַד־כָּה סוֹפָא דִי־מִלְּתָא אֲנָה דָנִיֵּאל שַׂגִּיא ׀ רַעְיוֹנַי יְבַהֲלֻנַּנִי וְזִיוַי
יִשְׁתַּנּוֹן עֲלַי וּמִלְּתָא בְּלִבִּי נִטְרֵת׃ פ

Ps 34:9; 16:3

Isa 6:1

Ezek 12:13; Jer 51:64

INTRODUCTION

Dan 7 is not a continuation either of chapter six or of the entire unit, 1-6. It does not continue after chapter six either chronologically or logically. It goes back to a date earlier than chapter 5. The unit to which it belongs, however, is Dan 2-7. It forms an inclusion to Dan 2. Miller listed D 7:1-2a as one of the editorial additions. The terminology in these verses is not the same as the rest of the chapter. The expression "dreamed a vision" is a strange combination. Normally prophets see visions, and others dream dreams. The chiasm of Dan 2-7 does not need these verses to make the passage a chiasm. Miller believed that originally there were two complete books of Daniel, one in Hebrew and one in Aramaic. Then some later editor compressed them into one, taking part of one manuscript and part of the other.[1]

---

[1] J. E. Miller, "The Redaction of Daniel," *JSOT* 52 (1991):115-24.

ENGLISH TEXT

Daniel	First Testament Intertexts

7:1During the first **year** of [the reign of] Belshazzar, **king** of Babylon, Daniel dreamed a **vision**, and [there were] **visions**

in his head [as he lay] on his bed. Then he wrote down the dream.

The beginning

of his **words** said, **2"**Daniel answered and said,

'I was seeing visions at night,

and **four winds of heaven** came forcing [the waves] of the [Mediterranean] Sea to bend over when **3four** huge **beasts** came up

from **the sea**, different one from the other.

Isa 6:1 **In the year** that **king** Uzziah died **I saw** the Lord, sitting on his throne.

Gen 1:1 In **the beginning** God created the heaven and the earth.

Deut 1:1 These are **the words** which Moses spoke to all Israel.

Ezek 1:1 **I saw visions** of God.

Zech 2:10(M) I have scattered you abroad as **four winds of heaven**, says Yehowah.

Ezek 1:5 From its midst were something like **four beasts**.

Jer 52:17 The bronze pillars that were in the house of Yehowah, the stands, and **the** bronze **sea** which was in the house of Yehowah, the Chaldeans broke, and they took all the bronze to Babylon.

Ezek 14:21 How much more when I send upon Jerusalem my **four** bitter acts of judgment: sword, famine, evil **beasts**, and pestilence.

Lev 26:21 If you walk contrary to me I will bring more plagues upon you, seven times for all your sins. 22I will release wild **beasts** among you that will rob you of your children.

COMMENTARY

Belshazzar, king of Babylon. There seems to have been some conscious imitation of vision-style here from the vision of Isaiah in relationship to **King** Uzziah. Belshazzar was the son of Nabonidus. He never was **king**, but he was given authority to administer the eastern part of the **Babylonian** government while his father took charge of the western region for many years. **Belshazzar's** rule took place shortly before Cyrus invaded **Babylon** (539 BIA). Belshazzar may have been called **king** here to call attention to **King** Uzziah in Isa 6:1.[2]

Daniel dreamed a vision. This time after five chapters where Daniel was pictured as an interpreter of the dreams of kings, it was Daniel himself who had the **dream** that is under consideration.

He wrote down the dream. This is a good policy for all dreamers. Those who write down their **dreams** before they have forgotten them have the opportunity later to study them and gain insights from them.

The beginning of his words. The author used terms taken from **the beginning** of entire scripture (Gen 1:1). **The beginning** of Deuteronomy (Deut 1:1) also starts with these **words**. The last paragraph of Dan 7 includes the **words, Here is where the word ends. The words** in between are the message of Dan 7. Dan concludes with **words** from Jeremiah and Ecclesiastes (Jer 51:64; Eccles 12:13). This is a way of announcing the introduction, the beginning of the narrative.

I was seeing visions. The introductory expression "**I was** watching" or **I was seeing** occurs eight times in Dan 7 (also Dan 4:7, 10). There were **visions** that were **seen** by others in Dan 2-6, but this is the first time the prophet himself was pictured as having had a **vision**. The prophet Amos **saw** things that gave him insights into God's message. Some of these may have been **visions,** and some may not. The first item Amos saw was locusts consuming crops (Amos 7:1-2). The second was fire destroying the land (Amos 7:3-6). These were events Yehowah showed Amos (Amos 7:1, 4), but he may have showed them through an actual threat of famine rather than **visions**. The third experience, however, Amos saw the Lord stationed on a wall with a plumb line (Amos 7:7). This must have been a **vision**, because the Lord was the object that was **seen**. Seeing the Lord is no every day experience. In all cases, the importance of the insight was Amos' interpretation. He **saw** something that Amos thought was a message from the Lord.

The prophet Zechariah reported ten **visions** that he **saw**. In each of these visions the prophet failed to understand what they meant. Then an angel appeared to Zechariah and told him what they meant (Zech 1:7-6:15). These **visions** differed from those of Amos in that Amos had no angel giving him the interpretation involved. It was the Lord, according to Amos, who showed him the event, and it was the Lord with whom Amos spoke. With Zechariah, the **vision**

---

[2] See further G. G. Nicol, "Isaiah's Vision and the Visions of Daniel," *VT* (1979):501-504.

came to him, and the angel interpreted the meaning of the **visions**. In all of these cases, it was the interpretation that was important. Ezekiel saw a **vision** that was related to the altar in the temple at Jerusalem. This vision prompted him, just as it had prompted Isaiah (Isa 6) before him to believe that God had commissioned him to prophesy. Ezekiel did not say who told him what this vision meant, but it involved a message from God. Some unidentified being spoke to Ezekiel and told him God's message (Ezek 1:1-7:27).

The **vision** that came to Daniel in Dan 7, however, was not accompanied by an interpretation. The author assumed that the reader could understand the drama provided. Although many have misinterpreted the meaning of the **vision** across the centuries, at the time that it was written it was assumed that local Jews would have no difficulty understanding the theater.

The four winds of heaven. This expression is found only in Zech 2:10(M) in the entire FT except in Daniel (Dan 8:8; 11:4). Perhaps this expression comes from the Babylonian document, *Enumma Elish*.[3]

Forcing [the waves] of the [Mediterranean] Sea. Literally this says, **Forcing the Sea**, but when the wind forces the sea to bend, the wind stirs up **the sea** and makes waves that bend. This sea is the one called the Mediterranean **Sea**, because that is **the sea** that is near Palestine. Montgomery agreed with those scholars who thought this was not the Mediterranean **Sea** but the great mythic chaos.[4] This assumes that it must be either the one or the other. Jews understood the threat of mythic chaos. They called the sea monster "Leviathan," the great dragon (Ps 74:13-14), but they related it to the dangers faced by Jews who sailed the Mediterranean Sea where their ships were sometimes capsized. In the same way they understood the Kingdom of God in relationship to their kingdom on the land of Palestine. They understood myths, but they mythicized their own scriptures. These abstract concepts were kept in practical perspectives.

Four huge beasts came up from the sea. The beasts were mythical monsters, and **the sea** is the place where terrible monsters resided (Gen 7:11; 8:2; Job 9:13; 25:12-13). The **beasts** were understood to have been part of the punishment God promised the Israelites if they broke their contract with him. If they kept their contract with God he would bless them with prosperity, posterity, and land. If they broke the contract, instead of blessings they would receive curses. The curses included **beasts.** Witstruck noted that **beasts** were normally listed as parts of curses that accompanied contracts. He gave two examples of Sefire treaties in which the curses included punishment by snakes, scorpions, bears, leopards, and lions (Sf I A, 9, 31).[5] He compared this with the curse God brought upon the Israelites after he had blessed them and they responded negatively. Because that

---

[3] So E. C. Lucas, "The Source of Daniel's Animal Imagery," *TB* 41 (1990):164, 185.
[4] J. A. Montgomery, *A Critical and Exegetical Commentary on the Book of Daniel* (New York: Charles Scribner's Sons, 1927), p. 285.
[5] T. Wittstruck, "The Influence of Treaty Curse Imagery on the Beast Imagery of Daniel 7," *JBL* 97 (1978):100-102.

was true, God would be to **them like a leopard lurking along the way, like a bear robbed of her cubs.** He would devour them like a lion and tear them apart like a wild **beast** (Hos 13:7-8).

The author of Dan 7 pictured the four empires that preceded Hanukkah as God's implementation of his curses. From the author's point of view it is important that the Mediterranean Sea is outside of the Promised Land, and it produces gentile monsters. The author was having a vision, just like Ezekiel, so, like Ezekiel, he saw **four beasts**. This was part of his homiletic program. These words became texts for his exegesis. His exegesis involved transforming these beasts into symbols of kings of the **four** successive nations that ruled the Near East. The author even had some help in making this deduction, because Ezekiel had earlier compared the people of Israel to sheep who had been taken from their own pasture and scattered without a shepherd among the wild beasts (Ezek 34:5-6). Ezekiel promised that God would rescue his sheep from the beasts and bring them back to the mountains of their own land in Israel (Ezek 34:11-14).

The **four beasts** here had the same literary function as **the four** metals in Dan 2. Also here the mixture of the horns plays the same role as the mixed metals in Dan 2. It is obvious that the two chapters constitute parables about the same situation and the same period in history. Ever since the insights of Swain, scholars have recognized that there had been the notion that **four** empires had ruled the ancient Near East in chronological succession. The **four** were: Assyria, Media, Persia, and Greece. [6] The authors of Dan 2 and Dan 7 recognized that list as Babylon, Media, Persia, and Greece. They thought the fifth nation would be Judah. Dan 2 and 7 have organized dramas around that conception. The difference between Dan 2 and Dan 7 is that much more attention is given in chapter 7 to the fourth beast with 10 horns, and especially the little horn which the tenth horn produced.

TEXT

Daniel	First Testament Intertexts
The first was **like a lion** with **wings** of an eagle. I continued to watch	Hos 13:7 I will be to them **like a lion.**
	Prov 18:15 **A lion** roaring or a **bear** roaming is a wicked ruler over a poor people.
until its **wings** were clipped and it was taken up from the earth and made to **stand** upright on **two feet**	Isa 6:1 There were seraphim **standing** above it, each having six **wings**. With **two** he covered his face; with **two** he covered his **feet.**

---

[6] J. S. Swain, "The Theory of the Four Monarchies Opposition History Under the Roman Empire," *CIP* 35 (1940):1-21. For analysis of succeeding interpretations of the four monarchies see E. C. Lucas, "The Origin of Daniel's Four Empires Scheme Re-Examined," *TB* 40 (1989):185-202.

	^{Ezek 1:5} From its midst was something like **four beasts**, and this was their appearance. It was something
like a human being, and a **human mind was given to it**. ⁵Now look! Another **beast**, a second one, was **like a bear**. It was raised on one side, and [there were] three ribs in its mouth, between its teeth, and this is what they [= God] told it: "Rise up and eat lots of flesh." ⁶After this I was watching. Now look!	**like** that **human being**. ⁶Each one had four faces, and each one had **four wings**. ⁷Their legs were straight legs, and the soles of their **feet** were like the soles of a calf's foot.
	^{Amos 5:19} **Like** a man [who] fled from **a lion** and he met **a bear**.
	^{Ps 8:5} What is **a human being** that you remember him / **the son of a human being** that you appoint him.
	^{Hab 1:6, 8} Look! I am rousing the Chaldeans . . . their horses are swifter than **leopards**
Another [beast] was **like a leopard**, and it	^{Hos 13:7-8} I will be to them **like a lion**, **like a leopard** I will lurk beside the way. I will fall upon them **like a bear** robbed of her cubs.
	^{Ezek 1:10} and the face of **a lion** to the right of all **four**.
had on its back **four wings** of a bird, and the **beast** had heads, and **dominion was given** to it.	^{Ps 8:7} You **give** him **dominion** over the works of your hands / you place all things under his feet /---⁸all sheep and cattle; / also **the beasts** of the field, / the birds of the heaven, / and the fish of the sea.

COMMENTARY

Like a lion with wings of an eagle. Jeremiah called Nebuchadnezzar a lion and compared his troops to **eagles** (Jer 49:19, 22). This monster had the appearance of a sphinx. This was a demonic figure that had special superhuman powers. It had teeth and claws **like a lion**, but it had **wings**, so that it could fly, but it had the mind of a human being, and it could stand upright like a human being. This was the clue to the reader that the beast was really a human being with monstrous qualities. It represented both the king of the beasts and the most majestic of the birds. The exegete manufactured these beasts from words he obtained from

Ezekiel's vision. Ezekiel's vision was describing the beasts in the temple in Jerusalem, one of which had **wings**. That gave the exegete the basis for providing **eagle's wings** for his beast that was **like a lion**.

The **lion** was the king of the beasts, and Jeremiah called kings of great countries **lions**. He applied this name to both the kings of Assyria and of Babylon (Jer 50:17). This coheres with chapter 2 where the first metal was the greatest and best.

A human mind was given to it. The word **human** was taken from Ezekiel's vision, which included the appearance of something like a **human** being. The author of this chapter attributed these **human** characteristics to the first of his beasts. This demonic character was transformed into **a human** being. This was intended to be an improvement, but it was still related somehow to the demon from which it originated. Giving the beast a mind like **a human** being did not remove its power.

Like a bear. The way in which some king appeared to be **like a bear** with three ribs in its mouth is an unsolved mystery. The author did not get his description of this beast from Ezekiel's vision. The monster might have been compared to **a bear** lying on its side because of the geographical outline of the country that lay alongside the Tigris river, reaching up into the northland of former Assyria. That would have been like the "boot" of Italy. Media may also have been called **a bear**, because its country was mostly mountainous, in contrast with the rich farmland in the Tigris-Euphrates Valley.

Herodotus said that the land was so rich in Assyria that wheat heads were four times as long as a person's finger, and the wheat produced 400 fold. In the mountains, instead of farmland, they raised animals, and there were wild animals for hunting. There may also have been **bears** in the mountains of Media. If we knew more about the details of Median history we would be able to understand this code. This beast, like Media, does not really fit into the four-nation succession scheme. The author of Dan 6 thought there was one law for both Medes and Persians (Dan 6:9, 13, 16). The author of Dan 8 treated Media and Persia as if they constituted one kingdom with two kings (Dan 8:20). The author of Dan 10 and 11, however, distinguished Persia as a separate kingdom (Dan 10:1, 13, 20; 11:1). This is one of the indications that different chapters of Dan were written by different authors.

Rise up and eat lots of flesh. This probably referred to Media's aggression in expanding its territories. It conquered Assyria and was a constant threat to Babylon. It extended its borders to the west, north, and south which might be symbolized by the three ribs that the bear had in its mouth (Dan 8:4), or the ribs may have symbolized the booty that Media had taken from many countries. But these are only guesses. Isaiah pictured the Medes as those who were cruel. They would slay the young men and also children and infants (Isa 13:17-18). The three ribs that were in the mouth of the **bear** may have represented kings, countries, or booty that Media had taken.

Like a leopard. It was swift like the Chaldean soldiers (Hab 1:6, 8). This was no ordinary **leopard**. It was equipped with four wings to fly, and it had four heads. This description came from his text. Ezekiel's beast had four faces, which the exegete assumed meant that he also had four heads to go with the faces. Ezekiel's beast had four wings, so the exegete's **leopard** also had four wings. It was evidently really a king, because it had dominion over some area, like the human being in Ps 8. It ruled like a king. This was another clue that the discussion was about kings rather than beasts. The **leopard** was the third beast, because it followed the second beast and preceded the fourth.

Hosea warned that the Ephraimites had been so wicked that the Lord would punish them by treating them as if God were cruel and powerful as **a lion**. He would **lurk by their way** and spring upon them from behind **like a leopard**. He would **fall upon** them like a bear robbed of her cubs (Hos 13:7). Dan 7 used this passage as an intertext to remind the Jews that their exile was no accident. The Lord had warned them in advance, through Hosea, that he would treat them this way. Now that they had experienced the exile and could look back upon it, the author of Dan 7 said this was just as Hosea promised. Babylon was **like a lion**; Media **was like a bear robbed of her cubs**. Persia was **like a leopard** attacking them from the rear as they walked on the way. Persia took the Jews by surprise. Like the first pharaoh, Cyrus had befriended them. Jews had helped him take Babylon without a battle, and he promised to return them to the Promised Land. They never expected him to treat them like an enemy. Hosea may not have thought of wild beasts in terms of foreign kings, but the author of Prov 28 and the author of Dan 7 did. The author of Dan 7 also probably remembered the judgment day Amos predicted which was like a man who fled from **a lion** and was confronted by a **bear** (Amos 5:19). There was no escape from the just judgment of Yehowah. After more than 400 years of submission to gentile rule, Jerusalem Jews knew this was true, and they dared to accept it—after it was over.

TEXT

Daniel	First Testament Intertexts
⁷After this **I was watching** in my **visions** of the night.	Ezek 1:1 The heavens were opened, and **I saw visions** of God.
Now look! A **fourth beast**, terrible, frightening, and very strong. It had large iron teeth. It consumed and shattered [most obstacles], and trampled the rest with **its feet**. It differed from all the **beasts** that came before it, and it had ten horns. ⁸I was pondering about the horns when look!	Ezek 1:5 From its midst was something like **four beasts**, and this was their appearance. It was something **like** that **human being**. ⁶Each of them had four faces and each had four wings. ⁷Their legs were straight legs, and the soles of their **feet** were like the soles of a calf's foot.

Another horn, a small one, grew up among them. Before it three of the earlier horns were uprooted. Now look! There were eyes **like** the eyes of a **human being** in this horn and a mouth **speaking extensively**. He made war with the saints.
⁹**I kept on watching** until **thrones** were set up and the Ancient of Days sat down.

Ps 12:4 Yehowah will cut off all flattering lips, the tongue **speaking extensively**

Isa 6:1 **I saw the Lord sitting** on **the throne.**

1Kgs 22:19 **I saw Yehowah sitting** on his **throne.**

Ps 55:20 God will hear [the case] and afflict them; **the Ancient one is seated** [for judgment].

COMMENTARY

Terrible, frightening, and very strong. The Danielic exegete still used words from Ezekiel's vision to describe this fourth beast. This monstrous creature was the last in the order of beasts, and clearly the worst. Instead of wings and teeth, this beast had horns and feet like a cow or goat. It was equipped to fight. It could trample and gouge.

It had ten horns. The **ten horns** are **ten** kings. Judas the Maccabee was called "the big **horn**" (*1Enoch* 90.9). Most beasts have only two **horns**, but this beast had ten, like a moose or reindeer, and they became human and in conflict with one another. One horn overpowered all of the rest. The identification of these **ten horns** cannot be absolute: Hartman followed Baumgartner in his selection: 1) Alexander the Great, 2) Alexander Aegus, 3) Seleucus I, 4) Antiochus I, 5) Antiochus II, 6) Seleucus II, 7) Seleucus III, 8) Antiochus III, 9) Seleucus IV, and 10) Antiochus IV Epiphanes.[7] Ginsberg has a different identification: 1) Alexander the Great, 2) Alexander II, 3) Seleucus I, 4) Antiochus I, 5) Antiochus II, 6) Seleucus II, 7) Seleucus III, 8) Antiochus III, 9) Seleucus IV, 10) Antiochus IV.[8]

Both scholars presume that Alexander the Great is both the fourth beast and one of **the horns**, but the beast **had the horns**. It was not itself a **horn**. The four beasts are four kings (Dan 7:17). The fourth of these beasts was the great king who conquered the ruling kings of the Near East, namely Alexander. He would not be classified among the ten because he was one of the four. Therefore he should not be considered among those who had already been counted. There

---

[7] L. F. Hartman and A. A. DiLella, *The Book of Daniel* (Garden City: Doubleday, 1978), p. 214, following W. Baumgartner, "Ein Vierjahrhundert Danielforschung," *TRu* 11 (1939):204.
[8] H. L. Ginsberg, "Studies in Daniel" *HUCA* 33, part 1 (1950-51):19-20; "The Composition of the Book of Daniel," *VT* 4 (1954):268.

were more **horns** than just Seleucids. There were the Ptolemies, Lysimachus, Antigonus, and their successors. It is not clear which of these were considered the **ten horns**. Before the little horn three of the earlier **horns** were uprooted. These three may have been Antiochus IV's older brother, Seleucus, Seleucus' son Demetrius, and Heliodorus, an imposter who was acting as king when Antiochus IV arrived from Rome. Caragounis is probably correct in saying that it is impossible to be certain of the analysis of the **ten horns**.[9]

Another horn, a small one. Here only in Dan 7 is the **horn** called "small." It is even called conspicuous (Dan 7:19), implying that it is large. Usually it is called "the horn" (Dan 7:8, 20-21). Dan 8 refers to the same character as a **little horn**.

Eyes of a human being. Like the first beast that had feet and a mind like a human being, this creature was also a **human being** with monstrous qualities.

A mouth speaking extensively. He was also accused of **speaking** very presumptuously (1Macc 1:24). In court the horn had to have been given permission to **speak** first. He was evidently the defendant in the trial, and he was allowed to defend himself with all the arguments he could muster.

In most Western courts the defense would not be allowed to **speak** until the plaintiff had made the accusation. The exception is when the defendant has admitted the plaintiff's facts, so that the burden of proof is the defendant's. Then the defendant is allowed to **speak** first.[10]

In ancient Jewish courts, either the defendant or the plaintiff might be allowed to begin, but if there was any possibility that the defendant might receive the death penalty then he or she was allowed to **speak** first, offering all the arguments available for his or her own defense. Since the defendant was here allowed to **speak** first, this implies that the trial might involve the death penalty (*mSan* 3.4)[11]

He made war with the saints. This sentence was added from the OG. It is clear that this was what Antiochus IV did.[12] This turned out to be the **war** between the Syrians and the Hasmoneans, led by Judas the Maccabee. **The saints** involved were the Jews who supported Judas in his revolt against the Syrians. Collins has insisted that the term for **saints** means "angels" instead. The subject of this clause is Antiochus Epiphanes. He surely did not make **war** on the heavenly angels! Collins claimed,

---

[9] C. C. Cargounis, "The Interpretation of the Ten Horns of Daniel 7," *ETL* 63 (1987):106-11.
[10] T. A. Mauet, *Trial Techniques* (United States: Aspen Publishers, Inc., c1996), p. 5.
[11] In Southern Tanzania in the twentieth century whenever the accusation is known by everyone in the court, the defendant is allowed to begin his rebuttal at once. So P. H. Gulliver, "Dispute Settlement without Courts: The Ndendeuli of Southern Tanzania," L. Nader (ed.), *Law in Culture and Society* (Chicago, c1969), pp. 24-59.
[12] C. F. Keil, B*iblical Commentary on the Book of Daniel* tr. M. G. Easton (Grand Rapids: William B. Eerdmans Publishing Co., c1976), p. 267, was one of the scholars who thought the fourth beast was Rome

In recent times, however, the phrase has given rise to extensive debate. The stimulus to this discussion lies in the observation that "holy ones" (קדושים) are usually heavenly beings in the Hebrew Bible and in other West Semitic texts and the realization that this understanding of the word is congenial to the worldview of Daniel.[13]

The word for **saints** is the same as the plural for "holy." There are several exceptions to this universal claim. For example: The Levites are holy (2Chron 35:3). The priests are commanded to be holy (Lev 21:6). The people of Israel are ordered to be holy (Lev 11:44, 45; Lev 19:2; 20:7, 26; Num 15:40). All the members of a congregation are to be holy (Num 16:3). The holy ones in the land are noble (Ps 16:3). When looking for an answer Job asked, **To which of the holy ones will you turn** (Job 5:1)? Was he talking about angels? The people whom God loves are the holy ones who are in his hand (Deut 33:3). Some of the holy ones are male prostitutes (1Kgs 15:12; 2Kgs 23:7). None of these would pass as heavenly angels, but they seem to have passed Collins' observation.

If Collins had demonstrated, rather than claimed, that there were never any holy people in any of the sects of Judaism or Israel and that the term always referred to angels in the FT, then it would be necessary to consider very carefully the use of this term in Dan 7. That clearly is not the case. Hasel has shown that *keh-doh-sheém* and its cognates appear not only in the FT and apocalyptic literature, but also in Akkadian and Ugaritic literature, both in reference to human beings and to heavenly beings.[14] Furthermore Brockelmanns has shown that of the 24 usages of *keh-doh-sheém* in the Dead Sea Scrolls, 13 refer to angels and 11 to human beings.[15]

The word can be applied either to heavenly beings or to human beings, so it does not matter very much whether the term in other documents and in other contexts means "angels" or "saints." It is the context of Dan 7 that is important. That context does not require heavenly beings. Antiochus Epiphanes fought with the Jews (saints) not the angels. His heavenly court trial was against Judas the Maccabee and not Michael or any of the angels.[16] Just because the mythical court trial was conducted in heaven does not mean that the "horn," the "Son of man," or the "saints of the Most High" were heavenly beings. They all belong to the category of human beings.

The court scene in Dan 7 is a unified drama. It is difficult to presume, as Collins did, that any author would compose a drama of a court scene in which the defendant (Antiochus Epiphanes) was an identifiable, historical, human being and the plaintiff (Son of man and the saints) consisted of unidentifiable, unhistorical, heavenly angels. It is still more difficult to imagine, as many scholars do, that an author of dramas would compose a unit in which part of the court scene would be

---

[13] J. J. Collins, *A Commentary on the Book of Daniel* (Minneapolis: Fortress Press, c1993), p. 313.
[14] G. F. Hasel, "The Identity of 'the Saints of the Most High' in Daniel 7," *Bib* 56 (1975):176-85.
[15] C. H. W. Brockelmans, "The Saints of the Most High and their Kingdom," *OS* 14 (1965):319-25.
[16] Contra J. J. Collins, "Son of Man and Saints of the Most High," *JBL* 93 (1974):64.

historical and the other part would be prophecy. Even Collins has admitted that Dan 7 is a unit, just as it is. It cannot be divided into two separate parts. He based this judgment on a comparison of the Canaanite myth in which the sea and the rider on the clouds belong to the same drama.[17] Hasel also holds that Dan 7 is a unified document.[18]

Furthermore the contestants in the court cases cannot be distinguished either. Either the plaintiff and the defendant would both be heavenly angels or both would be identifiable, historical human beings. They cannot be distinguished as two beings that are ontologically different. Collins also found it difficult to make the claim that he did. He said,

> The one point that is difficult to reconcile with the biblical tradition is the juxtaposition of two apparently divine figures, the one like a son of man and the Ancient of Days.[19]

Either the entire unit would be based on history or it all would be prophecy. The only way this could be coherent is to relate the plaintiffs to the defendants in a court scene. It all makes sense relating the court conflict to the historical conflict between the Jews and the Syrians, between Judas the Maccabee and Antiochus Epiphanes.

It is not likely that the author intentionally wrote a drama that was confusing, deceptive, or impossible without signaling in some way to the reader that he or she was doing it. The author made a point of explaining the identification of the characters of the drama (Dan 7:17-27) precisely so that the reader would not be confused. People usually write so that intentional readers can understand the message.

In his refutation of Collins, Beasley-Murray said,

> It seems to me to be evident beyond reasonable doubt that the persecution by Antiochus is in view and that the "saints of the Most High" denote the saints of earth, not of heaven.[20]

Thrones were set up. Many thrones were needed, because the judge in this drama had assistant judges. The text did not identify these further. They may have been members of the heavenly counsel, but they may only have filled the dramatist's need for assistant judges just because there were normally more judges than one to try a case where a death penalty might be given. When the Lord came from Sinai to the temple at Jerusalem he was accompanied with many chariots and troops (Deut 33:2; Ps 68:18).

---

[17] J. J. Collins, "Stirring Up the Great Sea: The Religio-Historical Background of Daniel 7," *The Book of Daniel in the Light of New Findings* (Leuven: University Press, 1993), p. 135.
[18] G. F. Hasel, "The Identity," pp. 176-85.
[19] J. J. Collins, "Stirring," p. 133.
[20] G. R. Beasley-Murray, "The Interpretation of Daniel 7," *CBQ* 43 (1983):53.

The Ancient of Days sat down. The Lord was often pictured as a king or a judge sitting on his throne, ready to begin a court judgment. His responsibility was that of judging the world with righteousness, the nations with fairness (Ps 9:8-9). **Yehowah is seated [on his throne] as king for the age** (Ps 29:11). His throne was established from early times (Ps 93:2). Therefore he was called **the Ancient of Days**. His appearance on the scene is the first clue that we have that all of these beasts were present in a mythical courtroom. The Ancient of Days sat down at the place where the judge belonged. The judge was described in poetry in relationship to his court room surroundings. Charles observed that Clement of Alexandria (Paed ii.10) was the only ancient source who called this figure "one like the Ancient of Days." Nevertheless, he added it to his translation, because he thought it was appropriate.[21] The basic scribes did not. In Ps 55:20, **the Ancient One**, does not have a comparative adverb before it, and the same was the case with the Ancient of Days. In the opinion of the authors and scribes, the heavenly judge involved was really God, not just a figure like God.

TEXT

Daniel	First Testament Intertexts
His clothes were white as snow, / and the hair of his head was like spotless wool. /	2Kgs 2:11 Look! A chariot of **fire** and horses of **fire** separated the two of them, and Elijah went up to heaven in a whirlwind.
His throne was surrounded with fire, / its wheels, **burning fire**. / [10]A river of **fire** took the lead / **and went out before him**. / **A million** [assistants] served him, / and a hundred **million** [court room observers]	Ps 97:2 Clouds and deep darkness surround him; righteousness and justice are the foundation of **his throne**; [3]**fire** **goes before him** and burns up his enemies round about.
	Isa 66:15 Look! Yehowah will come **with fire** and his chariots like storm-wind to turn in the heat of his anger and his rebuke like flames of **fire**, [16]for by **fire** Yehowah will execute judgment.
stood up [in respect] before him. / The court **sat** [in judgment], / and the books [of the contenders] were opened.[11]**I continued watching** then	1Kgs 22:19 I saw Yehowah **sitting on his throne** and all of the army of heaven **standing** alongside at

---

[21] R. H. Charles, *Critical and Exegetical Commentary on the Book of Daniel* (Oxford: Clarendon Press, 1919), pp. 181-82.

because of the sound of many words which the horn was speaking. **I watched** until the beast was killed, his body destroyed, given over to a burning **fire**. ¹² The rest of the beasts' kingdoms were removed, but they were allowed to live for a season and a time.

$^{Deut\ 4:24}$ Yehowah your God is a devouring **fire**.

$^{Ps\ 50:3}$ Our God comes; he will not keep silent. **A fire** consumes **before him**; a mighty tempest surrounds him. ⁴He calls the heaven above and the earth to judge his people.

$^{Ezek\ 1:4}$ A big cloud came from the North, with **flashing fire**, and its brightness **surrounded** it, and at its center was something like burnished bronze in the midst of the **fire**.

TECHNICAL DETAILS

Glasson correctly noted that there are very many verbal identities between Daniel 7 and 1Enoch 14. Both chapters include a vision, a throne, clouds, fire around the throne, many assistants to the one sitting on the throne who was wearing white garments. Glasson correctly concluded that there must be a dependency relationship between these two chapters. He thought 1Enoch was the original upon which Dan was dependent.[22] Glasson's main reason for thinking that Daniel was secondary was that 1Enoch made no mention of Antiochus Epiphanes. Therefore 1Enoch was written before the persecutions of Antiochus IV. Silence is a faulty basis for dating literature. Why does an author omit something from his or her manuscript? Does an author always write everything he or she knows in every document? The author of 1Enoch 14 lived late enough to have known about Nebuchadnezzar and Darius I but he did not mention either one. Why? Many NT writers failed to mention Antiochus IV as well. Glasson has not given an adequate reason for determining which document was the original and which was the secondary manuscript. Some of the factors to consider for dating are:

1. Dan 7:9-14 is a unified poem; *1Enoch* 14.1-25 is prose.
2. Dan 7:9-14 is a throne scene that includes the Son of man. *1Enoch* 14.1-25 has a throne scene without a Son of man.
3. The Son of man in 1Enoch is in a separate chapter (46.1-8). The Son of man in Dan 7:9-14 is the plaintiff in a trial. He was victorious, and his victory provided him authority to judge and rule, but he did not have that authority at the outset.

---

[22] T. F. Glasson, "The Son of God Imagery: Enoch XIV and Daniel VII," *NTS* 23 (1976):82-90.

4. The son of man in *IEnoch* 46.1-9 was an authorized judge and ruler who had authority to function. This means this poem came later than the poem in Dan 7, because it presumed the results of the earlier judgment scene.

Therefore it is more likely that Dan 7 is the original composition than *IEnoch* 14.1-25 and 46.1-8.

COMMENTARY

His clothes were white as snow. White was held to be the color of purity. Some monks and priests wore white when they entered sacred areas, such as the altar or the holy meal. Sokoloff has called attention to a variant text that would read "lamb's wool," rather than "spotless wool."[23] The message would be the same with either translation.

His throne was surrounded with fire. Fire, smoke, and cloud were symbols of the deity. God was believed to be present in all of these. Moses received the commandments on Mount Sinai under the cover of a cloud. Jesus was transfigured before his apostles on a mountain covered by a cloud (Matt 17:4). God accompanied the Israelites through the wilderness as a pillar of cloud by day and a pillar of fire by night (Exod 13:21; 14:19, 24). God spoke to his people out of the midst of the fire (Deut 5:4). A fire went before him and scorched his enemies (Ps 97:3). At his right hand was a flaming fire (Deut 33:2). The fire symbol was the clue to the reader that this scene was a heavenly scene in which God was the presiding judge.

Dan 7 is not a lesson plan for legal court proceedings in which all necessary steps of the procedure are included, together with instructions for proper ritual. Instead it is a visionary report, using those parts that were necessary for the drama. For example, no description was given in Daniel of the way the judge's presence was announced to those who were in the courtroom, but it has long been a custom in courts to announce the arrival of the judge. Today in the United States Supreme Court, for instance, before the judges enter the court room, at precisely the right moment, the marshal taps his gavel and calls all those present to stand and give their attention to the hearings that are about to follow. He then taps his gavel again and tells the people to be seated and come to order. This happens only after the judges are seated in their respective places.[24] Today, in lower courts, the clerk or bailiff announces the arrival of the judge in a courtroom and tells all the people present to rise and come to order.

A million [assistants] served him. In many courtrooms judges had a few assistants, such as secretaries, bailiffs, and legal counselors, but the huge number

---

[23] M. Sokoloff, "'*amar neqe*,' Lamb's Wool (Dan 7:9)," *JBL* 95 (1976):277-79.

[24] The marshal begins his call for attention with the words, "O yea! O yea! O yea!" without knowing that the expression comes from the French, "Hear!" (*oyez*--second person plural of the French verb *ouïr*). American courts inherited the expression from the English, who learned it from the French.

of assistants suggests the divine dimensions. See Deut 33:2. These were members of the Lord's council.

A hundred million stood up [in respect] before him. These were not angelic attendants accompanying the Son of man, as Justin thought (Justin, *Apol* 1.31). The Ancient of Days had assistants who might also have been considered attendants, but they belonged to the Ancient of Days and not to the Son of man. There were 1,000,000 of these but the 100,000,000 who stood as the Ancient of Days approached the bench were the observers who were present in court.

It is still considered court etiquette for everyone in the courtroom to stand up when the judge enters the courtroom. In a normal court room procedure in the USA, the bailiff or the clerk of court announces to everyone in the room that the judge is about to approach the bench, and everyone is required to arise and be silent. All remain standing in silence until the judge is seated, and people are told that they should be seated and give their attention to the honorable court. This tradition is very old and is evidenced in the scripture. The following is an exhortation for silence before the presence of the Lord in a court situation.

> The Lord is in his holy temple!
> Hush, before him all the land (Hab 2:20).

In this mythical kingdom, the judge was apparently seated in heaven, and the entire area constituted the court. How big was the area? The text does not say. It may have been the entire Promised Land or, more likely, the entire Near East, because all the people involved in the judgment were thought to have been present in the mythical court. Since the contest was between the Syrian Greeks and the Palestinian Jews, those involved in the court case were probably all of the Syrian Greeks and all of the Palestinian Jews. Many scholars agree with Hartman, who mistakenly said, "Without the slightest doubt, the figures here are angels."[25]

The court sat. This means that the Ancient of Days and the assistant judges all **sat** just as **the Lord sat on his throne** (Isa 6:1; 1Kgs 22:19), so that **court** procedure might continue. The thrones indicated exalted social status. Others in the **court** room either stood or sat on the ground or on the floor as Muslims do when they attend services at a mosque. The scene in Daniel began as thrones were set up in preparation for the arrival of the heavenly judge and his assistants.[26] The judge (the Ancient of Days or God) approached the bench and sat down. He was

---

[25] Hartman, *Daniel*, p. 94. The reason for this conclusion, of course, is that the court took place in heaven where there are supposed to be only angels. This is not as obvious as Hartman thought. When David was king of Israel, living on earth, he was claimed to have served in the counsel of God (Acts 13:36), and the Son of man in this chapter was evidently a human being who could be present in this mythical court. In mythology, the citizens of all the countries involved could also participate in the heavenly court case by fighting and suffering for their faith on earth.
[26] S. Mowinckel, *He that Cometh* (New York: Abingdon Press, c1954), p. 352, thought the chairs were for both the Ancient of Days and for the Son of man to come and assist in the judgment, but Mowinckel failed to notice that the Son of man was a plaintiff in this case, and therefore he could not also act as judge.

wearing a white robe, and flames of fire surrounded his throne. Although Daniel did not say that the marshal, clerk, or bailiff announced the Lord's arrival at the bench, and no call for attention like that given in Habakkuk was quoted, asking people in the courtroom either to stand or be silent, Daniel told of the response: **A hundred million stood up before him** (Dan 7:10). This suggests that the author of the myth was acquainted with court procedure that included the announcement that the judge was approaching the bench, and the people present were told to rise, as they were pictured as having done. It also implies that the original readers knew enough about **court** cases that the author did not have to retard the movement of the narrative to include all the details that took place.

The books [of the contenders] were opened. After the judge and all of the people had been seated (Dan 7:10), the next part of the agenda would have been for the judge to review the briefs of the contestants in court. This action was reported by the statement, **The books [of the participants] were opened** (Dan 7:10). Rabbis said that on New Year's Day **the books are opened** and fates recorded (b*RhShen* 16b). Rabbis said, "Know what is above you--a seeing eye and a hearing ear, and all your deeds are written in a **book**" (m*Aboth* 2.1). The Assyrians, the Babylonians, and Canaanites all celebrated New Year's Day festivals. These were related to the coronations and judgment liturgies. There are several small details of Dan 7 that resemble one or more of the other liturgies. There were evidently some mythology, art, birth omens, and liturgical forms that were in the air and could be used independently by authors from different nations.[27] There is not enough similarity to indicate direct liturgical borrowing. **Books** are part of the standard court materials that belong to any court trial.

The **books** mentioned in Dan 7, however, **were opened** before the trial, so they seem to have been lawyers' briefs rather than "**books** of the living ones," which would have come at the end of the trial as part of the verdict. Second Baruch looked forward to a judgment day when the **books** of all those who had sinned would **be opened**. At the same time all the treasuries in which the righteous were stored would be brought to trial as evidence (*2Bar* 24.1), but no one would know until that time what would happen to the enemies of the righteous. That would become apparent in the trial (*2Bar* 24.3-4). The **books** and the souls of the righteous were all brought to the trial as data to persuade the judge. The **books**, then, like the books in Dan 7:10, would have been the lawyers' briefs with the accusations presented to the judge before the trial.

The many words which the horn was speaking. The "horn" was one of the descendants of the political leaders who followed the fourth beast, namely Antiochus IV Epiphanes. Here he had spoken extensively in his own defense.

The beast was killed. Mythically, this means the **beast's** arguments in his own defense were not convincing to the judge who gave him a death sentence, decreeing further that his body should be burned. This addition was made because of the reference in the intertext to flaming fire. This intertext from Ezekiel, on the

---

[27] Lucas, "The Source," p.175.

one hand, motivated the description of the chariot that brought the Ancient of Days to the scene, and on the other hand, it led to the description of the death of Antiochus. Antiochus IV died shortly before or shortly after the victories of Beth-horon and possibly Beth-zur, just a few months before Hanukkah. This scene took place after that event.

The exact order of events and times is not clear. Many important things happened in a very short space, and it is not possible to be sure of the chronological order. According to 1Macc Hanukkah followed the Battle of Beth-zur, but according to 2Macc, after the victory of Beth-horon the general Nicanor fled to Antioch. The death of Antiochus occurred just before or just after that event.[28] Hanukkah followed the Battle of Beth-horon, and the Battle of Beth-zur was fought after Hanukkah when Antiochus V was king.

Doran noted that Timothy was reported to have been **killed** in 2Macc 10:37 and then reappeared in 2Macc 12:2. He suggested that these narratives have been misplaced, chronologically, and that 2Macc 12 really belongs, chronologically, before 2Macc 10:14-38. If these units are switched, the Battle of Beth-zur would occur before Hanukkah during the reign of Antiochus IV.[29] Although the Battle of Beth-zur was important, the crucial battle was the Battle of Beth-horon. Josephus said the victory at Beth-horon contributed "not a little" to the regaining of freedom (*Ant* 12.312).

At the same sentence (Dan 7:12), the first three beasts were allowed to survive, but their kingdoms were removed. Walters correctly said,

> There is no need for chapter seven to do more than deal with the fourth, which must therefore be whatever kingdom follows Persia, the kingdom of chapter six.[30]

The beast that was condemned in this trial was not the Syrian Empire, as Driver suggested, but the king of that empire.[31] It was not the empire, but the king, who was given a death sentence and burned with fire. This court trial was a mythical way of reporting a historical event--the death of Antiochus Epiphanes. He left the Promised Land to obtain more funds to support his military program. He went to Elymais where there was a temple containing a huge amount of gold and silver.

---

[28] According to A. J. Sachs and D. J. Wiseman (trs.),"A Seleucid King List," *Ancient Near Eastern Texts*, ed. J. B. Pritchard (Princeton: Princeton University Press, 1969), p. 567, Antiochus died in the month of Kisilmu, which is the same month as Hanukkah. The text does not say which year. It might have been the year before Hanukkah and before the Battles of Beth-horon and Beth-zur, after which Lysias fled to Antioch (*Ant* 12.315). Otherwise it would have occurred just before Hanukkah. Second Maccabees did not name the place of battle, but he told of the battle of Judas with Nicanor, after which Nicanor fled back to Antioch (2Macc 8:34-35). "At about that time" he described the death of Antiochus (2Macc 9:1-7). This, then, was followed by the purification of the temple (2Macc 10:1-5). The Battle of Beth-zur happened after the purification of the temple (2Macc 11:1-13). According to First Maccabees, however, it was after the Battle of Beth-zur that the Syrian general, Lysias, retreated to Antioch and plans were begun for the purification and dedication of the temple (1Macc 4:34-61).

[29] R. Doran, "2 Maccabees and 'Tragic History,'" *HUCA* 50 (1979):107-114.

[30] S. D. Walters, "The End (of What?) is at Hand," *TJT* 2 (1986):33.

[31] S. R. Driver, *The Book of Daniel* (Cambridge: University Press, 1912), p. 87.

He expected to conquer it and take its wealth, but he was defeated. He was called "Epiphanes," which means "manifest," "incarnate," or the legal agent of the deity.[32] Since he held this high office, he assumed that all of the money in all of the temples devoted to the deity of his empire belonged to him. Therefore he was justified in raiding them when he wished.

He became ill while he was either in Nanaea (2Macc 2:13-17) or in Elymais (1Macc 6:1-13) and died. He reportedly confessed that his misfortunes were caused by the wicked deeds he had performed in Jerusalem (1Macc 6:8-13; *Ant* 12.357-59). That was the Jewish interpretation. Josephus acknowledged, however, that Polybius thought the cause of Antiochus' death was his desire to defile the temple of Artemis (Polybius 31.9). Different historians make different judgments about these things. He probably did not make a confession at all. The fact that he died proved to the author of this story that God had decreed in the heavenly court that he should be killed and his body should be burned.

The rest of the beasts' kingdoms. These were **the kingdoms** of Babylon, Media, and Persia. At the time of this heavenly trial all of these **kingdoms** were hidden under the rule of the Seleucids, but they had not lost their identity. The author simply summarized them to show that they existed, but they were not primarily important to this trial. They continued to exist but not as great empires. They were no longer sovereign nations. They were subject to the fourth beast until the battles of Beth-horon and Beth-zur. Strabo, Herodotus, and Xenophon referred to these countries just as if they were still independent lands. The author of Dan 7 did not tell what happened in history to make one of these countries submit to succession by another, so Reid thought that meant

> Succession of the four world empires in Dan 7:2-7 is dependent, not on combat, but on the demise of the predecessor.[33]

Anyone who knows the history of these empires, however, knows that one empire did not just wait around to be taken over by another. Babylon was taken with the least military activity of all, but there were violent wars among these countries. The author of Dan 7 did not mention the events of all of these wars, because that was all past history and readers would have known it. The author was no pacifist; he believed that the Lord of armies had directed the wars in such a way that Israel would win.

The judgment proclaimed that all four countries would vanish, sooner or later. With the death of Antiochus IV the disintegration of these kingdoms had begun. They were destined to continue for a short time under pagan rule, but after a while the Hasmonean government that ruled over Palestine would also extend

---

[32] Antiochus was not the only king who thought of himself as an agent of the deity. Anarchus the sophist told Alexander the Great that justice sat on the throne of Zeus so that whatever Zeus did was held to be just, and that whatever was done by a great king should be considered just (Arrian, *Anabasis* 4.8, 7). Alexander the Great claimed that he was the son of Zeus (Arrian, *Anabasis* 7.2, 3; further 7:29, 3).

[33] S. B. Reid, *Enoch and Daniel* (Berkeley: BIBAL Press, c1989), p. 82.

its borders to include all of these. The empire was beginning to be passed on to Palestine. In the future the Jews would rule the large empire that had been controlled at one time by the Persians and later by the Greeks. That was all part of this trial, in the judgment of the author. After the success of the Battle of Beth-horon and possibly Beth-zur, the author visualized the future of Palestine as a successor to the line of huge empires in the Middle East. First there was Assyria (which Daniel overlooked), then Media, followed by Persia, which was followed by Greece.

Alexander had begun his campaign by defeating the Persian forces at Hellespont in 334 BIA. He annexed all of Asia Minor by November, 333 BIA. He conquered Tyre, Palestine and Egypt in 332 BIA In 331 he crossed the Euphrates and overthrew Persia at Arbela, east of Nineveh. He then took Babylon and Susa, and then crossed the Indus in 327 BIA and subjugated the adjoining territory.[34] In twelve years and eight months Alexander moved his entire empire from a city-state in Macedonia to a vast empire that included part of India. Jews in Hasmonean times visualized a similar expansion from Jerusalem. The image in Dan 2 of the rock that crushed all four parts of the statue claimed that all four empires were destroyed at once. They were not, but the image was such that it would have been difficult to have the rock fall selectively or slowly, so as to crush only certain empires or just one at a time.

The fifth **kingdom** to rule the area from Asia Minor to India, in the judgment of the author, would be Judah. The author did not live to see this take place, because it never happened. History did not follow exactly as the author thought it would. All of these nations that the author of Daniel thought would soon be subject to Jerusalem instead became subject to Rome. Rome was really the fifth great **kingdom** in succession, as later Roman historians claimed.

Jews did not give up the expectation that some day they would become the fifth great nation to rule the world from India to some point in the west. There continued to be rebellions against Rome led by various Jewish and Christian terrorists. It was not until the fourth century IA, when Constantine became emperor of Rome with the aid of Christians, that Christians believed that the vision of Dan 7 had been achieved. That was when the Holy Roman Empire began, and Christian Church fathers wrote about this victory just as the author of Dan 7 wrote about the victory of Beth-horon and possibly Beth-zur. Rome became the new Jerusalem, and Christians were the new saints of the Most High. The old age of the beasts was over. The age to come had come. One sect of Jews (Christians) negotiated with Constantine just as another sect of Jews had earlier negotiated with Cyrus of Persia.

This was the eschatological fulfillment of Daniel according to Christians, just as Beth-horon and Beth-zur constituted the eschatological fulfillment for Jews at an earlier date. In both cases the end of the age of beasts had come; the new age had arrived. In each instance the expectation was only for further expansion of the age that had already arrived. Neither the Jews after Beth-horon and Beth-zur nor the Christians after Constantine looked forward to the end of the cosmos or of

---

[34] So Driver, *Daniel*, pp. 113-114.

time. Why would anyone want that to happen? Daniel was composed as a victory drama--not a lamentation.

TEXT

¹³I kept on observing in the visions of the night--now look!

Daniel	First Testament Intertexts
With the **clouds** of heaven **came**	ᴱᶻᵉᵏ ¹:⁴ A big **cloud came** from the North, with flashing fire, and its brightness surrounded it, and at its center was something like burnished bronze in the midst of the fire.
	ᴾˢ ⁹⁷:¹⁻² Rejoice! Yehowah is king. Let the land rejoice. Let many islands be happy. A **cloud** and thick darkness surrounds him. Righteousness and justice are the dwelling place of his throne.
	ᴵˢᵃ ¹⁹:¹ Look! Yehowah is riding on a swift **cloud**. He is going to Egypt.
one like a Son of man (כבר אנש), / He came to the Ancient of Days, / and they presented him [the son of man] before him [the Ancient of Days]. /	ᴱᶻᵉᵏ ¹:⁵ From its midst was something like four beasts, and this was their appearance, **like** that **man** (אדם)
	ᴱᶻᵉᵏ ¹:²⁶ Above the firmament which was over their heads was something like the appearance of sapphire stone, like a throne, and upon the appearance of the throne was **something like the appearance of a man** (אדם) on it.
	ᴱᶻᵉᵏ ⁸:² Look! Something **like the appearance of a man** (איש)

¹⁴To him [the Son of man] was given ruling authority,
    power, and a kingdom,
and all peoples, nations, and languages would serve him.
His ruling authority was a ruling authority of an age,
    that would not pass away,
        and his kingdom would not be destroyed.

COMMENTARY

I kept on observing in the visions. This was an interruption to remind the reader that this was all a **vision**, and the author was writing a myth, a play which dramatized a teaching that had recent historical facts as its basis.

With the clouds of heaven. **The clouds of heaven** were symbols of God. They were present wherever God's presence was known--on Mount Sinai (Exod 24:15-16), when the 70 elders were authorized (Num 11:25) on the Mount of Transfiguration (Matt 17:5), and in the pillar of fire and cloud which led the Israelites through the wilderness (Exod 14:24). Fletcher-Louis said,

> On Mount Sinai, God appears in a **cloud**, Exod. 24:16-17, just as God speaks to Jesus from a **cloud**. Both Moses and Jesus are the only humans to enter the cloud.[35]

Fletcher-Louis overlooked the Danielic Son of man, the Maccabee who entered the **cloud** and appeared before the Ancient of Days after the Battle of Beth-horon and possibly Beth-zur.

Mendenhall has shown that the "**clouds**" imagery is related to the ancient symbol of the winged sun disk that indicated the manifestations, glory, power, and dignity of gods like Re, Horus, Zeus, Ahura Mazda, and Baal Shamem.[36] In some ancient art, the winged sun disk provides a frame for the king himself, with his bow and arrow drawn against the enemy. This winged disk was held to precede the kings into battle to terrorize and destroy the enemy. Victory scenes showed the king coming back with booty with the flying sun disk nearby. This flying disk was the manifestation of the deity's power and was frequently related to victorious kings. It was also reflected in the famous Israelite victory poem, after Jael had pounded a tent stake through Sisera's temples: **So may all your enemies perish, O Lord, but your friends like the sun [disk] rising in its power** (Judges 5:31). The rabbis applied Judges 5:31 to the sons of Mattathias, the priest, who stood firm, and their enemies perished before them (*ExodR* 15.6). When the Assyrians lost their power over Israel, the cloud (*ah-náhn*, ענן) of the Assyrian king came and rested on the Judaic king, Josiah.[37]

---

[35] C. Fletcher-Louis, "4Q374: A Discourse on the Sinai Tradition: The Deification of Moses and Early Christology," *DS* 3(1996):252.
[36] See also J. K. Hoffmeier, "Son of God: from Pharaoh to Israel's Kings to Jesus," *BR* (June, 1997):44-49, 54, and P. G. Mosca, "Ugarit and Daniel 7: A Missing Link," *Bib* 67 (1986):496-517.
[37] G. E. Mendenhall, *The Tenth Generation* (Baltimore: Johns Hopkins University Press, c1973), pp. 32-66, 210-11. A. Feuillet, "Le Fils de l'Homme de Daniel et la Tradition Biblique," *RB* 60 (1963):187, observed that the cloud frequently accompanies theophanies, but whenever angels are present, the cloud is absent (cf. Dan 8:15; 9:21; 10:5-16). A. LaCocque, *The Book of Daniel* tr. D. Pellauer (Atlanta: John Knox Press, 1979), p. 146, noticed that there are about a hundred references to clouds in the Hebrew Scripture. In 70% of these cases, the clouds refer either to Sinai or the temple.

Artwork by Norma Creel

© British Museum

The Hebrew *ah-náhn*, which is usually rendered **clouds**, played the same role for Hebrews that the flying disk did for other Near Eastern political powers. It was this *ah-nahn* which went before and behind the children of Israel when they crossed the sea. It had as its religious equivalent, the Hebrew *mah-láhk* (מלאך), which is a messenger, angel, or agent. The *ah-nahn* was transferred from Sinai to the tent of meeting and finally to Solomon's temple. It was associated with Moses and Solomon. Maccabees expected the kind of divine help that was normally associated with the sun disk, cloud, or angels. Judas and his followers entered into battle, **with the Lord going before them** (2Macc 10:1), just as the Lord had done when the Hebrews crossed the sea (Exod 14:19). In one of their battles a horse with a fearful rider wearing a golden suit of armor supporting the Jews in battle, was seen charging at the enemy (2Macc 3:25; *1QM* 12.8). In the myth of Dan 7 the cloud accompanied Judas in his victory at Beth-horon and possibly Beth-zur and was reestablished at the dedication of the temple about three years after the temple had been defiled.

The Son of man came before the Ancient of Days in or **with the clouds of heaven** just after Judas the Maccabee had won the famous battle of Beth-horon and possibly Beth-zur. The mythologist believed that the Lord's *ah-nahn* was present with Judas in that battle, so he symbolized it by showing Judas, as one like a Son of man, coming with the *ah-nahn* of **heaven**, just as Egyptian, Assyrian, and other ancient Near Eastern kings came home from battle with the flying sun disk in the sky just above them. This symbolized the divine presence and authority with the victorious leader--here Judas. Just as other ancient artists presented kings with drawn bows inside the sun disk frame, so the mythological artist of Dan 7 presented Judas arriving at the judgment scene with the *ah-nahn* or framed in the *ah-nahn*. In this court session the one like a Son of man became the Son of God and God's agent, who the Ancient of Days decreed would receive the kingdom, power, and glory. Jews believed that it was God who gave Judas his victories, and they went into war confident that God's presence would go before him, striking down his enemies, no matter how many there were. Therefore the presence of Judas before the Ancient of Days in a cloud was fitting symbolism. The Ancient of Days is a euphemism for God, the one who was enthroned of old (Ps 55:20).

The mythologists deliberately described the rule of the foreign power that governed the Jews from the first invasion of Jerusalem by Nebuchadnezzar in 605 BIA to 164 BIA as leaders under the control of demonic powers. They came up from the great deep, but the new kingdom Judas was establishing was pictured as having come with the power and authority from **Heaven.** It came from the Ancient of Days and was accompanied with the Lord's *ah-nahn*. This *ah-nahn* is often accompanied by fire, lightning, and thunder. Here the *ah-nahn* might be part of the atmosphere associated with the flames of fire that surrounded the seat of the Ancient of Days. When Moses went up Mount Sinai to receive the commandments, the mountain was wrapped in smoke, (or a cloud) and the Lord descended in the fire (Exod 19:18-20). The Lord was present in the pillar of cloud and fire at the tent of meeting (Exod 33:7-11).[38] On the Mount of Transfiguration, the Lord announced through the cloud that Jesus was his Son (Luke 9:34-35). In Daniel's judgment scene the fire and clouds were probably added to let the reader know that God was present in this entire judgment, and his influence surrounded, not only the throne, but also the one for whom the verdict was pronounced, Judas as one like a Son of man.

Came one like a Son of man. Gunkel and Gressmann thought that the Ancient of Days and the **Son of man** narrative were patterned after a Babylonian New Year's festival and enthronement ceremony.[39] This would imply that the Son of man became a king through this judgment ceremony. Emerton, however, believed that the origin of this drama comes from Canaanite New Year's festivals.[40] Rabbis said that on New Year's Day the books are opened and fates recorded (*RhShen* 16b). These may all be correct in thinking that the judgment scene involved in Dan 7 involves an enthronement event. If it does it would imply that the author of Dan 7 was trying to communicate to his readers that Judas was divinely enthroned as king. Even though the Seleucids never acknowledged it, God had made Judas king of Israel. Earlier kings, such as David and Saul, had been anointed in secret.[41] The exaltation of **the Son of man** was not prophecy. It was fulfillment. **The Son of man** was not a group of saints, as some scholars have held. Keil correctly said,

---

[38] See also J. VanderKam, "The Theophany of Enoch 1.3b-7, 9," ZAW 23 (1973):129-50; F. Schnutenhaus, "Das Kommen und Erscheinin Gottes im Alten Testament," *ZAW* 76 (1964):3; P. D. Miller, Jr., "Fire in the Mythology of Canaan and Israel," *CBQ* 27 (1965):256-61. F. Cumont said that in Mazdean faith legitimate kings rule by the will of the supreme god, and they are given a special divine grace, called *Hvareno*. This did not make the king a god, but it provided him a unique destiny and supernatural power. Cf. F. Cumont, "Mithra," *Dict. des antiquities grecques et romaines*, ed. Daremberg and Saglio; *Les religions orientales dans le repandit dans paganisme romain* (Paris, 1929), pp. 131 ff.; and *Les mysteres de Mithra*, (Dover: Dover Publications, 1956), pp. 91-96. M. Rissi, *The Future of the World* (Naperville: Allenson, 1972.), p. 19, said the white cloud was a sign of the parousia.
[39] H.Gunkel, *Schöpfung und Chaos* (Göttingen: Vandenhoeck & Ruprecht, 1895), pp. 327-28 and H. Gressmann, *Der Messias* (Göttingen: Vandenhoeck & Ruprecht, 1929), p. 153.
[40] J. A. Emerton, "The Origin of the Son of Man Imagery," *JTS* 9 (1958):230-34, 38.
[41] For further details of these anointings see Buchanan, *The Gospel of Matthew* (Lewiston: The Edwin Mellen Press, c1996) I, pp. 146-53.

But the delivering of the kingdom to the people of God does not, according to the prophetic mode of contemplation, exclude the Messiah as its king, but much rather includes Him, inasmuch as Daniel, like the other prophets, knows nothing of a kingdom without a head, a Messianic kingdom without the King Messiah.[42]

Mowinckel was one of those who thought that the Son of man was a symbol of the saints of the Most High, namely the people of Israel.[43] Sahlin took issue with Mowinckel. He held that there was nothing in the text to indicate that the **Son of man** was a personification of the Saints of the Most High.[44] Sahlin thought the **Son of man** was the angel Michael. For support of his position he noted in 1Enoch that there were similar things done by Michael and by the **Son of man**. Therefore the two were identical. He overlooked the logic of high school geometry: 1) objects that are similar to the same object are similar to each other.[45] 2) Objects that are equal to the same object are equal to each other. He took the data of rule 1 to prove rule 2. According to his logic, things that are similar to the same object are equal to each other. It is true that the Son of man was said to have some of the same kind of legal authority as Michael and some of the other angels. It is legally possible for a principal, in this case God, to have many agents. Each legal agent is legally identical to the principal so far as his or her assignment or area of authority is concerned. Sahlin knew this. He called attention to the fact that the angels Raphael, Gabriel, Michael, and Phanuel had different responsibilities.[46] They were all God's legal agents but they were not identical, and it would be absurd to think the Son of man was identical to all of them just because the Son of man and all four angels were legal agents.

Mosca compared the mythical character of Baal in Ugaritic studies to the mythical character of the **Son of man** in Dan 7:28. He thought the hyperbolic way Baal was divined was also the way David was referred to as the **most high and first born Son** of God in Ps 89.[47] It is true that there are points of comparison between Baalism and the religion of Israel. For both, Canaan is the land of life. For both the great sea is the spawning ground for the enemy. For both the deity had heavenly attendants. This does not mean that the Son of man was the same as Baal. There were some differences. The Son of man did not die as Baal did, according to the texts. He was not associated with the weather or the cycle of the year as Baal was. There are also differences of contexts.

---

[42] Keil, *Daniel*, p. 235. M. Girard, "Le Lemblant de Fils d'homme de Daniel 7, un personnage du monde d'en haut: approche structurelle," *Science et Esprit* 35 (1983):265-96, thought the saints of the Most High were angels, but they did not constitute the Son of man. The Son of man was the leader of this group. He said the leader of this group was much greater than angels, although thoroughly human.

[43] Mowinkel, *He That Cometh*, p. 350.

[44] H. Sahlin, "Wie Wurde Ursprünglich die Benennung 'Der Menschensohn' Verstanden?" *STh* 37 (1983):149.

[45] Sahlin, "Ursprünglich," pp. 156-57.

[46] Sahlin, "Ursprünglich," pp. 157-60.Following this logic, Sahlin also thought Jesus and Michael were identical (pp. 162-63, 174-76). According to this logic there could be many others who are identical to Michael.

[47] Mosca, "Ugarit, pp. 496-517.

Morgenstern said the saints of the Most High constituted the Jewish people, and the Son of man in Daniel was a god, patterned after the ancient Tyrian national deity, Ba'al shamem-Melcarth. The ceremony of Dan 7 would have taken place at the equinoctial New Year's Day (Dec. 18) in which the king played the role of god.[48] This would imply that the Jewish king, like Solomon, was not a god but an agent of God. He would have been Judas the Maccabee, and the solar ceremony would have taken place on Hanukkah. At that time the Ancient of Days gave the Son of man the kingship. Morgenstern, however, also thought this ceremony was a New Year's Day judgment scene. In Hasmonean times New Year's Day was celebrated in the autumn, usually in October. Gammie correctly noticed that texts from the scripture are more important for gaining insights into Daniel than the literature of Ugarit or Qumran.[49]

It is not necessary to look to the Chaldean Ea-Oannes, Enun Elish, Baal Shamem, Shaoshyant, Gayomart, or any of the other Babylonian, Tyrian, Canaanite, or Iranian mythological characters to learn what or who the Son of man was as it is used in Dan 7. None of them provided the source in which the author obtained this title.[50] The author of Dan 7 found his intertext in the Book of Ezekiel.

It is true that Hebrews, Israelites, and Jews used mythological concepts that were used by other peoples in the Near East. For example, the author of the poem in Exod 15 was familiar with concepts like "Leviathan" and "the great deep," but that was not the major point of the poem. The poet's main interest was the deliverance of the Israelites from the Egyptians at the border of Egypt. Some of the same mythology was used in Ps 74, but that poet's basic source was Exod 15, and his major concern was the destruction of Jerusalem with its temple. He was lamenting that tragedy.[51] In the same way, the author of Dan 7 relied principally on Ezekiel for his source material. That was the text on which he based his homily. In his vision of the altar in the temple at Jerusalem Ezekiel mentioned both beasts and a human being, so Dan 7 commented on both of these.

The author of Dan 7 used Ezek 1 which, in turn, was based on Isa 6. Isa 6 pictured the Lord on the throne accompanied by seraphim that had wings, feet, and faces. The whole temple scene was filled with a cloud. Ezekiel described this scene in greater detail than Isaiah did, and when he did so, he changed its meaning. The seraphim became beasts that had wings, feet, and faces, just as the seraphim did[52]. The cloud that filled the temple in Isaiah became a cloud from the

---

[48] J. Morgenstern, "'The Son of Man' of Daniel 7:13 f.: A New Interpretation," *JBL* 80 (1961):65-77.

[49] J. G. Gammie, "On the Intention and Sources of Daniel I-VI," *VT* 31 (1981):283.

[50] As H. L. Jansen, *Die Henochgestalt* (Oslo: I Kommisjon Hos Jacob Dybwad, 1939), p. 105, contended. For a survey of the various mythological concepts that different scholars have used to interpret the "Son of man" figure in Dan 7 see J. J. Collins, *A Commentary on the Book of Daniel* (Minneapolis: Fortress Press, 1993), pp. 280-94.

[51] For the justification of these claims see Buchanan, *Introduction to Intertextuality* (Lewiston: The Edwin Mellen Press, c1994), pp. 70-84.

[52] The Assyrian text (VAT 10057) also included beasts in its liturgy, but the beasts were not kings. They were gods. The author of Dan 7, if he knew of VAT 10057, may intentionally have reinterpreted the seraphim of Isa 6 to become kings to prevent seraphims' possible confusion with gods. See Lucas, "Source," p. 169.

North in Ezekiel. The coals of fire in Isaiah became something like moving torches in Ezekiel. The Lord seated on his throne (Isa 6:1) became something like a human being in Ezek, sitting on something like a throne (Ezek 1:26). This was not the only time Ezekiel redefined his terms when using texts.

Ezekiel often made such changes as this. For example Jeremiah expanded Ps 1. Ps 1 told **of a tree planted by water. It produces its fruit in its season, and its leaf will not wither** (Ps 1:3). That meant that it would never dry out, but would be productive every year. Jeremiah paraphrased that to say that it would never cease producing fruit (Jer 17:9), although he meant the same as Ps 1 did. Ezekiel took Jeremiah's words, **never cease producing fruit**, to mean that the tree would produce fruit every month of the year and that this tree would grow in the Kidron Valley nourished by the water that came from the temple (Ezek 47:12). It was on the basis of Ezek 47 that Jesus came looking for figs out of season (Matt 21:18-22).[53]

The expression **one like** was used to inform the reader that this was mythical, visionary language. It did not mean the character in the drama was a heavenly being who was only like a human being, as many scholars have thought.[54] The authors resorted to metaphorical language, because they were not trying to describe anything scientifically. This whole judgment scene was one that took place in the author's mind. This is the same type of language that Ezekiel used when he saw a vision of God (*mahr-óht eh-loh-heém*, מראות אלהים) (Ezek 1:1). He described this vision by using the following expressions: **something like four beasts, something like a human being** (Ezek 1:26; 8:2**), like the sole of the foot of a cow** (Ezek 1:7**), like the face of a human being** (Ezek 1:10**), like the beasts was their appearance, like the flames of fire burning was like the appearance of torches** (Ezek 1:13). In the same way, the author of Dan 7 used mythic terms when he described the main character in his vision as **one like a Son of man**.[55]

Using Ezek 1 as an intertext, the author of Rev 4:4-8 pictured the throne scene more explicitly than Ezekiel did. He described a huge basin in the temple, which he called "**something like a glassy sea**" that was supported by four beings, functioning as legs of a table.[56] According to Ezekiel there were four monsters, each one of which was like a sphinx. Each had parts of cows, lions, eagles, and human beings. The author of Dan 7, however, took these words from Ezekiel and separated them into separate beasts.

---

[53] Buchanan, "Withering Fig Trees and Progression in Midrash," C. A. Evans and J.A. Sanders (eds.), *Studies in Scripture in Early Judaism and Christianity* (Sheffield: Sheffield Academic Press, c1994), pp. 249-69; *Matthew* I, pp. 816-18.

[54] Such as Keil, *Daniel*, p. 234.

[55] Several scholars have suggested that the expression "Son of man" comes from the Persian savior "Saoshyant," but it seems unnecessary to go that far afield in search of a meaning that reflects an intertext from Ezekiel.

[56] See further Buchanan, *Revelation: Its Introduction and Prophecy* (Lewiston: The Edwin Mellen Press, c1993), pp. 134-40.

A Modern "Sea" in the Court of the Lions in Spain

Ezekiel described the Isaianic seraphim as sphinx-like beings that had body parts like different beasts, domestic animals, and birds. The author of Dan 7 took the parts of beasts to be individual beasts, some of which were not mentioned in Ezek 1. The author of Dan 7 identified three of the beasts. The lion was Babylon; the bear was Media; the leopard was Persia. The fourth beast, which was too monstrous to be compared to a known beast, was Greece. All of the beasts that held up that basin were foreign nations. Isa 6 said it was **the Lord** that was sitting **on the throne**. Ezek 1 interpreted this to mean **something like a man** sitting **on a throne**. The author of Dan 7, however, knew from Isa 6 that the one seated **on the throne** was not one **like a human** being. It was **the Lord**, so he corrected Ezekiel and called the one sitting **on the throne the Ancient of Days**. The one that Ezekiel described as one who was **something like a human being** sitting **on the throne,** the author of Dan 7 placed in a different role. Instead of one sitting **on the throne,** he became one **like a Son of man**, the plaintiff who came with the **clouds** before **the Ancient of Days,** who was sitting **on the throne**. The **cloud** that filled the temple in Isa 6 which Ezekiel took to be a **cloud** coming from the North, Dan 7 interpreted to be the **cloud** that accompanied the one **like a Son of man** as he approached the bench before **the Ancient of Days**.

Ezekiel spoke in visionary terms describing the temple in Jerusalem, where God's presence dwelled. The word "sea" does not appear in Ezek 1, but Jeremiah said there was a bronze sea in the temple that the Babylonians broke into pieces and carried away to Babylon (Jer 52:17). Like the author of Dan 7, the author of Rev 4 used Ezek 1 as an intertext while describing a heavenly temple scene, which, of course, would resemble the temple at Jerusalem. In a similar description of the temple there was a **glassy sea like a crystal** (Rev 4:6), apparently held up by four beasts. This may have been the name for the basin in the throne room of the temple. Ezekiel described the firmament that was above the beasts as **shining like a crystal** (Ezek 1:22).

The author of Dan 7 seems to have understood that the basin involved was called a sea, and he may have taken from this notion the clue for suggesting that the beasts he was describing came out of the sea. No one in the twentieth century has seen this throne room in the temple, and both Ezekiel and the author of Rev 4 were speaking in terms of visions, but Jeremiah was not speaking of visions. He reported the actual furniture of the temple that was removed to Babylon. Part of the furniture consisted of a **bronze sea.** That which is conjecture is the description of the sea, its function in the temple, and its relationship to the beasts.

Since Ezekiel had once lived in Jerusalem and had seen the temple, his vision may have been close in description to the actual appearance of the throne room of the temple. The author of Rev 4 may also have seen the temple. The author of Daniel probably also was familiar both with the text of Ezekiel and the appearance of the temple. His task, however, was to relate the text of Ezekiel to the situation he wanted to describe. There may have been a tradition that identified the beasts that held the large basin with foreign nations, but that was not necessary. The author of Daniel was free to make this identification himself. Jewish and Christian interpreters sometimes made strange identifications. For example, Rabbi Eleazar of Modi'im was commenting on a verse of scripture referring to the time the Israelites fought in war with Amalek. Moses stood on the top of the hill and watched the battle as it raged. The rabbi took the phrase, **On the top of the hill** (Exod 17:9), and interpreted, "**The top**—these are the deeds of the fathers. **The hill**—these are the deeds of the mothers" (Mek *Amalek* 1.96-98).

There was nothing inherent in the text to indicate that **top** meant fathers or that **hill** meant mothers, but the rabbi needed to discuss the merits of the ancestors, so he found a text and interpreted it very freely. The author of Dan 7 was free to interpret Ezekiel in the same way. He could decree that the body parts of beasts in Ezekiel were entire beasts, which he interpreted to be the kings of the nations that the Jews resented. He could also decree that the **man** mentioned by Ezekiel was the leader of the Maccabean rebellion. He not only could do this; he did. The scripture existed to meet his needs. The author of Dan 7 lived through the Maccabean rebellion, and he needed to interpret that event in terms of scripture. He could visualize Judas the Maccabee as the Son of man the same way Rabbi Akiba decreed that Bar Cochba was the king Messiah (y*Ta'an* 68d).

The author of Daniel used Ezek 1 and Isa 6 because he wanted to describe a heavenly court scene, and he expected the heavenly court to look like a royal throne room. Ezek 1 and Isa 6 described the throne room in the temple, so he took his intertexts from there. His emphasis, however, was not on the furniture of the throne room but upon the court case being tried there, and that was the trial in heaven reflecting the Maccabean revolt on earth. God functioned as the judge of all the earth, but this was a vision, so the interpreter used the same kind of literary expressions that Ezekiel used. Ezekiel contrasted **something like four beasts** to **something like a human being** (Ezek 1:5). Homiletically, the author of Dan 7 described the beasts in detail, identifying them with the kings of the four gentile nations that ruled exiles from Judah to the leader of Palestine, using basically the same expressions. Ezekiel's expression, **something like a human being** (*duh-moót ah-dáhm*, דמות אדם) was the intertext for the Danielic expression **like a son of man** *(kuh-váhr eh-náhsh,* כבר אנש). Both of these terms were synonyms. Both the expression **man** and **son of man** have the same meaning. They are synonyms that are sometimes used in parallel (Job 25:6; Ps 8:5). This is true both in Hebrew and Aramaic[57] and even if other words are used. For example *béhn eh-nóhsh*

---

[57] They were even used as synonyms in pre-biblical Ugaritic. See Mark Smith, "The 'Son of Man'

and Aramaic[57] and even if other words are used. For example *béhn eh-nóhsh* (בן אנוש) means the same as *eh-nohsh*, and *behn ah-dahm* (בן אדם) means the same as *ah-dahm*. *Bahr-eh-nahsh* (בר אנש), *bahr-náhsh* (בר נש), and *bahr-náh-shah* (בר נשא) mean *eh-nashh*. They are all synonyms. They all mean "human being." Sometimes the expression *eesh* (איש) and *géh-vehr* (גבר) also have this meaning, although they usually mean "man" as distinguished from "woman." Since Ezekiel often spoke in terms of vision, he described these visionary figures as being like something that could be seen with the naked eye. This means whatever term he used following "that which appeared to be..." or "like.." or "like the appearance of..." it is necessary to learn from the context of the drama what it was that he was comparing to something human.

Just because the author of Dan 8 compared Gabriel to **something like a man** (גבר, Dan 8:15) does not mean that the author of Dan 7 could compare Gabriel only to **something like a son of man**.[58] Angels are not the only creatures that can be compared to human beings. There are also some ways in which apes are "something like" human beings. The etymology of the expression or the way other authors used the term or even the way the author of Dan 8 used it in another context is of no value in learning the meaning of the expression as the author of Dan 7 used it in the heavenly court case.

In Isa 6, the angelic figures were the **seraphim**—not the **saints of the Most High** or **the son of man**. Ezekiel described these angelic figures in terms of animals, birds, and domestic animals, but he probably continued to think of them as angels. It was not the angelic beings but **the Lord** that Ezekiel called the one **like a son of man**. The angelic figures of Isa 6 and Ezek 1 were taken by Daniel to be **beasts**—not **sons of man**. The author of Dan 7 had Isa 6, Ezek 1, and the throne room in the temple in mind as he composed a new drama, using characters from both of these earlier dramas. He had to reorganize the characters, however, to fit the situation in Jerusalem after the Battle of Beth-horon and possibly Beth-zur, assuming that the battle on earth corresponded to the judgment in the courtroom of the temple in heaven.

Isaiah treated the angelic figures as agents of the Lord. Dan 7, however, used the angelic figures as if they were demonic beasts who were in conflict with the one like a Son of man (Ezek 1:5; Dan 7:13). The beasts came from the sea, and the Son of man came with the clouds of heaven. The demonic beasts symbolized the gentile kings who ruled Judah after the Babylonian captivity, the last of which was Antiochus IV. The Son of man, then, was Judas the Maccabee, the adversary of the greatest of the beasts. In the heavenly court case Antiochus was the defendant and Judas was the plaintiff. Ezekiel wrote in Hebrew, and the author of Dan 7 wrote in Aramaic. That which Daniel did that was more extensive than either Isaiah or Ezekiel was to give these terms a homiletic interpretation to fit his court drama. The roles of the various characters used by the different authors are as follow:

---

[57] They were even used as synonyms in pre-biblical Ugaritic. See Mark Smith, "The 'Son of Man' in Ugaritic," *CBQ* 45 (1983):59-60.
[58] Contra Collins, *A Commentary*, pp. 304-10.

	Isaiah 6	*Ezekiel 1*	*Daniel 7*
	The Lord	One like a human being	The Ancient of Days
The messengers	The Lord's Seraphim	Angelic beasts	Demonic beasts
		One like a human being	One like a Son of man

This means etymologizing the expressions is not a useful way of determining their meanings. The characters in the visions are to be identified by their function in the drama and their relationship to their intertexts. In Dan 7, from the category of "beasts" emerged the "horn" which the dramatist used to play the role of Antiochus Epiphanes, the defendant. The "one like a Son of man" functioned as Judas the Maccabee, the plaintiff in the visionary court trial.[59] Because the visions of Isa 6 and Ezek 1 constituted the textual basis for the vision of Dan 7, it is necessary to know how both Isaiah and Ezekiel used the expression to learn how Daniel used it. Both Ezekiel and Daniel were commentators who built their homilies on earlier texts. Ezekiel based the narrative of his vision on the report of Isaiah's vision (Isa 6) and probably the poem of creation (Gen 1). Daniel based his vision-story on the accounts of Isaiah's and Ezekiel's vision.[60]

Charles mistakenly insisted that the **Son of man** came riding *on* the clouds, rather than *with* them. He pictured the Son of man using the clouds as a heavenly chariot as transportation.[61] Keil also thought the clouds implied that the **Son of man** came from heaven.[62] Both scholars overlooked the mythological significance of the clouds. The **Son of man** did not come *on* the clouds or *from* the clouds, or *down to* the clouds but *with* the clouds. This means that, like Moses, the **Son of man** came with God's endorsement. As with the experience on the Mount of Transfiguration, God showed his approval by surrounding the situation with a cloud (Matt 17:1-7). Prior to this event, the fourth beast, the horn, had

---

[59] Driver, *Daniel*, pp. 87-88, was at least consistent. He thought the "horn" was the entire empire of Syria, and he thought the "Son of man" was "the glorified people of Israel." He did not suggest, however, that "Moses" was only a symbol of the Hebrew people.

[60] This also means that the on-going arguments J. Fitzmyer and G. Vermes have had were dealing with moot subjects. They agreed that the Son of man was not a messianic title in pre-Christian Judaism. It was not a messianic title *per se*. It pointed directly to Judas the Maccabee—not just to any messiah or any king. It was Dan 7 that identified Judas with the term "human being" in Ezekiel. After that it became a title for Judas and later for any antitype of Judas. Any figure who later was called a Son of man, without meaning just "human being" in general, was an antitype of Judas the Maccabee. This was true of Jesus in the gospels. For him the Son of man was a code name to remind those who had ears to hear that he was the new Judas the Maccabee. When he identified himself with the "Son of man," Jesus did not use this expression as a general term suggesting his human ontology or as a circumlocution for the pronoun "I." For a list of articles by Fitzmyer and Vermes on this subject see J. R. Donahue, "Recent Studies on the Origin of 'Son of Man' in the Gospels," *CBQ* 48 (1986):486, fn. 9.

[61] Charles, *Daniel*, p. 186.

[62] Keil, *Daniel*, p. 235.

presented his own defense before the Ancient of Days, and he lost. The fact that he lost proved that he belonged to the category of the monsters who came out of the great deep. This is quite a change of roles for the angelic figures of Isa 6 who appeared as messengers of the Lord. The next person to approach the Ancient of Days was the **one like a Son of man**, who was evidently the plaintiff in this court case. His victory in this court trial proved that he had come with divine approval **with the clouds**.

The death of Antiochus Epiphanes took place a very short time either before or after Judas won either the Battle of Beth-horon (2Macc) or the Battle of Beth-zur (1Macc) (164 BIA). All of this bad news for the beasts and good news for the saints seemed too miraculous to be accidental. God must have designed the entire program. Since this was the case, it was the obligation of the author to dramatize the theological dimension of the event. This phenomenon evidently convinced the mythologist that God had held a heavenly court session during which the plaintiff was Judas the Maccabee who was given the favorable verdict. After all, one of the things God did was to hold court and pass judgment (Ps 82:1; 94:2; 96:13). The only way human beings had of knowing how God judged cases was to observe how events happened on earth.

Antiochus must have been the defendant, because he died. That was a good sign that he had been given a death sentence in this heavenly trial. Although he reflected his demonic origins, in the opinion of the author of Dan 7, Antiochus Epiphanes was not a demon or an angel. He was an identifiable human being, and he was not on trial against an angel but against another human being. Furthermore his death took place very near to the time of Judas' famous victories. Therefore Judas and Antiochus must have been participants of the same divine judgment. Just as Antiochus and Judas were in military conflict together, so in the heavenly court it was they who were the legal contestants. Just as Judas won the Battles of Beth-horon and Beth-zur, so he won the heavenly court case. Antiochus not only lost in the military conflict; he also died at about the same time, and the author of Dan 7 wrote after both the death of Antiochus and the victories of Beth-horon and possibly Beth-zur. Neither the **little horn** nor the **one like a Son of man** was an angel, even though the **little horn** had an angelic figure for its Isaianic intertext. Both were human beings. One was Antiochus IV and the other was Judas the Maccabee. Montgomery was right when he said of **the Son of man**,

> It is not a beast, nor a divinity, "a Son of God," but a man who is raised to the empire of the world.[63]

The myth of Dan 7 provides a theological and religious dimension to the Hasmonean Rebellion, just as the Passover provides the religious dimension of the exodus from Egypt. Jews learned what God was doing in heaven by studying what was happening on earth. At the end of three years of guerrilla warfare, Judas gained the position of national leadership. That meant that in the heavenly court case he was given the rulership, the glory, and the kingdom (Dan 7:14). Names were not given of the historical characters involved. The contest in court was

---

[63] Montgomery, *Daniel*, p. 319.

between the **little horn** and **one like a Son of man**, but it is not difficult to identify the characters in this drama. The characters were not empires but personalities. They were contemporaries who were tried in the same heavenly court scene. The **little horn** was Antiochus Epiphanes, and the **one like a Son of man** was Judas the Maccabee. Bevan, however,[64] refused to think of that possibility. He said,

> Thus in the chapter itself there is nothing which suggests the idea of a personal Messiah, and it is particularly important to observe that the rest of the book bears out this conclusion . . .

Montgomery disagreed. He thought the Son of man was a symbol of the saints of the Most High, but he said,

> It must be admitted that the earliest interpretation of "the Son of man" is Messianic. The term is frequent in the Parables of Enoch, En. 37-71, where it occurs 14 times. The dependence upon Dan. 7 is patent from the first reference, En. 46^1 ff [65]

Frölich was so sure that the **Son of man** was identical to the saints of the Most High that she did not even mention the term **Son of man**. She simply spoke of the judgment scene between the tenth horn and the holy ones of the Most High,[66] just as if the saints did not have a leader to fight the little horn. She also understood the "man" in *1Enoch* 93.4 to be "humankind and the chosen ones of Israel."[67] Delitzsch thought the fourth beast was Rome, because Rome was the first nation to extend its boundaries all the way from the East to the West,[68] and that Jesus was the Son of man of which Daniel spoke. He said,

> If Jesus speaks of himself as the Son of man, He means thereby not merely to say that he was he Messiah, but he wishes to designate Himself as the Messiah of Daniel's prophecy, *i.e.* as the Son of man coming to the earth in the clouds of heaven. He thereby lays claim at once to a divine original, or a divine pre-existence as well as to affirm true humanity of His person, and seeks to represent

---

[64] A. A. Bevan, *A Short Commentary on the Book of Daniel* (Cambridge: University Press, c1982), p. 119.
[65] Montgomery, *Daniel*, p. 320. He also noted that the rabbinic interpretation of the Son of man was messianic. His own interpretation is on p.323.
[66] I. Frölich, *"'Time and Times and Half a Time',"* (Sheffield: Sheffield Academic Press, 1996), pp. 70-71.
[67] Frölich, *Time*, p. 166. Frölich overlooked the obvious midrashic relationship between 1 Enoch and Dan 7, which shows that 1Enoch is secondary (*1Enoch* 14, 62). In Daniel, the Son of man is the plaintiff in the case and the Ancient of Days is the judge. At that trial the Son of man was given the authority that goes with becoming a ruler and a judge. In 1Enoch 62 that Son of man functioned as a king and judge, using the authority he received in Dan 7.
[68] So Keil, *Daniel*, p. 268.

Himself, according to John's expression, as the Logos becoming flesh.[69]

That is more than the Book of Daniel ever intended. Jesus probably considered himself an antitype of the Danielic Son of man, but the author of Dan 7 did not have Jesus in mind when he wrote this drama. Montgomery wrote too early to have added another early reference to Daniel. One of the recently released Dead Sea Scrolls is a poetic midrash on the Book of Daniel, which clarifies the meaning of the term "Son of man" and "the kingdom." This will be shown here in parallel columns. In this case Daniel is the intertext, and *4Q246* is the commentary. When these two columns are placed side-by-side and compared, it is apparent that *4Q246* is a midrash based on various words and themes of Daniel. If the lacunae in *4Q246* were all filled in with the original words, all conjectured solutions to this passage could be judged more accurately. From the words and lines that have been preserved, however, it seems obvious that *4Q246* is a poetic piece that has compressed the message of Daniel into a few short lines. The reader was expected to know Daniel and understand all of the themes that the poet summarized. If we are to understand the message in the twentieth century, we must learn from Daniel the message of *4Q246*.

4Q246	Ezra, Daniel, 1Enoch, and 4Ezra
page 1	
	Dan 2:46 **Then King** Nebuchadnezzar **fell down** on his face **before** him, and he worshiped Daniel.
¹[. . .] settled over him. **He fell down before** the throne	
	Dan 3:10 Everyone who hears . . . **shall fall down** and worship the golden statue.
² [. . .] **King of the age**. You are trembling and you change	Dan 3:9 **King, live for ages** (מלכא לעלמין חיי).
	Dan 5:10 **King**, live **for ages**! Do not let your thoughts frighten you or your color change.

---

[69] Keil, *Daniel*, p. 274.
[70] Most scholars, like J. A. Fitzmyer, "*4Q246*: 'The Son of God' Document from Qumran," *Bib* 74 (1993):155, 157, 160, render the Aramaic word *ah-thoór* (אתור) "Assyria," because that is what the word means in most of the rest of the scripture. Here, however, as in the War Scroll, its context requires the term to mean "Syria." In the War Scroll the Kittim are called the *keet-ee-ay ah-shoór* the Battle (כתיי אשור) (*1QM* 1.2). The Kittim in the War Scroll are sometimes mentioned in relationship to *ah-shoór* in ways that either mean that the Kittim are Ashurim or are coterminous with them (*1QM* 1.6; 11.11) and once in relationship with Japeth (18.2). They are all enemies of the sons of light. The word Kittim comes from Cyprus, which was under control of the Syrian Greeks before the Battle of Magnesia and again before the Romans forced Antiochus IV to remove his troops from Cyprus. The Kittim were clearly the Romans in the Habakkuk

³[...] your **vision** and everything

You are until **the age**
⁴[. . .] there will be a depression upon the land
⁵[. . .] and a great sifting among the cities

⁶[. . .] **the king of Syria**⁷⁰ **and of Egypt**
⁷[...] to be great over the land⁷¹
⁸[...] will make and everyone will serve

⁹[...] he will be called (ויתקרא) and in his name he will be designated (יתכנה).

^{Dan 6:7} **King** Darius, live **for ages**!

^{Dan 2:28} Your dream and **the visions** of your head on your bed are these.

^{Dan 4:1} I had a dream, and it frightened me . . . **the visions** of my head alarmed me.

^{Dan 6:27} He is the God of life, and he exists (קים) **for ages. His kingdom** will not pass away, his government [will endure] until the end.

^{Dan 11:11} **The king of the South [Egypt]** will become angry, and he will go out and engage in battle with him, with **the king of the North [Syria]**

Page 2

Buchanan, *Intertextuality*, pp. 82-83). During the time when the Jews were in military conflict with the Greeks and the Romans there no longer existed a nation called Assyria. Assyria had been conquered by the Medes, which, in turn, was conquered by the Persians. Then the Greeks ruled that area until the Romans took control of the whole territory. During the period when Daniel and the scrolls were written Jews were in conflict with the Syrians and the Romans. *Ergo Ashur* (*11QM*) or the *Atur* (*4Q246*) means Syria rather than Assyria. The only difficulty is with a prosthetic *alef*. The struggle during Hasmonean times was between Egypt and Syria—not between Egypt and Assyria.

⁷¹ Throughout the document Fitzmyer, "Son of God," rendered *ah-reh-ah* (ארעא) "the earth." The term is sometimes used to mean the entire earth. At other times it means "land"—i.e., the Promised Land. It is the Promised Land that is the subject here. That is why it is translated "land" here.

⁷² S. L. Mattila, "Two Contrasting Eschatologies of Qumran, (*4Q246* vs. *11QM*)," *Bib* 75 (1994):529, followed by Fitzmyer, "Son of God," p. 155, in his interpretation of the "comets." He said this metaphor was to indicate the shortness of the term of the various rulers. That is a possible interpretation. Here it is translated as if the emphasis was upon the glory of the kingdom. There was a famous Halley's comet in 164 BIA.

⁷³ This means the people will rise up in rebellion, and the "rest" involved is rest from the sword that they used until they obtained peace. First they had to fight the war that God had made for the Son of God before he could rule in peace. It is the peace that follows a victorious war. Joshua and David both fought until the land had rest. *Contra* Mattila, "Eschatologies." p. 536.

¹**Son of God** (ברה די אל) he will be labeled (יתאמר).	ᴰᵃⁿ ⁷:¹³ **Look! With the clouds, One like a Son of man** (בר אנש) is coming.
	ᴰᵃⁿ ⁷:¹² The people of the saints **of the Most High.**
Son of the Most High they will call him. Like comets of vision⁷² ²their kingdom will be. For years they will rule over ³the land. They will trample over everything. [One] **people** will trample [another] **people**;	⁴ᴱᶻʳᵃ ¹³·³¹ They will plan to make war against one another—**city** against **city**, place against place, **people** against **people**, and kingdom against kingdom.
[one] **city** will trample [another] **city** ⁴until **the people of God** arise,⁷³	ᴵˢᵃ ⁹:² [Egyptians will fight one another], city against city, kingdom against kingdom.
and everything **will rest** from the sword.	¹ᴱⁿᵒᶜʰ ⁶²·¹⁴ They **will** eat, **rest**, and rise with that **Son of man**.
	ᴰᵃⁿ ⁷:²⁷ The kingdom, the government, and the greatness of the kingdoms under the entire heaven will be given to **the people** of the saints **of the Most High**.
	ᴰᵃⁿ ⁸:²⁴ **The people of** the saints.
	ᴰᵃⁿ ²:⁴⁴ The elect ones the God of heaven **will raise up a kingdom of the ages**.
⁵**His kingdom will be a kingdom of the age;**	ᴰᵃⁿ ⁷:¹⁴ **His government is a government of the age.**
all of his ways will be **in truth**.	ᴰᵃⁿ ⁴:³⁴ **All of his deeds are true**, and **his ways** are **just**.
He will **judge** ⁶the land with **justice** and **everything** will achieve **peace** (שלם). The sword will cease from the land.	ᴰᵃⁿ ⁶:²⁶ Then King Darius wrote . . . "May your **peace** (שלמכון) be multiplied.

⁷**Every city will worship** (יסגדהן) **him**. A great God is in these things, ⁸and he makes war for him. **Peoples will be given into his hand** (ינתן בידה); all of them ⁹will be thrown down before him	Dan 7:28 **All the governments will worship** (ישתמעון{) **him**. Dan 11:11 He will raise up a great multitude, and the multitude **will be given into his hand**. Dan 7:26 The kingdom, the government, and the greatness of the kingdom **will be given** to the people of the saints of the Most High. 1Enoch 62.9 Kings, governors, and high officials . . . shall fall down on their faces and **worship** and raise their hopes in that Son of man.
his government is a government of the age, and all the depths [. . .	Dan 7:27 **His kingdom is a kingdom of the age**.

Page 3

¹**will obey** (ישמעון) **him**.	Every **government will** worship and **obey** (ישתמעון) **him**.

When these two columns are placed side-by-side and compared, it is apparent that *4Q246* is a midrash based on various words and themes of Daniel. The allusions are not to just one chapter of Daniel but to chapters 2, 3,4,5,6,7, and 11. This means that Daniel was probably a complete unit by the time this Dead Sea fragment was composed. From the words and lines that have been preserved it seems obvious that *4Q246* is a poetic piece that has compressed the message of Daniel into a few short lines. The reader was expected to know Daniel and understand all of the themes that the poet summarized. If we are to understand the message in the twentieth century, we must learn from Daniel the message of *4Q246*.

As in Daniel also in *4Q246* there are two opposing political powers and two historical ages. During the first age, reflected mostly in page 1, a foreign king was in power, and Daniel was the interpreter of his dreams. In Daniel, the foreign king was Nebuchadnezzar, Darius, or one of the Seleucids. In *4Q246* the king was either the same or some later typological equivalent. During this age of foreign control, the kings of Egypt and Syria fought and trampled under their feet the people on whose land the battles raged. Page 2 is mostly dedicated to the following age, or the age to come after the gentile age would be over. During this age, the chosen people lived in peace under their own national leader, which was probably Judas the Maccabee. For Daniel this was the Hasmonean age. In both of these documents the word "age" or "ages" was important. This discussion will concentrate primarily on page 2 of 4Q246 and the Book of Daniel.

Both documents deal with a government or a kingdom that belongs to the age; these political entities belong both to the people and to the king who rules over the land. The citizens whom Daniel called **the people of the saints of the Most High** (Dan 7:18, 27; see 8:24) the author of *4Q246* called "the people of God" (*4Q246*). First Maccabees 14:27 called Simon **the prince of the people of God** (*ah-sahr-ahm-ayl*, ασαραμελ = *sáhr ahm-áyl*, שר עם אל). First Enoch referred to the people of God **as the holy and elect ones** (*1Enoch* 62.7) or **the righteous and elect ones** (*1Enoch* 62.13). All of these names are suitable titles for the chosen people who live on the Promised Land. Daniel called the leader of the chosen people **one *like* a Son of man**. He did not call him a king, because Judas the Maccabee was never officially anointed as a king.[74] The character which Daniel called **Son of man** the author of *4Q246* called **Son of God, Son of the Most High**, and also **king**.

The title "Son of God" is a well-known title for a king.[75] Alexander the Great was called "the son of Zeus"; the Egyptian pharaoh was called "the son of Re"; Solomon was known as God's son when he sat on Yehowah's[76] throne ruling Yehowah's kingdom from Jerusalem (1Chron 28:5-7; 2Sam 7:14). Fourth Ezra called God's son "the Messiah" (*4Ezra* 7.28). It is evident that the reference to a king as "God's son" was a legal, rather than an ontological, title, from the fact that an Egyptian pharaoh could be the son of two gods, Horus and Seth,[77] at the same time. This is what Paul meant when he said Jesus was from the family of David, according to the flesh, but the Son of God, according to the spirit (Rom 1:3-4). His designation, "according to the spirit," was his legal status. As legal agents of the deity, these monarchs were held to be legally identical to the principal who was the deity. They spoke and acted in the name of, at the authority of, and at the responsibility of the deity.

A second fragment (*4Q521*.1) said heaven and earth would obey his [=God's] messiah.[78] This was because of the Messiah's legal status. Anyone who obeyed the principal would also have to obey his legal agent. Since the Messiah was God's legal agent, heaven and earth would have to obey him, just as they would obey God. A third Dead Sea fragment (*4Q448*) offered a prayer to God for the king, God's people Israel wherever they were scattered, and for God's kingdom (*mahm-lékh-tuh-kháh*, ממלכתך) (*4Q448.B*, 8). The kingdom that was considered God's was also clearly Judah, the land ruled by King Jonathan (*Yóh-*

---

[74] This identification was first proposed in Buchanan, *To the Hebrews* (Garden City: Doubleday, 1972), pp. 38-51.

[75] It did not originate in the Jewish-Christian church, as W. Kramer, *Christ, Lord, Son of God* (Naperville: A. R. Allenson, 1966) tr. B. Hardy, p. 111, claimed. Kramer also misunderstood the role of a legal agent when he said God was the agent in Gal 4:4-5. God was the principal who sent the apostle or agent; Jesus was the agent who was sent (pp. 112-13).

[76] For a justification of this pronunciation see Buchanan, "Some Unfinished Business with the Dead Sea Scrolls," *RevQ* 13 (1988):411-20.

[77] Frankfort said the King of Egypt was the god Horus incarnate, although the deity was not exhausted by his incarnation. This implies that the god Horus was the principal, and the king was the legal agent. The relationship seems to have been legal (H. Frankfort, *Kingship of the Gods* [Chicago: Chicago University Press, c1948], p. 19).

[78] M. O. Wise and J. D. Tabor, "The Messiah at Qumran," *BAR* 18 (1992):62.

nah-thahn hah-méh-lehk, יונתן המלך) (*4Q448*.B, 2; C, 8), otherwise known by his Greek name of Alexander Janneus. He was the king who ruled Palestine from 103 to 76 BIA.[79] As the king of Israel Janneus was probably called also the Son of God at the same time. This was an *ex officio* title that was recognized as a legal designation. Long before these Dead Sea Scroll fragments were published, Aalen concluded,

> The kingdom of God corresponds to the Jewish expressions: the world to come, the new Jerusalem, and the Great Feast, where the content of the concept is salvation, conceived in local categories.[80]

Like judges, who were also legal agents of the deity, kings could even be addressed as gods, but, as the Psalmist reminded them, they were not ontologically God, because they would die like other human beings (Ps 82; *Ber* 6a; *Mid Ps* 82; *11QMelch*).[81] If these national leaders had been elected by ballot by the people of the country, then they would have been representatives or "sons" of the people, as Collins claims.[82] Then they would not have been called sons of God at all but sons of the people. These leaders, however, were monarchs, and their anointing or enthronement ceremonies made them legally sons or agents of the deity. As agents they were legally accountable to the deity rather than to the people. This provided them with great authority, Herodotus said, "The king's decree makes every action right." (Herodotus 3.31). Appian also echoed, "The law which is common to all [is] what the king determines is always right" (Appian, *Roman History* 11.10, 61).That meant that the Persian king could do whatever he wished. All of this means that the Son of man in Daniel cannot be fairly identified with the saints of the Most High, as Fitzmyer holds.

When the author of *4Q246* interpreted "Son of man" to mean both "king" and "Son of God," it is clear that he understood the title "Son of man" to be the office of a national leader. The Danielic ruler was given the governing authority,

---

[79] Buchanan, "4Q246 and the Political Titles of Jesus," *QC* 4 (1994):84. R. Otto, *The Kingdom of God and the Son of Man*, tr. Floyd V. Filson and Bertram Lee-Woolf (London: Lutterworth Press, c1951), p. 31, did not have the benefit of these Dead Sea fragments when he defined the Kingdom of Heaven as "the higher, transcendent, holy, and blessed world in contrast to this world; the otherworldly and supramundane existence which awaits us as the wholly future state; heaven, the heavenly Jerusalem, Paradise, or whatever mythical images we may choose as idiograms for this *wholly other* [emphasis his] existence and this wholly other realm of being." Now, however, that we have more data we should correct this misunderstanding.

[80] S. Aalen, "'Reign' and 'House' in the Kingdom of God in the Gospels," *NTS* 8 (1962):27. This disagrees with R. Bultmann, *Jesus and the Word* tr. L. P. Smith and E. H. Lantero (New York: Charles Scribner's Sons, c1958), p.35, who said the Kingdom of God "is that *eschatological* [emphasis his] deliverance which ends everything earthly." He thought that the expectation of the Kingdom of God "excluded the question of practical regulations for nation and state from the centre of his thought" (p. 107). Of course Bultmann wrote this before these Dead Sea fragments had been published.

[81] See further Buchanan, *Biblical and Theological Insights from Ancient and Modern Civil Law* (Lewiston: The Edwin Mellen Press, 1992), pp. 127-35.

[82] J. J. Collins, "A Pre-Christian 'Son of God' among the Dead Sea Scrolls," *BAR* 9 (1993):36, said, "The figure who is called the Son of God is the representative or agent *of the people* [emphasis added] of God."

the glory, and the kingdom; all peoples, languages, and nations would serve him (Dan 7:14). The Qumran ruler would have a kingdom that would be as spectacular as a comet; cities would bow down before him; and peoples would be given into his hand. All of these would throw themselves down before him in subjection.

Prior to the composition of Dan 7, the term "Son of man" was a very general term that meant a "human being." After the author of this drama identified this term with a very specific person, namely Judas the Maccabee, it quickly became a royal term. This early Qumran fragment already identified the expression "Son of man" with "Son of God," "Son of the Most High," and "king." Jesus used the term "Son of man" as a code name to identify himself with the Messiah without exposing himself to the Roman authorities. When Jesus asked Peter who the Son of man was he said, "You are the Messiah the son of the God of life" (Matt 16:13-16). Like the author of *4Q246* Matthew knew that a messiah was also the Son of God and the Son of man. These all became synonymous after the publication of Dan 7.

All of the political entities that Daniel said were "given" to the people of the saints of the Most High were "given" into the hands of the Son of God, according to *4Q246*. The same is true of Daniel 7. Because of this Mowinckel said,

> In the present form of Daniel's visions of the beasts, the Son of Man is a pictorial symbol of the people of Israel, not an individual figure and not a personal Messiah of any kind.[83]

Muilenburg echoed the same basic opinion,

> No fewer than three times we are told that it [the Son of man] is the "saints of the Most High" or "the people of the saints of the Most High" (עם קדישי עליונין; vs., 18, 25, 27).[84]

Muilenburg was trying to be syncretistic, showing that the various conflicting opinions about the Son of man might be reconciled. Although he said the Son of man was the Saints of the Most High, he also said it was the Messiah, king, eschatological king and that the "messianic interpretation seems to us not only permissible, but probable."[85] He thought the Son of Man was the king of the new age, the king of the *Endzeit*, the Messiah, and the judge of the end time. None of these designations describes "the saints of the Most High," which he said was the definition given in Dan 7.

Just because the Son of man and the saints of the Most High were both recipients of the kingdom does not mean that the two were identical. When a kingdom is given to a king it is also given to the people who give him allegiance. When Daniel said the kingdom, government, and greatness of the kingdom were

---

[83] Mowinckel, *He that Cometh*, p. 350.
[84] J. Muilenburg, "The Son of Man in Daniel and the Ethiopic Apocalypse of Enoch," *JBL* 79 (1960):198.
[85] Muilenburg, "Son of Man," p. 201, 204, 205.

given to the people of the saints of the Most High and also to the Son of man, he did not think they were identical, as Mowinckel, Fitzmyer, and others have presumed.

Paul was fair to Daniel when he said God had transferred Christians into the kingdom of the Son of God's love so that the Christians might be made worthy of a portion of the saints of light (Col 1:12-14). The kingdom belonged to God's Son. The Christians had the privilege of becoming citizens of that kingdom. The Christians were not identical to God's Son; they were members of the saints of the Most High. The same relationship existed between the Son of man and the Saints of the Most High in Dan 7. Saint Augustine also understood the typology of Daniel. He wrote after Constantine and concluded that the church that then existed was the kingdom of God and the kingdom of Christ, because Christ's saints were there ruling with him. Augustine did not try to identify the saints with Christ anymore than Daniel tried to identify the saints with the Son of man, but Augustine thought both Christ and his saints were necessary for the kingdom of God (*de Civitate dei* 20.9, 35-45).

Collins did not agree with Fitzmyer. He thought the Son of man was an indvidual, but he argued,

> The decisive objection against the messianic interpretation [of the Son of man] is that nowhere in the book do we find either support for or interest in the Davidic monarchy.[86]

Of course we do not. The Hasmoneans were Levites who supported themselves. They never supported Davidic messiahs. It was the Hasmoneans who directed the events that took place at the first Hanukkah. It was the Hasmoneans who were responsible for the victory which the Book of Daniel celebrated. Why would anyone expect Hasmoneans to promote a Davidic monarchy? They became monarchs themselves and were in competition with the Davidic candidates for messiahship.

Caquot thought the Son of man was a collective figure for the saints of the Most High, which he held to be the pious Jews of Maccabean times.[87] The word for "saints" means the "holy ones." The Israelites were called a "holy people" (Deut 7:6) and a "holy nation" (Exod 19:6). The name of Yehowah was "holy" (Ps 106:47). The saints were those who feared Yehowah (Ps 34:10). The Saints were not only those who were dead or in heaven. This was a title given generally to the people who had made a treaty with Yehowah, namely the Jews, the Samaritans, or the Israelites. Paul later called Christians "saints." Saints were also called "the sons of light" (*1QM* 1.9), "the people of the saints of the contract" (*áhm kuh-doh-*

---

[86] Collins, *A Commentary*, p. 309. Although the Son of man in Dan 7 was not a son of David, H. M. Teeple, "The Origin of the Son of Man Christology," *JBL* 84 (1965):213, was mistaken in saying "In Jewish eschatology the Son of man was distinct from the Son of David." Rabbis often identified the two. For examples see Buchanan, *Revelation and Redemption: Jewish Documents of Deliverance from the Fall of Jerusalem to the Death of Nahmanides* (Dillsboro: Western North Carolina Press, c1978; sold by Mercer U. Press), pp. 317, 346, 403, 505, 572.

[87] A. Caquot, "Les Quatre Betes et le 'Fils d'Homme,'" *Sem* 17 (1967):37-71.

sháy buh-reét, קדושי ברית עם) (*1QM* 10.10), and "the sons of his pleasure" (*buh-náy reet-zoh-nóh*, בני רצונו)

Caquot was right in thinking that the saints were the Jews who supported Judas, but he was mistaken in identifying the Son of man with the saints. Rhodes argued that the Son of man in Dan 7 corresponds to the son enthroned in Ps 2.[88] This identification pictures the judgment scene in Dan 7 as also an enthronement ceremony. Neither the saints nor the Son of man were angelic figures, as some scholars hold. The one like a Son of man was Judas the Maccabee, and the contemporary Jews were the saints. Charles thought that the people of the saints of the Most High were to be understood as the faithful remnant of Israel, but he believed that they were "transformed into heavenly or supernatural beings."[89] Some of the people of the saints were those who composed parts of the Book of Daniel right there in Palestine. They had not been transformed into any kind of heavenly beings that could not have celebrated the first Hanukkah in Jerusalem.

The authors of Daniel, and *4Q246* were writing about the same God whom both addressed as **the Most High**.[90] Their topic of interest was the same land, the same kingdom, citizens of the same kingdom, and rulers over the same nation. The two authors had the same political aspirations and the same conquest theology. Consistent with all of these parallels "the people of God" in one document are citizens of the same country as **the people of the saints of the Most High** in the other,[91] and the **one like a Son of man**[92] held the same position as "the Son of God" or the "Son of the Most High."[93] They are therefore both

---

[88] A. B. Rhodes, "The Kingdoms of Men and the Kingdom of God. A Study of Daniel 7:1-14," *Int* 15 (1961):411-430.

[89] Charles, *Daniel*, p. 187.

[90] A name also used by Luke, 1Enoch, 2Baruch, and 4Ezra. J. Goldingay, "'Holy Ones on High' in Daniel 7:18, *JBL* 107 (1988):495-97, argued that because the word for Most High in Aramaic is plural (*ehl-yoh-neen*, עליונין) that it must refer to heavenly beings, "high saints." If that were so, the translators of OG and q did not know that, because both rendered the expression in the singular (*heep-sis-too*, ὑψίστου). The Damascus Document (CD 20.8) used the term in the singular, referring to God (*ehl-yohn* עליון), and the Syriac for 2Bar 80.1 (*muh-ree-mah*, מרימא) is singular. The term "Most High" is a name frequently used for God whether it was used to modify "angels" (*2Bar* 80.1), "saints" (Dan 7:18; CD 20:8), or "prophet" (Luke 1:76).

[91] This refutes T. H. Gaster, *The Dead Sea Scriptures* (Garden City: Doubleday & Co., 1956), pp. 142, 147, who translated עם as *im*, "with" or "in" rather than *ahm*, "people." There are still a few scholars like J. J. Collins *The Apocalyptic Imagination* (New York: Crossroad, 1984), pp. 82-83; *Daniel* (Grand Rapids: Crossroads, c1984), pp. 78-79, C. L. J. Proudman, "Remarks on the 'Son of Man,'" *CJT* 12 (1966):128-31; M. Noth, "Zur Komposition des Buches Daniel," *TSK* 98/99 (1926):143-63, who think the Son of man in Daniel is an angel. In opposition to these, LaCocque, *Daniel*, p. 127, observed that there is no mention of an angelic kingdom in this literature. R. Hanhart, "Die Heiligen des Höchsten," *VT Suppl* 16 (1967):90-101, concluded that there were very few passages where *koh-duh-sheém*, (קודשים) might be translated either as pious human beings or angels, but the great majority would make sense only as "saints," and should not be rendered "angels."

[92] Hartman, *Daniel*, pp. 89-90, fns. 212-213, has competently shown how ridiculous the notion is that the Son of man was an angel. For a further analysis of the Son of man see Buchanan, *To the Hebrews* (Garden City: Doubleday, 1972), pp. 38-51 and *Insights*, pp.96-112.

[93] The title "Most High" was used by Daniel, 1Enoch, *4Q246*, and 4 Ezra as a title for God.

political names, and the **Son of man** in Dan 7 is a mythical name for Judas the Maccabee.[94]

In Dan 7, the **Son of man** was presented as the victorious plaintiff in a court case. In 1Enoch the **Son of man** was a king who would sit on his throne and rule the people of Israel while judging and avenging Israel's enemies. This means the testimony in 1Enoch is later than Dan 7. The **Son of man** was not the judge in Dan 7. He was the plaintiff. It was after that heavenly judgment that the Son of man was given royal and judicial authority that enabled him to conduct the judgments reported in 1Enoch.

Fourth Ezra's commentary on Dan 7 calls the one who came with the clouds "the Man" (*homo* or *virum* in Latin) or **Son of man** (*bahr násh-ah*, בר נשא in Syriac). Like the king (Ps 2), this man stood on Mount Zion and was called God's son (*4Ezra* 13.1-38). Like the shoot from the stump of Jesse (Isa 11) he was a military leader who destroyed his enemies with the breath of his mouth. Like other kings he had the authority of Moses after he came down from the mountain. Like other kings he was God's legal agent whose words became law (*legem, 4Ezra* 13.38). He did not have to kill his enemies with his own hands. He had only to order that it be done, and his order was carried out.

To the Ancient of Days. Instead of **to the Ancient of Days** Rahlfs' edition of the OG reads **and as an Ancient of Days** (OG Dan 7:13). This would imply that the Son of man appeared **as the Ancient of Days** rather than **to the Ancient of Days**. Struckenbruck argued that this was an intentional translation change to avoid the understanding that there were two deities—the **Ancient of Days** and the Son of man.[95] That is not very likely. If the Son of man had been understood to be a deity it would have been *legal* identity, as an agent of the deity. As a king he might have been considered an agent of the deity but not as the principal. Initially the Son of man would not have been confused as the **Ancient of Days,** because they played different roles in the drama. The Ancient of Days was the judge, and the Son of man was the plaintiff. If the Son of man had been Judas the Maccabee, and this had been a coronation ceremony, as some scholars have held, he might secretly have been accepted as king, even though the Syrians would not have allowed that to have happened knowingly.

To him was given. That which was given the plaintiff was the victory in this court case. The court decreed that he would be given the ruling authority, power, and a kingdom. That which the court took from the fourth beast was given to the Son of man. He was to function as a national leader, having honor, glory, and power similar to that of Nebuchadnezzar or Belshazzar. All peoples, nations, and

---

[94]This discussion of Daniel and *4Q246* was first published as Buchanan, "*4Q246* and the Political Titles of Jesus," *Mogilany* 1993, ed. Z.J. Kapera (Krakow: The Enigma Press, 1996), pp. 77-87. The relationships of these insights to the title "Son of man" to Jesus are discussed there. See further Buchanan, *Hebrews*, pp. 38-52. F. L Anderson, *The Man of Nazareth* (New York: Macmillan, 1914), p. 45, concluded that the terms Son of man, Son of God, and messiah had the same meaning.

[95] L. T. Struckenbruck,"'One Like a Son of Man as the Ancient of Days' in the Old Greek Recension of Daniel 7,13: Scribal Error or Theological Translation," *ZNW* 86 (1995):268-77.

languages would serve him, just as they had served Nebuchadnezzar and other earlier beasts. This was the stone that crushed the statue in Dan 3.

The judge in this court case decreed against the defendants. He determined that the ruling authority would be taken away from the four beasts, but that they would escape with their lives, at least for the time being (Dan 7:12). The horn received special treatment. The judge's decision meant, mythologically, that the horn would receive the death penalty, and his body would be burned (Dan 7:11). The idea of burning came from the intertext in Ezekiel. Burning a person's bones was a specially despicable punishment (Lev 20:14; 21:9; Josh 7:25). Historically, all of this meant that it was God who hardened the heart of Antiochus Epiphanes as he had previously done with Pharaoh. This was done so that Antiochus IV would leave the Palestinian scene to make war in the eastern colonies, hoping to plunder the temple of Artemis in Elymäis so as to gain enough spoils to pay for the military costs of his battle against Judas the Maccabee. His campaign was unsuccessful; he lost the battle; he became ill and died in the eastern colonies (*Ant* 12.354-59; Polybius 31.9).

Ancient peoples often attributed excessive torture to the deaths of the people they hated. They assumed that God must hate them, too, and therefore would have made them suffer for their sins before they died. This was part of the trial the dying person faced when he or she appeared before the divine judge. He or she would have been "put on the rack" and tortured until forced to make a confession. When a person in antiquity was a defendant in court who was suspected of lying, the prosecuting attorney could request the judge to have the person tortured to evoke a confession. This is one of the ways they tried to discover the truth. This was basic to the tortures God made Job face. God permitted Satan to have him "put on the rack."

It was assumed that God used the same court procedure. For example, Herod the Great is reported to have died with a raging fever, itching of the skin, pains in the intestines, tumors of the feet, inflammation of the abdomen, and gangrene of the genitals creating worms. He had asthma and convulsions. This was all part of the trial he faced before God. At his death he faced God's judgment, and God "put him on the rack" to force a confession from him. Jews believed this treatment was God's judgment on Herod, because of the cruelty he had shown the rabbis whose students tried to chop down the Roman eagle over the gates of Jerusalem (*War* 1.656). Josephus also said Antiochus died after a severe illness, confessing that these tortures came as divine punishment for his sacrilege in defiling the temple at Jerusalem. Other historians reported differently. Polybius said Antiochus died because he tried to plunder the temple of Artemis in Persia (*Ant* 12.357-58). These were contradictory opinions of the same divine judgment.

From the mythologist's point of view, the best part of the myth was saved for the last. He did not introduce the plaintiff to the scene until after the judgment had been made against the defendant. After the defendant had been sentenced, the plaintiff, who was introduced as the **Son of man**, came with the clouds of heaven.[96] The text does not say that the **Son of man** was a plaintiff, but he clearly functioned as a plaintiff and received the verdict as a plaintiff would. Furthermore, since Antiochus was the defendant, and Judas was the one who opposed him in actual warfare, it seems most likely that the mythologist understood Judas the Maccabee to have been the one in the divine court who accused Antiochus Epiphanes before the Lord. The judge decreed in favor of the Son of man, announcing that he would receive **the ruling authority, glory, and a kingdom** that was under contest in the Hasmonean rebellion (Dan 7:14).

The same trial that decreed a death sentence for the horn awarded a kingdom to the **Son of man**. Antiochus died at about the same time that Judas had the temple cleansed. At the same time the judgment was also granted to the saints of the Most High, namely the Jews contemporary with Judas (Dan 7:22), who were to receive the kingdom at the very time Judas was to receive it--they as citizens, and Judas as the ruler.[97] This refutes Casey's position that the Son of man

---

[96] See Buchanan, *Hebrews*, pp. 38-51. It is ridiculous to presume, as W. S. Towner, *Daniel* (Atlanta: John Knox Press, c1984) pp. 108-15, does that Daniel 7 is mythologized history right up to the point where the Son of man and the saints receive the kingdom, and then suddenly, without warning, ceases to be mythology and is to be taken literally. This provides Towner many obstacles, as he admitted. It meant he had to admit that this "prophecy" was false, which he was reluctant to do.

[97] M. Casey, *Son of Man: the Interpretation and Influence of Daniel* (London: SPCK, 1979), p. 34, tried to dismiss this possibility by saying, 1) "The fact that the author never mentions Judas Maccabaeus is a fatal objection to this view." 2) He admitted, however, that the suggestion ". . . fits so beautifully into the Syrian tradition of interpretation, which saw the Maccabean victory under Judas as the meaning of the triumph of the Saints of the Most High, and could easily have seen Judas Maccabaeus as a type of Christ." Casey's second objection was that he thought this was *too* neat to be true. If Judas had really been the intended Son of man the church would have perpetuated the tradition. That might have been so if Christians and Jews had been in defensible positions in the Roman Empire after the two revolts of the Jews against Rome (66-70 and 132-35 IA). After the Bar Cochba defeat, Romans inspected Jewish and Christian materials to learn if they contained any subversive material. This is evident from an early rabbinic report. Once the [Roman] government sent two officials and said to them, "Go and become [false Jewish] proselytes, and examine the Torah of the Jews, what its nature is." They went to Rabban Gamaliel at Usha, and they read the Hebrew Scripture. They studied the Mishnah, midrash, halachot, and haggadoth. When they left they said to them [the rabbis], "All of your teachings are good and admirable, except for one item. Stealing from a pagan is permitted, but from a Jew it is forbidden, but we shall not disclose this matter to the government" *(Sifre Deut* 33.3, Piska 344. 143b).

In order to survive, Jews and Christians had to censor their literature to conform to Roman demands. They quickly learned the importance of their success in proving to the Romans that they had no aggressive or subversive ideals such as the Hasmoneans and the later rebellious Jewish nationalists had. This meant that it would not have been wise to picture Jesus as an antitype of the leader of the Maccabean revolt. Casey's first objection has no validity. Not only did Daniel not once mention Judas the Maccabee by name but he also did not mention Antiochus Epiphanes specifically. He was describing this history mythically and symbolically, as Casey has argued in many places. Casey, himself (pp. 51-70), observed that Syrian fathers identified the saints of the Most High with Hasmonean Jews, contemporaries with Judas, without mentioning the Son of man. Casey took this to mean they believed the Son of man was merely a symbol for the saints and had no reality. He overlooked the fact that, following the Bar Cochba war (135 IA), it was not wise to mention such nationalistic figures as Judas the Maccabee. Believers could safely mention the saints who were contemporary with Judas, who participated in the war and the victory, and pious Jews or Christians would know all the rest that was implied. This is the way people communicate as a fifth column.

is only a symbol of **the saints of the Most High**, without any essence of its own.[98] Both the one like a **son of man** and **the saints of the Most High** were characters in the drama, but both were identified with real people. The drama took place in heaven, but it was based on events that happened on earth.

When he was dealing with the question of **the saints of the Most High,** DiLella concluded that they could not have been angels because of their relationship to the Maccabean Revolt. This was a real war dealing with real people. He said,

> But Antiochus did fight against the Jews because of their adherence to the Mosaic law, and he did abolish the celebration of the Jewish feast days, and the Jews were in his control for some three years (1Macc 1:41-63; 4:26-55). Thus "the holy ones of the Most High" must refer to the faithful men, women, and children who were being done in by the Syrian tyrant.[99]

Had DiLella been consistently logical, he would have continued to say that Antiochus also opposed **the Son of man.** He would have noticed that Antiochus was a real human being who did fight with **the Son of man**, who was also a human being, named Judas the Maccabee. Instead DiLella argued that **the Son of man** was only a *symbol* for the Jews.[100] Antiochus probably thought that Judas was more than a symbol.

The identification of the one like a Son of man with Judas the Maccabee and the claim that Daniel was composed in its final form in close relationship to the Hanukkah of 164 BIA were made and published in 1972.[101] Many scholars have since ignored the suggestion, but DiLella[102] and Hartman set out to refute the position, using two arguments:

1) Daniel was written before 164 BIA, Hartman said. This was evident to him, because there were some inaccuracies in the prophecies. He pointed out a few of these. There were even more than he noted, but that does not prove the text was written earlier. The author's misidentification of Nebuchadnezzar with Nabonidus and Jehoiakim with Jehoiakin, for example, were mistakes made about much earlier history that had already happened, without any question. The same is true of the restoration of Judah in the time of Ezra and Nehemiah, which the author by-passed with hardly a mention. Would Hartman claim that the author had never heard of them, and that therefore he must have written before the sixth century BIA? Hartman presumed that an author could not make a mistake or would not

---

[98] Casey, *Son of Man*, p. 28. "Moreover he is a pure symbol, that is to say, he is not a real being who exists outside Daniel's dream; he is only a symbolic being within the dream" (p. 25). "There are no previous examples of purely symbolic beings coming with the clouds in the OT because there are no previous examples of purely symbolic beings coming at all" (p. 28).

[99] A. A. DiLella, "The One in Human Likeness and the Holy Ones of the Most High in Daniel 7," *CBQ* 39 (1977):12.

[100] DiLella, "One," pp. 16-17.

[101] Buchanan, *Hebrews*, pp. 38-51.

[102] DiLella, "One," pp. 12-19.

distort history from an apologetical point of view. This does not follow. The author's tendential doctrine is evident in many places.

2) The author could not have been pro-Maccabean, Hartman held, because Judas and his followers did some violent things, and the author was a pacifistic Hasid. How did Hartman know that he was a pacifistic Hasid? Because many earlier secondary sources said so. Hartman listed several of these. This presumes that "ten thousand Frenchmen cannot be wrong." Following the same logic Collins said,

> Third, a considerable number of authors have remained persuaded that the "one like a human being" is individual but understand him as a heavenly, angelic being rather than the messiah.[103]

Of course many millions of people for many centuries believed that the earth was flat, but that did not prove that it was. Some people are capable of believing six impossible things before breakfast. It is not numbers of people who hold opinions, but data and logic that decide the case.

The scholars who think the Book of Daniel is anti-Maccabean have overlooked the fact that it was the Hasmonean leaders that preserved the Book of Daniel in their canon together with 1 and 2 Maccabees. The canon has passed through the censorship of the Maccabees, just as it earlier passed the approval of David's court historian, Ezra and Nehemiah, and the later Palestinian rabbis. According to a pro-Maccabean source,

> Likewise Judas also gathered for us all the reports that had been distributed because of the war, and they are still with us (2Macc 2:14).

Among those reports was probably included the Book of Daniel which was not rejected because it was anti-Maccabean. There have been many books written during the history of the Hebrews, Jews, Samaritans, and Christians that have not been preserved. Our biblical canon is a collection preserved by partisan editors, such as the court secretaries of David, Ezra and Nehemiah, and first century IA rabbis. Among these partisan editors were the Hasmonean scribes and secretaries who determined which books would be preserved from that time on and be included in the canon and these preserved the Book of Daniel.

More recently there have been other scholars who acknowledge this and notice that the victory themes of Daniel match the Hasmonean victories.[104] All of the dates prophesied in Daniel point to the year 164 BIA when the horn

---

[103] Collins, A *Commentary*, p. 310.

[104] M. Casey, *Son of Man*, p. 34, dismissed the idea that the identification of Judas with the Son of man was just too neat to be true. J. Coppens and L. Dequeker, *Le Fils d'homme et les Saints du Tres-Haut en Dan 7, dans Les Apocryphes et dans le Nouveau Testament* (Bruges-Paris: Publications Universaires, 1961), p. 54, held that in its present form the Book of Daniel is pro-Hasmonean. H. Sahlin, "Antiochus IV Epiphanes und Judas Mackabäus," *ST* 23 (1969):42-43, argued that Judas the Maccabee was the Son of man in Daniel.

(Antiochus Epiphanes) died and Judas overpowered the Syrian Greeks at Beth-horon and Beth-zur. The victories were celebrated by establishing a new pro-Maccabean feast, still called Hanukkah and mythologized as a divinely directed court scene in Dan 7.

There are still scholars who hold that the **Son of man** was an angel,[105] because they understand the clouds literally. This requires them to ignore the fact that they are dealing with a myth. This myth is a complete unit,[106] beginning with the judge approaching the bench and concluding with a verdict that gave the kingdom to **the saints of the Most High** (the Jews) and the **Son of man** (Judas) while giving the death penalty to **the little horn** (Antiochus).[107] Historically, Antiochus died before the first Hanukkah, so that it was reasonable for a mythologist to include both events as part of the same divine judgment.

Wenham correctly claimed that Daniel provides the primary background for the gospel teaching about the Kingdom of God and Jesus' identification with the Son of man. The two concepts, Kingdom of God and Son of man, belong together and are related to the restoration of Israel.[108] Hanhart said further, "The heavenly kingdom is the earthly Israel."[109] Caird said,

> According to Daniel, it was the Ancient of Days who sat in judgment, and the phrase 'judgment was given to the saints' meant that the verdict went in their favor, so that the imperial power was taken from the fourth bestial kingdom and given to Israel (Dan vii.9, 22).[110]

---

[105] Like Collins, *Apocalyptic*, pp. 82-83; *Daniel* (Grand Rapids, c1984), p. 82; *Daniel, First Maccabees, Second Maccabees* (Wilmington, Delaware: Michael Glazier, c1981), pp. 78-79. Although Collins, "The Son of Man in First Century Judaism," *NTS* 38 (1992):451, still thinks the Son of man was an angel, he also realizes that later Jewish commentators (1Enoch and 4Ezra) identified the Son of man with the son of David and the Messiah. These commentators considered him an individual, rather than a collective personality or symbol (p. 457). Others who thought the saints were angels are C. L. J. Proudman, "Remarks on the 'Son of Man,'" *CJT* 12 (1966):128-31; Towner, Porteous, Noth, *et al.* In opposition to these, LaCocque said, "Let us add that in Dan. 7 the dominion and the royalty are given to the Saints while we nowhere find any mention of an angelic kingdom" (p. 127). LaCocque, however, had in mind a "wholly spiritual sanctuary" (p. 126). N. W. Porteous, *Daniel* (London: SCM Press, 1965), p. 15, said the saints of the Most High were not all Jews in general but only the non-collaborators, those who resisted Antiochus Epiphanes. Porteous did not notice that the greatest of these resisters were the Hasmoneans and their following. For a list of scholars who hold that the Son of man was an angel, see Hartman and DiLella, *Daniel*, pp. 89-90, fns. 212-213. They have also competently shown the ridiculousness of such an idea as this (pp. 90-95).

[106] For a list of those who did not think Dan 7 was a unit see Collins, *A Commentary*, pp. 278-80.

[107] R. Hanhart, "Die Heiligen, pp. 90-101, after analyzing the views of other scholars, dealing with the use of the expression, *koh-duh-sheém*, (קודשים) in the FT, apocryphal literature, and the Dead Sea Scrolls, concluded that there were a few passages that might be translated either as human beings who were pious or angels, but in the majority of cases, the Hebrew and Greek expressions could only make sense as "saints," and they were not to be translated as heavenly angels.

[108] D. Wenham, "The Kingdom of God and Daniel," *ET* 98 (1987):132-34.

[109] Hanhart, "Heiligen," p. 100.

[110] G. B. Caird, *A Commentary on the Revelation of St. John the Divine* (New York: Black, c1966), p. 252.

Scholars, like Collins, who emphasize the heavenly existence of the Son of man, the Messiah, and the Son of David, confuse legal and mythical identity with ontological identity and assume that a human being, such as David, Judas the Maccabee, or Jesus, could not be described as a member of the heavenly council (Acts 13:36) or associated with clouds (Matt 17:5) while still being a political leader on earth.[111]

Once scholars allow themselves to entertain this close relationship between the Kingdom of God or of Heaven and the Son of man, both in Daniel and in the NT, and the identity of the Kingdom of Heaven to Israel, the parallels become obvious. Jesus, as the antitype of the Danielic Son of man, was seen as a new Judas the Maccabee. Like Judas he was called the Son of man; like Judas he wanted to obtain possession of the kingdom; like Judas he **was led like a sheep to the slaughter**, and was killed by the enemy for his people, giving his life as a ransom for the many. As the new Judas Jesus was expected to do the same things Judas had done, and the later church was able to explain his death in terms of type-antitype. Like Judas the new Son of man was also expected to suffer and die (Matt 16:21; 17:22-23; 20:18-19; 20:28).

Coppens and Dequeker held that Jews had been expecting a savior who would establish a new kingdom, the Kingdom of Heaven. God would establish this kingdom at the time when the Son of man came. They correctly argued that the author of Daniel (whom they believed was a redactor of an earlier text) was a Maccabean who clearly reinterpreted this expectation nationalistically. For the so-called redactor,

> The promised Kingdom of God would be no more in the first place the Kingdom of Heaven or the domination of angels, but instead the earthly rule of the Jewish people, after the victory which it had already won over Antiochus Epiphanes, thanks to the decisive intervention of the Lord in favor of his elect.[112]

Coppens and Dequeker were correct in noting that Daniel, as it now is preserved, was understood to apply to the Maccabean victory, and the establishment of the Jewish kingdom which followed. They were also correct in thinking that this conclusion was reached and this literature written after the victory of the Battles of Beth-horon and Beth-zur and the death of Antiochus Epiphanes. There is no good reason to be distracted by the clouds into shifting from myth to history, as many scholars have done. Clouds were frequently used, mythically, to depict the presence of God in a theophany.

Montgomery disagreed with Dalman who thought the Hebrew *mahl-koót* (מלכות) never meant kingdom (*Königsregiment*). He said,

> The Last Kingdom replaces the first Four in the dream, and is, in the idea of the scene, specifically bound, as are its predecessors;

---

[111] On this see further Buchanan, *Insights*.
[112] Coppens and Dequeker, *Le Fils de l'Homme*, p. 54.

the Mountain that fills the whole earth, is not a spiritual Kingdom of Heaven.[113]

1Enoch was probably describing the same court scene that was detailed in Dan 7, in a still more exaggerated fashion. The Son of man appeared before the judge (the Head of days). The judge gave the Son of man a name and authority needed to rule the land. This means God appointed Judas to be the ruler of Palestine. The Son of man became a hope to the holy and elect ones, as Judas surely did, a light to the gentiles, and a cause for misery to the kings and mighty ones who were delivered to the hands of the elect ones, according to the author. 1Enoch meant that the gentile powers who had ruled the Promised Land were overthrown by the Jews under the leadership of Judas the Maccabee (*1Enoch* 48.1-10; 62.7-12). This was really giving Judas and the Jews more credit than they deserved. The Roman power, wealth, arms, guidance, and imperialistic designs influenced the whole movement. The Romans were using the Hasmoneans to weaken the power of the Syrian Greeks and eventually to take over their kingdom completely.

The Romans eventually succeeded in doing exactly that, ruling all of the territory from Great Britain at one end to India at the other, including all of Europe and North Africa. At a crucial point in history, the Hasmoneans were instrumental in weakening the Greeks enough so that Rome could later push still farther. The Syrian Greeks never recovered from this blow. During the seventh decade BIA, when Pompey took over Jerusalem, marking the beginning of the end of Jewish freedom, Romans also put an end to the Seleucid rule.[114] The hyperbole of the Jewish description was normal for an author with a doctrinally subjective point of view, but it is not an objective report of the facts.

Ruling authority of an age. **An age** was a period of indefinite duration. When a new administration began, a new **age** began, and it lasted as long as the dynasty involved. In the ancient Near East the four great **ages** were **the ages** of the Assyrians, the Medes, the Persians, and the Greeks. From the author's perspective, the **age** of pagan rule began with Nebuchadnezzar (605 BIA). From a closer perspective, the Greek age lasted from the time of Alexander the Great (327 BIA) until the end of the Seleucid dynasty (Appian, *Roman History* 11.11, 70, 63 BIA). The authority that began with Judas (164 BIA) continued until the time of Herod the Great (38 BIA). That was the extent of the Hasmonean **age**.

His kingdom would not be destroyed. The **kingdom** mentioned here is the **kingdom** that reigned over Palestine after the victory of Judas at the Battle of Beth-horon. It was God's **kingdom**, but it was also the **kingdom** ruled by his legal

---

[113] Montgomery, *Daniel*, p. 178.
[114] For forty years Mithridates of Pontus had been conducting a war against Rome on various levels. Pompey learned of Mithridates' death on his way to Jerusalem. Romans celebrated his death with a public festival for ten days. After forty years of trying to fence him in Rome was finally successful. In the process of defeating him, Romans also conquered all of Asia Minor and Syria as well and toppled the Seleucids at the same time. So F. E. Peters, *The Harvest of Hellenism* (New York: Simon & Schuster, 1970), p. 320-22.

agents, the Hasmoneans. At the time of this composition the new **kingdom** was just beginning to take shape, but the author expected it to continue and get stronger for a long time. The claim made here was a confession of faith rather than a predetermined fact.

TEXT

Daniel	First Testament Intertexts
¹⁵[As for me], I Daniel, my **breath** within me **was choked**, and the visions in my head alarmed me, ¹⁶so I came up to one of those standing there and asked about all of this. He spoke to me, and made known the interpretation (פשר) of the words to me.	Gen 41:8 Pharaoh had a dream. . . ⁸In the morning his **spirit was troubled.**

COMMENTARY

I Daniel. Reid has made an interesting comparison between pseudepigraphical prophecy in Jewish and Christian studies and pseudepigraphy in African cults. In Zambia a seer often takes the name of an earlier seer who has died. It is called "Bansanga possession." It is done to perpetuate the spirit of the earlier seer and to deny individual identity. When a medium introduces himself or herself in the Bansanga spirit possession this is done with the formula, "I am Monze." Reid has astutely noted the similarity between that formula and the one used here, "**I Daniel.**" Reid correctly said, "Pseudonymity is not literary forgery."[115] The various authors of dramas in **Daniel** composed their works in the name of that expression "I Nebuchadnezzar" in Dan 4:1. This earlier wiseman was named Daniel.

My breath. The word for "breath" is *roó-akh* (רוח), the same word that is translated "spirit" in the similar idiom in Genesis. The Pharaoh's spirit was troubled, which means he was emotionally upset. Daniel was emotionally upset, too, but the idiom had a different emphasis. His breath was choked. He nearly became unconscious. With both, the experience was prompted by a dream or a vision. Both personalities were frightened.

The visions in my head alarmed me. This reminds the reader that this story is a myth. It came in a dream. There were no actual beasts that could be photographed.

---

[115] Reid, *Enoch and Daniel*, p. 113. This raises the question about the meaning of "I Nebuchadnezzar." It seems to imply that the expression might also be attributed negatively to someone. This may mean that the author of Dan 4 knew Nebuchadnezzar did not have the dream attributed to him, but that he presented the dream as if some later seer had done it in his name.

One of those standing there. **Those standing there** were new characters in the play. They were introduced here to give the author a chance to interpret the roles of the characters in the play. It was from this unknown character that Daniel learned the meaning of his dream. Daniel did not interpret his own dream. He had the dream, and the anonymous character told him what it meant. In real life most people would not turn to just anyone **standing** nearby to be able to provide competent religious counsel, but this is a drama dealing with visions and dreams.

TEXT

Daniel	First Testament Intertexts
[17]"These **huge beasts**, of which there are **four**, are four kings rising up from the ground,	Ps 34:9 Let his **saints** fear Yehowah.
[18]but **the saints of the** Most High will receive the kingdom, and they will possess the kingdom until the age and until the age of ages."	Ps 16:3 As for **the saints of the** land, they are noble. I am delighted with all of them.

COMMENTARY

Are four kings. Now the story begins to unravel. At this point Daniel began to interpret his dream, point-by-point. His dream began with four huge beasts, so his midrash began by interpreting the meaning of the four beasts. Those beasts that had minds and eyes like human beings really were human beings. The myth gave the author an opportunity to tell how he felt about these particular human beings. They were all kings, to be sure, but they were monstrous. The OG referred to these beasts as "kingdoms." Since they were contrasted to the Son of man, which was a human being, it is reasonable to conclude that the MT was correct.

The mythologist portrayed Judas as one like a Son of man who was the plaintiff, and God, as supreme judge who was the Ancient of Days. The Son of man *received* power and authority in this mythical judgment scene. God, as the Ancient of Days, gave him this power and authority. The Son of man and the saints were not judges here. Later, after the authority had been in force, they could function as judges--the Son of man as the supreme judge, and the saints as subordinate judges (so also Matt 19:28). This is where Paul got the notion that the saints were destined to judge the world (1Cor 6:2).

Scholars often confuse the function of the participants in this court trial. By mythologizing this important period of history, Jews were expressing their belief that God had decreed the Hasmonean victory over the Greeks. The Battle of Beth-horon or Beth-zur was their day in court, just as there had been a judgment day in 586 BIA at which the verdict had been pronounced against the Jews. The rule of the "beasts" was of demonic origin; the rule of the one like a "Son of man" was of divine origin. It was accompanied by God's *ah-nahn*. This vision mythologized historical events shortly after Judas won decisive victories over the Greeks at Beth-horon and Beth-zur. At the mythical court session, Jews were vindicated (*Ant* 12.285-312).

Rising up from the ground. The word rendered "**ground**" here might also be translated "land" (*ah-ruh-áh*, ארעא). At the beginning of the dream, these were supposed to have **come up from the** sea (*yah-máh*, ימא). The importance of the sea origin probably was intended to show that they were the great monsters of the sea, the abyss, the symbol of chaos. Actually, the first three were Easterners. They originated from the Fertile Crescent area, so they rose up from the ground or the land. These were the kings that ruled the Jews after they had been taken into Babylon as exiles. The first of these was Nebuchadnezzar. Others were Nabonidus and his son Belshazzar, Darius, and the Greek kings.

The saints of the Most High will receive the kingdom. Since the discovery of the Dead Sea Scrolls where holy war soldiers were described as "**saints,**" many scholars have stopped thinking of **the saints of the Most High** as angels.[116] The Israelites who feared Yehowah were called saints (Ps 34:10). **The saints of the Most High** are **the saints** of Yehowah, the people of God, or **the saints** of the land. The noble ones in whom Yehowah takes delight are **the saints** of the land (Ps 16:2). They were not called the angels of heaven. Their residence was on the Promised Land. Charles said that **the saints** were God's people. They were called the saints of the Most High to express the supernatural character of God's people in contrast to the beasts.[117] They were the holy people as distinguished from the common people who were the gentiles or pagans (Lev 10:10). Hartman has almost ridiculed the idea that the saints were angels out of discussion. Among his many good arguments are the following:

> If we substitute "the angels" wherever "the holy ones (of the Most High)" appear, we shall see that there would be small comfort for the persecuted community to be promised that "[the angels] will receive the kingdom" and "possess it forever" (vs. 18); and that "dominion was given to [the angels]. Thus the time came when [the angels] "took possession of the kingdom" (vs. 22). "The kingship and the dominion and the grandeur of all the kingdoms under the heavens will be given to [the people of the angels, or angelic people]. Their royal rule will last forever, and all dominions will serve and obey it" (vs. 27). Moreover, the Jews on hearing or reading the apocalypse would surely have been baffled by vss. 21-22, "that horn [= Antiochus IV] waged war against [the angels] and was prevailing against them until the Ancient One arrived"; and by vs. 25, "He [Antiochus] will utter words against the Most High, and [the angels] he will devastate, planning to

---

[116] But not all of them. There is still Goldingay, "'Holy Ones, pp. 495-97.
[117] Charles, *Daniel*, p. 191. Charles followed Bevan, *Short Commentary*, p. 125, in this deduction.

change the feast days and the law; they will be handed over to him for a year, two years, and half a year."[118]

If The holy ones (of the Most High) were to be understood as angels, then Antiochus is being said to fight against angels, and to change the feast days and the law of the angels, and to have control over the angels for three and a half years. It hardly seems plausible that the author of Daniel 7 meant to imply that Antiochus was capable of such activities.[119]

TEXT

[19]Then I wanted [to know] the truth about **the fourth beast** who was different from all the rest--more terrible, with teeth of iron, claws of bronze, who consumed and shattered [most obstacles], and trampled the rest with its feet [20]and about **the ten horns** which were on its head and the other [horn] of which three [horns] fell and the horn which had eyes and a mouth that spoke extensively and which appeared greater than its fellows. [21]I continued to watch, and this horn made war with the saints and overpowered them [22]until the Ancient of Days came and the verdict was given to the saints of the Most High. Then the time arrived, and the saints possessed **the kingdom**. [23]This is what he said:

TECHNICAL DETAILS

These four verses were written to introduce the poem that follows (Dan 7:23-27). The poem was one that the author of Dan 7 already had in his possession, and he chose to use it near the end of his document, beautifully integrating it into his narrative. The poem identified **the fourth beast**, **the ten horns**, and **the kingdom**. The author not only introduced them in these four verses, but also interspersed the first two items into the poem itself as topics the author of Dan 7 did not want the reader to miss. That was not necessary for **the kingdom**, because it was part of the poem itself and appeared as a conclusion. Concluding an essay with a poem of confession is not a unique feature for Dan 7. There are also concluding confessions of a king as poems in Dan 2:20-23, 3:33, 4:31-34, and 6:27-28.[120]

COMMENTARY

I wanted [to know] the truth. Since he wanted to know the truth, he probably asked the one standing there who answered the rest of his questions. Many scholars assume that the one standing there was an angel, but the text does not say

---

[118] Hartman, *Daniel*, p. 91.
[119] Hartman, *Daniel*, p. 95
[120] So also G. T. M. Prinsloo, "Two Poems in a Sea of Prose: The Content and Context of Daniel 2:20-23 and 6:27-28."

that. He was a character that was introduced into the drama to make a conversation possible.

Different from all the rest. Daniel skipped the detail of the first three beasts, because it was the fourth beast that demanded the most of his attention. He did not explain, for example, the significance of the bear who had three ribs in his mouth and lay on his side (Dan 7:5). The fourth kingdom to rule the Middle East was the Greek kingdom. It came into power under the leadership of Alexander the Great, who, in a few short years conquered all of the land from Macedonia to India, including Egypt and Arabia. He had the latest of iron weapons, armor, and heads of battering rams. He plundered the land as he went, confiscating property and supplies for his army. He was not different in kind from the other kings; he was different in degree--greater and more powerful.

The ten horns which were on its head. These **ten horns** had to have a special significance in the dream. The monster was pictured as a beast, like a cow or goat, which had horns for fighting, but instead of two he had ten, perhaps like a moose or male deer. These horns were all human kings, but again, it was the last of these horns that affected Judah, so it received the most of the dreamer's detail.

The horn which had eyes and a mouth. This was the king who appeared in court and spoke extensively in his own defense. He was tried by the Ancient of Days and given the death sentence.

Made war with the saints. Noth correctly said that **the saints** mentioned in Dan 7:21 are the righteous of Israel,[121] but he thought Dan 7:21 was a later insertion. This is the way many scholars dismiss meanings they do not like in scripture. Insertions have been made, but modern scholars are not always able to identify them. Original authors could write as poorly as later editors. Here there is little to suggest an author who differs from the one who wrote the verses around it. Coherence requires that the saints in Dan 7:21 were the same as the saints of the Most High in Dan 7:22, 25, and 27. They were probably not **the** identical **saints** mentioned in Ps 16:3 and 34:10, but they are of the same definition. They are the saints of the land who fear Yehowah and in whom Yehowah takes delight.

There are other testimonies telling of the opposition of the horn to the saints: 1) **He will speak words against the Most High. He will exhaust the saints of the Most High** (Dan 7:25). 2). **He will destroy powerful people, including the people of the saints** (Dan 8:24). 3) **He will be furious against the holy treaty, so he will act and give instruction for those who abandoned the holy treaty** (Dan 11:30). He also supported those who broke the treaty they had made with God (Dan 11:32).

---

[121] M. Noth, "The Holy Ones of the Most High," *Laws of the Pentateuch and Other Essays* (Philadelphia: Fortress, 1967), pp. 215-38.

TEXT

The fourth beast—
>There will be a fourth kingdom on the land,
>>which is different from all the [other] kingdoms.
>
>It will consume all the land,
>>trample, and shatter it.

²⁴**The ten horns—**
>From that kingdom ten kings will arise,
>>and another [king] will arise after them.
>
>He will be different from the preceding ones.
>>He will subdue three kings,
>
>²⁵and he will speak words against the Most High.
>>He **will exhaust** the saints of the Most High
>>>and try to change the calendar and the religion.
>
>They will be given into his hand
>>for a time, two times, and half a time.
>
>²⁶Then the court will sit [in judgment],
>>and his ruling authority will be removed,
>>>finally to be reduced and destroyed.
>
>²⁷**The kingdom,** ruling authority, and
>>the greatest kingdom under all the heavens
>>>will be given to the saints of the Most High.
>
>**Its kingdom** is a **kingdom** of the age [to come],
>>and all ruling authorities will serve and obey it.

Daniel	First Testament Intertexts
²⁸**Here is where the word ends.** As for me, Daniel, my thoughts alarmed me very much. My appearance changed, and I kept the words in my mind."	Eccles 12:13 **The word ends.** Jer 51:64 **The words** of Jeremiah **give out here.**

COMMENTARY

Then the time arrived. This was the predestined time of the end, which was mentioned several times in the Book of Daniel. This was the time that had already taken place. The critical battles of the war with the Syrian Greeks were over; the Seleucids were being driven out of the land or they already had been driven, and the saints received the kingdom. This means the land of Palestine was successfully taken from the Syrian Greeks and given to the Jews who were contemporary with the Hasmoneans. Collins continues to argue, however, that the saints who received the kingdom after the Battle of Beth-horon victory were angels.¹²² Jews did not celebrate Hanukkah because angels received the kingdom,

---

¹²² Collins, *A Commentary*, p. 319.

but because they, themselves, had received it. They initially received it after Judas' famous military victory (164 BIA) and fully received it after the tax was removed during the reign of Simon (142 BIA).

The mythologist who wrote Dan 7 believed that this was all predestined from the time when Nebuchadnezzar first entered Jerusalem. This was the end of **the "time**, two times, and half a time." There is no logical way in which this completed end can be turned into a prophecy that applies to the twentieth century. Nor does it seem reasonable to assume this text was written in a time of constant crisis so that people expecting the end would move their expectation from 3½ years to 70 years (Dan 9), then finally looking forward to the end of all history (Dan 2, 8, 10, 11, and 12), as Stahl proposed.[123]

Dan 7 was a celebration essay, rejoicing in the victory of the Son of man and the saints of the Most High over the little horn. It seemed too good to be true. This was not a suicidal note from depressed people who were so badly crushed that they wanted to escape from existence in the world. The message of Daniel was a message of survival from past pressure—not pressure "of life in history" or "of life at the end of history" as Goldingay held.[124] **The** predestined **time** actually arrived back in 164 BIA. The kingdom that they inherited was the Davidic kingdom, which they originally captured from the Canaanites under the leadership of Joshua, various judges, Saul, and David. Driver correctly noted,

> The age of Antiochus Epiphanes is in fact the *limiting horizon of the book* [emphasis his]. Not only does the revelation of chs. x-xii culminate in the description of that age, which followed, without interval, by a period of final bliss, but the age of Antiochus himself is in viii.19 (as the sequel shows) described as the 'time of the end.' 'Can there then,' asks Delitzsch, 'have been for Daniel a "time of the end" *after* [emphasis his] that which he himself expressly describes as the "end"?[125]

Another king will arise after them. Some of the ten kings were Seleucids. One of the Seleucids was Antiochus Epiphanes (175-164 BIA). He was this "another king" who arose. The identification of the kings is not clear. There are two possibilities:

1) He apparently advanced himself ahead of his normal schedule, displacing a) his older brother's son, Demetrius, who was supposed to be in line for the kingdom ahead of him, b) Antiochus IV's sister, Cleopatra's son, Ptolemy VII, and c) Heliodorus, chief minister of Seleucus. Another possible identity is a) his brother Seleucus and Seleucus' two sons, b)Antiochus and c)Demetrius.
2) The other possibility is that he subdued other neighboring foreign kings in military conflicts. Ginsberg identified the three kings as Ptolemy VI and VII and

---

[123] R. Stahl, "'Eine Zeit. Zeiten und die Hälfte einer Zeit.'" Die Versuche der Eingrenzung der bösen Macht im Danielbuch," *The Book of Daniel*, pp. 480-94.
[124] J. E. Goldingay, *Daniel* (Dallas: Word Books, c1989), p. 183.
[125] S. R. Driver, *The Book of Daniel* (Cambridge: University Press, 1905), p. 100.

Artaxias of Armenia,[126] but the text implies that those Antiochus subdued were "horns," and other scholars have noted that Antiochus IV did not really subdue these kings.

He will exhaust the saints of the Most High. These were not the angels of God, as Collins has argued.[127] They were the Jews in Judah who were the victims of Antiochus' persecution. Some of these were the soldiers who joined ranks with Judas to oppose the Syrian Greeks. The author of Dan 7 used the same verb here as that of the Chronicler: **The wicked will not again exhaust them** (1Chron 17:9). The object of the exhausting for the Chronicler was the people of Israel. The object for Dan 7 was **the saints of the Most High.**

He will try to change the calendar and the religion. The topic continues. Antiochus not only exhausted the saints of the Most High, but he tried to change their **calendar and** their **religion**. He was not concerned with the calendar or the religion of the angels. There was not anything that he could do about **the religion** of the angels. It was the saints to which he directed his energies. Ever since his forced retreat from Egypt, after this confrontation with the Romans, Antiochus IV tried to enforce Hellenism on the Jews. This meant forcing them to give up their Sabbath observance, reading of the scriptures, circumcising males, offering sacrifices, observing festivals (1Macc 1:44-49) and other Jewish traditions.

December, 168 BIA, either Antiochus or his Syrian or Jewish agents erected a pagan altar on top of the sacred altar of the temple, or placed an idol on the wing of the temple. Either way, they polluted the temple (1Macc 1:54-55). This is the act that finally stirred up the Maccabean Revolt. This was not, however, the beginning of Hellenistic influences in Palestine. Centuries before Greek merchants spread Greek culture with their products all over Asia Minor, Egypt, Palestine, and Syria. When Palestine was under Egyptian domination, Egypt used Greek mercenary soldiers to police Palestine. Jewish merchants also went abroad and returned with Greek products and culture. There were also many Jews who lived in the diaspora who spoke Greek, accepted Greek culture, and returned to Jerusalem to the feasts regularly. When Alexander the Great conquered Palestine he found a country that had already been extensively infiltrated with Greek culture.[128] There were also, however, many very conservative Jews who considered this influence in Palestine to be pagan, and held that those who accepted it had abandoned the treaty made with God.

They will be given into his hand. Not the angels, but the saints. The passive voice is used here to avoid the blasphemy of using the divine name. It means "**God will give them into his hand**." This was the period of God's wrath. Jews did not think it was Antiochus who successfully subdued them. It was God who allowed him to do it. It was the Jews who had sinned, and not the angels. It was the saints who

---
[126] Ginsberg, "Composition," p. 270.
[127] Collins, *A Commentary*, p. 322.
[128] See further M. Smith, *Palestinian Parties and Politics that Shaped the Old Testament* (New York: Columbia U. Press, c1971), pp. 57-81.

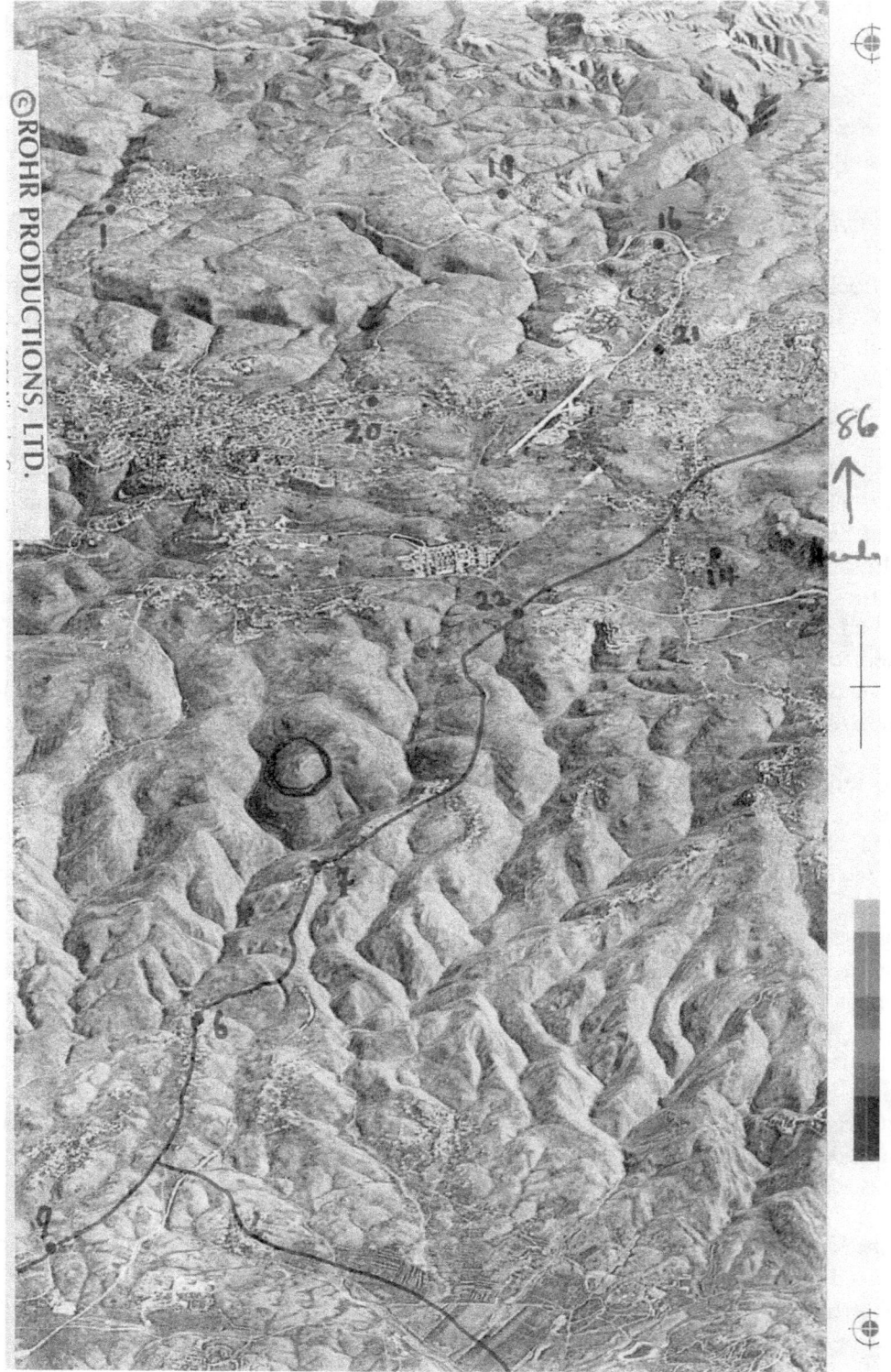

Beth-horon is the encircled hilltop, near the modern road that follows the hilltops from Jerusalem to the Mediterranean shore. The old road went through the valley between the modern road and Beth-horon. From this strategic point Judas and his troops were able to lock in the Syrians and prevent them from reaching Jerusalem.

consequently had to pay for their crimes before they could be restored to the Promised Land.

The time that they were "imprisoned" was from the beginning of the exile into Babylon until the cleansing of the temple in 164 BIA. God's fiercest anger was the three year period between the defilement of the temple by Antiochus IV Epiphanes and its cleansing by the order of Judas the Maccabee. The three years were those years spent during the most crucial part of the Maccabean Rebellion. They constituted the time spent from the beginning of the war until the dedication of the temple.

There were some discrepancies in the exact time spent. Did it begin with the defilement of the temple or with the first military battle? It might have begun with the legation of Apollonius (June 168, 1Macc 1:20, 29). Did it conclude with the last Day of Atonement before the Battle of Beth-horon? with the Battle of Beth-horon itself? or with the first Hanukkah? Different calculators used different dates at both ends. From the defilement of the temple until its dedication was almost exactly three years (ca 1,095 days), but according to Dan 8:4 it was 2,300 morning and evening sacrifices, which equals 1,150 days. According to Dan 12:11 it was 1,290 days, but in Dan 12:12 it was 1,335 days. The author of Dan 7 rounded things off to fit into Sabbath year reckoning, three and a half years or about 1,278 days, one half of a Sabbath of years. All of the various authors of different dramas in the Book of Daniel who spoke of this period, however, were speaking of the same period. It was the period of the Hasmonean war before Hanukkah. The author of the prophetic section of the Book of Revelation described this period as 42 months (3½ x 12 = 42) (Rev 11:2; 13:5) and called the same period 1,260 days, calculating on the basis of a 30 day month (30 x 42 = 1,260). Dan 7:25 and Dan 12:7 refer to this period as "A time, times, and half a time." This is another way of saying 3½ years.

In a different situation, after the temple had been burned, when the Psalmist was in distress, lamenting the terrible destruction, he complained

> We do not see our signs.
> There is no longer a prophet.
> There is not among us anyone who knows how long (Ps 74:9)

There was no such distress as that in Dan 7. The author knew how long. It was to be no more than three and a half years, because the time had already elapsed. The judgment had been held; the horn had been killed; the Jews had been victorious at the Battle of Beth-horon. This chapter was not a lamentation or a hope "against all hope that God would make it all right in the end," as Burkitt understood.[129] It was not a tract for hard times. It was a success story, a song to celebrate.

Although different contemporary editors used different dates for their calculations, they all were dealing with the same fact. The so-called 3½-year period was measured from the beginning segment of the Hasmonean War. The crucial battle was the Battle of Beth-horon; the significant celebration was Hanukkah (164 BIA). The author of Dan 9 had some further adjustments: He had

---

[129] F. C. Burkitt, *Jewish and Christian Apocalypses* (London: Oxford Press, 1914), p. 16.

to determine when the Babylonian exile began and how to fit Jeremiah's prophecy to balance the time until 164 BIA. He did this also according to Sabbath rules and scripture. This took some stretching to satisfy all of the dogma. Modern scholars have worked as arduously and as creatively as ancient calculators to make all of these figures cohere and satisfy modern dogma.

The court will sit in judgment. The heavenly **judgment** could not have taken place before Antiochus' death and the establishment of Judas the Maccabee as the legitimate leader of Palestine, because the **judgment** took all of these events into consideration. The horn and the Son of man were the main characters in the drama. Second Isaiah anticipated a time when Israel would no longer drink the cup of staggering or the bowl of wrath. These would be put in the hand of Israel's tormentors (Isa 51:22-23). According to the Dramas of Daniel this would happen when God held court in heaven on a great Day of Judgment. This was the time of the great transfer. In history, this was the time when the rule of Palestine was transferred from the Syrian Greeks to the Jews, from the horn to the one like a Son of man, from Antiochus Epiphanes to Judas the Maccabee.

Reid said the fourth beast was brought to judgment (Dan 7:26). This meant that "there is no combat myth in Daniel 7."[130] Mattila forced a contrast between the military eschatology of the War Scroll with the passive, peaceful eschatology of Daniel and 4Q246. The War Scroll, on the one hand, anticipated a time of peace, joy, blessing, and long life (*1QM* 17.7; 1.9), but that would take place only after a victorious war in which the enemy would be annihilated. Daniel, on the other hand, like 4Q246, also expected peace after "all the nations and 'abyses' are to be brought into submission to the people of God." She said that this would be done "without human military force." On the one hand there would be a war followed by peace. On the other hand there would be peace, preceded by chaos, but "the chaos is only a rebellion after which the true order of nature will be restored."[131] In both cases there is the expectation of peace following a war. The one is called war, and the other is called "rebellion." In the one the enemy was defeated, and in the other it submitted. The rebellion, however, turned out to be the Maccabean Rebellion which was a war between the Maccabees and the Syrian Greeks. The submission was the retreat of the Syrian Greeks after they had been defeated in the battles of Beth-horon and Beth-zur. Changing names does not alter history.

Reid overlooked the fact that this judgment day took place in heaven and was only deduced by the author of this drama on the basis of that which happened on earth. That which happened on earth was the Maccabean Rebellion, and that was a serious combat. The author knew the result of the heavenly judgment, because Judas won the Battle of Beth-horon. This meant God gave the victory to the Jews, and the Greeks were defeated. The author of Dan 7 knew more about the events of this crucial period of history than Reid presumed.

---

[130] Reid, *Enoch and Daniel*, p. 83.
[131] Mattila, "Eschatologies," pp. 536-38.

His authority will be removed. The **authority** of the little horn, Antiochus IV was **removed** by the divine judgment that took place at his death in Persia, shortly before or after the battles of Beth-horon and Beth-zur. This was the predetermined end mentioned several times in the Book of Daniel. This poem telling of the end of Antiochus Epiphanes had to have been written after the death of Antiochus. The entire judgment scene was written after the event.[132]

The greatest kingdom under all the heavens. This was not an objective analysis. Even at the time that this was written, the small Davidic kingdom that was finally attained by the time of Simon (142 BIA) was not anywhere nearly as great as the Roman Empire, or its predecessors, the Assyrian Empire, the Median Empire, the Persian Empire, or Alexander's empire. At its largest size it extended from the Gulf of Aqaba on the south to the northern border of Lebanon on the north, but even if it was small it was the greatest, in the view of its citizens.

Furthermore Jews dreamed of Judah's expansion. This is the only prophecy that occurs in the Book of Daniel. Like the ancient prophets the author of Dan 7 made a general prediction that was not limited to a precise time. It was that this little country would sometime be bigger. After Maccabean times Jews knew about the expansion of the little country of Persia under Cyrus and the extension of the small nation of Macedonia to as far east as India under Alexander the Great. Jews could surely do as much as any other country had ever done. Following Second Isaiah, Jews looked forward to the time when foreign kings would minister to them (Isa 60:10), when foreign kings would be their babysitters, and queens would be household servants for Jews, and kings would bow down in humility before Jews (Isa 49:23). These are some of the advantages that would come when Judah became **the greatest kingdom under all the heavens.**

To the saints of the Most High. The same trial that decreed a death sentence for "the horn" awarded a kingdom to "the Son of man." Antiochus died very close to the time Judas had the temple cleansed. The primary plaintiff in this trial was the Son of man. Here, that character is just as easy to identify as the defendant is. The "horn" was Antiochus Epiphanes; the "Son of man" was his opponent in war, Judas the Maccabee. Neither one was the angel Collins claimed. At the same time the judgment was given to Judas the Maccabee it was also granted to **the saints of the Most High**, who were not angels, but were the anti-Hellenistic Jews who were contemporary with Judas (Dan 7:22). Contemporary Jews were to receive the kingdom at the very time Judas was to receive it--they as citizens, and Judas as the ruler. **The saints of the Most High** were not Hellenists and not the angels. The Hellenists who had been first were suddenly last, and the Hasmoneans and their followers, who had been cave-dwelling guerrillas had become leaders in the government.

Probably not all Palestinian Jews were included among **the saints**. Throughout the Maccabean Revolt and throughout the Book of Daniel the nations

---

[132] For some reason Frölich, "'*A Time and Times,*'" p. 76-77, said this was prophecy, "a predicted event" that happened "before the latter's death." Then, in direct contradiction, she said it was "subsequent to the successful battles of Judas Maccabeus." The later judgment was correct.

were contrasted to Israel. The hellenizers were the powerful ones who abandoned the treaty with God by making a treaty with Antiochus. It was the high priests—Jason and Menelaus--who led the Hellenistic movement. It was the Hasmoneans who opposed them by leading the revolution. With the Battle of Beth-horon, the tables were turned. The last became first and the first became last. The Hasmonean brothers became high priests, and their supporters were given the chief seats in the government. These were **the saints of the Most High.**

When Mattathias declared the beginning of the revolt, he cried, "Whoever is zealous for our nation's traditions and the worship of God, let him be with me" (*Ant* 12.271). An early Jewish historian compared the action of Mattathias to that of their forefather Phineas who took the law into his own hands and thereby turned away the wrath from Israel and received the promise. His action was reckoned to him as righteousness (1Macc 2:54; 3:8; Num 25; Ps 106:31). There were enough of these zealots who followed Mattathias to turn back the troops of Antiochus Epiphanes. Their numbers were small but their zeal was great.

Like many others, Bickerman mistakenly held that Daniel was a book of resignation and that Daniel represented the position of the Jews of Hasmonean times, because they "showed no zeal in its defense."[133] He thought the one who would come with the clouds like a Son of man would rule over the world forever, but that would take place without any human act.[134] Bickerman missed the point of Dan 7 which was not a message of resignation but of celebration in which the zeal of the Jewish soldiers had been vindicated, and Antiochus IV had been killed. Dan 7 shows the theological interpretation of the Hasmonean war in which the Lord had given his blessing to the zealous leadership of Judas the Maccabee. It is not a chapter of resignation but of God's judgment. It is true that there were a thousand Hasidim who accepted death rather than break the Sabbath, but that does not mean that they were unwilling to defend their nation on the other six days of the week. Neither is there much evidence to suggest that one of these wrote the Book of Daniel.

This refutes Casey's position that the Son of man is only a symbol of **the saints of the Most High**, without any essence of its own.[135] It also refutes Driver, who thought the Son of man figure could not be held by an individual messiah, when it was the saints who should receive the kingdom.[136]

The **saints of the Most High** were the pro-Maccabean Jewish citizens who were contemporaries in Palestine with Judas.[137] They were not angels, as some have thought, but pious Jews who supported the Maccabean Revolt. The Damascus sect described the "men of knowledge" (*ahn-sháy day-óht*, אנשי דעות)

---

[133] E. J. Bickerman, *From Ezra to the Last of the Maccabees* (New York: Schocken, 1970), p. 95
[134] Bickerman, *From Ezra*, p. 95.
[135] Casey, *Son of Man*, "Moreover he is a pure symbol, that is to say, he is not a real being who exists outside Daniel's dream; he is only a symbolic being within the dream" (p. 25). "There are no previous examples of purely symbolic beings coming with the clouds in the OT because there are no previous examples of purely symbolic beings coming at all" (p. 28).
[136] Driver, *Daniel*, p. 103.
[137] Montgomery, *Daniel*, p. 87, evidently thought the saints were Jews contemporary with Judas the Maccabee, but he argued that they would receive the kingdom, but not by force. It would be a gift of the Highest.

and the "men of perfect holiness" (*ahn-sháy tah-meém hah-kóh-dehsh*, אנשי תמים הקודש) as "all the saints of the Most High" (*kóhl kuh-dohsh-áy ehl-yóhn*, כל קדושי עליון) (*CDC* 20B.4-8)--clearly not a group of angels. Even though angels are not mentioned in this context, Collins argued, "Unfortunately the context here is compatible with a reference either to angels or to men."[138]

To import angels into this picture is perfect eisegesis. The context does not deal with angels at all. It deals with the way the members of the sect should treat a backslider. It is the members of the group, the **men** of knowledge, the **men** of perfect holiness, to whom the instruction is given. Those qualified to act were "all the saints of the Most High." The community into which men were admitted was called the "council of the **men** of perfect holiness" (*CDC* 20B.1, 5, 7). Backsliders were to be tested by "the **men** of knowledge" (*CDC* 20B.4-5). If they were to be excluded from the community, it was "all the saints of the Most High" who would curse them as they left (*CDC* 20B.8).

At the admission ceremony in the Scroll of the Rule those admitted were to be blessed, and those rejected to be cursed. This blessing and cursing was not done by angels but by priests and Levites (*IQS* 2.1-18). This ceremony was probably patterned after the directions in Deut 27:11-26 to place half of the tribes on Mount Gerizim and half on Mount Ebal. Those on Mount Gerizim would bless the people and those on Mount Ebal would utter the curses. Joshua reportedly fulfilled this command (Josh 8:30-35). No angels were involved either in the blessing or the cursing. Collins' basis for thinking that the report given in CDC is "unfortunate" is not that it is ambiguous but that it argues against his position.

At the same time that Judas received the kingdom, administrative authority, and glory of his position, the saints of the Most High, i.e., the men of perfect holiness, also received the same benefits. The kingdom over which the horn and the Son of man fought was the Promised Land, the Davidic kingdom, which the Hasmoneans finally recovered completely. This was not done by resignation or absence of zeal in the nation's defense.

All ruling authorities will serve and obey it. This would be only a fulfillment of the prophecy of Second Isaiah. That prophet promised that the land of Palestine would have to become much greater than the Solomonic kingdom (Isa 49:19-20).

At this early stage of the recovery of Palestine from the Syrian Greeks, Jews looked forward to the fulfillment of Second Isaiah's prophecy. When Judah had only recently been captured from the Greeks, Jews dreamed of ruling the world, but their concept of the world did not constitute the cosmos. It was as big as the empire of Alexander the Great. The mythologist here believed that in time all governments--the Assyrians, Medians, Persians, Greeks, Egyptians, and others would come under Jewish domination. After all these other empires at one time or another had been so powerful that all surrounding kingdoms had been under their domination. Jews would simply take their place as the next empire in the line of succession. Porteous said

---

[138] Collins, *A Commentary*, p. 316.

> His [Heaton's] own probably correct interpretation of their [Babylon, Media, and Persia] reprieve is that they are to become part of the nations who will become vassal to the saints of the Most High (vv. 14 and 27). That this hope was not fulfilled does not in the least prove that it was not entertained.[139]

This was an extension of the conquest theology that motivated the Israelites to take control of Palestine in the first place. World domination, however, did not become a part of Jewish doctrine until the upper class Jews had been taken into Babylon and exposed to the empire building politics associated with great countries. That changed Canaan conquest theology into world conquest theology. That theology has continued in Judaism and Christianity until this very day and has justified many wars and ethnic cleansings (See 1Cor 6:2).

Here is where the word ends. These are the concluding **words** of the narrative that began with the words, **The beginning of the words** (Dan 7:1). At **the beginning of the words Daniel said** he was **seeing a vision at night**. At the **end of his words** he reported that he remembered **the words, keeping** them **in his mind**.

These headings form an *inclusio*, circumscribing the narrative of Dan 7. This marks the end of the drama in Dan 7, showing that Dan 7 is a complete unit. Whatever sources were used in the composition of this chapter, there was one human being who organized the document and set it apart by an introduction and conclusion. This does not refer to the end of history, as some scholars think.[140]

DANIEL 7 AND ANCIENT COURT SESSIONS

Introduction. Dan 7 is the central chapter in the Book of Daniel,[141] both in position and in importance. Other chapters in Daniel have been shown to be myths. There is no doubt that this is so. The authors themselves of the other chapters first told the story and then told what it meant, just as was true of Dan 7. For example, the author of Dan 2 said that the image which was made of four different kinds of material was really a myth representing four different kingdoms that followed each other in chronological sequence—Babylon, Media, Persia, and Greece. The male goat that ran so fast that his feet did not touch the ground and who came to overthrow the ram with two horns was Alexander the Great, king of the Greeks who overthrew the Medes and the Persians.

There has been little debate that these stories are myths intended to explain the theological meaning of a known period of history. Although scholars do not all agree about Dan 7, the same logic applies. This chapter consists of a court room scene, depicting God's verdict against the Greek kingdom. This scene had many of the features usually found in a court trial: There was a judge together with his assistant judges; there were people in the courtroom; there was a plaintiff

---

[139] Porteous, *Daniel*, pp. 109-110.
[140] Keil, *Daniel*, p. 245.
[141] This claim has been recognized by many, e.g., P. R. Raabe, "Daniel 7: Its Structure and Role in the Book," *HAR* 9 (1985):267-75.

and a defendant. There were attorneys' briefs for the judge to examine. There were thrones for the judge and his assistants, and there was a verdict made by the judge which affected both the plaintiff and the defendant.

This chapter has a structure similar to Ps 82. There God is pictured as one seated on a judgment bench, judging the national leaders, who are also called sons of the Most High. They had failed to vindicate the poor and needy, they had stumbled around ignorantly, so they were destined to fall dead like other human beings. The poet encouraged God to judge the land, because he was able to take possession of all the gentiles. The Ancient of Days in Dan 7 also entered into a court judgement, vindicating the saints of the Most High and bringing death sentence to gentiles.

The mythologist, through the agency of the one standing there, told the reader who the *dramatis personae* were:

1. The four beasts were four kings who would rule until **the saints** received the kingdom (Dan 7:17-18).
2. The fourth beast was the fourth kingdom.
3. The ten horns are the ten kings of the fourth kingdom.
4. The horn that grew out of these horns was the most wicked of the kings. He was the one who suppressed the saints, and tried to change their religion and calendar.
5. The court would remove the kingdom from **the horn** and give it to **the Son of man and saints of the Most High**.

This court trial was never held on earth. This myth was a religious way of describing a heavenly court trial that determined the outcome of some specific historic events that took place on earth at a certain point in history. The author of the myth knew about the trial that had taken place on earth. That was the Maccabean Revolt. This myth was his deduction of what must have taken place in heaven to have caused all of this to happen. The point in history on which the author based his myth was the time of the Maccabean revolt against the Syrian Greeks.

Antiochus on Trial. The judgment day given in Dan 7 was portrayed with only a small amount of detail. It describes, theologically or mythologically, the eviction of the Greeks from the temple by Judas the Maccabee[142] and the establishment of

---

[142] I first read a paper identifying the Son of man in Daniel with Judas the Maccabee in Toronto, December, 1968. By that time the manuscript, containing the suggestion, was already in the hands of the publishers of *The Consequences of the Covenant* (Leiden: E. J. Brill, 1970), pp. 10-11. The paper read in Toronto was published as a note in my commentary, *Hebrews*, pp. 38-51. I first read Sahlin's article in 1987, even though he had published it in 1969. We had evidently been working at the same time with some of the same ideas, although with different emphases. Dealing with Dan 7, Sahlin said, "The point is unequivocal, that the tyrannic rule of Antiochus Epiphanes has now come to an end. Through the wonderful intervention of God will Israel finally be saved, and God will establish his final kingdom. This, however, will be carried out through a man who will be clothed by God with messianic power. That form, however, can be none other than Judas

the first Hanukkah, when the temple was cleansed and controlled by the Jews. This happened about 164 BIA, when Antiochus Epiphanes was ruler of the Syrian Greeks, and Judas was the leader of the Jewish rebels. Casey thought Porphyry was wrong in his analysis of Daniel, but he said,

> The only past event that Porphyry could reasonably have thought to be symbolized by the triumph of the man-like figure is the Maccabean victory over the Seleucids in 164 BC. This harmonizes perfectly with his exegesis of Dan 11:21-12[:13], and it is confirmed by his exegesis of the rest of Daniel 7, in that he saw in both passages the story of the persecution by Antiochus Epiphanes followed by the Maccabean victory.[143]

The historical events that happened then were told as if this military victory were really the results of a divine judgment scene. This will become clear when the parts of a court trial are identified in Dan 7.

The Participants. Then it was that the conflicting parties had their day in court. In normal twentieth century American procedure, the plaintiff would have presented his accusation at this point, but that was not standard Jewish practice. According to the rabbis, non-capital cases might begin either with the plaintiff or the defendant stating his or her case. In capital cases, however, as was the case in Dan 7, the defense was always allowed to speak first with all the arguments that could be mustered for acquittal (*mSan* 4.1). This is what happened when Daniel reported that he heard the horn (the defendant) speaking "extensively" (Dan 7:11). Only after that was the plaintiff allowed to bring in the arguments for conviction.

This was not only the approved court procedure, but it was the most dramatic way to tell the story. To have had the plaintiff enter first with the clouds of heaven would have revealed the verdict at the beginning and spoiled the suspense of the myth. The defendants were the **four beasts**--the mythical representation of the gentile kings who ruled Judah after the fall of the temple in 586 BIA. They were insultingly called "beasts" to describe the way the Jews felt about them.

One of the two main contestants from this group was **the horn**, which was a code name for Antiochus Epiphanes, the ruler of the Syrian Greeks at the beginning of the Hasmonean rebellion. He was the principal defendant in the case, and he spoke "very many words," which probably means he offered an extensive or exaggerated argument for his own defense. This does not necessarily mean that he represented himself *pro se*. Adequate legal counsel in the narrator's imagination may have represented him, as Herod and Archelaus were in actual

---

Maccabaeus, the man who generally stands before the reader of the Book of Daniel, even if his name is not mentioned." (Sahlin, "Antiochus IV," p. 49).
The facts are so clear, and this interpretation is so logical that it is strange that scores of scholars have not reached this conclusion generations ago. That, however, has not been the case. Scholars have continued to write articles on the Son of man, apparently without having noticed that these two articles have been published. For example see J. R. Donahue, "Recent Studies," pp. 484-98.
[143] Casey, *Son of Man*, p. 63.

trials nearly 200 years later. At least since the time of Aristotle, Greeks had trained rhetoricians for this function. In antiquity, historians often credited kings with winning battles fought by the national army and navy when the kings were not even present. Since **the horn** was a mythical name for a king, he may have been credited with the defense offered in his behalf. Since this was a mythical trial, these details are important only to show that there are enough to make it clear that this was understood as a trial scene.

Divine Symbols. Daniel said that the Son of man came before the Ancient of Days with the clouds of heaven (Dan 7:13). The text does not say that the Son of man was "coming *down*" [emphasis added], as Casey rendered the text.[144] It just says that he came to the Ancient of Days. He was not pictured as an angel coming to earth, but, more than likely, as a human being, coming up to God in heaven to be judged and found innocent. After this he was installed as the divinely appointed leader of the Jews. It is further unlikely that a subordinate figure would be interpreted as coming *down* to God, the Most High. The text does not say that the Son of man came upon the clouds or on the clouds, as Emerton and Charles have claimed,[145] but *with* the clouds (*eem*, עם). This is coherent with the concept that Jesus and his three apostles were surrounded by a cloud on the Mount of Transfiguration (Matt 17:5) and David served in the counsel of God while he was king of Israel (Acts 13:36).

It is clear that Daniel 7 and the judgment scenes in 1Enoch constitute a glorified mythologization of the history of the Jews from the first entrance of Nebuchadnezzar into Jerusalem in 605 BIA to the restoration of the temple in 164 BIA and the death of Antiochus Epiphanes at approximately the same time. This narrative was told in terms of a court scene in which the kings of the four countries that ruled Palestine after 586 BIA (Babylon, Media, Persia, and Syria) were characterized as the **four beasts** of Ezekiel's vision. Real beasts do not often appear in court, but these kings were being insulted *posthumously* as if they were monstrous characters. In this myth the animals had the same function that animals play in Aesop's fables. For example, the fox that could not reach the grapes he wanted and then deduced that they were sour, anyway, does not fit the character of foxes. Foxes do not eat grapes, but human beings do, and they sometimes behave like the hypothetical fox in Aesop's fable. The same principle is true of the fable of the dog in the manger that would not let the cow eat the hay.

The beasts in Dan 7 were intended to illustrate human character. They were presented in this court scene as if they all lived at the same time and appeared altogether, when, in reality, one king ruled at a time. The second king (= beast) did not begin to rule until the reign of the first king was over, but this provided no problem to the author of the myth any more than the passage of time provides an obstacle to a play writer. Scenes change, time passes with a few stage changes, and the play goes on.

---

[144] Casey, *Son of Man*, p. 28.
[145] Emerton, "The Origin," pp. 99-101. See also Zech 12-14; Joel 3; Ezek 38-39; Isa 17:12-14; and Isa 29:1-8 as New Year festivals. The OG renders the text "upon the clouds," probably misreading the *eem* (עם) for an *ahl* (על).

The mythologist portrayed Judas as one like a Son of man who was the plaintiff, and God, as supreme judge who was the Ancient of Days. The Son of man *received* power and authority in this mythical judgment scene. He and the saints were not judges here. Later, after the authority had been in force, they could function as judges--the Son of man as the supreme judge, and the saints as subordinate judges. Scholars often confuse the function of the participants in this court trial. By mythologizing this important period of history, Jews were expressing their belief that God had decreed the Hasmonean victory over the Greeks. The Battle of Beth-horon was their day in court, just as there had been a judgment day in 586 BIA at which the verdict had been pronounced against the Jews. The rule of **the beasts** was of demonic origin; the rule of **the one like a Son of man** was of divine origin. It was accompanied by God's *ah-nahn*. This vision mythologized historical events shortly after Judas won a decisive victory over the Greeks at Beth-horon. At the mythical court session, Jews were vindicated (*Ant* 12.285-312).

JUDGMENT DAY AND JEWISH FEASTS

Every autumn Jews celebrate three feasts that are closely related to important events of 164 BIA: 1) New Year's Day, 2) the Day of Atonement, and 3) Hanukkah The first of these is New Year's Day. Traditionally on New Year's Day not only Jews, but also other nations, believed that two important things happened: 1) God would judge the nation and determine the treatment the nation should receive the following year. 2) God would enthrone kings and give them the authority to rule the nation as the apostle of the deity during the following year.

God had made a treaty with Abraham, which included three promises. God, for his part, would give Abraham 1) posterity, 2) prosperity, and 3) the land, but there were two sides to the treaty. The children of Abraham would have to obey all of the rules included in the treaty. This treaty was a marriage contract in which Yehowah was the groom, and the children of Abraham formed a corporation that functioned legally as the bride. God could be counted on to keep his side of the agreement if the people kept theirs. If the children of Abraham broke the rules, they would be like a wife who was unfaithful to her husband. God would then divorce his people and annul the treaty. He would follow the rules quoted in the treaty: If a husband divorced his wife he had to give her a legal document stating the conditions and terms of the divorce. He had to put it in her hand and send her out of his house (Deut 24:1).

When the temple at Gerizim was destroyed and the North Israelites were taken captive into Assyria and Egypt, Jeremiah recognized that God had divorced his people, sending them out of their house and off the land. The same was true of Judah when the Babylonians burned the Jerusalem temple and took Jews captive into Babylon. With the treaty no longer in force, Jews and Samaritans had to take measures to reconcile themselves to God so that the treaty could be renewed. According to sabbatical rules for debtor slavery, they would have to pay double for all of their sins. According to Lev 25 they would be cursed and punished seven times for all of their sins.

With their huge national debt Jews and Samaritans had to take strong measures to avoid sinning and building up the national debt still further. They also were obligated to do good deeds to cancel earlier debts. Ten days after New Year's Day Jews established a Day of Atonement. These days were set aside for canceling debts, repenting of sins, forgiving one another, and obtaining reconciliation with each other and with God. The ten days between New Year's and the Day of Atonement were days of reckoning. At this time Jews were obligated to audit their books, review the activities of the year and pay for sins committed. Since God would not accept as parties to the contract a people that was not sinless, Jews had not only to pay all the fines they owed for crimes they had personally committed, but they had to pay for the accumulated iniquities of their ancestors to the third and fourth generation.

How could Jews know if they were in debt or not? They could notice whether they were living on the Promised Land, free from foreign rule or not. If they were subject to foreign powers, that means God was punishing them for their sins. If the land was restored, and they were living under the rule of their own king, then their debts were paid up. They even may have had a credit balance in the treasury of merits. Every Day of Atonement Jews hoped that their good deeds would allow God to restore them to their Promised Land. One of the rabbis said that if all Israel would repent for just one day, the kingdom would come. That one day, of course, would be the Day of Atonement.

In January or February of 164 BIA, just a few months after New Year's Day and the Day of Atonement, Judas won the Battle of Beth-horon, and the next months were spent having the temple cleansed and restored. This proved to contemporary Jews that the Day of Atonement had been effective. Not only was the temple rededicated, but also the nation's sins had been forgiven. The land was being restored. On the Judgment Day at New Year's God had given the Jews a verdict of "not guilty." On that Day of Atonement their sins had been forgiven. This evidence motivated the optimism that is reflected in the Book of Daniel. It was in this era of optimism that some Jewish scholar composed Dan 7. He deduced from the events of recent months that God's judgment on that particular New Year's Day was one on which God held court, and Antiochus and Judas were brought to trial. Antiochus received the death sentence, and Judas was declared innocent. He was also given the rulership of the nation.

The excitement of this period was enhanced by Halley's Comet that appeared in the sky from Sept 24 to Nov 10, 164 BIA. Wolters suggested that this might be the reason Hanukkah was called "the feast of lights." Josephus apparently did not know about the legend of the oil that miraculously burned for eight days. Instead, he said that he thought Hanukkah was called "the feast of lights" because of "the light that shone on us" or "enlightened us" (*hay-meén fah-náy-nai*, ἡμῖν φανῆναι (*Ant* 12.325). This appearance in this sky was probably interpreted as a favorable sign from God.[146] This may have been the inspiration for the expression, "Like comets of vision" (4Q246.2, 1).

---

[146] A. Wolters, "Halley's Comet at a Turning Point in Jewish History," *CBQ* 55 (1993):696. See also F. R. Stephenson, K. K. C. Yau, and H. Hunger, "Records of Halley's Comet on Babylonian Tablets," *Nature* 314 (1985):587-92.

The period between January or February and the following December, 164 BIA was a time of nationalistic excitement as the nation prepared for Hanukkah. Not only were contractors busy cleansing and redecorating the temple, but there was probably a good deal of study and composition during this period as scholars tried to explain this good news in terms of fulfillment of prophecy. The various chapters of the Book of Daniel were probably written during that time and presented before the audience gathered at the first Hanukkah. Even Dan 7 may have been composed for that time.

Antiochus IV may have died while either the Battle of Beth-horon or the Battle of Beth-zur was taking place, because the famous judgment scene of **Dan 7** depended on the death of the **little horn**. Although the first Hanukkah is the first likely time for the first presentation of Dan 7, there were later Hanukkah festivals that followed, and there was still another time of great excitement that might have motivated the composition of Dan 7. That would have been the release from taxes and declaration of complete independence during the third year of the reign of Simon in 142 BIA. This was a time of great celebration, the beginning of a new age. Contracts were prepared and dated according to a new calendar: "the first year of Simon" (*éh-toos próh-too eh-peé see-moh-naws*, ἔτους πρώτου ἐπὶ Σιμωνος). This means the first year of the Lord Simon as ruler of an independent country. We have no record of Simon being called "Lord," but he probably was. That was a title given to people of dignity, especially kings and rulers. Jewish messiahs during the Crusades were called "Lord."[147] Had Judah been a Latin country at that time the calendars would probably have been dated *anno domini Simoni* or AD. By this time Dan 7 would have been composed, and the entire collection of Dramas of Daniel was probably read again at that celebration (1Macc 13:35-14:15). Daniel may have been read at every Hanukkah celebration after the first Hanukkah.

Dan 7 has to have been written *after* both the major victory or victories of Judas and the death of Antiochus Epiphanes. If Antiochus did not die until a month before Hanukkah, this would mean some scholar reached the conclusions he did about the judgment and wrote it all into this coherent chapter in a very short time. The atmosphere surrounding that first Hanukkah might have motivated such creativity as that, but the more time that elapsed after Antiochus' death before Hanukkah, the more likely it is that Dan 7 was composed for the first Hanukkah. If it was not written for that very Hanukkah it may have been used at a later date—even possibly as late as 142 BIA when it would have been introduced at the special eight day feast celebrating complete liberty.

CONCLUSIONS TO DANIEL SEVEN

The mythical nature of Daniel 7 is clear because Daniel was mythologizing history that can easily be demythologized. Since the history is well known, and the dates all synchronize, there are not many questions about the figures involved. By noting the mythical nature of this entire chapter it is also necessary to acknowledge that Daniel was written *after* the victory of Beth-horon,

---

[147] Buchanan, *Redemption*, p 195.

the death of Antiochus Epiphanes,[148] and possibly the Battle of Beth-zur. Dan 7 does not reflect a "desperate situation," as Collins holds.[149] The victory of the mythical court session was composed after the desperate situation was over. This also makes its pro-Hasmonean *tendenz* obvious, refuting many other scholars who have tried to claim that the myth turns to prophecy at the point where the Son of man comes with the clouds before the Ancient of Days. Then it turns back again to myth at the beginning of Dan 8. This is not the logical way to read Dan 7, but scholars have argued this way partly because of the textual problems involved in Daniel 11.

Although Daniel was composed following a tense situation in conflect with gentiles, just as Esther was, Daniel does not reflect the terroristic glee and outburst of hostility related to Purim. Purim was allowed because of a decree of a gentile king. That was quite different from Hanukkah. Hanukkah came because of the realization that God had forgiven Israel's sins on the previous Day of Atonement. The Beth-horon victory inspired gratitude for God's forgiveness and stirred contemporary Jews to celebrate. That attitude is reflected in the Dramas of Daniel that emerged.

---

[148] This makes the dating of such scholars as G. Hoelscher, "Die Entstehung des Buches Daniel, *ThStK* 92 (1919):113-38 (third century BIA); M. Haller, "Das Alter vom Daniel 7," *ThStK* 93 (1920/21):83-87; M. Noth, "Komposition," pp.143-63 (fourth century BIA), and Collins, *A Commentary*, p. 324 (167 BIA) impossible.

[149] Collins, *A Commentary*), p. 33.

CHAPTER EIGHT

HEBREW TEXT

בִּשְׁנַת שָׁלוֹשׁ לְמַלְכוּת בֵּלְאשַׁצַּר הַמֶּלֶךְ חָזוֹן נִרְאָה אֵלַי אֲנִי 8:1   Ezek 1:1
דָנִיֵּאל אַחֲרֵי הַנִּרְאָה אֵלַי בַּתְּחִלָּה: 2 וָאֶרְאֶה בֶּחָזוֹן וַיְהִי בִּרְאֹתִי
וַאֲנִי בְּשׁוּשַׁן הַבִּירָה אֲשֶׁר בְּעֵילָם הַמְּדִינָה וָאֶרְאֶה בֶחָזוֹן וַאֲנִי   Ezek 8:3; 40:2
הָיִיתִי עַל־אוּבַל אוּלָי: 3 וָאֶשָּׂא עֵינַי וָאֶרְאֶה וְהִנֵּה ׀ אַיִל אֶחָד עֹמֵד   Ezek 1:3-4; 8:5
לִפְנֵי הָאֻבָל וְלוֹ קְרָנָיִם וְהַקְּרָנַיִם גְּבֹהוֹת וְהָאַחַת גְּבֹהָה מִן־הַשֵּׁנִית
וְהַגְּבֹהָה עֹלָה בָּאַחֲרֹנָה: 4 רָאִיתִי אֶת־הָאַיִל מְנַגֵּחַ יָמָּה וְצָפוֹנָה
וָנֶגְבָּה וְכָל־חַיּוֹת לֹא־יַעַמְדוּ לְפָנָיו וְאֵין מַצִּיל מִיָּדוֹ וְעָשָׂה כִרְצֹנוֹ
וְהִגְדִּיל: 5 וַאֲנִי ׀ הָיִיתִי מֵבִין וְהִנֵּה צְפִיר־הָעִזִּים בָּא מִן־הַמַּעֲרָב
עַל־פְּנֵי כָל־הָאָרֶץ וְאֵין נוֹגֵעַ בָּאָרֶץ וְהַצָּפִיר קֶרֶן חָזוּת בֵּין עֵינָיו:
6 וַיָּבֹא עַד־הָאַיִל בַּעַל הַקְּרָנַיִם אֲשֶׁר רָאִיתִי עֹמֵד לִפְנֵי הָאֻבָל וַיָּרָץ
אֵלָיו בַּחֲמַת כֹּחוֹ: 7 וּרְאִיתִיו מַגִּיעַ ׀ אֵצֶל הָאַיִל וַיִּתְמַרְמַר אֵלָיו וַיַּךְ
אֶת־הָאַיִל וַיְשַׁבֵּר אֶת־שְׁתֵּי קְרָנָיו וְלֹא־הָיָה כֹחַ בָּאַיִל לַעֲמֹד לְפָנָיו
וַיַּשְׁלִיכֵהוּ אַרְצָה וַיִּרְמְסֵהוּ וְלֹא־הָיָה מַצִּיל לָאַיִל מִיָּדוֹ: 8 וּצְפִיר
הָעִזִּים הִגְדִּיל עַד־מְאֹד וּכְעָצְמוֹ נִשְׁבְּרָה הַקֶּרֶן הַגְּדוֹלָה וַתַּעֲלֶנָה
חָזוּת אַרְבַּע תַּחְתֶּיהָ לְאַרְבַּע רוּחוֹת הַשָּׁמָיִם: 9 וּמִן־הָאַחַת מֵהֶם
יָצָא קֶרֶן־אַחַת מִצְּעִירָה וַתִּגְדַּל־יֶתֶר אֶל־הַנֶּגֶב וְאֶל־הַמִּזְרָח וְאֶל־   Ezek 20:6; Isa 14:12
הַצֶּבִי: 10 וַתִּגְדַּל עַד־צְבָא הַשָּׁמָיִם וַתַּפֵּל אַרְצָה מִן־הַצָּבָא וּמִן־
הַכּוֹכָבִים וַתִּרְמְסֵם: 11 וְעַד שַׂר־הַצָּבָא הִגְדִּיל וּמִמֶּנּוּ הרים [הוּרַם]
הַתָּמִיד וְהֻשְׁלַךְ מְכוֹן מִקְדָּשׁוֹ: 12 וְצָבָא תִּנָּתֵן עַל־הַתָּמִיד
בְּפָשַׁע וְתַשְׁלֵךְ אֱמֶת אַרְצָה וְעָשְׂתָה וְהִצְלִיחָה: 13 וָאֶשְׁמְעָה אֶחָד־   Zech 1:12
קָדוֹשׁ מְדַבֵּר וַיֹּאמֶר אֶחָד קָדוֹשׁ לַפַּלְמוֹנִי הַמְדַבֵּר עַד־מָתַי הֶחָזוֹן
הַתָּמִיד וְהַפֶּשַׁע שֹׁמֵם תֵּת וְקֹדֶשׁ וְצָבָא מִרְמָס: 14 וַיֹּאמֶר אֵלַי
עַד עֶרֶב בֹּקֶר אַלְפַּיִם וּשְׁלֹשׁ מֵאוֹת וְנִצְדַּק קֹדֶשׁ: 15 וַיְהִי
בִּרְאֹתִי אֲנִי דָנִיֵּאל אֶת־הֶחָזוֹן וָאֲבַקְשָׁה בִינָה וְהִנֵּה עֹמֵד לְנֶגְדִּי   Ezek 1:26
כְּמַרְאֵה־גָבֶר: 16 וָאֶשְׁמַע קוֹל־אָדָם בֵּין אוּלָי וַיִּקְרָא וַיֹּאמַר גַּבְרִיאֵל   Ezek 1:28
הָבֵן לְהַלָּז אֶת־הַמַּרְאֶה: 17 וַיָּבֹא אֵצֶל עָמְדִי וּבְבֹאוֹ נִבְעַתִּי וָאֶפְּלָה
עַל־פָּנָי וַיֹּאמֶר אֵלַי הָבֵן בֶּן־אָדָם כִּי לְעֶת־קֵץ הֶחָזוֹן: 18 וּבְדַבְּרוֹ   Ezek 3:24
עִמִּי נִרְדַּמְתִּי עַל־פָּנַי אָרְצָה וַיִּגַּע־בִּי וַיַּעֲמִידֵנִי עַל־עָמְדִי: 19 וַיֹּאמֶר   Isa 10:25; Isa 26:20;
הִנְנִי מוֹדִיעֲךָ אֵת אֲשֶׁר־יִהְיֶה בְּאַחֲרִית הַזָּעַם כִּי לְמוֹעֵד קֵץ: 1Macc 3:8; Ezek 1:28
20 הָאַיִל אֲשֶׁר־רָאִיתָ בַּעַל הַקְּרָנָיִם מַלְכֵי מָדַי וּפָרָס: 21 וְהַצָּפִיר
הַשָּׂעִיר מֶלֶךְ יָוָן וְהַקֶּרֶן הַגְּדוֹלָה אֲשֶׁר בֵּין־עֵינָיו הוּא הַמֶּלֶךְ
הָרִאשׁוֹן: 22 וְהַנִּשְׁבֶּרֶת וַתַּעֲמֹדְנָה אַרְבַּע תַּחְתֶּיהָ אַרְבַּע מַלְכֻיוֹת
מִגּוֹי יַעֲמֹדְנָה וְלֹא בְכֹחוֹ:
23 וּבְאַחֲרִית מַלְכוּתָם כְּהָתֵם הַפֹּשְׁעִים

יַעֲמֹד מֶלֶךְ עַז־פָּנִים וּמֵבִין חִידוֹת׃
24 וְעָצַם כֹּחוֹ וְלֹא בְכֹחוֹ וְנִפְלָאוֹת יַשְׁחִית וְהִצְלִיחַ וְעָשָׂה
וְהִשְׁחִית עֲצוּמִים וְעַם־קְדֹשִׁים׃
25 וְעַל־שִׂכְלוֹ וְהִצְלִיחַ מִרְמָה בְּיָדוֹ
וּבִלְבָבוֹ יַגְדִּיל וּבְשַׁלְוָה יַשְׁחִית רַבִּים
וְעַל־שַׂר־שָׂרִים יַעֲמֹד וּבְאֶפֶס יָד יִשָּׁבֵר׃
26 וּמַרְאֵה הָעֶרֶב וְהַבֹּקֶר אֲשֶׁר נֶאֱמַר אֱמֶת הוּא
וְאַתָּה סְתֹם הֶחָזוֹן כִּי לְיָמִים רַבִּים׃
27 וַאֲנִי דָנִיֵּאל נִהְיֵיתִי וְנֶחֱלֵיתִי יָמִים וָאָקוּם וָאֶעֱשֶׂה אֶת־מְלֶאכֶת
הַמֶּלֶךְ וָאֶשְׁתּוֹמֵם עַל־הַמַּרְאֶה וְאֵין מֵבִין׃ פ

ENGLISH TEXT

Daniel	First Testament Intertexts
8:1 In the third **year of the** kingdom of King Belshazzar, **a vision appeared to me**. I, Daniel, after it appeared to me, previously, **2I was watching in a vision**, and it happened while I was looking, I was in Susa, the capital of the province of Elam. **I was watching in a vision**, and I was **alongside the river of Ulai**.	Ezek 1:1 **In the** thirtieth **year of the** fourth month, in the fifth of the month, I was in the midst of the exile. The heavens opened, and **I saw a vision** of God. Ezek 8:3 It brought me to Jerusalem **in a vision** of God. Ezek 40:2 **In a vision** of God he brought me to the land of Israel. Ezek 1:3 In the land of the Chaldeans, **alongside the stream of Kebar** the hand of Yahowah was on him there. **4I was watching--Now look**! A windstorm came.
3I raised my eyes, and I saw—**Now look!**	Ezek 8:5 He said to me, "Son of man, lift up your eyes to the north. So **I raised my my eyes** toward the north. **Now look!**"
A ram standing before the bank. He had two horns, and the horns were large, one larger than the other, and the larger one came up last.	Ezek 39:17 They shall eat flesh and drink blood. 18The flesh of mighty men you shall eat, and the blood of the princes of the land you shall drink—of **rams**, lambs, goats, bulls—all of them fatlings of Bashan.

⁴I watched the ram, charging westward, northward, and southward, and no living creature could stand before him; nothing escaped from his hand. He did whatever he wanted, and he grew larger.

TECHNICAL DETAILS

The Hebrew phrase **I was paying close attention** (Dan 8:5) is basically the equivalent of the Aramaic word rendered **I was watching** in Dan 7:7. Both passages are dependent on Ezek 1:1. **And trampled him** (Dan 8:7) is the Hebrew equivalent of **and trampled** (Dan 7:7). The idiom **stand before** means to stand before an enemy without retreating (Judges 2:14; 2Kgs 10:4). There are other similarities between Dan 8 and Dan 7. Dan 8 is a kind of midrash on Dan 7, interpreting Dan 7. It is also closely tied to Dan 10-12. Doukhan has shown that most of the words and expressions that are typical of Dan 8 are also prominent in Dan 10-12.

COMMENTARY

The kingdom of King Belshazzar. **Belshazzar** was the son of Nabonidus who was king of Babylon. He delegated his son **Belshazzar** to administer the kingdom in the area around Babylon, while King Nabonidus himself went west to administer the distant regions of the country, that part that most kings ignored. In the judgment of the author of this chapter, this was a waste of time and talent. He considered **Belshazzar** the real king of the empire at that time.

A vision appeared to me. This chapter begins very much like the beginning of the prophecy of Ezekiel. The vision was given here to remind the reader that this is not objective history but drama.

I Daniel. Reid has made an interesting comparison between pseudepigraphical prophecy in Jewish and Christian studies and pseudepigraphy in African cults. In Zambia a seer often takes the name of an earlier seer who has died. It is called "Bansanga possession." It is done to perpetuate the spirit of the earlier seer and to deny individual identity. When a medium introduces himself or herself in the Bansanga spirit possession this is done with the formula, "I am Monze." Reid has noted the similarity between that formula and the one used here, **I Daniel**. Reid correctly said, "Pseudonymity is not literary forgery."[1] The author of Dan 8 evidently wrote this essay in the name of an earlier wiseman named Daniel.

I was in Susa the capital of the province of Elam. This was all part of the vision. The author **was** not **in Susa**, but he imagined that he was. This was at the southeastern corner of the Babylonian Empire. In his mind's eye, from there he was able to see all

---

[1] S. B. Reid, *Enoch and Daniel* (Berkeley: BIBAL Press, c1989), p. 113. This raises the question about the meaning of the expression "I Nebuchadnezzar" in Dan 4:1. This seems to imply that the expression might also be attributed negatively to someone. This may mean that the author of Dan 4 knew Nebuchadnezzar did not have the dream attributed to him, but that he presented the dream as if some later seer had done it in his name.

the way across the country to the north and the northwest. It seems quite likely, however, that he did not go to Susa physically. It was in a vision that he was brought there just as Ezekiel was brought to Jerusalem and to the Land of Israel in a vision. Susa was a large, beautifully constructed citadel, covering about 300 acres of land. It has been surveyed and excavated. **Susa** was founded by Darius Hystaspes (521-485 BIA) (Xenophon, *Cyrop* 8.6, 22).

Alongside the River of Ulai. This vision was patterned after parts of Ezekiel. Since Ezekiel had his vision near a **river**, it was necessary for the author of this chapter to develop his drama in the same kind of setting. **The River Ulai** is probably a canal near Susa which connected **the rivers** Choaspes and Coprates called Eulaeus. It is now dry, but at one time it carried a stream 900 feet broad.

A ram. Persia was under the zodiacal sign of Aries (the **ram**) and the Syrian Greek Seleucids were under the sign of Capricorn (the goat). The national symbols were chosen for this reason. **Rams** were not very fierce animals. The aggression described here is more characteristic of Persia and Media than the temperament of the animal. The ram was a king or general who was the leader of a flock (Ezek 39:18).

The larger one came up last. The horns were Media and Persia. At first Media was the larger, but after Cyrus Persia grew from a small portion of Media to a huge empire that included Media, Babylon, and parts of Asia Minor. So it was Persia that **came up last** and became **larger.**

Westward, northward, and southward. There is no mention of Cyrus' eastward expansion, probably because the author, whose interest was Palestine, was not interested in any eastward expansion.

TEXT

⁵I was paying close attention when look! A male goat came from the west across the surface of the entire land, and he did not touch the ground. The goat had a conspicuous horn between his eyes. ⁶He came to the ram with the two horns, which I saw standing before the bank. He ran against him with his power, in his anger. ⁷I saw him approach the ram. He attacked him, and he struck the ram and broke his two horns, and there was no strength in the ram to stand before him, but he threw him to the ground and trampled him, and no one could rescue the ram from his hand.
⁸The male goat did great things, but when he was strong, the large horn was broken, and there came up in its place four conspicuous ones toward the four winds of heaven.

Daniel	First Testament Intertexts
⁹From one of them went out a small horn, and it expanded more to the south, to the east, and to the **glorious land**. ¹⁰It grew until it reached the troops of	Ezek 20:6 A **land** which I searched out for them, flowing with milk and honey, the most **glorious** of all the **lands**.

Heaven. Some of the troops of **Heaven fell**, and some of the **stars**, and it trampled them.	^{Isa 14:12} How you **have fallen** from **heaven**, Day **Star**, son of the dawn . . . ¹³You said to yourself, I will go up to **heaven**, above the **stars** of God.

¹¹It expanded even to the military general, and from him the continual offering was discarded, and the [special] place of his temple was thrown down. ¹²An army was directed against the continual burnt offering because of transgression, and. truth was thrown to the ground. [The little horn] acted and became successful.

COMMENTARY

A goat came from the West. The **goat** (capricorn) that **came from the West** was Greece. It began at Macedonia and moved rapidly east. It moved so fast that the author said its feet did not touch the ground. Josephus interpreted this by saying that the goat was carried through the air **from the west** (*Ant* 19.270). Some scholars have compared the idiom to that which was applied earlier to Cyrus of Persia, but it is not the same. Cyrus also trampled kings under his feet. Of him it was said, **a path with his feet did not come** (Isa 41:3), meaning that he did not bother to follow the normal roads. He cut across fields to reach his destinations. Alexander the Great was said to have come so fast that he practically flew. Arrian said

> In uncertain situations he regularly acted with greatest courage, which planned to catch the enemy by surprise before they could become fearful (Arrian, *Anabasis* 7.27, 3).

It was not the paths that he avoided; it was lethargy. Alexander crossed the Hellespont in 334 BIA; he defeated Darius Codomannus at Issus in 333 BIA; he crossed Palestine, conquered Egypt, defeated Persia, and extended his empire north and east to include modern Afghanistan and Pakistan by 331 BIA. He moved as if he had wings on his feet. He was a skillful and judicious general, but he was also persistent, demanding, and unyielding. The only army before which he ever allowed himself to be defeated was his own troops when he refrained from conquering the rest of India, but at the soldiers' requests, instead turned back toward Macedonia (Arrian, *Anabasis* 5.29, 1).

He often undertook forced marches at night covering the amount of space that would normally take ten hours in four hours. When he and his troops arrived, they were expected to join in battle very soon after arrival. He, himself, led some of the most difficult maneuvers over the roughest terrain. He kept going after many of his horses and soldiers died of exhaustion.[2] Of the beasts that might be used to describe the activity of Alexander, a male goat seems appropriate.

Male goats are much more aggressive and defensive than rams. Nearly every flock of sheep in the Near East has--not a ram--but a male goat as its leader. Zechariah paralleled **shepherd** with **male goat**, because both were leaders (Zech 10:3). Isaiah paralleled **male goats of the earth** with **kings of the nations** (Isa

---

[2] On this see Arrian, *Anabasis Alexandri* (Cambridge: Harvard U. Press, c1946) in two volumes.

14:9). Sheep are very docile, unobservant creatures that do not look after themselves. They depend on a shepherd just as obedient citizens depend on a monarch. **Goats**, on the other hand, are observant. They know when to fight and when to flee. If danger arises, a male goat will run to safety, and all of the sheep will follow him. Even though the figure of the goat may have been chosen from the signs of the Zodiac, the symbol was very descriptive of the actions of Alexander the Great. When he took the lead many followed him.

A conspicuous horn between his eyes. There has never existed, to anyone's knowledge, a unicorn. The idea of an animal with one **horn** developed from an artist's drawing a goat from the side where one **horn** covered the other, and it looked as if the goat had only one **horn**. That is the way the capricorn appears in the Zodiac. No one had ever seen such a beast alive, but the same was true of Alexander the Great. No one had previously seen such military achievement as he conducted. This **horn** was Alexander the Great, the general who led the military campaign to the East. He attacked the ram (the king of Persia and Media), crushed it and trampled over the tops of the people on his way farther east.

He threw him to the ground and trampled him. When the Greeks moved east, under the leadership of Alexander, they moved rapidly and forcefully. Persia had been a great and powerful country until Alexander moved east. Alexander took it all. **Trampling** is a good term to describe what a large army does to the land through which it marches. It destroys the crops, loots the resources of the area, and leaves the land desolate. This is specially true if the army used elephants, as both the Persians and the Greeks did.

The large horn was broken. This means that Alexander the Great died (321 BIA)— only 12 years and 8 months after he had begun, he amassed and administered a huge empire. It bordered the Danube River in the Northwest, Ethiopia in the Southwest, and extended to India in the East, including what is now Pakistan, with the Taurus Mountains to the north and the Persian Gulf and the Erythraeun Sea to the south. He built a new city, Alexandria, Egypt, for his capital.

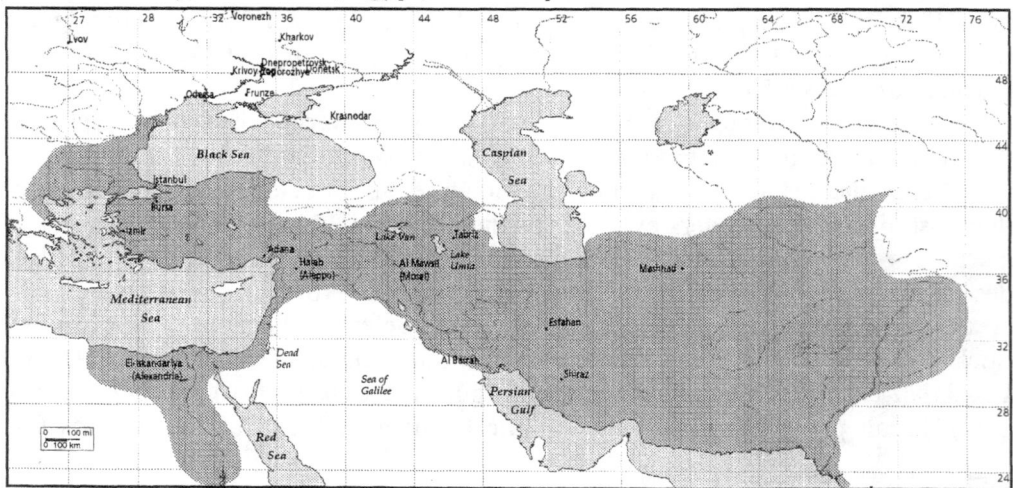

Arrian said,

> To Alexander, himself, and to those who were with him he appeared
> to be the lord of all the earth and sea (Arrian, *Anabasis* 7.15, 5)

Arrian defended Alexander for considering himself to have been born of a deity, holding that he was greater than Minos, Aeacis. and Radamanthus—all of whom traced their ancestry back to Zeus (Arrian, *Anabasis* 7.29, 3). Seleucus I said it was common knowledge that whatever the king did was always right (Appian, *Roman History* 11.10, 61).[3] That was because kings were thought to be legal agents of the deity. That belief was also applied to Alexander the Great. When he died he left the powerful Macedonian army. Whoever controlled that army would rule the world, as it was known at that time.

Many leaders vied for that position. The empire he had built was first divided among his generals. These fought against one another until the largest empire was overthrown and its king, Antigonus, killed. Then the remainder was divided among only four. These were the four concpicuous "horns" mentioned here. None of these called themselves "king" until there was no longer a legitimate heir to Alexander alive. That showed the respect they held for Alexander. After the Battle of Ipsus (301 BIA), however, all four of these leaders called themselves "king" of their respective territories (Herodotus 15.2, 13).

The four were Ptolemy, Seleucus, Callandrus, and Lysimachus. It was Seleucus and his posterity that effected the lives of the Palestinian Jews the most. Seleucus was one of Alexander's close companions whom he held in high respect. Seleucus accompanied Alexander in his initial invasion into Asia in 334 BIA and remained with him throughout his entire military campaign. (Arrian, *Anabasis* 5.13, 1; 7.22, 5). Two of the strongest opponents of Alexander when he was campaigning east of the Tigris River in Iran were Spitamenes and Oxyartes. After Alexander conquered this territory, he made peace with Oxyartes and took his daughter, Roxane, for his wife. Spitamenes was killed, and Alexander gave Apama, Spitamenes' daughter, to Seleucus for his wife (Arrian, *Anabasis* 4.19, 5).[4]

From one of them went out a small horn. Many details were omitted here. All the rest of the Seleucids were passed over, because the author was concentrating on the **small horn** that caused the most anxiety to the Jews and Jerusalem. The author moved quickly from Alexander the Great to Antiochus IV. The small horn was Antiochus IV Epiphanes. He was one of the descendants of the earlier Seleucus. Before he began to rule, the Seleucid dynasty had grown from the eastern border that reached India to the Taurus Mountains at the eastern end of Asia Minor. For 14 years he had been a hostage in Rome, following the Roman victory at Magnesia. His older brother, Seleucus IV, had him released. He returned to rule Syria after the death of his brother, Seleucus. He was the **horn** that was described as a "king of strong countenance." This **horn** was small, because Romans had reduced the Syrian Empire, power, and wealth. Like his father and brother, however, Antiochus IV was

---

[3] *Appian's Roman History* (Cambridge: Harvard U. Press, 1955) in 4 vols.
[4] E. R. Bevan, *The House of Seleucus* (New York: Barnes and Noble, Inc., c1902, 1966) I, p. 31.

aggressive, and unwilling to accept the limitations the Romans forced upon him. He was a principal character in the Book of Daniel, because he was the one against whom Judas fought the famous Maccabean Rebellion.

To the south, to the east, and to the glorious land. Antiochus IV also extended the empire in every direction possible. **To the east** was Persia; **to the south** was Egypt; **and to the glorious land** was the country in between Egypt and Antioch. Antiochus IV's father had already moved the capital city from the eastern part of the empire farther west to Antioch on the Orontes River. He then moved still farther west into parts of Greece and Europe, but the Romans stopped him and forced him to retreat to lands east of the Taurus Mountains. The treaty made with the Romans prohibited Antiochus from moving further west from the boundary set by the Romans, so he could expand only eastward and southward.

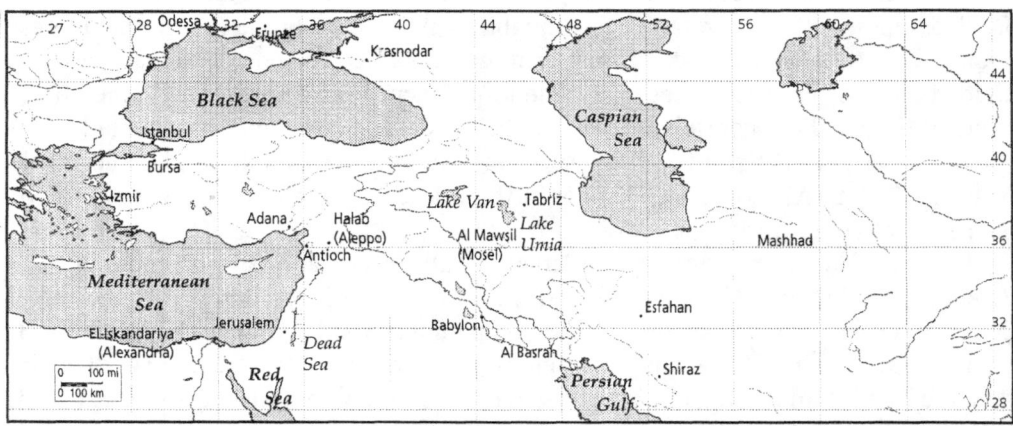

When the large armies marched either north or south they trampled over cities in Palestine. This made warfare a way of life for Jews and Samaritans. Ezekiel called Palestine **a land flowing with milk and honey, the most glorious** (*ts-veé*, צבי) **of all the lands** (Ezek 20:6). Jeremiah presented the Lord as saying, **I said, "How shall I place you among the sons?" Then I gave you a precious land, a glorious heritage of the armies of the nations** (Jer 3:19). The word that means **glorious** also means "gazelle." Just as the king of Media-Persia was called a ram, and the king of the Greeks was called a goat, so Palestine may have been called a gazelle. Whether or not that was part of the implication, there is no doubt about the identity of the land involved.

It grew until it reached the troops of Heaven. The little horn was compared homiletically to the subject in the Isaianic text. That was the king of Babylon, who was called the day star.[5] Before he fell, he had become so highly exalted that he

---

[5] This is the usual translation. *Hay-láyl behn sháh-khahr* (הילל בן שחר) (Isa 14:12). *Sháh-khar* can either mean "darkness" or "dawn." Therefore it refers either to the first star of the evening or the last star at night. It either stirs up the dawn or it stirs up the night (Ps 108:3). The OG (Ps 109:3) renders this term *heh-ohs-phór-aws* ἑωσφόρου). Bar Cochba may have taken his title, "son of a star." from Isa 14:12 as well as Num 24:17. That which is important is that these heavenly titles were applied to human beings on earth.

thought he could **reach heaven** and be above the stars (Isa 14:12-15). Of course Isaiah was speaking in hyperbole to ridicule the arrogance of his enemy. Ezekiel accused the king of Tyre of claiming that he was god, seated in the throne of the gods, but he was only a man and not a god (Ezek 28:2; also *PsSol* 2.28-29). Many kings in antiquity thought of themselves as gods or sons of gods. Even Solomon was called God's son (2Sam 7:14).

The author of Dan 8 applied the Isaianic text to the Maccabean Rebellion just as hyperbolically as Isaiah had intended it originally. Antiochus IV was also supercilious, and the author of Dan 8 agreed hyperbolically with the author of 2Macc who said Antiochus IV was so arrogant that he thought he could comand the waves of the sea and weigh the high mountains in a scale. He even thought he could **reach** the stars of **heaven** (2Macc 9:8, 10).

Neither the author of Dan 8 nor the author of 2Macc believed for one minute that Antiochus could command the waves of the sea, weigh the mountains in a scale, or go up to **heaven** and join battle with the angels. They were describing their feelings about his arrogance rather than reporting actual fact. That is the intent of hyperbole. It expresses feelings of Antiochus' enemies rather than fact. When the author of 2Macc interpreted Dan 8:10 he expanded the concept hyperbolically. Most readers and hearers recognize hyperbole and distinguish it in their minds from historical event, the way the author of 2Macc did. Using the words from Isaiah, the author used the expression **stars of God** and **troops of Heaven** to apply to the Jewish troops.[6] The "horn" (daystar) expanded his territory geographically in every direction possible until finally he got as far as **the glorious land** (Palestine). At that point, **he reached the troops of Heaven** instead **of heaven** itself.

Many scholars agree that the term expressed here means the army of God, but others take it to mean heavenly bodies, like stars in the sky.[7] The latter appeal to the Greek texts, one of which renders this passage **the stars of heaven** (OG), and the other calls the expression **the powers of heaven** (Th). Both interpretations are possible. The MT seems the most likely, and its meaning takes **Heaven** to mean "God," and **troops** to mean "military forces." The word *tsah-váh* (צבא) is used many times in the FT with the meaning of "war," "military," "army," and **troops**.[8]

The troops of Heaven were the **stars of God**. The term "son of God" described a king, such as Solomon (2Sam 7:14). Nevertheless, in the Torah, that which the MT called **the children of Israel**, the OG names **the sons of God** (Deut 29:26). In a similar way the term "star" was used to refer to the general or leader of an army, probably King David (Num 24:17). Ben Cozebah, the general who led the

---

[6] So also C. F. Keil, B*iblical Commentary on the Book of Daniel*, tr. M. G. Easton (Grand Rapids: William B. Eerdmans, n.d.), p. 296, who said the term "stars" was a fitting designation for the holy people (Exod 19:6). They were also called the "troops of Yehowah" (Exod 7:4; 12:41) and the "holy ones." A. A. Bevan, *A Short Commentary on the Book of Daniel* (Cambridge: University Press, 1892), p. 132, said, "The '*host of heaven*' represents the people of God . . . By the casting down of some of the stars are meant the cruelties perpetrated at Jerusalem by Antiochus and his agents (1Macc i.24, 30)."

[7] So J. J. Collins, *A Commentary on the Book of Daniel* (Minneapolis: Fortress Press, c1993), p. 320.

[8] R. H. Charles, *A Critical and Exegetical Commentary on the Book of Daniel* (Oxford: Clarendon Press, 1929), p. 204, said that the troops of heaven were the people of God.

Jewish rebellion against Rome (132-135 IA), was called a star and identified with the star of Num 24:17 (*yTaan* 68d).

The Jewish **troops** whom the horn attacked were fighting a religious war, and therefore might have been called the army of God or the army **of Heaven**. These were the guerrilla forces that rebelled against Antiochus IV and his Greek army. There were many casualties on both sides, so some of stars and some of **the troops of Heaven** fell, but they were soldiers who lived on the earth. Collins said,

> In all of these passages, of course, the empirical data lie in the persecution of the Jews by Antiochus Epiphanes.[9]

He thought this was a description of a war that was going on in **heaven** just as the Maccabean Revolt was taking place on earth. In other words, Collins acknowledged that the point of focus for the Book of Daniel is the Maccabean Revolt. It is rather difficult to evade that interpretation.

It trampled some of them. Every time the large armies of Syria or Egypt fought one another, one of the nations led hundreds of soldiers over the land of Palestine. When that happened, they **trampled** over farmland, villages, and people, looting the land as they went.

The military general. That was probably Judas the Maccabee, the leader of the Jewish forces. He was a guerrilla leader, and at the first he had no royal title. But in the eyes of the Jewish militants he was the general of the army of God. This was a religious war that was being fought. Judas was the one who brought **the troops** of the "small horn" to a halt. He turned away God's anger from Israel and became famous to the ends of the earth (1Macc 3:8-9).[10] First when Apollonius organized **troops** to crush Jerusalem and the surrounding territory, Judas and his **troops** forced the Syrians to flee, and he killed Apollonius (1Macc 3:10-12). When Seron, the general of the Syrian army, learned of this defeat he sent out forces again to annihilate Judas' troops and raze Jerusalem with its temple, but Judas defeated them badly, and recovered their weapons as booty (1Macc 3:13-26).

With still more **troops**, the Syrians came against Judas with Nicanor and Gorgias as officers (1Macc 3:38-41). After much maneuvering of **troops**, Jews and Syrians locked horns in the rugged terrain around Beth-horon where the Syrians were badly beaten and Judas' **troops** took much valuable booty back to Jerusalem and made plans for rededicating the temple (1Macc 4:1-25). There was still another battle, probably before the first Hanukkah, when the Syrian general, Lysias, attacked Judas and was again defeated at Beth-zur. Lysias, probably after hearing of the death of Antiochus Epiphanes, then retreated north to Antioch with the remnant of his troops. The precise dates and order of events is not certain. The order suggested here is based on 1Macc and a reorganized 2Macc.

---

[9] Collins, *A Commentary*, p. 320.
[10] Of course, the ends of the earth in those days from a Near Eastern point of view extended from India in the east to Spain in the west. The Americas and Australia were not known.

After Judas' strategic victories, Judas paused to have the temple cleansed, and Jews celebrated their first Hanukkah (1Macc 4:26-36). This was probably the series of events which the author of Dan 8 described when he said Antiochus IV expanded his action even up to the military general. He joined battle with the **troops of Heaven**. It was Judas the Maccabee against whom Antiochus sent his best military **troops**.

The place of his temple was thrown down. The word rendered **his temple** here is *meek-dahsh-óh* (מקדשו), something that is sanctified. This word usually is applied to the **temple**. It must have a more specific meaning here, because the **temple** was not destroyed by the Syrians. This may have referred to the holy of holies in the **temple**, the place where people other than priests entered, plundered, and defiled. Rabbis frequently used the expression **the place** as a euphemism for God. **The place** called attention to the place where God lived, either in heaven or in the **temple**. Here it described the location of the destruction that took place in the **temple** at Jerusalem.

An army was directed against the continual offering. This passage is difficult to translate, because the subjects are not certain. The words *tsah-váh tee-nah-táyn ahl hah-tah-meéd* (צבא תנתן על התמיד) could also be rendered 1) **an army** was surrendered because of **the continual offering** or 2) **an army** was set over **the continual offering**. The first alternative (1) would mean that the Jewish troops were forced to surrender to the Syrian Greeks at this point. The second, (2) that a Syrian garrison was set up there to ward off all Jews who resisted. The result would be the same. It seems that the troops of Antiochus, rather than Jewish troops, are still the subject of the discussion.

It was the Syrian army that brought about the defilement of the altar and the cessation of the **continual offering**. It was the Syrian **army** that was in charge, even if Hellenized Jews had actually carried out the commands, acting sinfully (*buh-péh-shah*, בפשע). According to 1Macc 1:47 this involved sacrificing pork on the altar in the temple. It threw truth to the ground, and acted with success. First they came into the temple and stole all of the valuable furniture and equipment. Two years later Antiochus sent an officer to Jerusalem with armed troops, to destroy much of the city, kill many people, defile the temple, loot the city, and arm the city against the local inhabitants (1Macc 1:29-40). This was the event Dan mentioned here.

Collins thought that both here and in Dan 7:25 the **army** involved was a heavenly **army**, an **army** of angels that functioned in heaven.[11] The idea that Antiochus IV might overpower an **army** in heaven, throw heavenly angels to the ground, and trample over them requires special pleading, and Collins acknowledged that the heavenly events had their counterpart on the land. It is true that Jews deduced the events of heaven from the events on earth, but that philosophy works two ways. The geography and government of heaven were thought to be like the ones at Jerusalem. God dwelled both in the temple at Jerusalem and also in the temple in heaven. The temple in heaven and its occupants were holy, but so was the temple at Jerusalem and its worshipers. The faithful members of the contract with Abraham were both holy and heavenly. Jerusalem was called both the holy city and

---

[11] Collins, *A Commentary*, p. 335.

the heavenly city,[12] and Palestine was called the holy land. Therefore it takes more than an adjective or a name to determine that something does not actually take place on earth.

The author of this narrative was not in heaven observing events there and consequently deducing what was happening on earth. He was on earth describing things that took place on the earth. The author wrote about events that took place in the glorious land, including the destruction of a temple area and troops being thrown to the ground and trampled. This happened just the way Alexander the Great threw Media and Persia to the ground and trampled on them (Dan 8:7). The author of Dan 8 was very likely talking about local events rather than heavenly deductions.

He acted and was successful. At the beginning Antiochus and his agents exercised frightful activity in Judah. They forced Jews to abandon their Jewish practices. Jews were not able to stop them. Many Jews submitted to Antiochus' demands. Others died rather than obey. This was when truth was thrown to the ground, and Antiochus was free to do almost everything he wanted.

TEXT

Daniel	First Testament Intertexts
[13]I heard a holy one speaking, and a holy one said to someone [else] who was speaking, "**How long** is the vision of the continual offering	Zech 1:12 The angel of Yehowah answered and said, "Yehowah of armies, **how long** will you not comfort Jerusalem and the cities of Judah with whom you have been angry these 70 years?"
	Hab 1:2 **How long**, Yehowah, will I scream and you not listen?
	Ps 79:5 **How long**. Yehowah? Will you be angry forever? Will your jealousy burn like fire?
	Ps 80:5 Yehowah, God of armies, **how long** will you burn with anger with the prayers of your people?
	Ps 90:13 Return, Yehowah! **How long**? Comfort your servants.
and the transgression that desolates, and the giving up of the sanctuary and the troops to be **trampled**?" [14]He said to me,	Isa 10:5 Assyria, the rod of my anger... I have commanded him to plunder and

---

[12] See further Buchanan, *To the Hebrews* (Garden City: Doubleday, c1972), p. 222.

"Until 2,300 evening and morning sacrifices, and the sanctuary will be vindicated." ¹⁵When I, Daniel, saw **the vision**, I requested instruction. ¹⁶Now look! There was standing before me **something like the appearance of a man**, and I heard the voice of a man between [the banks of] the Ulai. It called and said, "Gabriel, make this man understand **the vision**." ¹⁷Then he came to where I was standing, and when he came I was torn apart [with fear], and **I fell on my face**. He said to me, "Understand, **Son of man**, that the **vision is for the time of the end**." ¹⁸While he was **speaking to me**, I fell into a deep sleep, with my face to the ground. Then he approached **me and stood me up into a standing position**. ¹⁹He said, "Look! I am informing you what will be at

the last of the anger, for it applied to **the appointed time of the end**."

Ezek 1:26 It was **something like the appearance of a man.**

Ezek 1:28 When I saw it **I fell on my face**.

Hab 2:3 For there is still a **vision for the** appointed **time**, and it **speaks** of **the end**. It will not deceive.

Ezek 3:24 The spirit entered into **me and stood me upon my feet**.

Ezek 1:28 He said to me, "**Son of man, stand on your feet**, and I will **speak to you**."

Isa 10:25 Just a very little time, and **the anger will be finished**, and my wrath [will be directed] at their [Assyria's] destruction.

1Macc 3:8 He turned away **the anger** from Israel.

Isa 26:20 Wait a short time until **the anger passes**.

COMMENTARY

How long is the vision? The vision was extended as long as the temple was defiled. At this point the discussion was turned away from the military activity that was taking place and turned to religious interpretation. What was God doing all of this time? What would be the predestined outcome? This was a question that would have been asked many times during the three years after the temple had been defiled and before the Battle of Beth-horon and the rededication of the temple. How long would the temple be defiled? When would God's anger subside? During that three-year period, no one in Judah knew. The battle was raging, and Syria's troops were strong. The author turned to Habakkuk to find scriptural expressions. Habakkuk had asked the same questions, and he wanted also to learn, "When will there be an end to this violence? When will God's anger cease?"

The difference between Habakkuk's situation and the author of Dan 8 was that Habakkuk cried out in desperation. The author of Dan 8, however, was writing a drama. He really knew how long the anger lasted, because it was already over when he wrote.

He said to me. The speaker was the "holy one" mentioned earlier (Dan 8:13). The character in this drama was selected to give the message the author wanted communicated. The character in Zechariah who functioned in the same capacity was called an angel (*mah-láhk*, מלאך) (Zech 4:1; 5:5). Since the Danielic character was entrusted with communicating a similar special message the holy one was probably a heavenly angel.

Here is the answer to that anxious question. By the time this chapter was written, the battles described had already been fought, and the temple either was in the process of being cleansed and rededicated or it had already been cleansed and rededicated. The Lord's anger had ceased. The appointed time of the end had come. The author knew about all of the events, but he presented the historical account in terms of vision and prophecy. The time was 2,300 morning and evening sacrifices. This was the number of sacrifices that would not be offered because the temple was defiled. Transferred into days, this means the temple was defiled for 1,150 days. Perhaps that time was reckoned from the time Menelaus purchased the high priesthood for himself (171 BIA) until the rededication of the temple (164 BIA). But it could have been from the defilement of the temple (168 BIA) until the victory of Judas at Adasa, near Beth-horon (164 BIA). First Macc 4:52-54 claimed that the period was exactly three years.

The sanctuary will be vindicated. The word translated **vindicated** here is *neets-dahk* (נצדק). That means "made right, righteous, or just." In real terms it means that the temple was cleansed so that it could function again. The word *tseh-dehk* means "innocent" after a court trial. It has no crimes against it. When the people were prohibited from using the temple, not only were the people being punished, but the temple itself was suffering. When the temple was cleansed, God's anger was removed. This means God judged the temple favorably. It was no longer blamed for anything. It was not embarrassed; it was highly respected again.

The vision is for the time of the end. **The end** involved is the last of the anger (Dan 8:19), meaning God's anger. Jews believed that they had been sent into exile because God was angry with them. They had been unfaithful to the contract they had made with God, so God was punishing them. Habakkuk and Zechariah both told the Jews why God was angry and urged them to reform and turn around. That would be necessary to satisfy God's anger. Whenever God's anger ceased, their punishment would cease. They would be restored to the Promised Land after they had been rescued from the exile. The wrath would **end** after the Lord had become completely reconciled to his servants (2Macc 8:29). Bevan said,

> The angel informs Daniel of what will take place "in the last days of wrath," i.e. at the end of the heathen domination, for the period of the subjection of Israel to the gentiles is the period of the divine wrath (chap. xi.36).

This all makes sense, but for some reason Bevan also said,

> for the vision is for the time of the end," i.e. it refers to *the final crisis of the world's history* [emphasis added], and is therefore worthy of peculiar attention.[13]

The "period of the subjection of Israel" and the "period of the divine wrath" could have begun with the beginning of the exile to Babylon. That would be 605 BIA, 597 BIA, or 586 BIA. The last 3½ years of that wrath would have begun near June, 168 BIA (1Macc 1:20, 29) when the legation of Apollonius began, or possibly a few months later when the temple was defiled (Dec. 15, 168, 1Macc 1:54).

Things were going well for the Jews at the time Dan 8 was written. Why would victorious Jews between 164 and 142 BIA have wanted history to come to an **end**? Bevan has imported a doctrine into the text that had its origin in some non-biblical theology and is unrelated either to the composition or the meaning of the Book of Daniel. Montgomery correctly said,

> What the 'end' is appears from 9:26, 'his end,' i.e. 'Antiochus'.[14]

There is nothing in Habakkuk, Zechariah, Ezekiel, or the Book of Daniel to suggest that the issue involved was the final crisis of the history of the world. Neither was there any implication that they were anticipating **the end** of time or the cosmos. These suggestions were all invented by Western theologians, many centuries after Daniel had been written. All the text meant was that it was **the end** of God's anger with Israel, and this was certain to have many consequences for the chosen people on earth. It meant that the Syrians would be defeated; the Promised Land would be restored; the temple would be cleansed and rededicated. All of this happened and was completed by 142 BIA. Keil correctly refuted those who thought this meant **the end** of history. He said it was **the end** of the time of Antiochus.[15] Even though Goldingay suggested in other passages that Daniel was pointing to **the end** of history, in relationship to this passage, he corrrectly said,

> But Daniel is not thinking of "the absolute eschatological 'End,' of "the final and absolute End for all events" when "human history comes to a close" (against Welch; contrast Jones, 178-219). If anything, further human history on earth is *presupposed* by talk of the restoration of the sanctuary, as it was by the talk of a new

---

[13] Bevan, *Short Commentary*, p. 137.
[14] J. A. Montgomery, *A Critical and Exegetical Commentary on the Book of Daniel* (New York: Charles Scribner's Sons, 1927), p. 346. Keil, *Daniel*, p. 313, also said it was "the period of the oppression of of the people of God by Antiochus." See also p. 316.
[15] Keil, *Daniel*, p. 310.

kingdom in 2:44; 7:14, 18, 27. The end in Daniel is not so different from the day of Yahweh in the prophets.

That which was finished was the gentile rule over Israel. The last ruler was Antiochus IV, and **the end** was **the end** of his rule over Israel. Smith-Christopher said,

> Apocalyptic writing, it must be remembered, remains a popular literature precisely because of the frequently recurring sense in history that 'ours *must be* the last age.'[16]

The **end** used in the Book of Daniel was not just a typical expression that finds natural expression among all people in every age as if every people thought the world or the cosmos was coming to an **end**. Words like "Benedict Arnold," "Watergate," and "Waterloo" have their origin in certain specific situations. The same is true of **the end** used in the Book of Daniel. **The end** was something that had already happened. It was not just a normal feeling of a situation that *must* happen soon. It was **the end** of the life of Antiochus IV, **the end** of the Seleucid power over Judah, **the end** of God's anger with his people (Dan 8:25; 11:35, 45). This was a very special designation.

Something like the appearance of a man. This whole narrative was cast in terms of a vision and exegesis. Where did the author go for intertexts of visions? To Ezekiel, of course, so in Ezekiel's vision was a figure that was **something like the appearance of a man**. That was a text, and the Danielic exegete took that figure to become a character that would tell Daniel how long God's anger would last.

I fell on my face. The author of this chapter knew the facts of history. He knew how long the temple was defiled. His task was to cast all of this into a drama that was theologically valid. He turned to Ezekiel to learn how visions were narrated. There he found the characters for his cast, and the order of events. One of the characters was one **like the appearance of a man**. He would be the one to inform Daniel of the predestined order of events. Daniel was the character who had the visions, and he was made to do the same things Ezekiel did with his vision. He **fell on** his **face**. Then he was invited to stand up. At that point he told Daniel about the end of God's anger.

In ancient courts the defendant was expected to **fall on** his **face** before the judge in humility after all of the arguments had been given, waiting for the judge to give the verdict. If the judge asked the defendant to stand up and face the judge, this was good news. It meant that the judge was prepared to declare the defendant innocent of the accusations made. Daniel was pictured as having fallen before the one who appeared to be like a human being as if that being were a judge and Daniel was the defendant waiting on his face for the verdict.[17] When Daniel was invited to

---

[16] D. L. Smith-Christopher, *The Book of Daniel* (Nashville: Abingdon Press, c1996), p. 115.

[17] See further Buchanan, *Biblical and Theological Insights from Ancient and Modern Civil Law* (Lewiston: The Edwin Mellen Press, c1992), pp. 57-61.

stand, that meant God had judged Israel favorably. There would be an end to God's anger, and that end was already on God's predestined schedule.

TEXT

[20]The **ram**, which you saw with two horns, were the kings of the Medes and the Persians. [21]The **male goat** was the king of the Greeks. The **large horn**, which was between his eyes, is the first king. [22]It became **broken** and **four** arose in its place. **Four** kingdoms will arise from the nation, but not with his strength.

[23]At the end of their kingdoms
   transgressors will weaken them,
and a king of a defiant countenance,
   who understands riddles, will arise.
[24]His strength will become great,
   but not by his own power.
He will be frightfully destructive;
   he will succeed and act.
He will destroy powerful people,
   including the people of the saints.
[25]Because of his cleverness
   deceit will prosper in his hand.
He will plan great things,
   and he will easily destroy many [people].
He will take a stand against the leading military general,
   but he will be broken through no [human] power.

COMMENTARY

The ram which you saw with two horns. One of the reasons it is not very difficult to demythologize the myths in the Book of Daniel is that the author began the process of demythologization himself. First he told the myth and then he told what the symbolization meant. Here he said that **the ram with two horns** represented two kings of the Medes and the Persians. **The ram** apparently represented the Medes and the Persians, and the horns represented the kings. The vision showed that the horns were large, one was larger than the other was (Dan 8:3). During the time of the Babylon independence, Persia was a small country at the south of Media. Media had grown to be a large country, including Persia in the south and Assyria to the north. Later, Cyrus conquered Media from Persia and began to extend his empire from that point. Many years later Roman historians still referred to these two countries together as if there had been a union of the two countries rather than a conquest on the part of Cyrus. Like **the** visionary **ram** Cyrus pushed in every direction until he had an empire that reached from India to Greece, including parts of Europe. Although Media was much larger than Persia, initially, later Persia was larger than Media had ever been. The larger "horn" in this case was apparently Cyrus, the great king of Persia.

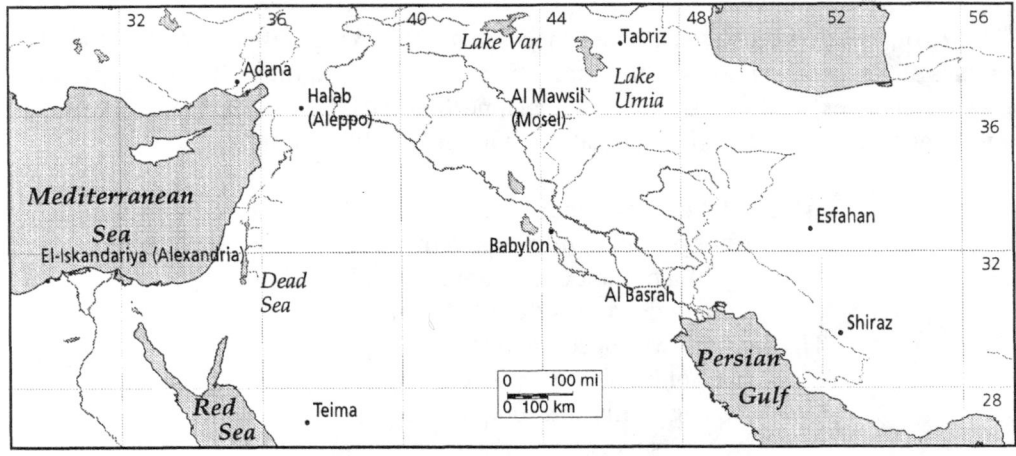

The male goat was the king of the Greeks. The entire **goat** represents Greek royalty, including all of **the kings** involved. The big horn was **the** big **king**. This, of course, was Alexander the Great. He was the first of those who extended their influence into the Middle and Far East. The author practically says that. When Alexander came to Jerusalem the high priest and other Jewish leaders went out to welcome him. He made concessive promises to the Jews, and the Jews were prepared to cooperate with him in his battle against the Persians, just as Jews had done earlier when Cyrus of Persia entered Babylon. Their cooperation with Cyrus gained Jews many benefits, and their cooperation with Alexander would also have been beneficial if only Alexander had lived long enough to fulfill his promises. After his death, Jews wandered back and forth between Egypt and Syria, casting their lot first with one country and then with another, whichever seemed to offer the most benefits. Hellenistic Jews negotiated with Hellenistic Syrians or Hellenistic Egyptians. Sometimes one sect of Jews was pro-Egyptian at the same time another was pro-Syrian. While this was going on, Palestine was becoming increasingly Hellenistic.

At the end of their kingdoms. That is **the end of** the Greek **kingdoms,** the four **kingdoms** of the four kings that succeeded Alexander the Great. After the Battles of Beth-horon and Beth-zur it seemed clear to the Jews that the days of the Seleucids were over. The reason was not that the Greeks were incompetent in military strategy but that there were transgressors who would weaken them. That is the reading of the MT.

The Hebrew could be pointed differently, however, and the meaning would be that their own transgressions would weaken them, and so they would be punished by the king described in the following poem. The OG has **their sins having been**

filled up. The explanation in any case is that the Greek **kingdoms** were coming to an **end**, and the cause of this was the sinners who sinned.

Since the **kingdoms** that were coming to an **end** were gentile **kingdoms** rather than the Jewish **kingdom**, it was the gentile sinners who committed the transgression. The doctrine of the treasury of merits is consistent throughout the Book of Daniel. In the first place, it was the sins of the Jews that made God angry and caused him to punish the Jews. As soon as Jews had paid for all of these sins and iniquities God's anger subsided, but at the same time the gentiles' sins had increased and deserved punishment (Gen 15:16; 2Macc 6:14). Jews expected the judgment of God on New Year's Day, and the Day of Atonement was the day when the books would be audited to determine whether Jews were in a moral and fiscal position to receive God's anger or favor. The victory of the Battle of Beth-horon convinced them that their sins had been paid in full, and that God's anger was over. This line is an introduction to the poem that follows.

A king of a defiant countenance. This king was Antiochus IV Epiphanes, the subject of this poem.

Not by his own power. The author may mean by this that he was more deceitful and clever than mighty, but another possibility is that God controlled Antiochus' actions. He succeeded because God wanted him to. This was a part of God's wrath. God hardened Antiochus' heart just as he had hardened Pharaoh's heart, but in both cases this was part of a larger plan to allow his people to escape.

He will be frightfully destructive. This describes his military advances. Antiochus expanded his empire as much as he could, crushing the nations that stood in his way. These words also report the treatment the Jews felt at his dominion after he had been forced by the Romans to end the war in Egypt and go back to Syria.

Including the people of the saints. These were some of **the people** whom Antiochus destroyed. They were not angels, as Collins assumed. **The people of the saints** were also called **the saints** of the Most High (Dan 7:18). They were **the saints** over which Antiochus (the horn) had prevailed in war (Dan 7:21). They were the orthodox Jews who resisted the forced Hellenization introduced by Antiochus Epiphanes. They were persecuted in many ways. When mothers had their sons circumcised, Syrians killed the baby boys and hanged them around their mothers' necks as the Greeks paraded the mothers around the city. Jews were killed for owning scriptures or observing any of their traditional Jewish customs. They were also killed in war.

Deceit will in his hand prosper. This refers to the time Antiochus sent the Mysian officer to the cities of Judah. He came with a large army. At first he craftily spoke to leaders in peaceful terms until he gained their confidence. Then he attacked Jerusalem by surprise, plundered it, killed many people, destroyed houses, looted possessions, and constructed a citadel to control the population (1Macc 1:29-40).

Take a stand against the leading military general. This is sometimes rendered "prince of princes" (*sáhr sah-reém*, שר שרים). This was only one of the exalted names given to Judas the Maccabee, the commander in chief of the military forces. He directed the **army of Heaven** (Dan 8:10), also called the **stars** (Dan 8:10). Judas was in charge of all of the troops, and after he had won many battles, he was treated as if he were the king of Judah. He directed the government. He was the one against whom Antiochus sent his troops to annihilate.

He will be broken. The detail is clear, even though it is not consistent. The horn that **was broken** was Antiochus IV. He was **broken** at his death in 164 BIA. When the horn **was broken** it was not **broken** into other horns. Neither was he killed in battle. He went east to plunder a temple and acquire money to continue his military activities. He failed in his attempt, became ill, and died there in the east. No human being killed him. Literally, the text says **without a [human] hand he will be broken**. He suffered the fate that Job promised would come to wicked kings: **In an instant they die; in the middle of the night people are shaken and pass away; the mighty are removed by no human hand** (Job 34:20).

TEXT

^{26}The vision of the evening and morning
    which has been told is true,
but you, seal up the vision,
    for it belongs to many days [from now].

^{27}I, Daniel, became [exhausted] and was ill for days. Then I rose up and I went about the work of the king. I was astonished by the vision, and I did not understand [it].

COMMENTARY

The vision of the evening and morning. That which is true may be **the** entire **vision** which may have come to Daniel at **the evening and morning** sacrifices. The other possibility is that the answer given to the question about the time when all of these things would come to an end was answered in terms **of morning and evening sacrifices**, namely 2,300. It was true that the waiting period would be that long.

Seal up the vision, for it belongs to many days. **The vision** was treated as if it were a legal will. It was to be written down, notarized, and **sealed** to be opened and made effective in the future when the predestined conditions and time were fulfilled. It was sealed up to be preserved. In the future the **seals** would be broken, and the terms written in the will would become known and become effective. The time that was predestined was 164 BIA when Judas the Maccabee and his troops would overwhelm the Syrian army, and the temple would be cleansed and rededicated.

The work of the king. This was evidently Belshazzar. His administration as co-regent was part of the time between 555 and 539 BIA. Daniel was reported to have been employed by the king and continued in office until the invasion of Cyrus in 539 BIA (Dan 1:21; 1Macc 6; 2Macc 9; *Ant* 12.9, 1). This was 66 years after Daniel was reported to have been taken into Babylon for his education.

CHAPTER NINE

HEBREW TEXT

9:1 בִּשְׁנַת אַחַת לְדָרְיָוֶשׁ בֶּן־אֲחַשְׁוֵרוֹשׁ מִזֶּרַע מָדָי אֲשֶׁר הָמְלַךְ עַל מַלְכוּת כַּשְׂדִּים: 2 בִּשְׁנַת אַחַת לְמָלְכוֹ אֲנִי דָּנִיֵּאל בִּינֹתִי בַּסְּפָרִים מִסְפַּר הַשָּׁנִים אֲשֶׁר הָיָה דְבַר־יְהוָה אֶל־יִרְמְיָה הַנָּבִיא לְחָרְבוֹת יְרוּשָׁלִַם שִׁבְעִים שָׁנָה: 3 וָאֶתְּנָה אֶת־פָּנַי אֶל־אֲדֹנָי הָאֱלֹהִים לְבַקֵּשׁ תְּפִלָּה וְתַחֲנוּנִים בְּצוֹם וְשַׂק וָאֵפֶר: 4 וָאֶתְפַּלְלָה לַיהוָה אֱלֹהַי וָאֶתְוַדֶּה וָאֹמְרָה אָנָּא אֲדֹנָי הָאֵל הַגָּדוֹל וְהַנּוֹרָא שֹׁמֵר הַבְּרִית וְהַחֶסֶד לְאֹהֲבָיו וּלְשֹׁמְרֵי מִצְוֹתָיו: 5 חָטָאנוּ וְעָוִינוּ וְהִרְשַׁעְנוּ [וְהִרְשָׁעְנוּ] וּמָרָדְנוּ וְסוֹר מִמִּצְוֹתֶךָ וּמִמִּשְׁפָּטֶיךָ: 6 וְלֹא שָׁמַעְנוּ אֶל־עֲבָדֶיךָ הַנְּבִיאִים אֲשֶׁר דִּבְּרוּ בְּשִׁמְךָ אֶל־מְלָכֵינוּ שָׂרֵינוּ וַאֲבֹתֵינוּ וְאֶל כָּל־עַם הָאָרֶץ: 7 לְךָ אֲדֹנָי הַצְּדָקָה וְלָנוּ בֹּשֶׁת הַפָּנִים כַּיּוֹם הַזֶּה לְאִישׁ יְהוּדָה וּלְיוֹשְׁבֵי יְרוּשָׁלִַם וּלְכָל־יִשְׂרָאֵל הַקְּרֹבִים וְהָרְחֹקִים בְּכָל־הָאֲרָצוֹת אֲשֶׁר הִדַּחְתָּם שָׁם בְּמַעֲלָם אֲשֶׁר מָעֲלוּ־בָךְ: 8 יְהוָה לָנוּ בֹּשֶׁת הַפָּנִים לִמְלָכֵינוּ לְשָׂרֵינוּ וְלַאֲבֹתֵינוּ אֲשֶׁר חָטָאנוּ לָךְ: 9 לַאדֹנָי אֱלֹהֵינוּ הָרַחֲמִים וְהַסְּלִחוֹת כִּי מָרַדְנוּ בּוֹ: 10 וְלֹא שָׁמַעְנוּ בְּקוֹל יְהוָה אֱלֹהֵינוּ לָלֶכֶת בְּתוֹרֹתָיו אֲשֶׁר נָתַן לְפָנֵינוּ בְּיַד עֲבָדָיו הַנְּבִיאִים: 11 וְכָל־יִשְׂרָאֵל עָבְרוּ אֶת־תּוֹרָתֶךָ וְסוֹר לְבִלְתִּי שְׁמוֹעַ בְּקֹלֶךָ וַתִּתַּךְ עָלֵינוּ הָאָלָה וְהַשְּׁבֻעָה אֲשֶׁר כְּתוּבָה בְּתוֹרַת מֹשֶׁה עֶבֶד־הָאֱלֹהִים כִּי חָטָאנוּ לוֹ: 12 וַיָּקֶם אֶת־דְּבָרָיו [דְּבָרוֹ] אֲשֶׁר־דִּבֶּר עָלֵינוּ וְעַל שֹׁפְטֵינוּ אֲשֶׁר שְׁפָטוּנוּ לְהָבִיא עָלֵינוּ רָעָה גְדֹלָה אֲשֶׁר לֹא־נֶעֶשְׂתָה תַּחַת כָּל־הַשָּׁמַיִם כַּאֲשֶׁר נֶעֶשְׂתָה בִּירוּשָׁלִָם: 13 כַּאֲשֶׁר כָּתוּב בְּתוֹרַת מֹשֶׁה אֵת כָּל־הָרָעָה הַזֹּאת בָּאָה עָלֵינוּ וְלֹא־חִלִּינוּ אֶת־פְּנֵי יְהוָה אֱלֹהֵינוּ לָשׁוּב מֵעֲוֹנֵנוּ וּלְהַשְׂכִּיל בַּאֲמִתֶּךָ: 14 וַיִּשְׁקֹד יְהוָה עַל־הָרָעָה וַיְבִיאֶהָ עָלֵינוּ כִּי־צַדִּיק יְהוָה אֱלֹהֵינוּ עַל־כָּל־מַעֲשָׂיו אֲשֶׁר עָשָׂה וְלֹא שָׁמַעְנוּ בְּקֹלוֹ: 15 וְעַתָּה ׀ אֲדֹנָי אֱלֹהֵינוּ אֲשֶׁר הוֹצֵאתָ אֶת־עַמְּךָ מֵאֶרֶץ מִצְרַיִם בְּיָד חֲזָקָה וַתַּעַשׂ־לְךָ שֵׁם כַּיּוֹם הַזֶּה חָטָאנוּ רָשָׁעְנוּ: 16 אֲדֹנָי

Jer 25:12; 29:10; Amos 8:12
2Chron 36:21; Zech 1:12; Neh 9:1
Esth 4:1; Isa 7:16 ; 37:16-17
Neh 1:5, 6; 9:32; 10:1 1Kgs 8:23-24
1Kgs 8:46-47; Deut 6:2; 7:9
Deut 11:13-14; Neh 1:6; Ezra 10:1
Jer 26:4; 44:21; Neh 9:33-34
Ezra 9:7;1 Kgs 8:47 Isa 37:18
Deut 30:1; 2Chron 6:36
Ezra 9:7, 17; Neh 1:6, 8
1Kgs 8:34; Deut 4:30; Jer 4:4
Jer 26:4; Neh 9:17; Ezek 17:20
Deut 4:30; Jer 7:20; 2Chron 12:7; Neh 9:34
1Kgs 8:15, 31; Neh 10:30
1Kgs 8:26; Deut 29:20; Ezra 9:11
Jer 35:17; 36:31; 31:28; Exod 15:26
Exod 9:18

Jer 1:12; 11:4
Deut 29:11; Neh 1:8
Isa 37:16-17; Jer 32:20-21
Neh 9:2, 32-34; Num 25:4
Jer 26:4; 44:21,27; 42:18
Neh 9:33-34; Ezra 9:7
Ps 44:14//79:4; Isa 37:17
1Kgs 8:30; Num 6:25
1Kgs 8:28-29, 52
Neh 1:6
1Kgs 8:15, 32; Deut 28:15
Ezra 9:7
2Chron 6:36; Deut 30:1

בְּכָל־צִדְקֹתֶ֔ךָ יָֽשָׁב־נָ֤א אַפְּךָ֙ וַחֲמָ֣תְךָ֔ מֵעִֽירְךָ֥ יְרוּשָׁלַ֖͏ִם הַר־קָדְשֶׁ֑ךָ כִּ֤י
וּבַעֲוֺנ֣וֹת אֲבֹתֵ֔ינוּ יְרוּשָׁלַ֥͏ִם וְעַמְּךָ֖ לְחֶרְפָּ֑ה לְכָל־סְבִיבֹתֵֽינוּ׃
בַחֲטָאֵ֙ינוּ֙

17 וְעַתָּ֣ה ׀ שְׁמַ֣ע אֱלֹהֵ֗ינוּ אֶל־תְּפִלַּ֤ת עַבְדְּךָ֙ וְאֶל־תַּ֣חֲנוּנָ֔יו וְהָאֵ֣ר פָּנֶ֔יךָ
עַל־מִקְדָּשְׁךָ֥ הַשָּׁמֵ֖ם לְמַ֥עַן אֲדֹנָֽי׃ 18 הַטֵּ֨ה אֱלֹהַ֥י ׀ אָזְנְךָ֮ וּֽשֲׁמָע֒
[פְּקַ֣ח] עֵינֶ֗יךָ וּרְאֵה֙ שֹֽׁמְמֹתֵ֔ינוּ וְהָעִ֕יר אֲשֶׁר־נִקְרָ֥א שִׁמְךָ֖ עָלֶ֑יהָ כִּ֣י ׀
פְקֹחָֽה

לֹ֣א עַל־צִדְקֹתֵ֗ינוּ אֲנַ֨חְנוּ מַפִּילִ֤ים תַּחֲנוּנֵ֙ינוּ֙ לְפָנֶ֔יךָ כִּ֖י עַל־רַחֲמֶ֥יךָ
הָרַבִּֽים׃ 19 אֲדֹנָ֣י ׀ שְׁמָ֙עָה֙ אֲדֹנָ֣י ׀ סְלָ֔חָה אֲדֹנָ֛י הַֽקְשִׁ֥יבָה וַעֲשֵׂ֖ה אַל־
תְּאַחַ֑ר לְמַֽעֲנְךָ֣ אֱלֹהַ֗י כִּֽי־שִׁמְךָ֤ נִקְרָא֙ עַל־עִ֣ירְךָ֔ וְעַל־עַמֶּֽךָ׃
20 וְע֨וֹד אֲנִ֤י מְדַבֵּר֙ וּמִתְפַּלֵּ֔ל וּמִתְוַדֶּה֙ חַטָּאתִ֔י וְחַטַּ֖את עַמִּ֣י יִשְׂרָאֵ֑ל
וּמַפִּ֣יל תְּחִנָּתִ֗י לִפְנֵי֙ יְהוָ֣ה אֱלֹהַ֔י עַ֖ל הַר־קֹ֥דֶשׁ אֱלֹהָֽי׃ 21 וְע֥וֹד אֲנִ֖י
מְדַבֵּ֣ר בַּתְּפִלָּ֑ה וְהָאִ֣ישׁ גַּבְרִיאֵ֡ל אֲשֶׁר֩ רָאִ֨יתִי בֶחָז֤וֹן בַּתְּחִלָּה֙ מֻעָ֣ף
בִּיעָ֔ף נֹגֵ֣עַ אֵלַ֔י כְּעֵ֖ת מִנְחַת־עָֽרֶב׃ 22 וַיָּ֖בֶן וַיְדַבֵּ֣ר עִמִּ֑י וַיֹּאמַ֔ר
דָּֽנִיֵּ֕אל עַתָּ֥ה יָצָ֖אתִי לְהַשְׂכִּילְךָ֥ בִינָֽה׃ 23 בִּתְחִלַּ֣ת תַּחֲנוּנֶ֗יךָ יָצָ֣א דָבָ֔ר
וַאֲנִי֙ בָּ֣אתִי לְהַגִּ֔יד כִּ֥י חֲמוּד֖וֹת אָ֑תָּה וּבִין֙ בַּדָּבָ֔ר וְהָבֵ֖ן בַּמַּרְאֶֽה׃
24 שָׁבֻעִ֨ים שִׁבְעִ֜ים נֶחְתַּ֥ךְ עַֽל־עַמְּךָ֣ ׀ וְעַל־עִ֣יר קָדְשֶׁ֗ךָ
לְכַלֵּ֨א הַפֶּ֜שַׁע וּלַחְתֹּ֤ם [וּלְהָתֵם֙] חַטָּאוֹת֙ [חַטָּ֔את] וּלְכַפֵּ֖ר עָוֺ֑ן
וּלְהָבִיא֙ צֶ֣דֶק עֹֽלָמִ֔ים וְלַחְתֹּ֥ם חָז֖וֹן וְנָבִ֑יא וְלִמְשֹׁ֖חַ קֹ֥דֶשׁ קָֽדָשִֽׁים׃
25 וְתֵדַ֨ע וְתַשְׂכֵּ֜ל
מִן־מֹצָ֣א דָבָ֗ר לְהָשִׁיב֙ וְלִבְנ֤וֹת יְרֽוּשָׁלִַ֙ם֙ עַד־מָשִׁ֣יחַ נָגִ֔יד שָׁבֻעִ֖ים שִׁבְעָ֑ה
וְשָׁבֻעִ֞ים שִׁשִּׁ֣ים וּשְׁנַ֗יִם תָּשׁוּב֙ וְנִבְנְתָה֙ רְח֣וֹב וְחָר֔וּץ וּבְצ֖וֹק הָעִתִּֽים׃ 26 וְאַחֲרֵ֤י הַשָּׁבֻעִים֙ שִׁשִּׁ֣ים וּשְׁנַ֔יִם יִכָּרֵ֥ת מָשִׁ֖יחַ וְאֵ֣ין ל֑וֹ
וְהָעִ֨יר וְהַקֹּ֜דֶשׁ יַ֠שְׁחִית עַ֣ם נָגִ֤יד הַבָּא֙
וְקִצּ֣וֹ בַשֶּׁ֔טֶף וְעַד֙ קֵ֣ץ מִלְחָמָ֔ה נֶחֱרֶ֖צֶת שֹׁמֵמֽוֹת׃
27 וְהִגְבִּ֥יר בְּרִ֛ית לָרַבִּ֖ים שָׁב֣וּעַ אֶחָ֑ד
וַחֲצִ֨י הַשָּׁב֜וּעַ יַשְׁבִּ֣ית ׀ זֶ֣בַח וּמִנְחָ֗ה
וְעַ֨ל כְּנַ֤ף שִׁקּוּצִים֙ מְשֹׁמֵ֔ם וְעַד־כָּלָה֙ וְנֶ֣חֱרָצָ֔ה תִּתַּ֖ךְ עַל־שֹׁמֵֽם׃ פ

	Neh 1:7-9; 9:17; Ps 15:1
	Isa 37:17;1Kgs 8:28-29;Neh 1:6; Deut 28:15;1Kgs 8:15
	Isa 6:9
	Exod 29:36-37; Isa 43:25
	Zech 13:4
	Isa 6:11;Jer 25:12
	Lev 26:33;Isa 10:23

INTRODUCTION

Daniel was busily at work in his study, trying to learn how long the exile would last until the chosen people are returned to the Promised Land. His first text was the prophecy of Jeremiah. Before he became deeply engrossed in his study he was interrupted by a prayer for forgiveness and deliverance of the city of Jerusalem. After the prayer Daniel was able, with the assistance of an angel, to deduce the time of the end. This is the message of the ninth chapter of the Book of Daniel.

ENGLISH TEXT

Daniel	First Testament Intertexts
9:1 **In the first year**	Isa 6:1 **In the year** that King Uzziah died, I saw the Lord.
	Ezra 4:5-6 All the days of Cyrus, king of

of Darius, son of Ahasuerus, who was born a Mede, became king over the kingdom of the Chaldeans, ²I, Daniel, was studying in the books the number of years, which, according to the word of Yehowah which came to Jeremiah the prophet to fill up the destruction of Jerusalem— 70 years.

Persia to the rule of Darius, king of Persia, and in the reign of Ahasuerus, at the beginning of his reign, they wrote an accusation against the citizens of Judah and Jerusalem.

Jer 25:12 The word of Yehowah, which came to Jeremiah the prophet to fill up the destruction of Jerusalem 70 years.

Jer 29:10 For thus says Yehowah, "When 70 years are filled up for Babylon, I will visit you."

2Chron 36:21 . . . to fill up the word of Yehowah in the mouth of Jeremiah . . . to fill up 70 years.

Zech 1:12 The angel of Yehowah said, "Yehowah of armies, how long will you not comfort Jerusalem and the cities of Judah against whom you have been angry these 70 years?"

COMMENTARY

The first year of Darius. Following the style of Isaiah's vision, the author of this chapter began by relating the vision to the reign of a certain king (Isa 6:1).[1]

Scholars have not been able to identify this **Darius** who was born a Mede. Colless argued that this is just another name for Cyrus of Persia who was born a Mede.[2] **Darius** was probably a fictional character patterned after the same **Darius** mentioned in Dan 6:1, although Dequeker argued that this was **Darius** II, rather than **Darius** I Hystaspes.[3] His existence is coherent with the division of history into four nations (Babylon, Media, Persia, and Greece) rather than three (Babylon, Persia, and Greece), but there is no evidence that Media ever conquered and ruled Babylon. This was more than likely an invention of an editor who was obligated to transform a pattern from 1) Assyria, 2) Media, 3) Persia, and 4) Greece to one that began with Babylonia rather than Assyria and still reached the number four. Since the second number was Media, and Media did not follow Babylonia in the sequence of great nations, the editor devised one and invented a ruler to fit the

---

[1] G. G. Nicol, "Isaiah's Vision and the Visions of Daniel," *VT* 29 (1979):501-504, noted other similarities between Isa 6 and Dan 9.
[2] B. E. Colless, "Cyrus the Persian as Darius the Mede in the Book of Daniel," *JSOT* 56 (1992):116.
[3] L. Dequeker, "King Darius and the Prophecy of Seventy Years," *The Book of Daniel in the Light of New Findings* (Leuven: University Press, 1993), pp. 187-210.

program. Since **Darius** seems not to have been a historical character, we are not able to determine when he lived. Smith-Christopher blamed this on "Daniel's own idiosyncratic chronology,"[4] as if the author of the Book of Daniel had only one author with one peculiar philosophy of history. It is much more likely that several different authors who were writing historical dramas rather than history composed the book. Therefore the kinds of historical knowledge exhibited in the book are not completely coherent with one another.

I, Daniel, was studying in the books. The Hebrew for **was studying** is *bee-noh-teé* (ביןתי). This word is from the Hebrew *been* (בין), which means "know," "learn," **study**, "teach," or "understand," depending on its form and context. This is a word that occurs frequently in Dan 8 and 9 (8:17, 23; 9:1, 22, 23), but not at all in Dan 2-7.[5] The books that **Daniel was studying** were the books of the scripture. Wilson argued that the **books** were only the letters contained in Jer 29.[6] Jeremiah was certainly one of the books of scripture to which the author went for information. There are many quotations and allusions to Jeremiah in this chapter, but only one obvious reference to Jer 29 in Dan 9.

Some scholars propose a late date for **Daniel** on the basis that **Daniel was studying the** scripture. They argue that there was not a collection of biblical books until very late in the biblical tradition. There are many reasons for thinking that this chapter was written late, but this is not one of them. Since scholars have begun to work on scripture intertextually, they have discovered that many FT books have been composed, like **Daniel,** depending on many earlier biblical sources, showing that there was an early collection. We cannot know exactly how large the collection was at any one time, but we can be sure that eighth century Isaiah had access to earlier sources, and that he already knew methods of rhetoric for using them.

The Book of Deuteronomy was composed with Genesis and Exodus at the author's disposal. By the time of Jeremiah, Ezekiel, and Second Isaiah these authors had the entire Torah, as well as Hosea and some of the Psalms. All of these **books** were available to the author of Dan 9, even if the chapter had been written as early as it pretends to have been. There were probably several times when books were collected and authorized. One of these may have been at the time of Jeremiah, when Deuteronomy became Judaized. Another occurred under the leadership of Ezra and Nehemiah. Still a third was performed under the Hasmonean rule when **Daniel** was added to the canon. There was still a fourth after the fall of Jerusalem when books like the Song of Solomon, and Ps 74 were included.[7]

Daniel was not really a historical character, who **studied** the scripture, but the author of Dan 9 was, and he mythologized Israelite history, using **Daniel** as his hero. **Studying the** scripture was a reasonable thing for a Jew to do. Jews and early Christians believed the FT contained the only data available for arguing a case in

---

[4] D. L. Smith-Christopher, *The Book of Daniel* (Nashville: Abingdon, c1996), p. 121.
[5] Noticed by J. Doukhan, "The Seventy Weeks of Dan 9: An Exegetical Study," *AUSS* 18 (1980):5.
[6] G. H. Wilson, "The Prayer of Daniel 9: Reflection on Jeremiah 29," *JSOT* 48 (1990):91-99.
[7] Buchanan, "The Fall of Jerusalem and the Reconsideration of some Dates," *RevQ* 53 (1989):31-48.

court and for deducing the future. By studying cycles, typology, and some basic rules of Jewish rhetoric Jews thought they could predict the future. They also believed that everything that was in the world was in the scripture and that all prophecy would be fulfilled in the days of the Messiah. Those who prophesied almost always wrote at a time when they thought they lived in the messianic age.

By the time Dan 9 was written Jeremiah and Zechariah were both accepted as prophets. Therefore everything they wrote was the word of God and would be fulfilled. Jeremiah said the Jews who had been taken captive would be permitted to return in 70 years. Just a little mathematical calculation should provide the necessary date, according to Jeremiah. Supposing the 70-year period began with the full captivity in 586 BIA. Then the 70 years would be up about 516 BIA. There was a lot of nationalistic activity in Persia at that time, related to the return of Ezra and Nehemiah and the first return to the Promised Land after the exile to Babylon. The midrash on Jeremiah, however, shows that the author of this chapter did not have that date in mind (Dan 9:24). He was thinking of a date sometime after the Greek kingdom, "the kingdom of iron" (Dan 2:40).

Dan 9 is a midrashic narrative whose initial text was Jeremiah's prophecy that the Jews would be permitted to return to the Promised Land. Since **Daniel** was presented as one who had **studied** the terms of the contract that had been made between God and his people, and he thought that the prophesied time was up, he decided to take the case to court. The rest of the chapter dealt with **Daniel's** prayer for relief. Although **Daniel's** initial text was Jeremiah and the Torah, his prayer for relief was based primarily on Solomon's prayer in 1Kgs 8 and Hezekiah's prayer in Isa 37.

Daniel was not the only one to have imitated Solomon's prayer. So did Nehemiah (Neh 1:5-11). The author of **Daniel's** prayer clearly took words from Jeremiah, 1Kgs, Isaiah, and Nehemiah, and wove them into his midrash. Nehemiah's prayer was itself a midrash that used 1Kgs and Jeremiah as intertexts. 1Kgs had also been constructed on the basis of passages taken from the Pentateuch. Jeremiah also based his prophecy on an earlier Torah text (Deut 15:12-13). The author of this prayer in Dan 9 used all of these intertexts to produce his supplication.

TEXT

Daniel	First Testament Intertexts
³**I turned my face** to the Lord God	Lev 26:18 **I will turn my face** against you, and you will be smitten before your enemies.
to request	Amos 8:12 They will run back and forth **to request** the word of Yehowah.
with prayer, supplication, **fasting, sackcloth,**	Neh 9:1 The people of Israel were gathered **with fasting and** in **sackcloth** with dirt on their heads.

and ashes.	^{Esth 4:1} Mordecai tore his garments and wore **sackcloth and ashes.**
⁴**I prayed to** Yehowah, my God.	^{Neh 1:6} Hear the prayer of your servant which **I pray before you**, day and night, concerning the children of Israel, your servants,
I confessed	**making confession** for the sins.
and **I said**,	^{Isa 6:5} **I said**, "Woe is me! I am silenced, for I am a man of unclean lips, and I live in the midst of a people of unclean lips."
	^{Ezra 10:1} When Ezra **prayed** and when he **confessed**, weeping and falling on his face before the temple a very great crowd of Israelites gathered.

COMMENTARY

Fasting, sack cloth, and ashes. This was a traditional practice, employed by Mordecai, Ezra, Nehemiah, and others. It was designed to gain approval from God. When Judas, the Maccabee, was leading guerrilla Jews into battle against Nicanor and his Greek troops, he commanded his soldiers to pray to God dressed in **sack cloth** (*Ant* 12.300). Both prayer and **sackcloth** were court customs in most countries in the Near East. Defendants were expected to appear in court unshaved, with hair uncombed, dressed in black, shabby clothing. This was designed to obtain pity from the judge.

Prayed to Yehowah. In the Book of Daniel, the word **Yehowah** is seldom used for the deity. Instead God is referred to as "God of heaven," "The Most High," "God," "God of the fathers," and "Lord." This suggests that the **prayer** in this chapter is of separate composition. That possibility is further supported by the fact that this **prayer** used better literary Hebrew than the other parts of Daniel. It is entirely free of Aramaisms. The prayers of Ezra and Hezekiah, both of which addressed God as Yehowah, also motivated it.

The request made to the judge in court after the arguments had been given was called a **prayer** in those days. Still today in courts in U.S.A., the plaintiff's request to the judge or jury is called the "**prayer** for relief." When Judas and his troops **prayed** to God in sackcloth they considered themselves to be appearing before the heavenly court. Their **prayer** for relief was for victory over the Greek troops who came against Judas with overwhelming odds. When they gained the victory, Jewish troops believed it was not because of their military skills but because God had judged the trial in their favor.

Many scholars have noticed that the **prayer** of Daniel in Dan 9 does not quite fit the setting provided for it in Dan 9.[8] Daniel was ostensibly studying the scripture for the purpose of learning how long the exile would last. When would the prison sentence be over so that Jews might return to the Promised Land? Before he became deeply engaged in his project, the author offered the following **prayer**. This **prayer** was not suitable for a worshipper wanting guidance for study, but it is an excellent **prayer** to celebrate the first Hanukkah after the temple was cleansed in 164 BIA.

The first clue that this was a Hanukkah **prayer** is that many of its intertexts come from 1Kgs 8, the chapter that contains Solomon's Prayer for the initial dedication of the first temple. He also used the **prayer** of Nehemiah before the restoration of Jerusalem, following the Babylonian exile. Especially appropriate was Isa 37, where Hezekiah's **prayer** was effective in forcing the Assyrians to retreat to Nineveh. The situation at Jerusalem in the time of Hezekiah was similar to the situation during the time of Judas the Maccabee. With thousands of Assyrian troops at the gates of Jerusalem, the situation looked hopeless for Hezekiah, but after Hezekiah **prayed**, 185,000 Assyrian soldiers died during the night (Isa 37:36). The remaining ones went back to Nineveh, crushed. At the time of Judas, Antiochus IV had sent half of his military force under his best general to Jerusalem to destroy the Jews once and for all and raze the city of Jerusalem to the ground. After the bitter defeat in the Battle of Beth-horon, and possibly after the victory of Beth-zur, and the news of Antiochus' death, the remnant of the Syrian troops retreated north to Antioch, just as the Assyrian troops had earlier retreated north to Nineveh. After this success, the **prayer** of Dan 9, like the **prayer** of Hezekiah, was appropriate for Hanukkah.

The events that happened before the Hasmonean Hanukkah prompted Jews to think of all of these earlier occasions. Charles thought this **prayer** was added before 145 BIA,[9] sometime after Hanukkah. The time involved depended on the use of Hezekiah's **prayer** and the retreat of the Syrian remnant after the Battle of Beth-horon or possibly Beth-zur. That retreat may have taken place early in 164 BIA. Hanukkah happened several months later. The time between Beth-horon and Hanukkah would have been a suitable time to compose such a **prayer** as this. The **prayer** was not a suitable **prayer** for the kind of insight for which Daniel was supposedly **praying**, but it was suitable for Hanukkah, as was all the rest of Dan 9. The prayer was composed independently, and there are obvious editorial seams that connect it to the rest of the chapter, but the motivation for the **prayer** was the same as the motivation for the rest of chapter 9.

---

[8] So E. W. Heaton, *The Book of Daniel* (London: SCM Press, c1956), p. 203. A. A. Bevan, *A Short Commentary on the Book of Daniel* (Cambridge: University Press, 1982), p. 145, disagreed, insisting that the meaning of the prayer should first be interpreted in relationship to the text that preceded it. G. H. Wilson, "The Prayer of Daniel 9: Reflection on Jeremiah 29," *JSOT* 48 (1990):91-99, related it to Jer 29.
[9] R. H. Charles, *A Critical and Exegetical Commentary on the Book of Daniel* (Oxford: Clarendon Press, 1929), p. 222.

PRAYERS OF SOLOMON AND DANIEL

Daniel	First Testament Intertexts
$^{9:4}$O, Lord, **God, great and terrible, who keeps treaty and shows contractual faithfulness** to those who love him and keep his commandments,	$^{Neh\ 15;\ 9:32}$Now, our **God, the great**, mighty, **and terrible God, who keeps treaty and shows contractual faithfulness**, do not minimize all the hardship that has come upon us.
	$^{1Kgs\ 8:23}$ O Yehowah, **God** of Israel, there is no God like you in heaven above or on earth below **who keeps treaty and shows contractual faithfulness to** your servants who walk before you with all their heart.
^{5}**we have sinned, committed iniquity, and behaved wickedly**. We have rebelled and turned away from your commandments and your traditional rules. ^{6}We have not paid attention to	$^{1Kgs\ 8:47}$ . . . repent and make . . . requests to you in the land of their captivity, saying, **We have sinned, committed iniquity, and behaved wickedly.**
	$^{Jer\ 7:25}$ From the day when **our fathers** went out from the Land of Egypt **until this day**, and I sent to you all **the servants the prophets.**
your servants the prophets who have spoken in your name,	
to our **kings**, our **generals**, and **our fathers**, and to all **the people of the land**. ^{7}Yours, O Lord, is righteousness, but ours is the shame, **to this very day** to the **men of Judah, those who live in Jerusalem,** and	$^{Jer\ 44:21}$ Is it not the incense which you have burned in the cities of Judah and in the streets of Jerusalem, you, your **fathers**, your **kings**, your **generals**, and **the people of the land**.
	$^{Jer\ 4:4}$ Remove the foreskins of your hearts, O **men of Judah** and **those who dwell in Jerusalem**
	$^{1Kgs\ 8:46}$ You give them before the enemy and take them captive into the land of the enemy
all of the Israelites, both **near and far**, in all the lands	**far or near**.
where you have pushed them, **because of** the **treachery which** they	$^{Ezek\ 17:20}$ I will bring him [the king] to Babylon, and I will judge him there **because of** his **treachery which** he **has**

have committed against you.
⁸Yehowah, ours is the shame for
our kings, our generals,
and our fathers by which we have sinned against you.

⁹To the Lord our God belongs mercy and **forgiveness** because we have rebelled against him, ¹⁰and we have not

listened to the voice of **Yehowah, our God**,
to **walk in** his **teaching** which he has given before us through the hand of his servants, the prophets. ¹¹All **Israel** has transgressed your **teaching** and turned away from **listening** to your voice. You poured out upon us the curse and the **oath** that is written in the Torah of Moses,

the servant of **God**, because we have sinned against him.
¹²He **confirmed** (ויקם) his **word that** he **spoke** against us

¹⁴For **Yehowah, our God, is just in all** his actions which he has done,
but we have not paid attention to his voice.
¹⁵Now, **O Lord**
our **God, who**

brought your
people out of the land of Egypt

with a mighty hand

and **made yourself a name as of this day**,

committed against me.

^(Neh 9:34) **Our kings, our generals**, our priests, **and our fathers** have not kept the Torah or paid attention to your commandments, and the warnings which you gave them.

^(1Kgs 8:34) **Forgive** your people Israel and bring them again to the land which you gave to their fathers.

^(1Kgs 8:31) A man is forced to take an **oath**, and he comes and takes his **oath** before the altar in this temple.

^(1Kgs 8:26) Now, **God** of **Israel**,

make valid (יאמן) your **word that** you **spoke** to your servant, my father, David.

^(Neh 9:33) You **have been just in all** that has come upon us, and you have acted faithfully, **but we have** acted wickedly.

^(1Kgs 8:15) Blessed be **Yehowah**,
the **God** of **Israel, who with** his **hands** has fulfilled what he promised . . . ¹⁶since I **brought** my **people out of Egypt**.

^(1Kgs 8:21) He **brought them out of the land of Egypt**.

^(Neh 1:10) They are your servants, your people whom you redeemed with great strength and **a mighty hand**.

^(Neh 9:10) You **made for yourself a name as of this day**.

¹⁷**Now pay attention to the** prayer **of your servant** and to his **requests**.	1Kgs 8:30 **Now, therefore, our God, pay attention to the requests of your servant** and of your people Israel.
¹⁸Incline your ear, **my God, and pay attention**!	1Kgs 8:28 Yehowah, **my God, pay attention** to the cry . . . which your servant prays . . ²⁹ that
Open your eyes and look at our desolations, and the city over **which** your **name** has been called.	**your eyes may be opened** night and day toward this house and place of **which** you have said, "My **name** shall be there."
¹⁹O Lord, **listen**; O Lord, **forgive**; O Lord, pay attention, **and act**; do not delay.	1Kgs 8:32 Now, **listen** Heaven, **and act.**

TECHNICAL DETAILS

The reader has only to scan down the pages and notice the close parallels between these two documents to realize that one is heavily dependent upon the other. It does not take a great deal of analysis to learn which way the dependence lies. Dan 9 is dependent upon 1Kgs 8. Solomon's prayer is a very important literary work. It points out the importance of the temple in every area of life. In situations of war, famine, drought, travel, sin, exile, and oaths, it became a source and example for later prayers. Since it was associated with the dedication of Solomon's temple, it was a source for Nehemiah and Ezra when they anticipated the restoration of the temple in Jerusalem in the sixth century. It was also an indispensable intertext for a Hanukkah prayer in 164 BIA.

Another prayer that was important to later worshipers was the prayer of Hezekiah (Isa 37:16-20; 2Kgs 19:15-19). It is only 4 verses in length, but its effectiveness was so great that it was remembered by later generations. The king of Assyria had sent his general, Rabshakeh, to subdue Judah. He first offered only terms of complete surrender, and he had thousands of troops to support his speech. Hezekiah followed Isaiah's advice and resisted. He knew the situation was serious, so he offered a prayer for deliverance. That night a disease went through the Assyrian troops and killed 185,000 Assyrian soldiers.[10] Hezekiah began his prayer

---

[10] The angel who slew the Assyrian soldiers (Isa 37:36) may have had a little assistance, because Isaiah was confident in advance that the general and his troops would never enter Jerusalem. What was his military line of defense? Thousands of Assyrian troops were stationed on Mount Scopus and the Mount of Olives. They had only one place from which to obtain water, and Hezekiah had tried to exclude that possibility (2Chron 32:4). That was the spring of Siloam. Hezekiah had probably begun his tunnel, but the spring was evidently still available to the Assyrians at the time of the attack. They had to have water, but there was an underground passage from the city of Jerusalem to the spring. All the people of Jerusalem would have had to do was to poison the water

saying, **Yehowah of armies, God of Israel, who dwells [with] the cherubim; you alone are God over all the kingdoms of the earth. You created the heavens and the earth** (Isa 37:16). He concluded the prayer with the words, **You alone are Yehowah** (Isa 37:20). Ezra began his prayer, **You are Yehowah alone; you created the heavens** (Neh 9:6). The prayers of Solomon and Hezekiah became classics in Judaism, and they were specially appropriate intertexts for a Hanukkah prayer in 164 BIA.

Solomon's prayer was important, because it was part of the dedication ceremony for the original temple. Hezekiah's prayer was important because the events related to his prayer were very similar to the situation surrounding the Battle of Beth-horon and Beth-zur just before the rededication of the temple in 164. Syrian troops had set out just as confident as Rabshakeh on the walls of Jerusalem. After three battles, however, the general turned back to Antioch with the remnants of his army in much the same way Rabshakeh had led his reduced army back to Nineveh. Some pious Jew who was rejoicing that the temple was being cleansed and prepared for continued worship composed this prayer recorded in Dan 9 that echoed words from both Solomon's prayer and Hezekiah's. He would not have been able to relate Hezekiah's deliverance to the situation in Jerusalem in 165 BIA until the Battle of Beth-horon had been fought and the Syrians had fled north just as the Assyrians had done years before.[11]

THE PRAYER OF HEZEKIAH

TEXT

Daniel	First Testament Intertexts
[4]Oh, Lord God, great and terrible	Isa 37:16 Yehowah of armies, **God of Israel, who dwells [with] cherubim, you are God alone to whom belongs all the kingdoms of the earth. You created the heaven and the earth**
[18]extend, O God, **your ears and listen**!	[17]**extend your ear and listen**!

---

during the night, and 185,000 Assyrian soliders would have been poisoned. That would have caused a disease to go though the Assyrian army. It might have happened, but the author of the prayer used in Dan 9 would not have known that. For an analysis of this period of history see W. W. Hallo, "Jerusalem under Hezekiah: An Assyriological Perspective," *Jerusalem* (New York: Continuum, 1999), pp. 36-49.

[11] J. J. Collins, *A Commentary on the Book of Daniel* (Minneapolis: Fortress, c1993), p. 38, overlooked the comparison of this prayer to the prayer of Hezekiah and the similarity of the historical circumstances involved. Therefore he concluded that this was an older prayer that was included into a Maccabean document.

COMMENTARY

God, great and terrible. The God of Israel was not a mild deity. The adjective that was used most to describe him was "of armies," or "of the troops." He was believed to be a God of war. His was not the power of persuasion. The poet said, **Yehowah is a man of war; Yehowah is his name** (Exod 15:3). His **right hand shatters the enemy** (Exod 15:6); he overthrew his adversaries, destroying them with the sword (Exod 15:7, 9). Israelites had faith in this God because he was so devastating to Israel's enemy. It was his strength and military skills that provided Israel comfort.

Extend your ears. This pictures God bending over with his **ears** toward the ground and cupping them with his hand so that he could hear the distant prayers of his people.

TEXT

Daniel	First Testament Intertexts
[18]**Open your eyes and look** at our desolations--	Isa 37:17 **Open**, Yehowah, **your eyes and look! Listen** to all the words of Senacherib who has sent [them] to ridicule the God of life. [18]It is true, Yehowah, that the kings of Assyria have destroyed the kingdoms of **all the lands.**
[7]all Israelites, **near and far,** in **all the lands** where you have pushed them.	2Chron 6:36 **They are carried away captive** to a **land far or near**.

COMMENTARY

Open your eyes. The anxious worshiper suspected that God was taking a nap, resting his **eyes**, or looking in another direction. His cry was intended to attract God's attention.

Look at our desolations. When Hezekiah was praying he called God's attention to all the insulting words that the Syrian general had said. The threat had been made verbally and orally. He asked that God both **look** and listen, but it was the listening that received the most attention. He also pleaded for deliverance, because the situation was desperate. The worshiper who wrote the prayer after the Battle of Beth-horon, however, was in a different situation. He and his contemporaries had already been delivered. Like Hezekiah, the prayer of Dan 9 asked that God both **look** and listen, but **looking** was more important than listening, because there were no Assyrians calling threats from the wall. He wanted God, instead, to *see* the desolations around the temple that the Syrians had caused during the previous three years.

All the lands. **All the lands** for the Maccabean worshiper were not Assyrians lands, but places where Jews lived, because they had been taken to those places as captives.

Many scholars have wondered why this prayer had been inserted into the prose section of Dan 9. It seemed not to be the kind of a prayer that was proper for that particular situation. They are right in thinking that the same person who wrote the prayer had not written the rest of the chapter. This Hanukkah prayer, however, was suited to a chapter that was studying mathematically how the prophecy of Jeremiah could be fulfilled in the way it really was, at the very time the end involved was taking place.

The editor of Dan 9 had many sources at his disposal that might have been related to the victory theme that was on all Jewish minds as plans were being made to celebrate a new Hanukkah. The OG has some extensive texts that are not included in the MT. The editors of the two different texts employed different methods of editing. Both editors selected the passages they thought were best and organized them the way that seemed right to them. Neither of them, however, in good conscience omitted this good prayer that was closely related both to Hanukkah and to the Jewish victory over the Syrians. It was only a question of determining where it should be put.

Having considered the purpose of the prayer in Dan 9, our next step will be to go back to the beginning of the prayer in Dan 9 and study the text, verse-by-verse.

TEXT

Daniel	First Testament Intertexts
$^{Dan\ 9:4}$"O, Lord, **God, great and terrible, who keeps treaty and shows contractual faithfulness to those who love him and keep his commandments,**	$^{Neh\ 1:5}$ O Yehowah, The **God** of heaven, the **God** who is **great and terrible, who keeps treaty with those who love him and keep his commandments**.
	$^{Neh\ 9:32}$ Now **God, the great**, mighty, **and terrible God, keeping treaty and contractual faithfulness.**
	$^{1Kis\ 8:23-24}$ O Yehowah, **God** of Israel, . . . **who keeps treaty and contractual provision** to your servants who walk before you with all their heart.
	$^{Deut\ 7:9}$ He is the trustworthy **God, keeping treaty and contractual provision with those who love him.**

^{Deut 6:2} You shall fear Yehowah your **God, keeping** all his laws **and his commandments**.

^{Deut 11:13-14} If you really **obey the commandments** which I am **commanding** you today, to **love** Yehowah, your God, to serve him with all your mind and with all your soul I will give your land rain in its season.

^{1Kgs 8:46} . . . repent and make . . . requests to you in the land of their captivity, saying,

⁵**we have sinned, committed iniquity, behaved wickedly,** rebelled, **and** turned away from your **commandments** and traditions.

^{1Kgs 8:47} **We have sinned, and behaved wickedly**.

COMMENTARY

O Lord, great and terrible. This is the beginning of Daniel's prayer. Like other prayers for relief in any of the ancient courts, it began with an address to the deity, following the very words used at the beginning of Nehemiah's prayer. This was the prayer Nehemiah offered to God before he confronted the king to ask permission to return to Jerusalem to rebuild the city of Jerusalem (Neh 1:5-11). The prayer was addressed to God, because the author believed that God was the judge who was able to grant the request being made. Daniel played the role of a plaintiff, pleading his case in behalf of the community he represented. Like Solomon and Nehemiah, Daniel was the lawyer who took his case to the heavenly court, where God was both the judge and the defendant. This two-fold role of a judge was not as unusual in ancient courts as it would be today.[12] The case being tried was the contract made between God and his chosen people. In order to fulfill this prayer, God would have to be **great and terrible**, and he would also have to be a god who had made a contract or treaty with the people whom the worshiper represented and could be trusted to keep his side of the agreement.

Who keeps treaty. The legal agreement between two individuals in U.S.A. courts is called a contract. That made between two countries is called a **treaty**. In sixteenth century England, both of these agreements were called "covenant." The Hebrew word for both kinds of agreement is *buh-reét* (ברית). There is no special meaning to the word "covenant" that is not expressed by either a **treaty** or a contract. It is just antiquated. Most people know what a contract or a treaty is, so one of those terms

---

[12] See further Buchanan, *Biblical and Theological Insights from Ancient and Modern Civil Law* (Lewiston: The Edwin Mellen Press, c1992), pp. 44-45.

will be used here. Because God's relationship to his people is considered a marriage, perhaps it should be called a contract. On the other hand, since it is an agreement made with a nation of people, it probably is best to call it a **treaty**.

A person who is a party to a contract and faithfully upholds the terms of the contract in ancient Semitic cultures was said to have *khéh-sehd* (חסד), which is sometimes rendered "steadfast love." "Steadfast love" is also an accurate translation, since love is also a legal term that applies to the relationship of parties to a contract.[13] This also applies to **treaties**. Here it is rendered "contractual provision" to call attention to its legal dimension in relationship to contract or a **treaty**. The *khéh-sehd* that God shows is not free grace to all, distributed impartially. In Jewish and Christian theology it is understood to apply only to those who are parties to the **treaty**, which means that they are members of some Jewish or Christian denomination.

Who love him. **Love** is a legal term, related to a contract or treaty. Those who keep the contract or treaty **love**. Hosea complained because Israel had made treaties with foreign countries that became Israel's **lovers**. When couples took marriage vows the husband agreed to **love** his wife, which meant he would provide for her as her father had done previously. The wife, in turn, agreed to be submissive. Since she had no earning power, she was unable to **love**. A king who **loved** his citizens provided for them and protected them from enemies. Citizens, in turn, obeyed the king. When God **loved** his people he provided for them according to the stipulations of the treaty. Parties to the treaty who **loved** God kept the commandments that were contained in the treaty. This means loving was the same as keeping the commandments that are the terms of the treaty.[14]

We have sinned. **Sin** is a legal term that would be called "crime" today. It means the person involved has broken some national law and was obligated to pay some kind of fine or be punished in some way. In NT times there was no separation of church and state, so a crime against the nation was a crime against God.

We have committed iniquity. A crime that has not been punished is a fine that remains unpaid. If it is not pardoned or forgiven by the court it is kept both on the national books and also in the heavenly record. If a person did not pay this fine to reconcile his account, this obligation was passed on to his children to the third or fourth generation. This unpaid fine was called an **iniquity**. It is debt recorded in the heavenly books because of some sin committed.

We have behaved wickedly. The Hebrew verb, *rah-sháh* (רשע) refers to action that has been taken to court and given a negative verdict. The opposite term, *tseh-deh-káh* (צדקה) is **behavior** that has won a positive verdict in court. *Rah-sháh* is usually rendered **wicked** or "unrighteous," and *tseh-deh-káh* is generally translated "righteous" or "just."

---

[13] Buchanan, *Insights*, pp. 82-87.
[14] See further Buchanan, *Insights*, pp. 74-87.

Turned away from your commandments. God's **commandments** were Israel's responsibility to the treaty between God and his chosen people. None of them was written by God. They were all preserved in the FT. People who were understood to have been God's legal agents wrote all of the scripture that was accepted as canon. A legal agent is a person who acts in behalf of the principal, in the name of the principal, and at the principal's responsibility. Legally, the agent is the principal, and those things he or she either does or says are attributed to the principal. God's legal agents were Moses, the kings, and the prophets whose words had proved to be accurate. When they wrote the books that were canonized they legally wrote the word of God. The commandments designed by the king and his staff of legal advisors were understood to be God's commandments. Whenever citizens of the state broke national laws, those contained in the FT, they turned away from the treaty and were unfaithful to the terms of the treaty to which they agreed.

TEXT

Daniel	First Testament Intertexts
	Neh 1:6 Let your ears be **attentive**, please, and your eyes be opened to hear the prayer of **your servant**.
6We **have not paid attention**	Jer 26:4 If you **do not pay attention** to me to walk in my Torah, which I have given before you, 5**to listen to** the words
to your servants, the prophets who have	of **my servants the prophets** . . .
spoken in your name to **our kings, our generals, our fathers**, and to all	Neh 9:33-34 We are guilty—**our kings, our generals**, our priests, **and our fathers**—have not kept your Torah.
	Jer 44:21 You, your **fathers**, your **kings**, your **generals, and**
the people of the land.	**the people of the land**.
7**Yours, O Lord, is righteousness**, but ours is the	Exod 9:27 Yehowah **is righteous**; I and my people are guilty.
	Ezra 9:7 From the days of our fathers we have been in great guilt. . . and with
shame to this very day, to the men of Judah, those who live in Jerusalem, and **all of the** Israelites, both	**shame of face as to this very day.**
near and far	2Chron 6:36 They are taken captive to a **land far or near**.

	^{Deut 30:1} When **all of the** words of the blessing and curse which I have given before you come upon you, and you return with all your mind **in all of the**
in all the **lands where** you **have pushed** them	**countries where** Yehowah your God **has pushed** you (also Jer 16:14; 23:3, 8; 32:37).
because of the treachery **which** they **have committed against you.** ⁸Yehowah, ours is the **shame**. It belongs to our **kings**, our **generals**, and our **fathers** who	^{Neh 1:6} **Because of the sins** of the children of Israel **which** we **have sinned against you,** I and my **father's** house.
have sinned against you.	^{Neh 1:8} If you **commit treachery**, I will scatter you among the peoples, ⁹but if you return to me and keep my **commandments** and perform them, **even if you are pushed** to the end of heaven, from there I will gather you.

COMMENTARY

The prophets who spoke in your name. When Moses appointed subordinate judges to assist him, he told them to be cautious in judgment, because their judgments were God's (Deut 1:16-17). For these judges to have been legal agents of God, Moses had also to have been a legal agent of God. That meant that all of the works attributed to Moses were accepted as God's word. When he dealt with **prophecy**, however, Moses reportedly said Israelites should not accept the word of **prophets** as the word of God until they learned that the **prophecies** had come to pass. Following this directive, Israelites canonized those **prophets** like Amos, Hosea, Micah, and Isaiah, who **prophesied** the fall of Samaria, and Jeremiah and Ezekiel, who **prophesied** the fall of Judah. These were the **prophets** which Daniel claimed spoke in God's name. Therefore, it was the people's obligation to pay careful attention to their words. The commandments, which they made, were considered part of God's contract with the Israelites. The restoration of the temple and the land was their assurance that the new treaty Jeremiah promised had in fact been reestablished.

Our kings, our generals, and our fathers. According to treasury of merit theology the sins or crimes that citizens of a nation committed were lumped into one great national debt. **Kings** and **princes** had more opportunity to be either blessed or destructive than any of the citizens. Therefore their crimes involved greater heavenly debt than other citizens did. The **fathers** were those citizens who were already dead and who died without reconciling their obligations, so their iniquities were transferred to their heirs.

All the people of the land. Here this expression probably refers to **all** the citizens of Israel who lived in the Promised Land, without class distinction. The expression, **people of the land** (*ah-máy hah-áh-retz*, עממי הארץ) also has a pejorative meaning. When Nebuchadnezzar conquered Palestine he took into Babylon all of the professional leaders, government leaders, craftsmen, businessmen, and landowners, leaving only the unskilled **people**. These were the **people of the land** in contrast to the upper class **people** who were taken into Babylon. Nebuchadnezzar left the land that had been owned by the wealthy **people** who were taken into Babylon to become the possession of these local **people** who had never owned land before. When the wealthy returned to Palestine they wanted to claim their land, and the local **people** did not want to surrender it. There was a naturally developed hostility between the redeemed wealthy **people** who had been exiled to Babylon and the local **people** of the land.

Yours is righteousness. **Righteousness** is a condition determined by courts. Even if a person has committed a crime, if the court declares him or her to be innocent, that person is **righteous**. Since God is the highest judge, no one can take him to a higher court, even though Job would like to have done just that. Since he made the judgments, **righteousness** is in his hands. It belongs to him. He is free to give this verdict to whomever he will. Paul said, **It is God who justifies. Who can condemn** (Rom 8:33-34)? The pope is legally infallible when he speaks from his judgment bench, because no one can take him to a higher court to prove that he is wrong or **unrighteous**. Since God is the judge, by definition, he is always **righteous**. Here Daniel was simply calling the judge's attention to his authority.

Ours is the shame. It was considered proper etiquette in court for the defendant to appear humble and disgraced by being forced to appear as a defendant in court. This attitude was undertaken in the hope that the judge would feel sorry for him or her and grant the prayer for forgiveness and mercy.

Both near and far. This means **both near and far** from Jerusalem—not from Babylon or Persia. This suggests that the author wrote this while he was in Jerusalem, or at least Judah.

In all the lands where you have pushed them. These are **lands** that are far from Jerusalem and Judah. Before the Babylonian exile there had been an Assyrian exile when the Assyrians had taken North Israelites captive. Israelites had also lived in Egypt for more than 400 years before the exodus from Egypt, and there were Israelites who remained there and did not participate in the exodus. It was assumed that the Lord as punishment for sins designed the crises that forced Jews and Israelites to leave Palestine and live in foreign lands. In addition to Egypt, Assyria, and Babylonia, there were Jews and Israelites who were engaged in shipping, commerce, and business in other **lands** who had voluntarily moved to foreign locations. Because of these situations Jews and Israelites had been widely scattered before the invasion of Alexander the Great.

The prayer was for all the Israelites **both near** to Jerusalem and **far away from** Jerusalem in **all the lands** of the diaspora. This expression was obviously made from Palestine and not from Babylon. It was the diaspora Jews who had been pushed into **lands** where God had pushed them into exile as punishment.

TEXT

Daniel	First Testament Intertexts
⁹To the Lord our **God** belongs **mercy and forgiveness**, because we have rebelled against him, and	Neh 9:17 You are a **God** of **forgiveness**, gracious, **and merciful**.
¹⁰we have not **listened to the voice of Yehowah, our God**, to walk in his teachings which he has given before us through the hand of	Deut 4:30 You will return to **Yehowah your God and listen to his voice.**
	Neh 1:7 We have dealt very corruptly with you; we have not kept **your commandments**, your statutes, and your traditions which you have commanded **your servant** Moses. ⁸Remember, please, the word, which you commanded.
his servants, the prophets.	Ezra 9:11 Which you commanded through **your servants the prophets**.

COMMENTARY

To the Lord our God belongs mercy and forgiveness. Since God is the greatest judge. He is the one who makes final judgments. This is his privilege and official duty. Just as righteousness **belongs to** him, so also **mercy and forgiveness belongs to** him. He determines who will receive it. One of the rhetorical skills taught by Aristotle and Quintillian was the art of flattering the judge. This was done by reminding the judge of his ability, authority, and power to grant the kind of decision the participant wanted. The prayer given here was planned to gain **forgiveness and mercy** from God, because the chosen people were not in a position to list their virtues and argue that they deserved the decision they wanted the judge to give. **To God belongs** means that **God** has the ability to **be merciful and forgiving**.

We have not listened to the voice of Yehowah. **The voice of Yehowah** could be heard only through the voices of his legal agents. These were Moses, the prophets, Solomon, and David. The only way they could be "heard" was to read the scripture. Those who heard "walked" in God's teachings, which were mediated through the scripture, just as shepherds who led their sheep, walked in paths that were familiar. This was an important part of the confession. It was repeated three times in one paragraph (Dan 9:10, 11, 14).

TEXT

Daniel	First Testament Intertexts
¹¹All Israel has transgressed your teaching and turned away from **listening to** your **voice.**	Exod 15:26 If you **really listen to the voice** of Yehowah and do that which is right in his eyes . . .
	Jer 7:20 Look! My anger and my wrath will **be poured out upon** this place.
You **poured out upon us**	2Chron 12:7 My wrath will **not be poured out upon Jerusalem** by the hand of Shishak.
the curse and the oath that is written in the **Torah of Moses, the servant of God,** because we have sinned against him. ¹²He confirmed his word that he has spoken against us, against our judges who have judged us	Neh 10:30 Enter into a **curse and an oath** to walk in God's **Torah** which was given in the hand **of Moses, servant of God.**
	Deut 29:20 Yehowah will divide him for **evil** from all the tribes of Israel, according to all **the curses** of the treaty **which is written in the** book of this **Torah.**
to bring against us great **evil,**	Jer 35:17 Look! **I am bringing to** Judah and to all of the inhabitants of **Jerusalem all the evil** that I have spoken over them.
	Exod 9:18 Look! About this time tormorrow I will rain very large hail stones **which has not occurred** anything like it in Egypt from the day it was founded until now.
which has not occurred under all heaven such as has happened in Jerusalem. ¹³Just as it **is written in the Torah of Moses. All this evil** has come upon us, but we have not	Jer 36:31 I will **bring upon them** and **upon** the inhabitants of **Jerusalem** and to the people of Judah **all the evil** that I have spoken to them.

pleaded before **Yehowah** our God to turn away from our iniquities and acquire insight into your faithfulness.
¹⁴**Yehowah has watched over**

evil, and he **has brought** it upon us, **because Yehowah** our **God is righteous** in all his actions which he has done, but we

have not **listened to** his voice.
¹⁵Now, **O Lord** our **God, who brought your people from the land of Egypt**

with a mighty hand and

made yourself a name, as of this day, we have sinned and we have done wickedly.

---

^(Ps 2:11) Serve **Yehowah** with fear; with **trembling** kiss his feet.

^(Jer 31:28) Just as I **have watched over** them to pull up and break down to overthrow, destroy, and **do evil**, so I **will watch over** them to build and to plant.

^(Jer 44:27) Look! I **am watching over** them for **evil** and not for good.

^(Jer 1:12) I am **watching over** my word to perform it. **Yehowah, God** of Israel, you **are righteous, because** you have left us a remnant as of **this day**.

^(Jer 11:4) **Cursed** be the man who does not **listen to** the words of this contract which I commanded your fathers on the day when I **brought** them **from the land of Egypt.**

^(Jer 32:21) You **brought your people** Israel out **from the land of Egypt** with signs and miracles,

with a mighty hand and an out-stretched arm and with great fear.

^(Jer 32:20) You have **made for yourself a name as at this day**.

^(Deut 29:11) So that you will pass into the contract of Yehowah, your God, with the **curse**, which Yehowah your God **made.**

^(Neh 1:8) **Moses, your servant**, saying, "If you **are traitorous**, I will scatter you among the peoples."

COMMENTARY

All Israel. Throughout the prayer of Solomon, the worshipers were called "the people of **Israel**." When the first temple was built, and Solomon was king, Judah and North **Israel** were united into one nation called **Israel**. After the division the northern kingdom continued to be known as **Israel**, and the southern kingdom was called "Judah." After two captivities, Jews continued to hope for a reunification of the two divisions, with North **Israel,** submissive to Judah, of course, and with Jerusalem as the capital city. That never happened, but the author of this prayer used the term **all Israel** to include both kingdoms and **all** Jews and Samaritans in the diaspora.

Poured out upon us. The author pictured curses being **poured out upon** the Jews like water being poured from a pitcher, over their heads. Being **poured out upon** the people meant being **poured out upon** the city of Jerusalem.

The curse and the oath which is written in the Torah. **The oath and the curse** given here are those taken upon admission into the contract between God and his people (Deut 29:11, 13). The agreement made was that the Israelites would be God's people, and Yehowah would be their God. Being God's people meant keeping the commandments written in the scripture. The contract also included both blessings that the people would receive if they were faithful to the contract, and curses that would come upon them if they broke the contract (Deut 30:1). The contract made was a wedding contract, in which Yehowah was the groom and Israel was the bride.

If the people failed to observe the commandments associated with the contract they were considered unfaithful, and their action was called **whoring after other gods**. Unfaithfulness to the oath and contract that the Israelites made prompted God to divorce them, following the rules for divorce **in the Torah** (Deut 24:1). This means God would give them a legal divorce document and send them out of his house. Jeremiah said this was what had taken place when the Assyrians burned the temple at Mount Gerizim, and the Babylonians destroyed the temple at Jerusalem. Jeremiah understood both incidents as those in which God had sent his people out of his house. Other **curses** that accompanied the contract were 1) famine, 2) pestilence, 3) wild beasts, 4) sword.[15] They were also required to pay sevenfold for all of their sins. These seven **curses** are listed in Lev 26:27-45. It was on the basis of these sevenfold **curses** that the author of Dan 9 understood that the 70 years of punishment Jeremiah promised was increased to 490 years.

Watched over evil. Nothing escaped the **watchful** eye of the Lord. He **watched over** Israel's **going out** and **coming in** (Ps 121:8). He did not **slumber or sleep** (Ps 121:3-4). He protected his chosen people from harm, but he did not turn a blind eye to Israel's wickedness. Israelites had made a contract with God to behave in certain prescribed ways. If they broke these commandments, God would observe that as well and bring upon them his promised curses. God had become famous by delivering Israel from Egypt long before. The author of this prayer was reminding God of all his mercy, forgiveness, and protection.

---

[15] These curses were known by other nations as well. Hesiod said that the gods from heaven would bring punishment to evil people—calamity, famine, and pestilence all at once, followed by war (Hesiod, *The Works and Days* 1.236-50).

As of this day. It appeared to the worshiper that God was beginning to repeat his earlier performance of delivering his people. The evidence of this was shown in the events that led up to Hanukkah. The prayer was composed after Solomon's dedication of the temple; after Hezekiah's prayer had been composed; after the reconstruction and rededication of the temple under the leadership of Ezra and Nehemiah. These were all intertexts that had been used in the formation of Daniel's prayer.[16]

TEXT

Daniel	First Testament Intertexts
¹⁶O Lord, according to all your righteous deeds, **please turn away** your **anger and** your **wrath** from your city,	Num 25:4 Take all the leaders of the people and hang them before the sun before Yehowah, and **the** fierce **anger of Yehowah will turn away** from Israel
	Jer 42:18 My **anger and** my **wrath were poured out on** the inhabitants of **Jerusalem** (See also Jer 23:20//30:24).
Jerusalem, the mountain of your holiness, because in	
our **sins and the iniquities of** our **fathers, Jerusalem** and your people have become **a mockery to** all **those who surround us**.	Neh 9:2 They stood and they confessed their **sins and the iniquities of** their **fathers.**
	Ps 44:14 You have made us **a mockery** to our neighbors, laughter and derision **to those who surround us** (//Ps 79:4).
¹⁷**Now, pay attention to the** prayer **of your servant** and to his **requests,**	1Kgs 8:30 **Now,** therefore, our God, **pay attention to the requests of your servant** and of your people Israel . . .
	Num 6:25 May Yehowah **make** his **face to shine toward** you and be gracious to you.
and **make your face to shine upon** your desolate temple, for the sake of the Lord.	Ps 80:4 O God, restore us, **make your face shine** and let us be saved.

---

[16] C. F. Keil, *Biblical Commentary on the Book of Daniel*, tr. M. G. Easton (Grand Rapids: William B. Eerdmans Co., n.d.), p. 32, assumed that the Book of Daniel had been composed in the sixth century BIA, and reasoned accordingly that Nehemiah and Ezra had both used Daniel as a source.

COMMENTARY

Please turn away your anger. Every time Israelites or Jews experienced pain or difficulty of any kind, they assumed that the pain has come, because God was **angry** with them and was punishing them for something. They then tried to think of ways to appease God so that their fortune would change for the better. In the wilderness, when Israelites were mingling with the Midianites, the Israelites were afflicted with a plague. The proposal was made that all of the leaders be crucified, supposing that that would **turn away** God's **anger**. During the Maccabean rebellion Jews were battling with the Syrians and with the Hellenizing Jews, just as Phineas had done in the wilderness (2Macc 2:54), thinking that this would **turn away** God's **anger**. When Judas won the famous battle of Beth-horon, Jews believed that God was pleased with all of the sacrifice that had been made. Therefore he **turned away** his **anger** and made his face to shine upon Israel.

Make your face shine. This is a Hebrew idiom that means "show favoritism." It is part of the priestly benediction, which was evidently very old and very popular. Parts of this benediction are woven into at least 16 of the Psalms and were paraphrased in 2Macc and *1QS*.[17] The entire doctrine of election that is affirmed by every Jewish and Christian sect presumes that God favors these chosen people and wants them to have better treatment in life and greater prosperity than all others. This prompts them to expect lighter punishments and greater blessings than others. This is the basis for Jewish and Christian doctrines of apartheid and discrimination.

TEXT

Daniel	First Testament Intertexts
[18] **Incline your ear, my God, and pay attention. Open your eyes and look** at our desolations and the city over which your **name** has been called. It is not because of our righteousness that we throw our supplications before you, but according to your great mercy.	Isa 37:17 **Incline, your ear, Yehowah, and pay attention; open your eyes and look.**
	1Kgs 8:28 Yehowah, **my God, listen** to the cry . . . **which your servant** prays . . .[29] that **your eyes may be opened** night and day toward this house and place of **which** you have said, "My **name** shall be there."
	Neh 1:6 Let **your ears be attentive**, please, and **your eyes be opened** to hear the prayer of your servant.

---

[17] Buchanan, *To the Hebrews* (Garden City: Doubleday, 1972), p. ix; *Introduction to Intertextuality* (Lewiston: The Edwin Mellen Press, c1994), pp. 25-26.

¹⁹O Lord, **listen**! O Lord forgive!

O Lord, **pay attention** and act. Do not delay, for your sake, my God, because your **name** has been called over your city and on **your people**.
²⁰While I was still speaking, praying, and confessing my sins and the sins of my **people Israel,** and throwing my

supplications before **Yehowah**, **my God**, concerning **the holy mountain of my God,**

^(Deut 28:15) It will happen if you do not **listen to** the **voice** of Yehowah so as to be careful to do all his commandments and statutes which I am commanding you today, all the curses and **the oath** . .

^(.1Kgs 8:15) Blessed be **Yehowah**, the **God** of Israel, . . . **who with** his **hands** has fulfilled what he promised . . . ¹⁶since I **brought** my **people** Israel **out of Egypt**. Now, therefore, our God, **pay attention to the requests of your servant** and of **your people Israel.**

^(Ps 15:1) **Yehowah** who will live in your tents, and who will inhabit **your holy mountain**?

COMMENTARY

Open your eyes. Solomon's prayer, which is the intertext for this request, asks God to look upon the temple that had just been built and watch over it day and night. Daniel, on the other hand, asked God to look at the tragedy that has taken place. The temple where God's name was to dwell was in ruins. Antiochus Epiphanes in about 168 BIA had defiled the temple when he entered the holy of holies and robbed the temple of its vessels and treasures. After this it had been left desolate for more than three years. After the victorious Battle of Beth-horon, Judas returned to Jerusalem with his troops. There he observed that the temple lay in ruins. The gates had been burned, and weeds had grown in the sanctuary (*Ant* 12.317-18). This is the situation to which the worshiper called God's attention.[18]

The intertext the author used was Hezekiah's prayer when Rabshakeh and the huge Assyrian army were gathered at the walls of Jerusalem. Hezekiah prayed, asking God to look at the situation the Jews in Jerusalem were facing. Unless God acted quickly Jews were going to be annihilated by this foreign army. God acted, and 185,000 Assyrian soldiers died that night (Isa 37:36). When this prayer was composed the city had already been ravished, and the temple was in ruins.

The Danielic prayer reflects the temple in ruins. That was the situation after the Battle of Beth-horon and possibly the Battle of Beth-zur when the Syrian army had been driven back to Antioch, and before the Jews had time to reconstruct the temple and cleanse it for continued worship. The situation after Hezekiah's prayer and the situation after the Battle of Beth-horon are very similar. After Hezekiah's prayer the remnant of the Assyrian army headed north in defeat. After the Battle of

---

[18] For the justification of the claim that Daniel was written after the rededication of the temple in 164 BIA see Buchanan, *New Testament Eschatology: Historical and Cultural Background* (Lewiston: The Edwin Mellen Press, c1993), pp. 121-59.

Beth-horon, the remnant of the Syrian army also headed north in defeat. The prayer in Dan 9 may have been composed after Beth-horon as if Beth-horon had been the result of this prayer.

Listen. When an attorney stands before the U.S. Supreme Court, the first thing he or she says is, "Mr. Chief Justice, and may it please the court." That formal statement is always used to initiate an argument. This is a practice also in some of the lower courts in U.S.A. Counsel in the Supreme Court asks the justices to **listen** attentively to the argument that will follow, and the attorney hopes that they would act favorably on his or her request. This is a very old custom. In an ancient prayer asking for forgiveness, the worshiper first reminded God of his greatness and the justness of all of his laws, admitting that the worshiper had no excuse for breaking any of them. Then he asked that he might be forgiven any transgressions that he had made in error or had forgotten to correct. He finally concluded his prayer with the litany,

> **May the words of my mouth and the thoughts of my mind be acceptable in your sight** (Ps 19:14).

This is basically the same request made by the author of this chapter of Daniel. Addressing his message to the heavenly judge, he said, **Listen!** (Dan 8:18-19) "Pay attention!" (Dan 9:17, 19). Even though it is called a "hearing" it is not really a hearing if the judge does not **listen**. In position before a judge, the plaintiff and defendant both want the judge to **listen** to their arguments and requests. That is also true of the prayer offered here.

O Lord, forgive. **Forgiveness** is a fiscal term. Banks and other loaning agencies may become reconciled with a borrower by **forgiving** the loan, thus exempting the borrower of any requirement to pay the amount owed. Pardoning is a legal concept. A judge may pardon a criminal, relieving the criminal of the responsibility of serving out the determined prison term or paying the assessed fine. In a treasury of merits doctrine, pardon and **forgiveness** became almost synonymous, because it was assumed that every crime that did not require excommunication or a death penalty might be satisfied by the payment of money or goods (Exod 22:1).

Since it was held that God also kept track of all the crimes committed and the penalties that had not been paid, it was money by which crimes could be reconciled. Therefore crimes could be **forgiven** just as loans could. The worshiper was not asking that financial loans might be **forgiven**, but that the fines accumulated for crimes that had not been paid be **forgiven**, without demanding payment of all the unpaid fines that had accumulated, generation after generation. These were the iniquities of the fathers which were mentioned (Dan 9:16). The Israelites were incapable of paying all of the fines they owed. They had become experts in rebelling and committing crimes, but they had done little to satisfy the obligations they had to correct these. But God was like a rich banker. He was able to have mercy and **forgive** (Dan 9:9). If God should **forgive**, that would relieve the Israelites of ever having to pay this enormous debt. From the debtors' point of view this was the best way to handle the situation. All debtors would like to have their debts managed in the same way.

Over your city and over your people. When someone's name is called over something it means he or she owns it. On one occasion Joab sent a message to King David asking him to appear before Joab took the city and Joab's name, rather than David's, be **called over** it (2Sam 12:28). Since Yehowah's name had been **called over** Jerusalem that meant this was Yehowah's **city.**

The way the prophets explained the destruction of Jerusalem and the exile of the most prominent people of the nation away from their homes was that the people had been so unfaithful that God carried out the curses contained in the treaty God had made with his people. These punishments included destroying Jerusalem, his "house," and sending the Jews out of his house, captive, into Babylon (Deut 24:1).

TEXT

Daniel	First Testament Intertexts
^{21}again I was speaking in prayer when the man Gabriel, whom I had seen in a vision at first, **came to me flying** swiftly, at the time of the evening sacrifice. ^{22}He was instructing, and he spoke to me. He said, "Daniel, now I have come to **enlighten** you. ^{23}At the beginning of your supplication the word went out, and I came to report that you are beloved. **Understand** through the word and **learn** through the vision.	$^{Isa\ 6:6}$ One of the seraphim **flew to me** with a coal in his hand, which he had taken from the altar. $^{Isa\ 6:9}$ Then he said, "Go! Say to this people, 'Listen and listen but do not **understand**. Look and look, but do not **learn**. . . .its mind understands and it turns and is healed.'"

COMMENTARY

The man Gabriel. This **man** seems at first to be no more than any other **man** standing nearby, conveniently, to answer Daniel's questions. Then, in the same sentence, we learn that he could fly like a bird. This was intended to imply that the **man** was a divine messenger with a special message from God. **Gabriel** in the Daniel passage performed the same function as the seraph in Isaiah's vision. Both divine messengers were commissioned to give directions to the person receiving the vision. Isaiah was commissioned to prophesy to a people who could not understand, and Daniel was enlightened so that he could understand.

The word went out. This means that Daniel's prayer was heard. The message from Daniel went flying up to the Lord who sent a messenger back with an answer at once. It was through **the word** and the vision that Daniel would receive the enlightenment that he needed. The information Daniel needed came to him in poetry. This was an answer to the question that Daniel was asking at the beginning of the chapter.

TEXT

Daniel	First Testament Intertexts
24Seventy weeks are determined / over your people / and over your holy city to complete [the penalty payment] for **transgression**, / to **seal** the **sins**, /	Exod 29:36 You shall offer a bull for a sin offering on the day for **atonement**, and you shall offer the **sin offering** on the altar when you perform atonement for it. You shall **anoint** it for its **holiness**. 37**Seven** days you shall **atone** over the altar, and you shall make it **holy**, and the altar will be
to atone the iniquity, / to introduce ages of righteousness, / to seal **the vision and the prophet**, / and to anoint the holy of holies.	the holy of holies. Everyone who approaches the altar must be **holy**.
	Isa 43:25 I, I am he who **seals** your **transgressions** for my own sake. Your **sins** I will not remember.
	Zech 13:4 On that day each one of **the prophets** will be ashamed of **his visions** and of his prophecies.
	Zech 13:1 There will be a fountain opened for the house of David and the inhabitants of Jerusalem for [cleansing] of **sin** and for menstrual defilement.

COMMENTARY

Seventy weeks are determined. This means that **70 weeks** of years were predestined. For this length of time nothing could be changed; it was completely scheduled, and Gabriel was going to tell Daniel how this period of time would be divided. This **70 weeks** was the period from the beginning of the exile until the death of Antiochus IV and the institution of Hanukkah in 164 BIA, but Keil tried to extend it until the time of Christ. This requires overlooking some real difficulties.[19]

Hasel has considered carefully the problem that arises in Dan 9:24 where the word for **seventy** is *sheh-voo-eém* (שבעים) rather than the more frequently used term *sheh-voo-óht* (שבעות). After studying many words that have both masculine and

---

[19] Keil, *Daniel*, p. 375.

feminine plural endings, he learned that the masculine ending in Daniel was normal. When there are two plural possibilities, the feminine was used to refer to the individual parts of the group, whereas the masculine plural always dealt with the entire plural group in its unity and entirety. Therefore the **70 years** in Daniel was intended to concentrate on the entire passage of time, **70 weeks** of years. It was the whole period of time between the destruction of Jerusalem in 586 BIA to its restoration in 164 BIA that was important. It was not intended to be split up into one 69 weeks of years report of history and another one week of years prophecy.[20] Hardy supported Hasel, providing still further reasons to render the relevant passage, **seventy weeks**.[21]

When an ancient Jew or Samaritan loaned money to another, he or she was not allowed to charge interest. If, however, the debt was not paid on time, the debtor was obligated to work off the debt at half wages. Every seven years, all debts were cancelled and all debtor slaves were allowed to be released, debt free, even though he or she had not completely paid the debt. Jeremiah reasoned that God followed the same rules of the contract. This meant that when God demanded that all of the debts of the nation be worked off at half wages, as debtor slaves must do, he could do that for only seven years. After seven years, the Jews must be released and be allowed to return home (Deut 15). Jeremiah was so firmly convinced of this that he bought a field at Anathoth from his cousin, just before Jews were to be taken into debtor slavery in Babylon (Jer 32:9-44). He believed that he would be back on the land to claim his property within seven years.

Seven years went by, but the Jews had not been returned. Jeremiah died without becoming liberated to build on his property, and the exiles were not released. Jews did not lose faith in Jeremiah, however, because he prophesied the fall of Jerusalem, the destruction of the temple, and the Babylonian exile. Therefore he was a legitimate prophet, according to Deut 18:22. Jews probably just up-dated the prophecy further. At that point Babylonian Jews probably thought that they would be returned on the Jubilee. That happened every 49 years. At that time, not only were the debtor slaves set free, but also their lands that had been sold were returned to the original owners. Dating from 586 BIA it would have been 537 BIA when the next Jubilee would have occurred. By that time Cyrus had captured Babylon and promised to liberate the Jews to return to Palestine (539 BIA). Some creative scribe of that period probably reasoned that Jeremiah's prophecy really meant seven weeks of years.

If it had not been for Cyrus, Jews would probably have by-passed the Jubilee and updated Jeremiah's prophecy still further. In fact, even though Cyrus had promised to allow the Jews to return, it was not until the second year of Darius (ca 519 BIA) that the temple was rebuilt, when Zerubbabel was governor, and Joshua was the high priest. That was when **70 years** had elapsed between the destruction of the temple and the restoration. That meant that Jeremiah's prophecy of 7 years was then understood to mean 70 years. No one questioned Jeremiah's

---

[20] G. H. Hasel, "The Hebrew Masculine Plural for 'Weeks' in the Expression 'Seventy Weeks' in Daniel 9:24," *AUSS* 31 (1993):105-118.

[21] F. W. Hardy, "The Hebrew Singular for 'Week' in the Expression 'One Week' in Daniel 9:27," *AUSS* 32 (1994):197-202.

validity as a true prophet. It was necessary, however, to adjust the years to the facts. Seven years at first meant seven years; later it meant seven weeks of years; still later it meant **70** years. By the time Dan 9 was written, it was necessary to update it to **70 weeks** of years. If you are a convinced dogmatist, you first discover the facts and then readjust the prophecy to fit, but you never question the validity of a true prophet. That allows you to show that the prophecy has been fulfilled—just as the prophet promised!

Your people and over your holy city. Doukhan has called attention to the twofold emphasis in these verses: 1) concerning **your people and** 2) concerning **your holy city**.

Your People	Your Holy City
1) To complete the [punishment required for] transgression	1) To introduce ages of righteousness
2) To seal the sins	2) To seal the vision and the prophet
3) To atone the iniquity	3) To anoint the holy of holies

The parallelism of these concepts is obvious. When the punishment required for transgression was completed, the ages of righteousness would be introduced. When the sins were sealed, the vision and the prophet would be sealed. After iniquity was atoned, it would be possible to anoint the holy of holies.[22]

To complete [the punishment required] for transgression. Jewish and Christian theology is contractual theology. It is based on the belief that God made a treaty with his people. God agreed to be their God, and they agreed to be his people. The terms were that God would provide 1) posterity, 2) prosperity, and 3) land. The other party to the treaty was the chosen people who also agreed to certain provisions. They would keep all of the laws written in the scripture. If Israelites failed to keep their conditions of the treaty, then God would annul the agreement and instead of blessings he would provide curses—famine, pestilence, wild beasts, and the sword. He would drive them off the land, and punish them seven times for all of their sins. When Nebuchadnezzar entered Jerusalem (605 BIA) that was a sign that God had noticed that the Israelites were not living up to their side of the treaty. When Nebuchadnezzar entered Judah with troops, later, burning the temple, looting the city of Jerusalem, and taking thousands of upper class Jews captive into Babylon (586 BIA), Jews realized that God had annulled the contract and was enforcing the curses. They expected to be left in Babylon until they had paid for their past offenses.

The 70 weeks of which Gabriel spoke was the time required **to complete** the payment levied to compensate for their earlier transgression. The fine was the

---

[22] J. Doukhan, "Seventy Weeks," pp. 10-11. See also W. H. Shea, "Poetic Relations of the Time Periods in Dan 9:25," *AUSS* 18 (1980):59-63.

required compensation. That meant that they had to pay double for all of their debts and iniquities (Deut 15:18). Or, from another proof-text, they would have to pay seven times for all of their sins (Lev 26:18-28). It is on the second basis that 70 years becomes transformed into 70 weeks of years.

One of the fragments from among the Dead Sea Scrolls is a small commentary on Lev 25, dealing with the release of debtor slaves and property on Jubilee. The text is badly fragmented, but there are certain terms that survive and are related. The Jubilee involved is called "the last Jubilee" (*11QMelch* 6). It is the "end of days" for the captives (*11Q Melch* 4). It is not only the last Jubilee, but it is the tenth Jubilee (*11QMelch* 7), when the children of light are atoned (*11QMelch* 7), and liberty for the captives is proclaimed (*11QMelch* 4, 6). The commentator related the text from Leviticus to that of Isa 52, which promised good news to Jerusalem. Among other allusions from scripture seems to be one from Dan 9—the reference to a last Jubilee that is also the tenth Jubilee, it was the end of days after 490 years. The release of captives reflects the kind of excitement and celebration as that associated with Hanukkah. It is not clear from the fragment whether all of these signs of victory and restoration are celebration for a current experience or a prophecy for the future.

Because the Jubilee is related to the Day of Atonement and the tenth Jubilee, the fragment either belongs to the same period as the Book of Daniel or else it originated far enough later than Hanukkah to have used Daniel 9 as a type and a prophecy that might later be fulfilled. It might have originated between the Hanukkah of 164 BIA and the release of the taxation during the reign of Simon in 142 BIA. That would have been the time when celebration was in order. If not, then it would have to come enough later to allow for a joyous interpretation that might be counted as the tenth Jubilee—at least 49 years after 164 BIA. The argument could be made that it was late enough to recognize that the gain before Hanukkah had been lost (63-37 BIA). If so it would have to be still late enough to promise another Maccabean victory.

> Its interpretation is: that he will proclaim them to be among the children of Heaven and of the inheritance of Melchizedek . . . for he will restore (their patrimonies?) to them and proclaim freedom to them and make them abandon all of their sins. This will take place during the sabbatical cycle (*shabu'a*) of the first jubilee following the ni[ne] jubilees, and on the D[ay of Atone]ment f[alling] at the en[d of the ju]bilee, the tenth (11Q 3.2).

Wacholder said further

> Any lingering doubt that this is so disappears when one reads in line 18 of our fragment: "And the herald of good tidings (Isa 52:7a) refers to the messiah, the Spirit concerning whom it was

said by Dan[iel (9:25): 'Until the coming of the messiah, the prince 7 sabbatical cycles . . .'" (11Q 3.2, 18).[23]

Zusman claimed that there had been five times when the Lord punished the Israelites for their sins, and he always punished them on Tisha be Av.

1. The first took place in the wilderness after the Israelites sinned by spying out the land. On Tisha be Av the Lord decreed that they would be punished for generations.
2. The second was the destruction of the first temple [586 BIA].
3. The third was the destruction of the second temple [70 IA].
4. The fourth was the day Beitar was captured by the Romans [135 IA].
5. The fifth was when Hadrian ploughed Jerusalem like a field.[24]

Jewish belief in cycles and typology sometimes motivated scholars to alter the facts of history to fit the doctrinal needs. For example, Rabbis held that Israel would not be redeemed except during a Sabbath year (*yBer* 2.4, 4d-5a; *bMegilla* 17b). This was because Israel's punishment and redemption was calculated in terms of Sabbath and Jubilee justice. If redemption happened not to fall on a Sabbath or Jubilee year, there was a strong motivation to recalculate the figures to force the facts to fit the doctrine. Once the redemption of 164 BIA was interpreted in Dan 9 in terms of Sabbaths and Jubilees, this provided a further basis for later rabbis to argue that redemption would always come in that way, as an antitype of the Maccabean redemption.

LaCocque said, "In brief, Daniel announces the coming of the ultimate Jubilee, the Eschaton."[25] He was correct in this judgment, but the eschaton of which Daniel was concerned came with Hanukkah in 164 BIA.

Seal the sins. On the great day when the Lord promised to destroy the surrounding nations, he also promised to open up a fountain to cleanse the inhabitants of Jerusalem from sin and uncleanness (Zech 13:1). **Sealing sins** may not have involved baptism, but it was probably some legal ceremony whereby **sins** were disabled so that they could not be activated against the sinners. Job said that when God **sealed** the stars they would not shine (Job 9:7). **The sins** may have been written down in a scroll and **sealed** in such a way that they could not have a legal claim. They were considered "paid in full." This may have been carried out in court liturgy in Palestine or in a court in heaven.

One of the possible ways Jews may have **sealed** their **sins** to make them irrevocable may have been to **seal** them liturgically in bowls. That was done with evil spirits in charge of misfortunes, sicknesses, and accidents. Incantations were

---

[23] B. Z. Wacholder, "Chronomessianism: The Timing of Messianic Movements and the Calendar of Sabbatical Cycles," *HUCA* 46 (1975):210-211.See the Qumran texts in J. T. Milik, "Milkî-sedeq et Milkî-resha dans le anciens écrits Juifs et chrétiens," *JJS* 23 (1972):95-144.

[24] L. E. Zusman, *With Respect to Jerusalem: Your City* (Chokhmah: c1989, ולירושלים עירך הוצאת חכמה , ירושלים), pp. 8-9.This is interesting rhetoric, but it is not likely that all of these events happened on the same day of the year.

[25] A. LaCocque, "The Liturgical Prayer in Daniel 9," *HUCA* 47 (1976):121.

inscribed into the inside of bowls, which were then closed with a lid. Then the seam between the bowl and the lid was sealed to keep the demons in charge of causing various curses closed into the bowl so that they could not function against the people for whom the incantation was inscribed. For example Solomon reportedly overpowered a demon that caused shipwrecks and other problems at sea by having the demons **sealed** into a broad, flat bowl. He then poured seawater over it and strengthened it with marble, pitch, and hemp around the mouth of the bowl. He then **sealed** it with a magic ring and stored it in the temple (*TSol* 16.6-7). Bowls like this were kept **sealed** in temples or in the foundations of houses to keep any of the listed evil things from taking place.[26] Jews may have had similar liturgies to declare bankruptcy and **seal** off sins to keep them from being punished. There is no record of this, so this may not have been the case.

Second Isaiah offered comfort to Jews in Babylon who already had received the promise from Cyrus that they would be permitted to return to Jerusalem. Second Isaiah argued that the Lord said, **I, I am he who seals your transgressions for my own sake. Your sins I will not remember** (Isa 43:25). When **sins** were **sealed** they ceased to exist in the mind of the one against whom **the sins** had been directed. They were legally forgotten. They could no longer be brought to court and punished.

Atone the iniquity. On the Day of Atonement (*mYoma* 8.9) sins were cancelled providing that the proper actions were taken. For every iniquity there was a required payment. This had to be brought to the altar of the temple to pay the offense against the nation and God. When a Jew injured someone he or she was required to pay the court-assigned fine, but the offense was not just a civil offense against the state; it was an injury against a fellow citizen. Both had to be satisfied before **the iniquity** was atoned. For example, when Jacob came to Peniel, he was on his way to Hebron to claim his birthright and blessing that he had obtained from Esau by improper means. He had to wrestle with an angel all night. This wrestling experience was with his own conscience and his knowledge of the terms of the treaty and the Day of Atonement (Gen 32-33).

He had enough wealth to pay God for his offense against God, and he probably had enough military power to overthrow Esau and take over the family property at Hebron. The problem was that he also was reminded that God's promise of the land would be cancelled if he did not get his sin atoned. To remain on the land and receive blessings of posterity and prosperity he had to atone for all of his sins. If not, God would annul the treaty and replace blessings with curses—famine, pestilence, wild beasts, and the sword.

He finally realized that he could not receive God's blessings unless he became reconciled to his brother, Esau. This was an essential part of the Day of Atonement activities. So he sent many gifts ahead to Esau, saying to himself, **I will atone** (*ah-kah-puh-ráh*, אכפרה) **him with a gift, and maybe he will forgive me** (Gen 32:21). When he met Esau he did not confront him arrogantly with military force and power. Instead he bowed before him humbly and pleaded with Esau to accept both his gifts and **his blessing** (*beer-káh-tee,* ברכתי) (Gen 33:11), which

---

[26] See further Buchanan, *The Book of Revelation: Its Introduction and Prophecy* (Lewiston: The Edwin Mellen Press, c 1993), pp. 398-401.

means he offered to return both the birthright and the blessing and give many punitive gifts to pay for his offenses. The brothers were reconciled; Jacob met the terms of atonement; Esau went back to Hebron to claim his birthright and blessing; Jacob went north to Shechem and settled in another area of the Promised Land, where he purchased land from Chamor (Gen 33:14-19). There was room on the land for both brothers, and because of Jacob's experience at Peniel, they were reconciled without warfare.

The rules for divorce were that a man must give his wife a written legal document, put it in her hand, and drive her out of his house (Deut 24:1), as Abraham did when he divorced Hagar (Gen 21:14). When Jews were driven from the Promised Land and God's house was burned, Jews believed that God had divorced them, annulling the treaty, so that they were no longer the recipients of the blessings of the treaty. They would have to perform the correct liturgy on the Day of Atonement before they could be atoned, and have the treaty renewed. While the temple was not standing or defiled and unavailable for use, they had to compensate with good works and repentance.

The only way Jews could learn whether or not they had fulfilled the requirements of the Day of Atonement was to wait to see what happened after the Day of Atonement. If the land was restored, it would mean that the people had been atoned. The famous Battle of Beth-horon was fought about four months after the Day of Atonement. The fact that the battle was won, and later the temple was cleansed, proved to the Jews that their **iniquity** had been atoned, and their land was being restored.[27]

Introduce ages of righteousness. This does not mean "everlasting **righteousness**," as some scholars interpret.[28] An **age** was a period of time, just as a week or a year was a period of time. An **age** had a beginning and an ending, just as other units of time do. **Ages** involved more units than one, but they did not mean forever. Actually, these **ages** all came to an end after Pompey entered Jerusalem (63 BIA), and Herod became king (38 BIA).

Whenever the transgression had been completed, the sins had been sealed up, and the iniquity atoned, then God was expected to bring the exile to foreign powers to an end, renew the treaty, and give the Jews back the Promised Land. Soon prosperity and posterity would follow. That would bring the old evil **age** of gentile rule to an end and begin the **age** to come. The **age** to come would be an **age of righteousness**, and it would take place on the Promised Land, free from foreign rule with Israel's own king on the throne at Jerusalem. That which made the new **age righteous** was that it removed the taxes levied by foreign powers against the nation. Jews would be judged by their own legal system and their own courts so that **righteousness** based on its own laws would be in effect. They would be vindicated in the light of all nations.

All of this began to take place when Judas won the Battle of Beth-horon. Judas was followed by his brother Jonathan, who was held in favor for most of the

---

[27] According to 1Macc the Battle of Beth-zur was also fought before Hanukkah. According to 2Macc Hanukkah occurred before the victorious battle of Beth-zur, but see the solution on p. 182.
[28] Keil, *Daniel*, p. 343.

time by weak kings of Syria. Under his leadership the borders of Judah were extended. He was allowed to wear the crimson robe and golden clasp of the king's kinsmen and was made high priest. His brother, Simon, was made *strategos* (commander of the army) **from the Ladder of Tyre to the borders of Egypt** (1Macc 11:57; *Ant* 13.145). Those were the national borders at the death of Joshua. Tryphon finally executed Jonathan, but Simon opened negotiations of peace again with Syria, and Syria granted Judah release from all tribute and taxation. The yoke of the heathen which had been imposed with the death of Josiah 466 years earlier was removed, and Jews were completely independent of foreign rule. Simon was high priest and ruler; the garrison of the Syrians in Jerusalem was removed. In May, 142 BIA there was a great eight day celebration with palm branches, musical instruments, and hymns (1Macc 13:34-35, 41-43; *Ant* 13.215). The predestined "end of days" had arrived. This was the **righteousness** that came from heaven as a gift of God (Ps 85:11-12). The prophecies that had been made earlier were then fulfilled during these days of the Messiah; the new **age of righteousness** had begun; and a new calendar was instituted. The spirit of this celebration was reflected over and over again in the Book of Daniel.

Seal the vision and the prophet. When the Lord promised to cleanse the inhabitants of Jerusalem, he also promised to remove from the land **the prophets** and the unclean spirit. On that day **the prophet** would be ashamed of his **visions**. When these **prophets** prophesied they were supposed to be killed (Zech 13:2-5). **Sealing the vision and the prophet** may have meant making them inactive, so that they could not prophesy falsely. The author of Dan 9, however, might have interpreted Zechariah differently.

The vision is that which Gabriel told Daniel. The prophecy that was included in **the vision** was to be written down in a scroll, rolled up, and **sealed** with seven metal seals so that no one was permitted to open it until the prescribed time was up. It had the authenticity of a will. It may have been **sealed** not to be dismissed but to be preserved.

Fig. 3. Papyrus 1 before its seven seals were cut and the papyrus unrolled. Photo: Palestine Archaeological Museum.

Anoint the holy of holies. **The holy of holies** was the room in the temple where the altar was kept, the inner sanctuary. The expression occurs many times in the FT. **Anointings** were undertaken to install leaders, like David and Solomon into royalty. On this occasion, however, it was the temple itself that was to be

anointed, just as God commanded Moses for the holy of holies of the tent of meeting (Exod 29:36; 30:26-29; 40:9-11).[29] It was scheduled to happen a few months after Judas and his army returned to Jerusalem. During those months the temple was properly cleansed and reconstructed. After New Year's Day, Sukkoth, and the Day of Atonement came Hanukkah, 164 BIA. That was the festival at which **the holy of holies was anointed** and sacrifices began again to be offered morning and evening every day. When Saul and David were **anointed** (1Sam 10:1, 6, 10; 16:13-14) the spirit of the Lord came upon them, and they were authorized to function as leaders of the nation. When the temple was **anointed** it also was cleansed and authorized to function.

TEXT

Daniel	First Testament Intertexts
[25]Know and understand: From **the going out of the word** / to repopulate and rebuild Jerusalem / until the anointed leader [appears], / seven weeks ./ For 62 weeks / it will again be rebuilt / with streets and suburbs,[30] / but in difficult times. / [26]After 62 weeks / the Messiah will be cut off / and have no [help]. / The people of the leader to come / will destroy the city and the temple, / but its end will be with a flood. Until **the end** of the war / **desolations** are predestined. / [27]He will enforce a treaty / on the many for a week. / For half a week / he will cause meat offerings and grain offerings to cease. / On the wing [there will be] an abomination / of **desolations** until the **decreed end / will be poured out**	Zech 12:1 **The word** of Yehowah concerning Israel. Jer 25:12 **The word of Yehowah, which came** to Jeremiah the prophet to fill up the destruction of Jerusalem 70 years. Isa 6:11 Until the cities lie waste without inhabitant, and houses without human beings, and the land lies **desolate.** Lev 26:33 Your land shall become a **desolation**, and your cities shall be a waste. Isa 10:23 Destruction **is decreed, pouring out** righteousness, for **the end** and the **decree** the Lord Yehowah of armies will perform in the midst of all the land.

---

[29] There is no record that Solomon's temple had been anointed or that the new temple after the return from Babylon had been anointed, but they might have been. Even if they had not been, there was the command with reference to the tent of meeting which second century Jews understood must be fulfilled.

[30] The word rendered here as "suburbs" is *khoots* (חוץ) rather than the MT *khah-roóts* (חרוץ), omitting the *resh* (ר), following the suggestion of Bevan, *A Short Commentary*, p. 156-57. *Khoots* means something outside, Bevan called it "public places." *Khah-roóts* means "trenches" or "moats," neither of which applies to the topography of Jerusalem.

on the **desolator**.

$^{Isa\ 1:7}$ Your land lies **desolate**; your cities are burned with fire. In your presence aliens consume your land. It is **desolate**, as overthrown by foreigners.

TECHNICAL DETAILS

Doukhan has analyzed the poetry in this passage as follows:

1. Dan 9:25a: Construction of the city	1. Dan 9:25b: Construction of the city
From the going out of the word / to repopulate and rebuild Jerusalem / until the anointed leader [appears], / seven weeks ./ For 62 weeks	It will again be rebuilt / with streets and suburbs, / but in difficult times.
2. Dan 9:26a: Destruction of the city	2. Dan 9:26b: Destruction of the city
The Messiah will be cut off / and have no [help].	The people of the leader to come / will destroy the city and the temple, / but its end will be with a flood.
3. Dan 27a: Cessation of sacrifice and offering	3. Dan 9:27b: Cessation of sacrifice and offering
^{27}He will enforce a treaty / on the many for a week. / For half a week / he will cause meat offerings and grain offerings to cease.	On the wing [there will be] an abomination / of desolations until the decreed end / will be poured out on the desolator.[31]

COMMENTARY

From the going out of the word. The restoration of Jerusalem following the victory of Cyrus in Babylon was almost ignored by all of the narratives in Daniel. The reason for this was that the editor did not want any restoration to minimize the restoration at Hanukkah in 164 BIA and possibly the fulfillment of prophecy and the beginning of the new age of righteousness in 142 BIA. The reference to the **going out of the word** was so clearly a reference to **the word** that went out to Jerusalem in the sixth century that Laato argued that this little poem was pre-Maccabean and based on Zech 12-14.[32]

The word that came to Jeremiah was to be fulfilled in the days of Second Isaiah. This was the good news from Babylon that came to Jerusalem announcing that Cyrus had control of the city of Babylon, and that he would fulfill his promise

---

[31] Doukhan, "Seventy Weeks," pp. 12-16.
[32] A. Laato, "The Seventy Yearweeks in the Book of Daniel," *ZAW* 102 (1990):212-25.

to rebuild Jerusalem and allow Jews to return to the Promised Land. Second Isaiah anticipated this event and wrote the word that "went out," **saying with respect to Cyrus, "[He is] my shepherd, and he will pay up all of my desires," and saying with respect to Jerusalem, "It will be built," and the temple, "It will be founded"** (Isa 44:28). There was joy in Babylon when **the word went out** to Jerusalem:[33]

> **How beautiful upon the mountains**
> **are the feet of him that brings good news,**
> **who publishes peace,**
> **who brings good news of good,**
> **who announces salvation,**
> **who says to Zion, "Your God has become king!"**(Isa 52:7).

But **the word that went out** was not fulfilled for several years. Zechariah complained that the anger of the Lord had continued for 70 years (Zech 1:12). Smith-Christopher was correct when he said, "No matter how you calculate it Jeremiah was wrong,"[34] but so far as the early Jewish interpreters were concerned, by definition, he could not have been wrong. He was an approved prophet. It required only the task of discovering how he could be proved to be correct. This required some dogmatic forcing of figures and facts to fit the prophecy. Interpreters have been calculating in rather bizarre ways to show that Jeremiah's prophecy is being fulfilled 2,000 years later.[35]

Seven weeks. The **weeks** mentioned here are "**weeks** of years," each one seven years long. **Seven weeks** of years is a Jubilee—49 years. Counting from 605 BIA this would be about 554 BIA. If it had been counted from 586 BIA, when the temple and Jerusalem were destroyed, it would be 537 BIA. Cyrus conquered Babylon in 539 BIA. That would have happened just two years before the Jubilee of years. That is close enough for dogma. It means the author of Dan 9 calculated from 586 BIA, rather than 605 BIA, as was done in chapters one and two. It was about 20 years longer before Ezra and Nehemiah led settlement movements when Jews from Babylon came back to reconstruct Jerusalem and its temple and build up its walls. For Dan 9, however, those events were assimilated into the 62 weeks of years after the **seven weeks**.[36]

Until the anointed leader. **The anointed leader** was probably Zerubbabel as a son of David who was accompanied by Joshua, the high priest. Both the high priest and the king would have been **anointed** (Hag 1:14; 2:4, 23). They were called "sons of oil" (Zech 4:14). The first Israelite king to be **anointed** was Saul (1Sam 10:1). The

---

[33] Keil, *Daniel,* p. 380, argued that this decree could not refer to the promise of Cyrus, because there is no express mention of the rebuilding of the city of Jerusalem. There were many things involved in the reports in Daniel that were not included. Authors and editors choose which things they will include and which things they will omit.
[34] Smith-Christopher, *Daniel,* p. 121.
[35] For examples see the introduction.
[36] Charles, *Daniel,* p. 245, noted that there was a mathematical error here.

second was David (1Sam 16:13). Other kings were referred to as **the anointed** ones (2Sam 1:14; Ps 2:2; 20:6; 84:9, 38; 132:10).

Laato was of the opinion that Dan 9:24-26 was originally composed with Zech 12-14 in mind. He thought this was a pre-Hasmonean poem to which Dan 9:27 was added in Hasmonean times.[37] There is almost no midrashic relationship between these verses and Zech 12-14, but the general themes are thought provoking. Laato corrected Shürer's conclusion that the authors of Daniel, like Josephus, did not know history very well and could not be trusted when they noted dates and times.[38] Laato said scholars should check every reference to learn how valid each date was.

For 62 weeks it will again be rebuilt. This was the temple that was built during the time of Haggai and Zechariah (Neh 2; Hag 2:1-5). It was nothing like its former glory, but it existed, and it was possible to function as a temple. If **62 year weeks** had been accurate, then this poorly maintained temple would have lasted for 434 years, until 103 BIA.

With streets and suburbs. This was not a glorious time for Jerusalem, but it was inhabited. There were **streets** in the city **and suburbs** at the outside.

In difficult times. **The difficult times** were reported by Nehemiah. The city lay in ruins; the walls were broken down; and local Samaritans irritated the workers and obstructed their progress in building (Neh 3:33-4:23).

The Messiah will be cut off. The author suddenly jumped more than 400 years to the Hasmonean times. This probably refers to the murder in Antioch of the high priest (an **anointed** official) Onias III at the instigation of his brother, Jason (2Macc 4:7-9, 23-38). It probably happened about 171 BIA. **The Messiah** was to have been **cut off** after 62 weeks from the return of Jews to Palestine after the conquest of Babylon by Cyrus. That places it in the area of the Maccabean Revolt and Hanukkah. Keil assumed that **the Messiah** was Jesus and that the 70 weeks concluded with 70 IA. This is mathematically impossible. In order for him to justify this conclusion he had to place "a wide blank space" between the numbers used in the calculation reported in the text. He further argued that no one could know how long these "times" were.[39] Keil has begun with a conclusion he wanted and modified the data to satisfy his dogma. Laato agreed that this now refers to Onias III, but he thought it originally alluded to the son of David for whom all Israel mourned after he had been killed (Zech 12:10-14).[40]

And have no [help] These words reflect the nonsensical Hebrew words, *wuh-ayn loh* (ואין לו). Something seems to have dropped out of the text. It probably originally had an object, "**He had no** . . . ". Doukhan seems to have offered the best suggestion

---

[37] Laato, "Yearweeks, " pp. 221-25.
[38] Latto, "Yearweeks," p. 214; E. Shürer, *Geschichte des jüdischen Volkes im Zeitalter Jesu Christi* (Leipzig: J.C. Heinrichs, 1909).
[39] Keil, *Daniel*, p. 382, 394, 400.
[40] Latto, "Yearweeks," p. 223.

here. He noted that in Dan 11:45, the expression was "*wuh ayn oh-záyr loh.*" (ואין עוזר לו), **there was no one to help him**. Therefore he thought the best word to supply here was the same, because it makes good sense and it appears to be a normal Danielic expression.[41]

The people of the leader. These were the Syrian Greeks who came under the direction of Antiochus IV Epiphanes, the leader.

Will destroy the city and the temple. This seems to refer to the time Antiochus plundered **the city and the temple** after he had been turned back from his invasion of Egypt by the Romans, but that did not happen until after the treaty had been negotiated between Antiochus and the Jews. Perhaps the word **destroy** is a little strong to describe what happened. The result was that **the temple** was defiled, and the gold and money from **the temple** were plundered and confiscated. Many people were killed in **the city**, but after the Syrians left, there were still Jews living in Jerusalem. Three years later they were able to repair all of the damage done to **the temple** in a few months. This damage was also reported in other chapters: 1) **Then the powerful ones among us will rise up and plunder the temple and the fortress. They will turn away the continual offering and provide the abomination of desolations** (Dan 11:31). 2) **From the time when the continual sacrifice is removed and the provision of the abomination of desolations, 1,290 days** (Dan 12:11).

Its end will be with a flood. This does not mean Antiochus was caught in a heavy rainstorm. It means he was overwhelmed by the situations that confronted him. First he had successfully invaded Egypt and practically had it under his own control when the Romans met him and forced him to leave Egypt. This was a crushing defeat. His military expenses were so high that he went to Persia to plunder a temple to get more money. This was an unsuccessful venture, and while he was there he learned that Judas had won one victory after another, even though he confronted half of Antiochus' military force. With all of these depressing experiences, he became ill and died. So he came to **his end.**

Until the end of the war. **The war** described here is the Maccabean Revolt. It lasted about three years before Antiochus died. During this time the temple was defiled and the situation surrounding it was called desolation. Antiochus was a thoroughly Hellenized leader. He was convinced that Hellenistic culture was the very best. Like Alexander the Great he wanted to unify a huge empire geographically, linguistically, and culturally. When Palestinian Jews resisted his pressures Antiochus used military and police force to bring his ideals into reality. That was the cause **of the war.**

Desolations are predestined. **Desolations** were **predestined**, because they had been prophesied by Isaiah.

---

[41] Doukhan, "Seventy Weeks," pp. 18-19.

He will enforce a treaty on the many for a week. **A week** here is **a week** of seven years—not **a week** of seven days. This story was not being told in chronological order. One of the first things Antiochus did was make **a treaty** with the liberal Jews of Palestine. This was not **forced** on them; they asked for it, initiating the action (1Macc 1:11-15). It involved financial advantages as well as cultural improvements. Antiochus at first gave Jews special privileges other nations were not allowed. It was about 3½ years after the treaty had been confirmed that the Romans forced Antiochus to retreat from Egypt. It was at that time that Antiochus plundered the city of Jerusalem, defiled the temple, and **forced** uncooperative Jews to give up their traditional religious practices. That was the cause of the war that resisted the desolations mentioned earlier in the narrative. This war had gone on about three years before Antiochus died.

It evidently shocked Antiochus and made him very angry to learn that there were two groups of Jews in Judah who had very divergent views. There were many Hellenized Jews who spoke good Greek and had accepted Greek customs and culture. These were so eager to make **a treaty** with Antiochus that leaders were in competition to offer Antiochus better terms for **the treaty**. He made **a treaty** with this group and confidently invaded Egypt, thinking that he had the support of the Jews of Palestine. What a shock it would have been to learn that there was another group of Palestinian Jews supporting Egypt and possibly negotiating with Rome at the same time. It was the group that had not participated in the treaty with Antiochus that led the Maccabean Rebellion and finally brought Antiochus to his death in defeat.

For half a week. This is **half a week** of years--3½ years. It was an important period. During these years Antiochus forced Jews to stop their traditional worship and discontinue their regular sacrifices. It was also the period during which the most difficult part of the Maccabean Rebellion was fought. The altar was changed and used for pagan sacrifice.

These 70 weeks of years do not add up correctly. There were many subjective factors involved in the calculation. Two figures were roughly correct: 1) The 49 year period between the beginning of the Babylonian captivity and the reconstruction of the temple, providing the beginning of the captivity is considered to be 586 BIA rather than 605 BIA 586 - 49 = 537, just 2 years after Cyrus conquered Babylon.[42] 2) The last week of years.

> The treaty was signed about 171 BIA
> The treaty was broken about 167 BIA
> The temple was cleansed about 164 BIA

---

[42] There is very little reason to think that the author would force the beginning date of the exile back to 609 BIA when Nebuchadnezzar first became king, as Charles, *Daniel*, p. 55, argued. That would allow 70 years to pass before 539 BIA when Cyrus captured Babylon and released the Jews to return to Palestine. Charles, himself, observed, however, that Nebuchadnezzar did not become king until 604 BIA (p. cix). The dates involved were the beginning and ending dates of the Jewish exile. Nebuchadnezzar was involved only because the exile began sometime *during* his reign.

To come out perfectly, then, there would be 62 weeks of years between 537 and 164 BIA 62 X 7 = 434 years, but instead of 434[43] years there are 373 years in between these two dates. How do we explain this? The calculator was an apologist rather than a mathematician. He was writing drama rather than science. He wanted to show that this entire period was predestined to fall into sabbatical concepts, so he interpreted the beginning and end of the period correctly and hid all of the rest in the middle figure of 62 weeks of years.[44]

There were some thought-provoking possibilities here, and different calculators worked on different bases. For example, the authors of Dan 1 and 2 calculated on the basis of nine Jubilees. In order to make that work out right they had to begin the exile with Daniel and his friends in Babylon by 605 BIA, even though there had been no Babylonian invasion by that time. In order to make nine Jubilees (441 years if the 50th years are not counted) and have the end of the exile at 164 BIA, the exile had to start at 605 BIA (605 minus 164 = 441). Both the authors of chapters 1 and 2 and the author of chapter 9 agreed to ignore the Jubilee years when counting Jubilees. The author of Dan 9 is not unique in this. The Book of Jubilees counted 49 years as a Jubilee. The authors of chapters 1 and 2 counted 49 years to a Jubilee and came out with 441 for nine Jubilees. The author of chapter 9 counted 49 years to a Jubilee and obtained 490 years with ten Jubilees. Authors or editors of chapter 12 calculated on still other bases. It required some inventive calculations to make the facts agree with the doctrine. That which is obvious is that all of the calculators knew that the exile was over by 164 BIA, because they wrote after it had happened. The Battle of Beth-horon had been fought.

There is no complete consistency in the Book of Daniel, because there were several different hands at work, some writing in Hebrew and others writing in Aramaic. Each one was trying to explain the theology of the exile. They all had some basic assumptions: 1) Jewish exile was the beginning of a turn of events for Jews. 2) The Battle of Beth-horon was the end of this period of punishment. 3) The Babylonian Captivity was like the Egyptian Captivity; 4) The earlier events that would provide prophetic texts necessary to explain the historical phenomena were

    a) Joseph of Egypt
    b) Hezekiah's prayer
    c) Nehemiah's prayer
    d) Solomon's prayer
    e) Isaiah's and Jeremiah's prophecy
    f) Rules of Sabbath and Jubilee (Deut 15 and Lev 25)

---

[43] According to *Ant* 20.10 there were only 414 years. For a justification of Josephus' deduction see Laato, "Seventy Weeks," 214-216.

[44] Wacholder, "Messianic Movements," p. 208, correctly noted, "Daniel's dates, as they related to the remote past, were often approximate or artificial, made to fit into a more or less arbitrary chronomessianic structure."

5) The modified succession of empires was God's predestined order of history, which concluded with Israel.

With these data before them, the authors of these dramas used dreams and visions as frameworks through which they could express their doctrinal beliefs. The various authors apparently agreed in advance on the basic assumptions around which to compose their essays. 1) They all were expected to deal with some or all of the period of the Babylonian exile. 2) They would write in terms of dreams and visions. 3) They would relate these dreams and visions to gentile kings and governments. 4) They would all write success stories that would relate to the experiences of Hanukkah celebration. 5) They would deal with the question of typology and prophecy fulfillment. 6) The main hero character in their dramas would be called Daniel.

These were not prepared to provide an objective report of the historical events that occurred between the fall of Jerusalem and the latest cleansing of the temple. Instead they were preparing dramas to entertain nationalistic Jews at the greatest celebration of their lives. The dramas were composed to elicit applause, gratitude, and celebration. Since most Jews of the Hasmonean period spoke and read both Hebrew and Aramaic, authors wrote in whichever language they preferred. Modern scholars who have tried to make these languages cohere and all of these confused calculations fit have failed miserably.[45]

On the wing [there will be] an abomination of desolations. **The wing** here is **the wing** of the temple as in Matt 4:5 and Luke 4:9, but that does not tell us what that abomination was. It might have been some statue that would satisfy the Hellenizers, such as a statue of Zeus. That which is clear is that whatever was constructed there was abhorrent to the fundamentalist Jews. One report is that an altar was installed on top of the altar in the temple and used to sacrifice hogs rather than goats, sheep, and cattle (1Macc 1:47; 2Macc 6:5). Both may have been done. The "abomination of desolations" was the *shee-koot-zeém meh-shoh-máym* (שקוצים משמם). It was an intentional ridiculing of the Syrian deity, the "Lord of heaven" (*bah-áhl shah-máh-yeem*) (בעל שמים), a name given to the Greek deity Olympian Zeus.

Collins was of the opinion that Dan 9 must have been composed "shortly after the installation of the 'abomination.'"[46] That depends on how much time is given as "short." Three years lapsed after the abomination before Hanukkah. The author would not have known how long the war would last before the strategic battle would be fought at Beth-horon two years before it happened—or even one year. The warfare was risky and uncertain until the famous Battle of Beth-horon was fought. That was the battle that turned the tide. The author of Dan 9 knew of that event. Collins was right in noting the "specificity of the prediction."[47] Indeed,

---

[45] For a list of attempts see S. R. Driver, *The Book of Daniel* (Cambridge: University Press, 1912), pp.143-52. He said, "*The prophecy admits of no explanation, consistent with history, whatever*"[emphasis his]. Charles, *Daniel*, however, argued for a single author and explained the various different styles as later intrusions, misorganizations, or translator's mistakes.
[46] Collins, *A Commentary*, p. 359.
[47] Collins, *A Commentary*, p. 360.

the specificity of such a prediction under such circumstances would be amazing. It is not difficult, however, to record it after the fact. There is always 20-20 vision when looking toward the past. Hindsight is often scientifically accurate.

The decreed end. After the "exile" was over, everything turned out so favorably to the Jews that it was easy for Jews to understand that the whole period of 490 years was designed and executed by God. The chosen people had a period of suffering, but by the time they celebrated Hanukkah they were all in the process of living "happily ever after," and that is the way the story ends. Furthermore this predetermined plan was poured out on the desolator, Antiochus IV Epiphanes. He was the satanic figure in this drama, and he got what he deserved. Try to imagine what one of those first Hanukkahs would have been like when dramas like this one were read before a celebrating congregation. The congregation probably responded with many "Amens," standing applause, and shouts of "Hallelujah!" No one among the authors or in the audience thought **the end** described in some of the dramas had anything to do with events in the twentieth century. **The end** they celebrated was **the end** of Antiochus IV and the Syrian rule.

Two other chapters make the same testimony: 1) **But he will be broken through no [human] power** (Dan 8:25). 2), **But they will not succeed, because there is still an end at the appointed time**" (Dan 11:27). **At an appointed time . . . the ships of the Kittim will come against him, and he will be emotionally crushed and turned back.** (Dan 11:29-30). **Until the time of the end, for there is still the appointed time** (Dan 11:35). **He will succeed until the wrath is completed, for the action is predestined** (Dan 11:36). Each of these writers was certain that this would happen to Antiochus IV, because they wrote after it had all happened.

CHAPTER TEN

HEBREW TEXT

10:1 בִּשְׁנַ֣ת שָׁל֗וֹשׁ לְכ֙וֹרֶשׁ֙ מֶ֣לֶךְ פָּרַ֔ס דָּבָר֙ נִגְלָ֣ה לְדָֽנִיֵּ֔אל אֲשֶׁר־נִקְרָ֥א שְׁמ֖וֹ בֵּלְטְשַׁאצַּ֑ר וֶאֱמֶ֤ת הַדָּבָר֙ וְצָבָ֣א גָד֔וֹל וּבִין֙ אֶת־הַדָּבָ֔ר וּבִ֥ינָה ל֖וֹ בַּמַּרְאֶֽה׃ 2 בַּיָּמִ֣ים הָהֵ֔ם אֲנִ֥י דָנִיֵּ֖אל הָיִ֣יתִי מִתְאַבֵּ֑ל שְׁלֹשָׁ֥ה שָׁבֻעִ֖ים יָמִֽים׃ 3 לֶ֣חֶם חֲמֻד֞וֹת לֹ֣א אָכַ֗לְתִּי וּבָשָׂ֥ר וָיַ֛יִן לֹא־בָ֥א אֶל־פִּ֖י וְס֣וֹךְ לֹא־סָ֑כְתִּי עַד־מְלֹ֕את שְׁלֹ֥שֶׁת שָׁבֻעִ֖ים יָמִֽים׃ פ 4 וּבְי֛וֹם עֶשְׂרִ֥ים וְאַרְבָּעָ֖ה לַחֹ֣דֶשׁ הָרִאשׁ֑וֹן וַאֲנִ֣י הָיִ֗יתִי עַ֣ל יַ֧ד הַנָּהָ֛ר הַגָּד֖וֹל ה֥וּא חִדָּֽקֶל׃ 5 וָאֶשָּׂ֤א אֶת־עֵינַי֙ וָאֵ֔רֶא וְהִנֵּ֥ה אִישׁ־אֶחָ֖ד לָב֣וּשׁ בַּדִּ֑ים וּמָתְנָ֥יו חֲגֻרִ֖ים בְּכֶ֥תֶם אוּפָֽז׃ 6 וּגְוִיָּת֣וֹ כְתַרְשִׁ֗ישׁ וּפָנָ֞יו כְּמַרְאֵ֤ה בָרָק֙ וְעֵינָיו֙ כְּלַפִּ֣ידֵי אֵ֔שׁ וּזְרֹֽעֹתָיו֙ וּמַרְגְּלֹתָ֔יו כְּעֵ֖ין נְחֹ֣שֶׁת קָלָ֑ל וְק֥וֹל דְּבָרָ֖יו כְּק֥וֹל הָמֽוֹן׃ 7 וְרָאִיתִי֩ אֲנִ֨י דָנִיֵּ֤אל לְבַדִּי֙ אֶת־הַמַּרְאָ֔ה וְהָאֲנָשִׁים֙ אֲשֶׁ֣ר הָי֣וּ עִמִּ֔י לֹ֥א רָא֖וּ אֶת־הַמַּרְאָ֑ה אֲבָ֗ל חֲרָדָ֤ה גְדֹלָה֙ נָפְלָ֣ה עֲלֵיהֶ֔ם וַֽיִּבְרְח֖וּ בְּהֵחָבֵֽא׃ 8 וַאֲנִי֙ נִשְׁאַ֣רְתִּי לְבַדִּ֔י וָאֶרְאֶ֗ה אֶת־הַמַּרְאָ֤ה הַגְּדֹלָה֙ הַזֹּ֔את וְלֹ֥א נִשְׁאַר־בִּ֖י כֹּ֑חַ וְהוֹדִי֙ נֶהְפַּ֤ךְ עָלַי֙ לְמַשְׁחִ֔ית וְלֹ֥א עָצַ֖רְתִּי כֹּֽחַ׃ 9 וָאֶשְׁמַ֖ע אֶת־ק֣וֹל דְּבָרָ֑יו וּכְשָׁמְעִי֙ אֶת־ק֣וֹל דְּבָרָ֔יו וַאֲנִ֛י הָיִ֥יתִי נִרְדָּ֖ם עַל־פָּנַ֑י וּפָנַ֖י אָֽרְצָה׃ 10 וְהִנֵּה־יָ֖ד נָ֣גְעָה בִּ֑י וַתְּנִיעֵ֥נִי עַל־בִּרְכַּ֖י וְכַפּ֥וֹת יָדָֽי׃ 11 וַיֹּ֣אמֶר אֵלַ֡י דָּנִיֵּ֣אל אִישׁ־חֲמֻד֡וֹת הָבֵ֣ן בַּדְּבָרִים֩ אֲשֶׁר֙ אָנֹכִ֜י דֹבֵ֤ר אֵלֶ֙יךָ֙ וַעֲמֹ֣ד עַל־עָמְדֶ֔ךָ כִּ֥י עַתָּ֖ה שֻׁלַּ֣חְתִּי אֵלֶ֑יךָ וּבְדַבְּר֥וֹ עִמִּ֛י אֶת־הַדָּבָ֥ר הַזֶּ֖ה עָמַ֥דְתִּי מַרְעִֽיד׃ 12 וַיֹּ֣אמֶר אֵלַי֮ אַל־תִּירָ֣א דָנִיֵּאל֒ כִּ֣י ׀ מִן־הַיּ֣וֹם הָרִאשׁ֗וֹן אֲשֶׁ֨ר נָתַ֧תָּ אֶֽת־לִבְּךָ֛ לְהָבִ֥ין וּלְהִתְעַנּ֖וֹת לִפְנֵ֣י אֱלֹהֶ֑יךָ נִשְׁמְע֣וּ דְבָרֶ֔יךָ וַאֲנִי־בָ֖אתִי בִּדְבָרֶֽיךָ׃ 13 וְשַׂ֣ר ׀ מַלְכ֣וּת פָּרַ֗ס עֹמֵ֤ד לְנֶגְדִּי֙ עֶשְׂרִ֣ים וְאֶחָ֣ד י֔וֹם וְהִנֵּ֤ה מִֽיכָאֵל֙ אַחַ֣ד הַשָּׂרִ֣ים הָרִאשֹׁנִ֔ים בָּ֖א לְעָזְרֵ֑נִי וַאֲנִי֙ נוֹתַ֣רְתִּי שָׁ֔ם אֵ֖צֶל מַלְכֵ֥י פָרָֽס׃ 14 וּבָ֙אתִי֙ לַהֲבִ֣ינְךָ֔ אֵ֛ת אֲשֶׁר־יִקְרָ֥ה לְעַמְּךָ֖ בְּאַחֲרִ֣ית הַיָּמִ֑ים כִּי־ע֥וֹד חָז֖וֹן לַיָּמִֽים׃ 15 וּבְדַבְּר֣וֹ עִמִּ֔י כַּדְּבָרִ֖ים הָאֵ֑לֶּה נָתַ֧תִּי פָנַ֛י אַ֖רְצָה וְנֶאֱלָֽמְתִּי׃ 16 וְהִנֵּ֗ה כִּדְמוּת֙ בְּנֵ֣י אָדָ֔ם נֹגֵ֖עַ עַל־שְׂפָתָ֑י וָאֶפְתַּח־פִּ֗י וָאֲדַבְּרָה֙ וָאֹֽמְרָה֙ אֶל־הָעֹמֵ֣ד לְנֶגְדִּ֔י אֲדֹנִ֗י בַּמַּרְאָה֙ נֶהֶפְכ֤וּ צִירַי֙ עָלַ֔י וְלֹ֥א עָצַ֖רְתִּי כֹּֽחַ׃ 17 וְהֵ֣יךְ יוּכַ֗ל עֶ֤בֶד אֲדֹנִי֙ זֶ֔ה לְדַבֵּ֖ר עִם־אֲדֹ֣נִי זֶ֑ה וַאֲנִ֤י מֵעַ֙תָּה֙ לֹא־יַעֲמָד־בִּ֣י כֹ֔חַ וּנְשָׁמָ֖ה לֹ֥א נִשְׁאֲרָה־בִּֽי׃ 18 וַיֹּ֧סֶף וַיִּגַּע־בִּ֛י כְּמַרְאֵ֥ה אָדָ֖ם וַֽיְחַזְּקֵֽנִי׃ 19 וַיֹּ֜אמֶר אַל־תִּירָ֧א אִישׁ־חֲמֻד֛וֹת שָׁל֥וֹם לָ֖ךְ חֲזַ֣ק וַחֲזָ֑ק וּֽכְדַבְּר֤וֹ עִמִּי֙ הִתְחַזַּ֔קְתִּי וָאֹֽמְרָ֛ה יְדַבֵּ֥ר אֲדֹנִ֖י כִּ֥י חִזַּקְתָּֽנִי׃ 20 וַיֹּ֗אמֶר הֲיָדַ֙עְתָּ֙ לָֽמָּה־בָּ֣אתִי אֵלֶ֔יךָ וְעַתָּ֣ה אָשׁ֔וּב לְהִלָּחֵ֖ם עִם־שַׂ֣ר פָּרָ֑ס וַאֲנִ֣י יוֹצֵ֔א וְהִנֵּ֥ה שַׂר־יָוָ֖ן בָּֽא׃ 21 אֲבָל֙ אַגִּ֣יד לְךָ֔ אֶת־הָרָשׁ֖וּם בִּכְתָ֣ב אֱמֶ֑ת וְאֵ֨ין אֶחָ֜ד מִתְחַזֵּ֤ק עִמִּי֙ עַל־אֵ֔לֶּה כִּ֖י אִם־מִיכָאֵ֥ל שַׂרְכֶֽם׃

Ezek 1:1

Ezek 9:2
Jer 10:9; Ezek 1:26
Ezek 1:7, 24
Ezek 1:1

Ezek 1:1
1Sam 28:20
Ezek 1:24
Ezek 1:28
Ezek 2:1
Ezek 2:2; 3:24

Deut 31:6; Ezek 2:6

Ezek 1:28, 26
Isa 6:7

1Kgs 17:17
Ezek 2:6; Deut 31:6, 7, 29
Josh 1:6, 9; Ezek 3:14

ENGLISH TEXT

Daniel	First Testsment Intertexts
^{10:1}**In the** third **year** of Cyrus, king of Persia, the word was revealed to Daniel, who was called Belteshazzar. The word was valid, and the war was extensive. He understood the word and the **vision** became clear to him	^{Ezek 1:1} It happened **in the** thirty fourth **year** on the fifth of the month I was in the midst of the exile alongside of the river Chebar, when the heavens opened, and I saw a **vision** of God

COMMENTARY

In the third year of Cyrus, king of Persia. **Cyrus** conquered Babylon in 539 BIA. He had been **king of Persia** for many years before then, long enough to have conquered all the land from Sardis to Babylon. Cyrus, however, was seldom called **King of Persia** in ancient contracts. He was more often called **King of Persia and Media**.[1] It was as if Media did not become a part of Persia. Instead the new kingdom became called Media and Persia or Persia and Media.

Jews did not become interested in **Cyrus** until he turned his attention to Babylon. Since Daniel was hypothetically one of the exiles that came to Babylon as a foreign student, **the third year of Cyrus** was probably dated from the conquest of Babylon; i.e., ca 536 BIA. This would have been 50 years after Nebuchadnezzar conquered Judah (586 BIA), so it would have been considered a Jubilee year. If this were really history rather than myth, Daniel would have been an old man by the time **Cyrus** took Babylon. Rather than a historical person, Daniel seems to have been only a character in the plays that were composed around him. In other chapters Daniel interpreted other people's dreams. Here he both had the vision, and he understood it. This was the fourth vision. It did not begin until the reign of **Cyrus** over Babylon, and the story moves with increasing exactness as it approaches the Seleucid era.[2]

The war was extensive. The word rendered **War** here was translated "power" in Th. MT has "army" or **war**. OG has "multitude." The text may be corrupt. The word "army" or **war** does not make sense in the immediate context. Neither does any of the textual variants. The basic text is **the word was revealed** (Dan 10:1). The following words should be a further explanation of the "word" and the "revelation." If this were so the text would read, "**The word was revealed to Daniel.** The word was true, and the revelation was great," but none of the texts allows this. It is not the

---

[1] So R. H. Charles, *A Critical and Exegetical Commentary on the Book of Daniel* (Oxford: Clarendon Press, 1929), pp. 254-55.

[2] A. A. Bevan, *A Short Commentary on the Book of Daniel* (Cambridge: University Press, 1892), p. 162, says that the fact that chapter 11 ends in a way that could not follow historically, proves that the book was composed before the reign of Antiochus IV was over. He did not notice that Dan 11:40-45 is a second account of Dan 11:14-19 rather than a prophecy of the future.

immediate text, however, that determines the meaning. Dan 10 is only an introduction to Dan 11 and 12. It is Dan 11 and 12 that provide the content of Daniel's vision. That vision tells about an **extensive war** that went on for many years between Egypt and Syria. Therefore that is the translation given here.

TEXT

²I, Daniel, was mourning for three weeks. ³I ate no gourmet food. No meat or wine entered my mouth, and I did not anoint myself until three weeks were completed.

Daniel	First Testament Intertexts
⁴**On the** twenty-**fourth of the** first **month I was** beside **the** great **river**, which is the Tigris. ⁵I lifted up my eyes **and I was watching.**	Ezek 1:1 **On the** thirtieth year, **in the** fourth **month,** on the fifth **of the month, I was** in the midst of the exile beside the river Chebar, **and I** saw a vision of God.
Now look! [There is] **a man dressed in linen,** and **his waist** was girded	Ezek 9:2 **Now look! . . . A man . . . dressed in linen.** Whose [ink] horn was at **his waist.**
with the **gold of Uphaz.** ⁶His body was beryl, and his face was **like the appearance of** lightning, and his eyes were like lamps of fire. His arms and his **legs were**	Jer 10:9 Beaten silver is brought from Tarshish, and **gold from Uphaz.**
	Ezek 1:26 …something **like the appearance of** a human being.
	Ezek 1:7 Their **legs were** straight legs; the bottoms of their legs **were like** the bottoms of a cow's legs, and they sparkled **like bright shining bronze** [hooves].
like bright shining bronze,	
and **the sound of** his voice was **like the noise of** a mob.	Ezek 1:24 I heard **the sound of** their wings **like the noise of** much water [cascading].
⁷I, Daniel, alone **saw the vision.** The men who were there with me did not **see the vision.**	Ezek 1:1 **I saw a vision of God.**

COMMENTARY

I Daniel. Reid has made an interesting comparison between pseudepigraphical prophecy in Jewish and Christian studies and pseudepigraphy in African cults. In Zambia a seer often takes the name of an earlier seer who has died. It is called "Bansanga possession." It is done to perpetuate the spirit of the earlier seer and to deny individual identity. When a medium introduces himself or herself in the Bansanga spirit possession this is done with the formula, "I am Monze." Reid has astutely noted the similarity between that formula and the one used here, "I Daniel." Following Reid's suggestion this would mean that the author of Dan 10 accredited his message to an earlier wiseman, named Daniel.[3]

I was in mourning for three weeks. The text does not say why **Daniel was lamenting**. He was obviously fasting. He was not avoiding all water and food, but he had put himself on limited rations of basic foods.

Beside the great river which is the Tigris. **The Great River** that was the border **river** of the Promised Land is now called *Náh-hahr eel kah-beér* in Arabic. It is the border river between Lebanon and Syria. In antiquity it was also called **The Great River** (*náh-hahr hah-gah-dóhl*, נהר הגדל). This was later misinterpreted as **the river Euphrates** (Gen 15:18; Josh 1:4; Deut 1:7).[4] The exegete who misinterpreted the "Great River" as the Euphrates, probably did this after the Babylonian captivity—after the Jews had expanded their concept of the Promised Land from the kingdom of David and Solomon to an empire that reached to Babylon and could be compared with the empires of Nebuchadnezzar, Cyrus, or Alexander.

The great river that is in close proximity to Babylon is **the Tigris**, so that is where Daniel was stationed for this narrative. He was placed there as an antitype of Ezekiel who also had a vision alongside a **river**. Ezekiel's vision was near the **River** Chebar, which was evidently some small river near Babylon. The author of Daniel did not recognize **the river**, so he changed it to **the Tigris**. Porteous, Collins, and others thought the author made a mistake in identifying **the great river as the Tigris**, since everyone knows it was the Euphrates.[5] This is just one more bit of evidence that the adjective **great** was applied to any comparatively large **river**. It was not an official name for only one **river**. The Euphrates river seems great to one who has never seen a river bigger than the Jordan, but it does not seem **great** to one who has seen the Mississippi or Amazon rivers. The river that forms the northern border of Lebanon seemed big enough to the local people to be called **the Great River**.

---

[3] S. B. Reid, *Enoch and Daniel* (Berkeley: BIBAL, c1989), p. 113. This raises the question about the meaning of the expression "I Nebuchadnezzar" in Dan 4:1. This seems to imply that the expression might also be attributed negatively to someone. This may mean that the author of Dan 4 knew Nebuchadnezzar did not have the dream attributed to him, but that he presented the dream as if some later seer had done it in his name

[4] See Buchanan *The Consequences of the Covenant* (Leiden: Brill, 1970), pp. 91-109.

[5] N. W. Porteous, *Daniel* (London: SCM Press LTD, c1965), p. 151; J.J. Collins, *A Commentary on the Book of Daniel* (Minneapolis: Fortress Press, c1993), p. 373.

A man dressed in linen. This was not really a human being. He was the antitype of Ezekiel's divine communicator who was called "something like a human being." All of this was visionary both for Ezekiel and for Daniel. It was described in fantastic colors and clothing to lead the reader to understand that this was a divine being. This was written in the language of dreams and visions. Pagan idols were frequently described in similar ways, and their appearances resembled these descriptions.

The sound of his voice. Following Ezekiel the author of Daniel reasoned that this being would have had a tremendous voice. Ezekiel said he sounded like much water cascading. For Daniel this was like the roar of a mob. The idea is the same.

The men who were with me. This is the first that the reader learns that Daniel was initially with a group. No matter how large the group, it was Daniel alone to whom the divine message was directed. Moses, however, was always alone with God, but there were people who stood at a distance. Maybe that was the situation implied here. This verse was an intertext for the account of Paul's conversion on the Road to Damascus, at which time Paul saw Jesus in a vision, but the men who were with him saw nothing (Acts 8:4-9).

TEXT

Daniel	First Testament Intertexts
But a great trembling fell upon them, and they fled into hiding. ⁸I was left alone when **I saw** this great **vision, and no strength was left in me**. The glory that appeared over me was changed to dread, **and I retained no strength**.	Ezek 1:1 The heavens opened, and **I saw visions** of God. 1Sam 28:20 [Saul] was very much afraid because he feared the words of Samuel, **and he retained no strength**.
⁹**I heard the sound of** his **words**, and when **I heard the sound of** his **words** I became unconscious **on my face** with **my face** to the ground.	Ezek 1:24 **I heard the sound of** wings. Ezek 1:28 When I saw it I fell **on my face.**

COMMENTARY

I saw this great vision. This was a classical description of the revelation of a vision. Daniel, like Saul, was stunned and afraid. Like Ezekiel he saw a vision and heard sounds. Like Ezekiel Daniel fell to the ground with his face downward. According to Acts the apostle Paul experienced the same kind of vision and responded similarly.

My face to the ground. The author of Dan 10 knew exactly how Daniel would have behaved in the presence of a vision, because he had read how Ezekiel acted in the presence of a vision. He prostrated himself before the messenger with his face to the ground.

TEXT

Daniel	First Testament Intertexts
¹⁰Now look! A hand touched me and made my knees and hands tremble.	
¹¹**It said** to me, "Daniel, beloved **man**, understand the **words** which **I am speaking to you**,	Ezek 2:1 **He said**, "Son of **man**,
and stand on your feet, because **I** have been sent **to you** now." While he **was speaking** this	**stand on your feet, and I will speak to you**."
word to me, I **stood** trembling. ¹²He said to me,	Ezek 2:2; 3:24 The spirit came to me **and stood** me **upon** my **feet**.
"**Do not be afraid**, Daniel, because from the first day that you devoted your mind to understand and to humble yourself before your God your **words** were heard, and I have come because of your **words**."	Ezek 2:6 You, son of man, **do not be afraid** of them nor **be afraid** of their **words.**
	Deut 20:1 When you go out to war against your enemy, and you see horses, chariots, and people, more than you, **do not be afraid** of them.
	Deut 31:6 Be strong! Be courageous; and **do not be afraid**.

COMMENTARY

Do not be afraid. The words came directly from Ezekiel rather than Deuteronomy. The fear involved was not fear of facing the enemy in battle. It was fear of the **words** that Daniel heard in his vision. The term **words** does not occur in the relevant passages in Deuteronomy, but it is present in Ezekiel. In this context in Dan, the term **words** occurs five times in four verses (Dan 10:9-12). There are also other words, **He said**, **man**, **stand on your feet**, and **I will speak to you**, that also come from Ezek 2:1-6. This means that the author of Dan 10 had Ezekiel right before him as he composed this passage and described the vision in Ezekielian terms.

It was normal in antiquity for citizens to be afraid of judges and kings. These were all thought to be legal agents of the deity with unlimited powers to ravish, injure, and punish citizens at will. The king was free to confiscate anyone's property that he chose and have the owner and family killed (1Kgs 21:5-14). People trembled before these leaders with authority. The natural consequence of this feeling was to assume that God also used his powers in ways that were damaging to people. One of the teachings of Epicurus that was good news to his followers was that there were no gods. People did not have to fear the irresponsible behavior of the gods.

Stand on your feet. The words were taken from Ezekiel's experience. In antiquity, in a court scene, the defendant normally humbled himself, fell on his face before the judge, and awaited the verdict. He was trying by his humility to evoke pity from the judge. If the judge asked him to stand on his feet and face the judge, this was a sign the judge was prepared to give a positive verdict. The divine being acted as a judge and invited Daniel to stand and receive his judgment, which was positive.

Humble yourself before God. When Daniel was mourning and fasting (Dan 10:2), he was prostrate before the divine being with his face to the ground. This was the way that he **humbled himself before God.**

TEXT

¹³The general of the Persian kingdom **stands** over against me for 21 days. Now look! Michael, one of the first generals, came to help me, but I remained there near the Persian kings. ¹⁴I came to inform you what will happen to your people in the final days (*buh-ah-khar-eét hah-yah-meém*, באחרית הימים) because there is still a vision for the days."

COMMENTARY

General of the Persian kingdom. The word rendered "general" here is *sahr* (שר). This was an ancient leader that is sometimes rendered "prince," but this official is almost always directly related to an armed force. In this case he was in charge of the military force against which the angel was opposing. The battle took place on earth in the Persian kingdom. The angel was probably from heaven, but he was active on earth. According to this narrative he came to earth while he was communicating with Daniel. Daniel probably did not go to heaven to meet the angel.

At the beginning of the rule of Cyrus over Persia, the Jews were on his side; they thought of him as the Messiah anointed to restore the Jews to the Promised Land. He was called the Lord's anointed. The Lord was the one who had grasped Cyrus' right hand and subdued nations before him (Isa 45:1). Cyrus did not realize that it was for the sake of Israel that God had leveled mountains, broken down iron bars and bronze gates for Cyrus (Isa 45:2-4). Cyrus was the one who would rebuild Jerusalem and set the Jewish exiles free to return (Isa 45:13). During this time Jews were active assistants in Babylon helping Cyrus overpower the forces of Babylon and gain control of the city. During this time Jews had visions of grandeur. They thought there was nothing they wanted that Cyrus would not supply. Evidently there came a time when Cyrus failed to do exactly that which Jews thought he would do for them, so they began to think of Persia as an enemy and were engaged in an effort to overpower the Persians.

This probably involved giving support to the Greeks under Alexander's leadership as he moved east to take over Persia. Indeed, Josephus said that this is exactly what happened. Alexander sent an embassy to Jerusalem and negotiated an arrangement with the Jews whereby they would assist him in his program. In turn, he assigned them to positions in his military plan and gave them equal civic rights with the Macedonians (*Ant* 12.8).

The messenger that told Daniel to **stand** upon his **feet** also told him **The general of the Persian kingdom "stands" over against me.** The author of Dan 10 found the word **stands** in the same Ezekiel passage as the other words mentioned in this context.

What will happen to your people. All of the chapters of Daniel are tendentious. They are not devoted to the future of people in general. The question is always, "**What will happen to** these Jews, in the immediate future?" Here the information given was pertinent to the final days, meaning the final days of the exile from the Promised Land. Driver said that the idiom here means the last days of the age of Antiochus Epiphanes.[6] There was no anticipation at all that was relevant to the last days of the world, the end of time, or the end of the cosmos.

Michael, one of the first generals. This was probably a heavenly angel who was understood to lead Israel's wars. If **Michael** was engaged in warfare against the Persians, it is likely that other Jews were as well. Either they were soldiers engaged in battle or they were intelligence officers coaching the military movement from the outside.

I remained there with the Persian kings. The RSV renders this clause, "I left him there," meaning that since Michael was there to fight with the Persian kings, the messenger who was speaking to Daniel was no longer necessary there, and he was free to come to Daniel. That seems to make sense, but it adds the pronoun "him" to the text and changes a passive verb to an active one. The best reading seems to mean that he stayed there with Michael, fighting **the Persian kings**. After remaining there for an undisclosed time, he came to Daniel.

TEXT

Daniel	First Testament Intertexts
[15]While he was speaking to me, according to these words, **I turned my face** to the ground and was silent.	Ezek 1:28 When I saw it **I fell on my face.**
[16]Now look! **Something like a human being**	Ezek 1:26 Seated above **something like a** throne was **something like a human being**.

---

[6] S. R. Driver, *The Book of Daniel* (Cambridge: University Press, 1912), p. 159.

touched my lips, and I opened **my mouth and said** to the one standing across from me, "My Lord, in the vision pains came upon me, and I could not retain strength. ¹⁷How can a servant of my lord speak with this my lord, since now no strength exists in me,

and **no breath is left in** me?" ¹⁸Again one that **was something like a human being touched** me, and he made me **strong**,
¹⁹and he said, "**Do not be afraid**, beloved man. Peace be upon you;

be **strong**! Be **strong**!"

^{Isa 6:7} Then he **touched my mouth and said**, "Look! This **has touched** your **lips**; your iniquity is turned away and your sin is atoned."

^{1Kgs 17:17} After these words the son of the woman [of Zarepath], the mistress of the house, became very ill until **no breath was left in** him.

^{Ezek 2:6} You, son of man, **do not be afraid** of them nor **be afraid** of their **words**.

^{Deut 31:6, 7, 23; Josh 1:6, 9, 18} **Be strong**; be courageous; and **do not be afraid**.

^{Ezek 3:14} The spirit lifted me and took me, and I went with a bitter spirit, but the hand of Yehowah was **strong** upon me.

COMMENTARY

Something like a human being. This is typical analogical language that appears frequently in Ezekiel. The being was a character with the responsibility of providing a revelation to the recipient. It means that the being was something like a human being in some way—in a vision. This one was enough like a human being to be able to speak in a language Daniel could understand in his vision. The author of this passage took these words from the same verse in Ezekiel (Ezek 1:26) from which the author of Dan 7 obtained the expression "**like a** Son of man" (Dan 7:13), but the characters did not play the same roles, and they were actors in different dramas.

Dan 7 was a dramatic court play in which one of the characters **was like a human being** in some way. He did not have a speaking part but he was **like a human being** in contrast to other characters that were like beasts and he was able to receive power, glory, and a kingdom the way a human king receives it. The last of the beasts was given a death sentence in the trial. The character **like a human being** played the opposing role, so he was obviously the plaintiff in the trial. The one **like a human being** in Dan 10 had a role in a preamble only. He had no part in the drama itself. The function of the preamble of Dan 10 was to alert the reader to the belief of the author that the events that followed in Dan 11 and 12 were divinely predestined.

The author began his narrative by using divinely inspired words from Ezekiel who spoke of someone **like a human being** and created a role for him that prepared the reader for the next two chapters. In Dan 11 and 12 the characters are easily identified with individual, historical **human beings**. The one **like a human**

being in Dan 10 was only instrumental in preparing Daniel to receive the vision. It had no role in the historical function of the drama. Both characters were **like human beings** but they were different kinds of characters in different dramas.

To illustrate the point in modern theater, let us assume that there are two actors. Actor number 1 is Patrick Stewart. He has played the role of Othello in Shakespeare, but he also played the role of Captain Ricardo in the second version of Star Wars. That does not mean that Captain Ricardo is Othello. The same actor was involved, but the characters he played are different. Then there is another actor, actor no 2, named Red Skeleton, who played the role of Freddie the Freeloader. Freddie the Freeloader was different from either Othello or Captain Ricardo. It would be foolish to assume that Freddie the Freeloader was Othello just because it was a role played by an actor, and Red Skeleton was an actor. Actors are different and roles are different, even though both Red Skeleton and Patrick Stewart are called actors and the roles they play are called characters.

Similarly, there are two characters in the Book of Daniel that are called "one **like a human being**," one in Dan 7 and one in Dan 10. Both are characters in dramas. If the one in Dan 7 were called character number 1 and the one in Dan 10 were called charactor no 2, and they play different roles in different dramas, it would be foolish to assume that character number 1 equals character number 2, just because both are roles in dramas. It is necessary to study the drama to find out what the role of each character is before assuming that both characters are the same or that the same actor played both roles. It is then that the reader can easily see that character number 1 functions as the plaintiff in a court trial (Dan 7:13) and that character number 2 acts as a divine messenger that brings a vision to a visionary (Dan 10:18).

One of the rules in geometry is "things that are equal to the same thing are equal to each other." That does not mean "things that are **something like** the same thing are equal to each other." That means that characters in different dramas, probably composed by different authors, that are "**something like a human being**" are not necessarily equal to one another. An examination of the roles that both play shows that they are clearly different.

Touched my lips. Following the vision of Isaiah when he saw the Lord in the temple (Isa 6:1), some divine being **touched** Daniel's **lips** just as the seraph took coals off the altar to **touch** Isaiah's **lips** and cleanse them. That prepared Isaiah to speak; after this Daniel began speaking.

My Lord, in the vision. The address, **My Lord**, occurs many times in the discussion, just as it does in the visions of Zechariah (Zech 1:9; 4:4, 5, 13; 6:4)

Touched me and made me strong. This was the same divine being that did the **touching**. This **touching** was accompanied by the same exhortation Moses and Joshua gave to the Israelites before they entered the Promised Land. They needed to be **strong** and courageous. The same was true of Daniel.

TEXT

Just as he was speaking with me, I gained strength, and I said, "Let my lord speak, because you have strengthened me." [20]Then he said, "Do you know why I have come to you? Now I will return to fight with the Persian general, and when I leave, look! the Greek general will come, but I will tell you what is written in the Book of Truth. [21]No one is supporting me against these except Michael your prince."

COMMENTARY

I will fight the Persian general. This means Jews were at war with **the Persians**. They probably did not have troops in the battlefield, but they may have had intelligence officers both in **Persia** and in other places, working on the problem of overthrowing **the Persians**. The Jewish divine informant would not have been fighting **the Persians** if the Jews did not believe it should be done.[7]

The Greek general. This was Alexander the Great who led a rapid conquest from Macedonia to India. On his way, he also took Egypt and Persia. Jews were probably supporting him in his endeavor at first, because he was an enemy of Persia, as were also the Jews. They later changed their feelings toward **the Greeks**, just as they had toward the Persians earlier.

The Book of Truth. It is not certain that such a book ever existed. This was a heavenly being that was supposedly counselling Daniel and giving him authoritative information. **The book** of authority was called **the Book of Truth**. It may have been the same **book** as the one referred to as "Your **book**" (Ps 139:16). **The Book of Truth** was supposed to be a **book** of prophecy that would inform its readers of the predestined future. Of course, this was not really prophecy but a historical report of events that happened in Palestine.[8] This hypothetical book contained the truth, because the author included in it only events that had actually taken place. Since this is near the end of the introductory chapter, the author probably intended the reader to think that the following message, in Dan 11 and 12, came from **the Book of Truth**. On the other hand, this may not have been a hypothetical book at all. There may really have existed in Maccabean times a document called **The Book of Truth** to which the author of Dan 10 referred and from which material that is now in Dan 11 and 12 was taken.

---

[7] For an ancient document showing the wars that occurred among the gods, see E. A. Speiser (tr.), "The Creation Epic," *Ancient Near Eastern Texts*, ed. J. B. Pritchard (Princeton: Princeton U. Press, 1969), pp. 60-72.

[8] Porteous, *Daniel*, p. 156, said, "In the commentary the fiction of prophecy will be dropped and the references treated as references to past events."

CHAPTER ELEVEN

HEBREW TEXT

11:1 וַאֲנִ֞י פ

בִּשְׁנַ֨ת אַחַ֜ת לְדָרְיָ֣וֶשׁ הַמָּדִ֗י עָמְדִ֛י לְמַחֲזִ֥יק וּלְמָע֖וֹז לֽוֹ: 2 וְעַתָּ֕ה אֱמֶ֖ת אַגִּ֣יד לָ֑ךְ

הִנֵּה־עוֹד֩ שְׁלֹשָׁ֨ה מְלָכִ֜ים עֹמְדִ֣ים לְפָרַ֗ס וְהָֽרְבִיעִי֙ יַעֲשִׁ֣יר עֹֽשֶׁר־גָּד֣וֹל מִכֹּ֔ל וּכְחֶזְקָת֣וֹ בְעָשְׁר֔וֹ יָעִ֣יר הַכֹּ֔ל אֵ֖ת מַלְכ֥וּת יָוָֽן: 3 וְעָמַ֖ד מֶ֣לֶךְ גִּבּ֑וֹר וּמָשַׁל֙ מִמְשָׁ֣ל רַ֔ב וְעָשָׂ֖ה כִּרְצוֹנֽוֹ: 4 וּכְעָמְדוֹ֙ תִּשָּׁבֵ֣ר מַלְכוּת֔וֹ וְתֵחָ֕ץ לְאַרְבַּ֖ע רוּח֣וֹת הַשָּׁמָ֑יִם וְלֹ֣א לְאַחֲרִית֗וֹ וְלֹ֤א כְמָשְׁלוֹ֙ אֲשֶׁ֣ר מָשָׁ֔ל כִּ֤י תִנָּתֵשׁ֙ מַלְכוּת֔וֹ וְלַאֲחֵרִ֖ים מִלְּבַד־אֵֽלֶּה:

5 וְיֶחֱזַ֥ק מֶֽלֶךְ־הַנֶּ֖גֶב וּמִן־שָׂרָ֑יו וְיֶחֱזַ֤ק עָלָיו֙ וּמָשָׁ֔ל מִמְשָׁ֥ל רַ֖ב מֶמְשַׁלְתּֽוֹ: 6 וּלְקֵ֤ץ שָׁנִים֙ יִתְחַבָּ֔רוּ וּבַ֣ת מֶֽלֶךְ־הַנֶּ֗גֶב תָּבוֹא֙ אֶל־מֶ֣לֶךְ הַצָּפ֔וֹן לַעֲשׂ֖וֹת מֵישָׁרִ֑ים וְלֹֽא־תַעְצֹ֞ר כּ֣וֹחַ הַזְּר֗וֹעַ וְלֹ֤א יַעֲמֹד֙ וּזְרֹע֔וֹ וְתִנָּתֵ֨ן הִ֤יא וּמְבִיאֶ֨יהָ֙ וְהַיֹּ֣לְדָ֔הּ וּמַחֲזִקָ֖הּ בָּעִתִּֽים: 7 וְעָמַ֛ד מִנֵּ֥צֶר שָׁרָשֶׁ֖יהָ כַּנּ֑וֹ וְיָבֹ֣א אֶל־הַחַ֗יִל וְיָבֹא֙ בְּמָעוֹז֙ מֶ֣לֶךְ הַצָּפ֔וֹן וְעָשָׂ֥ה בָהֶ֖ם וְהֶחֱזִֽיק: 8 וְגַ֣ם אֱ‍ֽלֹהֵיהֶ֡ם עִם־נְסִֽכֵיהֶם֩ עִם־כְּלֵ֨י חֶמְדָּתָ֜ם כֶּ֧סֶף וְזָהָ֛ב בַּשְּׁבִ֖י יָבִ֣א מִצְרָ֑יִם וְהוּא֙ שָׁנִ֣ים יַעֲמֹ֔ד מִמֶּ֖לֶךְ הַצָּפֽוֹן: 9 וּבָ֗א בְּמַלְכוּת֙ מֶ֣לֶךְ הַנֶּ֔גֶב וְשָׁ֖ב אֶל־אַדְמָתֽוֹ: 10 וּבְנ֤וֹ [וּבָנָיו֙] יִתְגָּר֔וּ וְאָסְפוּ֙ הֲמוֹן֙ חֲיָלִ֣ים רַבִּ֔ים **וּבָ֥א ב֖וֹא וְשָׁטַ֣ף וְעָבָ֑ר** וְיָשֹׁ֥ב וְיִתְגָּרֶ֖ה [וְיִתְגָּר֗וּ] עַד־**מָֽעֻזֹּה** [**מָעֻזּֽוֹ**]:   Isa 8:7-8

11 וְיִתְמַרְמַר֙ מֶ֣לֶךְ הַנֶּ֔גֶב וְיָצָ֕א וְנִלְחַ֥ם עִמּ֖וֹ עִם־מֶ֣לֶךְ הַצָּפ֑וֹן וְהֶעֱמִיד֙ הָמ֣וֹן רָ֔ב וְנִתַּ֥ן הֶהָמ֖וֹן בְּיָדֽוֹ: 12 וְנִשָּׂ֥א הֶהָמ֖וֹן יָר֣וּם [וְרָ֣ם] לְבָב֑וֹ וְהִפִּ֥יל רִבֹּא֖וֹת וְלֹ֥א יָעֽוֹז: 13 וְשָׁב֙ מֶ֣לֶךְ הַצָּפ֔וֹן וְהֶעֱמִ֣יד הָמ֔וֹן רַ֖ב מִן־הָרִאשׁ֑וֹן וּלְקֵ֨ץ הָעִתִּ֤ים שָׁנִים֙ יָב֣וֹא ב֔וֹא בְּחַ֥יִל גָּד֖וֹל וּבִרְכ֥וּשׁ רָֽב:

14 וּבָעִתִּ֣ים הָהֵ֔ם רַבִּ֥ים יַֽעַמְד֖וּ עַל־מֶ֣לֶךְ הַנֶּ֑גֶב וּבְנֵ֣י ׀ פָּרִיצֵ֣י עַמְּךָ֗ יִֽנַּשְּׂא֛וּ לְהַעֲמִ֥יד חָז֖וֹן וְנִכְשָֽׁלוּ: 15 וְיָבֹא֙ מֶ֣לֶךְ הַצָּפ֔וֹן וְיִשְׁפֹּ֖ךְ סֽוֹלְלָ֑ה וְלָכַ֖ד עִ֣יר מִבְצָר֑וֹת וּזְרֹע֤וֹת הַנֶּ֨גֶב֙ לֹ֣א יַעֲמֹ֔דוּ וְעַם֙ מִבְחָרָ֔יו וְאֵ֥ין כֹּ֖חַ לַעֲמֹֽד: 16 וְיַ֨עַשׂ הַבָּ֤א אֵלָיו֙ כִּרְצוֹנ֔וֹ וְאֵ֥ין עוֹמֵ֖ד לְפָנָ֑יו וְיַעֲמֹ֥ד בְּאֶֽרֶץ־הַצְּבִ֖י וְכָלָ֥ה **בְיָדֽוֹ**: 17 וְיָשֵׂ֣ם ׀ פָּ֠נָיו לָב֞וֹא בְּתֹ֧קֶף כָּל־מַלְכוּת֛וֹ וִישָׁרִ֥ים   Sir 36:8
עִמּ֖וֹ וְעָשָׂ֑ה וּבַ֤ת הַנָּשִׁים֙ יִתֶּן־ל֣וֹ לְהַשְׁחִיתָ֔הּ **וְלֹ֥א תַעֲמֹ֖ד וְלֹא־ל֥וֹ**   Isa 7:7
תִהְיֶֽה: 18 וְיָשֵׁ֧ב [וְיָשֵׂ֧ם] ׀ פָּנָ֛יו לְאִיִּ֖ים וְלָכַ֣ד רַבִּ֑ים וְהִשְׁבִּ֨ית קָצִ֤ין חֶרְפָּתוֹ֙ ל֔וֹ בִּלְתִּ֥י חֶרְפָּת֖וֹ יָשִׁ֣יב לֽוֹ: 19 וְיָשֵׁ֣ב פָּנָ֔יו לְמָעוּזֵּ֖י אַרְצ֑וֹ וְנִכְשַׁ֥ל וְנָפַ֖ל וְלֹ֥א יִמָּצֵֽא: 20 וְעָמַ֧ד עַל־כַּנּ֛וֹ מַעֲבִ֥יר נוֹגֵ֖שׂ **הֶ֣דֶר**   Sir 36:6
מַלְכ֑וּת וּבְיָמִ֥ים אֲחָדִ֖ים יִשָּׁבֵ֔ר וְלֹ֥א בְאַפַּ֖יִם וְלֹ֥א בְמִלְחָמָֽה:

21 וְעָמַ֤ד עַל־כַּנּוֹ֙ נִבְזֶ֔ה וְלֹא־נָתְנ֥וּ עָלָ֖יו ה֣וֹד מַלְכ֑וּת וּבָ֣א בְשַׁלְוָ֔ה וְהֶחֱזִ֥יק מַלְכ֖וּת בַּחֲלַקְלַקּֽוֹת: 22 **וּזְרֹע֥וֹת** הַשֶּׁ֛טֶף יִשָּׁטְפ֥וּ מִלְּפָנָ֖יו   Sir 36:6
וְיִשָּׁבֵ֑רוּ וְגַ֖ם נְגִ֥יד בְּרִֽית: 23 וּמִן־הִֽתְחַבְּר֥וּת אֵלָ֖יו יַעֲשֶׂ֣ה מִרְמָ֑ה

וְעָלָה וְעָצַם בִּמְעַט־גּוֹי: 24 בְּשַׁלְוָה וּבְמִשְׁמַנֵּי מְדִינָה יָבוֹא וְעָשָׂה
אֲשֶׁר לֹא־עָשׂוּ אֲבֹתָיו וַאֲבוֹת אֲבֹתָיו בִּזָּה וְשָׁלָל וּרְכוּשׁ לָהֶם יִבְזוֹר
וְעַל מִבְצָרִים יְחַשֵּׁב מַחְשְׁבֹתָיו וְעַד־עֵת: 25 וְיָעֵר כֹּחוֹ
וּלְבָבוֹ עַל־מֶלֶךְ הַנֶּגֶב בְּחַיִל גָּדוֹל וּמֶלֶךְ הַנֶּגֶב יִתְגָּרֶה לַמִּלְחָמָה
בְּחַיִל־גָּדוֹל וְעָצוּם עַד־מְאֹד וְלֹא יַעֲמֹד כִּי־יַחְשְׁבוּ עָלָיו מַחֲשָׁבוֹת:
26 וְאֹכְלֵי פַת־בָּגוֹ יִשְׁבְּרוּהוּ וְחֵילוֹ יִשְׁטוֹף וְנָפְלוּ חֲלָלִים רַבִּים:
27 וּשְׁנֵיהֶם הַמְּלָכִים לְבָבָם לְמֵרָע וְעַל־שֻׁלְחָן אֶחָד **כָּזָב** יְדַבֵּרוּ וְלֹא   Hab 2:2
תִצְלָח כִּי־**עוֹד קֵץ לַמּוֹעֵד**: 28 וְיָשֹׁב אַרְצוֹ בִּרְכוּשׁ גָּדוֹל וּלְבָבוֹ   Isa 10:23; 28:22; Sir 36:8
עַל־בְּרִית קֹדֶשׁ וְעָשָׂה וְשָׁב **לְאַרְצוֹ**: 29 **לַמּוֹעֵד** יָשׁוּב וּבָא   Num 24:24; Sir 36:8
בַנֶּגֶב וְלֹא־תִהְיֶה כָרִאשֹׁנָה וְכָאַחֲרֹנָה: 30 **וּבָאוּ בוֹ צִיִּים כִּתִּים** וְנִכְאָה
וְשָׁב וְזָעַם עַל־בְּרִית־קוֹדֶשׁ וְעָשָׂה וְשָׁב וְיָבֵן עַל־עֹזְבֵי בְּרִית קֹדֶשׁ:
31 וּזְרֹעִים מִמֶּנּוּ יַעֲמֹדוּ וְחִלְּלוּ הַמִּקְדָּשׁ הַמָּעוֹז וְהֵסִירוּ הַתָּמִיד וְנָתְנוּ   Deut 33:35-36
הַשִּׁקּוּץ מְשׁוֹמֵם: 32 וּמַרְשִׁיעֵי בְרִית יַחֲנִיף בַּחֲלַקּוֹת **וְעַם יֹדְעֵי**   Sir 36:5, 17
אֱלֹהָיו יַחֲזִקוּ וְעָשׂוּ: 33 וּמַשְׂכִּילֵי **עָם** יָבִינוּ לָרַבִּים **וְנִכְשְׁלוּ** בְּחֶרֶב
וּבְלֶהָבָה בִּשְׁבִי וּבְבִזָּה יָמִים: 34 וּבְהִ**כָּשְׁלָם** יֵעָזְרוּ עֵזֶר מְעָט וְנִלְווּ
עֲלֵיהֶם רַבִּים בַּחֲלַקְלַקּוֹת: 35 וּמִן־הַמַּשְׂכִּילִים **יִכָּשְׁלוּ** לִצְרוֹף בָּהֶם   Sir 36:8 (Heb)
וּלְבָרֵר וְלַלְבֵּן עַד־**עֵת קֵץ** כִּי־עוֹד **לַמּוֹעֵד**: 36 וְעָשָׂה כִרְצוֹנוֹ
הַמֶּלֶךְ וְיִתְרוֹמֵם וְיִתְגַּדֵּל עַל־כָּל־אֵל וְעַל אֵל אֵלִים יְדַבֵּר נִפְלָאוֹת
וְהִצְלִיחַ עַד־כָּלָה זַעַם כִּי נֶחֱרָצָה נֶעֱשָׂתָה: 37 וְעַל־אֱלֹהֵי אֲבֹתָיו   Sir 36:4,5
לֹא יָבִין וְעַל־חֶמְדַּת נָשִׁים וְעַל־כָּל־אֱלוֹהַּ לֹא יָבִין כִּי עַל־כֹּל
יִתְגַּדָּל: 38 וְלֶאֱלֹהַּ מָעֻזִּים עַל־כַּנּוֹ **יְכַבֵּד וְלֶאֱלוֹהַּ** אֲשֶׁר לֹא־**יְדָעֻהוּ**   Sir 36:5, 8
אֲבֹתָיו **יְכַבֵּד** בְּזָהָב וּבְכֶסֶף וּבְאֶבֶן יְקָרָה וּבַחֲמֻדוֹת: 39 **וְעָשָׂה**   Sir 36:3, 4
לְמִבְצְרֵי מָעֻזִּים עִם־אֱלוֹהַּ **נֵכָר** אֲשֶׁר הִכִּיר (וַיִכִּיר) יַרְבֶּה **כָבוֹד** וְהִמְשִׁילָם
בָּרַבִּים וַאֲדָמָה יְחַלֵּק בִּמְחִיר: 40 וּ**בְעֵת קֵץ** יִתְנַגַּח עִמּוֹ מֶלֶךְ   Isa 8:7-8
הַנֶּגֶב **וְיִשְׂתָּעֵר** עָלָיו מֶלֶךְ הַצָּפוֹן בְּרֶכֶב וּבְפָרָשִׁים וּבָאֳנִיּוֹת רַבּוֹת   Sir 36:6
וּבָא בַאֲרָצוֹת **וְשָׁטַף וְעָבָר**: 41 וּבָא בְּאֶרֶץ הַצְּבִי וְרַבּוֹת יִכָּשֵׁלוּ
וְאֵלֶּה יִמָּלְטוּ **מִיָּדוֹ** אֱדוֹם וּמוֹאָב וְרֵאשִׁית בְּנֵי עַמּוֹן: 42 וְיִשְׁלַח יָדוֹ
בַּאֲרָצוֹת וְאֶרֶץ מִצְרַיִם לֹא תִהְיֶה לִפְלֵיטָה: 43 וּמָשַׁל בְּמִכְמַנֵּי
הַזָּהָב וְהַכֶּסֶף וּבְכֹל חֲמֻדוֹת מִצְרָיִם וְלֻבִים וְכֻשִׁים בְּמִצְעָדָיו:
44 וּשְׁמֻעוֹת יְבַהֲלֻהוּ מִמִּזְרָח וּמִצָּפוֹן וְיָצָא בְּחֵמָא גְדֹלָה לְהַשְׁמִיד
וּלְהַחֲרִים רַבִּים: 45 וְיִטַּע אָהֳלֵי אַפַּדְנוֹ בֵּין יַמִּים לְהַר־צְבִי־
קֹדֶשׁ וּבָא עַד־קִצּוֹ וְאֵין עוֹזֵר לוֹ:

TEXT

¹¹:¹I, in the first year of Darius the Mede, stood to make him strong and to support him.

TECHNICAL DETAILS

Scholars usually divide the Book of Daniel into two halves: 1-6 and 7-12, the first six chapters being a collection of essays and the last six chapters called the apocalypse. There is more difference, however, between chapter 11 and the 10 earlier chapters than there is between chapter 7 and the six earlier chapters. Furthermore Dan 7 seems to belong to the unit Dan 2-7. This unit has been organized into a *chiasm*, and Dan 7 forms an *inclusio* with Dan 2. Dan 7 forms a conclusion to the unit, Dan 2-7, and it also forms a hinge to connect that unit to the following chapters. Dan 7 begins something new. Earlier chapters in the Book of Daniel have been homilies based on earlier intertexts, but that is not so for Dan 7.

Dan 10 provides an introductory setting to Dan 11, which holds the message of the second unit (Dan 10-12).

Instead of a homily created on the basis of texts and typologies, Dan 11 is a story. It is the story introduced at the beginning of Dan 10 as **the word was revealed to Daniel, who was called Belteshazzar. The word was valid, and the war was extensive. He understood the word, and the vision became clear to him** (Dan 10:1). It also either is taken from, or itself is, **The Book of Truth** introduced at the end of Dan 10 (Dan 10:21). The author of Dan 10 wanted his readers to know that the message in Dan 11 and 12 is a valid report of an **extensive war** that was reported in **The Book of Truth**.

The story that follows does not begin with the words, "Once upon a time," but it has a similar style form. The characters in the story are given only vaguely as **the king of the South** or **the king of the North**.[1] Although it is not poetry its style is something like Spencer's "Fairie Queen." The story involved is based on historical events in the Near East following the division of Alexander the Great's kingdom, first into several parts, then into four parts, and later into three kingdoms. These were Antigonus in Macedonia, Ptolemy in Egypt, and Seleucus in Asia.

Delcor compared the philosophy of history of Dan 11 with that of the philosophical historian Polybius. He noticed that Polybius attributed to "Fate" that which the author of Dan 11 credited to God.[2]

The Book of Daniel has little interest in Macedonia, so from the Jewish point of view, history continued with the conflict between Egypt and Asia. Since this history covers a period of many years, the characters changed. Kings of both countries died, and sons and grandsons carried on the wars. Nevertheless, the names of the kings were never given, and sometimes it is not absolutely clear which of the Ptolemies and which of the Seleucids were described by Dan 11. They have to be deduced from external historical sources, such as the histories of Dio, Livy, Polybius, and Josephus. Following a brief introduction to provide the historical background and setting (Dan 11:1-2), the expansion of Alexander is the place where Dan 11 begins. The narrative deals with the experiences of Alexander the Great and his successors especially as they were related to the Jews and the Promised Land.

COMMENTARY

Darius the Mede. Dan 11:1 seems to be part of Dan 10. It may have been misplaced at the beginning of Dan 11. Throughout the Book of Daniel, there is the supposition that there was a time when **the Medes** had overthrown the Babylonians and ruled the Near East, and **Darius** was the king at that time. The implication is that Babylon ruled the area at one time, and Media ruled it at a later time when Babylon no longer existed. That is not really the way Near Eastern countries were arranged at that time. Daniel is the only ancient scribe to mention **Darius the Mede**, but it is true that

---

[1] One of the Greek texts (G) consistently interpreted "the king of the South" as "the king of Egypt." The kings of the North in the War Scroll are also probably Seleucids (*11QM* 1.4).
[2] M. Delcor, "L'Histoire selon le Livre de Daniel Notamment au Chapitre 11,"*The Book of Daniel in the Light of New Findings* ed. A. S. Van der Woude (Leuven: University Press, 1993), pp. 381-86.

Media was a strong and large kingdom until the time Cyrus captured the country and added it to his Persian Empire. Instead, however, of following Babylon as a ruler of the entire Fertile Crescent, Media existed at the same time Babylon was strong. It never conquered Babylon and included Babylon as part of its empire, as Jeremiah and Isaiah prophesied, but at one time the Persians were subject to Media (Herodotus 1.127). Media was adjacent to Babylon to the north and the east having conquered Persia and part of Assyria.

The source of the author's history, however, was almost entirely confined to the scripture. Jeremiah and Isaiah both prophesied that Media would come out of the North and destroy Babylon (Jer 50:1-3, 8-10; Isa 13:17-22). Since both of these great prophets were accepted as true prophets, their prophecies must have taken place. According to the accepted Jewish rhetoric of the day, the author was justified in placing Media after Babylon in the succession of great empires.

Media and the Succession of Empires. Media was brought into the picture because it was the second of a series of four countries that ruled the countries surrounding the Tigris-Euphrates rivers. The original order was Assyria, **Media**, Persia, and Greece. Babylon was not included in the list. Daniel, however, substituted Babylon for Assyria, because Jewish exile was into Babylon rather than Assyria. Nineveh was included within the borders of **Media**, and Nineveh was the place where the North Israelites had been taken into captivity. Nineveh was to Samaria what Babylon was to Judah. The expression "The Medes and the Persians" was common and used as if the two groups belonged to one tradition. Herodotus referred to Xerxes as "the king of the Medes" (*bah-see-loós hah-may-dóhn*, βασιλεὺς ὁ Μηδῶν) (*Hist* 9.7, 19), when he was really the king and leader of the Persians. Cyrus was cited in Persian contracts as the king of **Media** and Persia, as if there continued to be two separate countries or a union of the two countries and Cyrus was king of them both.

There continued to be a country called **Media**, however, that was independent and formerly part of greater **Media**. This country lay alongside the western shore of the Caspian Sea and was distinguished as Atropatian **Media**. It had its own king. Parthia and Armenia frequently invaded it, but Atropatian **Media** always recovered its borders. When Rome and Parthia were in war, the king of Atropatian **Media** continued to negotiate with both countries. Rome never succeeded in annexing this country. (Strabo 11.13.1-2), although Mark Anthony had to deal with this country as late as 36 BIA (Dio, 49.25-44). Atropatian **Media**, however, would never have been confused for one of the great empires of Asia.

The rest of **Media**, known as "greater **Media**," however, became a part, first of Persia and then of Syria, and finally, Rome. Even though boundary lines changed, and other countries encompassed countries, their original territories held to the old names, similar to the Soviet Union in the twentieth century. As soon as military force was withdrawn, those small countries that existed within the union claimed their original identity and independence. They had never stopped being whatever they were before they became part of the Soviet Union. So it was with **the Medes** and the Persians. When Cyrus conquered **Media**, he did it without much need for military confrontation. He persuaded the **Median** soldiers to abandon their current positions and join his army. This meant that there continued to be a friendly relationship between Cyrus and the **Medians**. They voluntarily became part of his empire.

TEXT

²Now I will disclose the truth to you: Look! Three more kings will arise in Persia, and the fourth will be much wealthier than all [the others will]. As he becomes strong through his wealth he will stir up everything against the Greek kingdom.

COMMENTARY

The truth. This **truth**, which hypothetically came from the **Book of Truth** mentioned in Dan 10, was a report of historical events that took place in the Near East that were important to Palestinian Jews. Because they actually happened, the author presumed that God had predetermined them long before and had written them down in this special book of his.³

Three more kings will arise in Persia. Darius was a stage character that was not really involved in the history himself. The author was reporting the **kings** of Persia and not Media. The three **kings** who followed Cyrus, would have been Cambyses (529-522 BIA) Gamata (522 BIA), Darius the Great (522-486 BIA), and Xerxes (486-465 BIA). Because Gamata ruled only seven months, he might not have been included in the "Book of Truth." Xerxes may have been considered the third. The only names of Persian **kings** given in FT are 1) Cyrus, 2) Darius, 3) Xerxes, and 4) Artaxerxes, but no order is given (Ezra 4:5-7).

As he becomes strong. This refers to Xerxes who was famous for his wealth and military strength (Herodotus 7.20-99).

---

³ E. R. Bevan, *The House of Ptolemy: A History of Egypt under the Ptolemaic Dynasty* (Chicago: Argonaut, Inc., Publishers, 1968), p. 230, like many scholars, thought the author of Dan 11 was reliable. He either was alive at the time some of the reported events happened or he had reliable sources. One of his sources might have been *The Book of Truth*.

He will stir up everything against the Greek kingdom. This was the action begun by Darius the Great and continued by his son Xerxes who fought against the Greeks in the famous Battle of Salamis (480 BIA). At that time the Persians had become such a threat to **the Greeks** that they succeeded in burning Athens (Herodotus, 8-9). Persians were finally forced to retreat (479 BIA), but there continued to be a contest between the East and the West over Asia Minor. At a later time Antiochus III, the Great, succeeded in conquering most of the coastal cities of Asia Minor,[4] Thrace, most of the Mediterranean Islands, and some of **the Greek** cities. That was before the Romans crushed the Cartheginians and began their expansion to the East under the leadership of Scipio.

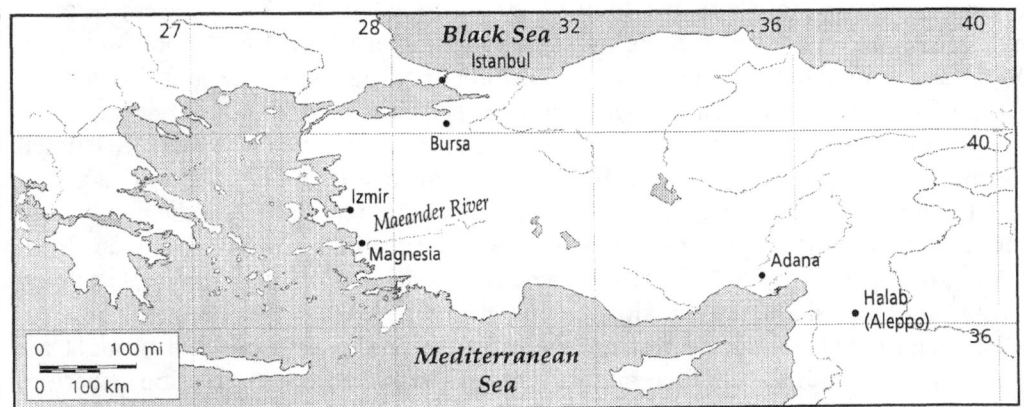

TEXT

³A mighty king will arise and will rule a large dominion, and do as he pleases. ⁴When he has arisen, his kingdom will be broken into the four winds, but not to his posterity, and not according to his dominion which he rules, because his kingdom will be taken and belong to others, and not these alone.

COMMENTARY

A mighty king will arise. A warrior **king** (*gee-bóhr*, גבור). This was Alexander the Great who ruled a large dominion, all the way from Macedonia to India, including Egypt. Justin said of Alexander:

> He met no enemy that he did not conquer; he besieged no city he did not capture; he attacked no people he did not overpower (Justin 12.16).

---

[4] Seleucids were never able to conquer the tribes in the mountains of the north. These were finally subdued by the Romans.

Alexander the Great was a student of Aristotle, and he spread the use of the Greek language and culture wherever he conquered, but the philosophy, which is related to him and called Hellenistic, was a mixture of Persian and Greek.[5]

Will be broken into the four winds. When his empire had reached the peak of its size and power, Alexander died. Initially the empire was divided among several generals, some acting in behalf of Alexander's two sons. After 25 years of military shuffle, however, it was divided into four parts, ruled by **four** of Alexander's former generals. 1) Antigonus ruled Macedonia and Anatolia in the Northwest. 2) Thrace, and the western part of Asia Minor in the North belonged to Lysimachus. 3) Ptolemy ruled Egypt, Cyrene, Palestine, and Syria in the Southwest. 4) Babylon belonged to Seleucus. There were **four** generals, in very roughly **four** directions. The land was divided approximately into the **four** winds, geographically. Antigonus apparently extended his kingdom to include most of the cities of all of Asia Minor and even Syria and Babylonia (Polybius 28.20, 7), forcing Seleucus to flee and Ptolemy to retreat. At that time his position overshadowed all of the others.

Later the **four** kings (Cassander, Lysimachus, Ptolemy, and Seleucus) formed an alliance to curb Antigonus' advances. Ptolemy did not actually participate in the war that followed, leaving Antigonus dead, so the treaty that followed was made without Ptolemy. Syria and Palestine were taken from Antigonus and given to Seleucus, rather than Ptolemy (Polybius 5.67, 8). Ptolemy objected. He had entered the alliance only on the condition that he would recover Syria and Palestine, but he was not there for the battle. Seleucus had brought the most soldiers into the conflict, and he emerged from battle with the lion's share of territory. Seleucids called this moment the birthday of the Empire.[6]

There were many battles fought later between the Ptolemies and Seleucids over this territory, as Ptolemies tried to gain it back and the Seleucids tried to maintain it. Seleucus later defeated Lysimachus in a war in which Lysimachus was killed, and Antiochus' sons, Seleucus II and Antiochus III acquired most of the cities of Asia Minor (Polybius 18.51, 3-4; Livy 34.58, 5). Antiochus III ruled all of the land from India to Europe,[7] with the exception of Egypt and the mountainous regions of Asia Minor. He planned to annex Egypt at his earliest opportunity and to move west through Greece and conquer Rome. Soon Alexander's kingdom was divided into two parts, with the Seleucids to the North and the Ptolemies to the South. These are the two contestants that are significant in this chapter. Each of them wanted to rule all of Alexander the Great's kingdom.

But not to his posterity. Alexander had two sons, but neither obtained any of the empire. Initially some of the generals held some of the territory in the name of the two sons, but that was soon usurped.

---

[5] For the theory that Dan 11:3-45 constitutes a dynastic prophecy like those in Babylonia, see A. K. Grayson, *Babylonian Historical-Literary Texts* (Toronto: University of Toronto, 1975), p. 21, and W. G. Lambert, *The Background of Jewish Apocalyptic* (London: Athlone, 1978), pp. 9-10.

[6] E. R. Bevan, *The House of Seleucus* (New York: Barnes & Noble, 1966) I, p. 54.

[7] See further F. E. Peters, *The Harvest of Hellenism* (New York: Simon & Shuster, c1970), pp. 66-85; M. Hengel, *Jews, Greeks and Barbarians* tr. J. Bowden (Philadelphia: Fortress Press, c1980), p. 1-20.

Not according to his dominion. None of the generals who ruled the empire that Alexander left was able to rule with his leadership skills or military power. When Alexander died, the empire weakened.

TEXT

⁵The king of the South will become strong, but from among his generals [one] will become stronger than he,[8] and he will rule from a dominion that is a great dominion.

COMMENTARY

The king of the South was Ptolemy I, pharaoh of Egypt. He extended his borders until he had included all of Syria as part of his kingdom. That also included the territory between Syria and Egypt, including Jerusalem. He took Jerusalem by deceit. He pretended he was coming to Jerusalem on the Sabbath to offer sacrifice. After he had been admitted into the city, he took it by military force at a time when the Jews would not fight, because of the Sabbath. He conquered territory around Samaria, Gerizim, and the hill country of Judah. He then took many people from all of these territories back to Egypt as slaves (*Ant* 12.3-7). Palestinian Jews were unhappy in their relationship with Egypt, even though many Jews who had not been brought as slaves moved voluntarily to Egypt for economic reasons. From that time on Egypt continued to be an important diaspora center for Jews and one of the strong forces that increased the Hellenization of Palestine.

THE PTOLEMY FAMILY TREE

Ptolemy I (305-283)

Ptolemy II (283-247)

Ptolemy III (247-221)

Ptolemy IV (221-203)

Ptolemy V (203-181)

Ptolemy VI (180-146)

When Seleucus was forced to flee from Antigonus, he found refuge in Egypt, where he was appointed as one of Ptolemy's generals. He persuaded Ptolemy to send him with a small force to regain Babylon. He was successful, and was again a leading force in the Middle East, the strongest of Alexander's surviving generals. The Seleucid era was dated from the time Seleucus recovered his country (312 BIA).

---

[8] Seleucus was one of Alexander's marshals who became a general in Ptolemy I's army when Ptolemy became king of Egypt. Seleucus himself later became king of the eastern portion of Alexander's empire. Of Seleucus, Arrian, *Anabasis* 7.22, 5, said, "he had the royalest mind of them all, and after Alexander himself, ruled over the greatest extent of territory" (taken from Porteous, p. 159).

TEXT

⁶After some years they will make an agreement, and the daughter of the king of the South will come to the king of the North to make peace, but she will not retain the strength of her arm. His arm will not endure, and she will be surrendered--she, those who brought her, her child, and the one who possessed her at the time. ⁷A branch from her roots will arise in his place, and he will come against the army and enter the fortress of the king of the North. He will act against them and prevail. ⁸Also their gods, their images, and their precious vessels of silver and gold he will bring into captivity to Egypt. He will stay away from the king of the North for several years.

COMMENTARY

After some years they will make an agreement. There were several attempts at peace treaties between the Seleucids and the Ptolemies. The first was the marriage of Ptolemy II's (283-247 BIA) daughter, Berenice, to Antiochus II (261-246 BIA). This is probably the treaty mentioned in Dan 11:6.

The daughter of the King of the South. There were three Ptolemy-Seleucid marriages. 1) Berenice married Antiochus II. She was the daughter mentioned here. 2) Another was Antiochus III's daughter, Cleopatra, who married one of the Ptolemies. She was the sister of Antiochus IV. This means that Antiochus IV was a relative of the Ptolemies, and presumably would have kindly, unselfish feelings toward them. That was not the case.

She will not retain the strength of her arm. **Arm** is a term frequently used to mean military "power" or "authority." Weapons were often called **arms**. The terms of the Berenice-Antiochus II marriage required Antiochus II to divorce his wife, Laodice, and for their two sons to renounce their claim to the Syrian throne. This angered Laodice. Two years later Ptolemy died, so Antiochus divorced Berenice and remarried Laodice. Laodice no longer trusted her husband so it was probably she who had Antiochus poisoned. She also persuaded her son, Seleucus, to secure the throne for himself by killing Berenice and her infant child. This act of vengeance guaranteed that none of Berenice's posterity would ever sit on the throne of Syria. This all evidently took place in Syria. Berenice had been brought to Syria to marry Antiochus. Those who brought her to Syria remained as her attendants. Seleucus, Laodice's son, then had the whole party killed—mother, infant child, and all of Berenice's attendants. There was another person who was singled out for special attention, **the one who possessed her** (*mah-khah-zeé-kah*, מחזקה) or **held her**. This might have been a new husband or it may have been the person in whose protection she had been placed at the time. It appears as if Seleucus had everyone killed who was in Berenice's presence at the time. This was a tragic ending to a treaty that was intended to establish peace.[9]

---

[9] E. R. Bevan, *Ptolemy*, pp. 1967-69.

A branch from her roots will arise in his place. This was Ptolemy III, Euergetes, Berenice's brother, who took his father's (Ptolemy II's) place in avenging his sister's death. As soon as possible he had Laodice killed.

He . . . enter the fortress of the king of the North. Ptolemy III came from the sea and captured the port city of Antioch, Seleucia, and then went inland to take Antioch itself. This happened in 238 BIA, and Egypt controlled this territory for 26 years. Seleucia was a port that was made by human construction. It lies adjacent to Kissel Dagh (a mountain) on the south and to the north of the place where the Orontes River runs into the Mediterranean Sea. The outlines of this port can still be seen.

A Current Picture of the Abandoned Port of Seleucia

He will bring into captivity to Egypt. Jerome quoted Porphyry in reporting the extent of the booty Ptolemy took from Syria to Egypt: 40,000 talents of silver and 2,500 precious vessels and the images of gods that Cambyses had taken from **Egypt** to Persia, 280 years earlier.[11] These were taken back to **Egypt** in grand procession, and as a result of this victory Ptolemy was given the name Euergetes, "the benefactor." All of this happened to avenge the death of Ptolemy's sister, Berenice. Vessels and gods were often taken as trophies to show off the victory one country had over another. They held a symbolical value. That was why Syria took **Egypt's** gods and vessels in the first place.[12] Babylon also took the temple vessels from Jerusalem when it conquered that city. Rome also carried the candelabra and vessels in

---

[11] MPL 25.706.
[12] E. R. Bevan, *Ptolemy*, pp. 197-99.

procession in Rome after they burned Jerusalem in 70 IA. When Jacob and his family left the habitat of Laban, they also took the family gods (Gen 31:30-35).

He will stay away. For about 20 years Ptolemy **stayed away** from conflict with the Seleucids. This gave the Seleucids time and opportunity to recover Antioch and northern Syria.

Another treaty involved Ptolemy III and probably Seleucus II (246-226 BIA). A third treaty involved Ptolemy V, Epiphanes, who received Antiochus III's daughter, Cleopatra, as Ptolemy's wife (193 BIA). Cleopatra was Antiochus IV's sister. As dowry she brought into the marriage the revenue from Coele-Syria, Samaria, Judah, and Phoenecia (*Ant* 12.154). Antiochus IV was reminded more than once that he was related to the Ptolemy family (Polybius 28.20, 5, 9; 23. 2). The power over the Ptolemies Antiochus III hoped to gain by the wedding of his daughter to Ptolemy V was not effective. Cleopatra became a faithful Egyptian queen. The fact that Antiochus IV's sister was queen of Egypt also did not have much influence over Antiochus IV. He was not restrained from engaging in war against his family members.

Ptolemy VI also gave his daughter, Cleopatra, to King Alexander in marriage (152-151 BIA) as part of a treaty (1Macc 10:51-58), but later he took her back and gave her instead to Demetrius (1Macc 11:9-12). Very shortly after, the Arabs killed Alexander, and Ptolemy VI died (1Macc 11:17-19) about 147-46 BIA.

None of these treaties was lasting; the kings of Egypt and Syria continued to fight over Palestine, the buffer state between them. Whenever Syria and Egypt discussed the question of a treaty, the subject always arose about the agreement that Cassander, Lysimachus, and Seleucus made after Antigonus was defeated. At that time the three decided that all of Syria should belong to Seleucus, including Palestine. Ptolemies always argued that this was an unfair treaty, because Ptolemy I had previously annexed Syria and Judah to Egypt. Ptolemy also argued that Antiochus III had given these lands to him as dowry with his daughter, Cleopatra, but Antiochus insisted that he gave only the revenues from these countries to Ptolemy. Because the two sides could never agree in negotiation sessions, they continued to settle the argument by military means (Polybius 5.3-13). This meant that the armies marched back and forth over Palestine again and again, each time causing suffering for the Palestinians (*Ant* 12.129-31). The king of the North was one of the Seleucids whose capital city was Antioch; the king of the South was one of the Ptolemies whose capital city was Alexandria.

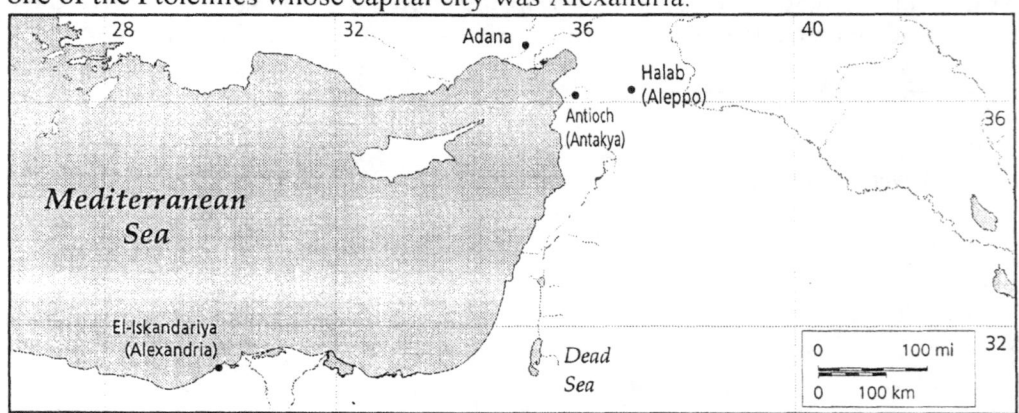

TEXT

Daniel	First Testament Intertexts
⁹Then [the king of the North] will come into the kingdom of the king of the South, but he will return to his own land. ¹⁰His sons will assemble and gather a mob of many troops. They **will** come forcefully, **spread out, and pass over**, and again gather troops as far as his fortress.	$^{\text{Isa 8:7}}$ The Lord is bringing up against them the waters of the river, mighty and many, the king of Assyria, in all his glory **will** rise over all its sources, and overflow all of its banks. ⁸It **will pass** through Judah. It **will spread out and pass over** until it reaches the neck.

¹¹Then the king of the South will become angry and he will come out and join battle with the king of the North. He will raise a great multitude, and the multitude will be given into his hand. ¹²When the multitude is raised, his mind will become overconfident. He will make tens of thousands fall, but he will not become strong. ¹³Then the king of the North will return and raise a still bigger mob than the first. After a few years he will come forcibly with a great army and many supplies.

COMMENTARY

He will return to his own land. Since Ptolemy remained inactive Seleucus had an opportunity to rebuild his army. When he thought he was capable, Seleucus moved south to oppose Ptolemy, but he was badly defeated and **returned** home sooner than he had planned. This was the conclusion of the events that were to follow. The next step was the important Battle of Raphia (217 BIA). Antiochus III was a young, inexperienced king at the time. He came against the equally young and inexperienced Ptolemy IV (221-203 BIA). Both kings had troops and equipment provided by supporting countries. Antiochus had 62,000 foot soldiers, 6,000 cavalry, and 102 elephants (Polybius 5.81, 13).

His sons will assemble and gather a mob of many troops. Two sons of Seleucus were Seleucus III (226-223 BIA) and Antiochus III (223-187 BIA). Antiochus III was especially active and aggressive. Seleucus III was murdered after three years of rule, but Antiochus III became Antiochus the Great. He was the one who expanded the country to its greatest extent. He not only extended the kingdom East as far as India, but he also conquered the territories west, taking the seashore towns of Asia Minor, Thrace, all of the Mediterranean islands, and some of the cities of Greece.

Spread out and pass over. This idiom was used to remind the reader of Isaiah's threat to the people of Judah. He compared the invasion of the king of Assyria to a gigantic flood that would overwhelm everything that gets in its path. This flood would enter Judah like a gushing stream that was so deep that it would reach a person's neck. The author of this chapter pictured the invasion of Antiochus III as being as powerful and extensive as the invasion of Tiglath Pileser when he conquered Samaria in the eighth century BIA.

This was the beginning of Antiochus the Great's efforts to annex Syria and Palestine to his empire. After negotiations had been ineffective, Antiochus recruited a large army and moved south (218 BIA), taking important areas as he went. He took Beruth, the Golan Heights, Scythopolis, and all of the Transjordan, including Rabbat Amman. Then he captured Samaria and Sidon before moving further south to Raphia (Polybius 68.1-78.6). After he conquered Mount Scopus, Jerusalem surrendered to him (Polybius 16.39, 3-5).

As far as his fortress. The **fortress** was probably Raphia, and it was probably considered to be Antiochus' **fortress**. Raphia was south of Gaza, and the two **fortresses** were only 20 miles apart. Antiochus apparently gathered his troops together at Gaza. Then he went farther south until he put Raphia behind him. After the battle was over, Antiochus returned to Raphia as a refuge, which implies that the **fortress** belonged to Antiochus rather than Ptolemy and that it was the **fortress** mentioned here.

He will make tens of thousands fall. It was Ptolemy who won the battle, **making thousands** of the enemy **fall**. While Antiochus was stationed in Palestine, Ptolemy gained time by pretending to be considering negotiations. During this time Ptolemy was strenghening his troops in numbers and training. When he was prepared, he broke off negotiations and waited for Antiochus' advance.[13]

Antiochus lost 10,000 foot soldiers, 300 cavalry, and 5 elephants, while more than 4,000 of his soldiers were taken prisoner by the Egyptians. Ptolemy lost 1,500 soldiers, 700 cavalry, and nearly all of his elephants were either killed or captured (Polybius 5.86, 5-6). Antiochus asked for terms of peace and returned with what was left of his army to his own country. Ptolemy continued to hold possession of Palestine and Syria. Polybius said the Jews were always more closely aligned to the Egyptians than to the Seleucids (Polybius 5.86, 10-11), but that was not invariably so. Jews were quite willing to switch sides when it seemed to their advantage. Sometimes one group of Jews fought on one side while other Jews were supporting the other.

But he will not become strong. Ptolemy did not take advantage of his victorious position to extend his power and territory. He gave Antiochus the opportunity to build up his own forces undisturbed.

Return and raise a still bigger mob. Although Antiochus III was defeated in the Battle of Raphia and forced to make a treaty with Ptolemy and **return** to his own land, he did not relax his zeal or efforts. He turned his attention to the East and extended his borders in that direction. It was from that success that he acquired the title "the Great."

---

[13] E. R. Bevan, *Ptolemy*, pp. 226-29.

After a few years. It was nearly 20 **years** later. After Ptolemy IV had died and was succeeded by the infant Ptolemy V (203-181 BIA) Antiochus moved south again and defeated the Egyptians soundly at the Battle of Panias in the Golan Heights (198 BIA).

TEXT

[14] In those times many will arise against the king of the South, and the sons of the violent ones of your people will rise up to make the vision stand, but they will stumble. [15] Then the king of the North will come, and he will pour out a mound and capture the fortified city. The forces of the South will not stand, not even the people of his choice troops, because there will be no strength to stand.

Daniel	First Testament Intertexts
[16] The one who comes will do to him as he wishes, and he will not be able to stand before him. He will stand in the glorious land, and everything will be in his **hand**. [17] He will turn his face to come with the authority of his entire kingdom, it will go well with him, and he will carry it out. He will give him the daughter of women to destroy it, but **it will not stand; it will not be** his.	Sir 36:6/OG [5] Make glorious the **hand** and courageous the right arm. Isa 7:7 Thus said the Lord, Yehowah, **"It will not stand; it will not be."**

TECHNICAL DETAILS

Schechter was the first to identify the Geniza Hebrew version of Ben Sira. He recognized that the book is packed with quotations and allusions to passages in the FT. He found 340 phrases, idioms, and typical expressions. Others have recounted and reached slightly different conclusions. Schechter said that there were references in Ben Sira to every book of the FT with the exception of Daniel.[14] Schechter and Taylor actually found two similar parallels between Daniel and Ben Sira (Sir 3:30 // Dan 4:24; Sir 36:17 // Dan 9:17), but these did not seem enough to show dependence. Torrey found another parallel that seemed more significant: Sir 36:10 // Dan 8:19; 11:27, 35. This included the expression, **The time of the end**.[15] Fox was intrigued by the possibility that there might be enough parallels to show that Ben Sira actually used Daniel as a source. Since Ben Sira wrote about 190-180 BIA, Fox

---

[14] S. Schechter and C. Taylor, *The Wisdom of Ben Sira: Portions of the Book of Ecclesiasticus from Hebrew Manuscripts in the Cairo Genizah Collection, Presented to the University of Cambridge by the Editors* (London: C. J. Clay & Sons, 1809).

[15] C. C. Torrey, "The Hebrew of the Geniza Sirah," *The Alexander Marx Jubilee Volume*, ed. S. Liebermann (New York: Jewish Theological Seminary of America, 1950), p. 597.

thought that if a relationship could be demonstrated it would show that at least parts of Daniel were composed before the Maccabean era.[16] He concluded that

> The book of Daniel most certainly deserves to be dated earlier than 165 B.C., the date that is traditionally given.[17]

There are even more points of contact between Ben Sira and Daniel than Fox noticed, but they do not lead to the conclusions Fox suggested. The dependence between these two documents is almost entirely between the prayer in Sira 36:1-17 and Dan 11:16-12:13. The big question is, "Did Daniel use Ben Sira or did Ben Sira use Daniel?" The major parallels will be shown in the passage that follows.

The prayer in Ben Sira is poetry; Dan 11-12 is prose. Except for Ben Sira there are few references in Dan 11 to earlier scripture. Readers will notice that Dan 11:17-12:13 echoes the theme of the appointed end over and over again, as if this were its primary text. The expression appears only once in Ben Sira: **Hasten the end time and establish the appointed time** (*hah-kheésh kaytz oo-pah-kóhd moh-áyd*, החיש קץ ופקוד מועד) (Sir 36:8). Furthermore there are other words that appear in the Ben Sira poem that seem to have been picked up by the author of Dan 11 and 12 and woven into the manuscript. Such words are **hand**, **glory**, **honor**, **knowledge** or **understanding**, **hear**, and **time**. The presence of the same words in two documents does not prove conclusively that one document had to be the primary text and the other document had to be the commentary. There are other data to consider before reaching a decision.

COMMENTARY

Many will rise up against the king of the South. The **many** involved here were **many** Palestinian Jews who still resented the time Ptolemy I entered Jerusalem under the pretense of offering sacrifice and then took the city on the Sabbath day (320 BIA). At that time he took **many** Jews and Samaritans into Egypt as slaves. Jews had long memories and welcomed a chance for revenge. That came when they had the opportunity to support the Syrians in their war against the Egyptians. These were violent Jews who had studied the prophecies, the typologies, and other signs, and from them believed that the time had come when God would deliver them from subjection. This belief was strengthened by the knowledge that Egypt did not have strong political leadership at the time. The Pharaoh of Egypt was still an infant. Jewish rebels were able to obtain enough military support from those Jews who believed their calculation to risk an open battle with Egypt. They were taking action to enable the prophecy and the vision to be fulfilled, but it failed.

The sons of the violent ones of your people. These were the rebellious Jews of the time. They took part in Antiochus' attack on Egypt. The author lived many years after this event and was himself anti-Seleucid, so he spoke of those who supported

---

[16] D. E. Fox, "Ben Sira on OT Canon Again: The Date of Daniel," WTJ 49 (1987):335-50.

[17] Fox, "Ben Sira," p. 50.

the Seleucids in negative terms. It was not their violence that disturbed the author but their allegiance to Syria.

Capture the fortified city. This might have been Gaza that was taken after a long siege, but the same was true of Sidon, which Antiochus subdued after the Battle of Panias. This was an important battle. The Egyptian general Scopus had taken refuge at Sidon with 10,000 soldiers (Jerome 25.709, p. 563), but was defeated by Antiochus.

The forces of the South will not stand. This refers to the battles that followed the Battle of Panias (198 BIA) where Antiochus defeated the Egyptians, then took Sidon, and moved farther south with his troops, taking the strategic cities of Palestine as he went. One of the cities that surrendered to Antiochus was Jerusalem (Polybius 16.39, 3-5; *Ant* 12.3, 3). Egypt was no match for the Syrians at that time. Antiochus was strong enough to do as he pleased and no one could stop him.

He will stand on the glorious land. This is Palestine, and the king involved was Antiochus III, the Great, after he had crushed the Egyptians at the Battle of Panias (198 BIA). He then moved south, taking all of Palestine on his way. Afterward **he stood** on the shores of Palestine, looking over his achievements. This, however, happened more than three years after the Romans had finalized the Carthaginians' defeat and signed a treaty with them. The handwriting was already on the wall. The Romans were then free to turn their attention east and begin the movement that later defeated Antiochus III.

Everything will be in his hand. The **hand** and arm are often used in scripture to refer to power. In the prayer of Ben Sira, the Lord is asked to **glorify [your] hand and strengthen [your] right arm** (*Sir* 36:6). In the text from Daniel the reference is to Antiochus Epiphanes who, at that time, had complete control of things.

He will give him the daughter. This is a reference to the time Antiochus III **gave** his **daughter**, Cleopatra, in marriage to the youthful Ptolemy V Epiphanes (193 BIA). As dowry she brought into the marriage half of the revenues of Coele-Syria, Samaria, Judah, and Phonecia (*Ant* 12.154). Antiochus IV Epiphanes was Cleopatra's brother. From this marriage were born both Ptolemy VI Philometer, (174-146 BIA), and Ptolemy VII, Physcon (146-117 BIA). These sons were Antiochus IV's nephews.

The daughter of women. This expression has puzzled most scholars. Why was Cleopatra called **the daughter of women**? Most **daughters** and sons are born from **women**. The best suggestion seems to be that she was a queen *par excellence*. When her husband died she acted as ruler of Egypt for eight years (182-174 BIA). She was highly respected. Although she had Syrian royal blood in her veins she was loyal to Egypt.

To destroy it. Antiochus III's real motive in arranging this marriage and treaty was to protect himself from Roman interference while he gained a footing in Egypt. The implied, but unwritten, antecedent of the pronoun, **it**, which he planned **to destroy** was probably either Egypt itself or Egypt's close relationship with Rome. Antiochus had hoped that his daughter would use her influence to sabotage Egypt's treaty with Rome. If he could just break up the Egypt-Rome alliance he could more easily take Egypt. His plan failed, however, because his daughter, Cleopatra, became a loyal Egyptian and advised her husband to maintain an alliance with Rome. This proved to be beneficial to Judas and the Maccabean Rebellion.

Antiochus IV was Cleopatra's brother, and he was reminded more than once that he was related to the Ptolemy family (Polybius 28.20, 5, 9; 23. 2). The power over the Ptolemies that Antiochus III hoped to gain by the wedding of his daughter to Ptolemy V failed, but neither he nor his son, Antiochus IV, had any intentions of giving up hope of taking over Egypt completely. The blood relationship between the later Ptolemies and Seleucids did not make peace any easier.

But it will not stand, and it will not be his. The pronoun here reflects the same noun as the preceding pronoun. That which Antiochus intended to destroy is that which **would not stand** and that to which he could not claim possession. This seems most likely to have been his plot to control Egypt. The author remembered another time when Syria was a threat to the region. When Ahaz was king of Judah, Syria was plotting to unite with Israel to conquer Judah and install its own puppet king over Judah. This terrified Ahaz and the people of Judah, but Isaiah assured Ahaz that if he would only wait this threat would vanish. That which Syria threatened would not happen (Isa 7:7). After the fact, the author of Dan 11 thought the way in which the Syrian plot was upset was a fulfillment of Isaiah's prophecy. To anti-Hellenizers like the author, Antiochus was the new Rezin who was threatening Judah, and true to Isaiah's prophecy, his plan failed.

TEXT

[18]He will turn his face to the islands and capture many, but an officer will put an end to his insolence. Nothing but his insolence will return to him. [19]He will turn his face to the fortresses of his own land, but he will stumble and fall and will not be found.

COMMENTARY

Put an end to his insolence. The word for "**end**" was not *kaytz* (קץ) or *moh-áyd* (מועד), the terms used for **end** in the Ben Sira prayer. It is rather *heesh-beét* (השבית), "to destroy" or "to finish." It was not just an **end** of a certain period of time. It was an **end** to his power and authority, and with it his **insolence**. It means that many of the things that were in his hand were gone. The officer who **put an end to** Antiochus' **insolence** was Lucius Scipio, who stopped him at Magnesia. Scipio did not really **put an end to** Antiochus' **insolence**. After Scipio left. Antiochus continued to be **insolent,** but the basis for his **insolence** was greatly diminished. Rome was anxious about Antiochus' advances. He had been closing his forces slowly around Rome. He wanted Egypt so that he could move from Egypt to Carthage. He wanted Greece so that he could easily move across the sea to Rome at the same time that he would attack Rome from the south with his base at Carthage. (Livy 35.60 1-6). Rome accurately anticipated his movements and determined to stop him as soon as it could.

He will turn his face to the islands. After Antiochus the Great had conquered Palestine, he moved farther west. He added to his empire many of the cities of Asia Minor. These were the seacoast areas and plains. He was never able, however, to conquer the Gauls and the tribal chieftains in the mountains of the north. He took Thrace and most of **the islands** of the Mediterranean Sea. At the invitation and encouragement of the king of Aetolia, Antiochus entered with troops into Greece. Macedonia, however, objected and went to Rome for assistance. Important Greek cities in Asia Minor also asked Rome for help. The Aetolian league welcomed the expansionistic moves of Antiochus III. Flamininus told Antiochus that he would help Antiochus acquire all of Greece and then move on to take Italy. The Aetolians preferred being subject to the Greek Antiochus than to accept Roman rule, which they feared (Dio 19, Zonaras 9, 18). One of Antiochus' statues was set up in the temple of Athena in Coronea, Greece (Livy 36.20, 2-3).

When Antiochus reached Aetolia, however, he found the promise of help from Aetolia unfulfilled. The soldiers were few and unenthusiastic. The guards appointed slept during the night and allowed the Romans to enter unobserved. When the war was over, and Antiochus was driven out of Greece, the Romans accused the Aetolians of inciting Antiochus into the war (Livy 38.8, 7; 34.60, 1-6)

With the counsel of Hannibal, Antiochus planned to make a treaty with Carthage, obtaining military support from there, and undertaking a two-fold attack on Rome, both from the east and from the south. If he had succeeded in this he would have become master of an empire larger than that of Alexander the Great (Dio 19, Zonaras 9,18; Livy 34.60, 1-6). These plans were stopped when the Scipios turned their attention to Antiochus after the defeat of Carthage.

After he had been victorious in Palestine and Egypt, Antiochus III was stationed in Asia Minor, preparing to move farther west. He had heard, however, that one of the Ptolemies had died, leaving the government in Egypt temporarily weak. He thought this was a good time to annex Egypt to his empire, so he left his oldest son, Seleucus IV, to administer the program in Asia Minor while he took many troops toward Egypt. When he learned, however, that the rumor was false, he withdrew, and tried to sail to Cyprus on his way back to Asia Minor to strengthen the military position he had left with Seleucus. This was probably the time **he turned his face to the islands**. He ran into a storm, and he had to return to the Palestinian shore. This refers to the confrontation of Antiochus III with Scipio, first at Thermopylae and secondly at Magnesia. That western end of his empire that Antiochus had built up carefully over many years suddenly came crashing down like a house of cards.

Will not be found. This is a Hebrew idiom, which means, "he will not exist." As he was commanded, he went back to Syria, and then to Elymais, Persia, where he hoped to plunder the temple treasures there, but the local people killed him (187 BIA). The Danielic author expressed it: "Nothing but his insolence will return to him" (Dan 11:18; see Livy 37.45; Polybius 21.14; Diodorus 29.15).

TEXT

Daniel	First Testament Intertexts
[20] One will arise in his place, and he will make an oppressor go through the **glory** of his kingdom. In a few days he will be broken, neither in anger nor in war, [21] A despised person will arise in his place, but the **glory** of the kingdom will not be given to him. He will come quietly and seize the kingdom with flatteries. [22] The **troops** will be utterly swept before him and crushed. Also the leader of the treaty.	Sir 36:14 Fill Zion with your majesty and your temple with your **glory.** Sir 36:6 **Glorify** [your] hand and strengthen [your] right **arm**.

THE SELEUCID FAMILY TREE

Seleucus I Nicator

Antiochus I Soter (280-261)

Antiochus II Theos (261-246)   (Cleopatra)

Seleucus II Callinicus (246-226)

Seleucus III (226-223)   Antiochus III the Great (223-187)

(Antiochus)   Seleucus IV (187-175)

Antiochus IV Epiphanes (175-164)

COMMENTARY

One will arise in his place. This was Seleucus IV, the oldest son of Antiochus III. Some of the support Antiochus III had in his war with Rome came from the Gauls. Romans knew that they were not through with problems in the Taurus Mountains when they forced Antiochus to stay east of this mountain range. The Gauls were still in these mountains, and it was probably in support of the Gauls while attempting to recover part of the territory his father surrendered to the Romans that he was killed in a battle, trying to cross the Taurus Mountains. Dio only reported his death. He did not say he was killed in battle. Livy reported that Seleucus was involved with the Gauls in the military conflict (Livy 38.12, 3-6; Dio 19, Zonaras 9,21).

The glory of his kingdom. **The glory** is of Antiochus' **kingdom**. It was destined to be broken. The glory of Ben Sira's prayer is for **the glory** that would come to God if he established the Jewish kingdom at his holy city, Zion.

In a few days he will be broken. There seems to be a confusion of kings here. It was Seleucus IV who followed Antiochus III, but it was Seleucus III who had a short reign before Antiochus III. He ruled only 3 years (226-223 BIA). According to Jerome (on Daniel 11:10, 20), he was killed in Phrygia through the treachery of his own generals, Nicanor and Apaturius. The discussion continues in relationship to Seleucus IV.

Seleucus IV learned that there was a large amount of silver and gold in the sacred treasury of the temple in Jerusalem. He sent one of his agents, Heliodorus, to Jerusalem to confiscate it. Heliodorus was the oppressor mentioned (Dan 11:20). When he made the attempt, mobs of women and men appeared and lamented the attempt, weeping and calling upon God to protect his own treasury. In the process, Heliodorus apparently had a heart attack or stroke. He fell helpless to the ground Jews believed that God had sent an angelic force to strike him down. When he recovered, he returned to Seleucus and told him that the place was haunted (2Macc 3:3-40). Perhaps this failure was reported as Seleucus being broken.

Heliodorus later killed Seleucus IV (175 BIA) in an attempt to obtain his throne, but he died after **a few days, neither in anger nor in war**. Antiochus IV succeeded him (as Dan 11:21 reported).

A despised person will arise in his place. This was Antiochus IV Epiphanes, the second son of Antiochus the Great. He had been a hostage in Rome for 14 years after the Battle of Magnesia (Dio 19, Zonaras 9,20, 21). This was to guarantee to the Romans that Syrians would pay the heavy war indemnity they had accepted in the treaty after the Battle of Magnesia. Antiochus IV's brother, Seleucus, secured Antiochus' release from the Romans by substituting his own son, Demetrius, **in his place**. By normal succession, Seleucus' son should have succeeded him, but he had been left a hostage in Rome, and Antiochus was aggressive and resourceful. He soon removed Heliodorus from the throne, bypassed Seleucus' son, and placed himself on the throne. He followed immediately after Seleucus and ruled in the **place** of Seleucus. Orthodox Jews referred to him as a "sinful shoot" (1Macc 1:9). Palestine had been under control of the Seleucids ever since the Battle of Panias (198 BIA). Antiochus IV wanted to Hellenize Palestine to make it fit into the culture and administration of the rest of his empire, and there were some leading Jews who were in favor of the idea.

Will not be given to him. Antiochus IV was not a prisoner at Rome. He was a hostage, but he was treated royally and educated by Rome's best standards. After this training he returned as a skilled diplomat. He did not inherit the kingdom by normal means. He got it by the intrigues of two men, Eumenes and Attalus of

Pergamos, two brothers who met Antiochus on his way from Rome and provided him military support of Pergamos needed to secure the throne. He evidently moved very quickly, removed obstacles and people that were in his way, and took control. By the time the people of Antioch could express their opinions it was too late.

He will come quietly and seize the kingdom with flatteries. Antiochus had been educated in Rome. From there he learned diplomacy and political skill. He did not enter Antioch until he had powerful political and military support from other countries. Before the people of the country realized he was going to be king he had killed all the people that stood in his way and had taken his place on the throne.

The **troops** *will be utterly swept before him.* The word rendered **troops** is *zeh-roh-óth* (זרעות), which literally means "arms." The term has a wide range of meanings. It can mean power, wealth, military arms, etc., depending on its contexts. When the prayer of Ben Sira used the term "arm" it referred to the Lord's right arm that would be necessary to subdue the enemy. The author of Dan 11 used the term in a way that was consistent with the prayer.

Also the leader of the treaty. (*Neh-geed buh-reet*, נגיד ברית). Compare with *bah-ah-lay buh-reet ahv-rahm* (בעלי ברית אברם)—"the parties to the contract of Abram."

At the beginning there would not have been a **treaty** with Antiochus, so **the treaty** involved was **the treaty** of the Jews with God. **The leader of this treaty** may have been the high priest, Onias III, a pro-Egyptian, who was killed. Onias was first removed from office in 175 BIA by Antiochus, thanks to a bribe of 400 talents of silver offered by Joshua the brother of Onias (2Macc 4:7-9), who had changed his name to the Greek name of Jason. After Jason had been high priest for three years, another Onias, who had taken the Greek name, Menelaus, offered Antiochus 300 more talents than Jason had bid, but he failed to produce the money. Menelaus then stole golden vessels from the temple to win the favor of Andronicus, one of Antiochus' courtiers. When Onias heard of this he censored Menelaus severely. Menelaus responded by persuading Andronicus to kill Onias, who would have been **the leader of the treaty** mentioned here. Bevan said,

> It is curious that our account does not represent Antiochus himself as hostile at this time to any section of the Jews. So far from being the inhuman monster we expect in a book written to glorify the Maccabean revolt, he is depicted as weeping at the death of the inoffensive Onias.[18]

After Antiochus IV returned from his disappointment in Egypt, when he was confronted by the Romans, he appeared to the Jews as furious and cruel (Dio, 19, Zonaras 9,18).

---

[18] E. R. Bevan, *Seleucus*, p. 171.

TEXT

²³From the time the treaty is made with him he will act deceitfully. He will grow in strength with a small nation.

Daniel	First Testament Intertexts
²⁴He will **come quietly** with the richest men of the region, and he will do that **which his fathers had never** done, neither his grandfathers nor his great grandfathers. He will plunder and scatter booty and their possessions. He will make plans against the fortresses, **but up to a time**.	ᴰᵉᵘᵗ ¹³:⁷ If your brother or . . . **entices** you **secretly**, saying, "Let us go and serve other gods **which** you **have not** known, you nor **your fathers** have known, . . . ⁹you shall not obey him. ˢⁱʳ ³⁶:⁸ Hasten the end, and establish the **appointed time**.
²⁵Then he will stir up his **power** and his mind against the king of the South with a huge army, and the king of the South will assemble for battle with a large and very powerful army, but he will not stand, because they will design plans against him. ²⁶Even those who eat his gourmet food will break him down. His army will be swept away, and many will fall wounded.	ˢⁱʳ ³⁶:³ Shake your [fist] over a foreign people, and they will see your **power.**

COMMENTARY

With a small nation. Charles thought the sentence implied that Antiochus used his own powers to become strong. Therefore, he rendered this passage, "He shall take the field and become strong with a small force,"¹⁹ but the word Charles rendered "force" is the Hebrew *goy* (גוי) or the Greek *éhth-naws,* (ἔθνος) which means either **nation** or "gentile." The sentence must mean something different from what Charles understood. It was not that Antiochus was a king who became strong by means of a small guerrilla army. He actually had a strong army with elephants, chariots, and cavalry. The strength involved was the strength he acquired over or in relationship **with a small nation**, once he succeeded in forming a treaty with this **small nation**.

      The **small nation** was Palestine; the large nation was Syria. In behalf of Syria, Antiochus signed the treaty. In behalf of Palestine, it was the high priest and his wealthy colleagues who signed. Both were officially authorized to make treaties

---

¹⁹ R. H. Charles, *A Critical and Exegetical Commentary on the Book of Daniel* (Oxford: Clarendon Press, 1929), p. 299.

in behalf of their respective **nations**. Once this was accomplished Antiochus exercised strong influence over Palestine.

With the richest men of the region. These were the ones the orthodox called "lawless men" who initiated the negotiations with Antiochus.[20] It was they, rather than Antiochus, who made the first move to obtain a treaty with Antiochus. Chief among these was Joshua, who changed his name to the Greek, "Jason." He became high priest, and asked that Jerusalemites might be called Antiocheans and have a gymnasium in their **city** (2Macc 4:7-12). When Antiochus IV visited Jerusalem Jason gave him a grand welcome (2Macc 4:21-22). Hellenizing Jews signed a treaty with Antiochus that would probably grant Jerusalem the status of a Greek *polis* with the same privileges that other Hellenistic cities had.

Greeks presented a greater threat to Judaism than Babylonians or Persians had ever attempted. The latter nations allowed Jews to practice their own religion and treated them favorably. It was not the military force or the economic deprivation of the Greeks that made the difference. It was the intellectual and cultural pressure that made conservative Jews shudder. Greeks entered the country to compete in the battle of the mind.

When Alexander moved east to conquer as much territory as he could, he not only took military troops and supplies with him. He also included philosophers, educators, artists, scientists, writers, and others that were necessary to spread and establish Greek culture into all the areas he conquered. The Greeks founded and rebuilt cities in every country. They built gymnasia and introduced a whole new way of life to provincial areas. The Greeks founded 30 new **cities** in Palestine alone.

It was not just the introduction of a new way of worship or a new deity. The Greeks brought with them a whole new way of thinking.[21] This whole universalistic movement tended to swallow up provincial countries like Judah. There was an inevitable conflict between this universalism of the Greeks and the exclusivism and apartheid of primitive Judaism. From the Pentateuch, Jews had learned not to make treaties with other nations. Even Israelite tribes were forbidden to intermarry. Being holy meant being segregated from other peoples (Lev 10:10). After the Maccabean victories, however, the Greek culture overwhelmed Judaism and later Christianity. The strong effort made both by Judaism and Christianity to win converts, make proselytes, and spread their religion and culture to the whole world was learned from the Greeks and not the isolationists such as Hosea, Ezekiel, Ezra, and Nehemiah.

Although conservative Jews fought hard against the Greek culture in the Maccabean Rebellion to defend their identity, it was precisely the Greek culture that they first fought and later embraced that enabled both Jews and later Christians to expand the way they both have done. Had they both observed the apartheid doctrines of the Torah they would probably have isolated themselves out of existence.

---

[20] E. R. Bevan, *Seleucus* II, p. 168, also noted this: "It is a cardinal fact to be grasped in estimating the policy of Antiochus Epiphanes that *the initiative* [emphasis his] in the Hellenizing of Jerusalem was not on the side of the King, but of the Jews themselves."

[21] C. C. Cargounis, "Greek Culture and the Jewish Piety: The Clash and the Fourth Beast of Daniel 7," *ETL* 65 (1989):299, 305.

The Hellenistic **cities** that Greeks established had varying privileges. It meant the constitutions had to be changed along Greek lines. **Cities** were allowed to govern themselves by their own representatives according to a revised system. They escaped having royal governors. Being under this program was economically expedient, and allowed more status to the **city**.[22] Many **cities** found this an attractive alternative to being ruled directly by a foreign governor. Greek learning was encouraged, but this also involved abandoning traditional Jewish faith and practices (1Macc 1:11-16) and becoming a member of the world community. Many Jews entered into this new opportunity with great enthusiasm (2Macc 4:13-17). This was the event which was reported as **He shall make a firm treaty with the many for one week [of years]** (Dan 9:27). It was not an unusual political policy.[23]

When trying to conquer a country, it was ordinary military policy to bribe and gain the support of strong, wealthy leaders in the country to support the attack from the inside. This was involved when the Syrians set out to take Palestine away from Egypt. **The richest men of the city** were those Jews who had been taxed the most heavily by the Egyptians and would have welcomed relief. In American history it was the wealthy English colonists in America who added their support to the French as the French fought the English. Wealthy colonists were the ones who had paid the heavy taxes to England and quartered English soldiers. When they entered into a rebellion against the English they pledged to the movement their lives, their fortunes, and their sacred honor. They had all three.

That which his fathers had never done. It is difficult to discover or deduce what things Antiochus did that some of the Seleucids had not already done before him. Antiochus' brother, Seleucus IV, had tried to confiscate the wealth of the temple treasury in Jerusalem, but did not succeed. Although Antiochus the Great had conquered Jerusalem along with other Palestinian cities, he had not attempted to Hellenize the country or plunder the temple in Jerusalem. Antiochus the Great was finally killed trying to plunder a temple of Bel at Elymais. Antiochus IV later made the same attempt and also failed. They both plundered temples, because nations kept their national treasuries in temples, which were also fortresses, and both emperors needed the money to pay for their military programs. Polybius thought this was sacrilegious (Polybius 30.26, 9), but he also reported that Antiochus IV was more generous in honoring the gods at city sacrifices than all of his predecessors (Polybius 26.1, 10-11). He spent money lavishly in ways his ancestors had never done. They were careful in their expenditures, because they were usually short of money. Antiochus IV gathered more booty that enabled him to give generous gifts to those whom he favored. His greatest offense from the viewpoint of Palestinian Jews occurred when he plundered the temple in Jerusalem and confiscated its treasures.

It was not just military acts he committed, however, or different deities that Antiochus worshiped that bothered the Jews. More than other Seleucids he promoted Greek culture in a way that uprooted all earlier cultures, including those

---

[22] E. J. Bickerman, *From Ezra to the Last of the Maccabees* (New York: Schocken Books, 1970), p. 75; Jones, *Cities*, pp. 251-52; "Urbanization." So M. Smith, *Palestinian Parties and Politics that Shaped the Old Testament* (New York: Columbia U. Press, c1971), p. 65.

[23] See further Smith, *Parties*, pp. 57-81.

of **his forefathers**. The author took a Deuteronomic text that had been given in condemnation of Israelites who had wandered from the faith of *their* fathers (Deut 13:6-9) and applied the condemnation to Antiochus in relationship to *his* forefathers. Misappropriating texts to serve the needs of the author was customary for ancient Jewish exegetes. For example, commenting on the passage, **How beautiful upon the mountains are the feet of the one who announces good news, reporting peace** (Isa 52:7), the Dead Sea exegete interpreted the text to mean "**The mountains**. These are 'the prophets,' whose words are **the feet**" (11QMelch 3.II, 15-16; See also Mek *Amalek* 1.96-98).

But up to a time. This was the **time** Ben Sira wanted the Lord to hasten, to hurry and put an end to the expansionist designs of the Seleucids. This is the first time Dan 11 used this expression which became a theme of Dan 11.

Some fortresses were also temples and national treasuries. Antiochus had plans to take these and confiscate their contents. He also conquered fortresses to expand his empire. Some of these plans had already been fulfilled, because all of that which was in the future for Ben Sira was all in the past for the author of Dan 11. The author of this chapter knew that all of the devices and plundering of Antiochus were over. The **time** the author had in mind was the predestined **time** that God had set for Antiochus to be allowed to advance with his plans. After that **time**, he was destined to fail. The author of Dan 11 knew that, because he wrote after the events he "prophesied" had already happened.

Babylonian records tell of the oppressive rule of the Assyrians over Babylon, because of the anger of the gods, but after the predestined **time** of the Assyrians had run out, the gods, Marduk and Nabu, delivered King Nabopolassar from Assyrian bondage.[24] This means that Babylonians, like Jews, attributed their national victories and losses to the deity's anger or pleasure. They also believed the gods predestined the term of office of kings and the length of empires' dominion over other countries. Like the authors of Daniel, they knew that which the gods had predestined after the events had taken place.

He will stir up his power. Antiochus did this because of his plans to engage the king of Egypt in battle. The king of Egypt moved north with a large army, but the king of Egypt had some internal problems that inhibited his progress. His chief advisors were Eulaeus and Lenaeus, and they encouraged him to conquer Syria, assuming that he could. Antiochus, however, **stirred up his power.** That is, he organized his military resources to confront Ptolemy and overpowered the Egyptian army.

---

[24] D. C. T. Sheriffs, "'A Tale of Two Cities'—Nationalism in Zion and Babylon," *TB* 39 (1988):26-27.

TEXT

Daniel

²⁷These two kings [will set] their minds to do evil. Over one table they will speak **deceit**, but they will not succeed, **because there is still an end at the appointed time.**

²⁸He will return to his own **land** with much booty. His mind is against the holy treaty. He will act and return to his **land.**

First Testament Intertexts

^{Hab 2:2} **Because there is still** a vision **for the appointed time**. It will hurry to the end, and it will not deceive.

^{Sir 36:8} Hasten the **end**, and establish the **appointed time**.

^{Isa 10:23} For the Lord Yehowah of armies will make a full and definite **end** in the midst of the land.

^{Isa 28:22} I have heard a full and definite **end** from the Lord Yehowah of armies concerning all the **land.**

COMMENTARY

These two kings. **The kings** involved were precisely the ones that had been at war. One was Antiochus IV, and the other was his nephew Philometer. At a time when Cleopatra's **two** sons, Ptolemy Philometer and Ptolemy Physcon were quarreling over the position of leadership of Egypt, Antiochus IV entered Egypt, pretending to defend the elder brother, the 15 year old Ptolemy VI Philometer, but really plotting to annex Egypt to his empire. Both Antiochus and Ptolemy VI met in a peaceful discussion. Antiochus was pretending that his only reason for being in Egypt was to defend his nephew Ptolemy VI Philometer, and Ptolemy VI pretended that he believed him.[25] That was probably the time when, after Antiochus had successfully occupied Egypt, negotiations between Ptolemy and Antiochus took place.

It is important that the kings failed in their plot. The authors thought they failed because God had all the events of history predestined and a time appointed for the end of all of these adverse activities. The **kings,** of course, could not have known that, and neither could the author, until all of the succeeding events had taken place. Everyone has 20-20 vision when looking toward the past. At this point in time. King Antiochus IV was gaining momentum. He had made a successful military campaign to the south, and he had returned with much booty (1Macc 1:19).

While he was in Egypt, Antiochus captured Pelusium, marched to Memphis, and then sailed down the Nile to Alexandria. At this point Physcon came with Greek

---

[25] J. A. Montgomery, *A Critical and Exegetical Commentary on the Book of Daniel*, (New York: Charles Scribner's Sons, 1927), p. 454, thought the two were Ptolemy's counselors, Eulaeus and Lenaeus, who advised him to go to war with Antiochus, but these counselors were not kings.

envoys to try to settle problems peacefully and determine how Palestine and Syria might be divided without further war (Polybius 28.20-23). Antiochus could not be persuaded. When Antiochus left Egypt, he left a garrison of soldiers at Pelusium and another at Cyprus. When the brothers saw that no matter which of them won the crown, Antiochus was going to rule Egypt, they quickly became reconciled (Livy 45.11). It was in desperation that Physcon sent an embassy to the Roman senate, appealing for immediate help (Livy 44.19).

At an appointed time. A major theme in the narrative about Antiochus IV is that all of his activity was under the control of God who had **appointed a time** to bring this activity to an end. The expression was used several **times** (Dan 11:27, 35, 40; also Dan 12:4, 6, 9, 13). It was Habakkuk who created the terms **appointed time** *(moh-áyd,* מועד*)* and "end" *(kaytz,* קץ*)*, which were applied here to the situation with Antiochus IV. Ben Sira got the line about hastening the end **time** and strengthening the **appointed time** from Habakkuk. The author of Dan 11 probably used both texts to compose his manuscript.

The **appointed time** and **the end** involved was **time** Antiochus IV chose, in his opinion, but according to the author, these events had all been predestined and **appointed** by God long before. The author of Dan 11 knew that because Habakkuk and Ben Sira had prophesied it. Antiochus IV again began a raid toward the South. He wanted to extend his territory to include Egypt for several reasons: 1) He had a huge war debt to pay to the Romans according to a treaty his father had signed with Scipio. He needed more countries to tax so that he could obtain money to pay that debt. 2) In that treaty Antiochus III agreed to give up all of the islands, cities, and lands in the Mediterranean and west of the Taurus Mountains. Antiochus III was further forbidden to try to annex them again. Even if they should choose to desert Rome and come to him, he was not allowed to accept them (Polybius 21.42). This did not allow Antiochus IV much room to expand. The only possibility was Egypt, so Antiochus IV moved south, but in so doing Antiochus IV was taking a risk.

He had already made one successful raid on Egypt, ostensibly with peaceful intentions, and seemed to succeed without Roman interference, but Rome was observing all of his activities. Rome was slow to interfere, because Romans and Greeks were involved in a separate military encounter that required Roman thought and military resources. If Antiochus IV had been sincere in having no purpose for being in Egypt other than to help Philometer obtain his throne, he would have left as soon as Philometer had been admitted into Alexandria, and the brothers had been reconciled. Instead he entered Egypt again with a still greater military force

TEXT

Daniel	First Testament Intertexts
²⁹At an **appointed time**, he will again go south, but the latter [experience] will not be like the first,	Sir 36:8 Hasten the end, and strengthen the **appointed time**. Num 24:23-24 Woe! Who will survive the

³⁰for **the ships of the Kittim** will come against him, and he will be emotionally crushed and turned back.

determination of God?
The ships from the hand of the Kittim [will come] and afflict the Syrians and the Hebrews.

¹ᴹᵃᶜᶜ ¹:¹ It happened after Alexander, the son of Phillip of Macedonia, who went out from the land **of the Kittim**, had defeated Darius, king of the Persians and Medes, he ruled in his place as first [in power] over the Greek Empire.

COMMENTARY

An appointed time. The **appointed time** is not the one planned by Antiochus. It was the one planned by God and revealed to the prophets Habakkuk and Ben Sira.

The latter [experience] will not be like the first. The second invasion into the South (169 BIA) resulted in an encounter with Rome, but not before Antiochus had occupied Egypt, taken Pelusium, Memphis, and Cyprus and moved into Alexandria. He had left a military garrison at Pelusium before he was stopped (*Ant* 12.242-44). He had attacked Egypt both from the sea and the land. Egypt had no defenses to withstand him. Ptolemy Physcon then sent an embassy to Rome, pleading for help (Livy 44.19, 6-14). When the Roman senate learned that Antiochus IV had become the master of Egypt, they had to turn their attention to that problem. They realized that Antiochus' success in Egypt provided a serious danger to Rome. They assigned Popilius to deal with the problem (Polybius, *Frag* 29.2, 1-4). Antiochus was on his way to make another invasion into Egypt. He had already reached Eleusis, just four miles from Alexandria, when he met the Roman envoy, Popilius Laenas.

The ships of the Kittim. In dealing with the crucial passage, Dan 11:29-35, scholars are generally agreed that the reference to **the ships of the Kittim** coming against "him," forcing "him" to withdraw (Dan 11:30), refers to the confrontation of the Roman envoy (**the Kittim**) (1Macc 1:1; 8:5; *Jub* 24.28-29; 37:10; *Ant* 1.128) under the leadership of Popilius with Antiochus Epiphanes ("him") after Antiochus had conquered Egypt.

Instead of mentioning the ships of the Romans, the author recalled a passage from the Torah that began **Woe! Who will survive the determination of God** (Num 24:23)? This was the threat that confronted Antiochus IV, because **the ships of the Kittim** were coming against him (Num 24:24). The author was glad the Romans had come and put a stop to Antiochus IV. He understood it to be a fulfillment of the prophecy in the Torah. It was not just the Romans who brought the **ships of the Kittim** against Antiochus IV. It was God. He determined this action years before. It was a trap that God had set to catch Antiochus at precisely this **appointed time**.

The name **Kittim** is probably taken from the name of a city of Cyprus, called Citium. It is the city from which the philosopher Zeno, the founder of Stoicism, originated. **The ships of the Kittim** came east under the leadership of Popilius to bring Antiochus Epiphanes ("him") to a halt, after Antiochus had conquered Egypt (Livy 45.12, 1-6). Josephus said the name **Kittim** was given by Jews to all the islands of the sea and most of the sea coast areas (*Ant* 1.128.). This is supported by Jerome, *Commentary on Daniel* 11:30-31 (PL 25:569 = CCSL 75A, 922, 11) who said,

> By the terms '*siim*' and '*chethim*' we have rendered as '*triremes*' and 'Romans,' the Hebrews would have us understand 'Italians' and 'Romans.'

Rowley was chief among the scholars who have resisted accepting Romans as the people meant by the Kittim,[26] thinking the Kittim mentioned in the Habakkuk Commentary were more likely the Syrian Greeks.[27] His strongest argument for this position was that the author of the Habakkuk Commentary had used Ps 74, and that the "sign" mentioned was taken from Ps 74:4. He presumed that Ps 74 was a Maccabean psalm, but there is very little reason for that assumption, since the destruction mentioned in that Psalm was the total destruction of the temple, which was not destroyed in the Maccabean period. The most probable date for Ps 74 is after the fall of Jerusalem in 70 IA.[28] Other scholars have found problems with Rowley's identification as well.

There is some reason for confusion, but not very much. The case depends on the direction toward which the Kittim were moving. The Seleucids had moved their capital city to Antioch so that it would be at the center of their kingdom. In the time of Antiochus III (the Great), Syrians controlled many of the islands of the Mediterranean; they held all of coastlands of Asia Minor; they had subjugated part of Europe, north of the Bosphorus (Thrace); and they were extending their influence into Greece. Antiochus III had planned to form a league with Carthage so that he might have military support from Carthage and then move into Italy both from Greece and from Carthage (the east and the south). Had he succeeded in his plan and taken all of Italy and Greece as well as Egypt, his empire would have been greater than that of Alexander the Great.[29] This activity had not gone unnoticed by Rome, which was occupied with Hannibal and the Carthaginians, and was therefore unable to stop the movement **west** by Antiochus. Rome concluded its treaty with Carthage three years before the Battle of Panias (198 BIA).

---

[26] R. North, "Kittim," *Bib* 39 (1948):84-93, for example, argued that the word "kittim" came from the Hebrew *kat, kty(y)m* that means "sect." Therefore, he held there is no need to identify the kittim with the Romans, the Greeks, or any other group. The word means "sectarians," and the War Scroll is liturgy rather than a political document.

[27] H. H. Rowley, *The Zadokite Fragments and the Dead Sea Scrolls* (Oxford: Basil Blackwell, 1952), pp. 72-76.

[28] So Buchanan, "The Fall of Jerusalem and the Reconsideration of Some Dates," *RevQ* 14 (1989):31-48.

[29] See further Buchanan, *New Testament Eschatology* (Lewiston: Mellen Biblical Press, c1993), p. 146.

As soon as Romans had settled things with Hannibal, leaving Rome in charge of North Africa and Spain, they turned directly and steadfastly toward the **east**. They first moved into Greece, then they drove Antiochus out of western Asia Minor, away from the Mediterranean islands, and kept the Syrians out of Egypt. This was an extensive war that took place both on sea and on land, as the Romans moved from one victory to another. The first major sea battle was at Thermopylae, and the last defense of the Syrians was at the Battle of Magnesia. Although Antiochus had extensive designs, when Rome started to move into Asia Minor, Dio said that Antiochus and his generals were doomed to destruction at the beginning (Dio 19.62). Antiochus' loss was tremendous.

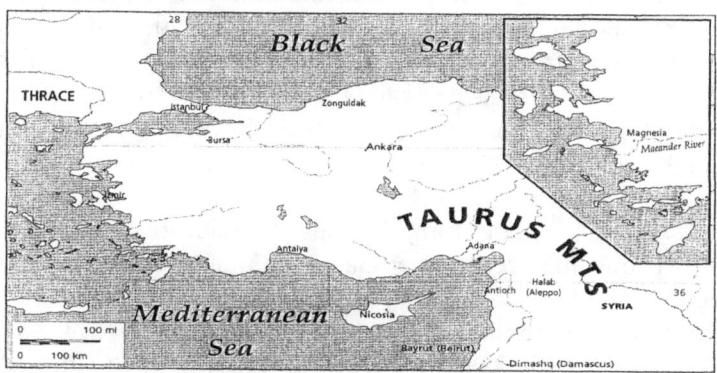

Romans imposed on Antiochus III cruel terms. He had to pay 15,000 Euboean talents, 500 at once and 1,000 each successive year until all was paid. He was not allowed to have more than ten decked ships of war nor any galley rowed by more than 30 oars. He was forbidden to make any aggressive wars with many specified cities or accept any cities that wanted to desert to him (Polybius 21.42, 1-27). Polybius said fortune had made Romans rulers and masters of the civilized world (*oi-koo-méh-nays*, οἰκουμένης Polybius 21.16, 8), and they were extending this empire toward the east.

Unfortunately the crucial passage in Pesher Habakkuk is at the ragged bottom edge of page three, so it is not certain that Pesher Habakkuk actually mentioned the word "east" in its commentary. From the text of Habakkuk are the words, **They fly like eagles, swift to consume. Everyone comes for violence; the direction of their faces is toward the east** (Hab 1:9). Methodologically, the author of this commentary commented on texts from Hab 1:8-9 in a basically sequential order. In his comment on Hab 1:8-9 he had already interpreted **from far away** (Hab 1:9), **to consume** (Hab 1:9), and **like an eagle** (1:9). The next two logical steps would deal with **violence** and **toward the east** (Hab 1:9). He seems to have done just that, but the fragmented bottom of the page quotes it as follows: "With anger [and f]ury of nostrils and rage of nostrils they speak with [all the people, f]or he is the one who said, **the di[rection of their faces is toward the east, and it gath]ers captives [like sand]**" (Hab 1:9; p Hab 3.13-14). This is the way most scholars have filled in the lacunae here.[30] It is not very likely that the author of the Habakkuk

---

[30] M. Burrows, *The Dead Sea Scrolls* (New York: Viking Publishing Co., 1955), p. 366; A. Dupont-Sommer, *The Essene Writings from Qumran*, tr. G. Vermes (New York: The World Publishing Co., c1961), p. 260.

Commentary would have chosen a text that said, **toward the east** if he wanted to describe a movement that was going west, so the Kittim seem most likely to have been Romans.[31] The author of Dan 11 described the Roman activity as a movement that was going **east**, because it really was. He called the Romans **the Kittim**, because it was the Kittim who were determined by God to stop Antiochus. It was both the Torah text and the text from Habakkuk that fit perfectly into his exegesis.

Of course, it is not certain that the Habakkuk Commentary actually said **toward the east**, because the conjectured text is not really there, but it is no longer valid to presume a Syrian movement or date on the basis of Ps 74 as has been done in the past.[32] That which is certain is that by the time of Antiochus III, the Seleucids had already been seriously crippled by Rome, and Antiochus IV was trying to recover some of his country's lost power and prestige when he encountered Rome on the shore of Palestine. It is also certain that the author of Dan 11 appropriately utilized two scriptural texts to report this historical event—one from the Torah and the other from the prophets.

Will come against him. Although the Egyptians could not stop Antiochus IV, the Romans could. The Roman senate sent Gaius Popilius to bring the war in Egypt to an end (Polybius 19.1, 2-4).

Polybius and Livy both thought the event that followed was rather rude on the part of Popilius (Polybius 29.27, 2-13; Livy 45.12). While King Antiochus was on his way to Alexandria, the Roman envoy, Popilius, and his troops arrived. Antiochus greeted him, but before returning his greeting, Popilius handed Antiochus a decree from the senate for him to read. This was obviously an order for him to end the war with Ptolemy at once. Antiochus asked for time to consult with his advisors, but Popilius took a stick cut from a vine that he was carrying.[33] He drew a circle around Antiochus in the sand and told him not to move out of the circle until he had made a decision about the contents of the letter.

Antiochus had little choice. He said he would do that which the Romans demanded. After that statement, Popilius grasped him by the hand, returning his

---

[31] In the War Scroll the Kittim are called the *keet-ee-ay ah-shoór* (כתיי אשור) (*11QM* 1.2). The Kittim in the War Scroll are sometimes mentioned in relationship to *ah-shoór* in ways that either mean that the Kittim are Ashurim or are coterminous with them (*11QM* 1.6; 11.11) and once in relationship with Japeth, and the Kittim (18.2). They are all enemies of the sons of light. The word Kittim comes from the city Citium in Cyprus, which was under control of the Syrian Greeks before the Battle of Magnesia and again before the Romans forced Antiochus IV to remove his troops from Egypt and Cyprus. The Kittim of the Habakkuk Commentary were clearly Romans. During the time when Jews were in military conflict with the Greeks and the Romans, there no longer existed a nation called Assyria. Assyria had been conquered by the Medes, which, in turn, was captured by the Persians. Then the Greeks ruled that area until the Romans took control of the entire area. During the period when Daniel and the scrolls were written Jews were in conflict with the Syrians and the Romans. *Ergo, Ah-shoór* (*11QM*) or the *Ah-toór* (*4Q426*) means Syria, rather than Assyria. The conflict during Hasmonean times was between Egypt and Syria—not between Egypt and Assyria.

[32] See further Buchanan, "The Fall of Jerusalem," pp. 31-48.

[33] This "stick" was probably not just some vine Popilius cut with his pocketknife. Roman officers often carried a twisted vine stick as an emblem of office. See further G. Webster, *The Roman Imperial Army* (Totowa, N.J.: Barnes & Noble Books, 1985), p. 130.

original greeting. Popilius gave Antiochus a fixed number of days to move all of his troops into Syria, and he later ordered him to move his troops out of Cyprus.[34] Antiochus had been badly hurt, and he complained bitterly, but he had to comply (Polybius 19.27, 2-10). Antiochus stopped at Jerusalem on his way back from this experience. This was one of the times he offended the Jews by his actions there.

He will be emotionally crushed and turned back. This was a terrible shock to Antiochus. He had planned these movements for years. He had been succeeding, step-by-step. He was on his way to Egypt to to conduct the final campaign that would put Egypt under his control. Then, just four miles from Alexandria, the Romans stopped him. What a revolting experience! Polybius said that before the Romans interfered, Ptolemy's kingdom had almost been crushed out of existence (Polybius 19.27, 11-13).

TEXT

[30b]He will become furious against the holy treaty, so he will act and give instruction for those who abandoned the holy treaty.

COMMENTARY

He will become furious against the holy treaty. The details are not given. Antiochus IV was moving toward annexing Egypt when Rome interfered. He had previously made a **treaty** with the Jews. Details of that **treaty** are also not spelled out in detail in any of the literature. That was **the treaty** made about 171 BIA which probably made Judah a Hellenistic *polis*, with all of the economic privileges associated with that cultural institution (1Macc 1:11-15; Dan 9:27). Voluntary treaties between nations usually have terms on both sides. One nation agrees to do some things and in exchange the other nation agrees to do other things. It is understandable why Antiochus IV should have been angry against the Romans and the treaty his father had made with the Romans, but here it says that he became angry with the Jews and **the holy treaty**. **The holy treaty** was not the Hellenistic **treaty** Jews had made with Antiochus; it was **the treaty** the pious Jews had made with God. Something happened in his dealing with the Romans that made him realize that the fundamentalist Jews were his enemies.

The picture became complex as soon as Egypt slipped out of his hands. From then on his southernmost territory was Judah, and he began to realize that Judah was divided with many Jews being pro-Egyptian. Not only that but there were many pro-Egyptian Samaritans at the same time as well as pro-Egyptian trans-Jordanian Tobiads.[35] Tobiads had been strong pro-Egyptian leaders in Trans-Jordan, Samaria, and Judah. With the rise of Antiochus IV the Tobiad brothers of Hyrcanus

---

[34] The Romans had forbidden Antiochus III to occupy any of the islands in the Mediterranean Sea. Antiochus IV had obviously ignored that command.
[35] On this see M. Daise, "Samaritans, Seleucids, and the Epic of Theodotus," *JSP* 17 (1998):31-51 and V. Tcherikover, "The Tobiads in Light of the Zenon Papyri," *Emerging Judaism* ed. M. E. Stone and D. Satran (Minneapolis: Fortress Press, c1989), pp. 77-99.

turned pro-Seleucid. The high priest Onias III supported Hyrcanus and was pro-Egyptian. The high priest Jason was a Tobiad, but he became pro-Seleucid. These new converts might easily be turned back.

There had been much resistance to Alexander the Great's invasion of Samaria. Samaritans burned Alexander's praetor, Andromachus, alive, while Alexander was in Egypt.[36] There continued to be at least two groups of Samaritans, just as there were two competing groups of Jews. One of these became pro-Seleucid, but the other remained pro-Ptolmaic. After Antiochus had plundered Jerusalem and taken the wealth of its temple, Antiochus appointed two governors over the area: 1) Philip over Jerusalem and 2) Andronicus over Gerizim (2Macc 5:22-23). It would not have been necessary to appoint a governor over Gerizim if all of the Samaritans had been pro-Seleucid. When being pro-Ptolmaic meant being pro-Roman Antiochus IV became anxious for his own national security. Some of these pro-Egyptian Jews and possibly Samaritans may have been stirring up trouble for him with the Romans.

Prior to this time Jews in Palestine seemed eager to participate in the new Hellenism that was proposed in the treaty. The high priest, Jason, even sent money to sacrifice to Hercules at Hellenistic games (2Macc 4:18-20), and many Jews did not hesitate to participate in pagan worship (1Macc 1:52; 2Macc 4:13-20). Jews had been Hellenized before the time of Antiochus IV. As early as the fourth century BIA Aristotle told of a certain Palestinian Jew he met who was a Greek "not only in language, but also in soul."[37] Several cities and villages in Palestine had become Hellenized by Maccabean times. Bickerman said,

> Even in the villages there must have been persons able to draft a contract in Greek, or to write a request in the style required for a Greek Petition.[38]

This was not classical Greek culture but a culture that had been mingled with Oriental culture. Antiochus had many reasons for thinking things were going well in Jerusalem. He thought the Jews were supporting his program and upholding his treaty. So long as he ruled Egypt he did not have to worry about a group of Jews being pro-Egyptian. According to Smith,

> In the 260 years from Alexander's death to the conquest of Jerusalem by the Roman general Pompey, there were at least two hundred campaigns fought in or across Palestine. This military history alone shows that no part of the country can have escaped Greek influence.[39]

---

[36] So Quintus Curtius Rufus, *History of Alexander* 4.8, 10.
[37] Josephus reported this from one of Aristotle's students, Clearchus (*Contra Apion* 1.180)
[38] Bickerman, *From Ezra*, p. 59.
[39] Morton Smith, "Hellenization," *Emerging Judaism*, pp. 111-112.

During the Ptolmaic period, prior to 198 BIA Jerusalem was captured ten or twelve times.[40] It was hardly possible for Jerusalem to avoid becoming a cosmopolitan city, but it always contained conservative, orthodox Jews. Jerusalem recovered from its many military lootings primarily because of the extensive financial support it received from wealthy Jews in the diaspora.

Those who abandoned the holy treaty. **Those** are the ones who were guilty of having broken **the treaty** Moses made with God. They were treaty-breakers. Here a clear distinction was made between the ones who observed **the holy treaty** and the ones who had **abandoned the holy treaty** (1Macc 1:11-15). **Those who abandoned the holy treaty** embraced **the treaty** made with Antiochus. Among **those who abandoned the holy treaty** were the priests, including the high priests (2Macc 4:13-15). Since there was no Jewish governor or king at that time, the high priest was the local ruler who functioned in behalf of the Syrian king, Antiochus, according to **the treaty** made with him.

Jason, the former Tobiad high priest, heard a false rumor that Antiochus had died, so he took advantage of the time. He entered Jerusalem with 1,000 soldiers to attack Menelaus, the acting high priest. In the conflict many Jewish citizens were killed (1Macc 5:5-10). Shortly after this Antiochus entered Jerusalem with troops. Antiochus was furious against the observers **of the holy treaty**, and he organized and instructed his local supporters. These were **the ones who had abandoned the holy treaty**.

The civil war in Jerusalem, however, was fought between the followers of Jason and those of Menelaus, both of whom had been involved in making a **treaty** with Antiochus. The first blood in the streets of Jerusalem was not drawn by Antiochus, but by the Jews themselves. Neither party to the civil war consisted of observers of **the holy treaty** Jews had made with God. Both Jason and Menelaus had been pro-Seleucid Hellenizers. It is possible that Jason was able to organize the anti-Seleucid, pro-Egyptian Jews in his war against Menelaus, and these may have coincided with the conservative Jews, but that is not reported. If something like that had not happened, Antiochus came to Jerusalem without taking part in the war between Jason and Menelaus. He started a new conflict. His conflict was with the Jews who were faithful to **the holy treaty**. These had apparently done something that irritated him very much.

Both Menelaus and Jason were his friends, and they were the ones who had made **the treaty** with him. He may have entered Jerusalem under the pretense that he was supporting the faction that he thought was justified. Here it was Menelaus; in Egypt it was Ptolemy Philometer. The war that had gone on in Jerusalem, however, was between two Hellenizers, Jason and Menelaus, so that should not have made Antiochus angry with the conservative Jews, because apparently they were involved only as victims.

Antiochus was very angry with Rome, and he may have simply transferred his hostility from Rome to Palestine at this point. If that was so, he already knew there were two groups of Jews in Palestine. If he had not realized that earlier, then something happened in this experience, other than Jason's rebellion, which drew his

---

[40] Smith, "Hellenization," p. 110.

attention to the pious Jews. If he was going to function according to **the treaty** he had made with Jews he would have to fight those who observed **the holy treaty** instead. That problem became more evident to him as the conflict became more serious.

Some Jews had evidently broken the firm **treaty** other Jews had made with Antiochus, and he had just suffered the consequences. What had they done? Some of them supported Egypt at the time Antiochus was trying to annex Egypt to his empire.[41] Even without a **treaty**, when Antiochus III fought against the Egyptians, the Jews had come to his aid. Since Antiochus III's son had a **treaty** with the Jews, he thought he had a right to expect at least as much support as his father received, but he evidently did not receive it. They may even have opposed Antiochus IV in another way.

According to Josephus and the Books of the Maccabees, there were powerful, wealthy Jews in Judah who made a treaty with Antiochus, but there were also at the same time in Judah other orthodox Jews who resented **the treaty** and never intended to observe it. There were also many pious, orthodox Jews in Rome at the time. These were Jews who observed **the holy treaty** and would have supported the faithful observant Jews in Palestine in their conflict with the Hellenizers.

What did the pious Jews do to arouse Antiochus' anger? Was it only that they supported the Egyptians when they were in conflict with Antiochus? How did they support the Egyptians? Did they inform the Romans about his activities? Did they break their **treaty** of support for Antiochus and instead support his enemies? Did they actually give the Romans military support and intelligence? When Physcon came to Rome to get aid from Rome in putting a stop to Antiochus (Livy 44.19), there were there already Jews in Rome. Were some of these complaining against the activities of Antiochus? Did they support the Egyptians in their appeal to the Roman Senate? The literature does not say, so the reader can only wonder. When Jason and Menelaus, both friends of Antiochus, killed many innocent citizens of Jerusalem, where could the injured Jews have gone for support? Surely not to Antiochus.

It is clear that the author of Dan 11 was on the side of the Romans. He interpreted their movement as the predestined activity of God. It was the fulfillment of scripture both from the Torah and from the prophets. He represented those Jews who supported both Rome and Egypt in opposition to Antiochus IV.

Antiochus had made a treaty with the nation. This **treaty** was made with legally authorized leaders of Palestine, namely the high priests. He expected the entire nation to observe it, but when he met the Romans near the border of Egypt, he may have realized that there were some Palestinian Jews that either never accepted the terms of **the treaty** emotionally, or if they did, they later abandoned it. When Antiochus was confronted by the Roman delegate he learned that Egypt had turned to Rome for help. He may have learned that at the same time the orthodox Jews and orthodox Samaritans had been helping Egypt and had also turned to Rome for help. Rome was Antiochus' problem, but Rome was ready to force him to leave Egypt because Egyptians and possibly nationalistic Jews in Rome had asked the Roman government to do it. In which case Antiochus would have been angry with the pious

---

[41] So E. R. Bevan, *Seleucus* II, p. 171.

Jews as well as the Egyptians and the Romans. Since he had a **treaty** with the Jews he would have considered this action unfaithfulness to the treaty and sabotage.

Treaties that have been mutually made are expected to be broken mutually and not just abandoned without notice. Faithfulness to **treaty** has long been considered a virtue among Israelites, Jews, and Samaritans. It is called "steadfast love" (*ah-hav-áh*, אהבה and *khéh-sehd*, חסד), but orthodox Jews would have argued that they were not responsible for **the treaty** with Antiochus, because they had never made it in the first place. They were too faithful to **the treaty** made with God to have participated in a **treaty** with Antiochus. It was only after his experience with the Roman delegate that Antiochus IV began his severe enforcement of the terms of **the treaty**, which involved Jewish conversion to Hellenistic practice. This may have resulted from the insight he had learned from his experience in Egypt. Whatever the details of orthodox, pro-Egyptian activity were at that time, it is clear that there was a subversive group at work. Antiochus IV learned of it if he had not known it before. He tried to suppress it, and the longer he resisted it the stronger it became.

There was still another factor involved in all of these events. Antiochus needed money. He had expected to annex Egypt to his empire and tax it heavily to obtain this money. Once the Romans put an end to that scheme, he still needed money, and he knew that there was lots of gold in the temple at Jerusalem. He hardly needed any other excuse for plundering the temple at Jerusalem. He had plundered temples before to obtain money for his military activities. He entered the conflict already started in Jerusalem partly, at least, to gain access to the finances available there.

After he had settled the war in Jerusalem and plundered the temple, Antiochus left Jerusalem undisturbed for two years (1Macc 1:29). By that time he knew of the factions in Judah. He also probably learned that one faction of Jews was aiding and abetting the Romans and the Egyptians. Politically this provided a problem for him, because he had worked zealously to bring some unity into his empire that had many diverse languages, customs, and political views. The unifying factor was Hellenism and religion. Prior to his confrontation with the Roman delegation, he had been rather moderate in his expectations of Judah, but after he had lost all control of Egypt, Palestine became his southern-most state and a necessary defense for Syria. It was important that this state be absolutely loyal to him. It was with this realization that he sent a delegation to Jerusalem to begin his religious cleansing. He knew he had a loyal base of Hellenizers in Jerusalem with whom to begin.

Once he learned what the situation was, he organized the Hellenizers and instructed them in the action that must be taken to make **the Hellenizing treaty** effective. This meant a declaration of war between Antiochus and the Hellenizers, on one side, and those who observed **the holy treaty**, on the other. The Maccabees were in the forefront of the second group. During his rebellion, Judas was able to make a **treaty** with Rome and elicit Roman support. One of the reasons that this was easy for Judas to do may have been that Judas had not been the first to talk with Rome about Roman support of the Jewish rebellion.

While Rome was in war, first with Carthage and then with Phillip, Antiochus IV had a lot of freedom to expand his empire, knowing that the Romans were too deeply involved in another war to interfere. He ignored **the treaty** his father had made with Rome and added many elephants to his army and ships to his navy. He also fortified Cyprus (Appian, *Roman History* 11.7, 46). Rome had noticed this, but could not prevent it until the war with Phillip was over. That occurred just before Popilius provided Antiochus with the letter from the senate. During that time, however, Romans might have been making secret negotiations with some Jews in Rome to encourage rebellion against Antiochus.

Whatever happened pointed up a clear and hostile division among Palestinian Jews. Antiochus' supporters were the Hellenizers; his enemies were the pious conservative Torah-observing Jews. The latter ones were pro-Egyptian and participated in the Hasmonean rebellion. While one group of Jews was negotiating with Antiochus for a gymnasium in Jerusalem, the other may have been negotiating with Rome to drive the Syrian Greeks out of the country.

Jewish loyalty to foreign **treaties** had no long-term record of being impeccable. Jewish ancestors had previously supported Cyrus against the Babylonians and later Alexander the Great against the Persians. By Maccabean times Jews had become skilled subversives. It is also not a new experience for Jews to be divided on a political issue. As early as the time of Jeremiah there were pro-Egyptian and pro-Babylonian Jews in Palestine at the same time. Also in pre-Maccabean times there were pro-Ptolmaic and pro-Seleucid forces contesting for the high priesthood. In Daniel we have only the orthodox Jewish report, because it is always the victors who determine what literature will be preserved. They canonize the literature. If we had a Hellenistic Jewish report and also a Syrian report of the feelings and justification Antiochus had, we might judge the situation more objectively. When there is only one-sided evidence it is necessary for historians to conjecture the other side, but conjectures should never be confused with facts.

Jews and Christians have both been famous for their sectarianism and lack of unity.[42] The Jews who made **the treaty** with Antiochus were undoubtedly happy with it. It represented advancement, culture, civilization, and economic advantages, but the happier one party became the more resentful another party became. Those who made **the** firm **treaty** with Antiochus IV did not speak for all Judaism.

TEXT

Daniel	First Testament Intertexts (Samaritan)
[31] Then the **powerful ones** among us will rise up and plunder the temple and the fortress.	Sir 36:6 Glorify the hand, and strengthen the right **arm**

---

[42] Jews sometimes exaggerate these divisions by saying wherever there are two Jews there are three opinions. The same tendency applies also to Christians.

347

They will turn away the continual offering and provide the abomination of desolations

³²Those who break the treaty he will seduce with deceptions, but the **people** that **knows** its

God will be strong and **act**.

³³Those who **instruct** the **people will teach** the many,

and they **will stumble** with the sword, in flames, in captivity, and with plunder for a time, ³⁴but when they **stumble**, they will receive a little help. Many will join them with deceptions, ³⁵and some of the

instructors **will stumble** to test, purify, and whiten them until

^{Sir 36:5} They will **know** just as we **know**.

^{Sir 36:8} Who can say to you, "What **are you doing?**"

^{Sir 36:17} All the ends of the earth **will know**.

^{Deut 32:35} For the day of vengeance and reckoning, / for a time when their foot **will stumble** / for near is the day of their calamity, / and haste is destined for them. / ³⁶for Yehowah will judge his **people**, / and he will comfort his servants.

^{Lev 26:37} They **will stumble**, each man with his brother, as if from before the sword, although no one pursues. None of you will be able to stand before your enemies.

^{Isa 3:8} Jerusalem has **stumbled**; Judah has fallen.

^{1Sam 2:4} The bows of the mighty will be crushed; those who **stumble** will gird on strength; ⁵ those who are satisfied with bread will **stumble**, and those who are famished will cease [being hungry].

the time of the end, because there is still the appointed time.

^{Hab 2:2} **Because there is still** a vision **for the appointed time**. It

will hurry to the **end**, and it will not **deceive**.

^{Sir 36:8(Heb)} Hasten **the end time**, and establish **the appointed time**.

COMMENTARY

Powerful ones. Literally, the "arms" (*zeh-roh-eem*, זרעים). In Dan 11:15, 22 this expression refers to forces or troops, and it probably means that here, but it is not clear who these **powerful ones** were. The confusing preposition is *mee-méh-noo* (ממנו) which can mean either "from us" or "from him." It could mean that the troops that were from Antiochus were the ones who acted, or it could mean the forces of the Jewish nation who supported Antiochus were themselves the ones who actually committed these acts, which were offensive to orthodox Jews. The text says that Antiochus **gave instruction for those who had abandoned the holy contract. The powerful ones among us arose and defiled the holy fortress. They turned away the continual burnt offering and provided the abomination of desolations** (Dan 11:30-31). This probably happened in late December 168 BIA(1Macc 1:54; 4:42-47).

The powerful ones could have been the same as the lawless ones (1Macc 1:11) and the **wealthiest men of the region** (Dan 11:24) who were impious in other ways, according to the orthodox law observers among the Jews. It was the orthodox Jews who won the struggle and edited the literature. We have only their point of view. The liberal Jews who had supported Antiochus in his program were the ones who behaved like gentiles, abandoning their traditional practices, breaking the holy treaty, and modifying their way of life to accommodate to their needs to work together with gentiles. At the same time others believed the Hellenizers were breaking the treaty made with God in order to keep the treaty made with Antiochus. Whether this action was actually performed by the Syrians, themselves, who were with Antiochus or by the Jews in Jerusalem who supported Antiochus, the author of Dan 11 was an orthodox Jew who believed that which was done was terribly wicked.

Plundered the temple. **Plundering the temple** meant that Antiochus entered **the temple**, stripped **the temple** of valuable things, such as vessels, the golden altar, the table for shew bread, and all of the silver and gold that was stored or hidden there (1Macc 1:20-24). This was not the only time one of the Greek kings **plundered** a **temple** or palace. Before Antiochus IV was born Antigonus **plundered** the treasures of Ecbatana and stripped the palace of its silver tiles.[43] Other Seleucids **plundered temples**, because they were the national treasuries where the money was kept. Antiochus Epiphanes was known as the "manifest deity." This means that he was the human agent or apostle of the deity, or the deity incarnate. Since he held this office he thought that he deserved the treasures of all of **the temples** in his empire. During his reign he confiscated the wealth of other **temples** in Syria.[44] **The Jerusalem temple** was just another national treasury to add to his list.[45]

---

[43] E. R. Bevan, *Seleucus* II, p. 47.
[44] E. R. Bevan, *Seleucus* II, p. 172.
[45] Antiochus IV was not the only, or even the first, Hellenistic king to be accepted as an agent of the deity. Before him were Alexander the Great, Antigonus (310 BIA), Demetrius (307 BIA), Ptolemy, Seleucus, and Antiochus II. (Bevan I, p. 126, 174-75).

They will turn away the continual offering. These powerful ones defiled the temple so that faithful Jews could no longer offer their daily sacrifices there. Liberal Jews were willing to replace traditional Jewish sacrifices with pagan sacrifices (1Macc 1:52). The holy temple had become a temple dedicated to the Olympian Zeus (2Macc 6:2). The powerful Hellenistic Jews may have been the ones who actually **turned away the continual offering** and put an "abomination of desolations" in its place. The fundamentalist Jews probably resented the Hellenizing Jews as much as the Syrian Greeks themselves.

The expression, here translated "abomination of desolations," *hah-shee-koóts meh-shoh-máym* (השקרץ משומם) is an intentional distortion of a non-Jewish religious term so as to defame the worshippers. Olympian Zeus was known as the "Lord of Heaven" (*bah-áhl hah-shah-máh-yim*, בעל השמים). The implication was that this so-called "Lord of Heaven" was really an abomination of desolations. In a similar way Jonathan's son's name was *eésh bah-áhl* (איש בעל), which means, "man of Baal." Later Jewish editors changed it to *eésh bóh-sheth* (איש בשת), "man of shame." The Olympian Zeus was the victim of similar defamation.

According to the rabbis the abomination of desolation was a statue (*tséh-lehm*, צלם) that was set up in the temple (*mTaan* 4.6). Others said that the offense was set up on the altar (1Macc 1:54). This may have been a statue of Zeus. When the Roman emperor Caligula (Gaius) tried to use military force to set up a statue of himself in the temple at Jerusalem, it created a national resistance that attracted tens of thousands of Jews to Ptolemais to prevent the Roman delegate, Petronius, from executing his orders. That Roman attempt may have been the cause of Gaius' own death (*War* 2.184-203).[46] Jews of that day identified the proposed action to have been an antitype of the abomination of desolations set up by the instructions of Antiochus IV Epiphanes.

Those who break the treaty. These were not the ones who **broke the treaty** with Antiochus, but those who **broke the treaty** with God. The proximity of the plural subjects here suggests that the ones **who broke the treaty** were also the **ones who** turned away the continual offering and put up an abomination of desolations. That is not the only possibility. First Maccabees blamed Antiochus himself for having set up the abomination of desolations (1Macc 1:54), and the OG translated these words "the powerful ones from him." Even if local Jews actually performed this offensive act, they would have done it as agents of Antiochus, so Antiochus, as the legal principal, would correctly be blamed for it.

Whatever the precise meaning of the ambiguous preposition (*mee-méh-noo* ממנו), the facts are that Antiochus wanted all of this done, and there were liberal Jews in Jerusalem who were eager to promote the program. After the confrontation with the Romans Antiochus probably enforced vigorously the treaty that had been made earlier. Prior to that time most Jews without any open revolt were rapidly accepting the treaty. Liberal Jews may or may not actually have performed the offense, but they seemed not to have objected to it. There were also orthodox Jews who were

---

[46] See further Buchanan, *The Book of Revelation: Its Introduction and Prophecy* (Lewiston: The Edwin Mellen Press, c1993), p. 335.

horrified by the defilement of the temple who were willing to die rather than participate in the program. The resignation of which Bickerman wrote effected only the Hellenizers.[47] Historians have to conjecture from the one-sided reports the feelings of the other side, and this cannot be done with confidence.

The people who knows its God. Ben Sira made a distinction between the faithful and the gentiles **who** did **not know** that there was no **God** except Yehowah. The author of Dan 11 was true to the intertext when he used this expression to distinguish between those who broke the treaty and the **people who knows its God.** These are the ones who were encouraged to **be strong and act**. Ben Sira's prayer urged **God** to hasten the end time, so that people could not ask what **God** was doing with his time. Where was his action? Correspondingly, those who know their **God** should hurry and act as well.

Smith-Christopher thought that during the midst of the Maccabean war, when Jews were fighting for their independence, that the author meant by "action" the work of rabbis who sat in their swivel chairs and studied scripture, encouraging passive resistance. The use of the term "sword" here means nothing more violent than "policing power," and "plunder" meant "massive taxation," according to Smith-Christopher.[48]

However much twentieth century Christians wished that all of our religious ancestors were quietistic pacifists, and all teachers and rabbis were opposed to violence, Jews and Christians have thousands of years of history to prove the contrary. In NT times many military leaders were called such academic names as sofists, "scholars" or "teachers" (*soh-fees-tai*, σοφισταί, *War* 1.648-56). For example, the Jewish teachers, Judas and Mattathias, whose disciples chopped down the Roman eagle were labeled "sophists." They had reputations of being astute experts on the law (*War* 1.648, 56). Another military leader, Judas of Galilee was also called a "sophist" (*War* 2.117-18). His son, Menahem, led some followers to Masada where they broke into Herod's arsenal and took the needed weapons for a military rebellion. They returned to Jerusalem where Menahem directed the siege of the palace and conducted himself like a king of Jerusalem until he was put to death by another pretender, Eleazar. The military leader, Menahem, like his father, Judas, was called a "sophist" (*War* 2.433-45). This is not surprising. The scripture which they studied to become sophists defined their God as "Yehowah of armies," and rules for conducting war are given in the Torah (Deut 20:1-21:14).

There was no separation of religion and the state in those days, so political leaders were also expected to be religious teachers, and teachers left their legal research while war was going on to become involved in military action. Becoming strong did not mean they were obtaining more graduate degrees. The action taken by the teachers reported here was not academic. They were clearly involved in the use of the sword for a more active role than "police power," and "plunder" was not the equivalent of "taxation." The Book of Daniel was being written while the Maccabean Rebellion was going on. It was almost impossible for anyone in the little

---

[47] Bickerman, *From Ezra*, p. 95.
[48] D. L. Smith-Christopher, *The Book of Daniel* (Nashville: Abingdon, c1996), pp. 143-44.

state of Judah at that time to have been emotionally removed from it all. Describing the attitudes of Jews evident in the Dead Sea Scrolls. Eisenman and Wise said,

> The violence, xenophobia, passionate nationalism and concern for Righteouness and the Judgements of God are evident throughout. Though these may have a metaphoric meaning as well as an actual one, it is impossible to think that those writing these texts were not steeped in the ethos of a militant army of God, and hardly that of a peaceful, retiring community. Their spirit is unbending, uncompromising.[49]

During the Maccabean period there were in Palestine strongmen in some of the smaller cities that were away from the major roads and cities. These strongmen had their own military support and sometimes had enough power to drive away tax collectors and other foreign groups that wanted to control the nation. One of these well-known strongmen was the Ammonite, Tobias. Another was Herod the Great's father, Antipater. A third was probably Mattathias, the father of the five Hasmonean sons.[50] He evidently had enough military power to begin a resistance movement and had enough influence to gather additional volunteers from the pious law abiding Jews of the nation to keep it functioning as a guerrilla military force. The first of his sons to lead the military troops was Judas the Maccabee.

This group of individuals is contrasted to the impious ones who broke the treaty with God. Throughout the Hasmonean period these two groups were fighting among themselves while the Hasmoneans were warring against the Syrian Greeks. While some Jews were breaking treaty with God others were standing firm and acting to vindicate their beliefs. Some of these were Hasmoneans and their followers. Collins noted defensively, "Daniel never refers unambiguously to the armed struggle."[51] That is true to the extent that he also never refers unambiguously to Antiochus IV Epiphanes, Antiochus the Great, the Romans, Alexander the Great, any of the chief priests, or Cyrus of Persia. That is the nature of the literature. It is gauged in terms of drama, employing characters like "horn," "male goat," "ram," "king of the North" "or "king of the South," "beasts," "human beings," and other such code terms as these.

Instead of military conflicts battles are described in terms of court cases and rocks that break up statues. It does not take much ingenuity, however, to realize that the Book of Daniel is very closely related to the Hasmonean Rebellion. The Hasmonean Rebellion could hardly have been ignored by contemporary authors who wrote about events of their day. Jews held Judas in a status similar to Moses who was leading the sheep during the wilderness period (*1Enoch* 89.31). Later Judas was recognized as one of the sheep who had a great horn (*1Enoch* 90.9). In the eyes of

---

[49] R. H. Eisenman and M. Wise, *The Dead Sea Scrolls Uncovered* (Rockport: Element, c1992), p. 30; See also Buchanan, *The Gospel of Matthew* (Lewiston: The Edwin Mellen Press, c1996) I, pp. 497-98.
[50] See further S. Schwartz, "A Note on the Social Type and Political Ideology of the Hasmonean Family," *JBL* 112(1993):305-309.
[51] J. J. Collins, *A Commentary on the Book of Daniel* (Minneapolis: Fortress Press, c1993), p. 3; Eisenman and Wise, *Scrolls Uncovered*, 85.

his contemporaries he was destined to be one whose memory would be for a blessing "until the age [to come]" (1Macc 3:7).

Even Collins noticed the practical, earthly dimension to holy war theology. On the Day of the Lord, the Lord would punish the troops and kings both in heaven and on earth (Isa 34:21), but Collins called this "pre-Israelite mythology."[52] He thought the War Scroll, in its earliest stages, reflected political, nationalistic theology,[53] but he evidently thought later Jews transcended this narrow, nationalist point of view. He admitted that there seemed to have been a coincidence between Israel's religion and the political and national boundaries of the nation, but nevertheless,

> The group to which the author of Daniel belonged did not wish to identify with the nation Israel either in a political or ethnic or geographical sense.[54]

Collins did not prove this. He just decreed it. He offered only two reasons for his opinion:

1) In Dan 12, he said, those who are raised to life in the resurrection are not identified with the nation of Israel. The text does not say that they are not. It just assumes the reader realizes that the resurrection is only for believers. The silence on the subject, however, gave Collins an opportunity to import his own desires into the text. The mother whose seven sons were killed by Antiochus was sure that they would be raised up on the resurrection, but for the pagan Antiochus, **there will be no resurrection to life** (2Macc 7:14).
2) "There is a wide agreement that Daniel refers to the Maccabeans in a derogatory manner as 'a little help' in xi 34."[55] This assumes that if many people hold any opinion, they must be right, no matter what their reasons are. Facts and logic, however, will finally win, and the "wide agreement" with which Collins identifies himself is getting narrower. Years ago there was "a wide agreement" that the world was flat. That agreement is also becoming smaller.

Those who instruct the people will teach the many. Ben Sira's prayer wanted all **people** to know. Knowledge, however, would not increase unless some would **teach** or **instruct**. The expression **the many** is a technical term that means "the congregation." Among those who stood firm were the orthodox rabbis who taught the congregations. They were not the same rabbis as those who had left their synagogues early on the Sabbath to take part in the Hellenistic activities of the gymnasium. Instead, by the orthodox, they were called the *mahs-keé-lay áhm* (משכילי עם) **those who make the people shine**. These were the ones who encouraged

---

[52] J. J. Collins, "The Mythology of Holy War in Daniel and the Qumran War Scroll: A Point of Translation in Jewish Apocalyptic," *VT* 25 (1975):598.
[53] Collins, "Mythology," p. 610.
[54] Collins, "Mythology," p. 603.
[55] Collins, "Mythology," p. 603.

the faithful to hold fast by instructing them in the Zionistic meaning of the scriptures.

Charles thought the wise could not have been **teachers**, because they were the Chasidim.[56] He assumed, of course that Chasidim could not have been **teachers**.[57] By the same logic he also assumed that Chasidim could not have been pro-Hasmonean soldiers. Collins, on the other hand, thought Chasidim could not have been **teachers** because they were **mighty warriors** (1Macc 2:14).[58] This all assumes that warriors could not be wise, and pious people could not also be **teachers** and warriors as well. This is not borne out by Medieval Jewish literature which pictures many messiahs who were **teachers** and also military leaders.[59]

Among the militants whom Josephus described as zealots, zealot chiefs, and sicarii who opposed the rule of Rome were the **teachers**, Judas and Matthias, who prompted their students to cut down the golden eagle at the gate of Jerusalem. Some of these were the ones who fought in the war and taught the Torah and Jewish traditions against the dictates of the Hellenists. Some of these warriors were **teachers**; some were Chasidim.

They will stumble. This does not mean these instructors would **stumble** in the faith but that they would suffer and die for their faith. They would teach the forbidden scriptures, encourage mothers to circumcise their sons. They would be caught doing these things and so they would die by the sword, being burned at stake, and being plundered. The Hebrew word for **stumble** is *neék-sheh-loó* (נכשלו). There is an intentional phonetic play on words here, the *mahs-kee-leém neék-sheh-loó*. The liberal Jews who broke their treaty with God and cooperated with Antiochus IV opposed these instructors and tried to lure them away from their rigorous positions with flatteries. The rabbis **stumbled** and fell in their suffering but this suffering was believed to cancel sins and lay up treasures in the heavenly treasury. This would purify and whiten both the rabbis and their congregations.

For **stumble** the intertext has *tah-moót* (תמוט) (Deut 32:35), rather than *neék-sheh-loó*, so the author may not have used that text. The reason for associating Deut 32:35-36 with Dan 11:33 is that both deal with judgment, **stumbling**, and the Lord's people. Instead of **the day of vengeance** (*luh-yóhm nah-káhm,* ליום נקם) the MT has **mine is vengeance** (*leé nah-káhm,* לי נקם). The Samaritan text, however, is followed by the OG, so it appears that the MT reflects a scribal copying error. The Day of Vengeance is another name for the Day of Yehowah, which is the day when Yehowah is scheduled to judge his people. That was to take place on New Year's Day. It is also the day when the books would be audited, sins and virtues were counted. It is a day of accounting.

Daniel's discussion contrasts the powerful ones who plundered the temple, turned away the continual offering, and abandoned the treaty made with the Lord

---

[56] That is like saying that United Methodists could not be teachers, because they are Protestants.
[57] Charles, *Daniel,* p. 309.
[58] Collins, *A Commentary,* p. 385.
[59] See the index for "Messiah" in Buchanan, *Revelation and Redemption: Jewish Documents of Deliverance from the Fall of Jerusalem to the Death of Nahmanides* (Dillsboro: Western North Carolina Press, c1978; sold by Mercer U. Press).

with the ones who had **stumbled** and had suffered warfare, flames, captivity, and plunder. The latter group was composed of the people who knew its God. It included the ones who instructed the many. On the day of vengeance the tables would be turned. That would come at the appointed time when all of this suffering and plundering would end. After that day of vengeance there would be a Day of Atonement when the Lord would comfort his servants, and forgive the people who knew its God. This was written as if it were all foreseen and would hurry to arrive. Actually it was all probably written after the fact in preparation for Hanukkah after the victories of Beth-horon and Beth-zur (1Macc 4:6-36).

For a time. Literally, **for days**. It has no verbal dependence upon Ben Sira's prayer. There is a frequent reminder given in Dan 11. God's anger, the people's suffering, and the wickedness of pagan kings all took place for the same reason. The people who had made a treaty with God had sinned, and they would be punished **for** only **a predestined time.** Then the sentence would be over. That would be the **time** of the end, which God had appointed for them. The **time** mentioned here is the **time** of the end, and the end to which he referred is the same end mentioned in Dan 11:27, 35, 40. It was also the end mentioned in Dan 8:17, 19 and in other ways was discussed in Dan 7:25; 8:14; 12:6, 11; 13. The author of Dan 11 knew God had an appointed end, because the author was writing history. This end had come by the **time** Dan 11 was written. The orthodox rabbis and their fundamentalist congregations would stumble and fall during this **time** of God's wrath, but when they stumbled, they would receive some help. From what source would that come? That is the next question.

They will receive a little help. When Jews were under control of the Babylonians, they negotiated with Cyrus of Persia, agreeing to assist in the capture of Babylon. For this cooperation they received some help in restoring the Promised Land and returning. After Cyrus succeeded, there evidently became tension between him and the Jews, so Jews were soon ready to assist the Greeks in taking Persia. After Alexander the Great had taken Gaza, he went at once to Jerusalem. The high priest together with other priests and leading citizens of the city went out to meet him before he reached Jerusalem. They welcomed him into the city, and he, in turn, allowed the Jews in Palestine, Babylon, and Media to observe their own laws and be exempted from taxes on the Sabbath year (*Ant* 11.338-39). At the point of time described here in Dan 11, Jews were ready to cooperate with any other nation that promised them good terms to help overthrow the Greeks.

Alexander began treating Jerusalem with some of the same kind of generosity that he showed to the Greek cities that had earlier experienced autonomy. He may have done this because Palestinian Jews had already become very much influenced by Hellenism. The autonomy of Greek cities could be violated in any one of three ways: 1) taxation, 2) imposition of a garrison, and 3) commands of a superior power interfering with the local constitution or administration. Alexander and his successors made a pretense of honoring all of these, but it was only fiction. Alexander allowed some cities to draw up their own constitutions, *but they had to be submitted to him for approval*. He removed the taxation that had been imposed by the Persians, *but asked cities for financial and military support as allies*. He removed Persian garrisons, *but if trouble arose he provided his own garrison in its place*. These were usually called "temporary." Sometimes they were and sometimes they were not.[60] Alexander and his successors considered it prudent to extend the privileges of Greek temples, to make large contributions to them, and to enable them to be reconstructed in a more grandiose size and beauty. It gained favor from the populace who, in turn, were more willing to accept their loss of autonomy. [61]

If Alexander had lived to a ripe old age and continued to govern all of the territories he had conquered, Jews would probably have resisted his rule as much as they resisted the rules of the Ptolemies and the Seleucids. He learned democracy from his Greek schooling, but he learned the expedience of the monarchy from the Persians and from necessity. He began under the claim that he was liberating all of these countries that he conquered and establishing democracies. He actually remitted many of the tributes that the Persians had imposed on the cities. This, however, was the case only for a certain number of years. The remission lost its value when Alexander demanded special financial gifts of allies in support for his wars. His Hellenistic successors acted accordingly (*Diod* 18.52, 6; 72, 2).[62]

When Alexander set foot on Palestinian soil, Jews were ready to cooperate with any other nation that promised them good terms to help overthrow the Persians. By the time of the Maccabean Rebellion, however, Jews had felt the force of Seleucid monarchy. The promise of liberation was recognized as a fraud, and they were ready to make an alliance with some other nation that would free them from the Syrians. Bevan said,

> The real fact of the Macedonian sovereignty, which had been cloaked in so many decent political fictions, is here brutally unveiled.[63]

The only nation to which Jews might turn for relief from Seleucid oppression was Rome. Judas the Maccabee had observed that the Romans were moving east. They had already conquered Greece, Thrace, and Macedonia, and they defeated Antiochus III, driving him east of the Taurus Mountains, almost completely out of Asia Minor, and making a very costly treaty with him that restricted the military movements of the Greeks severely. Judas noticed all of this while he was himself fighting Antiochus III's son. Acting on his knowledge, he initiated a treaty with the Romans whereby they would assist him in his war with the Syrian Greeks, and he, in turn, would help them move east in their plans to extend their empire (*Ant* 12.414-19).[64] Both sides were to receive help, as in most international treaties.

---

[60] E. R. Bevan, *Seleucus* I, pp. 104-106.
[61] Bevan, *Seleucus*, I, p. 109.
[62] Bevan, *Seleucus* I, pp. 104-106, 111.
[63] Bevan, *Seleucus* I, p. 107.
[64] J. E. Goldingay, *Daniel* (Dallas: Word Books, c1989), p. 303, said that the Romans could not be considered the help mentioned, because that did not come until later. There is no way Goldingay could know that. The cursory reports do not tell of all the discussions that took place in Rome before Popilius brought Antiochus IV to a halt. Nor does it tell of the activity of the pro-Egyptian Jews during this time. These anti-Seleucid Jews who lived in Palestine, Rome, and Egypt were

According to Mandell, Rome made only a friendship pact (ahm-ee-keé-tee-ah, amicitia; fee-leé-ahn, φιλίαν) with Judas (War 1.38). The author of 1Macc, and probably Judas, however, thought the treaty was more than that. Jews thought it was a treaty that involved military support (fee-leé-ah kai soo-mah-kheé-ah, φιλία καὶ συμμαχία, 1Macc 8:17).[65] It was because of Rome's military power, however, that Judas wanted a treaty with that country (1Macc 8:1-11). Rome's treaty with Egypt and forceable action against Antiochus IV was good news to Judas.

Whatever treaty Judas and Rome actually signed it was one that permitted Rome to assist the Jews in their war with Antiochus when they needed it. There is no detailed information about the kind of help that was, but the Syrian generals were surprised by the military force of the Jews at Beth-horon and Beth-zur. Where did Judas get the weapons to overpower one half of the entire Syrian army at those battles? That is where the treaty with Rome may have entered the picture. Rome may have provided the weapons Judas needed to win the battles at Beth-horon and Beth-zur. Mandell correctly noted that Rome made only treaties that were to its own advantage, but the suppression of the Seleucids was to the mutual advantage of the Jews, Egyptians, and of Rome. Rome needed Judas the same way it later needed Herod the Great, and it may have supported Judas the way it supported Herod.[66]

Whatever the **help** was that Rome gave to Judas, the author of Dan 11 was not willing to give Rome much credit for it. After all, this drama was being prepared for a Hanukkah celebration of Judas' victories—not Roman assistance. It was the **little help** Judas obtained, however, in his conflict with the Syrian Greeks, that guaranteed his success. It must have been a shock to the Syrians to learn how much help Judas suddenly had at his disposal. Previously Antiochus had enough military power to ovewhelm the Maccabean guerrillas at Judah if he would just direct it to the campaign. Then, suddenly he felt the force of a well-armed enemy.

Porteous disagreed with most scholars, like Driver, Heaton, Towner, LaCocque,[67] and others who claim the **little help** was the entire Maccabean Revolt. Montgomery said, "In 11:34 there is a solitary reference to Judas' enterprise."[68] The

---

probably not waiting around passively to see what was going to happen. It is likely that Roman and Egyptian Jews had opened the way for Judas to negotiate with the Romans.

[65] S. R. Mandell, "Did the Maccabees Believe that They Had a Valid Treaty with Rome?" *CBQ* 53 (1991):204-205.

[66] Mandell, "Valid Treaty," p. 215, was probably correct in observing that Judas sent only ambassadors to Rome who had Greek names, and was holding a double standard. While to the Jews he was a great anti-Hellenist, when he dealt with Rome he represented himself as Hellenistic.

[67] S. R. Driver, *The Book of Daniel* (Cambridge: University Press, 1912), p. 190; E. W. Heaton, *The Book of Daniel* (London: SCM Press, c1956), p. 237; N. W. Porteous, *Daniel: A Commentary* (Philadelphia:Westminster Press, 1965), pp. 145-73; W. S. Towner, *Daniel* (Atlanta: John Knox Press, c1984), pp. 147-71; A. LaCocque, *The Book of Daniel* (Atlanta: John Knox Press, 1979), p. 48, said, "The message implied . . . (v. 34) is that God acts independently of human politics, including undoubtedly that of the Maccabees, which moreover is qualified as being 'of little help' in Dan 11:34." Nevertheless, he also said, "Between the statue and the stone there is the conflict between kingdoms made by human hands and the Kingdom of God. Yet this latter kingdom is not an extraterrestrial kingdom, for its reign will not pass over to another people" (p. 52).

[68] Montgomery, *Daniel*, p. 87.

identification of the **little help** with the Maccabean Revolt came to all of these scholars, through a long line of secondary sources, from the third century IA pagan philosopher, Porphyry. Porphyry thought of the Hasmoneans as a small family from the little village of Modein (Jerome 25.717, p. 569). He did not identify the **little help** with the entire rebellious movement but only the activity of the family itself.[69]

Porteous thought the **help** would have come from the deaths of other martyrs who died for their faith. These he understood to be the pious law observers who faced death rather than break the Sabbath or deny their faith. Porteous seemed to have forgotten that many of those who were killed for their faith were Hasmoneans and their followers in the military revolt.[70] Collins thought that the author of Daniel would not have identified the Hasmoneans as those who provided the **little help**, because he would not have thought that their revolution had been any **help** at all![71] He has insisted that

> Daniel must be distinguished from that of the Maccabees and even from that of the *Animal Apocalypse*.[72]

The word "must" used here is more of a command or a plea than a logical requirement. Heaton thought the **little help** was the might of human beings. Salvation came from God.[73] Goldingay thought the **little help** was only the first successes of the Judaean activists as distinguished from their final success. He assumed the author divided the successes of the Maccabees into major and minor, earlier and later.[74]

One of the questions Collins left unanswered is: If the Book of Daniel had been planned and composed by those who had been either hostile to or disinterested in the Hasmonean revolution, why does the book reflect all of its hopes, aspirations, and victories surrounding the success of the Maccabees? Why is the Book of Daniel so optimistic if the authors of Daniel opposed the victorious Hasmonean Revolt? Why do all of Daniel's time schedules conclude about the time when Judas dedicated the temple? When Judas was collecting and censoring the books that should be preserved in the canon (2Macc 2:14), why did he, and later his brothers, include such books as 1 and 2Macc and Daniel if they had been anti-Hasmonean? All of these scholars, as well as many more,[75] held that the myth (pseudo-prophecy) became real prophecy at Dan 11:40, because they noticed the incoherence of that which followed with that which preceded it. Heaton said,

---

[69] Porphyry was called a pagan by Christians. He knew an amazing amount of Jewish history and religion to have been a secular philosopher. He may have been a Jew.

[70] Porteous, *Daniel*, p. 168.

[71] J. J. Collins, *Daniel, First Maccabees, Second Maccabees* (Wilmington: Michael Glazer, Inc., c1981), p. 107. He modified his position a little by the time he wrote *A Commentary*, p. 386. There he said, "Whether the author of Daniel saw the Maccabees as a help at all is nonetheless doubtful."

[72] J. J. Collins, *Commentary*, p. 67; "Inspiration or Illusion, Biblical Theology and the Book of Daniel," *ExAud* 6 (1990):35.

[73] Heaton, *The Book of Daniel*, p. 79

[74] Goldingay, *Daniel*, p. 303.

[75] Such as Driver, *Daniel*, p. lxvi; Heaton, *Daniel*, p. 240; Montgomery, *Daniel*, p. 470; and Smith-Christopher, *Daniel*, p. 147.

> His [the author's] ignorance of Antiochus' eastern campaigns begun in 165 B.C. left him free to invent another expedition against Egypt and to present the death of the tyrant in a setting which accorded with prophecy and the expectations of his own lively faith.[76]

They did not suspect that the second ending had been misplaced and really occurred under the leadership of Antiochus the Great, whose "end" did not refer to his death.[77]

The **little help** was not very **little**. Of course, Jews did not want to give Romans any credit for their contribution to the Hasmonean revolt, but without the Romans the Hasmoneans could never have succeeded in driving the Greeks out of their country. It was the Romans who struck the first blow in defeating the Seleucids. Before the Hasmonean rebellion began, the Roman ambassador met with Antiochus IV on the shore near Egypt and forced him to retreat. From then on everything led to the defeat of the Seleucids. When the Seleucids were finally brought to an end it was the Romans that made it happen (ca 66 BIA).

According to Charles and Bickerman, the Hasmoneans were the ones who offered a **little help** and were joined by flatterers who followed the Hasmoneans because of their fear (Dan 11:34-35).[78] Montgomery said those were "adherents of doubtful character" who joined Judas' group.[79] No doubt Judas had supporters of both descriptions, but that does not mean they were the ones mentioned in Dan 11:34-35. Most scholars agree with Charles but there were very few contemporary Jews who would have considered that help **little.** That is specially true of all the authors who composed an entire book that interpreted the Maccabean Revolt in victorious terms of God's foreordained and pre-scheduled plan and other Jews who joined Judas in celebrating the first Hanukkah.

The **help** which the Romans provided was called **little**, because it was from the outside, and understandably considered small in comparison to the force of the Jews themselves and their God.[80] Furthermore there were many influential Jews in Rome at the time who probably exerted much influence in persuading the Romans to support the Hasmonean movement. Palestinian Jews would have given Roman Jews more credit than non-Jews in the Roman government.

Those who joined themselves with flattery to those who provided **the little help** might have been the opportunists who profiteered by dealing with the Romans

---

[76] Heaton, *Daniel*, p. 240.

[77] Collins, *Daniel*, p. 105; Porteous, *Daniel*, pp. 169-73; Towner, *Daniel*, pp. 164-71. A. A. Bevan, *A Short Commentary on the Book of Daniel* (Cambridge: University Press, 1892), p. 163, noted that Von Lengerke and Hitzig both thought that "in v.40 the author suddenly goes back to describe events anterior to 168 B.C.," but he thought they were mistaken.

[78] Charles, *Daniel*, p. 310; Bickerman, *From Ezra*, p. 101.

[79] Montgomery, *Daniel*, p. 459.

[80] Calling this help "little" was like calling the assistance of the French fleet at Jamestown, Virginia, "little" in the colonists' war against the English. It was after the French had soundly defeated the English in a sea battle that Cornwallis was prepared to sign a peace treaty, granting the colonists the liberty for which they were fighting. Roman help was little only in the sense that American help for Israel since 1947 has been little.

as they dealt earlier with the Seleucids and prior to that with the Persians. The authors of Daniel may have been suspicious of the consequences of transferring loyalty from Syria to Rome. There was in Judaism an ancient tradition of warning against foreign alliances. The anxiety was justified. The Rome that provided **a little help** later controlled the entire nation of Israel as well as that of Syria.

Rome was not specially interested in the Jews for their own worth, but Rome was also expanding its own borders and found the Seleucid designs an obstacle. After the Battle of Magnesia (190 BIA), the Romans imposed a treaty on Antiochus III that moved his boundary to the east of the Taurus Mountains. The fact that they could force the Seleucids to retreat was impressive. Any nation that could thoroughly defeat such a powerful leader as Antiochus the Great could also defeat his son, Antiochus Epiphanes. Judas needed such strong assistance as this.

Many will join them with deceptions. The **many** involved here were probably those who broke the treaty with God and joined the rebels. They apparently infiltrated the Hasmonean camp with malicious objectives. They were the Hellenizers who wanted to weaken the Hasmonean followers from within. The word rendered "deceptions" here is often translated "flatteries." Since the word does not appear anywhere else in the FT, we are left with only the context to determine its meaning. It apparently comes from the word *khah-lah-káh* (חלקה) which describes the activity of the treaty breakers. It alludes to something smooth or slippery. Therefore it is rendered "flatteries" or "deceptions." From the point of view of the rebel nationalists, Hellenizers were deceptive, untrustworthy heathen.

The appointed time. This expression, which is used repeatedly in Dan 11 (Dan 11:24, 27, 29, 35, 36), was intended to call the reader's attention to Hab 2:2 and Sir 36:8. The first is an answer from God to Habakkuk's question. It assured Habakkuk that **the appointed time** was on schedule. If it seemed to Habakkuk that it was being delayed, he should wait for it. It would surely come. The second is a poem addressed to God. It urged God to act promptly as he had done in the past and assert his right arm as he had done at the exodus. He should overthrow the enemy and put an end to the enemy's arrogant leaders. In agreement with Habakkuk, Ben Sira assumed that all things were predestined, and that God had an **appointed time** for everything, including the defeat of the enemy. This would take place at the time of the end, and Ben Sira prayed that God would bring that about soon. The author of Dan 11 understood that the enemy's arrogant leader was Antiochus IV. At the time of the end, Antiochus' career would be over. The end involved was the end of the rule of Antiochus IV and the end of God's anger with Israel. It all happened in 164 BIA. Bickerman thought that the author was really prophesying rather than mythicizing history, so he said,

> He [the author of Daniel] felt that the end of time was approaching, and he could see no salvation for the people other than through the direct intervention of God.[81]

---

[81] Bickerman, *From Ezra*, p. 94.

The author of Dan 11 was not writing only about his feelings and hopes, but rather about his knowledge of the facts of history that had already taken place. It was not the end of time of which he was writing but the end of Syrian oppression. He knew by that time that God's intervention had already taken place through the agency of the Maccabean revolt.[82]

TEXT

Daniel	First Testament Intertexts
³⁶The king will do whatever he wants, and he will trample and exalt himself over every **god**, and he will say astonishing things against the **God of gods**. He will succeed until the wrath is completed, for the action is predestined. ³⁷He **will not acknowledge** the gods of his fathers nor the one beloved of women, nor any **god will** he **acknowledge**, because he will exalt himself over all. ³⁸He will **glorify** the **god** of fortresses instead of these, the **god** whom his fathers did not know. He will **glorify** with gold, silver, precious stones, and precious things. ³⁹He will act in relationship to strong fortresses with a **foreign god**. The ones whom he recognizes he will increase in **glory**. They will be rulers over the many, and he will divide the land for a price.	Sir 36:5 They will know, as we know, that there is no **God** except you. Sir 36:17 All the ends of the earth **will know** that you are the **God** of the age. Sir 36:4 As you have sanctified us before their eyes, thus **glorify** yourself before our eyes. Sir 36:3 Shake [your fist] at **a foreign** people. Sir 36:14 Fill Zion with your majesty and your temple with your **glory**.

COMMENTARY

The king will do whatever he wants. This is **King** Antiochus IV. The author of Dan 11 used this expression when a **king** won a significant battle (Dan 11:3, 16). It meant that no one could interfere with him. His power was compared to God's.

---

[82] R. Bultmann, *The Presence of Eternity* (New York: Harper and Brothers, 1957), p. 23, said "Eschatology is the doctrine of 'last things' or, more accurately, of the occurrences with which our known world comes to its end. It is the doctrine of the end of the world, of its destruction." Bultmann thought, however, that Daniel was the only book of the FT that had genuine eschatological expectations (p. 28). Contrary to Bultmann, none of the authors or editors of the Book of Daniel had any idea that the world was coming to an end. They were joyous because the life of Antiochus IV and his cruelty had come to an end.

Until the wrath is completed. This is another way of saying, **Up to a time** (Dan 11:24). The wrath was God's anger. Israel suffered because it had sinned, and Israel's sin made God angry. The suffering Jews endured at the hands of an enemy was at God's direction. Describing the same situation, 1Macc 2:64 said, **Great was the wrath that came upon Israel**. When Judas led armies successfully, he was credited with turning **the wrath away from Israel** (1Macc 3:8). When the author of 1Macc described the first Hanukkah he told of the joy and celebration surrounding the event. It lasted for eight days, because the **embarrassment** (*ohnay-dis-máws*, ὀνειδισμός) **caused by the gentiles was turned away** (1Macc 4:58). It was probably designed for eight days, because the celebration associated with Solomon's dedication of the first temple lasted eight days (1Kgs 8:65-66).

The battle of Beth-horon, followed by another victory at Beth-zur, was the turning point of the war. Those battles cleared the way for the cleansing and dedication of the temple (1Macc 4:6-36). They were signs that God's wrath was over. From this point on the king was not free to do whatever he wanted. God's predestined action consisted in exactly that which happened. It was after the events that the author of Dan 11 knew what was and was not predestined.

Will not acknowledge the gods. Ben Sira believed the **God** of the Jews was the only true **God.** Nevertheless, he prayed that **God** would so exalt himself and show his strength that all the gentiles would recognize him, and all the ends of the earth know that he alone was **God**. The author of Dan 11, however, held that the gentile Antiochus fell into the classification of those who did **not acknowledge** the greatness or the glory of God. He not only did not know the greatness of God. He did not even glorify any of the well-known pagan deities.

There are conflicting stories about Antiochus IV's religious activity. On the one hand, he honored the gods with more sacrifices than any of his predecessors and constructed magnificent temples in various cities (Polybius 26.1, 10-11), but on the other hand, he was famous for his sacrilegiousness in plundering other temples to obtain their wealth (Polybius 30.26, 9; Livy 41.20.5-10).

Charles noted that the coins reflected Antiochus' increasing arrogance. At the early part of his reign the coins showed a representation of Apollo and said, "**King Antiochus.**" Later a star appeared on his forehead, indicating his claim to deity honors. Still later the star vanished but the title given was "**King** Antiochus, god manifest." The latest title was a claim to be the legal agent of the deity. It had about the same significance as "god incarnate."[83]

It was neither the construction nor the destruction of pagan temples that disturbed the Jews. They were upset because of the way he treated the holy temple at Jerusalem. They described his arrogance by saying that he thought he could command the waves of the sea and weigh the mountains in a scale. He even thought he could touch the stars (2Macc 9:8-10). Offering sacrifices to foreign deities did not exempt Antiochus from censure, in the judgment of contemporary Jews.

The one beloved of women. This may have been Cleopatra, the sister of Antiochus IV Epiphanes. It was her sons against which he was fighting in Egypt. Although

---

[83] Charles, *Daniel*, p. 314.

negotiators reminded him that Ptolemy VI was his own nephew with whom he should be glad to reach peaceful terms, he was not convinced. Others have suggested that the beloved of women was one of the local goddesses. Bevan thought it was most likely Tammuz (Adonis) whose cult had been popular in Syria, especially among women (Ezek 8:4).[84]

He will glorify the god of fortresses. He had put his confidence in military strength. This involved fortresses, battering rams, and weapons.

The one whom he recognizes he will increase in glory. This may be a direct complaint against the high priests that competed for Antiochus' honor. The next sentence was, **They will be rulers over the many** (Dan 11:39). The many was the entire body of Jews, either of a congregation or of a nation. It was the high priests who ruled the nations when Syrians were in power. They were some of those whom Antiochus recognized, and they were chief among those who benefited from their offices.

He will divide the land for a price. The laws of Jubilee were established to prevent **land** from ever falling out of possession of the families who owned it. When the Israelites invaded Canaan, they took **the land** from the current owners and divided it among the tribes of Israel. Once it was thus assigned, families who "sold" their **land** received it back on Jubilee, when **the land** was restored to the original owners (Lev 25:25-28). That which the Israelites had done with **the land** of the Canaanites, Antiochus was evidently doing with **land** claimed by Jews. He could confiscate it and sell it to Jews who cooperated with him, probably at a favorable price, without the limitations of Jubilee. The ones who obtained **the land** were happy with this favorable situation, but the Jews whose **land** had been confiscated were probably some of those who joined Judas in his rebellion.

This is as far as the story goes in relationship to Antiochus IV Epiphanes, and it shows the kind of eschatology that is dominant throughout the book of Daniel. The end involved was the end of the activity of Antiochus IV and the beginning of the Hasmonean government. The next paragraph is an appendix about Antiochus III, the Great, that has been inserted here at the end of the story. It is clearly out of chronological order.

TEXT

Daniel	First Testament Intertexts
[40]**At the time of the end**, the king of the South will wage war with him, but the king of the North **will pass over** him with cavalry, chariots, and many boats. He will come into the lands,	[Sir 36:8] Hasten the **end time**; strengthen the appointed **time.** [Hab 2:2] Because there is still a vision for **the appointed time**. It will hurry to the **end**, and it will not **deceive**.

---

[84] A. A. Bevan, *Short Commentary*, pp. 196-97.

	^{Isa 8:7} The Lord is bringing up against them the waters of the river, mighty and many, the king of Assyria, in all his glory. It will rise over all its sources, and overflow all of its banks. ⁸It will pass through Judah.
spread out, pass over, ⁴¹and come to the glorious land.	**It will spread out and pass over** until it reaches the neck.
⁴¹Tens of thousands **will stumble**, but those who escape **his hand** are Edom, **Moab**, and most of the Ammonites. ⁴²He will extend his	^{Num 24:17/Sir 36:10} Destroy the head of the corners of **Moab**.
	^{Sir 36:6} Glorify [your] **hand**; and strengthen your **right arm.**
power into the lands, and the land of Egypt will not be able to escape.	

⁴³He will rule the treasuries of gold, silver, and all the precious things of Egypt, and the Libyans and Ethiopians in his footsteps. ⁴⁴Reports from the East and the North will frighten him. He will leave with great fury to destroy and utterly exterminate many. ⁴⁵He will plant his palatial tents between the sea and the glorious holy mountain. He will come to his end, and no one will help him.

TECHNICAL DETAILS

It was only after Antiochus III had failed in Asia Minor that he turned east to pillage a temple at Elam to pay his huge war debt, but he was killed there by the local Elamites. The mythical summary of this entire experience between 198 BIA and 187 BIA is reported in two parts of Daniel 11. The data contained in both five verse passages (11:14-19 and 11:40-45) is similar, as the following textual parallels will show:

Daniel 11:14-19	Daniel 11:40-45
1. Many rose against **Egyptians** (198 BIA)	1. **Egyptian** troops invade Judea and Coele-Syria.
2. Antiochus raised many troops.	2. Opposition had the support of Jewish rebels.
3. **Antiochus** surrounded **Panias.**	3. **Antiochus** won battle of **Panias.**
4. Egyptians forced to retreat.	
5. **Antiochus entered Palestine**	4. **Antiochus entered Palestine**

(glorious land).	(glorious land).
6. **Antiochus** made a treaty involving the marriage of his daughter to the Egyptian king (193 BIA).	5. **Antiochus** continued into Egypt and gained support of Libya and Ethiopia.
7. He **turned** to the coastlands of Palestine.	6. Bad news prompted **Antiochus** to **turn** north. He got as far as the coastlands of Palestine.
8. A commander put an **end** to his insolence.	7. Came to his **end** with none to help him.
9. Returned to his own land.	
10. Fell and was not found.	

Antiochus the Great. Keil noticed that Dan 11:40-45 was a separate section, divided from Dan 11:36-39 and Dan 12:1-3.[85] When Dan 11:40-45 is applied to Antiochus the Great, rather than Antiochus Epiphanes, its meaning makes good sense. Such good sense that Collins thought this second ending had a "legendary quality,"

> and the story of attempted temple robbery in Elymais is suspiciously similar to that of the death of Antiochus III.[86]

The two accounts vary in details. Account A (Dan 11:14-19) does not tell of the Egyptian attack of the North before being resisted by a Syrian force, as account B (Dan 11:40-49) does, but it tells of Jewish cooperation in the Seleucid resistance to Egypt. It also tells of the treaty between Egypt and Syria, which B omits, but does not report the extent of Antiochus' campaign, including support from Libya and Ethiopia, as B does. That, however, seems likely to have happened before the treaty was signed. Neither does account A tell of the bad news which prompted Antiochus to turn north. Both accounts tell of his reaching the coast lands of Palestine, probably the Gaza strip. According to Account A, a Roman commander, namely Scipio, forced him to give up the gains he had secured in Europe, Greece, and Asia Minor. B simply said he met his end there with none to help him.

Royal failure. In this context "his end" (Dan 11:45) is not his death, as scholars have assumed; it means only that Antiochus III was stopped in his tracks by the Romans, frustrated and embarrassed, and his expansion plans came to an end, as account A specifies. Account A omitted the rest of the story of Antiochus the Great before beginning the account of Antiochus Epiphanes. Account B was not discarded as an unnecessary duplicate by the editor who chose to put account A in its position. B

---

[85] C. F. Keil, *Biblical Commentary on the Book of Daniel* (Grand Rapids: Eerdmans Publishing Co., c1976), tr. M. G. Easton), p. 461.
[86] Collins, *A Commentary*, p. 389.

was added at the end of the Seleucid account as an appendix, somewhat like the second account of creation in Gen 1-3. Many scholars[87] now think Dan 11:40-45 is prophecy, even though some of them think it was ignorantly invented. The authors of both accounts in Dan 11 omitted many events that occurred during that period of history. Failure to report the death of either Antiochus the Great or Antiochus Epiphanes does not mean they had not yet died, but that accounts of their deaths were not necessary to these narratives. All authors choose what they will include and what they will omit, irrespective of their knowledge. Once B (Dan 11:40-45) is recognized as an alternative version of A (Dan 11:14-19) account B does not have to be used as a prophecy which was never fulfilled. It is a second summary of a historical event in the life of Antiochus III.

Relevance to dates. The entire Book of Daniel, then, was written after the fact as a mythologization of a very important period of history. Many of the chapters were completed and probably used in celebration at the first Hanukkah. Whatever chapters had not been completed by the first Hanukkah 164 BIA were added before 142 BIA. The entire document was available to be used in the special festival that was established at that time to celebrate the triumph of Judaism over Hellenism and the complete removal of dependence upon Syria (1Macc 13:43-52). The fact that there are two editions of these six verses suggests that chapter 11 once circulated separately and at one time had some variations.

Whenever all of the Daniel essays were gathered into one book some editor compared two different versions of chapter 11. Instead of taking parts of verses 14-19 and infusing verses from Dan 11:40-45 into the narrative, forming one composite report, he chose the essay that had the 14-19 version and put the variant version at the end of the chapter as an appendix. The editing process may have taken place between the festivities of 164 BIA and those of 142 BIA, but no one can be sure about this. This is not the only time parallel accounts have been included in the scriptures. There are reports in the Book of Isaiah that are identical to passages in Kings. There are two accounts of creation in Genesis. The author of Chronicles sometimes copied and sometimes modified the report of the same periods of history in Kings. The editors of the canon decided to allow variant parallel accounts of the same event to be included in the scriptures.

> *It is hard to overemphasize the importance these six verses (11:40-45) have had in confusing the function of the Book of Daniel in later Christianity and Judaism.*

The Seleucid narrative ends with Dan 11:39, and the account of Antiochus' defilement of the temple.[88] Without Dan 11:40-45, which was evidently added as an alternate reading for Dan 11:14-19, there would have been almost no basis for not reading Dan 7 as a unit and as a myth throughout. Sahlin, Casey, Porteous, Coppens and Dequeker were all impressed with the logic of following the chronology of the

---

[87] Such as I Frölich, *'A Time and Times and Half a Time'* (Sheffield: Sheffield Academic Press, 1996), p. 80.
[88] Montgomery, *Daniel*, pp. 466-70, was only one of many to think that prophecy began with Dan 11:40 and that because of that we knew that the book was written before the "predestined end."

beasts and the Son of man as being in the same sequence as the gentile kingdoms and Judas the Maccabee. It all fits perfectly, but only Sahlin concluded that this was actually the case. The rest were distracted by the confusion that followed Daniel 11:40.

One of the important analysts of the Book of Daniel was the third century IA philosopher, Porphyry. His works on Daniel are only extant through their quotation and report of St. Jerome. Jerome was an excellent early church scholar whose commentary on Daniel shows that he accurately and carefully studied the related works--Josephus, the Books of the Maccabees, Plotinus, Strabo, Dio, and other church fathers before writing his commentary. He included the works of Porphyry only to refute him, although he agreed with Porphyry's historical analysis most of the time.

According to Jerome, Porphyry said that all of the narrative of Daniel up to the time of Antiochus Epiphanes was authentic history. That is, all prior to Dan 11:40. The rest (Dan 11:40-45) was conjectured and false (MPG 25.617A). Jerome showed how Porphyry tried also to fit Dan 11:40-45 into history, but Jerome accurately held that these attempts failed. Porphyry thought Dan 11:40-45 was a historical continuation of Dan 11:1-39, and he tried to make sense of it but was unable to do so. Neither he nor Jerome thought that these verses were repetitious accounts of the same events related to Antiochus III rather than Antiochus IV. Jerome thought that these events which Porphyry tried to explain historically in relationship to Antiochus IV were really future prophecies to apply to the antichrist.

Charles followed Wellhausen in thinking that Antiochus IV made only two raids on Egypt, and that the so-called third campaign was unfulfilled prophecy. Keil also thought Dan 11:40-45 did not refer to any of the campaigns of Antiochus IV Epiphanes, but he thought it described the anticipated acts of the Antichrist.[89] None of these realized that there were two accounts of Antiochus III's campaigns reported in Dan 11.[90]

While the Hasmoneans were strong, the Dramas of Daniel were probably read at least annually at Hanukkah to celebrate the victory of the Jews over the Syrian Greeks. It was during that time that Daniel was added to the canon. Jerome studied scripture just the same way other Christians and Jews did. They believed that it was the word of God. That which was prophesied must be fulfilled. Nothing that was not in the scripture was in the world. It was not just the prophets whose works were considered prophecy. The Psalms, the Torah, and the wisdom writings were accepted as prophecy as well.

Once Daniel was added to the canon it was legitimate prophecy, and Jerome read it as such. He studied Daniel with the belief that part of it had been fulfilled, and the rest was still to be fulfilled. For example, Porphyry thought the "time, two, times and half a time" in Daniel was the time during which the Hasmonean war was fought from the time the temple was defiled until it was cleansed. Jerome disagreed, however, because only three years elapsed between those two dates rather than three and a half. Therefore that prophecy was still waiting for fulfillment.

---

[89] Keil, *Daniel*, p. 469, 472, 4 74.
[90] Charles, *Daniel*, p. 301, 318; J. Wellhausen, *Israels und Jüd. Geschichte* (Berlin: G. Reimer, 1897), p. 246.

The scholars who assumed that the Book of Daniel ceased to be myth and became prophecy with Dan 11:40 all obtained their lead indirectly from the ancient Jerome, although he was not the only one who believed as he did at the time he wrote. Most books of the NT who used the Book of Daniel understood it as a prophecy. Most scholars today hold that all of Daniel from Dan 11:40 to the end is prophecy and therefore inaccurate but is yet to be fulfilled. Porphyry provided a lasting contribution in showing the historical factor in the Book of Daniel. He also overlooked, as have most scholars since, the second report of the invasion of Antiochus III. Therefore he considered it to be false. It is not false when the key figure is recognized as Antiochus III the Great. That too is authentic history.

COMMENTARY

At the time of the end. This is not **the end** of the world about which the author was speaking. In context this is the time of **the end** of the Egyptian rule over Palestine. These words are probably editorial. They relate **the end** of Antiochus IV s activity (164 BIA) to the following pericope which turns us *back* to the leadership of Antiochus III who ruled several years earlier (223-187 BIA). They are not "*subsequent* [emphasis his] to the persecutions described in *v.* 35 which are to last 'until the time of the end,'" as Bevan thought.[91] It is also not correct that "There is nothing to indicate a change of subjects from the previous passage, so there can be no doubt that the reference is to Antiochus."[92] The discussion that continues is about Antiochus, but not about Antiochus IV, as Collins assumes, but about Antiochus III.

The narrative does not report all of Antiochus III's rule and expansion. Nor does it report only the final action of Antiochus III. It begins with his victory over Egypt at the Battle of Panias (198 BIA), but Antiochus III continued to live and rule until 187 BIA, eleven years more. The victory at Panias was a high point in Antiochus III's career, especially in relationship to Palestine. Nonetheless, it also marked the beginning of **the end**, so the editor used these few connecting words to relate **the end** of Antiochus IV to the last years of the rule of Antiochus III.

This was **the** predetermined **end** of Antiochus IVs activity. The editor knew what had been predestined, because it had already happened by the time he wrote. He also knew this literary unit that provided another account of the last years of Antiochus III.

The author of that unit knew enough about earlier history to compare the invasion of Antiochus III into Palestine with the invasion of Tiglath Pileser, many years earlier. He used the very words that he found in Isaiah to describe the action. This reports again the victory of Antiochus at Panias and Sidon in 198 BIA.

With cavalry, chariots, and many boats. Polybius said that Antiochus planned to invade Palestine both by land and by sea (Polybius 5.68, 1). This is a repeat account of the invasion of Antiochus III, prior to the Battle of Raphia. Antiochus started in

---

[91] Bevan, *Short Commentary*, p. 198.
[92] So Collins, *A Commentary*, p. 389.

the north, taking Lebanon, the Transjordan, Samaria, Gaza, and finally settling at Raphia where he planned his attack against Ptolemy. This is all *deja vu*.

Come to the glorious land. The glorious land, of course is Palestine, the land into which Antiochus moved after he had left Lebanon and the cities in the Transjordan.

Edom, Moab, and most of the Ammonites. After Antiochus III captured Rabbat **Ammon**, he crossed the Jordan and took Samaria. He did not go farther into the south of **Ammon** and enter into **Moab**, and once he crossed the Jordan he moved immediately toward Gaza, leaving Edom untouched. This is precisely the way Polybius described the invasion of Antiochus III (Polybius 5.68, 1-73, 16).

The land of Egypt will not be able to escape. Antiochus III's victory began with the Battle of Panias, but from there he conquered Sidon and moved farther south, by-passing the area east of the Jordan River, but continuing south as far as Egypt. He evidently proceeded farther into Libya and Ethiopia, taking much loot and booty as he went. Things were looking favorable for Antiochus III, but suddenly he learned of the events from the North and the East of his empire, and they alarmed him. The reports of the East did not interest the author of this unit, but the news of the North was that Scipio was moving east. Because Bevan still thought this discussion applied to Antiochus IV Epiphanes, he said, "What the '*tidings from the East and the North*' may be, we can only guess."[93]

He will leave with great fury. He was stationed in Egypt when the news reached him, so he quickly finalized his conquest there and headed north. This meant that he would march with his troops along the Eastern Shore of the Mediterranean Sea. There he camped temporarily between the sea[94] and Jerusalem, but he did not remain there. He went on into Asia Minor where Scipio at the Battle of Magnesia met and defeated him.

He will plant his palatial tents. Kings had several tents. Like Persian kings, Seleucids who went to war moved magnificant royal tents with them, and they had many smaller tents nearby for the king's personal servants.

Between the sea and the glorious holy mountain. This was on the plain between the Mediterranean Sea and the mountain on which the city of Jerusalem was located.

He will come to his end. Goldingay did not identify the king involved in this passage. He simply called him "the last northern king."[95] That probably meant that

---

[93] Bevan, *Short Commentary*, p. 199.
[94] According to the MT, the word is "seas" (*yah-meém*, ימים). Without the words "and Jerusalem," this would mean he camped between the Dead Sea and the Mediterranean Sea. That may have been the original text, to which someone later added "the glorious holy mountain." Antiochus' position would be correct either way. "Between the seas" is nearly the same as "between the sea and the glorious holy mountain."
[95] Goldingay, *Daniel*, p. 284.

this was a third invasion led by some Seleucid after the death of Antiochus IV. Delcor surveyed the problems many scholars had with the last 5 verses of Dan 11. He avoided reaching conclusions, but he assumed that the verses were applied to Antiochus IV.[96] Casey said Dan 11:40-45 was "inaccurate and inconsistent with those same primary sources [Dan 11:2-39]."[97] Lebram thought Dan 11 was composed on the basis of earlier pagan sources, some of which were legends. Dan 11:40-45, in Lebram's opinion, was an antitype of Cambyses, one time king of Asham (600-559 BIA).[98] Thinking, erroneously, that this end was the end of Antiochus IV Epiphanes, Bevan said,

> That Palestine, the scene of his greatest crimes, should also be the scene of his final overthrow, was, from the point of view of the persecuted Jews, a very natural expectation. No details are here given, but since in chap.viii.25 we read that Antiochus will "be broken without hand", we must suppose that the author looked forward to some divine intervention by which the great enemy would perish "with none to help him."[99]

But the text refers to Antiochus III, and not Antiochus Epiphanes, as Collins held.[100] There is a huge jump in time and events between Antiochus' placing his palatial tents between the Mediterranean Sea and Jerusalem and coming to his end. In between, he went on north to Asia Minor to meet Scipio. There was the terrible sea battle at Thermopylae in which Syria was defeated, followed by the famous battle at Magnesia where Antiochus III came to his end. This was not the end of his life, but it was the end of his expansion. It was a crushing defeat; it broke him militarily, economically, and emotionally. After he made a very unhappy treaty with the Romans, he returned to Syria and then led a battle in Elymais, Persia, hoping to capture the temple of Bel there and confiscate all of its treasure. There the local people killed him. So this was the second ending of the life of Antiochus III reported in Dan 11. The end of Antiochus III did not take place between Jerusalem and the Mediterranean Sea. The end of his expansionism took place at Magnesia in Asia Minor. His death took place in Persia.

---

[96] Delcor, "L'Histoire," pp. 374-75/
[97] M. Casey, "Porphyry and Syrian Exegesis of the Book of Daniel," *ZAW* 81 (1990):141.
[98] J. C. H. Lebram, "König Antiochus im Buch Daniel," *VT* 25 (1975):753-54, 68-71. See also H. Lewy, "The Babylonian Background of the Kay Kâûs Legend," *ArO* 17 (1949):28-109.
[99] Bevan, *Short Commentary*, p. 200.
[100] J. J. Collins, "Inspiration or Illusion, Biblical Theology and the Book of Daniel," *ExAud* 6 (1990):33.

When Antiochus also faced a crisis, there was "none to help him." When Judas later came to a strategic situation, he received "a little help." That was one of the reversals in the Danielic report.

After reading all of the militaristic activity of Dan 11, Reid still reiterated his basic doctrine: "The political stance of the text is unmistakably quietistic."[101] What would a military stance be like?

---

[101] S. B. Reid, *Enoch and Daniel* (Berkeley: BIBAL Press, c1989), p. 117.

CHAPTER TWELVE

HEBREW TEXT

12:1 וּבָעֵת הַהִיא יַעֲמֹד מִיכָאֵל הַשַּׂר הַגָּדוֹל		Jer 30:7
הָעֹמֵד עַל־בְּנֵי עַמֶּךָ וְהָיְתָה עֵת צָרָה		
אֲשֶׁר לֹא־נִהְיְתָה מִהְיוֹת גּוֹי עַד הָעֵת הַהִיא		1Macc 9:27; Exod 9:18
וּבָעֵת הַהִיא יִמָּלֵט עַמְּךָ כָּל־הַנִּמְצָא כָּתוּב בַּסֵּפֶר:		Joel 2:2; Ps 69:29; Isa 4:3
2 וְרַבִּים מִיְּשֵׁנֵי אַדְמַת־עָפָר יָקִיצוּ		Mal 3:16; Isa 26:19
אֵלֶּה לְחַיֵּי עוֹלָם וְאֵלֶּה לַחֲרָפוֹת לְדִרְאוֹן עוֹלָם: ס		
3 וְהַמַּשְׂכִּלִים יַזְהִרוּ כְּזֹהַר הָרָקִיעַ		Isa 52:13
וּמַצְדִּיקֵי הָרַבִּים כַּכּוֹכָבִים לְעוֹלָם וָעֶד: פ		Isa 53:11
4 וְאַתָּה דָנִיֵּאל סְתֹם הַדְּבָרִים וַחֲתֹם הַסֵּפֶר עַד־עֵת קֵץ יְשֹׁטְטוּ		Sir 36:8
רַבִּים וְתִרְבֶּה הַדָּעַת:		Sir 36:4, 17
5 וְרָאִיתִי אֲנִי דָנִיֵּאל וְהִנֵּה שְׁנַיִם אֲחֵרִים עֹמְדִים אֶחָד הֵנָּה		Ezek 1:1-3
לִשְׂפַת הַיְאֹר וְאֶחָד הֵנָּה לִשְׂפַת הַיְאֹר: 6 וַיֹּאמֶר לָאִישׁ לְבוּשׁ		Ezek 9:11
הַבַּדִּים אֲשֶׁר מִמַּעַל לְמֵימֵי הַיְאֹר עַד־מָתַי קֵץ הַפְּלָאוֹת: 7 וָאֶשְׁמַע		Isa 29:14; Sir 36:8, 17
אֶת־הָאִישׁ ׀ לְבוּשׁ הַבַּדִּים אֲשֶׁר מִמַּעַל לְמֵימֵי הַיְאֹר וַיָּרֶם יְמִינוֹ		Sir 36:6
וּשְׂמֹאלוֹ אֶל־הַשָּׁמַיִם וַיִּשָּׁבַע בְּחֵי הָעוֹלָם כִּי לְמוֹעֵד מוֹעֲדִים וָחֵצִי		Sir 36:8
וּכְכַלּוֹת נַפֵּץ יַד־עַם־קֹדֶשׁ תִּכְלֶינָה כָל־אֵלֶּה: 8 וַאֲנִי		Sir 36:6
שָׁמַעְתִּי וְלֹא אָבִין וָאֹמְרָה אֲדֹנִי מָה אַחֲרִית אֵלֶּה: פ 9 וַיֹּאמֶר		Sir 36:17
לֵךְ דָּנִיֵּאל כִּי־סְתֻמִים וַחֲתֻמִים הַדְּבָרִים עַד־עֵת קֵץ: 10 יִתְבָּרֲרוּ		Sir 36:8
וְיִתְלַבְּנוּ וְיִצָּרְפוּ רַבִּים וְהִרְשִׁיעוּ רְשָׁעִים וְלֹא יָבִינוּ כָּל־רְשָׁעִים		
וְהַמַּשְׂכִּלִים יָבִינוּ: 11 וּמֵעֵת הוּסַר הַתָּמִיד וְלָתֵת שִׁקּוּץ שֹׁמֵם		Sir 36:6
יָמִים אֶלֶף מָאתַיִם וְתִשְׁעִים: 12 אַשְׁרֵי הַמְחַכֶּה וְיַגִּיעַ לְיָמִים אֶלֶף		
שְׁלֹשׁ מֵאוֹת שְׁלֹשִׁים וַחֲמִשָּׁה: 13 וְאַתָּה לֵךְ לַקֵּץ וְתָנוּחַ וְתַעֲמֹד		
לְגֹרָלְךָ לְקֵץ הַיָּמִין:		

TECHNICAL DETAILS

One of the recurring themes in Dan 11 was that all of the evil things that had been occurring would continue for only a certain predestined time. Then they would end. The author of Dan 11:17-39 used very few earlier scripture passages in his narrative. His references to **the appointed** time or **the end** used Hab 2:2-3 and Sir 36:1-17 as intertexts. Dan 11:40-45 initially belonged in the narrative before Dan 11:17, so there were only accidental points of contact between these verses and either Habakkuk or Ben Sira.

Dan 11:39 concluded with Antiochus Epiphanes free to do as he pleased. He paid attention neither to gods nor to human beings. He exalted himself with precious metals military force. As a continuation of Dan 11:39, Dan 12 reminded the reader that these wonders would also come to an end at a specified time--just three and a half years after the temple was defiled. Antiochus' program would then come to an end, and the age of the Jews would begin. The author knew that would happen, because the Battle of Beth-horon, and possibly also the Battle of Beth-zur, had already been fought, Antiochus had already died, the temple either had already been cleansed or was in the process of being prepared for cleansing. The first Hanukkah either had been celebrated already or would have been the occasion for the first reading of the Book of Daniel.

Dan 11 began at the time of Darius the Mede, whenever that was, but one verse later the author told of Alexander the Great, whose empire was completed by his death (323 BIA). The temple was cleansed and Antiochus Epiphanes died about 164 BIA. Dan 11 is a mythological interpretation of that period of history in the Middle East. Repetitiously the author told of vicious things that the wicked foreign kings had done and the freedom they had to do as they pleased, but then he reminded the reader that all of this was part of God's predestined time schedule, and at a certain time--. . . **up to a time** (Dan 11:24), . . . **there is still an end at the appointed time** (Dan 11:27), **at an appointed time** (Dan 11:29), . . . **until the time of the end** (Dan 11:35), . . . **until the wrath is completed** (Dan 11:36), . . . **at the time of the end** (Dan 11:39)--all of this would be over. It is clear that the author of Dan 11 and 12 took these texts from Habakkuk and the Psalms of Solomon and constructed his essay around them.

At the end of the narrative, the chapters change, but the discussion about the predestined time continues and comes to a precise definition. This last unit of time that was completed during the reign of Antiochus Epiphanes would last only three and a half years. It was the last unit of time in an age that began, according to the author of Dan 2, when Nebuchadnezzar first entered Jerusalem in 605 BIA and took a few prominent Jews captive to Babylon. On that basis the captivity lasted 441 years (605 minus 164 = 441), exactly nine Jubilees (49 x 9 = 441).

According to the author of Dan 9, however, the captivity began at 586 BIA when the temple was burned, Jerusalem was sacked, and most of the prominent citizens were taken as captives into Babylon. It was necessary to use 586 BIA as a starting point, because that would allow the first 7 weeks of years to expire (49 + 586 = 537 BIA) just after Babylon fell to Cyrus in 539 BIA. Because his total needed to reach 70 weeks of years, he structured his mathematics dogmatically as 7 + 62 + 3½ + 3½ = 70 weeks of years, or 490 years.

In actual history the three and a half year unit lasted only three years, from December, 167 to 164 BIA, but the author who wrote Dan 9 was a dogmatist rather than an objective historian. He forced the time schedules to fit into his sabbatical eschatology. By making a few strategic changes in facts he was able to explain the events that took place during the previous 422 years in terms of Sabbath years and Jubilees.

ENGLISH TEXT

Daniel	First Testament Intertexts

^{12:1} At **that time** arose / Michael, the great general / who is stationed over all the children of your people. / **It was a time of such oppression /**

^{Jer 30:7} **That day** was so great that **there has never been any like it. It was a time of oppression** for Jacob; but he was saved from it.

^{1Macc 9:27} **The tribulation** was great in Israel **such as has not been from the** day the prophet was not seen by them.

as has never been / from the existence of

^{Exod 9:18} **Such as has never been** in Egypt **from** the **time** of its founding **until** now.

the nation **until** that **time**. /

^{Joel 2:2} **Such as has never been from the age.**

^{Joel 3:5} All who call upon the name of Yehowah **will escape.**

At that **time** your people **will escape,**

^{Ps 69:29} Let them be blotted out of **the book** of life.

/all that are found **written in the book.**

^{Isa 4:3} The one who is left in Zion, who remains in Jerusalem, will be called "holy," everyone who is **written** for life in Jerusalem.

^{Mal 3:16} May Yehowah pay attention and hear, and may a **book** of memory be **written** before him.

COMMENTARY

At that time arose. This little poem is about **at that time**. The **time** under discussion was the **time** of tribulation before the end of God's anger. It described the period of history in Judah after the defilement of the temple until its cleansing. This was the **time** that took place before the appointed **time** mentioned several times in Dan 11. The victory at Beth-horon, and possibly the one at Beth-zur, constituted a sign that Michael **arose** or **stood up** in defense of his people. There is a break in the narrative between Dan 11:45 and Dan 12:1. Dan 12:1 is not continuous with Dan 11:40-45. The reason for that is that Dan 11:40-45 is a second version of Dan 11:14-19. It applies to Antiochus III, rather than Antiochus IV. Dan 12:1, however, continues from the conclusion of Antiochus IV Epiphanes at Dan 11:39.

Michael the great general. The name **Michael** (*Mee-kuh-áyl*, מיכאל) means "Who is like God?" The military angel who led the Israelites against the enemies in war was called **Michael**. Like other angels, **Michael** was a theological concept. He was never seen with the physical eye. His actions were deduced from military action on earth. When Jews began to win battles they presumed that it was because **Michael** had come to them with invisible aid. He was an agent of God who was sent to provide God's legal presence in the situation.

It was a time of such oppression. This has Jer 30:7 as its intertext. That text refers to the destruction of Jerusalem and the Babylonian captivity, but Jeremiah promised that the nation would not end in oblivion. This **time of oppression** was **a time** in which Jacob would be delivered. At that **time** God would break the yoke of the **oppressor**, deliver Jews and Israelites from the lands of their captivity, and make a full end of the nations into which they had been scattered (Jer 30:7-11). The **time of oppression** discussed here recalled the text of Jeremiah. It was **a time of oppression** that had lasted for about three years, but it was one from which the Jews had been delivered at the Battles of Beth-horon and Beth-zur. It was a fulfillment of Jeremiah's prophecy. The yokes of Antiochus III and Antiochus IV had been broken, and both kings had come to an end with none to help them (Dan 11:45), and Jews were being delivered. This was fulfilled eschatology.

As has never been. The advent of the nation probably began with Saul as king. Until that time there was a loose organization of tribes but no identifiable kingdom. That means this was the worst oppression the Israelites had suffered in more than 800 years. This is an expression that the author took from Jer 30:7, Joel 2:2, and Exod 9:18.

Your people will escape. Even though the suffering would be terrible, the nation would survive. That is what Jeremiah had promised, but the promise was not for all Jews--only the ones whose names had been written in the book. The book involved was the membership book that God kept. That would not include the Hellenizers, the traitors, the mighty ones, the treaty breakers that supported Antiochus IV. The membership was probably identical to the citizens who were in good standing at the time. The **people** would **escape**, because it was predestined in God's plan. Daniel never told what happened to those treaty breakers who opposed the Hasmonean Revolt, but many of them probably continued to live in Palestine to irritate the Hasmoneans as much as they could. They had been the first in rank during the Seleucid regime, but during the Hasmonean rule, they would have held the last postions in the kingdom. Keil said,

> But the salvation which the people of God shall experience in the time of the unparalleled great oppression is essentially different from

the help which was imparted to the people of Israel in the time of the Maccabees.[1]

The most normal reading of the text is that they were not essentially different. The context that surrounds oppression and the victory is the one the **people** experienced during the Hasmonean revolt. Keil, however, thought the salvation mentioned here was exactly the same as that promised for those who **sleep in the dust** and would afterwards arise.[2] That implies that only the dead would be saved. Whereas those who celebrated the Hanukkah of 164 BIA probably thought they had been saved, as well.

TEXT

Daniel	First Testament Intertexts
	Job 14:11 A man lies down, and he **will not arise** / until the heavens wear out they will not get up; they will not awaken from their **sleep**.
²Many **who sleep / in the dust** of **the ground will arise**, / some	Isa 26:19 Your dead will live; the corpses **will arise**; those **who sleep in the dust will jump up** and sing.
	Gen 3:19 Until you return to **the ground**, for from it you were taken, for you are **dust**; to **dust** you shall return.
for life of **the age [to come]**, / and others to	Gen 3:22 He will take from the tree of **life** and eat and live **for the age.**
	Hos 6:2 After two days he will give us **life**; on the third day he **will raise** us up, and we will live before him.
	Isa 66:24 They will go out and view the corpses of the men who transgressed against me, because their worm will not die, and their fire will not be quenched.
the embarrassment / for **repugnance** of **the age [to come]**.	They will be a **repugnance** to all flesh.
³ But those who **provide knowledge**	Isa 52:13 Look! My servant will **provide knowledge**.

---

[1] C. F. Keil, *Biblical Commentary on the Book of Daniel*, tr. M. G. Easton (Grand Rapids: Eerdmans Publishing, 1976), p. 480.
[2] Keil, *Daniel*, p. 481.

will shine like the luminary in the heavens, / and those who **make the many righteous**, like the stars for the age [to come] and and to [its end].

^{Isa 53:11} My servant will **make the many righteous**; he will bear their iniquities.

TECHNICAL DETAILS

This little poem is a separate unit from the poem just before it (Dan 12:1). This poem is about death and resurrection (Dan 12:2-3).

COMMENTARY

Many who sleep in the dust of the ground. Because of Adam and Eve's sin they were cursed. They would return to **the dust** (Gen 3:19). Job said this was the human destiny. Human beings would lie down, but they would not arise. They would not wake up from their **sleep** (Job 14:11). It was Second Isaiah and Hosea who provided textual basis for the doctrine of resurrection (Hos 6:2; Isa 26:19).[3] In both cases the original meaning was the resurrection of the nation, not of the individual, but later Jews and Christians interpreted the resurrection individually.

The Day of Yehowah was the judgment which happened on New Year's Day. On that day the Lord judged both Israel's sins and virtues in relationship to those of her enemies. Joel said that the great Day of Yehowah would be fearful, but that those who called upon the name of Yehowah would escape (Joel 2:5). The victories of the Battles of Beth-horon and Beth-zur convinced contemporary Jews that the preceding New Year's Day and the following Day of Atonement (165 BIA) had obtained a favorable judgment from Yehowah. Those who called upon Yehowah had been delivered. This was not just an emotional deliverance. Those who escaped had been delivered from the rule of the Syrians against whom the Maccabean Revolt had been fought.

Jews of Hasmonean times believed that the faithful who died and were buried before their time (70 years of age) would be raised when the nation would be reestablished and have the reward of living out the rest of their days on the Promised Land, liberated from foreign rule. The doctrine of resurrection was based on scripture. According to Deuteronomic theology, God always punished the wicked and rewarded the righteous, if not immediately, then later. If a virtuous youth was killed in battle, without having received his reward for his virtue, it seemed reasonable to believe that God would reward him later by raising him from the dead and allowing him to live out the rest of his life in freedom and peace. A later Jewish scholar said that

> Those who fear the Lord will be raised to life of the age.
> Their life [will be] in the light of the Lord and will never end (Ps Sol 3.16).

---

[3] See further A. E. Gardner, "The Way to Eternal Life in Dan 12:1e-2 or How to Reverse the Death Curse of Genesis 3," *AusBR* 40 (1992):1-19.

There are also FT texts that can be interpreted as prophecies of a resurrection:

> Isa 26:19 Your dead will **live**;
> the corpses **will arise**;
> those who sleep in the dust
> will jump up and sing.

Day argued that Dan 12:1-2 was heavily dependent upon Isa 26:19. This is supported by the use of Isa 52:13 and 53:12 in the following verse (Dan 12:3). Day also believed that Isa 26:19 had used Hosea as an intertext. Hosea, for his part, had used an expression that was a normal Baalite conviction. Hosea borrowed the belief in personal resurrection from the Baal myth, according to Day.[4] Hosea first used it, but he did not use it as a personal resurrection. Israel had become guilty in relationship to Baal, so Israel died (Hos 13:1). This sin and guilt was called **stumbling**, (Hos 4:5; 5:5), **sinning**, (Hos 4:8), **playing the harlot** (Hos 4:10, 18), **being sick, wounded** (Hos 5:13), or **torn**. It was also called **death**, and when this condition was changed it was called **being raised up, bound up, becoming alive**, and being **healed** (Hos 6:1-2). All of these metaphors were used to describe Israel's waywardness and return. The death and resurrection involved here was not personal, but national. It was not physical, but metaphorical, mythical, or religious.

The words **life** and **death** in the scripture were often used to describe those who were members of the contract community or those who were not. Those who loved the Lord would live (Deut 30:6) whereas those who did not were dead. Life and Goodness were contrasted with death and evil (Deut 30:15). Israelites had the opportunity to choose between life and death, blessing and curse. Those who chose life would live long in the Promised Land (Deut 30:19-20). Death meant becoming scattered as outcasts among the nations (Deut 30:3-4). Those who believed in the Lord would be separate from the dead people (*1QH* 7.14-15).

Proselytes were those who at first did not know life. Later they learned to live and associated only with the elect (Philo, *De Fuga* 78, 97). Sin ruled in death but grace ruled through righteousness to life of the age [to come] (Rom 5:17, 21) When Jesus said, **Let the dead bury their own dead** (Matt 8:22; Luke 9:60), he did not mean corpses should bury corpses. He meant those who were not members of the contract community could be buried by the outsiders. The names of members were written in the Book of Life (Isa 4:3-5). The wicked were those whose names had been blotted out of the Book of Life, not written with the righteous (Ps 69:28).

Josephus said with liberty would come a happy and blessed life that would be lived in accordance with the laws and customs of their fathers (*Ant* 12.302-303). The evil person would be uprooted from the land of life in contrast to the Psalmist who would continue in the temple in the Promised Land (Ps 52:5-8). Rabbi Tanhuma said the Land of Israel was called the Land of Life (*wah-yáyt-zay*, ויצא 80b). While the suffering servant of Isaiah was in Babylon he was **cut off from the land of life** (Palestine). Gentiles **made his grave with the wicked** (in Babylon) **and**

---

[4] J. Day, "Resurrection Imagery from Baal to the Book of Daniel," *VT Supp Congress Volume*, ed. J. A. Emerton (Leiden: Brill, 1997), pp. 128-31.

the rich in his death (Isa 53:8). *Targ*Isa 53.8 has "land of Israel" as the translation for **land of life**.

In an early Jewish prayer, the worshiper asked that God's name be exalted in the age which he was about to renew when he made the dead live, built up the city of Jerusalem, completed the temple, uprooted foreign worship from his land and introduced the worship of the Holy One of Heaven in its place.[5] In this context, the resurrection was expected to take place when the Land was restored, with all of its traditional blessings.[6]

Judas the Maccabee reportedly took a collection from among his soldiers and sent it to Jerusalem when he learned that some soldiers who had been killed in battle had taken idols as booty from the battle. He sent this gift as a sin offering to blot out the sins of the soldiers who had sinned and died. He took the resurrection into account (2Macc 12:39-43). The mother's seven sons who were reported to have died rather than deny their faith believed that they would be raised up after death (2Macc 7:14), but for Antiochus Epiphanes there would be no resurrection into life (*ahnáhs-tah-sees ays zoh-áyn*, ἀνάστασις εἰς ζωήν). The reason for this was that "life" for Jews, Israelites, and Christians meant existence in good standing in the treaty God made with his people. Antiochus was not one of the chosen people while he was physically alive, so he would not be raised into the life of a Jew.

Day reported the following other religions that believed in the resurrection: 1) death and resurrection of Osiris two days after his death (Plutarch, *de Iside et Osiride* 13, 356 C; 19, 366 F), and 2) the resurrection of Attis, three days after his death (Firmicus Maternus).

Day pointed out eight ways in which Isa 26:19 was dependent upon Hosea. He was convinced, however, that Isa 26:19, like Ezek 37 and Isa 27, referred not to personal life after death but to restoration of the nation after it had been exiled.[7]

> He has torn, and he will heal us.
> After two days he will make us **live**,
> and on the third day he **will raise** us,
> and we **will live** before him (Hos 6:1-2).

> Look! I will open your graves, and I will raise you up from your graves, my people, and I will bring you to the land of Israel. You will know that I am Yehowah when I open your graves and when I raise you from your graves, my people. I will put my spirit in you and you will live, and I will give you rest upon your land (Ezek 37:12-14).

Day correctly concluded that Ezekiel was speaking only metaphorically. This message followed the parable of the valley of dry bones, which Ezekiel said constituted the whole house of Israel. These were the Jews in Babylon who thought

---

[5] D. de Sola Pool, *The Oldest Aramaic Prayer, the Kaddish* (Leipzig, 1929; New York, 1964), p. 12.
[6] See further Buchanan, *The Consequences of the Covenant* (Leiden: Brill, c1970), pp. 110-49.
[7] Day, "Resurrection," pp. 128-31.

their entire hope was gone (Ezek 37:1-12). In other words they were dead. When hope would be restored so that they could return to the Promised Land they would be revived. This means that their "death" was not physical but metaphorical, religious, and political. It was also a group reexistence rather than a resurrection of individuals.

Porphyry thought the resurrection that was spoken of in Dan 12 was intended metaphorically. Those who had been slumbering in the dust of the ground were the family of Mattathias who for a while waited and did nothing. They were hiding and slumbering in the caves of the earth. Then, those who "rose from the dead," arose and began the revolution. Those who possessed knowledge were the faithful teachers and rabbis who exhorted the people, on the basis of the law, to follow Judas in the rebellion. These were contrasted with the law breakers who sided with Antiochus (Jerome 25.725, p. 576). Jerome, however, thought this whole passage was prophecy about the coming of the Antichrist (Jerome 25.727, p. 577). The references from Hosea and Ezekiel were not intended to be understood as physical, individual resurrection in their own context. In both cases it was the nation that was revived after it had suffered defeat and severe injury.

Casey referred to Saint Ephraim's (306?-373) commentary on Dan 12:2 who said that the evil of the nation was the sleep of death. The revival came under the leadership of Zerubbabel. Casey commented,

> The reference to the revival under Zerubbabel prepares for the explanation of Daniel's use of the expression "those who sleep in the dust of the earth": this is that the evil which came upon the Jewish people in the post-exilic period was like the sleep of death. The next comment refers to the revival under the Maccabees.[8]

To the embarrassment of the repugnance for the age. The term **age** does not mean eternity. It describes a temporal period distinguished by its quality. Amos used the term to identify **the age** when David ruled (Amos 9:11). Neophyti said that after 430 predestined years were completed its end was redemption (*kahd ahl-mah keet-say luh-meet-pah-ruh-kah*, כד עלמא קציה למתפרקא) (*NeoTarg*Exod 12.41-42). The **age** that had reached its end was the 430 year age spent in Egypt. The redemption involved the exodus—not the end of the world or the cosmos.

"This age" usually refers to existence under foreign rule, because most of the literature dealing with **ages** was written while the authors were living under foreign dominion. From that temporal situation, Jews looked forward to the future **age** that was still to come. The "**age** to come" turned out to be the Hasmonean **age**, the **age** when Israel was free from foreign rule or taxation. When that **age** was actually realized, it was no longer "**the age** to come." It was called **the age**. That is the expresssion used here.

Isa 66 is a poem that is centered around Jerusalem and apparently used Ezek 9 as an intertext. It offers comfort for the faithful who mourn for Jerusalem and tremble at God's word (Ezek 9:4; Isa 66:2, 5). These were the ones that wore the sign of the *tau* (X) (Ezek 9:4; Isa 66:19). The wicked would be punished by

---

[8] M. Casey, "Porphyry and Syrian Exegesis of the Book of Daniel," *ZATW* 81 (1990):141.

death. The courts of Jerusalem would be filled with the slain (Ezek 9:7), and the righteous would gaze upon the dead bodies of those who rebelled against God (Isa 66:24) and whose end was **repugnance**. Both texts are judgment themes that provide inspiration for the judgment of Dan 12 that promises resurrection for the faithful and **repugnance** for the sinners.

There were two sides to the doctrine of resurrection, just as there were two groups of Jews in Palestine at the time of Antiochus Epiphanes. The followers of the Hasmoneans, who wrote this document, were the saints. The Hellenizers were the wicked ones.

The saints would be raised socially and politically to rule and receive the benefits of living in **the** Hasmonean **age** on the Promised Land, as the chosen people. The wicked, however, would be raised also, but not to life. The term "life" here is used metaphorically to mean the existence of those who were approved parties to the treaty made with the Lord. Instead of "life," for those contract breakers it would be to embarrassment, punishment, shame, and **repugnance**. In the new administration, those who had held exalted positions in the Seleucid government would be the ones in the least favorable positions. Then they would be ridiculed and have ample opportunity to repent, suffer, and be sorry.

There were some Jews who thought that **the age** to come would last forever. Others thought it would last only until the predestined cycle should come to an end. Maimonides said the resurrection was a miracle. It dealt with things outside the realm of nature. It could not be proved, but we just accept it (par 37). The reason for accepting it was that it was written in Dan 12:2, 13. This means that the soul would return to the body, but the resurrection life would not be eternal (par 6-7). It was only life in **the age** to come that was eternal and incorporeal (par 9). He thought Jews should teach the resurrection to the masses so that the doctrine of reward and punishment would prompt them to obey the Torah (par 11). [9]

Some Jews thought of resurrection as personal and individual; others thought it was national. According to Josephus, Mattathias reminded his sons that although their bodies were subject to death they would achieve immortality through the memory of their deeds (*Ant* 12.282). This was individual, but it was not bodily resurrection. Resurrection was rather consistently related to the Promised Land and to Jewish liberty in either case. Rabbis said that only those in the Promised Land would be raised. God, however, would provide a special tunnel to bring Jews who died outside the land in to the land for the resurrection (*bKet* 111b). One of the early commentators on Dan 12:3 interpreted the victory over the Syrians and the doctrine of the resurrection as follows:

> *1Enoch* 104.2 Take courage! Because you have wandered in evil times and in tribulations, as lights of heaven you **will shine** and become manifest. The gates of heaven will be opened for you.

This may mean only that God would look upon them favorably and that they would have many social, material, and political benefits. It may or may not mean they would ascend into heaven. When the gates of heaven are opened, so are the gates of

---

[9] Text is from R. S. Kirschner, "Maimonides' Fiction of Resurrection," *HUCA* 52 (1981):167-80.

Jerusalem. Jerusalem was called the city of God (Sir 36:13; Philo, *Som* 2.250; Dan 9:24) **heavenly Jerusalem** (Heb 12:22).[10]

It is not always clear when these terms are intended metaphorically and when they are to be understood physically and ontologically. Still today Orthodox Jews send the corpses of their loved ones to Israel so that they might be buried on the Mount of Olives, where the resurrection is expected to occur (Zech 14:1-15). They want their loved ones to be right there next to Jerusalem when that happens. They expect them to come back to life wearing the same garments in which they were buried (*bKet* 111b).

Those who provide knowledge. Ben Sira's prayer expressed the desire that all the ends of the earth would **know** that the Jewish god was the God of the age. He wanted all gentiles to **know**, just as God's people **knew** that there was no other deity except God. Ben Sira thought the way this would happen would be for God to threaten the gentiles and show them his great power. This would catch their attention and make them submissive.

Those who provide knowledge were the instructors, literally **those who make shine [the people]**[11] (*mahs-keé-leém*, משכילים). These were not classical, pagan philosophers who instructed people in basic education. They were the faithful orthodox rabbis who taught the forbidden scriptures and encouraged the congregation to fulfill the commandments of the scriptures even if it meant torture and death.

Jerome criticized Porphyry because he could not say who these were during the time of Antiochus IV. If the resurrection was historical as Porphyry thought then these should already have arisen and have been identified (Jerome 25.724, p. 575). Porphyry held that the time of Antiochus' persecution was the worst that had ever been, just as Daniel reported.

Josephus composed the speech he thought Eleazar would have given to those destined for death at the defense of Masada (72 IA). According to Josephus Eleazar, leader of the sicarii, thought of himself and his colleagues as teachers (*War* 7.329). Judas of Galilee was one of the teachers (*soh-fees-taí*, σοφισταί) who led the military resistance to Rome (*War* 1.648). His son, Menahem, was also a teacher (*War* 2.433), who commanded a group of guerrilla soldiers in an attempt to liberate Judah from Rome after the death of Herod.

These warriors thought of themselves as patriots who were antitypes of the rabbis in the Hasmonean times who made the people shine. The people who shone did not have to die and go to heaven. They became intelligent while they walked on the earth. As further evidence of Josephus' use of Dan 12 in his composition,

---

[10] See further Buchanan, *To the Hebrews* (Garden City: Doubleday & Co., 1972), p. 222.

[11] J. J. Collins, *A Commentary on the Book of Daniel* (Minneapolis: Fortress Press, c1993), pp. 388, 393, interpreted the term "people" as "*common* people," overlooking the fact that "common" is a pejorative term in Judaism. That which is common is not holy (Lev 10:10, S. Singer [ed.], *The Authorized Daily Prayer Book of the United Hebrew Congregations of the British Empire* [London: Eyre and Spottiswoodes, 1960], pp. 216-17). It is idolatrous, pagan, gentile. The people whom the teachers were teaching here considered themselves to be "holy people" (Deut 7:6; 14:2; Dan 12:7).

Eleazar's speech further reminded his fellow sicarii of the promise of life after death and of death as sleep (*War* 7.340-50).

During the first years of the Hasmonean Revolt, the instructors mentioned by Daniel were the people who were tortured and killed, along with members of their religious communities. In the new age, however, things would be different. These rabbis would be the ones honored for their faithfulness and heroism. They would shine like the sun in the sky, but that does not mean that they were angels with whom Jews had fellowship. During the oppression of the regime of Antiochus Epiphanes after he had defiled the temple these were lowest in the ladder of social recognition. But in the new age, the last would be at the top.

Like the luminary of heaven. Wolters noted that Halley's Comet appeared in the sky in 164 or 165 BIA, just after Antiochus IV's death. Therefore the author meant here that the teachers would shine like Halley's Comet in the sky.[12]

Those who justify the many. This is the second line of a beautiful poetic couplet in which the second line contains basically the same message as the first line. In the listing of heroes there were those who provided knowledge and those who justified the congregation. The instructors were the *mahs-kee-leém* (משכלים) of the people; the justifiers were the *mahtz-dee-keém* (מצדיקים) of **the many**. **The many** was a technical term for the congregation, so the "people" and **the many** were the same. The rabbis qualified for both titles. They were the teachers, but they were also the judges in court. Literally they **make innocent the many**.

Judges can both make people innocent, and they can make them guilty, depending on their judgments. They do not really train people to be guilty. They just declare them guilty after they have heard the evidence. Here the rabbis played two roles. During the rebellion, when observance of Jewish law was forbidden, they taught their congregations to observe the law. The rabbis were judges, in the legal system of the Jews, but they were not allowed to function in this capacity while the Syrians were in control. They could only teach their convictions and die for their faith. Then it was in the heavenly court that they removed the iniquities of the congregation, by their merits, so that the divine judge could declare them innocent. This couplet is a eulogy for the rabbis. Later rabbis commented on this verse in Daniel:

> *mAboth* 5.18 Everyone who makes **the many** virtuous,
>   no sin comes at his hand
> Everyone who makes **the many** sin,
>   there is no adequacy to accomplish repentance at his hand.

Many years ago Ginsberg, following Bevan,[13] argued that the words, **those who justify the many** (Dan 12:3) were based on the earlier text from Second Isaiah, **My servant will justify the many** (Isa 53:11), and the author of Dan 12 identified

---

[12] A. M. Wolters, "Zohar Harakîa (Daniel 12:3) and Halley's Comet," *JSOT* 61 (1991):111-120.

[13] A. A. Bevan, *A Short Commentary on the Book of Daniel* (Cambridge: University Press, 1892), p. 202.

those who justify the many with the suffering servant of Isaiah. To show this possibility further, the author of Isa 52:13 said the servant would **teach** (*yahs-keél*, ישכיל), which means that he would also be one of the instructors, rather than one of the angels. According to Daniel these would have been the Maccabean martyrs, who, like the suffering servant of Isaiah, died laying up treasures in heaven to remove the guilt of Israel.[14]

This made the survivors just, and prepared the way for an effective Day of Atonement celebration. This means that the rabbis praised in this couplet were no longer alive but that they died teaching the congregation while they were alive and justifying them through their deaths. When the rule of Antiochus IV was in force, these rabbis had no legal authority. After their deaths, however, they appeared in the heavenly court where their martyrdom canceled the iniquities of the community. On behalf of the congregation they enabled the heavenly judge to balance the books and declare the many just or innocent in the eyes of the court. In this way the rabbis justified **the many**. Had they been allowed to function as judges during the rebellion, they would have made the congregation just by declaring them innocent in court. Since they could not do this they acted as witnesses in God's heavenly court and, by their testimony, enabled God to declare **the many** innocent.

The Hasmoneans were the principal leaders in the entire revolt for freedom from pagan oppression and the observance of their traditional laws. They themselves may have been considered some of the instructors (*mahs-kee-leém*) who stumbled (*neek-sheh-loó*, נכשלו) (Dan 11:33-35) and fell by the sword in battle. If so, they would have acted to cleanse the community of its sin and make it white, or maybe they were some of the **ones who make the many innocent** (Dan 12:3) or **make the many understand** (Dan 11:33). If not, they at least were working alongside the faithful teachers and martyrs for the same cause.[15]

Eleazar, one of the Hasmonean brothers, had been killed before the first Hanukkah along with many other soldiers, and the temple was restored because of the martyrdom of these soldiers. The first Hanukkah occurred only a few days after the Day of Atonement, and the Battle of Beth-horon occurred only a few months after the previous Day of Atonement. Rabbis taught that if all Jews would repent for only one day, the kingdom would come. That day would be the Day of Atonement when all Jews had a chance to pay up the unpaid "fines" for all of their own sins and the inequities of their ancestors.[16]

After the victory at Beth-horon, there were several months before the first Hanukkah in which to cleanse and rebuild the temple so that sacrifice could continue. This was the beginning of the restoration of the kingdom. The authors and editors of Daniel evidently believed all of these coincidences proved that the

---

[14] H. L. Ginsberg, "The Oldest Interpretation of the Suffering Servant," *VT* 3 (1953):402-403.
[15] In Hebrew there seems to be a play on the words "the instructors stumble" (*mahs-kee-lay ahm neek-sheh-loo*, משכילי עם נכשלו). For an earlier version of this discussion see Buchanan, *New Testament Eschatology* (Lewiston: The Edwin Mellen Press, c1993), p. 156.
[16] See further Buchanan, "The Day of Atonement and Paul's Doctrine of Redemption," *NovT* 32 (1990):236-48.

kingdom was coming and that the Day of Atonement preceding the Battle of Beth-horon had been effective.

Just as the servant of Isaiah (the first generation of Jews in Babylon) had suffered and paid for the crimes their ancestors had committed, so Jews who participated in the Hasmonean Revolt suffered and thought that suffering redeemed Israel. The author of Second Isaiah was alive when plans were being made for Cyrus to overthrow the Babylonians and release the Babylonian Jews to return to Jerusalem. This current political success was the basis for his judgment that God had given the Jews a positive judgment. For the same reason the author of Daniel judged that the victory of the Jews at the Battle of Beth-horon proved that God had again redeemed his people on the previous Day of Atonement.

How did the Day of Atonement become effective? It functioned favorably because there were hundreds of Jews who died in battle, fighting for their faith. While they were defeating their foreign enemies in battle, they were laying up treasures in the treasury of merits to cancel the sins of Israel. This is the way they justified **the many** or **made the many innocent**. The fact that Judas won the Battle of Beth-horon, and the temple was cleansed, proved that their sacrifice was adequate in God's judgment. It was in the heavenly court[17] that this judgment was made, and it was there that both Judas and the saints of the Most High were vindicated. They were vindicated, according to Daniel, because of the teachers and the justifiers who suffered and died for their faith.

The servant of Isaiah was a personification of the generation of Jews that lived and died in Babylon. They were all Jews making their **death with the wicked** Babylonians, suffering so that the children could return to the **land of life** (Isa 53:8-9), namely Palestine, when Cyrus conquered Babylon and released the Jews to return. The suffering servant of Isaiah was a corporate figure, equivalent to **the saints of the Most High** in Daniel. It does not follow, however, that **the Son of man** in Daniel was a corporate figure. **The Son of man** was the ruler of the new kingdom; **the saints** were the citizens.

TEXT

Daniel	First Testament Intertexts
⁴Now you, Daniel, finish the words and seal **the book**	Ps 69:29 Let them be blotted out of **the book** of life.
	Mal 3:16 May Yehowah pay attention and hear, and may a **book** of memory be written before him.
until **the time of the end.**	Sir 36:8 Hasten **the end time**, and establish **the appointed time.**
	Hab 2:3 There is still another vision of **the**

---

[17] See commentary on Dan 7.

	appointed time and he will speak of **the end time**. He will not deceive.
Many will **wander**,	Zech 4:10 These seven [lamps] are the eyes of Yehowah—they **wander** in all the land
	Amos 8:12 They **will wander** from sea to sea, from north to east they will rove, looking for the word of Yehowah, but they will not find it.
and **knowledge** will increase.	Sir 36:5 They will **know** as we **know** that there is no God except you.
	Sir 36:17 All the ends of the earth will **know** that you are the God of the age [to come].

TECHNICAL DETAILS

Two independent poems have been inserted into the narrative between Dan 12:1-3. The first concentrated on the expression **in that time**, but in itself it is not clearly a message about the time of the end (Dan 12:1-2). It was placed where it is because it is associated with expressions like **until the time of the end** (Dan 11:35). The only message of the resurrection is contained in the one-verse poem (Dan 12:3). The narrative continues in prose and contains references about the time of the end.

COMMENTARY

The time of the end. This has been an important item of discussion throughout most of Dan 11, and it continues here until **the end** of Dan 12. Sir 36a and Hab 2 continue to be the intertexts for this discussion. **The end**, of course, is not **the end** of the world or the cosmos. It marks **the end** of foreign rule over Judah. This was **the end** of Antiochus Epiphanes.

Many will wander. The same word used here for **wander**ing (*yehsh-tuh-tóo*, ישטטו) was used by Zechariah (*meh-shoh-tuh-téem*, משוטטים) in relationship to a similar national situation. The **wander**ing that Zechariah was writing about had nothing to do with aimlessness or erring. It was not the sinners but the eyes of Yehowah that were doing the **wander**ing.

Knowledge will increase. The wanderers were probably the official spies who were agents of Yehowah. As here in Daniel, it was their task to spy out the land so that **knowledge** could **increase**. This was necessary for national intelligence. The

knowledge Ben Sira was concerned to propagate was the **knowledge** of God's greatness and uniqueness.

TEXT

Daniel

⁵I, Daniel, **was watching. Now look**! Two were standing, one on this side of the shore of **the river**, and the other on the opposite

shore of **the river**.

⁶I said to **the man** who **was dressed in linen**, who was above the water of **the river**, "How long [will it be] until the end of these

fantastic things?" ⁷I heard the man dressed in linen who was above the water of **the river**.
He **raised his** right **hand** and his left **hand to heaven** and swore **by the life of the age [to come]** that it would be for

a **time**, two **times**, and half a **time**, and when the one who breaks **the power** of the holy people is finished, all these things will be accomplished.

First Testament Intertexts

Ezek 1:1 I was in the midst of the exile, alongside **the river** Chebar. The heavens opened, and **I saw** visions of God. . . . ³The word of God came to Ezekiel . . . alongside **the river** Chebar. ⁴The hand of Yehowah was laid upon him there. **I was watching. Now look!**

Ezek 9:11 **Now look! The man dressed in linen** whose [ink] horn was at his waist replied, saying, "I have done just as you have commanded me".

Isa 29:14 Therefore, look! I will continue doing **fantastic things** with this people.

Deut 32:40 **For I will raise my hand to heaven**, and I will say, "**By my life for the age [to come]**, [May the following unmentioned curses come upon me] if I do [not] whet my glittering sword, and my hand seize judgment."

Sir 36:8 Hasten the **end time**, and establish the **appointed time**.

COMMENTARY

I Daniel. This is an expression that occurs many times in the Book of **Daniel**. It means that the author was writing in the name of **Daniel**. It does not mean that he was falsifying his identity.

Two were standing. There were two there, because a case cannot succeed in court without at least two witnesses.

The shore of the river. The setting here is consistent with that of Dan 8, where Daniel was at **the river** Ulai when he saw a vision. Both chapters in Daniel have the vision of Ezekiel alongside of a river as their intertext. There was one who appeared to be a man to whom Daniel asked the meaning of the vision. The man invited Gabriel to interpret the vision for Daniel. It happened that the vision applied to the time of the end (Dan 8:1-2, 15-17). When the being explained the vision in detail, he told Daniel to seal up the vision, because it applied to a time in the distant future (Dan 8:26).

In this setting, Daniel was also near **the shore of a river**, and he saw two men, one of whom was not Gabriel, but he was someone who was wearing white robes. One stood on one side **of the river**, and the other man stood on the opposite side. As in Dan 8, the vision at the side **of the river** was based on an intertext from Ezekiel.

Who was above the river. Since he was standing on a **river** bank, the bank was rather high. After Queen Nicotris reconstructed the Euphrates, she had the **river**bed lined with bricks and high banks as a defense against the Medes. In Dan 8 it was Gabriel who answered Daniel's questions. Here it was the man in white standing high **above the river**.

How long [will it be] until the end? This is the same question that was central in Dan 8. That vision applied to **the end**, and this chapter asks the relevant question about **the end**. This question would not have been asked if the author had not been prepared to give the answer.

These fantastic things. **The fantastic things** to which the author referred were those mentioned by Isaiah, and they were not good. Isaiah told the people that they were being surrounded by foreign nations who were attacking Jerusalem with war. There was moaning and lamenting, and the Jews were in distress. Isaiah said that was because the Jews honored God with their lips, but their minds were far from him. Their worship was vanity, but this would not be forever. It would continue for a little while. Then things would change and be better. They would stand in awe of the God of Israel, and they would not be ashamed (Isa 29:1-24).

The Jews contemporary with this Danielic author believed that they were living out Isaiah's prophecy. Like the **fantastic things** of which Isaiah spoke, the **fantastic things** Jews faced in Hasmonean times were the things that were evil to the Jews. They involved the suffering Jews faced, because some of them had not lived according to their laws. It was because of the Hellenizers, they thought, that they had been trampled over by marching armies that came either from Syria in the North or Egypt in the South. They consisted of the defilement and plunder of the temple, and all the other things Syrian Greeks did to Jews against their will under the rule of Antiochus Epiphanes. Long before the Battle of Beth-horon Jews were thinking about the wars and suffering of the Jews of Isaiah's time, and they were asking when all of this would end.

Swore by the life of the age [to come]. Oaths and vows were common in biblical times. An oath normally took this literary form: 1) The oath-taker took the name of someone or something sacred; 2) He or she listed curses that the deity might bring upon him or her; 3) if he or she did or did not do as claimed.[18] Sometimes these were minced to avoid mentioning the exact curses. Sometimes people added a negative or left out a negative because of their fear of the curses. Sometimes curses were called blessings. When that was done, the people involved understood what the curses would be, even though they were not spoken. In the example from Deut 32:40-41, the oath-taker (God) omitted the curses that were understood and left out the negative. With all of the mincing understood, God **swore** that he would sharpen his sword and act in the ways that followed.

A non-biblical liturgical example is that of Jupiter Lapsis, which Romans normally took when agreeing to a treaty. 1) The oath-taker took a stone; 2) in the name of the Roman state he said,

> 3) If, on the one hand, I keep this oath, may good things be mine, but if, on the other hand, I do otherwise in either thought or act, may all others live in their lands under their own laws safely, in their own possession of their own materials, temples, and tombs, but may I alone be cast away as this stone.

4) Then the oath-taker threw away the stone (Polybius 3.25, 6-9).

The oath taken on the shore of the river was taken in the name of life in **the age to come**. **The age to come** was the good **age** that was destined to follow the evil **age** under foreign rulers. That was considered a sacred **age** in contrast to the common era ruled by idolators (Lev 10:10). **The age** of the beasts would have been a common era; the end of which would have been the Hasmonean **age**. The Hasmonean age was believed to be a holy **age**.

A time, two times, and half a time. The word used for **time** here is the same one Sir 36:8 used for "appointed **time**" (*moh-áyd*, מועד).

In answer to the question, **When would these fantastic things end**?, the man clothed in linen said there would be still three and a half years more. The **fantastic things** mentioned were the things that were fantastically horrible that Antiochus IV had done in Judah. The three and a half years constituted the last half of a week of years since the treaty with Antiochus IV was broken. The man who swore that the time remaining was no longer than that, knew he was correct, because the author wrote after the period was over. Actually there were only three years between the defilement of the temple and its cleansing and restoration in 164 BIA.

Jerome said this proved that Porphyry was wrong. He thought this was the time of the Hasmonean rebellion, the period between the defilement of the temple and its cleansing. Jerome reminded the reader, however, that that was only three years, as Josephus said. Furthermore, Jerome reminded the reader that Daniel also said, **The kingdom, ruling authority, and the greatest kingdom under all the**

---

[18] See Buchanan, "Some Oath and Vow Formulas in the New Testament," *HTR* 58 (1965):319-26.

heavens will be given to the people of the saints of the Most High (Dan 7:27). This prophecy was never fulfilled in the time of the Maccabees, according to Jerome. Therefore it referred to the future coming of the Christ and the members of the Christian church. (Jerome 25.728, p. 578).

The one who breaks the power of the holy people. The word translated **power** here is the same word that means **hand**. **The one who** broke **the hand of the holy people** was Antiochus Epiphanes, **the one who** defiled the temple, confiscated its treasures, and enforced Hellenism onto the Jews in Palestine. He evidently ruled first for three and a half years without interference. Jews were apparently keeping the Hellenistic rules and customs to his satisfaction until something happened in relationship to the Roman interruption of his plans that made him angry with the traditional law abiding Jews. Whatever that was prompted him to change his attitude and enforce the terms of the treaty he had made with them three and a half years earlier.

He prohibited them from reading the scriptures, circumcising their males, or in any other way fulfilling the requirements of their religion. From his point of view, he had made a treaty with the Jews that they would adhere to the program he directed, but there were Jews in Palestine who did not approve of that treaty. They still believed they were religiously obligated to live according to the rules of the scripture and their tradition. Jews considered this civil disobedience. Antiochus Epiphanes would have called it something like "fifth columnist activity," "subversive movements," "threats to national security," or "unpatriotic movements."

In order to put an end to this disorder and bring unity and orderly administration into this community Antiochus IV was trying to **break the power of the** Jewish resisters completely. But his life came to an end shortly before the temple was rededicated (164 BIA). With his death and Judas' victory at the Battle of Beth-horon **all of these things** were accomplished. Porphyry understood that this all happened with the Maccabean rebellion, but Jerome held that this was related to the future coming of the Antichrist which would precede the coming of Christ (Jerome 25.729, p. 578).

Actually, many battles were fought under the leadership of Jonathan and Simon after the Battle of Beth-horon, and victory was not accomplished until 143-42 BIA. At that time Simon was high priest, general, and ruler of the Jews, and he obtained release from all foreign taxes. Jews reorganized their calendar at that time, **in the first year of Simon** (1Macc 13:42). Nevertheless, the Battle of Beth-horon was a decisive battle. The author of 2Macc said that battles were continuing even during the time of celebration (2Macc 8:33), according to the extant organization of 2Macc. But even if the present organization of 2Macc is valid, after the Battle of Beth-horon plans quickly began for Hanukkah. The cleansing of the temple was so important to the Jews that they thought they were on the winning side by 164 BIA.

TEXT

Daniel	First Testament Intertexts
⁸I **heard,** but I did not **understand,** so I said, "Sir, what will be the **end** of these things?" ⁹He said, "Go, Daniel, because the words are closed and sealed until **the time of the end.** ¹⁰Many will be purified, whitened, and tested, but the wicked ones will act wickedly. None of the wicked ones will **understand,** but the teachers will **understand.** ¹¹From **the time** when the continual sacrifice is removed and the provision of the abomination of desolations, 1,290 days. ¹²Blessed are they who **wait** / and arrive at the thousand / three hundred and thirty-five days. / ¹³You, go to **the end,** / and you will rest and stand in your portion / at **the end** of the days."	ᴿⁱʳ ³⁶:¹⁷ **Hear** the prayer of your servants according to your will concerning your people. Let all the **ends** of the earth **know** that you are God of the age. ᴿⁱʳ ³⁶:⁸ Hasten **the end time,** establish the appointed time. ᴴᵃᵇ ²:³ There is still another vision of **the appointed time** and he will speak of **the end time.** He will not deceive. If it is slow, **wait** for it, for it will surely come, and it will not delay. ⁴Look! the soul of the arrogant one in him is not righteous, but the righteous one will live faithfully.

COMMENTARY

I heard, but I did not understand. The prayer of Ben Sira asked the Lord to **hear** the prayer of his servants so that the Lord's will for his people would be performed. He wanted the ends of the earth to **know** or **understand** that the Jewish God was the God of the age. Daniel reported that he had **heard** the Lord's message, but he did not **understand** it. That which he did not understand was the meaning of the code expression **A time, two times, and half a time** (Dan 12:7), and **When the one who breaks the power of the holy people is finished, all these things will be accomplished.** (Dan 12:8). This unanswered question left an opening for further explanation.

The words are closed and sealed. This expression was rather rhythmic, like the expression, "signed and **sealed.**" In Hebrew the words are *seh-too-meém* (סתמים) and *khah-too-meém* (חתמים). They have similar sounds and similar meanings. This is expressed as if the future were predestined and written down into a will that would be closed and **sealed** until someone died. Then at the end of a person's life, the **seal** would be opened under legally approved conditions, and the contract would be executed. In that case the question, **How long [will it be] until the end of these fantastic things** (Dan 12:6)? would be answered, "Whenever the person mentioned in the will died." This might have been designed as if it were Antiochus IV's will, but it was not one he wrote. It was a divine will. The end involved came with the death of Antiochus. The national result was that with the death of Antiochus came the end of a traumatic national era. In this case, the end came whenever foreigners were driven from the land, and the land was restored to the Jews under their own ruler.

According to the author's myth, all of the events that happened during these 422 years had been prophesied and written down into a contract by a historical character in the time of Nebuchadnezzar. At that time the events were closed and sealed, and Jews had been required to wait 422 years to learn what was in the prophecy. By that time the "prophecy" had been "fulfilled." The mythologist, however, was no prophet. He lived after all of these events had taken place, so he knew very well what they were. He was simply reviewing the history and from it deducing the religious dimension of the events.

The time of the end. **The end** involved was **the end** of the exile that began with the entrance of Nebuchadnezzar to Jerusalem in 605 BIA, when Nebuchadnezzar took a few leaders captive (597 BIA), or when the temple was burned and 10,000 Jews were taken to Babylon (586 BIA). **The end** of those days took place when the temple was cleansed and rededicated in 164 BIA. This was **the end** of the defilement of the temple and **the end** of Antiochus IV Epiphanes. The land was not completely liberated and foreign taxation repealed until more than 20 years later. At that time Jews claimed that they lived during the time when God saved his people, gave back their *inheritance (klay-rawn-aw-meé-ahn,* κληρονομίαν), their kingdom *(bah-seé-lay-awn,* βασίλειον), their priesthood *(heh-ráh-too-mah,* ἱεράτευμα), and their sanctification *(hah-gee-ahs-máwn,* ἁγιασμόν) (2Macc 2:17). In their judgment they were completely reconciled to God (2Macc 8:29).

Many will be purified, whitened, and tested. Those who **would be purified, whitened, and tested** were the ones whose sins had been forgiven and atoned on the Day of Atonement just before the Battle of Beth-horon. These were the Hasmoneans and their followers. This was said prophetically, but it actually was a *fait accompli*. The author wrote after all of this had taken place. New Year's judgment day had already happened, and the people who had fought against the Hellenizers and the Seleucids had been judged innocent. That is why they were victorious in battle. But there were still the Hellenizers.

The wicked ones will act wickedly. **The wicked ones** were the Hellenizers. They were called the "powerful ones," the "wealthy ones," "contract breakers," and other disrespectful names. Among them was the one Habakkuk called "the arrogant one" whose soul was not righteous (Hab 2:4). They had cooperated with the Seleucids during the Maccabean rebellion. They suffered a severe defeat with the decisive Battle of Beth-horon, but they did not vanish. Neither did the Seleucids. The Seleucids still collected taxes from Judah. For the next 20 years there were many political and military engagements between Judah and Syria. From the nationalistic point of view these were some of the ways in which the **wicked ones acted wickedly.**

None of the wicked ones will understand. Ben Sira prayed that all the ends of the earth would **understand** that there was no other God except the God of the Jews. He asked God to shake his fist over the gentiles and let them see his power (Sir 36:3, 5, 17). The author of Dan 12 realized that this had not taken place yet. The Hellenizers did not realize that their cause was over. The decisive battle had been won. God's plan was predestined to succeed, and the Hasmoneans and their followers were on the right side. The Hellenizers were still acting wickedly, but they were fighting a losing battle.

But the teachers will understand. **The teachers** were some of those that Habakkuk said would live faithfully (Hab 2:4). **The teachers** had been the ones who had supported the revolution throughout the conflict, just as Rabbi Akiba supported Bar Cochba's Rebellion. They **understood** and taught the scriptures and explained how the current events fulfilled prophecies, such as those of Habakkuk, Isaiah, and Ben Sira. During the Syrian persecution the rabbis encouraged the congregation to **live faithfully** even in the face of torture and death.

The provision of the abomination of desolations. One of the worst and most wicked things the wicked ones did was to defile the temple. This was the final cause of the Maccabean Rebellion. When Antiochus Epiphanes plundered the temple he also constructed a heathen altar on top of the altar that was sacred to the Jews in their temple in Jerusalem (*Ant* 12.253). This was called **the abomination of desolations** (1Macc 1:54; Dan 9:27). It happened in December, 167 BIA, after Antiochus had forbidden the continual daily sacrifice to take place. This was the time when Antiochus Epiphanes began an all out campaign to destroy the Jewish religion altogether, but instead it was the beginning of a revolution that would conclude with the cleansing of the temple and the establishment of Hanukkah. It was the beginning of a time that would last 1,290 days. This was one of the great reversals shown in the Book of Daniel. That which Antiochus Epiphanes had planned was contrary to that which God had predestined. It was the international reversal that motivated the composition of the Book of Daniel.

1,290 days. This is roughly three and a half years, forty-two months, or half a week of years (Dan 12:7). Doctrinally this is the length of time that took place between the time the temple was defiled and the time it was cleansed and rededicated. The rededication, however, took place in December, 164 BIA, just exactly three years after the temple had been profaned (1Macc 4:54; 2Macc 10:3, 5; *Ant* 12.320), although, according to Daniel it was 3½ years. That was affirmed to make everything fit into a sabbatical time schedule. Because it did not exactly fit, Jerome refuted Porphyry on this point. Porphyry said that Antiochus was himself really the Antichrist, but Jerome insisted that he was only a type of the Antichrist who was to come in the future (Jerome 25.730, pp. 579-80).

Blessed are those who wait. These were the ones who had not given up their faith during the Hellenization of Palestine. They observed their holidays and dietary rules. They circumcised their males. They continued to study the scripture in secret. They had **waited** until God's anger passed over like a storm and vanished. When that happened the Syrians were defeated by the Hasmoneans, and the foreign tax was finally removed. Those who waited were rewarded. The end surely came; it did not deceive (Hab 2:2-3).

1,335 Days. Most scholars agree with Gunkel in thinking that this is all prophecy. They also follow his suggestion for explaining how this number got into the text. That which happened, Gunkel said, was that 1,290 days elapsed and the prophecy was not fulfilled. *Ergo,* some later glossator added 45 more days to the prophecy.[19] It is obvious that the Book of Daniel was not prophecy but rather a religious interpretation of history. The mathematics of the book was forced to yield to doctrine. The dates given and the names of rulers involved do not cohere, historically. Some authors calculated the exile starting from 605 BIA and others from 586 BIA, depending on their doctrinal design. Some arranged things according to a nine-Jubilee program and others according to a ten-Jubilee program.

Three years were treated as if they were three and a half years. A glossator probably added the 1,335 day period, but he probably did it on the basis of some other starting point. We cannot determine what that was, but that is probably the way he reasoned. If we were to think of Daniel as a prophecy, as Collins did, we would have to agree with him that some of Daniel's predictions were false, and then be surprised, as he was, that it was included in the canon.[20] Because it was drama, partly written as if it were prophecy, it was included in the canon, as all other prophetic books were included in the canon, because it was fulfilled.[21] It was not written in a time of distress when people were biting their fingernails, but a time of success, when the readers and hearers of this document were celebrating. Daniel was not a prophecy that was mistaken, but a collection of dramas whose authors were generous with the facts, exaggerating some of them and fitting dates around doctrine.

You will rest and stand in your portion. The term **rest** was used to describe the national condition of Israel when its borders were secure; it was ruled by its own king; and it was free from foreign taxation (Exod 33:14; Deut 3:20; 12:10; 25:19; 2Sam 7:11). It is a sabbatical term. Just as individuals had **rest** from their labors on the Sabbath day, so the nation had **rest** after its successful wars. At the dedication of the temple Solomon blessed Yehowah who had given **rest** to his people Israel (1Kgs 8:56). The **portion** or the lot in which Jews were expected to **stand** was the Promised Land. This was the **portion** of territory that God promised the Israelites as their share of the inheritance. Israel received all of this at the end of the predestined number of days, after the Battle of Beth-horon had been won, after Antiochus IV had died, and plans had been made for the cleansing and rededication of the temple.

---

[19] H. Gunkel, *Shöpfung und Chaos in Urzeit und Endzeit* (Göttingen: Vandenhoeck und Ruprecht, 1921), p. 269.One of the followers of Gunkel was J. J. Collins, "Inspiration or Illusion, Biblical Theology and the Book of Daniel," *ExAud* 6 (1990):34, who thought dates were recalculated when the first number expired.
[20] Collins, "Inspiration," p. 34.
[21] On this see Buchanan, *Biblical and Theological Insights from Ancient and Modern Civil Law* (Lewiston:The Edwin Mellen Press, 1992), pp. 19-29, 142.

In court a defendant was expected to **wait** with his or her face to the ground, prostrate, until the judge determined the fate of the person under judgment. If the judge asked the person to **stand** before him that was a sign the defendant would be liberated and released as innocent. Hasmonean Jews thought God was punishing them from the day their ancestors were exiled from Judah. For more than 400 years they had been humiliated. The battles of Beth-horon and Beth-zur proved to them that the previous Day of Atonement had been successful. They had been vindicated in the judgment that had taken place on the previous New Year's Day. They celebrated Hanukkah, liberated to **stand** in the Promised Land.

TECHNICAL DETAILS

Dan 11:17-12:13 and Sir 36:1-17. Fox was correct in thinking that there were enough points of contact between Daniel and Ben Sira to think that either one was dependent on the other or that they were both dependent on a third unknown, earlier document. Some bases for deciding which way the dependency lies are the following:
1. Proverbs, poems, and short sayings are more often the texts of larger, prose documents, than vice versa.
2. If there is one expression that is quoted in both documents, and it appears only once in the first document as an inherent part of the document, but is used repeatedly in the second document, the second document is more likely to be the homily based on the first than vice versa.
3. When several additional words from the poem, proverb, or short saying appear also in the prose document, distributed interpretively, then the prose document is more likely to be the secondary document than the poem, proverb, or short saying.

The prayer of Ben Sira is itself a midrashic poem based partially on Hab 2:2-3. The repetitious verse is Sir 36:8: **Hasten the end time, and establish the appointed end**. These words did not come from Daniel. They had as their intertext Hab 2:2-3: **For there is still another vision for the appointed end. It speaks for the end time, and it does not deceive. If it is slow, wait for it, for it will surely come. It will not delay.** Instead of **not delay**, Ben Sira has **Hasten**. The words **end time** and **appointed end** come directly from Habakkuk—not from Daniel. But there are other words in the prayer: **hand, know** or **understand, power, glory, that time, hear,** and **right hand**. It is not very likely that Ben Sira picked all of these words out of Dan 11:17-12:13 and formed them into a poetic prayer.

Dan 11:17-12:13 also used Habakkuk and Isaiah, but it did not get all of these words from either of those sources. There is still one more basis for judgment. Ben Sira was supposedly written about 190-180 BIA. Dan 11-12 reports the end of Antiochus Epiphanes, about 164 BIA. It would have been impossible for Ben Sira to have taken these words that were related to the end of Antiochus Epiphanes before he began to rule. This means Ben Sira's prayer was a source for Dan 11:17-12:13, and this knowledge helps to understand the meaning of these chapters of Daniel.

The last verse of Daniel and the scrolls. In one of the fragments from the Dead Sea Scrolls (*11QMelch*) describes the laws of Jubilee and the Day of Atonement. It contains some themes and some words used also in the last words of the Book of Daniel.

TEXT

Daniel	11QMelchizedek
¹³You, go to **the end**, and you will rest and stand in your **portion at the end of the days**."	⁴Its interpretaion is for **the end of the days** for the captives.
	⁷the tenth Jubilee, to atone on it for all the sons of light and men of **the portion** of Melchizedek.[22]

COMMENTARY

The commentator who wrote this passage understood correctly that the expression **end of days** applied to the tenth Jubilee. That means after 70 weeks of years. That happened after the exiled **captives** had completed their "servitude" in Babylon. It was **the end of** those particular **days**—not **the end of** the world, the cosmos, or of all time. It was to be followed by the celebration of Hanukkah and the Sabbath **rest** that came with self rule. That was to be their promised and predestined **portion at the end of the days.**

---

[22] "11Q Melchizedek and the New Testament," *NTS* 12 (1964/65):302. Translated from the Hebrew text of M. De Jonge and A. S. Van der Woude

CONCLUSIONS

INTRODUCTION

The significance of Daniel. Daniel has been one of the most influential books of the Bible. In nearly every study on eschatology, the Book of Daniel is used as an important source. This is no accident. From early times Daniel has held a position of trust in the area of eschatology. Josephus praised Daniel as one of the greatest of the prophets:

> The books he wrote and left [for posterity] are still read by us, and we are convinced by them that Daniel communicated with God, for he prophesied not only the things that were about to happen as the other prophets did, but he also gave the precise time *(kai-ráhn hóhr-mid-zehn,* καιρὸν ὥρμιζεν) when these things would take place. Furthermore, the [other] prophets foretold disasters and for this reason were out of favor with kings and people. Daniel, [however], was a prophet of good news to them, so for the praiseworthiness of his predictions, all held him in favor (*Ant* 10.267-68).

The Gospel of Matthew expected the fulfillment of the message spoken **by the prophet Daniel** (Matt 24:15). One of the Qumran fragments described a time of testing as that which was written **in the Book of Daniel the prophet** *(buh sáy-fur Dah-nee-áyl hah nah-veé,* בספר דניאל הנביא) (*4Qflor* 2.4). Medieval Jews claimed that Daniel was weightier than all the wisemen of the nations (*bYoma* 77a).[1] He was held as a great saint and example for Jews to follow. In the Protestant Bible Daniel is classed among the prophets. According to the Torah God agreed to speak to the prophets in dreams and visions (Num 12:6). The Book of Daniel majored in dreams and visions.

Prophetic deductions. Soon after there had been an exile from the Promised Land, Israelites began to deduce what this meant. They started to ask, "Why has God treated us this way?" "How, when, and under what conditions will God allow us to

---

[1] I counted 120 references in non-rabbinic medieval Jewish sources alone.

return?" Scholars of that day began to study the local laws, the treaty that God had made with his people, cycles of time, and the normal enforcement of Sabbath and Jubilee customs. As early as the composition of Isa 11 and 27, sometime between 701 BIA and about 675 BIA, prophets began to develop an Israelite and Jewish eschatology. Jeremiah, basing his prophecies on Deuteronomy and Leviticus, popularized the relationship of Sabbatical and Jubilee justice to national exiles.

After the Hasmonean victory, however, it was the Book of Daniel that became the principal source for eschatology. This was the document that ostensibly prophesied the destruction of the Syrian Greek kingdom and the establishment of the Hasmonean kingdom with borders as extensive as those of Solomon's. While the Hasmonean kingdom was in full force, the Book of Daniel was a national victory drama. After Pompey, Crassus, and Quirinius, however, it became a prophetic source for future expectations. With the death of Herod's wife, Miriam (29 BIA), the house of the Hasmoneans came to an end. By that time Rome had already conquered the mountains in Asia Minor and brought the house of Seleucus to an end (ca. 66 BIA). The joy of Hanukkah had faded, and when Romans instituted their own leaders to govern Palestine and collect taxes for Rome, the victories of the Hasmoneans had all vanished. It was during the Hasmonean rule that the Book of Daniel was added to the canon.

The Book of Daniel was composed around the Hasmonean victory and the rededication of the temple. This was not the only time the temple had been dedicated. After the exodus from Egypt and the conquest of Canaan, King Solomon dedicated the temple. Ezra and Nehemiah rededicated the temple after the walls had been rebuilt and the new temple completed. Nevertheless, Daniel almost ignored the dedication of Ezra and Nehemiah, even though the author of Dan 9 used parts of Nehemiah's prayer of dedication as an intertext. The same author claimed Solomon's dedication as the antitype for the first Hanukkah celebration. The reason for this omission is not difficult to understand. The Jewish feast of Hanukkah was not established to memorialize the dedication of Ezra and Nehemiah. It became an essential part of the Jewish calendar after the Hasmonean victory and rededication of the temple at that time. The Book of Daniel was very closely related to the celebration of Hanukkah and was widely and quickly distributed.

Purpose of this study. The goal of this study has not been simply to show the nineteenth century theological concepts on which twentieth century scholars based their eschatological hopes.[2] Nor is it a review of the creative interpretation of Daniel's symbolism by modern exegetes. Many others have followed that pattern. The object here has been to find out where all of this expectation of end times originated in the first place. One of the important biblical origins for contemporary eschatology is the Book of Daniel. Therefore this research has examined Daniel in enough detail to be able to understand what there is about Daniel that has given as much impetus as it has to modern beliefs about end times. This conclusion is a summary of the insights found in that study.

---

[2] For that see G. Maier, *Die Johannesoffenbarung und die Kirche* (Tübingen: Mohr, 1981).

Myth and history. History consists of events remembered that take place in time and geographical location. Historians often narrate these in relationship to certain countries, cities, forests, bodies of water, deserts, and fields. They also relate them in chronological sequence, listing the earlier events before the succeeding events. If a historian were compared to a photographer, then the mythologist, by analogy, would be an artist. An artist does not attempt to make his or her painting or sculpture exactly like the person, object, or scene that has captured his or her attention. The artist tries to communicate a message through the painting that shows what the artist sees. The camera can provide a technically accurate image of that which the artist paints, but it cannot show the artist's message or interpretation.

The mythologist does the same with history. The mythologist describes events of history in a dramatic, sometimes religious, way. Taking all of the history for granted, he or she sets out to tell what all of this means--what is the message of this accumulation of historical facts? What meaning does it convey to the one who examines this history from a certain point of view, namely the mythologist's? Taking the history out of normal, factual, historical form does this, and distorting its objective perspective to suit the mythologist's desired emphasis provides a religious, apologetic, dramatic literary mold.

The mythologist, like a cartoonist, feels free to distort and exaggerate certain parts of the myth in order to point out the intended message. In other words, he or she interprets or mythologizes history just as an artist or cartoonist paints or draws his or her own perspectives into a painting or a cartoon. When it is done, the author assumes that his or her intended readers know the history and can therefore grasp the meaning that has been dramatized, just as the cartoonist assumes that the people who see the cartoon will recognize the characters cartooned. The distortion is a necessary part of the message. Even later historians, who are adequately acquainted with the history, have little trouble demythologizing much of the narrative and recognizing the history slightly disguised in the myth preserved in the Book of Daniel.

The Book of Daniel is one of the canonical documents that is best known for its mythologization of history. This is comparatively easy to decode, because the author interrupted the myth from time to time to explain to the reader precisely what the myth meant in simple terms. In other cases the mythologist thought the myth was so simple and obvious that the reader could easily deduce it. The mythology of the Book of Daniel reflects Jewish feeling that was prominent during the Maccabean Rebellion and the cleansing and rededication of the temple. Therefore it is necessary for modern scholars to learn as much as possible about that period of Jewish history in order to understand that which the original readers already knew when they first read or heard these stories.

Many scholars have recognized the mythical character of Dan 2-6.[3] Some have argued that chapter 1 was written as an introduction to the chapters that follow. It provides a suitable setting, and it uses many of the terms and concepts that are

---

[3] One of the earliest to make this deduction (IA 1733) was Sir Isaac Newton, *Observations on the Prophecies of Daniel and the Apocalypse of St. John* in *Sir Isaac Newton's Daniel and the Apocalypse*, ed. W. White (London: Murray, 1992), p. 10.

found in other chapters.[4] Wills classified all of these myths as court legends and compared them to legends circulating around Cyrus, Croesus, and others.[5] Paton placed Dan 2-6 in the class with the Jewish romances such as Tobit, Judith, 1Esdras 3, and the story of Ahikar.[6] This helps the Westerner to understand Near Eastern concepts.

Once, when my wife and I were touring Syria in a station wagon, we stopped at a Syrian town of Qoussier. There we visited with a Syrian family under the grapevines that covered the space between their houses. At the right time, everything stopped, and they turned on the radio. For half an hour we all listened to a program in Arabic. My Arabic was not good enough to understand the entire program, but when it was over, we all turned our attention to the oldest man in the family. He then retold the same story that had been told on the radio. My Arabic was only good enough to realize that that was what he was doing. No one in the family was bored; everyone expected it. That man obviously was recognized for his skill in story telling, and they were all happy to listen to his repetition after they already knew the story.

Before there were radios there were old men who told stories while families and communities listened. At the time Daniel was written there were ancient Jews who told and listened to favorite legends and stories told over and over again. They did not have to be precisely true to be entertaining, and story tellers probably modified the stories a bit from time to time to fit the audiences. While modern story tellers tell stories to large groups of people, all of whom know the story, they will sometimes have members of the audience correct them on small points of detail. When that happens story-tellers listen attentively, modify the stories, and go on. Scriptures have been read aloud in synagogues for centuries as people listen for hours at a time, hearing that which they have heard before. Jews systematically read long passages from the Torah and prophets. After they have read the entire Torah they start all over again. They are accustomed to sitting and listening to scripture being read orally. Those who hear this done week after week become apt at memorization. In this community setting the myth and the drama of Daniel came into existence. The dramas of Daniel were introduced to the Jewish community that was accustomed to this setting and practice.

Texts. Parts of the Dramas of Daniel have been preserved in three different languages: Most of the book has survived in Aramaic; the rest is in Hebrew. There are two fragments in Greek, namely, Aquila and Symmachus. Theodotion has been preserved almost completely in Greek. These three texts do not all agree at every point. Some are translations of others, and it is no longer certain how these documents originated. It is not so simple as to assume that all of the Greek (OG =

---

[4] L. M. Wills, *The Jew in the Court of the Foreign King* (Minneapolis: Fortress Press, c1990), pp. 79-81.
[5] Wills, *Foreign King*, pp. 61-70.
[6] L. B. Paton, *A Critical and Exegetical Commentary on the Book of Esther* (New York: Charles Scribner's Sons, c1916), p. 75.

Old Greek [OG] and Theodotion [Th]) texts are exact translations of the Aramaic. The OG has extensive passages that are not included in the MT, including "Suzanna" and "Bel and the Dragon." The editor of the OG was more inclusive of his sources than the MT.

Some texts are translations into Greek and others might have been written in Greek.[7] Before the Dead Sea Scrolls were found, some scholars presumed that Aramaic was the only language spoken and written in Palestine, so that Daniel was originally composed entirely in Aramaic. That belief, however, no longer is valid. Scrolls have been found in all three languages and were evidently spoken in Palestine in Maccabean times by different communities. Many of the texts are garbled, and scholars like Charles[8] and Bevan[9] have devoted years of study in attempts to uncover the original text. Although textual study is useful, it is a mistake to think that all of Daniel represents one author whose style can be distinguished from the other styles also represented in the book. In some places the original text cannot be conjectured, but readers can learn the basic message of each chapter even though the text is not perfect. The next step here will be to see how well all of this mythology was composed.

STORIES OF REDEMPTION

Introduction

The conclusion will first call attention to the mythology in the chapters of Daniel. This will make clear the obvious mythological character of the entire Book of Daniel. After a survey of Daniel 1-7, it will be necessary to review Dan 10, 11, and 12 to answer questions other scholars have raised in relationship to the history that has been mythologized in those chapters. Essential to all of this is the ability to distinguish myth from historical narrative and show the function of myth in relationship to history. Chapter 7 introduces the mythical figure, "Son of man," which was later used in eschatological contexts.

The Success of Daniel

The book began with the introduction to the hero, Daniel, and his three Jewish friends (Dan 1, 2, and 3). Nebuchadnezzar brought them, as well as other leading young people from his empire, to Babylon to be trained in Babylonian language, culture, science, and other graduate studies. They were brought as captives from Jerusalem, but they succeeded so well that they were recognized as being superior to all of the wisemen of the empire. They were retained in the court of the

---

[7] There are more questions about textual relationships than there are answers. See S. Pace, "The Stratigraphy of the Text of Daniel and the Question of Theological *Tendenz* in the Old Greek," *Bulletin of the International Organization for Septuagint and Cognate Studies* 17 (1984):15-34.

[8] R. H. Charles, *A Critical and Exegetical Commentary on the Book of Daniel* (Oxford: Clarendon Press, 1919).

[9] A. A. Bevan, *A Short Commentary on the Book of Daniel* (Cambridge: University Press, 1892).

king. This story was constructed on the basis of the story of Joseph's success in the land of Egypt. When introduced to the Jews at Hanukkah it would have been greatly approved. Daniel matched the ideal that Jews have cherished. Medieval rabbis compared Jews to vines in a gentile forest. They seemed rather lowly in this age, compared to the huge gentile trees, but in the age to come they would have climbed over the top of the forest and taken possession of the entire world. They are like grapes that are first trampled under people's feet and then set at the table of kings. (*LevR* 36.2). Dan 1 set the pace for all the rest of the dramas under the theme of "The Great Reversal."

The King's Statue

Daniel's drama in stone. Daniel's myth is drama. Some scholars call it a collection of tales or stories. It reflects Jewish nationalistic theology, humor, and the kind of entertainment Jews of Hasmonean times enjoyed. It should be read the way a person reads Shakespeare's plays. Daniel's dramas took the literary forms of dreams and visions. This was to alert the reader to the fact that this was mythology and not to be read as factual history. One of the dreams (or myths) was that of King Nebuchadnezzar. He dreamed about a statue whose head was of gold, chest and arms of silver, midsection and thighs of bronze, whose legs were of iron, and whose feet were partly of iron and partly of pottery (Dan 2).

A stone not hewn by human hands appeared which shattered the image into pieces and grew so large that it became a great mountain that filled the whole earth (Dan 2:31-35). The author of Daniel himself demythologized this dream to show that the various kinds of metal signified four kingdoms that ruled over Palestine in succession. The fourth kingdom was the iron that became both iron and pottery. This was a strong kingdom that had overpowered previous kingdoms, but its king became involved in a mixed marriage, and the kingdom met its downfall. The mixed marriage was mythologized by two elements, pottery and iron, which do not mix very well. The fourth kingdom was followed by a fifth kingdom, that God would establish. This was the kingdom, symbolized by the stone not made by human hands, that would shatter the previous kingdoms and fill the whole earth (Dan 2:36-45). The expression **made with human hands,** like the word **common**, means it is pagan. The temple was defiled, for example, after the altar had been made a place for pagan sacrifice. At that time it would have been a temple **made with human hands**. As soon as it had been cleansed and rededicated it was a temple "not made with hands." This drama mythologized the period of history between the beginning of the exile into Babylon (605 BIA according to Dan 2) and the cleansing of the temple before the first Hanukkah (164 BIA).

Scholarly interpretations. Very few modern scholars think that this dream took place in the time of the Babylonian captivity.[10] It is generally accepted that this myth was

---

[10] Some of the earlier exceptions are E B. Pusey, *Daniel the Prophet* (Oxford: James Parker, 1978), p 1: "The Book of Daniel is especially fitted to be a battlefield between faith and unbelief. It admits no half-measures. It is either Divine or an imposture. To write any book under the other, and to give it out to be his, is, in any case, a forgery, dishonest in itself, and destructive of all

designed to point out the author's conviction that it was God who destroyed the idol through the kingdom that succeeded the statue. Most scholars also believe the parts of the statue symbolized Babylon, Media, Persia, and Grecian Syria--the four kingdoms that ruled Judah from the time of the destruction of the temple until the Hasmonean victory against the Seleucid kings of Syria, some of whom were involved in marriage with Egyptian royalty.[11] The author concluded, **A great God has made known to the king what will happen after this. The dream is certain and its interpretation is sure** (Dan 2:45). The reason the author was sure of the events conjectured to be in the future is that they had already occurred.[12] The word here translated **its interpretation** is the Aramaic *pish-reh* (פשרה).

In such Dead Sea Scrolls as the Habakkuk Commentary, the author quoted verses from Habakkuk and then began his commentary with the formula, **Its interpretation is** (*pish-roh*, פשרו). This term that was later used to mean the interpretation of Hebrew scriptural texts was first used in Daniel to introduce the commentator's interpretation of "dreams," which were really myths. Although this myth in Dan 2 was entirely cast as a description of future events from the point of view of Nebuchadnezzar at the end of the seventh century BIA, most scholars assume that the author was writing history as myth.

The history included the political affairs that took place with these four countries from the end of the seventh century to the middle of the second century BIA, and the myth is Daniel's conviction that these political events were God's design. Although he spoke mythologically of four parts of an image, the author was really talking about four kingdoms that had succeeded one another in history until a kingdom that God designed overthrew the last of them and became very great. At the conclusion of the interpretation Nebuchadnezzar was pictured as bowing down at the feet of Daniel. This represents gentile authority subject to Israel (Dan 2:46-49; Isa 49:23; 60:14; *Ant* 11.33). This is the end of this story, with a conclusion that is as formal as if the author had said, "and they lived happily ever after." At this point in

---

trustworthiness. But the case as to the book of Daniel, if it were not his, would go far beyond even this. The writer, were he not Daniel, must have lied on a most frightful scale, ascribing to God prophecies which were never uttered, and miracles which are assumed never to have been wrought. In a word, the whole book would be one lie in the name of God." Another scholar who argued for an early Babylonian origin was C. F. Keil, *Biblical Commentary on the Book of Danie*, tr. M. G. Easton (Grand Rapids: William B. Eerdmans Publishing Co., c1976). A more recent author is S. B. Ferguson, *The Communicator's Commentary: Daniel* (Waco: Word Books, c1988), p. 18: "This view of Daniel, which accepts a sixth-century dating, runs contrary to the trends of contemporary critical scholarship."

[11] This probably referred to the marriage of Ptolemy to the Syrian princess Cleopatra, the sister of Antiochus IV. On the basis of this union, the next generation of Egyptians claimed that Antiochus III agreed with Ptolemy of Egypt at the time of his marriage to Antiochus' daughter to give Palestine to Ptolemy as a gift (Polybius 28.20, 8-9).

[12] In response to the claim that if Daniel had really been composed in the Maccabean period it could not have been received into the Jewish canon, A. A. Bevan, *Short Commentary*, p. 13, said, "For the theory that the Jewish Canon was closed before the Maccabean period rests upon no evidence whatsoever." The earliest reference to the Book of Daniel is in 1Macc 2:59-60: "Hananiah, Azariah, and Mishael, because they had faith, were rescued from fire. Daniel because of his innocence was saved from the mouth of the lions."

the drama, the Hasmonean Jewish audience, celebrating Hanukkah, would have supplied lots of applause. The author would have received a standing ovation.

Mythic confusion. Scholars agree that the author was **certain** (Dan 2:45) of the events, because they had already taken place--that is, all except the last one. Scholars interpret that last event differently and vaguely, although Daniel was also **certain** that these four kingdoms that had ruled Palestine would be followed by another kingdom. There was, in historical fact, a fifth kingdom that followed the fourth, but scholars single out this item as if the author had *not* been **certain**--as if it *alone* were prophecy, and all the rest, mythologized history. To do this scholars had to split the author's myth into two time periods, even though the author gave it in only one.

The fifth kingdom, from a Jewish perspective, the one that followed the rule of the Greeks, was the Hasmonean kingdom. This was the kingdom the author thought God appointed to shatter the Greeks, as, indeed, that kingdom did. This would be the normal de-mythologization of the narrative, but for some reason, scholars follow this logic right up to the point of identifying the kingdom that succeeded the Greek kingdom--and stop! The author of Daniel, who interpreted the myth himself, said of his entire myth that the dream was certain and the interpretation was true (Dan 2:45), but modern scholars hold that this last interpretation is, instead, false prophecy. They said that the kingdom mentioned never really existed, but rather is one that people in the twenty-first century can still expect to come--*more than two thousand years later!* This overlooks the fact that the rule for including books into the canon was that they represented **fulfilled** prophecy (Deut 18:22), and Daniel was included in the canon.[13]

Porteous correctly observed that the stone that grew into a mountain that would stand forever symbolized the kingdom of which Daniel spoke.[14] He further identified this with the mountain of the house of the Lord (Isa 2:2; Micah 4:2) which would be established as the highest of the mountains. The author of Daniel probably also had Isa 30:29 in mind, which identified the Mount of Yehowah with the rock of Israel. This rock was also Jerusalem and was destined to be a rock of stumbling for all the gentiles (Zech 12:4). Although Porteous began correctly, he did not take the next logical step and identify the kingdom in Dan 2 with the Hasmonean kingdom that ruled from the mountain of the house of the Lord at Jerusalem immediately after the fourth kingdom ceased to rule Palestine. Sahlin said the stone was intended as a symbol of Judas the Maccabee.[15]

The Fiery Furnace

King Nebuchadnezzar had a huge statue erected in the capital city and decreed that everyone in Babylon was required to bow down and worship this

---

[13] F. C. Burkitt, *Jewish and Christian Apocalypses* (London: Oxford U. Press, 1914), p. 11, thought the only reason Daniel was accepted into the canon and Ben Sira and Baruch omitted was that Daniel had already been canonized before the fall of Jerusalem in IA 70. Esther was accepted because Rabbi Akiba fought for its admission. It reflected his nationalistic beliefs.
[14] N. W. Porteous, *Daniel* (Philadelphia: Westminster Press, c1965), p. 50.
[15] H. Sahlin, "Antiochus IV. Epiphanes und Judas Mackabäus," *ST* 23(1969):42-43.

statue whenever the musical instruments were played (Dan 3). Public officials observed that Daniel's three Jewish friends, Shadrach, Meshach, and Abednego had failed to respond as directed, so they reported this crime to the king. The king first gave the Jews an opportunity to redeem themselves by fulfilling the obligation. When they refused, he had them thrown into a fiery furnace that was so hot it burned the Babylonians appointed to throw them into the furnace. The flames, however, did not in any way effect the Jews. They emerged from the furnace without so much as a smudge or the smell of smoke on their clothes. The king was so favorably impressed that he confessed the God of the Jews and decreed that anyone who defamed this God would be torn to pieces and their houses destroyed. Such was one of the many great reversals of the Book of Daniel. In every reversal it was the Jews who always came out as victors. This essay was probably designed to mythicize the Babylonian exile where Jews were "imprisoned" and punished. Their captors planned to destroy them completely, but they were rescued, and their religion impressed the king.

Trees and Kingdoms

Nebuchadnezzar dreamed of a tree that grew so big that it reached from one end of the earth to the other (Dan 4). All birds and animals found shelter in and under this tree. Then a watcher from heaven commanded that it be cut down. Daniel's interpretation of this dream was that the tree was Nebuchadnezzar's kingdom. Although it was great, extending from the Euphrates River to the western border of Egypt, it could be destroyed in an instant by God who gives the kingdom to whomever he will. Even gentile kings of superpower countries were under the dominion of the Lord God of Israel who would change things whenever he chose (Dan 4:4-25).

This myth was probably created by someone familiar with Ezekiel's story of a shoot that an eagle brought from Lebanon to Babylon. It was planted by water but was later transplanted, and it dried up and died. After this the Lord took a shoot from a cedar tree and planted it on the top of the mountain height of Israel where it flourished and bore fruit (even though cedar trees do not bear edible fruit), so that all other trees and animals were dependent upon it. This was to show that the Lord could make dry trees flourish and green trees dry up. It also showed that this particular tree could not flourish by the rivers of Babylon. It belonged to the land the Lord had chosen for it (Ezek 17). The story from Ezekiel was called a "riddle" or a parable--not a historical report (Ezek 17:2), but Ezekiel told it in relationship to Jerusalem's king who was moved to Babylon and then broke a treaty with the Babylonians and tried to negotiate with Egypt (Ezek 17:11-21).

The "riddle" was Ezekiel's mythological way of telling the significance of some historical events. Most modern scholars also presume that the story in Dan 4 is also parabolic and not a historical report. They assume that it is a myth that the author composed to tell the religious significance of political rule of great kingdoms.[16] Sahlin believed that the message of this dream was to give comfort to the Jews in relationship, not to Nebuchadnezzar, but to Antiochus Epiphanes.[17]

Writing on the Wall

In Belshazzar's vision (Dan 5), while he was feasting with Judean temple vessels, a non-human hand wrote a message, *Muh-nah, muh-nah, tuh-kehl, oo-farh-seen* (מנא מנא תקל ופרסין) (Dan 5:17-25). Daniel's interpretation of this vision was that Belshazzar's kingdom would be taken from him and given to the Medes and the Persians (Dan 5:26-28). Since the Persians, at least, actually followed Babylon in ruling the Middle East, scholars have assumed that this was mythologized history and not just a report of factual events. The religious message came from the non-human hand that wrote. That was God who was pictured in control just as in the earlier story it was God who created the (Israelite) mountain and made it fall on the (gentile) statue. God was in control even of the enemy king who profaned Israel's sacred temple vessels. The non-human hand that took away the empire from the king of Babylon may reflect the easy way in which Cyrus of Persia captured Babylon. LaCocque said the death of Belshazzar at the end of this myth had the same mythical liberating function as the death of Antiochus Epiphanes in other myths.[18] Sahlin thought that Nebuchadnezzar in Dan 4 and Belshazzar in Dan 5 were both code names for Antiochus Epiphanes.[19]

The Lions' Den

Local government officials were jealous of Daniel, the foreign Jew, who held the highest government office in the land (Dan 6). This story began after Daniel had already achieved a status next to the king in prestige. Such a distinction as this aroused the envy of Babylonians of lower rank. They set a trap designed to remove Daniel from the king's court, permanently. They persuaded the king to make a decree that anyone who worshipped any god or human being for 30 days, except the king, would be thrown into a den of lions. Then they caught Daniel openly worshiping the God of the Jews and reported it to the king. When Daniel was thrown to the lions, not one of the lions injured Daniel, but when all of Daniel's accusers, their wives, and their children were thrown to the lions, they were consumed at once. The great reversal was when the king sent a decree throughout the land, confessing that Daniel's God was the true god, and Daniel continued to prosper.

---

[16] Scholars also think the author of Daniel used literary sources and attributed to Nebuchadnezzar the illness of Nabonidus. This is confirmed by materials found in Harran (*Nabon H2A*) and among the Dead Sea Scrolls (*4QOrNab*). On this see D. N. Freedman, "The Prayer of Nabonidus," *BASOR* 145:31 ff., E. Haag, *Die Errettung Daniels aus der Löwengrube* (Stuttgart: Verlag Katholisches Bibelwerk, c1983), pp. 62-79, and Wills, *Court of a Foreign King*, pp. 87-121.
[17] Sahlin, "Antiochus," p. 44.
[18] A. LaCocque, *The Book of Daniel*, tr. D. Pellauer (Atlanta: University of South Carolina Press, c1979), p. 92.
[19] Sahlin, "Antiochus," p. 45.

Dan 6 is very similar to Dan 5, just as Dan 7 is similar to Dan 2. This will soon become evident.

The Heavenly Court

Daniel's dream. After interpreting the dreams of others, in Dan 7, Daniel is reported as having had a dream himself. He dreamed that four monstrous beasts arose out of the sea. Three of these four beasts were patterned after three of the beings that upheld the water basin in the temple, according to Ezek 1. These three were the lion, the bear, and the leopard. In addition to the four beasts there was also in Ezekiel's vision a man who helped uphold the basin. When Daniel interpreted the myth of his dream, he said that the lion was the king of Babylon, the bear was the king of Media, the leopard was the king of Persia, and the fourth beast, that was the indescribable monster, was the king of Greece. The fourth beast replaced the human being as the fourth leg to hold up the basin. The human being was set apart. Corresponding to the man in Ezekiel's vision was the Son of man, according to Daniel.

In Daniel's vision was a heavenly trial, in which God was the Ancient of Days who acted as judge. The defendant in the case was Antiochus IV Epiphanes, who was a horn descended from one of the Grecian horns of the indescribable monster. After the proper court formalities were over, the defendant was allowed to defend himself. He did so extensively, but the judge decreed that he was guilty of the charge and should be given a death sentence, and his body should be burned. Then appeared the plaintiff, who was the Son of man. He came up to the heavenly judge with the clouds and he together with the saints of the Most High was given the kingdom, the glory, and the governmental authority. This was a mythical vision in which the characters of the drama are easy to identify. The vision was a theological interpretation of the events that had happened in Judah during the three-year Maccabean Rebellion, during which Judas the Maccabee and his troops battled Antiochus IV and his troops. This historical period ended with Judas winning the famous Battle of Beth-horon and Antiochus IV dying in Persia at about the same time. Therefore Antiochus was the defendant in the vision, and Judas was the plaintiff. This will be explained more fully.

The plaintiff's mythical title. The term "Son of man" seems to have been used in the FT to mean simply "man." For instance, Ezekiel was frequently addressed by the Lord as Son of man: **Son of man, stand upon your feet** (Ezek 2:1) or **Son of man, I am sending you to the children of Israel** (Ezek 2:3). The most likely meaning of "Son of man" in these passages seems to be simply "man."[20] Dan 7 obtained the term "Son of man" also from Ezekiel. Of the beings that upheld the large basin called the "sea" in the temple, three were beasts and one was a man. Daniel replaced

---

[20] Another possibility is that "Son of man" was a self-designation of Ezekiel by which he described his office as a messenger-prophet or eschatological prophet. In any event, it is not the same as the meaning in Daniel, which must be judged by its own context. For the possible relationship of Jesus' use of Son of man to Ezekiel's see E. Schweitzer, "The Son of Man Again," *NTS* 10 (1963/64):256-61.

the man with another beast, in his imagination. This fourth beast was more monstrous that any of the other beasts. The author of Dan 7 identified all four of these beasts, which Ezekiel pictured in the temple, with kings of the succession of great empires in the Fertile Crescent. He then set the "man" in contrast to the beasts. He called the "man" "Son of man." Since, however, he had already identified the beasts with kings, he also identified the contrasting being, the Son of man, with a national leader, a human being. The beasts were from the demonic deep, and the Son of man was associated with heaven. In the drama of Dan 7, the fourth beast was the "horn" and Antiochus IV. The Son of man was the contending party in the trial, Judas the Maccabee.

In Daniel, however, the "Son of man" was not just any human being. He played a special role and had a specific significance.[21] Not as a visible fact of history, but in a vision, Daniel saw one like a Son of man coming with the clouds of heaven up to the Ancient of Days. To this being who was like a Son of man was given ruling authority, glory, and a kingdom. All peoples, nations, and languages were to serve him. His ruling authority and kingdom were to continue for the age [to come] (Dan 7:13-14).

This expectation is coherent with the conclusion of other myths of the book that pictured kings of the great countries all acknowledging that the God of Israel was the true god. It would be only a matter of time before these countries would all be subject to Israel. At the same time the saints of the Most High were given the kingdom, ruling authority, and greatness of the kingdoms under the whole heaven; their kingdom and dominion was to be for the age [to come], and all other dominions were destined to serve the saints (Dan 7:27). Because the same privileges were given both to the saints of the Most High and also the Son of man many scholars have thought that the two terms were equivalent. The Son of man, they say, was really the saints who were Jews.[22] Since these were powers given to people who were responsible for a government, the one (Son of man) would have been the ruler and the rest would have been citizens of the same country.

The age to come at the end of the age of the beasts or the gentile age was the age of the Son of man or the Hasmonean age that followed the first Hanukkah. Collins was correct in refuting those scholars who thought that Jews had no concept of a title "Son of man" before or during the ministry of Jesus.[23] This title had its origin in Dan 7 whose author developed it in his drama based on Ezek 1. When Jesus used the title as a self-identification, he presumed a familiarity on the part of local Jews with the significance of the title, "Son of man." He claimed to be an antitype and fulfillment of the Son of man figure in Dan 7.

The Book of Daniel, written for or after the rededication of the temple and the restoration of worship in Jerusalem, was composed in terms of sabbatical release. Jeremiah had promised that the Jews were to be in captivity for seventy years. That

---

[21] Although even in Dan 8:17 and 10:16 *ben 'adam* (בן אדם) and *bene 'adam* (בני אדם) have a generic meaning. Following the text in Ezekiel, the "son of man" is a character in the drama in contrast to the beasts. His function shows the nature and identity of the character.

[22] U. B. Mueller, *Messias und Meschensohn in Juedischer Apokalypsen und der Offenbarung des Johannes* (Guetersloh: Gerd Mohn, c1972), p. 28.

[23] J. J. Collins, *A Commentary on the Book of Daniel* (Minneapolis: Fortress Press, c1993), p. 90.

time had long since passed, but probably on the basis of the seven-fold punishment threatened in Lev 26, the author deduced that the terms of the treaty required seven times 70 years or 70 weeks of years. He was able to manipulate this figure so as to coincide perfectly with the Maccabean victory.[24]

Jubilee justice. The author of Dan 9 interpreted the Maccabean victory in sabbatical terms. The Jubilee of ten weeks of years was the time when the "captivity" was over, "slaves" were set free, and the land was restored to the "original owners," as at Jubilee. This was a nationalistic interpretation of sabbatical justice. In this context, when the Maccabees were recovering the Promised Land from the Syrians, and Jews received a new national freedom, Daniel saw a vision during which the saints of the Most High received ruling authority and the kingdom, and a being like a "Son of man" also received ruling authority, glory, and a kingdom. The being "like a Son of man" would seem to have been the leader in charge of the Jewish saints who recovered control of the temple, cleansed it, and renewed sacrifice. The leader at that time was Judas the Maccabee, one who gave the initial impetus to the rebellion that finally succeeded in freeing the Jews from foreign rule and taxation and introducing the Hasmonean age to come. Complete national liberty was not obtained until 142 BIA during Simon's rule when the taxation was removed, and Simon was appointed high priest and leader (*War* 1.53; 1Macc 13:39-42).

Aristobulus I was the first Hasmonean to declare himself king (*War* 1.117), but earlier Hasmoneans, among their own people, were exalted higher than their official titles acknowledged. Simon, for instance, was called by the Hebrew name, "the general of the people of God" (Greek *ah-sah-rah-mehl* ασαραμελ) a transliteration for *sahr-ahm-áyl*, שר עם אל).[25] Judas, the leader when the temple was cleansed, was neither high priest nor king, officially, but he was highly respected by contemporary and later Jews. He was one *like* a Son of man. Judas' victory over the Greeks, the cleansing of the temple and its rededication were very important occasions in Jewish history.

These events proved to Jews that the sins they had committed before 605 BIA had been forgiven and their redemption was complete. Only three or four months after the Day of Atonement the victory of Beth-horon took place (January or February, 164 BIA). Approximately ten months after the Battle of Beth-horon had been fought the temple was rededicated, proving to Jews that they had been redeemed from their "enslavement" to the Greeks. This convinced the Jews that the Day of Atonement that occurred before the Battle of Beth-horon had been effective. It was probably in relationship to the following New Year's Day, just ten days before the Day of Atonement, that the drama of Dan 7 was designed. That was the day when God was believed to judge his people. The Battle of Beth-horon proved to them that this judgment was made in their favor.

---

[24] This manipulation involved assigning sixty-two weeks of years to the period from the return to Jerusalem until a certain treaty was made, with little concern for mathematical accuracy. See GenR. 85.2.

[25] A. S. Tedesche and S. Zeitlin, *The First Book of Maccabees* (New York: Harper and Brothers, 1950), p. 44, correctly suggested in relation to 1Macc 14:27. The initial *alpha* probably indicates a prosthetic *aleph* since the definite article ha would not have been present in this combination

The Day of Atonement. According to Jewish doctrine, God had made a treaty with Abraham, agreeing to provide for him 1) posterity, 2) prosperity, and 3) the Land of Canaan (Gen 15). The Israelite conditions to this treaty were that they would keep the laws prescribed in the Torah. If they failed to do this--that is, if they broke this treaty, then their blessings would be changed to curses, and they would be punished seven times for all of their sins (Lev 26). Instead of prosperity they would receive famine, pestilence, wild beasts, and the sword. Instead of the Land of Canaan they would be driven off the land and out of the Lord's house (Deut 24:1). The Day of Atonement was instituted to give Israelites and Jews the opportunity to pay the fines required for their sins so that the Lord would not dissolve their treaty with him. On the Day of Atonement every party to the treaty was obligated to come to the temple and pay the unpaid fines. These fines would not satisfy the Lord, however, unless the sinners first became reconciled to all of their fellow citizens against whom they had committed offenses (*mYoma* 8.9).

If all parties to the treaty were reconciled to one another, and if all fines to the Lord were paid in full, then the treaty would be retained and all Jews and Israelites would receive the blessings provided. When the Lord's house was destroyed both in Jerusalem and Gerizim, and the Israelites and Jews were all sent away from their land as captives, Jeremiah understood that God had divorced his people. Because the people had been unfaithful to their treaty, God nullified his treaty with his people. Jeremiah said that God would not restore his people to their former favorable position until they had paid double for all their sins. These were the terms of sabbatical eschatology (Deut 15:18; Jer 16:18). The only way Jews or Israelites could know if they had paid an adequate amount was their condition of life. If they were in exile that meant that they still owed more fines. If the Day of Atonement was effective, then the people would be restored to their land, and their treaty would be reinstituted.

The blessings of the Beth-horon and Beth-zur victories and the celebration of Hanukkah in 164 BIA proved to the contemporary Jews that the previous Day of Atonement had been effective. Their sins had all been paid or forgiven, and the treaty with the Lord was being restored. That was the occasion for their great celebration, and that was the mood reflected in the Book of Daniel.

Judas was their new leader--not the Greek kings. In contrast to the beasts he came as one like a Son of man, and to him God gave the kingdom, the authoritative power, and the glory of his position. The author of Dan 7 reasoned that God had accepted the martyrdom of the soldiers who had been killed in battle, the pious Jews who had been killed on the Sabbath day, and the mothers who died rather than leave their sons uncircumcised as an adequate atonement offering. The merits of their lives were enough to compensate for the sins of earlier Jews, whose crimes caused their captivity. These religious beliefs were confirmed on their first Hanukkah after the victorious battle of Beth-horon. Jews still pray on Hanukkah:

> I will mention your mercy in song and in happiness, because you delivered your people [the Jews] from hardship to well being; you have avenged our vengeance by your faithful priests [the Hasmoneans]. The Greeks tried to annul the Torah of our God. Your

hand has delivered us from hardship and oppression. Therefore, there has been appointed for us eight days of dedication to give thanks, to glorify, and to praise the mighty deeds of our God. Let us merit the consecration of the altar in our days . . ."[26]

Daniel Seven and the Date of Composition

Foresight is often mistaken, but hindsight is an exact science. When Isaiah and Jeremiah both predicted the fall of Babylon at the hands of Media, they were both mistaken. Media never overthrew Babylon. Kaufman observed further about Jeremiah's prophecies,

Many northern kings did not set up thrones at Jerusalem's gates ([Jer] 1:5); the people of Anathoth were not utterly destroyed (11:23; cf. Ezra 2:23). Jehoiakim did not receive 'the burial of an ass,' nor was his corpse thrown outside Jerusalem (22:18 f.; 36:30; cf. II Kings 24:6); Zedekiah did not die in peace (34:5), nor did God ever remember him in Babylon (32:5); the exiles were not compelled to worship other gods 'day and night' (16:13); Nebuchadnezzar did not destroy or exile Egypt (46:13 ff.); the seed of Jehoiakim—notwithstanding 22:30—was thought fit for kingship both by Ezekiel (17:22 ff.) and the restoration community, who pinned their hopes on Zerubbabel, a descendant of Jehoiakin (I Chron 3:15 ff.; Hag. 2:21 ff., Zech 3:8; 4:6 ff.; etc.).[27]

Daniel, however, "predicted" events with amazing accuracy. So amazing that it is obvious that the visions and dreams were composed after the historical events had taken place.

Although Josephus presumed that Daniel lived in Babylon during the Babylonian captivity, he observed that everyone liked Daniel, because his prophecies were not of doom, like those of other prophets, but of good things. Furthermore his prophecies proved to be true. His prophecy was recognized for its accuracy (*ah-kree-béhs* ἀκριβές) and trustworthiness (*ah-pah-ráhl-ahk-tahn*, ἀπαράλλακτον) (*Ant* 10.268-69). Josephus further spelled out how this prophecy was fulfilled: Daniel had said the temple would be defiled for three years, and that was what happened during the reign of Antiochus Epiphanes (*Ant* 10.275-76).

The Dramas of Daniel are presented as if individual Jews who lived in Babylon at the very beginning of the Babylonian captivity prophesied them all, but there are internal signs that make this impossible. Dan 2 contains Greek loan words that were nowhere discovered in Greek literature until the second century BIA that have been spelled in Aramaic. They would not have been known in Babylon until the conquest of Babylon by Alexander in 331 BIA. Dan 9 interprets Jeremiah's prediction of the end of the captivity to concur with the actual restoration of the temple in 164 BIA. The same chapter also includes a poetic

---

[26] Buchanan, *Revelation and Redemption: Jewish Documents of Deliverance from the Fall of Jerusalem to the Death of Nahmanides* (Dillsboro: Western North Carolina Press, c1978; sold by Mercer U. Press), p. 235.
[27] Y. Kaufman, *The Religion of Israel from its Beginnings to the Babylonian Exile*, tr. and abridged M. Greenberg (Chicago: University of Chicago Press, c1960), pp. 313-14; see further p. 429.

prayer that is based on the prayer of dedication of Solomon (1Kgs 8) and the prayer of Hezekiah that was followed by the destruction of the Assyrian soldiers and the return of the Assyrian general to Assyria.

These intertexts would not have been as pertinent as they are if the Battles of Beth-horon and Beth-zur had not been fought, and the Syrian soldiers had not been badly defeated, forcing the Syrian generals, Gorgias and Lysias, to take the remnants of their troops back to Syria. That seemed like a recapitulation of the Assyrian retreat following the prayer of Hezekiah after most of the Assyrian soldiers died in the Kidron Valley. Quotations from Solomon's prayer of dedication and Nehemiah's prayer before returning to restore Jerusalem would have been appropriate for the rededication of the temple at Hanukkah. The author of Dan 9 had two basic scripture passages with which to prove his case. These were the two witnesses needed to prove a case in court.

Dan 7 dramatizes the death of Antiochus Epiphanes and the installation of Judas the Maccabee as ruler of Palestine in a theological court scene that would have had no motivation before the death of Antiochus and the first New Year's Day before the Battle of Beth-horon. The Battle of Beth-horon was probably fought in January or February of 164 BIA. Antiochus IV died just before or just after the Battle of Beth-horon. Bevan holds that Antiochus died before the Battle of Beth-zur and that Lysias learned of it and retreated from Judas, partly because he had learned of this Syrian tragedy,[28] even though it was as late as October before Hanukkah. The Seleucid King List reports that Antiochus died in the month of Kislev, but it does not say which year.[29] That could have been the same month and year as Hanukkah or it might have been the year before Hanukkah. The witnesses do not agree on the order of events during this period. According to 2Macc the Battle of Beth-horon was fought first, then there was the purification, and the Battle of Beth-zur occurred after that when Antiochus V was king of Syria.

Doran's explanation of the problem with 2Macc is persuasive. He noted that Timothy was killed in 2Macc 10:37 and then reappeared again in 2Macc 12:2. His suggestion is that these narratives have been misplaced and that 2Macc 12 really belongs, chronologically, before 2Macc 10:14-38. If these units are switched, the Battle of Beth-zur would occur before Hanukkah during the reign of Antiochus IV.[30] This would also cohere with 1Macc. According to 1Macc, the battles of Beth-horon and Beth-zur were fought, and then Hanukkah was celebrated. Shortly after that Antiochus died. All of these events happened within a short time, and we cannot know for sure the exact dates of each one. That which is clear, however, is that the death of Antiochus and the Battle of Beth-horon and possibly the Battle of Beth-zur happened before Dan 7 was written.

Dan 7 was written as if the judgment day on the New Year's Day before these events took place was the time when God judged Judah favorably. The author of this drama thought Judas the Maccabee and Antiochus IV were the main human

---

[28] E. R. Bevan, *The House of Seleucus* (New York: Barnes & Noble, 1966) II, Appendix J, p. 299.
[29] J. B. Pritchard, *Ancient Near Eastern Texts* (Princeton: Princeton University Press, 1969), p. 567.
[30] R. Doran, "2Maccabees and 'Tragic History,'" *HUCA* 50 (1979):107-114.

characters in the heavenly judgment day, which he dramatized. Therefore it was written very shortly before Hanukkah or some time after Hanukkah.

Hanukkah was celebrated in December, 164 BIA. The various times given between the defilement of the temple and its rededication all roughly conclude at 164 BIA when Hanukkah actually occurred. The rock that crushed the gentile statue (Dan 2) and the Son of man that followed the four beasts (Dan 7) all presume the initiation of the country that followed the earlier four empires as Jewish Palestine.

Hartman objected to the obvious conclusion these facts suggest. He said,

> But since the author of the primary stratum of ch. 7 does not make even an obscure allusion to the king's desecration of the temple and the beginning of his bloody persecution of the Jews in 167 BC (I Macc 1:54-61), he surely did not write ch. 7 after these latter events.[31]

The reason they were not mentioned directly is that the entire myth of Dan 7 was written in code. Instead of kings the author spoke of beasts. Instead of war he spoke of a judgment day. He interpreted the events Hartman missed to give their theological dimension rather than their geographical and historical mention that was already known. It is not difficult to identify the historical events with the visions of Dan 7.

There is no possibility that Daniel was originally thought of as a prophecy that was written in the 7th or 6th century BIA. Nevertheless, there have been many scholars who have claimed that the entire book is prophecy, and that the author used Zechariah and Ezra as intertexts.[32] Patterson even presumed that Daniel was an intertext for Zechariah,[33] since it had been written before Zechariah. Patterson gave illustrations of court tales told as early as the third millennium BIA and showed that court tales continued to be written throughout the second and first millennium BIA. Therefore, court tales were not datable in and of themselves. He compared the court tales of Daniel with earlier and later tales and concluded that those in Daniel were closer to the earlier ones that he identified than the later ones.[34] Keil also argued that the contemplative, visionary style of the literature speaks against composition in the midst of a national crisis.[35] This means, he thought, that it was written much earlier when the author was not under stress. Keil recognized that the style of Daniel is contemplative, dramatic, and victorious. Keil was correct is noting the problem that this provides for anyone concluding that the document or documents were composed

---

[31] L. F. Hartman and A. A. DiLella, *The Book of Daniel* (Garden City: Doubleday & Co., Inc., 1978), p. 214.
[32] So, for example, Keil, *Daniel*, p. 43.
[33] R. D. Patterson, "The Key Role of Daniel 7," *GTJ* 12 (1991):258.
[34] Patterson, "Holding on to Daniel's Court Tales," *JETS* 36 (1993):452-54.
[35] Keil, *Daniel*, p. 46. There are others who still argue for a very early date for Daniel. D. W. Gooding, "The Literary Structure of the Book of Daniel and its Implications," *TB* 32 (1981):43-79; E. M. Yamauchi, "Daniel and Contacts Between the Aegean and the Near East Before Alexander," *EQ* 53 (1981):37-47; R. J. M. Gurney, "The Seventy Weeks of Daniel 9:24-27," *EQ* 53 (1981):29-36.; and B. L. Woodard, Jr., "Literary Strategies and Authorship in the Book of Daniel,"*JETS* 37 (1994):39-53.

in the midst of a life and death struggle. It more naturally fits in the celebration mood that took place after the victory of Beth-horon.

Some of the dramas of Daniel could have been written to be read at the very first Hanukkah celebration in 164 BIA. The final edition may have been as late as 142 BIA when the tax was removed, the Davidic kingdom completely restored, and the Hasmonean Simon had been installed as high priest and national leader. This was an occasion that called for celebration, and it was celebrated for 8 days. Calendars were dated beginning with that event. Dan 7 may have been composed specially for that celebration. It was completed early enough to have been employed by 1Enoch and one of the Dead Sea Scrolls.[36] This means that the entire Book of Daniel was probably composed for Hanukkah and for the celebration of liberty, between 164 and 142 BIA.

The time when there would have been the most excitement and motivation for literary creation to have taken place would have been the period between the Battle of Beth-horon and/or Beth-zur and the first Hanukkah (164 BIA). Many parts of the Dramas of Daniel might have been made public during the eight-day festival of Hanukkah. The optimism, success, braggadocio, and celebration reflected in the book belong to the festivity of Hanukkah; no matter at which Hanukkah it was introduced. Many chapters of Daniel might have been read during the first Hanukkah and also during later Hanukkahs. Chapter 7, however, might have required a later composition. Suppose, for example, that Antiochus Epiphanes did not die until a few weeks before Hanukkah. Could any author have written this chapter in two or three weeks? It is possible. When properly motivated, authors, musicians, and artists have been known to create important works in very short periods of time. Mozart and Bach were famous for this, and Handel wrote *The Messiah* in just a few weeks. There never was a time when the motivation would have been higher for the composition of Dan 7 than just after the death of Antiochus IV and before Hanukkah. If it had not been written before the first Hanukkah, it would have been an exciting drama to have been introduced in 142 BIA at the celebration of the complete liberation of Judah from Syria.

The Book of Daniel was collected after the Battle of Beth-horon, maybe even after the removal of the taxation (between 164 and 142 BIA). The book was unknown by Ben Sira who wrote about 200 BIA. The Hebrew of Daniel points to a late age in comparison with the known biblical literature. It resembles the Hebrew of the Chronicler, which was one of the sources used frequently by Daniel. Scholars have criticized the Book of Daniel for its careless style. It lacks the polish of the Psalms or Second Isaiah. It may have been rushed into the canon shortly after it was composed as part of the nationalistic excitement surrounding Hanukkah. There are more Persian loan words than Babylonian in the Daniel text. The Greek word *soom-phoh-neé-ah* (συμφωνία) first occurs in Greek literature as a musical instrument in the works of Polybius (2nd BIA). Daniel is not cited or alluded to in any work earlier than the 2nd century BIA.

---

[36] *4Q 174*.2, 3: "As it was written in the Book of Daniel the prophet" (*ah-shayr kah-toov buh-say-fehr Dah-nee-ehl hah-nah-vee*, אשֶׁר כתוב בספר דניאל הנבי א).

The Horns

The function of horns. Another myth (Dan 8) came as a vision to Daniel when he was in Babylon. He saw a ram standing on the bank of the river Ulai. This ram had two horns, one longer than the other. The longest one grew up last. This ram charged eastward, northward, and southward, and no one could resist his power, until a male goat with a single horn on his forehead came from the west so fast that he did not even touch the ground. He came against the ram, broke the ram's two horns and trampled upon him.

After the male goat became still stronger his horn was broken. Then the figure was changed from either a ram's two horns or a unicorn's one horn to a reindeer's tree of horns. The one horn was replaced with four horns, and from one of the horns grew a little horn. The little horn expanded his territory to the south, the east, and the (*hah-tsah-veé*, הצבי) glorious land (= Palestine). There he overpowered some of the army of Heaven (= army of God)[37] and caused some of the stars to fall to the ground, and trampled them. He took away the continual offering from the chief of the army and overthrew the place of the sanctuary. Then a holy one spoke and said that the continual burnt offering would remain desolate for two thousand, three hundred evening and morning sacrifices. Then it would be restored (Dan 8:1-14). Afterward Gabriel told Daniel that this vision was for the time of the end (Dan 8:15-17). Bevan said,

> The angel informs Daniel of what will take place "in the last days of wrath"; i.e. at the end of the heathen domination, for the period of the subjection of Israel to the gentiles is the period of the divine wrath (chap. xi.36),

which makes sense, but Bevan strangely also said,

> "for the vision is for the time of the end", i.e. it refers to *the final crisis of the world's history* [emphasis added], and is therefore worthy of peculiar attention.[38]

Daniel said only that the vision was for the time of the end, but he did not say the end *of history*. That was Bevan's interpretation. Gabriel promptly interpreted the vision to Daniel.

1) The two horns were the kings of Media and Persia.
2) The male goat was the king of Greece.
3) The four horns that grew up from the large horn were four smaller kingdoms that arose from one large Greek nation;[39] the smaller horn that

---

[37] Heaven was a euphemism for God. The army of Heaven, or the army of God was probably the Jewish army, just as Jerusalem is called the "city of God," "city of the living God," or "heavenly Jerusalem." Chinese worshiped Heaven as early as the 11th century BIA.

[38] A. A. Bevan, *A Short Commentary*, p. 137

[39] This is a brief summary of events. Initially, Alexander's kingdom was imprecisely divided among several generals, some acting in behalf of two of Alexander's sons. After about twenty-five years of military shuffle, 1) Ptolemy had Egypt, Cyrene, Palestine, and Syria; 2) Seleucus had

grew up was a monstrous king. He was destined to destroy mighty men and the people of the saints, but, like the image the rock destroyed, this king would be broken by no human hand (Dan 8:19-26).

Temple plundered. This dream (Dan 8:2-14) was a myth that Daniel demythologized enough so that Jews would understand it without difficulty. The male goat was Alexander the Great who overpowered the entire Near East, including Persia and Media. The four kingdoms that followed Alexander were later divisions of that kingdom given to Alexander's generals to administer in behalf of Alexander's heirs. The general who fell heir to the Tigris-Euphrates Valley was the first of the Seleucids. One of his descendants, Antiochus Epiphanes, inherited his father's conquest of Palestine (the glorious land) (Dan 8:9). There he overpowered the Jewish troops (the mighty men or the army of the stars) and their leader (the chief),[40] plundered the temple, and kept it out of use for pious Jews for three and a half years (2,300 morning and evening sacrifices). The chief of chiefs, whom Antiochus dared to resist, may have been Judas the Maccabee. Judas was never king, but he led the nation, and he was commander-in-chief of the Jewish forces when Jews gained their first step toward independence from Grecian Syria. Bevan is probably correct in saying that the "stars" and the army of heaven both represent the people of God. The expression, "casting some of the stars to the ground" alluded to the cruelties of Antiochus and his agents at Jerusalem (1Macc 1:24, 30).[41]

Antiochus stopped. Scholars are correct in understanding this as mythologized history that was then demythologized. Antiochus Epiphanes was a descendant of one of Alexander the Great's generals. He plundered the temple (ca. 168 BIA)[42] and prevented the temple worship from continuing for three or three and a half years

---

Babylon; 3) Lysimachus held Thrace and the western part of Asia Minor (modern Turkey); and 4) Antigonus ruled Macedonia and Anatolia in Greece. Later Seleucus overpowered Lysimachus in war and annexed to his kingdom all the land ruled by Lysimachus (Polybius 18.51, 3-4). He then ruled from Babylon to Europe. (See further F. E. Peters, *The Harvest of Hellenism* [New York: Simon & Schuster, c1970], pp. 66-85, and M. Hengel, *Jews, Greeks and Barbarians*, tr. J. Bowden [Philadelphia: Fortress Press, c1980], pp. 1-20.) By the time of Daniel, Lysimachus was only a memory. Daniel probably included him only to make four to correspond with the four beasts and the four parts of the statue. It made better narrative to have the fourth beast have four horns. The territory of Syria and Palestine was frequently a scene of conflict between the Seleucids and the Ptolemies. The Seleucid kingdom was the "fourth beast" of Daniel's myth. These "beasts" were personified kings of nations.

[40] So also LaCocque, *Daniel*, p. 162, who identified the stars with the saints. Porteous, *Daniel*, p. 125, says the imagery of the stars may have come from the Hebrew Scripture text where Isaiah accused the king of Babylon of claiming that he would "ascend to heaven above the stars of God" and make himself "like the Most High" (Isa 14:13-14; see also 1Macc 1:41-42).

[41] Bevan, *A Short Commentary*, p. 132.

[42] This was not the only temple Antiochus plundered. Polybius told of the lavish parties Antiochus held, financed from the money he robbed from Egypt when he attacked King Philometer. Polybius also noted that he sacrilegiously ruined most of the temples (Polybius 30.26, 9). Temples were often also state treasuries.

until Judas defeated the Greeks at the Battles of Beth-horon and possibly Beth-zur and rededicated the temple. This was the first Hanukkah.[43] Antiochus IV met his death in Persia where he went to plunder a temple. The temple was at Nanaea, according to 2Macc, but Elymais, according to 1Macc.[44]

The author of Daniel thought that this victory was more than a human event. This was God's design and execution. The historical events were all known; Daniel provided the religious interpretation for the background of Hanukkah. The comment about Antiochus being "broken" does not necessarily refer just to his death. It could symbolize his successive failures in conflict with Hasmoneans and also the Romans. He lost battles and became financially embarrassed. It was while he was in the East, trying to replenish his treasury by plundering another temple that he died of an illness or was killed by the local citizens, depending upon the source used.

Daniel's Exegesis

In one of the mythological settings the author portrayed, Daniel was studying the scripture to learn how long the captivity would last (Dan 9:2, 20-27). In Jer 25:12 he discovered that Jeremiah had predicted **70 years**--but 70 years had passed long before! While Daniel was praying, Gabriel told him that **70** meant **70 weeks of years** (Dan 9:24).[45] Gabriel probably gave Daniel that insight when he read Lev 26:17-28, which said if Israelites broke the treaty with the Lord that the Lord would punish them seven times for their sins. This meant Jeremiah's **70 years** should be multiplied by seven, resulting in 490 years. These were to be distributed after Nebuchadnezzar destroyed the temple at Jerusalem in 586 BIA as follows: 7 weeks [of years] in Babylon, 62 weeks until an anointed one was cut off, 3½ years under treaty of Jews with Greeks, and 3½ years of desolations (Dan 9:24-27). Total: 70 weeks of years until the end of the desolator.

This analysis of the data shows that it is more probable that the author of Daniel was pro-Hasmonean rather than anti-Hasmonean. It also points to the identification of Judas the Maccabee as the one **like a Son of man** who was divinely appointed to his role of leadership. To him was given the ruling authority, glory, and a kingdom (Dan 7:14). His was the government that followed the rule of Antiochus Epiphanes, the last remnant of the fourth beast, over the saints of the Most High after the temple had been cleansed and sacrifice restored (Dan 7:23-27). Although he was

---

[43] That is, it was the first Hanukkah after the Hasmonean Revolt. The first dedication was that of Solomon (1Kgs 8), and the second was that of Nehemiah. Hanukkah today is celebrated in relationship to the Hasmonean victory.

[44] B. Z. Wacholder, "The Letter from Judah Maccabee to Aristobulus: Is 1Maccabees 1:10b-2:18 Authentic?" *HUCA* 49 (1978):89-133, has argued persuasively that the letter presented as if it were from the Jews contemporary to Judas the Maccabee in Jerusalem to a certain Aristobulus in Egypt (2Macc 1:10-2:18) is authentic and that its account of the death of Antiochus is more reliable than that in 1Macc.

[45] Porteous, *Daniel*, p. 146. Bevan astutely observed that the author's logic in changing 70 to 70 times 7 may have come from the teaching in the Torah that Israelites were to be punished seven times for their sins (Lev 26:18, 21, 24, 28) and that the author combined the texts of Jer 25:11, 29:10; Lev 26:10 and Lev 26:18-28 to reach his conclusion.

not officially a king, he was **like a Son of man**, which may have meant that he was "like" a king.

The Kingdoms of the South and of the North

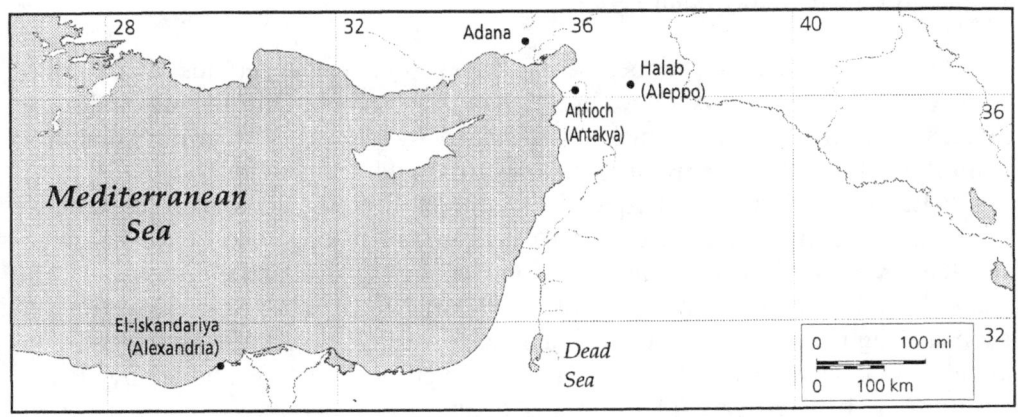

The battles rage. In another vision (Dan 11), Gabriel told Daniel that there would be three additional kings after Darius the Mede before a mighty king of Greece would arise and overpower that country. This king's empire would not go to his posterity, but it would be divided into four parts (just as the broken horn was replaced by four smaller horns [Dan 8:8]). Later one of the kings [Ptolemy] of the southern kingdom [Egypt] would make a treaty with the king [Antiochus III] of the northern kingdom [Syria]. In this treaty the king of the Northern Kingdom would give the king of the southern kingdom one of his daughters, but the treaty would not last. The daughter was the sister of Antiochus IV Epiphanes, who would later lead a successful war against the king [another Ptolemy] of the south.

There were many other battles between these two countries. In one of them, the king from the north conquered the southern kingdom and took his stand in the glorious land, but there he confronted a commander who put a stop to his expansions. Then he broke his treaty with the saints, defiled the temple at Jerusalem, and put an end to the continual burnt offerings (Dan 11:2-31). Some of the people of that land collaborated with him, but others took a stand in resistance. Many fell by the sword, but they received "a little help" when things became difficult (Dan 11:32-34). The myth of Dan 11 is a little more detailed and difficult to understand than others are, but scholars have been able to agree on the identification of most of the characters and incidents that are listed from Dan 11:1 to 11:39.[46]

---

[46] See Porteous, *Daniel*, pp. 145-73; W. S. Towner, *Daniel* (Atlanta: John Knox Press, c1984), pp. 147-71.

The narrative begins with Alexander the Great and his empire that was divided among his generals. It is also clear that the northern kingdom was the kingdom of the Seleucid Greeks and the southern kingdom was Egypt. Daniel represented a Judaic point of view. From Jerusalem Egypt was south, and Syria was north. The treaty formed which involved a marriage between these two royal lines was probably represented in another myth as the feet and toes of the image that were mingled iron with pottery (Dan 2:42-43).

The little help. The help mentioned here (Dan 11:34) is trivialized, just as the entire return of the captive Jews to restore the city and rebuild the temple under the leadership of Ezra and Nehemiah is trivialized by only the following summary: **From the going out of the word to restore and build Jerusalem** (Dan 9:25).

Egypt and Syria were frequently in conflict, from the division of Alexander's empire through the second century BIA. The northern king who broke his treaty with the Jews and defiled the temple at Jerusalem was Antiochus Epiphanes. The treaty he made was probably the one by which the Jews, under the negotiations of Jason the high priest, and Antiochus agreed to make Jerusalem a privileged city, probably a Grecian *polis*.[47] The treaty made was probably that mentioned by Daniel, **He made a firm treaty with the many** (Dan 9:27). This was a standard part of Alexander's administration that his successors continued. From an administrative point of view, Antiochus was generous in allowing Jews a few exceptions to normal *polis* administration to adjust to their religious rules. While Antiochus IV was king of Syria, Rome made an effort, with the cooperation of other nations, to negotiate a peace treaty between Syria and Egypt, but they were unsuccessful. Antiochus IV still hoped to recapture the entire kingdom once ruled by his father. This included all of Asia Minor, and part of Europe, including Thrace and some Grecian cities (Polybius 18.51, 4-6), but he was forbidden by treaty to extend his empire in the direction of Greece and Europe.

The treaty the Romans forced upon Antiochus III was that he must leave Europe, all of the Mediterranean islands, and all Asia Minor west of the Taurus Mountains. He also was required to make extensive financial payments, provide hostages, and was limited militarily (Polybius 21.17,1-9).

Still more important, he had to agree that he and his subjects would not pass through the territory of Rome or its allies with an army against the Romans or their allies. Syria would not furnish any supplies to the enemies of Rome or its allies. It would not make war on the inhabitants of the islands or of Europe. It would give up all of its war elephants and never keep any in the future. It would surrender all of its long ships with their gear, and in the future it would limit its navy to ten decked ships of war. It could not possess any galley rowed by more than thirty oars or any ship with more than one bank of oars in any aggressive war. Syria was forbidden to hire mercenaries from lands under Roman rule, and to receive any cities that wished to desert to it. It was allowed to retaliate if any of the cities or peoples involved in the treaty should initiate the war, but it was not allowed to exercise sovereignty over any of them or make a treaty with them (Polybius 21.42,1-27).

---

[47] See further Peters, *Harvest*, pp. 250-55.

In this entire treaty, no mention was made of Egypt, and Egypt was not a special ally of Rome at the time. Therefore Egypt was the only area around the Mediterranean Sea where Antiochus might expand his empire without openly breaking the treaty the Romans had made with his father. When Antiochus IV, invaded Egypt he may have strained this treaty. If not, he at least acted in a way that ran counter to Rome's goals of expansion toward the east.

Rome's response came after Antiochus had already made a successful campaign into Egypt and was then confronted by the Roman officer Gaius Popilius Laenas. That officer brought him a letter from the Roman Senate that ordered him to put an end to the war with Egypt at once and gave him a fixed number of days to take his army back to Syria. When he asked for some time to consider Popilius

> did something that was thought to be both offensive and very arrogant. He had in his hand a stick cut from a vine.[48] With this he drew a circle around Antiochus and ordered him to give a reply to the things written before leaving the circle (Polybius 29.27, 4-5).

Antiochus yielded to the Roman demand.

One of the reasons Antiochus invaded Egypt when he did was that at that time Egypt was under incompetent leadership, and Rome was deeply involved with a conflict in Macedonia. This conflict, however, was nearly over at the time Antiochus was confronted by Popilius. Polybius said if this had not been the case, Antiochus would never have acceded to the Roman demand. While there, Popilius drove all of the Syrians out of the island of Crete as well (Polybius 29.26-27,13) (168 BIA), since Antiochus III had agreed to stay out of the Mediterranean islands. The author of Dan 11 described Antiochus' interruption by saying that the ships of the Kittim would come against him (Dan 11:30).

The Kittim were probably the Romans who forced Antiochus Epiphanes to turn back after he had conquered Egypt. On his return from his second campaign against Egypt Antiochus IV pillaged the temple at Jerusalem, stirring up a great deal of animosity among the Jews. The people who led the resistance movement against the Greeks were the Hasmoneans. Some of them fell by the sword--not only troops but Hasmoneans themselves. The "help" they received was from the Romans, and it was not very "little." It was the Romans who prevented Antiochus IV from annexing all of Egypt to his empire, and it was Rome that continued to keep watch on Antiochus to see that he did not transgress against any of the conditions Rome had laid upon him. Actually he did transgress. He built more ships than he was allowed by treaty, and he acquired elephants, which was also a breach of treaty. Rome knew this was happening, and as soon as Antiochus died, Romans entered Syria, killed all of the elephants, and burned the prohibited ships (Appian, *Roman History* 11.8, 46).

---

[48] This "stick" was probably not just some vine Popilius Laenus cut with his pocket knife. Roman officers often carried a twisted vine stick as an emblem of office. See further G. Webster, *The Roman Imperial Army* (Totowa, N.J: Barnes & Noble, 1985), p. 130.

They were also watching Palestine and encouraging any rebellion there that might be developed to weaken Antiochus.

Judas undoubtedly needed more money, weapons, and supplies than he could obtain from local resources. He probably received financial support at first from wealthy Jews in Rome and later from the Roman senate, but the authors and editors of Daniel ignored all of this important data just as they ignored the restoration of Judah after Cyrus of Persia had taken Babylon.

Without Rome's support the Maccabean revolt would have failed, but a nationalistic author who thought this whole revolution was the work of God could not have been expected to give accurate credit to a foreign nation that provided the weapons, military advice, supplies, and other significant support. After all, the argument he was defending was that it was God who was the source of all the help needed in this war, and the essay was not designed to celebrate what Rome had done but what Judah had done. This was a nationalistic celebration.

ANTIOCHUS III AND THE SECOND ENDING

Problems. One of the reasons scholars have been distracted from the normal conclusions expected from decoding Daniel is that the long mythologized historical report of Dan 11 follows logically up to Dan 11:39, with Antiochus Epiphanes as the chief enemy character. Then the paragraph from Dan 11:40-45 is not a historically accurate report of the events that happened to Antiochus Epiphanes after he had defiled the temple at Jerusalem.[49] It does, however, provide a reasonably accurate account of some of the last ventures of Antiochus the Great, Antiochus Epiphanes' father.

Confusion of Kings. Josephus (*Ant* 12.129-55) reported the history that Daniel mythologized in relationship to Antiochus the Great without myth.[50] It is a summary of the history from 198 BIA to 189 BIA. About 198 BIA, when Palestine was under the rule of Egypt, Ptolemy V made military moves to extend his boundaries to the north of Judea into Coele Syria. This was territory that was under the control of Antiochus III. Ptolemy sent General Scopus north with troops to accomplish this mission, but Antiochus was ready for him. Antiochus the Great stopped the Egyptians at Panias, in the Golan Heights. Antiochus then advanced farther south, with many troops and elephants, taking all of Palestine--Judah, Samaria, and Phoenicia, leaving Edom, Moab, and part of the Ammonite land (Dan 11:41). He found little Jewish resistance, because Jews were eager to have the Egyptian yoke removed (*Ant* 12.131-54).

---

[49] LaCocque, *Daniel*, p. 8: "He alludes to the revolt of the Maccabees and the first victories of Judas (166). But he is unaware of the death of Antiochus autumn 164; (see Dan 11:40 ff.) and the purification of the Temple by Judas on 14 December 164. We can at least situate the second part of the Book of Daniel (chapters 7-12), therefore with a very comfortable certainty, in 164 BCE." Porteous, *Daniel*, p. 169: "At v. 40 the writer passes from pseudoprophecy to genuine prediction as is shown by the fact that he is speaking of the eschatological event or at least of events immediately preceding it." These are representative of the interpretation that is most widely held today.
[50] See also Polybius, *Hist* 18.49, 1-51, 10; 20.8, 1-5; 21.6, 1-43, 3, Dio 19, Zonaras 9.18-20, and Livy 36.41, 1-37.45.21

Before Antiochus had added Palestine to his empire he had already made extensive expansions to the west. He had ruled most of the cities of Asia Minor for 25 years. While Rome was in a life and death struggle with Hannibal of Carthage, Antiochus had moved increasingly westward colonizing Lysimachia, making political treaties with all of the major islands in the Mediterranean Sea and with several Greek cities. Some of the Greek cities were glad to see Antiochus moving west. The Aetolians, for example, requested Antiochus to move into Greece, promising that he could succeed in conquering both Greece and Italy. They feared the Romans more than the Seleucids, and fought on the side of Antiochus in some of the battles. Rumors in Rome were that Antiochus had taken all of Greece. Although they were deeply involved in war with Carthage, Romans were anxious about Antiochus' advances. (Dio19, Zonaras 9, 18-19).

By the time the Battle of Panias was fought Rome's conflict with Carthage had been over for three years, and Rome was apprehensive of Antiochus' activities. Rome started to set the stage to move eastward while Antiochus was planning to move farther west and south. After Carthage had made peace with Rome, Hannibal moved to Syria to assist Antiochus in his conquest of Rome. Antiochus planned first to negotiate a treaty with Carthage, so as to have support from the south, secure military support from the entire peninsula of Greece, and then move into Italy both from Greece and from Carthage. If he had been successful in overpowering Rome, he would then have ruled an even greater empire than Alexander the Great.

Several years after he had conquered Palestine, while he was settled in Asia Minor, Antiochus heard that one of the Ptolemies had died, leaving Egypt at least temporarily unstable. Antiochus seized the opportunity, left Asia Minor under the leadership of his son, Seleucus, and took a large force to conquer Egypt. Before he reached Egypt, however, he learned that the rumor had been false, so he withdrew. He tried to sail from there to Cyprus, but he ran into a storm and had to return to Syria. At that point Rome sent envoys to Antiochus to object to his behavior (Dio 19, Zonaras 9.18). This may have been the time that he returned from an advance toward Egypt because he had received the alarming news from the north and the east (Dan 11:44) or because of a certain commander [possibly Scipio] who put an end to his insolence (Dan 11:18), but that is only one of the possibilities. With political responsibility all the way from India to Greece, there were probably many interruptions during this tense period. Alarming news might have come from Rome or his eastern provinces.

Rome had been aware of Antiochus' threatening activities and acted to bring them to a halt as soon as it was free from its war with Carthage. Many envoys were exchanged between Rome and Syria before the war actually broke out. These were sometimes disturbing to both countries. On one of these occasions, when Antiochus was near Egypt, news reached him that caused him to move north, pitching his tents on the Palestinian coast (Dan 11:44). His final goal of conquering Rome was not successful. After losing many smaller battles in Greece and Asia Minor, he was defeated at Magnesia on the Meander River in Lydia. By the time the armies were joined at Magnesia, Dio said Antiochus was doomed before the battle began (Livy 37.39-45; Dio19.62, Zoneras 9, 18-20).

He will come to his end. Contrary to the supposition of most scholars the king that was mentioned here was not Antiochus IV but instead his father, Antiochus III. Scholars have been misled by the fact that Dan 11:40 follows the narrative telling about Antiochus IV. Scholars have not noticed that Dan 11:40-45 is a parallel text to Dan 11:14-19, and that both of these parallel texts report the activities of Antiochus III.

Daniel 11:14-19	Daniel 11:40-45
1. Many rose against **Egyptians** (198 BIA).	1. **Egyptian** troops invade Judea and Coele-Syria.
2. Antiochus raised many troops.	2. Opposition had the support of Jewish rebels.
3. **Antiochus** surrounded **Panias**.	3. **Antiochus** won battle of **Panias.**
4. Egyptians forced to retreat.	
5. **Antiochus entered Palestine (glorious land).**	4. **Antiochus entered Palestine (glorious land).**
6. **Antiochus** made a treaty involving the marriage of his daughter to the Egyptian king (193 BIA).	5. **Antiochus** continued into Egypt and gained support of Libya and Ethiopia.
7. He **turned** to **the coastlands of Palestine**.	6. Bad news prompted **Antiochus** to **turn** north. He got as far as **the coastlands of Palestine.**
8. A commander put an **end** to his insolence.	7. Came to his **end** with none to help him.
9. Returned to his own land.	
10. Fell and was not found.	

In this context "his end" (Dan 11:45) is not the death of Antiochus IV. It means only that the Romans stopped Antiochus III in his tracks, and left him frustrated and embarrassed, and his expansion plans came to a dead end. He then went to Persia to replenish his treasuries and was killed by the Elamites. Scholars know that Antiochus IV did not make a third attempt to take Egypt. Since they thought this text applied to Antiochus IV they believed that it had either to have been a false prophecy or a mistaken literary invention. Once it becomes clear that this is a second account of one of Antiochus' activities, it is also evident that there is no part of the

Book of Daniel that was originally prophecy. It was detailed history written in a dramatic style to celebrate the victory over the Seleucids.

SUMMARY

All of the chapters of Daniel have been studied up to this point (1-6, 8-12). They have all been shown to be mythologized history of the same period--that between Nebuchadnezzar's first entrance into Jerusalem in 605 BIA and the rededication of the temple in 164 BIA. An artist sometimes paints in broad strokes, painting out objects that distract from the message the artist wants observers to see. Similarly, the Danielic mythologists left out many details and overemphasized others to make their points, but the basic period and point of view is clear, and it was reported in one myth after the other. The mythologists also dealt with the same geography--the Davidic kingdom in relationship to the countries in the Fertile Crescent that ruled this country most of the time between the strategic dates.

To show how closely related to each other the relevant passages are in Dan 11, they are framed here so that the reader can easily exchange one for the other and notice how little difference that makes in the message of the entire chapter. This insight is important, not only for a correct understanding of this chapter, but also for the understanding of eschatology generally. For that reason Dan 11 is quoted here in its entirety to review the content for the reader before analyzing its meaning.

THE TEXT OF DANIEL ELEVEN

$^{11:1}$I, in the first year of Darius the Mede, stood to make him strong and to support him.
^{2}Now I will disclose the truth to you:

Look! Three more kings will arise in Persia, and the fourth will be much wealthier than all the others. As he becomes strong through his wealth he will stir up everything against the Greek kingdom. ^{3}A mighty king will arise and will rule a large dominion, and do as he pleases. ^{4}When he has arisen, his kingdom will be broken into the four winds, but not to his posterity, and not according to his dominion which he rules, because his kingdom will be taken and belong to others, and not these alone.

^{5}The king of the South will become strong, but from among his generals [one] will become stronger than he,[51] and he will rule from a dominion that is a great dominion. ^{6}After some years they will make an agreement, and the daughter of the king of the South will come to the king of the North to make peace, but she will not retain the strength of her arm. His arm will not endure, and she will be surrendered-- she, those who brought her, her child, and the one who possessed her at the time. ^{7}A branch from her roots will arise in his place, and he will come against the army and

---

[51] Seleucus was one of Alexander's marshals who became a general in Ptolemy I's army when Ptolemy became king of Egypt. Seleucus himself later became king of the eastern portion of Alexander's empire. Of Seleucus, Arrian, *Anabasis* 7.22, 5, said, "He had the royalist mind of them all, and after Alexander himself, ruled over the greatest extent of territory."

enter the fortress of the king of the North. He will act against them and prevail. ⁸Also their gods, their images, and their precious vessels of silver and gold he will bring into captivity to Egypt. He will stay away from the king of the North for several years.

⁹Then [the king of the North] will come into the kingdom of the king of the South, but he will return to his own land. ¹⁰His sons will assemble and gather a mob of many troops. They **will** come forcefully, **spread out, and pass over** and again gather troops as far as his fortress. ¹¹The king of the South will become angry and he will come out and join battle with the king of the North. He will raise a great multitude, and the multitude will be given into his hand. ¹²When the multitude is raised his mind will become overconfident. He will make tens of thousands fall, but he will not become strong. ¹³Then the king of the North will return and raise a still bigger mob than the first. After a few years he will come forcibly with a great army and many supplies.

> ¹⁴In those times many will arise against the king of the South, and the children of the violent ones of your people will rise up to make the vision stand, but they will stumble. ¹⁵After that the king of the North will come, and he will pour out a mound and capture the fortified city. The forces of the South will not stand, not even the people of his choice troops, because there will be no strength to stand. ¹⁶The one who comes will do to him as he wishes, and he will not be able to stand before him. He will stand in the glorious land, and everything will be in his hand. ¹⁷He will turn his face with the authority of his entire kingdom, but justice will be with him, and he will carry it out. He will give him the daughter of women to destroy it, but **it will not stand; it will not be** his. ¹⁸He will turn his face to the islands and capture many, but an officer will put an end to his insolence. Nothing but his insolence will return to him. ¹⁹He will turn his face to the fortresses of his own land, but he will stumble and fall and will not be found.

²⁰ One will arise in his place, and he will make an oppressor go through the glory of his kingdom. In a few days he will be broken, neither in anger nor in war. ²¹A despised person will arise in his place, but the glory of the kingdom will not be given to him. He will come quietly and seize the kingdom with flatteries. ²²The troops will be utterly swept before him and crushed. Also the leader of the treaty.

²³From the time the treaty is made with him he will act deceitfully. He will grow in strength with a small nation. ²⁴He will come quietly with the richest men of the city, and he will do that which his fathers had never done, neither his grandfathers nor his great grandfathers. He will plunder and scatter booty and their possessions. He will make plans against the fortresses, but up to a time. ²⁵Then he will stir up his power and his mind against the king of the South with a huge army, and the king of the South will assemble for battle with a large and very powerful army, but he will not stand, because they will design plans against him.

²⁶Even those who eat his gourmet food will break him down. His army will be swept away, and many will fall wounded. ²⁷These two kings [will set] their minds to do evil. Over one table they will speak deceit, but they will not succeed, because

there is still an **end** at the appointed time. ²⁸He will return to his own **land** with much booty. His mind is against the holy treaty. He will act and return to his **land.**

²⁹**At an appointed time**, he will again go south, but the latter [experience] will not be like the first, ³⁰for the ships of the Kittim will come against him, and he will be emotionally crushed and turned back. He will be furious against the holy treaty, so he will act and give instruction for those who abandoned the holy treaty. ³¹Then the powerful ones among us will rise up and plunder the temple and the fortress. They will turn away the continual offering and provide the abomination of desolations.

³²Those who abandon the treaty he will seduce with flatteries, but the **people** that knows its God will be strong and act.³³Those who instruct the **people** will instruct the many, and they **will stumble** with the sword, in flames, in captivity, and with plunder for a time. ³⁴When they **stumble**, they will receive a little help. Many will join against them with flatteries, ³⁵and some of the instructors **will stumble** to test, purify, and whiten them until **the time of the end**, for there is still **the appointed time**.³⁶The king will do whatever he wants, and he will trample and exalt himself over every god, and he will say astonishing things against the God of gods. He will succeed until the wrath is completed, for the action is predestined. ³⁷He will pay no attention to the gods of his fathers or to the one beloved of women, nor to any god will he pay attention, because he will exalt himself over all. ³⁸He will honor the god of fortresses instead of these. The god whom his fathers did not know he will honor with gold, silver, precious stones, and precious things. ³⁹He will act in relationship to strong fortresses with a foreign god. Whomever he recognizes he will increase honor. They will be rulers over the many, and he will divide the land for a price.

---

⁴⁰At the time of the end, the king of the South will wage war with him, but the king of the North **will pass over** him with cavalry, chariots, and many boats. He will come into the lands, **spread out, pass over**. ⁴¹and come to the glorious land. Tens of thousands will fall, but those who escape his hand are Edom, Moab, and most of the Ammonites. ⁴²He will extend his power into the lands, and the land of Egypt will not be able to escape. ⁴³He will rule the treasuries of gold, silver, and all the precious things of Egypt, and the Libyans and Ethiopians in his footsteps. ⁴⁴Reports from the East and the North will frighten him. He will leave with great fury to destroy and utterly exterminate many. ⁴⁵He will plant his palatial tents between the sea and the mountain of the glorious holy mountain. He will come to his end, and no one will help him.

The 490-year period was divided into four gentile periods--the Babylonians, Medians, Persians, and Greeks--which were followed by the Hasmonean kingdom, which God had established. The "end of days" was the three or three and a half years between the time Antiochus defiled the temple and the time Judas cleansed it (168-165/164 BIA). The end of days concluded the end of the foreign rule of Palestine, and it is the end mentioned throughout the book. As Heaton said,

> This view of the matter, although it must be said to fall short of certainty, is confirmed by the fact that throughout the book the time of the expected deliverance is always inextricably bound up with the end of Antiochus.[52]

The entire mythology was centered on the Maccabean rebellion from the point of view of a victorious pro-Hasmonean nationalist. Every myth in Daniel was written from the viewpoint of a victor celebrating a prophecy that had already been fulfilled, as would have been the case *after* the battle of Beth-horon, rather than from the perspective of someone whistling in the dark to keep up courage when the going was rough. Although LaCocque thought the "end" to which Daniel referred was "prophecy," he said,

> The kings are forced to recognize that they owed their sovereignty to the 'living God' of Israel (Dan 6:26). There is no parallel in the Bible to the optimism of these chapters concerning the nations."[53]

Walters thought the authors of Daniel wrote for people in the midst of their persecution, and he thought they were inappropriate,

> His friends were suffering cruel deaths for their faith, and he gives them stories in which God openly delivered the faithful from death. Antiochus arrogates to himself epithets of deity, and the writer produces stories in which the kings make a virtual *confessio fidei* in Daniel's God. Observance of the law is a capital offence in Palestine, but the writer reports that Daniel ate only kosher food and was recognized and promoted by the Babylonian king.
> In a way, Daniel A [Dan 1-6] seems awfully thin for a persecuted people, or, worse yet, too heartily optimistic.[54]

Walters is correct. The Dramas of Daniel do not fit into a situation of persecution. Optimism like this grows out of success. That is one of the reasons for thinking that this document was composed after the Battle of Beth-horon in anticipation of the first Hanukkah celebration after the Hasmonean victory. If they had been inappropriate they would not have been preserved for posterity.

SITUATION

The Dramas of Daniel, written after the fact, interpreted the theological basis for the establishment of the Hasmonean kingdom centuries after the Babylonian exile. Chapters were composed as dramas, rather than prophecies, and used to glorify the Hasmonean victories. No twentieth century commentator observed these

---

[52] E. W. Heaton, *The Book of Daniel: Introduction and Commentary* (London: SCM Press, c1956), p. 90.
[53] LaCocque, *Daniel*, pp. 8-9.
[54] S. D. Walters, "The End (of What?) is at Hand," *TJT* 2 (1986):38.

events, so all of us can offer only conjectured opinions of the details that might have taken place to bring together into one book all of these independent success stories that are recorded in the Book of Daniel. The possibility offered here is as follows:

After the death of Antiochus IV Epiphanes, the Battle of Beth-horon, and possibly the Battle of Beth-zur, Jews all over the world began making plans for the celebration of Hanukkah in Jerusalem, December, 164 BIA. They had a few months to prepare for this event. This meant that the building contractors were employed to clean up the court and rebuild damaged parts of the temple. The priests were assigned the tasks of performing the proper cleansing rituals. For three years Greeks had been killing Jews for owning biblical books in Palestine, and Bibles that were found were defiled and destroyed. Jews had sent their books to Jews in the diaspora for preservation. Among the plans for Hanukkah was the collection of these various books from the diaspora to restore them to the library at Jerusalem (2Macc 2:8-25).

Plans were made for the eight-day Hanukkah program at Jerusalem on Hanukkah, following the first dedication of Solomon's temple (1Kgs 8:65-66). To prepare for that occasion Judas might have assigned to the best scholars available the task of interpreting the theological dimensions of the exile and restoration to the gathered congregation. Each scholar was supposedly asked to interpret the history of the events from the beginning of the exile until Hanukkah, showing how the promises of God to Israel had been fulfilled. These would been written to entertain and exhilarate the Jews gathered at the celebration. After dramas had been presented at Hanukkah, they were edited and gathered into the book that is now the Book of Daniel, and widely circulated, to remind Jews of the blessings of Hanukkah. "Suzanna" and "Bel and the Dragon" are also dramas written about Daniel, and they are recorded in the OG, but they are not directly related to Hanukkah.. The authors fulfilled their responsibilities marvelously, and the original hearers probably gave standing ovations, applause, and shouts of "Amen!" The attitude reflected in the various chapters of the Book of Daniel seems best to fit the situation in preparation for Hanukkah. It is likely that some, at least, of the chapters were written for that occasion and were actually read at the first of Hanukkah. All of the chapters might have been written for that occasion, but that is not necessarily the case.

The death of Antiochus might have happened within weeks of Hanukkah. If so, it would require some rapid composition to get Dan 7 ready in time for Hanukkah, but zealous nationalists were properly motivated. Like other inspired artists, such as Mozart, Bach, or Handel when he wrote *The Messiah*, the author of Dan 7 may have put his inspiration into meaningful drama in a very short time.

It may be too much to expect a beautiful court drama to have been composed that rapidly. If not, then it was composed later. For instance, Dan 7 may have been specially prepared for the eight day celebration of Jewish liberation from taxes at 142 BIA. That which is certain is that Dan 7 was not composed before the death of Antiochus IV and the plans made for Hanukkah.

Like most other scholars Heaton interpreted the data differently. He said,

> As he was ignorant of the circumstances of Antiochus' death in 163 BC and the re-dedication of the Temple on 25 December 164 BC we may with some certainty say that he wrote before the end of 164 BC

and, therefore, that the whole book was produced within a period of five years.[55]

The death of Antiochus (the little horn) in the heavenly trial of Dan 7 shows that the author of that chapter was not ignorant of the death of Antiochus. The date for Antiochus' death is not known with certainty, but it was very close to the time of the Battle of Beth-horon and the Battle of Beth-zur. This was before the first Hanukkah--maybe very close or maybe a few months before Hanukkah. The author of Dan 7 did not spell out the details of Antiochus' death, because that was not the purpose of his drama. He was interpreting the theological meaning of his death.

It meant that God had held a heavenly court session on New Year's Day, as he customarily did, before the Battle of Beth-horon (165 BIA). At this court trial, those being judged were the Jews as plaintiffs, and the Seleucids as defendants. Antiochus IV acted as the defendant, the legal agent for the Seleucids, and Judas the Maccabee was the plaintiff, the legal agent for the Jews. At that trial God had judged Antiochus from heaven and declared him guilty of a crime that merited a death sentence. The author had to know all of the history that happened on earth to have dramatized the heavenly judgment day drama.

Heaton thought the book had been produced within five years. It might have been produced in ten or eleven months, between the Battle of Beth-horon and Hanukkah. The author did not mention Hanukkah because the dramas may have been composed for the very purpose of presenting them at the first Hanukkah. Since Hanukkah occurred near the end of 164 BIA, Heaton's conclusion that these chapters were composed before that time might have been accurate.

The basis for including books in the canon was the test to see if God's legal agents composed them. Since Moses and the kings of Israel and Judah were all accepted as God's agents, the books attributed to them, namely the four books of the Torah attributed to Moses, and the Psalms and wisdom writings, attributed to David and Solomon, were included. Since Moses had warned future generations not to accept the words of so-called prophets until their prophecies had been fulfilled (Deut 18:21-22), the prophetic books that predicted the fall of Samaria and Judah were accepted. That was true also of the historical books of Genesis, Joshua, Judges, and the books of Samuel, Kings and Chronicles, all of which were fulfilled in the kingdom ruled by David and Solomon.

The books associated with the restoration of the kingdom by Ezra and Nehemiah were also accepted into the canon, partly because Nehemiah had the authority to determine what was considered canonical at that time. After Hanukkah it was evident that the Book of Daniel was a report of fulfilled prophecy, so it was added to the collection, but not as a prophecy. The Book of Daniel was included

---

[55] Heaton, *Daniel*, pp. 50-51. Collins, *Daniel*, p. 36, thought that Dan 1-6 was all pre-Maccabean, and that the myth in Dan 2 which parallels Dan 7 in many ways contains some glosses which "do not require a date as late as the Maccabean era." He overlooked the fact that the rock crushed the toes of the statue which had not happened until Judas defeated the Syrians at Beth-horon.

only among the writings. Josephus, however, said that by his day it was accepted as the most accurate of the prophecies and the only one that prophesied good news.

The Book of Daniel quickly became part of libraries, such as the library at Qumran, and it became a source for other books, such as The Sibylline Oracles, 1Enoch,[56] and 1 and 2Maccabees.[57] The collection of success stories included in the Book of Daniel may have been read regularly, year after year, at annual Hanukkah celebrations. It was also probably read at the eight-day celebration in May, 142 BIA after the taxation and the Syrian garrison in the Acra in Jerusalem had been removed and the new calendar established. By that time even Dan 7 would have been composed.

Time periods. The time periods given in these myths are roughly consistent: a time, two times, and half a time (Dan 7:25; 12:7) is about the same as 2,300 morning and evening sacrifices (Dan 8:14), 1,290 days, or 1,335 days (Dan 12:11). This is the time destined to pass from the time the temple was defiled until the end of the 70 weeks of years (Dan 9:1-2, 24; 12:11-13), after which the temple was cleansed and rededicated. Josephus said the war between the defilement and the cleansing of the temple was exactly three years to the day in *Ant* 12.320, agreeing with some of his sources (1Macc 4:54; 2Macc 10:3-5) but in *War* 1.19 he concurred with Daniel's 3½ years. The 45 day difference between 1,290 and 1,335 probably means different people calculated on the basis of different beginning and ending dates. It may be the difference between the time of the Beth-horon victory and the death of Antiochus, or between the New Year's Day after the Beth-horon or Beth-zur victories and the first Hanukkah. These are only possible guesses, and the dogmatic character of the document does not require precision. It was on the basis of the dogma that the figures were adjusted.

A. A. Bevan is correct in saying that the question is obscure and that any explanation given should be offered with diffidence.[58] It is easy to reconcile the **time, two times, and half-a time** (7:25) to the **half week of years** (Dan 9:27). It is more difficult to reconcile 1,150 days (Dan 8:14) with 1,290 days or 1,335 days (Dan 12:11-12). It is clear that different authors reached these conclusions, but we cannot determine today the logic by which they reached different conclusions. All of these authors had the same end in mind. They may have reasoned, however, from different beginning dates.

---

[56] It is much more likely that 1Enoch, chapters 14, 46-69, is secondary to Dan 7 than vice versa. In Daniel there is a trial in which the Son of man was only the plaintiff. It was in Dan 7 that he was given the kingdom, glory, and authority he needed to rule and judge. In 1Enoch, however, the Son of man is also called the Elect one who already had the authority of the Messiah (*1Enoch* 52.4-6). He had been enthroned (*1Enoch* 61.7; 62.1-9) and therefore was authorized to judge on the Day of Judgment which he would do as the legal agent of the Lord of Spirits (*1Enoch* 63.8-12; 69.27-29). Several chapters in 1Enoch appear as interpretations of Dan 7. The text preceded the commentary.
[57] Wacholder, however, may be correct in thinking that 2Macc 1:10-2:18 consists of a genuine letter written while Judas the Maccabee was still alive
[58] A. A. Bevan, *Short Commentary*, p 127.

Beginning and end. The time period covered by the dreams, visions, and announcements by Gabriel or some holy one was the period between the appearance of Nebuchadnezzar in Jerusalem in 605 BIA or his destruction of the temple in 586 BIA, at the beginning, and its cleansing in 164 BIA, at the end. The term between these two dates actually amounts to 441 or 422 years, but mythologically that is close enough to 490 years to be religiously "accurate." If it were not for the dogmatic need to fit the story into sabbatical terms, the author might have made a good case in comparing the actual 441 or 422 years with the 400 (Gen 15:13) or 430 (Exod 12:40) years spent in Egypt. 441 is closer to either of the time periods reported in the scripture than the conjectured 490 years of Daniel. In fact 441 years is exactly nine Jubilees of 49 years. The author of Dan 1 evidently knew that, but the author of Dan 9 wanted everything to coincide with Sabbaths and ten Jubilees.

The authors of Daniel were not historical analysts; they were religious apologists who mythologized history to persuade others that God had acted in the way that they had dramatized it, and his dramatization was simply a recognition of the way scripture had been fulfilled. Their readers were Jews who were already convinced of the basic points of his myths. They needed only to dramatize their convictions satisfyingly. That was accomplished. If this collection had been played out as a drama or read before a Jewish audience at a Jewish celebration, the audience would have cheered, applauded, and shouted, "Amen!" The first listeners to these dramas were not people who "hoped against hope" that God would make everything all right in the end, as Burkitt suggested.[59] They were celebrating the end that had already come and the prophecy that had already been fulfilled.

AUTHORSHIP

There were probably two final editors for the Book of Daniel—one for the MT and the other for the OG. Both final editors of Daniel might have composed parts of the document itself, but not all of it. An earlier editor may have formed a unity of Dan 1-7. All editors were male orthodox Jews. The orthodoxy of which they were members would not have endorsed a woman's literary activity at that time. They were strongly nationalistic, pro-Hasmonean believers. They were the ones who selected which of the writings of others to include in the collection, and they chose only those who had the same points of view as their own. The editor of MT had a plan for the general outline. First, he chose only those units that were related to Hanukkah and the restoration of the kingdom. This meant he omitted such essays as "Suzanna" and "Bel and the Dragon," which were circulating about Daniel, but were unrelated to the Maccabean Revolt and the restoration of the Promised Land.

The authors of individual units of the drama, like the final editors, probably hated the gentiles and all Jews who mingled with gentiles and accepted gentile customs. They held the same views of gentiles and Jewish minglers as the authors of 1st and 2nd Maccabees and the Book of Esther did.[60] The hatred, however, is not so sharply expressed. These authors of Daniel belonged to the same party as the authors

---

[59] Burkitt, *Apocalypses*, p. 16.
[60] Collins, *Commentary*, p. 40, noted that Daniel and Esther resembled one another in some ways.

of the Maccabean books. They were all pro-Hasmonean; they were not all Hasidim. They had been engaged in the same nationalistic struggle against the Seleucids, but the emphasis in Daniel was on celebration more than hostility. The authors did not write in the midst of persecution, dreaming of a bright future long years ahead. They were committed to celebrate a victory that had already taken place after the persecution was over. Their moods were not the same as that reported in Esther, for example.

The author of Esther concluded with victory--the Jews had the freedom to kill all 70,000 of their enemies, and they took it, individual Jews joyously killing gentiles. The glee that comes from killing gentiles is still celebrated at Purim, in relationship to the Book of Esther, but Hanukkah has a different emphasis.

Daniel also celebrated the nation's victories, and they involved killing many gentiles, but Daniel painted the picture in broad strokes. The Beth-horon victory was dramatized against more than four centuries of history. The authors of the chapters in the Book of Daniel were not free from hatred. They did not come to the defense of the gentile officers who conspired against Daniel and his colleagues, but their concentration was on gratitude and joy that came with the freedom from the Seleucids and the blessings that came from the forgiveness of sins on the Day of Atonement. The death of Antiochus was not shown with the kind of glee associated with Haman's death. The author of Dan 7 pictured Antiochus as the victim of God's judgment, even though the Hasmoneans did everything they could to get him killed. When the final editors organized this document, the Battles of Beth-horon and Beth-zur had been fought. It was a time for cheering and giving thanks. The bitterness and hostility had been modified.

The Book of Daniel never spelled out the consequences that afflicted the Seleucid supporters whom the Hasmoneans hated. Since the Hellenizers were wealthy, upper class people who were free to travel as they chose and probably spoke the languages of the Mediterranean, the odds are that many of them moved to some country in the diaspora when their position became dangerous. This is only a conjecture.

Josephus told of the vengeance that the followers of Judas the Maccabee exacted against liberal Jews, but that is not told in the Dramas of Daniel. Like the author of 1 and 2Macc, the Danielic authors believed that those who cooperated with the gentiles were as sinful as the gentiles themselves were. They were saboteurs and traitors who were denying their true Jewish faith and betraying their country, in the authors' judgments. The glee shown in the individual units when Daniel and his colleagues outwitted the most intelligent and most powerful of the gentiles reflects the vindictiveness of the authors. The three friends of Daniel were not only saved from the flames, but their enemies were burned to death. The dramatist, however, could have created a scene that would have been crueler, if he had so desired. The author might have had Daniel acting out an Esther theme in which Daniel succeeded in having all the wisemen of Babylon killed, but he did not.

The optimism, joy, and celebration of the occasion tempered the hostility. The author of Dan 12 had not forgotten the sacrifices made by national leaders, and he was confident that God would further reward the faithful. The author of Dan 7 knew how important Judas the Maccabee was to the victory of the nation, and he interpreted his position as an appointment of God when Judas as the Son of man appeared before the divine judge on New Year's Day before the victory of Beth-horon. Dan 11 pictured the horrible wars that were fought on Palestinian soil, but Dan 12 followed it just as effectively as Rom 7 was followed by Rom 8. The authors and final editor of the Dramas of Daniel may have had much influence in shaping the character of Hanukkah--or, it may have been the other way around. The joy and celebration that thrilled the hearts of the Jews after the victory of Beth-horon may have carried over into the composition of the Dramas of Daniel.

THE ORIGINAL READERS OR HEARERS

Hasmoneans and the Hasidim. Those who first heard or read the Dramas of Daniel were the nationalistic Jews who survived the battles of the Maccabean Rebellion. They were the ones who were present at the first Hanukkah in 164 BIA. This group was not limited to the Hasidim. Neither were they those who refused to take part in any military resistance in times of persecution, as Collins claimed.[61] The suggestion that Judas was the leader whom the author of Dan 7 had in mind when he described him favorably as one like a Son of man implies that the author was favorable to the Maccabees and their movement. The calculation of the sabbatical chronology suggests this; but that has not been the view most widely accepted among scholars. Many, such as Charles,[62] Collins,[63] Hartman and DiLella,[64] Heaton,[65] LaCocque,[66] and Towner[67] have all understood the author of Daniel to have been in support of the Hasidim but depreciative of the Hasmoneans. This is true even though Charles acknowledged that the Hasidim later joined the Maccabean movement.[68] Welch said,

> The writer may have been a supporter of the Maccabees, but he would never have said that the Maccabean rising fulfilled his prediction. His hope for the end has a scope and a character which no rebellion, however motivated by religion, could ever claim.[69]

Welch overlooked the satisfaction with which the authors told of the way their enemies were killed. Anyone who defamed the religion of Shadrach, Meschach, and Abednego would be torn limb for limb, and their homes destroyed (Dan 3:29). The ones who accused Daniel were thrown to the lions together with their wives and children (Dan 6:24) There were no tears shed when Antiochus Epiphanes was killed

---

[61] J. J. Collins, "Daniel and his Social World," *Int* 39 (1985):131-43.
[62] R. H. Charles, *Daniel*, pp. 309-13.
[63] J. J. Collins, *Daniel, First Maccabees, Second Maccabees* (Wilmington: Michael Glazier, c1981), p. 107.
[64] Hartman and DiLella, *Daniel*, p. 97. See also their list of other scholars who hold this position, fn. 234.
[65] Heaton, *Daniel*, p. 24.
[66] LaCocque, *Daniel*, pp. 10-11.
[67] Towner, *Daniel*, p. 165.
[68] Charles, *Daniel*, p. 310.
[69] A. C. Welch, *Visions of the End* (Boston: Pilgrim Press, 1922), p. 50.

and his body destroyed and burned with fire (Dan 7:11). The divine messenger who told Daniel what was to happen was assigned the task of fighting with the king of Persia in war. His assistant was the great Jewish angel, Michael (Dan 10:20-21). There is no indication that the authors of these documents were lamenting the tragedies of these deaths and wars. Nevertheless, Montgomery said,

> The writer is not a Maccabean but an Asidaean, for he looks for help to God alone.[70]

This is not a fair distinction to make between the Maccabean movement and that of the Hasidim. It is not a fair claim to make either of the author or of the original listeners and readers. The pro-Hasmoneans also believed that Abraham, Joseph, Phineas, Joshua, Caleb, David, Elijah, Hananiah, Azariah, Mishael, and Daniel were glorified and blessed because of their faithfulness, obedience to God, zeal for the law, witness, mercy, and innocence--not because of their military skill (1Macc 2:51-60). The Hanukkah prayer called the Hasmoneans "faithful priests." The author of 1Macc quoted Judas as saying,

> Victory in battle does not depend on the size of an army, but rather on the strength that comes from Heaven. . . . He himself will shatter them before us (1Macc 3:19, 21; see also 4:8-10, 30-33; 7:36-38).

In comparable holy war theology, a Jewish poet echoed the following confessions (*1QM* 11.1-12):

> For yours is the battle, and with the strength of your hand. . (1),
> for yours is the battle, for the Philistines you subdued many
>   times through your holy name . . . (2-3);
> yours is the battle, and from you is the might, and it is
>   not ours . . . (4-5).
> For it is in your strength and in the power of your great
>   valor . . . (6),
> for from of old we have confessed the power of your hand
>   against the Kittim . . . (12).

The Hasidim were not opposed to war in principle, as LaCocque,[71] Collins,[72] and others have held. At the outset they joined forces with the Hasmoneans in their defense of the law (1Macc 2:42-48), and Judas was called their leader (2Macc 14:6). They were willing to fight to restore purified worship in the temple and law observance among the people. Once, however, that the temple had been cleansed and a candidate from the tribe of Aaron, namely Alcimus, had been appointed high

---

[70] J A. Montgomery, *A Critical and Exegetical Commentary on the Book of Daniel* (New York: Charles Scribners' Sons, 1927), pp. 458-59.
[71] LaCocque, *Daniel*, p. 11.
[72] Collins, *Daniel*, p. 107.

priest, they were prepared to make peace with the Seleucids and part company with Judas on this point (1Macc 7:4-14).

There is no further report in 1Macc of the activities of the Hasidim after Alcimus slew 60 Hasidim in one day (1Macc 7:15-18), but Judas was reported to have taken revenge on the supporters of Alcimus (1Macc 7:15-24). Charles[73] drew support for his position from 1Enoch (*1Enoch* 90.6-12), but this gives no clearer picture of the Hasidim after Alcimus' slaughter than does First Maccabees. There is not nearly as much evidence for the antipathy between the Hasmoneans and the Hasidim as scholars have implied. The latter were initially part of the Maccabean rebellion; their only rift with the Hasmoneans was over the matter of Alcimus, and after Alcimus slaughtered several of the Hasidim, Judas took vengeance on the followers of Alcimus. For all we can learn from available sources, the Hasidim may have returned to support the Hasmoneans after Alcimus' betrayal and to have been present with the other nationalists at the first Hanukkah. This, however, is also a conjecture. There certainly is not enough evidence to support the opposite conclusion, that the antipathy continued, and that the author of Daniel was one of their party who opposed the Hasmoneans.

Persecution and patriotism. When he returned from being humiliated by Popilius Laenas, Antiochus plundered the temple at Jerusalem (Dan 11:30-31; 1Macc 1:20-53). The abomination that makes desolate which he is reported to have set up (Dan 11:31) is the same as that reported in 1Macc 1:54. His attempts to seduce with flattery those who violated the treaty (Dan 11:32) were successful attempts made to persuade Jews to worship idols and profane the Sabbath (1Macc 1:42), withhold offerings, profane festivals, pollute the sanctuary and the saints, sacrifice pork, and leave sons uncircumcised (1Macc 1:45-47). This was done under threat of death and promise of reward (1Macc 1:50, 57; 2:15-18). **But the people who know their God shall stand firm and act** (Dan 11:32)! Among the group who stood firm were the **instructors** of the people (*mahs-kee-leém*, משכלים) who instructed and exhorted **the many** (*lah-rah-beém*, לרבים), i.e., the community, to hold fast to their faith even though they should fall by the sword, flame, captivity, and plunder (Dan 11:33).

Merits and militarism. Those who held fast faced precisely these consequences. The ones who owned scriptures were killed. Mothers who circumcised their sons were put to death with their babies hanging around their necks. Some died rather than eat food not approved by their dietary laws (1Macc 2:57-63). Those who held fast had to live in secret places as refugees (1Macc 1:53). Ginsburg followed Bevan who has cogently argued that the expression, **those who make the many righteous** (*matz-dee-káy hah-rah-beém*, מצדיקי הרבים) (Dan 12:3) was taken from Second Isaiah's, **My servant will make the many righteous** (Isa 53:11). Both the instructors of the people who make the many understand (Dan 11:33) and those who make many righteous (Dan 12:3) were identified by the author of Daniel with the suffering servant of Isaiah. In fact the author of Isa 52:13 said the servant would teach (*yahs-keel* ישכיל), which means he would be one of the instructors (*mahs-keel-eém*, משכלים).

---

[73] Charles, *Commentary*, pp. 309-10.

According to Daniel these were the Maccabean martyrs, who, like the suffering servant of Isaiah, died to lay up treasures in heaven so as to remove the sins of Israel, thus making the survivors righteous[74] and preparing the way for a valid Day of Atonement.

The Hasmoneans were the principal leaders in the entire movement for freedom from heathen oppression and maintenance of Jewish, traditional laws. They may themselves have been considered some of the instructors (*mahs-keel-eém*), who stumbled (*nik-sheh-loó*, נכשלו) (Dan 11:33-35) and fell by the sword in battle. Their sacrifices were necessary to purify and make [the community] white. The Hasmoneans may also have been some of the ones **who make the many righteous** (Dan 12:3). They were working alongside religious teachers and martyrs for the same cause.[75] One of the Hasmonean brothers was killed in battle before the first Hanukkah along with many contemporary soldiers fighting for the same cause. The temple was restored because of the Hasmonean martyrdom. The Beth-horon victory happened only a few months after the Day of Atonement. Therefore it seems reasonable to assume that the author of The Book of Daniel included all of those who died in the rebellion against the Greeks among those who made the many righteous. Smith-Christopher agreed that the Book of Daniel called for resistance, but he insisted, "nonviolent resistance."[76] The Maccabean Revolt was as violent as the Jewish resistors could make it. They were not just walking around in a circle carrying picket cards.

Making the many righteous, meant removing the legal guilt of the community for which it was being punished. The works of supererogation of the Maccabean martyrs accomplished this. Although there was some conflict in the ranks, those who were not pro-Seleucids were in basic unity. It was not as if one party was for Judas and the other for God. Some were compromisers with the Seleucids, and others were loyal, rigorous, law abiding nationalists, who were sabotaging the Seleucids for the Romans. The whole patriotic group, of which the Hasidim and the Hasmoneans were parts, was amazingly successful in fighting the Seleucids.

Following the Hasmonean War, the tables were turned. Those who were the national leaders under the dictates of the Seleucids were removed from office. It was not the Hellenizers who were high priests, but the Hasmoneans. Some of those who were opposed to the Seleucids were Hasidim and some were not. Those who celebrated the first Hanukkah were the first readers and hearers of the dramas included in the Book of Daniel.

THE STRUCTURE OF THE DOCUMENT

Unity problems. Rowley has analyzed scholarship for the last two centuries on the subject of the unity and disunity of the Book of Daniel. He noted scores of scholars who argued that Daniel was the result of many glossators and editors. These scholars

---

[74] H. L. Ginsberg, "The Oldest Interpretation of the Suffering Servant," *VT* 3 (1953):402-403.

[75] In Hebrew there seems to be a play on the words "the instructors stumble" (*mahs-kee-lay ahm neek-sheh-loo*, משילי עם נכשלו).

[76] D. L. Smith-Christopher, *The Book of Daniel* (Nashville: Abingdon, c1996), p. 144.

were trying to conjecture the original Book of Daniel by removing those passages that they believe had been added later. Most of these scholars disagreed among themselves while trying to date the various parts of the book.[77] Claiming that the book was unified in message and style, Rowley said,

> To resort to textual surgery whenever evidence is inconvenient is ruthless propaganda for a theory, rather than scientific study of evidence.[78]

After acknowledging the valuable results of critical scholarship generally, Smith said,

> The attempt to produce *exact* analyses of the present books, to indicate precisely the content of the original sources and the contribution of each glossator or redactor, has resulted in a cats' concert of conflicting accounts which discredit each other and may therefore be neglected.[79]

Part of the reason for this disagreement about the dissection of Daniel is that there have not been enough examples of the kind of literature that Daniel represents to make fair judgments. Until recently scholars have had only Daniel, 1Enoch, and the Book of Revelation to study together for structure. These are called "apocalypses" because the Book of Revelation begins with the word *ah-paw-káh-loop-sis* (ἀποκάλυψις), which, in context, refers to the opening of a scroll so that it can be read.[80] Because Daniel and Enoch are something like Revelation, they are also called apocalypses, even though they do not use the word. The visions in Daniel are as much like those in Zechariah as those in Revelation. If books were classified on the bases of their messages all of these might be called redemption literature, because they all are concentrated on the redemption of Israel and the restoration of the land to the chosen people. There are also other books that belong to that category.

Medieval insights. Since the translation of many medieval Hebrew documents has been made available, new insights have been gained.[81] Among this extensive

---

[77] The first to claim that there were two divisions in the book was Isaac Newton, *Tractatus theologico-politicus* (ed 1674), c. 10, p. 189. He said the Book of Daniel was a collection of papers that had been composed at several different times. He thought the first six chapters were written by different authors, but that the last six chapters were prophecy and written by Daniel himself.

[78] H. H. Rowley, "The Unity of the Book of Daniel," *The Servant of the Lord and other Essays on the Old Testament* (London: Lutterworth Press, c1952), pp. 237-68.

[79] M. Smith, *Palestinian Parties and Politics that Shaped the Old Testament* (New York: Columbia University Press, c1971).

[80] See further Buchanan, *The Book of Revelation: its Introduction and Prophecy* (Lewiston: The Edwin Mellen Press, c1993), pp. 31-35.

[81] The following documents and page references are to Buchanan, *Revelation and Redemption: Jewish Documents of Deliverance from the Fall of Jerusalem to the Death of Nahmanides* (Dillsboro: Western North Carolina Press, c1978; sold by Mercer U. Press).

literature are collections of smaller units that have been organized and edited into larger documents that resemble Daniel, Enoch, and the Book of Revelation in structure. Two examples are "The Book of Zerubbabel"[82] and "The Prayer, Secrets, and Mysteries of Rabbi Shimon ben Yohai" (pp. 387-417).[83] These documents are clearly anthologies. "The Prayer of Rabbi Shimon ben Yohai," "The Secrets of Rabbi Shimon ben Yohai," "The Mysteries of Rabbi Shimon ben Yohai," and "Future" are four separate collections that are synoptically related. Furthermore, there are units, such as the story about Armilos that are included in both "The Book of Zerubbabel"[84] and these collections attributed to Rabbi Shimon ben Yohai[85] with variations. They also appear in documents of Saadia Gaon,[86] and others.

These anthologies are so clearly collections of earlier materials that there are not always connecting sentences to tie them together. These authors and editors used units that were popular at the time, and different editors employed some of the same materials. Sometimes they quoted them exactly; at other times they expanded them, compressed them, or brought them up to date, but each fit these sources into whatever larger design the editor had in mind. It is so obvious that these literary forms are anthologies that scholars do not try to deduce later additions from original texts. Some units contained in these anthologies are available separately. There are enough variations between so-called parallel texts that sensible scholars would not try to discover which unit was dependent on which other parallel unit. These units were widely circulated and modified to suit the needs of those who employed them.

Biblical anthologies. Each collection has some sort of unity about it. They all are centered on the redemption of Israel, the return of Jews from the diaspora, the reconstruction of the temple, and the government of one or two Jewish messiahs. Therefore this is called "Redemption Literature" (*sif-roót hah-geh-oo-láh*, ספרות הגאולה). That is the name given by Ibn Shemuel in his collection of these materials.[87] To this classification belong also such biblical books as Daniel, Zechariah, Ezekiel, and Second Isaiah.[88] Not all redemption literature is included in anthologies. Some works are small units of poetry, letters, and prayers. Small units dealing with redemption were composed at different times, and they were circulated. Whenever it seemed to the editor that the times were right (the cycle had turned to the very point where a deliverance of the nation had occurred once before) then the editor gathered the relevant documents and formed an anthology.

---

[82] Buchanan, *Redemption*, pp. 338-82.
[83] Buchanan, *Redemption*, pp. 387-417.
[84] Buchanan, *Redemption*, pp. 351-52, 56-57, 63-81.
[85] Buchanan, *Redemption*, pp. 400-403, 414-16.
[86] Buchanan, *Redemption*, pp. 46-48, 122-23, 131-33.
[87] J. Ibn Shemuel, *Commentaries on Redemption* (Jerusalem: Bialik, 1954) in Hebrew: *Yeh-hoo-dáh ee-vehn Sheh-moo-áyl, Meed-reh-sháy Geh-oo-láh* (*Yeh-roo-sheh-láh-yeem:Moo-sáhd Bee-yáh-leek*, c1954). (יהודה אבן שמואל, מדרשה גאלה, ירושלים, מוסד ביאליק).
[88] J. A. Montgomery, *Daniel*, p. 79, said, "Ezekiel has a full-blown Apocalyptic, both in his Gog and Magog prophecy, cc. 38 f., and in his prospect of the Physical remaking of the Holy Land, cc47 f. From that time on we have an increasing stream of such apolcalyptic prophecy e.g., Joel, Zech. Is. 24-27."

Second Isaiah, for example, reflects the excitement of Jews after they had formed negotiations with Cyrus and received promises of restoration after he conquered Babylon. Zechariah was written after the restoration had begun. The prophecy of the Book of Revelation (Rev 4:1-22:5) was gathered during the war with Rome (66-70 IA). The Book of Zerubbabel and the collections of Rabbi Shimon ben Yohai were collected during the Crusades. This was about a millennium after the fall of Jerusalem in 70 IA. At that time Jews believed the war between the Christians and Muslims was the war of Gog and Magog mentioned in Ezekiel. Jews were waiting until these two nations destroyed one another. Then they expected to be able to gain military control of the civilized world. They were still trying to become the fifth nation in the succession of great nations: Babylon, Media, Persia, Greece, and Israel, or Babylon, Media-Persia, Greece, Rome, and Israel.

Daniel as redemption literature. The Book of Daniel has often been classified as "apocalyptic literature," and, depending on the definition, parts of Daniel may fit that classification.[89] Some of the dramas, however, are more noted for their narrative and wisdom style than their apocalyptic style, although they are not exactly like other wisdom literature, either. Wilson has shown, for example, that the typically "wisdom" words, found in Job, Proverbs, and Ecclesiastes, are scarce or not-existent in Daniel.[90] The earliest canon simply classified Daniel as one of the writings, without defining it more sharply. It is composed of dramas or stories. Daniel fits better into the classification of redemption literature than either wisdom or apocalypse. Redemption literature is a broader classification than apocalyptic that includes many kinds of literature that is directed toward the redemption of Israel and the liberation of the Promised Land. The Book of Daniel clearly belongs to that category.

Scholars who have believed that somewhere there must have been an original book of Daniel that was composed by one and only one author have had to wrestle with the question of language. Was the original written in Aramaic or Hebrew? How do you account for the wide differences there are between the Semitic document and the Greek document? Why is there no complete agreement among the various lengths of time mentioned in different chapters about the same period of history? The reason seems to be that there were many units originally composed by different authors in different languages, dealing with parts of the same period of history. There were probably more dramas composed than were accepted by the editors for canonization. Not all of these individual units belong to the same structure. All are dramas of some sort, but Dan 4 and 5 are different from Dan 7 or 11-12. There are some elements of comedy and tragedy in some of the chapters.[91] They were not all edited to form exactly one pattern.

Prompted by the Battle of Beth-horon, some editors collected a few of the choice units and formed a coherent anthology, without interfering with the units

---

[89] See further P. W. Coxon, "The 'List' Genre and Narrative Style in the Court Tales of Daniel," *JSOT* 35 (1986):95-121.

[90] G. H. Wilson, "Wisdom in Daniel and the Origin of Apocalyptic," *HAR* 9 (1985):373-81.

[91] See E. M. Good, "Apocalyptic as Comedy: The Book of Daniel," *Semeia* 32 (1984):41-70.

more than necessary. The editor of the MT left the Aramaic documents in Aramaic and the Hebrew documents in Hebrew. Editors did not change the units of time to make them all agree exactly. Lenglet has shown that there seems to have been a literary plan for at least part of its outline. The Aramaic section, Dan 2-7, seems to form a concentric unit framed by an inclusion:
1. Chapters 2 and 7 are visions of four empires.
2. Chapters 3 and 6 picture Jews being rescued from danger.
3. Chapters 4 and 5 are judgment scenes against the emperor.[92]

The first half, Dan 2, 3, and 4 are reversed in Dan 5, 6, and 7. Thus organized, Dan 7 is still the central document of the book, but it is tied more closely to the first 6 chapters than has been normally thought. This unit includes all of the Aramaic portions of the document. Lenglet held that one author or editor organized this entire portion which a later editor enclosed in the Book of Daniel by putting chapters 1 and 8-12 around it. The later editor, of course, wrote in Hebrew rather than Aramaic. Lenglet thought Dan 2-7 would have been composed about 167-164 BIA.[93] Since this unit included Dan 7, however, it could not have been composed or organized *before* 164 BIA when Antiochus IV was given his "death sentence." A more reasonable date would be 164-142 BIA. This does not mean that some or all of the individual units could not have been read originally at the first Hanukkah (164 BIA), but it means that the organization of the entire book may have gone through more steps than would otherwise be necessary. The steps at organization would have happened after Hanukkah. It was probably completely organized by the liberty celebration at 142 BIA.

Modern readers who first read the medieval Jewish redemption literature and then read the Books of 1Enoch, Revelation, and Isaiah will not be upset to find Daniel fitting into the same categories. FT scholars read in Gen 15:13 the prophecy that the Israelites would be oppressed (in Egypt) 400 years. Then they learn from Exod 12:40 that it was 430 years, but they don't assume that one text is mistaken or has been altered by some editor. They just notice that the texts were written by different authors and that they do not agree. In the same way they should not be disturbed to discover that "a time, two times, and half a time" is not exactly the same as 2,300 evening and morning sacrifices, "1,290 days," or "1,335 days." Neither should they exhaust themselves trying to find out the original text and the work of a later editor.

The Book of Daniel and the Book of Revelation are both literarily superior to these medieval anthologies, but they were similarly formed. The Book of Daniel is organized into chapters, many of which form independent narratives. Some chapters include independent poems and prayers that have been fitted into suitable places. The freedom with which medieval Jewish editors used their sources suggests that the final editor of Daniel may have modified his sources in similar ways to emphasize the message he wanted to convey.

---

[92] A. Lenglet, "La Structure Litteraire de Daniel 2-7," *Bib* 53 (1972):169-90.
[93] Lenglet, "Structure," pp. 188-90.

If we had the sources independently, as is true of some medieval Jewish anthologies, or if we had the same source appearing in two or more collections, one of which was Daniel, we might conjecture the original form of the units with more confidence. As it is, we should speak in terms of possibility and probability, and be satisfied with less than perfection. This means we should concentrate on the final document, the Book of Daniel, as it has been preserved and canonized. That does not mean that Daniel was written by one author, as Rowley claimed, but that the final editor had a message that he wanted to communicate. He used whatever sources were at his disposal, and organized them effectively into a larger unit.

Committee and composition. One conjecture is that there was a scholarly committee organized after the Battle of Beth-horon for the purpose of writing theological interpretations of the meaning of the events that took place during the time between the Babylonian exile and the Battle of Beth-horon. These were designed to be reported at the celebration of the first Hanukkah in 164 BIA. Some of the essays read are preserved in the Book of Daniel. The Battle of Beth-horon had been sufficiently successful to prompt scholars to begin their scholarly activity. Two things might have happened to make the Maccabean revolt much more optimistic. 1) The treaty that Judas made with Rome may have provided many more weapons than Jews had available previously, and 2) at the battle of Beth-horon Jewish troops gathered many weapons that the Seleucids were forced to leave behind. Either of these would have equipped Judas' army to fight more successfully at the Battle of Beth-zur, but the **handwriting was on the wall** after the Battle of Beth-horon.

DANIEL AND THE CANON

When forming the canon of the FT, the ancient editors evidently were guided by the directions for distinguishing true from false prophets. Those who really prophesied in the name of the Lord predicted things that actually happened later. If a prophet's words did not come true, Jews and Israelites should realize that he was false (Deut 18:21-22). It is probably not coincidental that of the many prophets mentioned in the FT, only those who made prophecies that were vindicated by history were accepted in the canon as the word of God. Isaiah, Micah, Amos, and Hosea all predicted the fall of North Israel, and it fell. Jeremiah and Ezekiel prophesied the fall of Judah, and it fell. Second Isaiah, Zechariah, and Haggai predicted the return of Babylonian Jews to the Promised Land, and that happened.

Daniel was written as if it were a prophecy, but it was probably accepted into the canon for the same reason that other prophets were--because the "prophecies" had already been fulfilled. The end "anticipated" had already taken place. Antiochus IV was already dead. The Hasmonean victory at Beth-horon was accomplished. The Book of Daniel could be entitled "Hanukkah and Israel's Fulfilled Prophecies." The Book of Daniel would not qualify as prophecy if the author and its readers had understood the prophecy made there had not been fulfilled. Then this would have been classed among the false prophets. This is one more reason for thinking that Daniel was written after the fact and that Judas the Maccabee was the Son of man in Daniel 7. The authors assumed that all events had been prophesied and would later be fulfilled. They knew what had been fulfilled, so they simply conjectured the prophecies that must have been made before the events happened.

The expression "Son of man" was used as the title for a king in both Daniel and 1Enoch. In Daniel this all fits together in a time frame concluding with the rededication of the temple at Jerusalem, following the famous victory of Judas over the Greeks at Beth-horon. The authors or final editors used whatever sources they had to put together a book of celebration. In myth after myth, the mighty gentile kingdoms were overthrown, and the Kingdom of God was established. The four beasts, the four metals, and the four horns as well as the ten days, the ten toes, the ten horns, and the ten kings were presented in such a way as to prove that God is in control of history. It was God who systematically broke down the foreign powers, one after another, according to a preordained plan that took seventy weeks of years, the last of which was divided into two half weeks before the new Hasmonean era was established. The time frame within which this was structured was organized according to sabbatical eschatological hopes and also cycles of time.

The end that was expected throughout the Book of Daniel was the end of the Syrian Greek domination of the Promised Land, followed by the Hasmonean kingdom.[94] The time frame dealt within this book was a period that began with either the entrance of Nebuchadnezzar into Jerusalem in 605 BIA or the destruction of the temple in 586 BIA. It reached its end in 164 BIA with the rededication of the temple after it had been defiled by Antiochus Epiphanes. This was a historical myth, written after the fact. The end "predicted" had already taken place. The victory of the Battles of Beth-horon and Beth-zur that followed the Day of Atonement in 165 BIA proved to Jews that they had already been redeemed; their prison sentence had been served; the end for which they longed had come. The celebration of this redemption took place at Hanukkah (164 BIA). There was no plan that was intended to transfer these years into centuries or any other units of time.

The Son of man was no angel or heavenly figure of some other kind. Neither were the saints of the Most High angels. The Son of man was Judas the Maccabee, and the saints were the Jews contemporary with him.[95] The "clouds" symbol, like the sun disk for other nations, indicated that the Lord was present; he went before them and confused and upset the enemy before the Jews began to fight in battle. When Jesus identified himself as the Son of man, he used this term as a code name for an antitype of Judas the Maccabee. The Son of man in all the literature was a figure that functioned like a king, messiah, or Son of God. The interpretation given in Daniel was religious and based on biblical concepts, like Sabbaths, Jubilees, cycles, types, and fulfillment of scripture. The end that carried the theme of the book throughout was political and national. It was the end of the Syrian Greek kingdom. It was not a personal end, not a mystical end, not a social end, not an end that took place only in heaven, not an end of history or the cosmos.

---

[94] So also P. R. Davies, "Eschatology in the Book of Daniel," *JSOT* 17 (1980):42.

[95] A. A. DiLella, "The One in Human Likeness and the Holy Ones of the Most High in Daniel 7," *CBQ* 39 (1977):1-19, insisted that the saints were the people of Israel, but said Judas the Maccabee could not be the One in Human Likeness, because Judas does not fit the pacifistic tenor of the Book of Daniel.

The dramas were collected and organized by some mythologist who believed that the Hasmonean victory was the fulfillment of biblical promises to the Jews in relationship to the Land of Canaan. Neither the individual authors nor organizing editors wrote with the intention that future generations would anticipate the future on the basis of this. They did not write about an end that might happen 2,000 years later. They wrote about an end that had already taken place, and the Jews had already won the Battle of Beth-horon and were celebrating the first Hanukkah because of it. In fact, one of the most likely reasons for the authorship and organization of this document was to interpret and celebrate Hanukkah--but that is not the opinion of most scholars.

If Daniel had been written as history it probably would not have been included in the canon. It was composed as if it were prophecy so that it would be accepted as the fulfilled word of God rather than the report of human beings. The reason for this was that Jews thought the events of Hanukkah were actually fulfilled prophecy that had been predestined. This claim was not made without any justification. Over and over again the authors of the essays included in this book searched the scriptures and found earlier types that were repeated as antitypes in the period of history of which they were reporting. They also found texts that became the bases for their arguments. They were showing that all that had happened from 605 BIA to 164 BIA had been prophesied earlier in scripture. All they did was provide a religious interpretation for these events. They did this by dramatizing their convictions in terms of dreams and visions and justifying them by scripture.

Since the Hasmoneans determined which books that had been written by the time of Hanukkah would be considered canonical, Daniel's centrality around the victory of the Hasmoneans allowed it to be included. Just as Nehemiah collected and canonized the works he considered worthy, including Ezra and Nehemiah, so Judas also had the materials collected that had been written or distributed for safe keeping because of the Hasmonean war and preserved them (2Macc 2:13-15). This included the canonical books which were restored (2Macc 2:22),[96] as well as Daniel and the books of Maccabees.

FROM DRAMA TO PROPHECY

Prophecy began with misfortune. It was not until the celebration of Jewish freedom was over; Roman governors and procurators replaced Jewish kings; Rome determined the selection of high priests; and foreign taxation was restored

---

[96] Ben Sira was familiar with all of the books now in the canon except Ruth, Song of Songs, Esther, and Daniel. S. Z. Leiman, *The Canonization of Hebrew Scripture: The Talmudic and Midrashic Evidence* (Hamden: Arcon Books, c1976), pp. 29-30, assumed that these all existed by that time, but that is not certain. At least they were not canonized by that time. Rabbis were still considering the wisdom of including the Song of Songs into the canon during the time of Rabbi Akiba. Ps 74 seems to have been composed after 70 IA (see Buchanan, "The Fall of Jerusalem and the Reconsideration of Some Dates," *RevQ* 53 [1989]:31-48). Leiman correctly concluded that one of the times when canonization was considered was during the leadership of Judas the Maccabee. Leiman thought it was either before or during 164 BIA. He was close. It was more likely either during or *shortly after* 164 BIA. The canonization process may have continued until 142 BIA. A later reevaluation took place during the 2d century IA.

that the Book of Daniel was discontinued as a book of celebration. There was no longer any national liberty to celebrate. Since Daniel was part of the canon by that time, however, it began to be used as a basis for future hope. It was a type upon which later antitypes might be conjectured, and that was done. From then until now hundreds of Jewish and Christian scholars have studied the signs of their times and tried to match them typologically with the last three and a half year period before Hanukkah.

Daniel has often been called the first and greatest of the apocalyptic documents, but scholars are not agreed on the definition of apocalyptic. It is also called the only apocalyptic book that was accepted in the FT canon. It was canonized before the idea of apocalypticism was invented. It was classified as one of the undefined "writings" in the canon into which it was admitted. Davies correctly said, "The word 'apocalyptic' has been detrimental to the Book of Daniel."[97] His complaint is that by classifying Dan 7-12 as apocalyptic and the first six chapters as court tales scholars drive a wedge between these two sections that prevents them from seeing their close relationship.

Since Daniel's "prophecy" was fulfilled, all later wishful Jewish and Christian eschatology has treated this book as if it were a prophecy (Matt 24:15; *4Qflor* 2.3). It is because of the way Daniel has been used that Koch could say that Daniel was not only a prophet but even more than a prophet. Jews and Christians have been able to recognize in the events of Roman days the completion of the words of Daniel. It has been useful as a warning in times of crisis.[98] The book was initially used for celebration. It was only later that it came to be used to encourage Jews to persevere in their faith and religious practice, as Walker suggested.[99] Jews and Christians have utilized this document as the bottom line by which God could be expected to act in relationship to his chosen people and the Promised Land. Therefore, the eschatology of the Book of Daniel will here be examined as the basis on which later eschatologists formulated their future predictions. Kvanvig looked upon Dan 7 as an interpretative model. It is a mirror that reveals the real dimensions of contemporary situations. It shows how close the present age is to the end time by pointing out signs that appear before the end.[100] Popular twentieth century Jewish and Christian millennialists as well as modern theologians still organize their eschatology on the basis of Daniel. In relationship to some of these, Heaton said,

> It would be a sterile and humiliating task to expound the tortuous exegesis, which has twisted the meaning of our text throughout the history of its Christian interpretation. The allegorizing of details is not so much exegesis as the exposition of dogmatic preconceptions.[101]

---

[97] Davies, "Eschatology," p. 37.
[98] K. Koch, "Is Daniel Also among the Prophets?" *Int* 39 (1985):117-30. For a survey of this use see J. G. Gammie, "A Journey through Danielic Spaces: The Book of Daniel in the Theology and Piety of the Christian Community," *Int* 39 (1985):144-56.
[99] W. O. Walker, Jr., "Daniel 7:13-14," *Int* 39 (1985):176-81.
[100] H. S. Kvanvig, "The Relevance of the Biblical Visions of the End Time. Hermeneutical Guidelines to the Apocalyptical Literature," *HBT* 11 (1989):35-58
[101] Heaton, *Daniel*, p. 96.

Faith and Nationalism after Daniel

The predestined time mentioned in the Dramas of Daniel many times was the time that was fulfilled--by 142 BIA, at the latest. By that time Jews had independent control of the entire Davidic kingdom, the complete Kingdom of God, the Promised Land. Jews no longer paid taxes to any foreign country. The land was at peace, and a new calendar was established by which contracts were dated from the first year of Simon, the great high priest and ruler of the Jews (1Macc 13:39-42). Had Jews spoken Latin in Palestine at that time, calendars would probably have been calculated from the year of our Lord Simon (*anno domini Simoni*). Coins minted during the Bar Cochba rebellion were dated, "Year one of the liberation of Israel." Jews did not object to calling human beings by respectful names like "lord." According to Daniel, Daniel called Nebuchadnezzar "My lord" (*Mah-ree*, מראי). (Dan 4:16). Medieval Jews justified their practice of calling the Messiah "Lord" on the basis of Jer 23:6. A twelfth century Jewish messiah called "David el David" and "Alroy," gathered thousands of Jewish troops in Persia to participate in the Crusades. He was called "Our Lord, our king, the Messiah of the Lord."[102]

In antiquity some calendars were based according to "the kingdom of our Lord Tiberius Caesar."[103] Christian practice of establishing a calendar according to "the year of our Lord" was following a standard tradition. The following poem was composed as a tribute to the Hasmonean, Simon (1Macc 14:6-15).

> [6]He extended the borders of the nation,
>   and ruled over the land.
> [7]He gathered many prisoners
>   and governed Gazara, Beth-zur, and the citadel.
> He removed its uncleanness,
>   and there was no one to oppose him.
> [8]They were tilling their land with peace,
>   and the land produced its products,
>   the trees of the plain their fruit.
> [9]Old men sat in the streets,
>   all of them discussing their good fortunes,
>   the young men, wearing their medals and military uniforms.
> [10]He provided food for the cities
>   and organized them with weapons of fortification

---

[102] For the Hebrew text see A. Neubauer, "Documents Inedits," *REJ* 4 (1882):174-77. For the English translation see Buchanan, *Redemption*, pp. 195, 518.

[103] "Addai, The Apostle of Edessa," in A. Ungnad, *Syrische Grammatik* (Munich: C. H. Beck'ische Verlage Buchhandlung, 1932), p. 24.

> until his glorious name was named
>> to the corners of the earth.
> ¹¹He established peace in the land,
>> and Israel rejoiced extensively.
> ¹²Each one sat under his own vine and his own fig tree,
>> and no one frightened them.
> ¹³War in the land vanished from them,
>> and kings were crushed in those days.
> ¹⁴He strengthened all of the humble ones of his people.
>> He searched out the law,
>>> and removed every lawless and evil person.
> ¹⁵He glorified the holy things
>> and multiplied the vessels of the temple.

The first readers or hearers of the Dramas of Daniel were in a mood to celebrate. They were enjoying peace, victory, and fulfillment. That which had been removed when the temple burned and the prominent Jews were taken captive into Babylon was then restored. The desired end had come. The function of the character "Daniel," in this drama was not that of a prophet. The authors were scribes, like Ben Sira. They were learned scholars who acted as advisers to the governing leader. Their tasks were not that of predicting the future but of interpreting dreams and visions—both those of kings and their own. The authors who wrote these chapters after the event cast them into a literary style to make them appear to be prophecies. The Dramas of Daniel were directed to celebration, to Hanukkah, and to independence, but that was not the whole story.

The Kingdom without End

The conservative, orthodox Hasmoneans and their followers were victorious, and the Dramas of Daniel were written by and for them. But what of the Jewish opponents? What happened to the pro-Seleucids, the Hellenizers? The poet said that Simon removed every evil and lawless person (1Macc 14:14). This probably does not mean that he killed them all but that he removed them from the chief offices. Those who had been the first in rank became last in rank. Daniel says nothing about them, but they did not go up in smoke. The divisions may not have been exactly the same, but divisions and sects did not vanish from the land. There never has been one Judaism any more than there has been one Christianity. "All one body we" is only an aspiration.

The Hasmoneans became the kings and high priests, but they were not always at peace with one another. They sometimes killed one another in contest for the throne (*Ant* 13.301-309). Furthermore they did not have the complete support of their citizens. The new orthodox Jews questioned the legitimacy of the new leaders. The Hasmoneans were not descendants of David or of Zadok. What right had they to rule the land?

One of the Hasmonean kings, whom one of the early Dead Sea documents called ruler of the Kingdom of God (*mahm-léhk-teh-kah*, ממלכתך, *4Q448*. B.8) was

"Jonathan II," (יונתן המלך, *Yóh-nah-than hah-méh-lehk, 4Q448.* B2, C.8) whose Greek name was "Alexander Jannaeus." At the Feast of the Tabernacles Jews brought palm and citrus branches into the temple. While the high priest, Alexander Jannaeus, was offering sacrifice those in the congregation who thought he was an illegitimate high priest pelted him with the citrus fruit. He later had a barrier constructed between himself and the congregation to protect himself from such attacks. He responded by killing 6,000 of his own citizens (*Ant* 13.372-73)

In traditional fashion each sect of Judaism negotiated with different foreign countries to gain military and financial support to overthrow the opposing sect. They turned to Egypt, Syria, Arabia, Parthia, or Rome for help. Some rebelled openly with Alexander Jannaeus in military battle. After one of these battles, the king ordered 800 of the opposing citizens to be crucified in Jerusalem. While they hung on crosses, he had their wives and children murdered before them while he feasted with his concubines (*Ant* 13.379-81).

While there was a conflict between two Hasmonean brothers, Aristobulus and Hyrcanus, the Romans were drawn into the fight. One of the Jewish factions invited Pompey into the city. There was a great slaughter in which 12,000 Jews were killed, and Pompey with his associates entered the temple and saw that which was prohibited for anyone to see except the high priest. He took nothing, and he ordered the temple cleansed afterward (*Ant* 14.58-76), but Romans later plundered the temple for its treasures.

After the battle of 63 BIA Pompey assigned a governor over the Jews, and the kingdom that was to have continued for ages had lost its autonomy (*Ant* 14.74-79). About 55 BIA, during the conflict between Aristobulus and Hyrcanus, the Roman general Crassus entered the temple at Jerusalem and carried off all of its gold and valuable possessions, valued at more than 10,000 talents (*Ant* 14.105-109). That which Antiochus IV Epiphanes did in one trip, it took Pompey and Crassus to do in two. Josephus said that the money and gold accumulated in the temple was sent there by Jews in the diaspora from Europe and Asia (*Ant* 14.110-114). This is another reminder that the Palestinian Jews depended heavily on Jews of the diaspora to provide them, not only with money, but also with political influence and military power when they were needed.

At that time the cycle of time would have looked like this: (605 BIA-63 BIA).

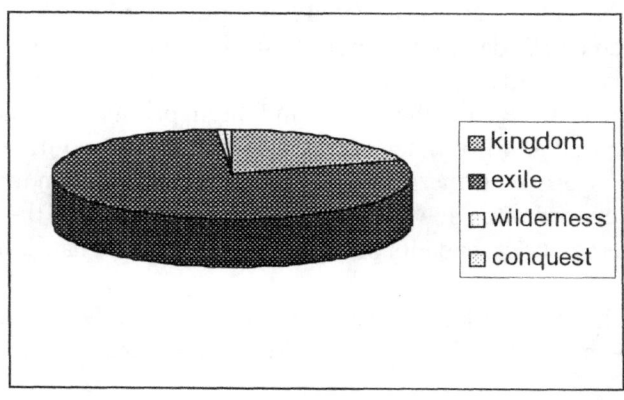

During the optimism of Hanukkah, when the Dramas of Daniel reflected the mood of the people, Jews believed that the kingdom that was being restored would never become subject to another nation. It would last for ages and would never pass away. Prior to the Dramas of Daniel, none of the earlier scripture promised an extension of the Promised Land beyond the United Kingdom ruled by David and Solomon. In fact some of the prophets objected to any attempts of Israel or Judah to become associated legally with other nations. Righteousness required being provincial and being party to only one treaty. That was the treaty Israel had made with the Lord.

The diaspora changed all of that. Before the exile Palestine was an all-class society. It was composed of the rich and the poor, the farmers, the artisans, shop keepers, lawyers, business magnates, priests, unskilled laborers, and slaves. When Nebuchadnezzar selected 10,000 of the most talented, best-educated, richest upper class citizens of Judah and took them to Babylon, an economic apartheid doctrine was developed and implemented as a religious doctrine and a basic philosophy. The religious leaders of Judaism were centered in the great city of Babylon. This group constituted a large, powerful, capable minority in Babylon. These were the redeemed of the Lord (Isa 35:9-10), the "good figs" (Jer 24) of which Jeremiah spoke, and they formed a political force that was able to negotiate with and influence leaders of large nations.

In every country Jews formed upper class ghettos (then called *politeuma*) by locating in a separate community in every city. Jewish law required this, because Jews were not allowed to travel more than 2,000 cubits on the Sabbath day. As the community became larger, houses were built at a distance greater than 2,000 cubits away from the synagogue, so Jews invented legal fictions by which they were permitted to extend the Sabbath limits so that they could attend the synagogue on the Sabbath. These rules were called *eh-roov-eén* (ערבין) and *shah-toof-eém* (שתפים) (*mErubin*). If there were no gentiles, Christians, or Samaritans between any Jewish houses it was legally permissible to perform liturgies to declare the entire community common property for the Sabbath. Once that was done it was permissible to walk to the end of the common property and still walk 2,000 more cubits on the Sabbath.

These rules had the sociological effect of segregating Jews from all other citizens of a community. It kept them well organized with special permission to live by their own laws. They also had their own political organization and goals. This special administration made Jews a strong political force in every nation. Because many Jews were merchants who traveled to other countries, messages were sent among various communities to keep the entire diaspora in communication with Jerusalem, Babylon, and among one another. Jewish scholars and leaders (called *gaonim*, גאונים) corresponded with various communities answering practical and legal questions and supporting them in their religious lives. Paul continued this practice among Christians. This kept the scattered communities unified.

In every country Jews bargained for special terms and often received them. They also began to think empirically. They dreamed, not just of a return to the little tribe of Judah, but of ruling a nation as big as Assyria, Babylon, Media, Persia, or

Greece had ever been. They were as well administered, internationally, as Greeks had been during the time of Alexander the Great. Palestine was as large as Macedonia. It seemed to Jews that they could do anything the Greeks had done. This expansionistic philosophy and theology had its early impetus in Babylon and has continued in Judaism and Christianity until this very day. The Book of Daniel has played an important part in this dream. With empirical goals such as these, the *politeumata* were seen as security risks for the nations in which they settled.

These minority groups became powerful, and the diaspora communities were always influential in determining policies of Jerusalem, but as Tcherikover said,

> These privileges were very great indeed, and they frequently aroused the envy and hatred of the Greeks. We shall see below that the existence of the Jewish community with its own authority, side by side with the Greek city, frequently caused a collision between the two forces and contributed not a little to fostering anti-Semitism among the Greeks.[104]

The authors involved in the composition of the Dramas of Daniel introduced a new expectation into Jewish thought--the succession of great nations in the Middle East. Secular historians had noticed that there were four great kingdoms in succession: 1) Assyria, 2) Media, 3) Persia, and 4) Greece. Jews modified that series and treated it as if God had ordained it. The new modification was forced to fit Jewish desires: 1) Babylon, 2) Media, 3) Persia, and 4) Greece. Jews added a further continuation of the succession, which would place their kingdom as the new successor to Greece. The optimism of Hanukkah under the leadership of Judas followed by the independence of Judah under the leadership of Simon led Jews to believe that their new nation would develop as rapidly as Persia under Cyrus or Macedonia under Alexander the Great. During the Hasmonean royalty the collection of Daniel's essays was accepted as one of the books of the canon (2Macc 2:14).

Pompey and the Roman control of the nation gave Jewish expectations a severe negative blow. Any outside observer would have noticed that the fifth kingdom that succeeded the Syrian Greeks was not Judah but Rome. At the time Pompey captured Jerusalem Rome controlled all of the territory west of the Euphrates, including Celica, Syria, Palestine, and Phoenicia—everything from the Euphrates to Egypt and the Mediterranean Sea (Appian, *Roman History* 11.8, 50).

Although this was a great discouragement, the Dramas of Daniel, which by then had become scripture, was transferred into a prophecy and treated as the word of God that would have to be fulfilled in the future. Nationalistic zeal did not come to an end. Following Jewish typology, the fourth kingdom was transferred from Greece to Rome. Pompey was the new Antiochus Epiphanes. When the Roman taxation was installed under the governorship of Quirinius (6-7 IA)[105] that which had

---

[104] V. Tcherikover, *Hellenistic Civilization and the Jews*, tr. S. Applebaum (Philadelphia: JPS, 1961), p.332.

[105] Appian (*Roman History* 11.8, 50) said that the Jews had been so rebellious that Rome taxed them heavier than other nations under Roman rule.

been gained during the leadership of Simon was clearly lost. Instead of becoming the fifth great nation in the succession, it had become a Roman colony, and the hostility that had once applied to Syrian Greece was then directed against Rome. Roman Caesars became the new Seleucids. The "little help" became the big obstacle, the "fourth kingdom."

Had they followed cyclical logic faithfully, Jews would have identified themselves with the Jews who had been taken into captivity to Babylon. This would have required them to anticipate another cycle of 490 years of captivity before there would be another Battle of Beth-horon and another Hanukkah, but they were not satisfied with being long distance eschatologists. They reorganized their succession of great nations to be as follows: 1) Babylon, 2) Media-Persia, 3) Greece, 4) Rome, and 5) Judah. Instead of looking for signs that would identify them with the beginning of the Babylonian captivity, they found signs that made them think that they were in the last 3½ years of the rule of Antiochus Epiphanes. The Jews involved were not primarily objective logicians. They were dogmatists, so they did not depend primarily on logic and facts. They bent the logic and selected as necessary facts only those that fit their needs and feelings.

There were several small military rebellions against Rome at the Jewish feasts, but it was not until one of the feasts in 66 IA that the gathered Jews fought the Romans in the rugged terrain near Beth-horon again, and again scored an astounding victory. This reminded the pilgrims of the decisive victory of Judas over the Syrian Greeks in this same rugged mountainside. In 66 IA, the situation between Rome and the Jews was similar to that of the Jews and the Syrians in 168 BIA when the Hasmonean rebellion began. Their defeat of the Roman general Cestius at Beth-horon proved to them that God was revisiting them with victory, so they declared war against Rome which lasted for 3½ years and concluded--not with a new cleansing of the temple, as they expected. Jews had fully expected God to interfere and overpower the Romans within 3½ years, just as it had happened before. Instead the war ended with a new destruction of Jerusalem and the burning of the temple. Josephus described several prophets that predicted the redemption of Israel right up to the time the Romans burned the temple (*War* 6.285-86; *Ant* 13.311-313; 20.97, 169). The writings from none of these, however, were included in the canon, because their prophecies were proved to have been false.

Jerome said that Jews believed that the real Antichrist was not Syrian Greeks and Antiochus Epiphanes but Rome and the generals, Vespasian and Titus (Jerome 25.716-17, pp. 569). Fourth Ezra, writing after the fall of Jerusalem, interpreted a vision in which the [Roman] eagle was the fourth kingdom in the succession of empires which appeared in a vision to Daniel (*4Ezra* 11.38-39; 12.10). Second Baruch prophesied that the kingdom that destroyed Zion would itself be destroyed (*2Bar* 39.3). Jews could not accept the possibility that cycles of time were not predictable. Nor could they believe that the cycle of time did not include a succession of empires in which Judah would be the last and the greatest. Neither could they think of the cycle which lasted 430 (Exod 12:40) years after exile in Egypt and 490 years (Dan 9:24) after exile in Babylon would have to start again and continue more than 400 years before the cycle would turn in Judah's favor.

Although Jews suffered a terrible defeat in 70 IA, the nationalism of Judaism was not finished. Jews read the signs of the times again in 132 IA and concluded that Julian was the new Antiochus Epiphanes. They fought for another 3½ years, trying to bring about the victory of 164 BIA, but it too failed. Jerome said Jews believed that at that time the Roman emperor Julian was the Antichrist (Jerome 25.717-18, p. 570). Both the battle of 66-70 IA and the one of 132-35 IA were fought in the belief that the Jews were reliving the Hasmonean days which ended in Hanukkah.

THE SECTS OF JUDIASM

Internal divisions. Throughout all of the wars that Jews fought with other nations there were inner conflicts among the sects of Jews themselves. In the days of Jeremiah there were pro-Babylonians and pro-Egyptians. Later there were pro-Persians and pro-Greeks; then there were pro-Egyptian Hellenizers and pro-Seleucid Hellenizers. During the Hasmonean war there were pro-Romans and pro-Seleucids. These were the conservatives and the Hellenists. When the Hasmoneans came to power, they changed. Some Hasmoneans became pro-Roman Hellenists, whereas others became pro-Parthian. It is not possible to trace these factions to identify them with later sects, but there were later sects--Pharisees, Sadducees, Essenes, and other sects. No one knows whether these were identified with earlier orthodox or Hellenistic groups or whether they were newly formed or regrouped.[106] However it followed, conflicts continued.

The Nazorean sect. One of the sects of Judaism, which originated during these times of upheaval, was probably called the "Nazoreans,"[107] at first, and later "Christians." It is not certain how the Nazoreans were related to earlier segments of Judaism. Did they emerge from the pre-Hasmonean orthodox? Were they anti-Hasmonean, sons of David, two-messiah orthodox? John the Baptist was a very rigorous law observer, and he appeared together with Jesus as one of the two expected Messiahs. On the other hand, however, the author of Hebrews was probably a pro-Hasmonean monk.[108] Later Christianity seems to have included all of the forces at work in Judaism of Hasmonean times. Judaism apparently regrouped and reorganized itself from time to time as situations changed.

Christians inherited the scriptures, traditions, and nationalistic expectations of other Jews. After the defeat of Bar Cochba (135 IA) all Jews and Christians were suspected by Romans of being potential saboteurs, fifth columnists, and terrorists. They were numerous enough and influential enough to be threatening. Josephus said

---

[106] R. T. Beckwith, "Daniel 9 and the Date of Messiah's Coming in Essene, Hellenistic, Pharisaic, Zealot and Early Christian Computation," *RevQ* 10 (1981):521-42, arbitrarily assigned various Jewish books to different sectarians as if there was no question about their authorship. To check the data for identifying and characterizing sects of Judaism see Buchanan, *The Consequences of the Covenant* (Leiden: Brill, 1970), pp. 238-81.

[107] See further Buchanan, *The Gospel of Matthew* (Lewiston: The Edwin Mellen Press, c1996) I, pp. 99-100.

[108] So Buchanan, *To the Hebrews* (Garden City: Doubleday, c1972).

that there was not a people in the world that did not have Jews in its midst (*War* 2.398) and that every Jew had more fear of the law of Moses than of any world ruler (*Apion* 2.277). This means they were not primarily loyal to the country where they lived. Although they became Syrian, Egyptian, or Roman citizens, they were not Syrians, Egyptians, or Romans first of all. According to Josephus, Ptolemy Philometer and his wife Cleopatra (2d century BIA) entrusted all of Egypt to the Jews and put their entire army under two Jewish generals, Onias and Dositheus (*Apion* 2.49). This large, influential group of Jews is reminiscent of the Jews in Babylon at the time of Cyrus.

Jews and Christians in the diaspora. Whenever Roman interests conflicted with those of Jews and Christians these citizens became anti-Roman. This was a serious security threat to Rome. When Jesus said there were many who would come from the East and the West and recline with Abraham, Isaac, and Jacob in the Kingdom of Heaven (Matt 8:11) he was speaking of faithful Jews in the diaspora who would support Palestinian Jews whenever the need arose. There were so many Jews in the Roman Empire that after the death of Herod more than 8,000 Jews appeared at Rome to influence the trial that would determine the successor to Herod's throne (*War* 2.80).

In order to survive in Rome after the defeat of Bar Cochba all Jews and Christians were on the defensive. They had to persuade Rome that they were loyal citizens. This involved removing all obvious terrorist themes from their literature. That which survived had been constructed in midrashic and parabolic code. There was in the scripture a doctrinal basis for passive ethics, but it was not anti-national.

The expectations in all of the scripture prior to the Babylonian exile applied only to the Promised Land, which was the Davidic kingdom. After Jews had lived and held political positions in large empires, like Babylon, Persia, and Alexander's kingdom, however, their expectations enlarged. They wanted Jerusalem to become the capital of a kingdom as large as any of these. Heaton said,

> When you read one of the great general histories of the ancient world, you discover that the Jews are scarcely more than footnotes to the main sweep of events so long as they occupy their native Palestine. It is only when they become exiles in Babylon that they enter civilization as the political historian reckons it.[109]

The war-torn land. For many years after the first Hanukkah, Jews thought they were in the process of obtaining such a kingdom as one of the great empires, but the kingdom quickly deteriorated. There continued to be wars between Syria and Jerusalem. While John Hyrcanus was high priest the strong wall built by the Hasmoneans around Jerusalem was pulled down (132 BIA; *Ant* 13.237-38), but after the death of Antiochus VII, Hyrcanus continued to push his frontiers in all directions, and Alexander Jannaeus continued this effort. It was the constant civil

---

[109] Heaton, *Daniel*, p. 63.

war in Syria that allowed Jews to expand without opposition, but Judah had its own civil wars. These wars led to the final destruction of the kingdom. Bevan observed,

> On the seaboard between Phoenicia and Egypt, cities where Hellenic culture had lately flourished, Gaza, Strato's Tower, Dora, were ruinous solitudes—monuments of the vengeance of the Jews.[110]

Not only was the landscape shattered, but also the nation's people suffered. During a six-year period Jannaeus killed at least 50,000 Jews (*Ant* 13.376). The situation went from bad to worse as Pompey was followed by Crassus, Crassus by Herod, and finally the Roman taxation of Quirinius.

By that time it was clear to the Jews that they were free from Syria. Pompey had put an end to the Seleucid leadership in that country, but Rome had emerged as the new antitype of Syria, and the combined work of two generals accomplished the same defilement as Antiochus IV. It was Rome that put Herod the Great into office and financed his program. His son, Archelaus, had 3,000 Jewish citizens killed while obtaining his position. After Rome deposed Archelaus, it replaced Jewish leaders with the Roman governor Quirinius and local procurators and, at the same time, introduced a new tax (6/7 IA). After Pompey, Crassus, Herod, and Quirinius it was obvious to the Jews that the kingdom had slipped out of their hands. The tax that was removed under the leadership of Simon (142 BIA) was restored (6/7 IA), and with it the celebrated freedom had vanished.

After Daniel had been composed and canonized, of course, Jews had scriptural proof that the succession was God's word. They continued to try to fit their current political program into some earlier favorable type, but after a bitter war of 3½ years Jews were crushed, and Rome retained its position as the fifth kingdom of the predestined succession of empires. By this time, one sect of Jews, distinguished as Christians, refused to enter into the rebellion, and they were persecuted by Bar Cochba. (*HE* 8.4).

Jewish and Christian conflicts. After that war, not only was there enmity between Jews and Romans, but there was also tension between Christians and other sects of Jews. Having Jews in violent disagreement with one another and on different political sides was nothing new. This was true from the time of Jeremiah. We have no detailed historical report of the history of Jews and Christians from the time of Bar Cochba until the time of Constantine. There were, however, apparently frequent uprisings in the Roman Empire, and both Christians and other sects of Jews constituted strong militant minorities that worried the Romans. Eusebius told about hundreds of Christians who were martyred. Other Jews were probably being martyred at the same time for the same reasons. That which was martyrdom from the Jewish and Christian point of view was national security from the Roman standpoint. This period of martyrdom lasted from the taxation of Quirinius (ca. 6-7 IA) to the victory of Constantine (ca 325 IA). The period of

---

[110] E. R. Bevan, *Seleucus* II, p. 264.

history between these two dates is roughly divided into four sections: There is 1) first the period from 164 BIA to 38 BIA when the Hasmoneans ruled, and the kingdom celebrated by Hanukkah was a reality. 2) Pompey opened up the way for Herodian rule (from 38-4 BIA). During this time Rome was really ruling Palestine, but under Palestinian leadership. 3) After the death of Herod, his son Archaeleus ruled Judah and Samaria for ten years (ca 4 BIA-6 IA). That was the end of all semblance of Jewish rule. Roman governors replaced Jewish kings. 4) This was followed by a long period of war, terrorism, and martyrdom.

The new Beth-horon. With Constantine the cycle of time was complete. Between the Battle of Beth-horon and the victory of Constantine the cycle would have looked something like this.

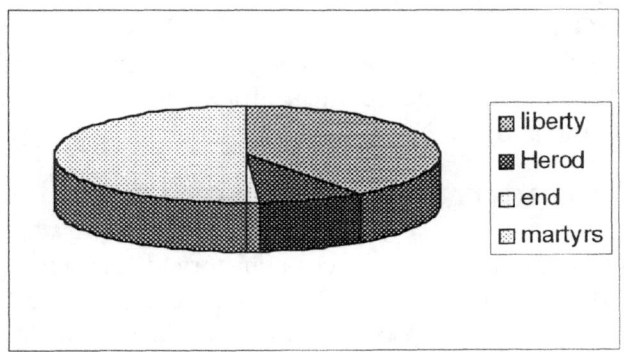

Jews and Christians continued to study the Book of Daniel to learn how the cycle of time worked. The cycle from the Babylonian exile to the Battles of Beth-horon and Beth-zur followed by Hanukkah had been successful. It lasted more than 400 years, but it concluded victoriously for Jews. Instead of studying the progress of events for more than 400 years, they looked for signs of the last 3½ years of that cycle. There was a three-year war before Judas won the Battles of Beth-horon and Beth-zur, so they fought for 3½ years to recover the nation in 66-70 IA and again in 132-135 IA. They might have given up at that point and reasoned that it failed two times out of three and was probably a mistaken deduction, but they did not. They continued to look for signs of the Messiah, and over a period of two millennia they conducted more than 75 identifiable messianic movements.[111] These messiahs were not just roving teachers, philosophers, or heavenly angels. They were real men, like Alroy, Abu Issa, Serenus, Ephraim, Obadiah, Bar Cochba, and others who actually gathered troops and fought battles with real political and military enemies.[112]

Daniel as prophecy. Renowned rabbis and scholars spent endless hours studying the scripture to calculate the end. Daniel's 490-year scheme was one of their basic texts. They looked for times that resembled the Maccabean Rebellion. For them

---

[111] So I. Zunz, *Gesammelten Schriften* III (Berlin, 1875-76), pp. 134-35.
[112] Buchanan, *Redemption*, p. 586.

bad times were good news, because these difficult times of persecution were designed to precede by only 3½ years the deliverance and the new Hanukkah. These bad times were called times of trouble (Dan 12:1; *1QM* 1.12; 15.1) and birth pangs of the Messiah by Jews (Mek *Vayassa* 5.76; *bSan* 98b), and days of tribulation by Christians (Matt 24:21, 29). These evil times were to be times of warfare between the children of light and the children of darkness—the Jews and the Romans (Kittim) (*1QM* 1.11-12).

Basic to their theology and purpose of calculations was the belief that time moved in predestined cycles and repetitious types and antitypes. Rabbi Samuel said that this age differs from the days of the Messiah only in respect to the servitude to foreign powers (*bSan* 99a). Neither Jews nor Christians were expecting to be taken up to heaven to become parts of a kingdom of Heaven there. They were trying to reproduce the signs so that there would be another Hasmonean kingdom on earth. Rabbi Eleazar of Modi'im said that if Jews would only keep the Sabbath, God would give them six goodly blessings. These were: 1) the land of Israel, 2) the age to come, 3) the new age, 4) the kingdom of the house of David, 5) the priesthood, and 6) the Levitical offices (Mek, *Vayassa* 5.71-73). These would all be integral parts of the redemption.

THE ETHICS OF CONQUEST THEOLOGY

Early Jews and Christians used their experiences in history to learn God's will. That which was successful, they reasoned, was God's design. Success was defined not in terms of getting along with other peoples in peace and equality but by success in warfare, expansion, and national superiority. They wanted peace on the land and good will toward the chosen people (Luke 2:14), but they wanted only the kind of peace that came with political superiority. They tried to form doctrines based on repeating past successes in expansion and national victory. Because they had been successful in driving out the inhabitants of Canaan and taking their land, they assumed that God had promised this to them. When they lost possession of the land, they tried to acquire it again by the same methods they had used before. In the scripture they reported only two methods of achieving righteousness, which was necessary for acquiring the land, one was active and the other was passive.[113]

Activist ethics. During their experience in the wilderness, the Israelites were afflicted with a dreadful disease, which killed many of them. This meant that God disapproved of something that they had been doing. Phineas believed God disapproved of their mingling and intermarrying with the local Midianites. Moses did nothing to stop the practice, so when the Israelite, Zimri, brought his new Midianite wife into his tent, Phineas entered the tent while the newly weds were engaged in sexual intercourse. He ran a spear through both of them, killing them. After that the plague stopped, so Israelites credited Phineas for this merit. (Num 25:1-9). The Psalmist who narrated this event said, **Then Phineas arose and judged**

---

[113] For a fuller discussion of this summary, see Buchanan, *The Consequences of the Covenant* (Leiden: Brill, 1970), pp. 1-41.

the case, and the plague was stopped, and that has been reckoned to him as righteousness from generation to generation to the age (Ps 106:30-31). That experience justified the use of arms to punish minglers and foreigners. On that basis Joshua, the judges, David, and Solomon used military means to overthrow the inhabitants of Canaan. The Hasmoneans led their revolt against the Syrians in the name of their forefather, Phineas (1Macc 2:23-28), and again they were successful.

Passive ethics. The second basis for ethics was based on Gen 15. During the treaty ceremony that Abraham made with God, he was promised posterity, prosperity, and the land of Canaan. He believed, and this was reckoned to him as righteousness (Gen 15:1-6). When the Jews were taken captive to Babylon, they were returned to the Promised Land without participating in any warfare. They suffered, did good deeds, and negotiated a treaty with Cyrus who conquered Babylon without a battle. Instead of concluding from this that they were clever negotiators who were skilled in international intelligence for which God rewarded them, they reasoned that they had fulfilled the terms of the treaty made with Abraham. They only believed. They did not organize a military rebellion. Their belief was reckoned to them as righteousness. The method worked, so that all future generations should know that belief was necessary for acquiring the Promised Land. It was not their negotiation ability but their faith that achieved their goal.

From the time of Second Isaiah there were two methods of fulfilling righteousness that the treaty required: 1) Taking up the sword in the name of the Lord, and 2) Doing good deeds and trusting God to fulfill his promises. The Book of Daniel reflects a familiarity with both methods. So do the books of the NT. After the death of John the Baptist, the temptations and the prayer at Gethsemane show that Jesus was struggling emotionally to learn which of these methods God wanted him to fulfill. When he came down from the Mount of Olives he was looking for a sign from God to tell him what to do. Ezekiel said that when the new age began there would be fruit on the trees in the Kidron Valley every month of the year (Ezek 47). Had Jesus seen ripe figs on the fig trees out of season, he would have understood that to be a sign from God that he should begin military action, but that did not happen, so he chose the passive method of ethics rather than the military.[114]

Finally, in the fourth century IA when Constantine was trying to overthrow Maxentius, Christians negotiated for terms with Constantine just as Jews had earlier done both with Cyrus of Persia and the Roman senate. With the aid of Rome (the little help), the Hasmoneans earlier defeated the Syrians, and in 142 BIA victory was complete. Taxation was removed; independence was acknowledged. Simon was the great high priest and national leader. Like most kings he would have been called "Lord." They began a new calendar, dating things from the "first year of Simon" (1Macc 13:42). When Constantine defeated Maxentius, Christians thought this was the fulfillment of the prophecy of Daniel. The Christian Roman empire was the fifth empire of the succession. It was the rock that crushed the pagan statue (Dan 2:34-35), the kingdom that should never

---

[114] Buchanan, "Withering Fig Trees and Progression in Midrash," C. A. Evans and W. R. Stegner (eds.), *The Gospels and the Scriptures of Israel* (Sheffield: Sheffield Academic Press, Ltd., 1994), pp. 249-69.

be destroyed (Dan 2:44-45). It was the fulfillment of Isa 35 (*HE* 10.46). Christians also began a new calendar, just as Jews had done during the reign of Simon. They numbered days from "the year of the Lord" meaning the Lord Jesus, rather than the Lord Simon.

At that time all other Jews might have joined the Christian sect and had a unified nation, but that was not the Jewish or Christian way of doing things. Inner conflicts continued. Other Jews did not accept Jesus as Lord or the Christians as the true recipients of the prophecy of Daniel, so conflicts persisted between Christians who were politically in positions of power in the Holy Roman Empire and other Jews who constituted a powerful, upper-class, minority in the nation. The Jews who had not supported Constantine were like the Hellenizers who had not supported Judas the Maccabee. Those who had been first became last, and the last became first. Just as the conflicts among Jewish sects did not come to an end with the rise of the Hasmoneans to power, so also the conflicts between Jews and Christians continued.

The conflict widened during the Crusades, which began about a millennium after the fall of Jerusalem. All three religious nationalities--Jews, Christians, and Muslims--were engaged in military conflict. Jews thought of Christians as the antichrists and Muslims and Christians as Gog and Magog, whom they tried to help destroy one another.[115]

Wars have been fought and people have been killed as both Christians and Jews have tried to gain possession of more territory and control. The Book of Daniel has been a motivating factor instigating much conflict, terrorism, and many ethnic cleansings. Christians and Jews might seriously examine the ethics involved in trying to become the fulfillment of the prophecy of Daniel, that did not originate as a prophecy but as a drama celebrating the victory of Judas and his brothers in the second century BIA.

A non-Palestinian illustration. There once was a celebration in Scotland, similar to Hanukkah in Jerusalem. The English had suppressed the Scots for years. Scots had been forbidden to wear their distinctive tribal tartans. When finally the English relented on this score, the Scots initiated a celebration in the Church of Scotland, every clan bringing its colors to the altar of the church for rededication. Scots have continued to celebrate the first Sunday in May as the Kirkin' of the Tartans. In Washington, D.C. there was no Church of Scotland or Presbyterian Church large enough to accommodate all of the local Scots that would participate in that celebration, so they negotiated with the Anglicans for the use of the National Cathedral on that particular Sunday each year.

When the National Presbyterian Church was constructed, this problem no longer existed, so the Scots moved to that church and held their celebration in the Presbyterian Church, but that did not last long. They had already established a tradition in the National Cathedral, so they moved back. They continue to celebrate the Kirkin' of the Tartans in the National Cathedral every year. This celebration originated as an anti-English, nationalistic festivity. It continues to be a joyous celebration, but the hostility is gone. The celebration is not used as a

---

[115] For example, see "That Day," tr. Buchanan, *Redemption*, pp. 291-93, 596.

means to stir up anti-Anglican feeling among the Scots. It has become a national festival without national hostility or military motivation.

Suppose Christians and Jews changed the use of Daniel from the false prophecy it has become to the celebration for which it began. What if we could celebrate this important period of history, as free of hostility and nationalistic warfare as the Kirkin' of the Tartans in Washington D.C.? Suppose Jews and Christians abandoned the hope of world dominion and ethnic cleansings. Would that make a difference in the world? We might give this some thought.

The Dramas of Daniel, when understood as they were initially composed, provide ocassions for further celebration. They were composed in better style than have usually been held and deserve more appreciation than they have received. There is nothing in the Dramas of Daniel, however, to indicate tht God intends the world to come to an end. Christians and Jews might advantageously stop planning for that to happen. It would be better if we would join forces with all of the other inhabitants of the globe in learning to live responsibly on the earth that has been entrusted to all of us.

APPENDIX I

SUZANNA

Introduction

Daniel is the hero of the drama of Suzanna, but it was not included among the dramas published in the Book of Daniel. There are probably two reasons for this: 1) In the Daniel dramas the hero was Daniel, but the villains were always gentiles who ruled the Jews during the Babylonian exile. In Suzanna, the villains were eminent, religious Jews, expert in law, whose responsibility was to judge the character of other Jews. 2) The dramas of Daniel were nationalistic and political. The villains were political leaders who caused problems for the Jews during the Babylonian captivity. There is nothing in the drama of Suzanna that is related to the political situation of the nation, the gentile ruling powers, or the celebration that could be related to Hanukkah. There is no fiery furnace, lions' den, king confessing to Judaism, statue of gentile powers, foreign beasts, crushing rock, Son of man, signs of the predestined end, or saints of the Most High. It is an independent Daniel drama, so it has been preserved independently. It exists only in the Greek. It has not been preserved either in Hebrew or Aramaic. The Greek texts also vary somewhat as will be evident in the following texts.

Text

Theodotion

$^{1:1}$There was a man living in Babylon whose name was Joakim. ^{2}He took a wife whose name was Suzanna, the daughter of Chelkias. She was very beautiful and feared the Lord. ^{3}Her parents were righteous, and they taught their daughter according to the law of Moses. ^{4}Joakim was very wealthy, and he had a garden adjacent to his house. Jews used to come to him, because he was the most highly respected of all. ^{5}Two elders were selected from among the people to be judges that year, concerning whom the Lord said, "Lawlessness went out from Babylon, from the elders, judges who seemed to guide the people."

Commentary

This is the introduction to the drama. These are the *dramatis personae*, the primary actors in the play. In these five verses the author has described both the virtuous ones and the villains. The only one omitted here is Daniel who was planned to be introduced later in the play. The wicked ones and the righteous were contrasted immediately, so that the readers would know at the outset what to suspect.

Although this story is mostly about the woman, Suzanna, it begins telling about her husband, Joakim, a wealthy Jew in Babylon. He had a garden that was a paradise (*pah-ráh-days-saws*, παράδεισος). A paradise was more than a flower or vegetable garden. It was a courtyard, a park. It was a place to entertain guests and to stroll for recreation. The garden of Eden was a paradise that apparently included all of the territory from the borders of Ethiopia to the Tigris-Euphrates rivers. This was the whole civilized world of the Middle East.

Joakim was one of the Jews moved from Palestine to Babylon during the exile, and he took Jeremiah's advice to settle down in Babylon and support the welfare of that city, because they would find welfare in its welfare. They should build houses, plant gardens, and eat their produce (Jer 29:5-7). The Jews who were taken captive to Babylonia had been upper class in Judah, and they soon also became wealthy and influential there in their new country.

Text

The Old Greek	Theodotion
⁷**These** men saw a woman who was pretty in appearance, ⁸the wife of their brother, from the children of Israel, named **Suzanna**, the daughter of Chelkias, the wife of Joakim, **walking around in her husband's garden** at evening time, and they wanted her.	**These** came frequently to the house of Joakim, and all those who were being judged came to them [there]. ⁷About noon, when the people had left, ⁸**Suzanna entered and walked around in her husband's garden**, ⁸and the two elders observed her every day, entering and walking around, and they became lustful of her.

Commentary

The author has started to paint a picture with words. The scene opens with the appearance of a legitimately married woman from a righteous family. She was a faithful Israelite, which means that she was from Samaria, rather than Judah. She was not only righteous and from a respected family, but she was beautiful. The author did not describe her beauty, saying that she was a blond or a brunette, tall or short. He allowed the reader to picture her according to his or her own imagination. The plot began to unfold when the two men were introduced having been attracted by her and lusting for her. The motivation for the crime that follows is already anticipated. The elders were there to conduct court trials in Suzanna's husband's courtyard.

Text

The Old Greek	Theodotion
[9] **They diverted their minds, and turned their eyes away from looking to heaven or remembering righteous judgments.** [10/11] **Both were overwhelmed by her, but they did not disclose to one another** the evil which held them concerning her, neither did the woman know this fact. [12] When it was dawn, they came eagerly, each without the other knowing, who would be the first to appear to her and speak to her. [13/14] Now look! She walked around the garden, according to her custom, and one of the elders came, and look! The other appeared. One answered and said to the other, "Why did you come so early without taking me along?" Then each **admitted** to the other **his pain**.	They diverted their minds and turned their eyes away from looking at heaven and remembering righteous judgments. [10] Both were overwhelmed by her, but they did not disclose their pain to one another, [11] because they were ashamed to tell of their lusts because they wanted to have intercourse with her. [12] They persisted in watching her lustfully, every day. [13] Then **one said to the other, "Let us go** home, because it is time for lunch," and as they left they were separated from one another. [14] Then they turned back and came to the same place. After they had confronted one another, they **admitted** the cause of **their lust**.

Commentary

The plot begins to unfold, first, by dealing with the consciences of the two prominent and highly respected judges. These super-righteous legal officers were ashamed of their lusts, because they knew they were forbidden by law. Nevertheless, they ignored their consciences and their responsibilites. This woman was so alluring to them that it was painful for them to control their lusts.

The Greek word for lust (*eh-pee-thu-meé-ah*, ἐπιθυμία) is the same word that means "covet." Coveting is not just wanting something. It means acting in some way so that you will receive it. For example, today in an Arab home, if a guest casually looked at something in the house, the host would immediately bring it to the guest and give it to him, saying, "*tuh-váh-dahl*, Please [take it]," even if it would make the host bankrupt to provide it. The social pressures associated with Arab hospitality require it. It is a good host's obligation to sense the wants and needs of his guest and provide them.[1] It is the good guest's responsibility to show no interest in anything that belongs to his or her host. To do so is to covet. It puts the host in the social position of having to provide. That has

---

[1] See further Buchanan, "The Spiritual Commandment," *JAAR* 26 (1968):126-27.

the same effect as stealing. Therefore it is forbidden in the ten commandments (OG Exod 20:17).

Different words and details were used by the variant texts to describe the way these lusts took control of the two men, but the facts are the same. They tried to disguise their lusts while looking for opportunities to express them. When they finally caught each other in their individual plots, they decided to corroborate their needs and work together to obtain the object of their lusts.

Text

The Old Greek	Theodotion
[19] **One said to the other, "Let us go** to her," and agreeing they went to her and were forcing her.	Then they planned a time when they could be with her alone. [15] Now it happened, when they were watching carefully for a suitable day when she entered, just as she had the day before and the day before that with only two maidens. She wanted to bathe in the garden, because it was hot. [16] No one was there except the two elders who were hidden and watching her carefully. [17] Then she said to her maidens, "Bring me the oil and perfume, and close the doors of the garden, so that I might bathe." [18] They did as she said, and closed the doors of the garden and left by the side doors to bring the things she had commanded them. They did not see the elders, because they were hidden. [19] When the maidens had left, the two elders rose up and ran to her, [20] and they said, "Look! The doors are closed, and no one will see us. We are lusting for you. Therefore, consent to us and be with us, [21] but if you don't we will testify that a young man was with you and because of that you sent your maidens away."

Commentary

The Theodotion text tells the story in great detail, whereas OG only summarizes the event. They planned to rape her. From these two passages alone, it is impossible to learn whether one author had access to the other and if so which was dependent on the other. OG may have summarized Theodotion or Theodotion may have developed the entire story from the OG summary. Theodotion tells what the situation was, who was involved, how the elders propositioned Suzanna. When they were unsuccessful it tells of their threats to her.

The picture of the elders peeking at Suzanna while she was bathing reminds the reader of David watching Bathsheba, lustfully, as she bathed on the nearby roof (2Sam 11:2-4). In both cases the respective lawless males acted to satisfy their lusts. Bathsheba was more cooperative than Suzanna. The elders first requested Suzanna's consensual agreement. When that failed they threatened to defame her.

Text

The Old Greek	Theodotion
²²The Jewess **said** to them, "I know that **if I do this I will die. If I do not do it I will not escape from your hands.** ²³It is better for me not to fall into your hands than to sin before the Lord."	²²Suzanna groaned and **said**, "I am crowded from every direction. **If I do this I will die. If I do not do it I will not escape from your hands.** ²³It is better for me not to act so as **to fall into your hands than to sin before the Lord."** ²⁴Then she cried out in a loud voice, and the two elders shouted against her. ²⁵As she ran, the one opened the doors of the garden. ²⁶When those who were from the house heard the cry in the garden, they entered through the side doors to see what had happened to her. ²⁷But when the elders said their words, the servants were very much embarrassed, because nothing like this had ever been said about Suzanna.

Commentary

Although she was earlier called a woman from Israel, which can mean either Samaria or Judah, Suzanna is here called a Jewess. There is obviously some textual relationship between the two texts, dealing with Suzanna's conversation. This seems to be really a conversation of her inner thoughts, but they are presented as if she spoke them out loud. Again it is the text of Theodotion that provides the detail of this confrontation, reporting all of the people involved and showing how the blame happened to be placed on Suzanna rather than the elders.

According to the scripture any woman caught in an adulterous situation was blamed if she were in the city where she could have called for help. If it happened in the country, only the male involved was blamed. Since she could not have called for help judges considered it to be rape (Deut 22:27). Here the victim called for help, and her servants heard. Nevertheless, she was not believed. There were two witnesses to the contrary.

Suzanna was afraid to sin before the Lord. This means she understood that the Lord was the final judge. Those who stood before a judge or a king were in a position where they could be judged.

Text

Old Greek	Theodotion
²⁸ Then these lawbreakers turned around and plotted **so as to put her to death**. They went to the synagogue of the city whre they lived and where all of the Israelites met in council. ²⁹ Then these two elders and judges **said,** **"Send for Suzanna, the daughter of Chelkias, who is the wife of Joakim."** At once they called her. ³⁰ When she **came,** with her were **her** father, her mother, **her children**, and her female servants, who numbered five hundred. The **children** of Suzanna were four.	²⁸On the next day, when the people came to her husband, Joakim, **the** two elders came filled with lawless designs against Suzanna **so as to put her to death.** ²⁹They **said** before all of the people, **"Send for Suzanna, the daughter of Chelkias, who is the wife of Joakim."** They sent [for her]. ³⁰She, **her parents, her children**, and all of her relatives **came.**

Commentary

There are many identical words between these two texts, which shows that there is some synoptic relationship between them. The men were properly described as lawless even though they were elders, who were themselves responsible for maintaining the law. The judgment was to take place at Joakim's house, because this was the place where court was normally held when the elders acted as judges. The judges who were trying to have Joakim's wife put to death were going to conduct the trial in Joakim's own courtyard.

In these few words it is clear that the two elders presented a verdict without ever having a trial. Suzanna was never invited to speak in her own defense. Her family and servants were all there, but there is no report that any of them challenged the elders when they made their accusation, even though this crime involved a death sentence. According to Jewish law, whenever a trial is entered into court and there is the possibility for a death sentence, the defendant always is permitted to speak as much as he or she chooses in defense before the plaintiff makes the argument for conviction (*mSan* 3.4). The judges in this case were not permitting that rule to be applied.

Text

The Old Greek	Theodotion

³¹Now the woman **was very delicate**,

³²**but the lawbreakers commanded that she be uncovered,**
so that they might be
filled with lust of **her beauty.** ³³Those who were with her and all who knew her **wept.** ³⁴**The elders** and judges **laid their hands on her head,** /

³⁵but **her mind trusted the Lord** her God, and **raising her** head, she said to herself, ³⁵ᵃ"Lord, **eternal God, who knows all things before they happen, you know that I did not do the things which these** lawless men **have wickedly [attributed] to me."** The Lord heard her prayer.

³¹**Now Suzanna was very delicate** and beautiful to see,
³²**but the lawbreakers commanded that she be uncovered**, because she was covered, **so that they might be filled with her beauty.** ³³All who were with her and all who saw her **wept,** ³⁴but **the** two **elders** rose up in the midst of the people, and **they laid their hands on her head.** ³⁵While she wept she **raised her** eyes to heaven, **because her mind was entrusted to the Lord.**

Commentary

The lawbreakers ordered Suzanna to remove her clothing. This was a customary procedure for a woman who had already been tried and condemned for adultery. Ezekiel prophesied that Jerusalem would be stripped and exposed in the same way (Ezek 16:35-39). The Psalmist also described the Edomites as if they had been lustful men screaming for Jerusalem to be stripped like an adulterous woman (Ps 137:7; also Hos 2:3, 10). The reason the elders ordered this exposure was not because she was really a condemned adulteress but because they wanted to gaze on her nakedness. Placing their hands on Suzanna's head was probably some kind of ritual which declared that she was guilty. When that happened all of Suzanna's friends and relatives wept, because they thought that this decreed Suzanna's death. Suzanna's prayer in OG is paralleled in Theodotion's text in the next paragraph.

Text

The Old Greek	Theodotion

³⁶**The** two **elders said, "We were walking in** her husband's **garden,** ³⁷and as we came around the stadium we saw **this woman** lying with

³⁶**The elders said,** "While **we were walking in** the **garden** alone,

this woman entered with two maidens.

The Old Greek	Theodotion
a man. We stood and watched them having sexual intercourse with one another. ³⁸ They did not know that we were standing. Then we discussed with one another, saying, 'Let us find out who they are.' ³⁹When we approached, we recognized her, but the young man covered himself and fled, ⁴⁰but when **we seized this woman, we asked** her, **'Who is the man?'** ⁴¹**But she would not tell us** who he was. We bear witness to these things." All **the synagogue believed them, because they were elders and judges of the people.**	Then she closed the door of the garden and dismissed the maidens. ³⁷**A young man** came to her who had been hiding, and he lay down with her, ³⁸but since we were in the corner of the garden, watching the lawlessness, we ran to them. ³⁹We saw them having intercourse, but we were unable to capture that man, because he was stronger than we were. He opened the doors and ran out. ⁴⁰ **We seized this woman and asked, 'Who was this young man?'** ⁴¹**but she did not** want to **tell us**, but we witnessed these things." The **synagogue**, however, **believed them, since they were elders and judges of the people,** and they gave her a death sentence

Commentary

Using different details the two texts give the same report. The elders were in the courtyard when Suzanna entered, met a young man, and had intercourse with him. The elders approached the couple so that they could identify them. They were unable to identify the man or capture him, because, according to the Theodotion text, he was young and strong. According to the OG he had his face covered. They recognized Suzanna, nonetheless. When they confronted her she refused to tell who the young man was. They bore witness before the court, which probably means that they witnessed under oath that their witness was the truth, the whole truth, and nothing but the truth. Because they were professional judges, whose responsibility was to see that justice was provided, the people all believed them. So they gave her a death sentence. This was the perfect crime that had apparently been completely successful. The story thus far reminds readers of the story of David's crime with Bathsheba. The deed was done, Uriah was killed, "But the thing David had done displeased Yehowah" (2Sam 11:27). David had overlooked that possibility, and so did the lawless elders.

Text

The Old Greek	Theodotion
⁴⁴/⁴⁵**Now look**! There was an angel of the Lord, while she was	⁴²Suzanna cried out in a loud voice, "**Eternal God**, who knows the secret things, **who knows all things before they occur,** ⁴³**you know** that

being led out to be destroyed,	they have testified against me falsely. **Now look! I am dying not having done any of the things which these have evilly done against me.**" [44]The Lord heard her voice, [45]**and as she was being led away to be killed**,
and the angel gave a **spirit of** understanding to **a young man who was Daniel**, just as he had been commanded. [48]After Daniel had commanded the crowd [to be silent],	God raised up the holy **spirit of a young** boy named **Daniel**. [46]He cried out in a loud voice, "I am innocent of this blood!" [47]All the people turned to him and said, "What is this word which you are speaking?"
he stood up in their midst and said, "Are you such fools, Israelites? Without interrogation or finding out clearly, have you condemned a daughter of Israel?	[48]After he stood up in their midst, he said, "Are you such fools, Israelites? Without interrogation or finding out clearly, have you condemned a daughter of Israel? [49]Turn back to the tribunal, for these have testified falsely against her." [50]Then all of the people turned eagerly. And the elders said to him, "Come! Sit in our midst and inform us, [51]because God has given to you the authoritative office." Daniel said to them,

Commentary

Suzanna's final plea to God is expressed in the Theodotion text here that was given in the previous paragraph by OG. This was her first vocal expression. It was not given to the people present nor to the lawless judges, but to God. According to OG it was an angel of the Lord who responded to her prayer. According to Theodotion text it was God himself. Since an angel can be a legal agent acting in behalf of, in the interests of, and at the responsibility of the principal, God, it is God in any case. It was just after they began to lead Suzanna away to be killed that Daniel appeared. No mention is made of his reason for arriving. No one asked who he was or by what authority he spoke.

Daniel knew before he arrived what had gone on before, because he declared his innocence to that event. He knew that there had been no trial, so Suzanna was being condemned unfairly. He also knew, however, that the judges had both witnessed and judged falsely. The author did not suggest how he might have learned all of that. Daniel began his address to the group by insulting them. For some surprising reason they liked being insulted and begged him to tell them more. His insults to them made them think that he was a messenger of God, and they encouraged him to assume leadership. He ordered them to reopen the court case, and they did. They had condemned Suzanna without a trial, and that surely was not fair. Although he would not gain praise and recognition for his diplomacy or tact, his object was correct.

Text

The Old Greek	Theodotion
⁵¹Now separate them for me a long distance from one another so that I might examine them." ⁵²When they had been separated, Daniel said to the synagogue, "Now do not take notice that these are elders, saying, 'They would never lie!' I will judge them just as things come to me. Now call one of them." They led in the younger of the elders, and Daniel **said to him, "Hear! Hear! You evil old man. Now the sins that you have committed previously have come [for punishment]**. ⁵³You have been entrusted to hear and judge judgments bearing the death penalty. On the one hand you have **condemned the innocent, and on the other hand, you have released the guilty**, while **the Lord says,** 'You shall not condemn to death the innocent and the righteous.' ⁵⁴**Now therefore, under which tree** and place of the garden **did you see them when they were together?**" The unrighteous one answered, "**Under the mastich tree.**" ⁵⁵ The younger man **said, "You have correctly falsified against you own soul, for the angel of the Lord will separate** your soul today."	"**Separate them a long distance from one another, and interrogate them.**" ⁵² As they **separated** them one from the other, he called one of them and said to him, "**Old man of evil days, now your sins that you committed previously,** ⁵³performing unrighteous judgments, condemning the innocent and releasing the guilty, **have come [for punishment].** The Lord says, 'You shall not condemn to death the innocent and the righteous.' ⁵⁴**Now, therefore,** if indeed you saw this woman, tell **under which tree** you saw them having intercourse together?" He said, "**Under a mastich tree.**" ⁵⁵Then Daniel said, "**You have correctly falsified against your own** head, **for an angel of God** has already received the sentence from God and **will split you** down the middle."

Commentary

Daniel began his interrogation in an unobjective way. Before he asked a single question, he insulted the witness, correctly accusing him of failing to give the accused due process of the law in court. He recited the law that the witness broke to justify his accusation. The method of separating witnesses in testimony is an ancient practice that is still continued today. Daniel accused the witness of lying under oath, however, before he heard the second witness and had a basis for that judgment. He decreed a fatal judgment after having heard only one witness.

Text

The Old Greek

⁵⁶**After he had** removed this one, he told [them] to bring the other. **He said to** this one, "Why is your seed scattered, as that of Sidon and not as of Judah? **Beauty has deceived you,** defiled **lust!** ⁵⁷**You have done this to the daughters of Israel, and they, being afraid, had sexual intercourse with you, but a daughter of Judah did not continue** the disease by supporting your lawlessness. ⁵⁸**Now then, tell me, under what tree** and what part of the garden **did you catch them having sexual intercourse together?" He said, "Under the oak."** ⁵⁹**Daniel said,** "Sinner! Now **the angel of the Lord** stands, **holding the sword** until the people destroys you, so that he might **saw you [in two]."** ⁶⁰⁻⁶²**Then all the synagogue cried out** against the younger man, since they had both admitted with their own mouth. **[Daniel] exhibited them** to be false witnesses, and as the law clearly states, **they treated them** just as **they wickedly did** against their sister.

Theodotion

⁵⁶**After he had** set him aside **he asked them** to lead in the other one. Then **he said to** him, "Seed of Canaan, and not Judah, that which is beautiful has deceived you, and lust has distracted your mind. ⁵⁷**You have done this to the daughters of Israel and they, being afraid, had sexual intercourse with you, but the daughter of Judah did not continue your lawlessness.** ⁵⁸Now, then, tell me under what tree did you catch them having **sexual intercourse together?" He said, "Under the oak."** ⁵⁹**Daniel said** to him, "You have accurately lied against your own head, for **the angel of God** remains, **holding the sword** to **saw you** down the middle. In this way he will destroy you." ⁶⁰**Then all the synagogue cried out** with a loud voice and blessed God who saves those who hope in him. ⁶¹They rebelled against the two elders, because **Daniel exhibited them,** after they had witnessed falsely from their own mouths, and **they treated them** in the manner in which **they wickedly did** to their

They gagged them, led them out, and threw them into a ravine. Then the angel of the Lord threw fire through their midst, **and innocent blood was saved on that day**.

neighbor. ⁶²Acting according to the law of Moses, they killed them, **and innocent blood was saved on that day**.

Commentary

Earlier in the text, the author identified being a Jewess with being an Israelite. Here, however, he distinguished the daughters of Israel, the Samaritans, with the daughters of Judah. Without showing any evidence Daniel accused both elders with having had sexual intercourse with the Samaritans who were promiscuous, in the author's judgment. This is an anti-Samaritan attack and may be a later editorial addition. It is in conflict with the rest of the document. Again Daniel condemned the witness before he had given him an opportunity to witness.

The Greek word for "oak" is *skeé-naws*, (σχῖνος) which sounds like the Greek word for "divide" (*skheéd-zoh*, σχίζω). Therefore Daniel formed a condemnation that was a play on words. Since the witness chose the "divide" tree he would be "divided" or sawed down the middle.

Since the elders had falsely accused in court an innocent woman, the same punishment that was designed for her should be given to the false witness (Deut 19:15-21). The text says, "Your eye shall show no pity" (Deut 19:21). Since the elders' witness was designed to bring a death sentence to Suzanna, Daniel decreed that both elders should be killed, and they were. So everyone except the elders lived happily ever after.

Text

The Old Greek

⁶³Because of this younger people are beloved of Jacob in their simplicity. Let us also watch for the competent young people, for younger people are pious, and they have the spirit of knowledge and understanding into the age of age.

Theodotion

⁶³Chelkias and his wife praised God for their daughter, Suzanna, together with Joakim, her husband, and all of her relatives, because there was not found in her anything disgraceful. ⁶⁴Daniel became great before the people from that day on.

Commentary

There have been both parallels and variations between the two versions of this story. That is why it has been shown in separate columns with the identical words in **boldface**. Basically, Theodotion's version is more expansive than the OG text. Generally the story is the same. The editor's conclusions at the end of the story are different. Theodotion's text concludes with Suzanna, Joakim, and their family becoming very happy and Daniel becoming famous. The OG text, however, concluded with an exhortation for older people to encourage young people, like Daniel, so that they can grow up to be pious and learned adults in every age.

Conclusions

Although this is an interesting hero story about Daniel, it does not belong among the Dramas of Daniel. That unit is composed of a collection of essays, all of which are national and political in nature, and all describe experiences that relate the Jews to the other nearby nations during the period from the beginning of the Babylonian exile until the restoration of the temple and the land. Suzanna does not fit into that category. This is an inner Jewish story in which all of the characters, both victims and villains are Jewish. The plot takes place in Babylon but Babylonian kings and governmental leaders are not involved. Suzanna is a success story but not for Jews in general. The success is only for Suzanna and her family. There is only one probably editorial anti-Samaritan statement in the story, and there is nothing specifically anti-gentilic. The content of the essay does not disclose the time of its composition. It was probably written about the time other Daniel legends were popular, perhaps sometime during the last half of the second century BIA. The author and original readers were both Jewish. The variations of the text suggest that it was originally told orally by story tellers who were free to alter the details.

APPENDIX II

BEL AND THE DRAGON

Introduction

Bel and the Dragon consists of two different stories, one of Bel and the other about a dragon. Each of these stories was centered on Daniel in relationship to the king, which was Cyrus of Persia. In both instances the king was encouraging Daniel to worship either Bel (Marduk) or a dragon. Daniel was obligated to explain to the king why he did not. In the process Daniel was placed in danger in a situation similar to Daniel in the Lions' Den (Dan 6). Different authors probably wrote the stories and each one was complete in itself. They have both been added to the Septuagint canon as appendices to the Book of Daniel. The stories are preserved in two texts: 1) Theodotion (θ) and 2) Old Greek.

Text of Bel

Old Greek	Theodotion
From Habakkuk, the son of Joshua from the tribe of Levi: ²A certain man who was a priest, whose name **was Daniel,** the son of Abal, **a companion of the king** of Babylon.	King Astyages was placed with his fathers, and Cyrus the Persian received his kingdom. ²**Daniel was a companion of the king** and he was honored above all of his friends.
³There was **an idol, Bel,** whom the Babylonians honored, **and every day there was squandered on it twelve measures of fine flour, four sheep, and six measures of**	³The Babylonians had **an idol,** whose name was **Bel, and every day there was squandered on it twelve measures of fine flour, four sheep, and six measures of**

Old Greek	Theodotion
oil. ⁴**The king revered it and used to go every day and worship it, but Daniel worshiped** the Lord.	oil.⁴**The king revered it and used to go every day and worship it, but Daniel worshiped** his God.

Commentary

The two versions in the columns given above tell the same story, but they have different beginnings. The Old Greek starts by identifying Daniel's family origin. Theodotion tells of the time the event took place in relationship to the royal leadership in Persia. As the story itself begins, however, there are identical verbal terms used by both versions. This is shown by the bold faced texts.

Text of Bel

Old Greek	Theodotion
⁵ **The king said to Daniel, "Why do you not worship Bel?"** Daniel **said** to the king, "**I do not** revere any [being] except **the** Lord **God who created heaven and earth and has governing authority over all flesh."** ⁶ **The king said** to him, "Then is not this one **a god**? **Do you not see** how many things are spent on it **every day?"** ⁷**Daniel said** to him, "Not at all! **Do not** let anyone deceive you, **for this [idol] is clay on the inside and brass on the outside**. I swear to you by the Lord God of gods that this [idol] **has never eaten anything."**	⁵ **The king said to Daniel, "Why do you not worship Bel?"** He **said,** "**I do not** worship idols made with hands, but I worship **the God** of life, **who created heaven and earth and has governing authority over all flesh."** ⁶**The king said**, "Do you not think that Bel is **a god** of life? **Do you not see** that it eats and drinks **every day?"** Daniel laughed and **said**, "**Do not** go astray, O king. **for this [idol] is clay on the inside and brass on the outside**, and it **does not eat** or drink **anything."**

Commentary

Babylon was the capital city of the nation, Babylon. This capital city was called the city of Marduk or the city of Bel, just as Jerusalem was called the city of God. These narratives quickly draw attention to the conflict between the two worshipers. The Bel worshiper, in this situation, was the king of Persia. The worshiper of Yehowah was Daniel, a close friend of the king and a contemporary Jew. The king thought Daniel should worship Bel, as other citizens of Babylon did, but Daniel refused. He argued that no one should worship Bel, because Bel was only an idol made with human hands of well-known material substances. It could not eat, drink, or do anything else, much less respond to worship.

Text of Bel

| Old Greek | Theodotion |

⁸ The king became angry and called the officials of the temple and said to them, "Show [me] the one **who eats** that which has been prepared for Bel. But **if not, you will die** or Daniel who alleges that the things are not eaten by it [will die]." They said, "Bel itself is the one who eats them."
⁹Daniel said to the king, "Let it be thus: If I do not show that it is not Bel who eats these things, all my associates and I will die."

There were seventy priests not counting women and children.
¹⁰ Then they led **the king** to the idol,

¹¹and they **placed the food** before the king and Daniel **and the mixed wine** was brought in and placed before Bel. ¹² Then Daniel said, "You, yourself, see that these things are laid out, O king. Then you seal the bolts of the temple when it is closed." The suggestion pleased the king.
¹⁴ Then Daniel commanded, after those who were with him had all left the temple, to sprinkle the entire temple with ashes, none of those on the outside knowing it. **Then he commanded**

that **they seal** the temple **with the king's signet ring** and with the signet rings of certain of the most honored priests. This was done.

⁸ The king became angry and called his priests and said to them, "If you do not tell me **who eats** and drinks this provision **you will die**, but if you show me that Bel consumes them, **Daniel will die**, because he has blasphemed Bel."
⁹Daniel said to the king, "Let it be according to your word."

There were seventy priests of Bel, **apart from women and children**.
¹⁰ **The king** went with Daniel to the temple of Bel. ¹¹The priests of Bel said, "Look! We will run outside, but you, O king, **place the food and the mixed wine**. Then close the door, and seal it with your signet ring. When you come early in the morning, if you find all the food under Bel, we will die or Daniel who is lying against us." ¹² They did not worry, however, because they had made under the table a hidden entrance, and through it they entered altogether and enjoyed the things [placed there].
¹³They left and the king laid out the food for Bel. ¹⁴**Then Daniel commanded** his slaves, and they brought ashes and scattered the whole temple before the king alone. Then after they left they closed the door and **they sealed** [it] **with the king's signet ring** and went away. ¹⁵The priests came at night, according to their custom with their wives and children, and they ate and

drank everything.

¹⁵⁻¹⁷It happened on the next day they arrived at the place, but the priests of Bel after they had entered through false doors, consumed all of the things laid before Bel, and they drank the wine. Then Daniel **said**, "Look at your **seals** [to see] if they are still there, O priests, and you, O king, examine [to see] that nothing that you disapprove has happened." They found the seal was [there], so they removed the seal, ¹⁸but **after they had opened the doors**, they saw that all of the things that had been laid out had been consumed, and the tables were empty.

The king was happy, and said to Daniel, "**Great is Bel, and with him there is no deceit.**"
¹⁹**Daniel laughed** extensively and said to the king, "Come here and see the deceit of the priests." Then Daniel said, "O king, **whose tracks are these?**" ²⁰ **The king said, "They are the tracks] of men, women, and children.**"

²¹Then he went to the house where the priests lived, and found the food of Bel and the wine,
and Daniel **showed** the king
the false doors through which the priests, after **they had entered, consumed the things that** had been set before Bel.
²²Then **the king** led them out from [the temple] of **Bel** and delivered them **to Daniel**, and that which had been spent for him, **he gave to Daniel, and he destroyed** Bel.

¹⁶Then the king set out early in the morning and Daniel with him.

¹⁷The king **said,**
"Are the **seals** secure, Daniel?" He said, "The **seals** are secure, O king."

¹⁸**As soon as they opened the doors**, and the king looked at the table, he cried out in a loud voice,

"Great are you, Bel, and there is not even one bit of deceit in you!"
¹⁹**Daniel laughed** and seized the king to prevent him from entering, and said, "Look at the floor, and find out whose tracks are these." ²⁰The king said, "I see **the tracks** of men, women, and children."
²¹Then the king became angry, and he brought together the priests, their wives,
and their children and they **showed** him **the hidden doors through which they entered** and consumed **the things that** were upon the table.
²²So **the king** killed them, and

he gave Bel as a concession **to Daniel, and** [Daniel] **destroyed** it and its temple.

Commentary

Daniel's challenge was put to the test. According to the Old Greek text it was Daniel who suggested that the test be made. Theodotion said it was the king who made the offer. The plan was to put the food out for Bel to eat and lock the temple doors and seal them with the king's seal so that no human being could disturb anything in the temple. Daniel, the priests, and the king were all present to witness the security. After the priests had left, however, Daniel and the king had the area covered with ashes so that footprints could easily be seen. The priests did not know of this. Then the doors were locked and sealed. Daniel had clearly set a trap for the priests. The details were a bit different but the narrative was the same in both versions.

In the morning, the king and Daniel went to witness again the situation at the temple. Just as before, the doors were locked and sealed, and when they were opened, the king saw that the food and wine were gone, and he praised Bel. Daniel, however, cautioned the king to look around before he entered the temple. Daniel pointed to the tracks in the ashes and asked the king who made them. The king observed that men, women, and children made them. After the trap door was exposed and the priests were called, it was obvious to the king that the priests and their families had eaten the food and drunk the wine. This also proved to the king that Bel was no deity. He gave the idol to Daniel. Daniel destroyed the idol, and according to Theodotion the king killed the priests, and Daniel also destroyed the temple.

The story of the Dragon was preserved on the same texts as the story of Bel. There are also edited statements in the story of the Dragon intended to relate the two stories and keep them together.

The Text of the Dragon

Old Greek	Theodotion
[23]**There was a dragon** in the same place, **and the Babylonians revered it.** [24]**The king said to Daniel, "You do not say** that this is brass, do you?" Look! It lives, eats, and drinks. **Worship it."** [25]**Daniel said, "O King, give me authority, and I will** overpower **the dragon** without iron **or rod."** [26]**The king** made the concession and **said to** him, **"It is given to you." After Daniel** had taken [27]minas of **pitch, tallow, and hair, he kneaded it, made a loaf and put it into the dragon's mouth. While eating, the dragon burst apart**, and [Daniel] showed it to the king **and said,** "Do you not worship these things, O king?"	[23]**There was a huge dragon, and the** Babylonians revered it. [24] **The king** said to Daniel, "You are not able to say that this is not a living god. Worship it."[25]**Daniel said, "I worship the Lord God, because this is not a living god, and if you will give me the** authority, O king, **I will** kill **the dragon without** sword **or rod."** [26] **The king said,** "I give it to you." [27]**Then Daniel** took pitch, tallow, and hair. He kneaded it, made a loaf and put it into the dragon's mouth. When he ate it the dragon burst into pieces, and he said, "Look at your revered pieces."

Commentary

There is here an editorial sentence connecting the story of the Dragon to the story of Bel. **The same place** was **the same place** where the story of Bel took place. The place is confirmed in the Theodotion text that referred to the citizens there as **Babylonians.** Like the story of Bel, this is a story of a discussion between Daniel and the king. In the story of the dragon as in the Bel narrative it was the Old Greek text that had Daniel initiating the test. Continuing the discussion of Bel in which Daniel proved that Bel was only an idol made of pottery and brass that did not eat or drink, the king pointed to the dragon that was obviously alive and did eat and drink. It was not just a brass idol. It was a living creature, and the Babylonians worshiped it. Why did not Daniel also worship it? Daniel argued that this dragon also lacked the qualities of a deity. It was so frail that Daniel could kill it without a military weapon if the king would only give him the authority to demonstrate. The king gave permission, and Daniel cooked up a mixture and made it into a loaf, like a loaf of bread. Then he put it in the dragon's mouth, and the dragon died. Surely a god would not die treated like this. The king had to admit that Daniel was correct again, but the plot thickens.

Text of the Dragon

Old Greek	Theodotion
²⁸Those from every region were gathered against Daniel, and they said,	²⁸When the Babylonians heard they became very angry, and they turned together against the king and said,
"**The king has become a Jew!** He has destroyed **Bel** and he has **killed the dragon**."	"**The king has become a Jew!** He dragged **Bel** down, **killed the dragon**, and slaughtered the priests." ²⁹They came and said to the king, "Give over Daniel to us. Otherwise we will kill both you and your family." ³⁰**The king saw that**
³⁰When **the king saw that** the crowd from the country had been gathered **against him**, he called his companions and said, "I will **give Daniel** up for destruction."	they were coming **against him** fiercely, and having been put under pressure he **gave** them **Daniel**.

Commentary

Daniel had defeated the king in two attempts. The king admitted defeat, but the citizens of the country were not happy about it. He had destroyed one of their gods as well as the temple associated with it. Then he killed their other god. That was too much. They accused the king of becoming a Jew. If the king allowed this to go unpunished his own people would kill him. When he saw them coming against him with force, he yielded. He would give Daniel up to them to be destroyed. It looked as if Daniel would finally lose this conflict, but that appearance did not take into consideration the God whom Daniel worshiped.

Text of the Dragon

Old Greek	Theodotion
	[31]They **threw** him **into** the **den of lions,** and **he was** there **six days.**
[31-32]**There** was a **den** in which **seven lions** were fed to which those who attacked the king were given, and **they** provided them **every day two bodies** of those condemned to death. The crowd **threw** Daniel **into** that **den** so that he might be eaten and find no tomb. Daniel **was** in that den **for six days.**	[32]**There** were in the **den seven lions.** They customarily **gave them two** [human] **bodies** and two sheep **a day.** Then, however, they did not give them [anything] so that they would consume Daniel.

Commentary

Based on the story of Daniel and the den of lions in the Dramas of Daniel, the method of destruction chosen was the den of lions. They were deliberately put on short rations so that they would be very hungry. The crowd threw Daniel into that den for six days, but he was not consumed.

Text of the Dragon

Old Greek	Theodotion
[33]Now it happened, on the sixth day, that **Habakkuk** had loaves broken up in a container, cooked and an earthen jar of mixed wine and **was going into the field to the harvesters.** [34]**An angel of the Lord spoke to Habakkuk, saying,** "Thus says the Lord God to you: '**The meal which you have, take away to Daniel** to the lion's den in **Babylon.**'" [35]**Habakkuk said, "Lord God, I have not seen Babylon, and the den** of lions--I do not know where it	[33]The prophet **Habakkuk** was in Judah. He kneaded, baked, and broke up pieces of bread into a container. Then he **went into the field to bring** [lunch] **to the harvesters.** [34]**An angel of the Lord said to Habakkuk,** "Take the meal which you have to Babylon to Daniel in the den of lions." [35]**Habakkuk said, "Lord, I have not seen Babylon, and** I do not know **the den.**"

Old Greek	Theodotion
is." ³⁶**After the angel of the Lord had taken** Habakkuk **by the hair of his head he set him in** the den in Babylon. ³⁷Habakkuk said to Daniel, "Arise and eat **the meal which** the Lord **God has sent you.**"	³⁶**The angel of the Lord took** the top of his head and lifted **him by the hair of his head and set him in Babylon** on the den with a whistle of his breath. ³⁷Then Habakkuk cried out, "**Daniel! Daniel! Take the meal that God has sent you.**"

Commentary

Habakkuk to the rescue! The lions were not giving Daniel any trouble, but after six days without food, Daniel would be getting hungry. Against any of his plans, Habakkuk was ordered by an angel of the Lord, on the sixth day, to take the food he had prepared for harvesters and give it to Daniel in Babylon. Habakkuk had never been to Babylon, but the angel of the Lord picked him up by the hair of his head and whisked him over to Babylon in the den of lions where Daniel was. Like Elijah when he was saved by the ravens, Daniel realized that the Lord had not abandoned him.

Text of the Dragon

Old Greek	Theodotion
³⁸**Daniel said**, "The Lord **God**, who does **not abandon those who love** him, **has remembered** me," ³⁹and Daniel ate. Then **the angel of** the Lord **took Habakkuk** and set him in the **place** from which he had taken him on the same day. The Lord **God remembered** Daniel.	⁸**Daniel said**, "**God**, **you have remembered** me. You **have not abandoned those who love** you." ³⁹Daniel arose and ate, and **the angel of** God **took Habakkuk** away to his **place**.
⁴⁰After this **the king went** out, **mourning for Daniel, and** after **he** had **looked into the den**, he saw him seated.	⁴⁰**The king went** on the seventh day **to mourn Daniel**. He came **to the den and he looked in**. Now look Daniel was sitting.
⁴¹The king **cried out and said**, "**Great** is the **Lord God, and there is none other except** him."	⁴¹He **called out** in a loud voice, **and said**, "**Great** are you, **Lord God** of Daniel, **and there is no other except** you!"
⁴²Then the king led **Daniel** out from the den, **and those who had asked for his destruction he threw into the den of lions** before Daniel, and they **consumed** [them].	⁴²He brought **Daniel** up, but those who requested his **destruction he threw into the den, and they** were **consumed** before him instantly.

Commentary

As Daniel ate his food he confessed that God never abandoned those who loved him. The next step of the story was to lead the king to make the same confession. When the king came to the den of lions and looked in, he saw Daniel sitting there comfortable and well fed. He confessed at once that Daniel's God was the true God, but that was not the end of the story. The king had the crowd that wanted Daniel killed themselves thrown into the den of lions where they were consumed immediately. This was the kind of great reversal that was typical of the Dramas of Daniel

GENERAL INDICES

WORDS

abyss 216
Acra 429
Akkadian 24, 59, 85, 117
allegory 7
altar 295, 348
Amilius Sura 68
Ammonite 18, 351, 362, 420
angel 92-95, 101, 116, 118, 130, 158, 160, 173, 174, 179, 193, 195, 205, 209, 211, 212, 216, 217, 221, 224, 243, 248, 253, 287, 305, 374, 383, 414, 441
Annuli 125
anoint 112, 282, 284
anointed 72, 187, 305, 416
anthologies 106, 437, 439
antitype   5, 7, 38, 110, 302, 381, 407, 441-443, 454
apartheid 23
apocalypse 357, 436
apocalyptic 8, 9, 104, 250, 443
apostasy 91
Arab 122, 134
Arabic 12, 86, 302, 399
Aramaic 12, 36, 43, 85, 108, 124, 140, 152, 155, 164, 192, 296, 297, 399, 410, 438
archaeological 87
ashes 259, 260

Assyrian 9, 67, 89, 93-95, 180, 186, 213, 224, 226, 264, 267, 272, 279, 334, 411
astrologer 53
astrology 24
Athenian 74
atonement 124, 222, 231-234, 253, 282, 285, 287, 288, 290, 354, 376, 383, 391, 394, 395, 408, 409, 431, 435, 441
Babylonian 24, 31, 33, 38, 39, 44, 48, 52, 56, 65, 72, 76, 78, 80, 85, 91, 94, 112, 116, 119, 121, 127, 153, 159, 166, 180, 187, 189, 193, 222, 237, 276, 296, 302, 334, 346, 354, 374, 384, 400, 404, 425-427, 440, 449, 451, 453
Bansanga 110, 214, 237, 302
Baptist 7, 138
Bar Mitzwah 48
bear 167, 168, 170
beast 167, 168, 176, 215, 217, 284
Behistan 67
benediction 2
birthright 124
blessing 124
breath 214
calendar 6, 13, 14, 102, 219, 233, 228, 397, 413, 429, 444
Canaanite 175, 180, 187, 189, 220, 362

canon 13, 270, 397, 402, 428, 438, 440, 443,
Capricorn 238
captive 22, 33, 38, 88, 146, 400, 418
captivity 4, 5, 23, 39, 65, 66, 69, 78, 94, 150, 193, 427, 449
Carthaginians 315, 338
cartoonist 398
Catholic 13
celebration 430
Chaldean 23, 25, 36, 45, 63, 87, 98, 109, 111, 136, 137, 143, 165, 168, 171, 189, 236, 256
Chasidim 353
chiasm 10, 11, 105, 311
circumcise 353, 434
citizens 46, 87, 96
cloud 117, 120, 175, 176, 178, 184, 186, 193, 207, 211, 212, 229, 230, 406, 407, 441
comet 197, 232, 382
commandment 2
common 14
concubine 446
confiscate 135
conquer 72
conquest 14, 40, 70, 84, 145, 149, 150, 152, 227, 421
contract 13, 26, 268
corporation 231
cosmic 62
cosmos 3, 7, 91, 98, 249, 306
court 8, 91, 173, 174, 178, 195, 206, 215, 223, 227, 228, 230, 272, 280, 386, 400, 405, 411, 427
Crusades 233, 438, 444
cuneiform 140
curses 167, 274, 276, 281, 284, 388
cycle 3-7, 37, 39, 40, 51, 66, 107, 259, 449
Davidic 220, 413, 423, 444, 451
defamation 12

defendant 8, 173, 174, 208, 229, 280, 428
defile 27, 373
demythologize 401
desolation 290, 347, 349, 392
diaspora 276, 343, 431, 437, 446, 447, 448
disk 186
dispensationalist 55
divorce 13, 31, 288, 318
dragon 400, 427, 430
dream 36, 41, 44, 54, 57, 59, 61, 65, 77, 105, 109, 111, 114, 116, 119, 120, 139, 165, 166, 200, 214, 218, 297, 300, 401, 403, 406, 415, 445
eagle 404
Ecclesiastes 2
Egyptian 3, 19, 38-40, 43, 95, 97, 135, 186, 226, 320, 322, 324, 334, 340, 341, 344, 363, 364, 367, 402, 420, 422
enchanter 45, 109, 136, 137
enemy 161, 178, 185, 186, 223, 346, 347, 359, 384, 418, 431, 441
English 333
Ephraimite 171
eschatological 51, 54, 55, 420
eschatologist 58
eschatology 150, 362, 372, 374, 396, 397, 441, 443
eschaton 286
Essenes 450
ethical 1
Ethiopians 363
Euboean 339
eunuch 21, 22, 31
executioner 46, 47
exile 9, 32, 43, 45, 222, 256, 272, 296, 297, 305, 396, 426, 440, 451, 453
exodus 2, 7, 93, 97
famine 165
fasting 259, 260, 302

fire............84, 90, 92, 94, 98, 101, 176, 178, 180
foreign........28, 31, 42, 56, 75, 94, 108, 126, 129, 156, 160, 191, 224, 232, 288, 290, 331, 333, 360, 378, 379, 384, 399, 441, 442, 446
French 333
furnace..... 84, 88-90, 92, 94, 98, 404
garrison 429
Gauls 327, 328
gentile 14, 28, 31, 39, 55, 58, 61, 77, 114, 162, 200, 213, 229, 250, 288, 331, 348, 361, 365, 377, 381, 401, 407, 412, 414, 425, 430, 431, 441, 447
gourmet........................... 25, 29, 31
Grecian 402, 406, 415
Greek............3, 10 12, 14, 18, 21, 38, 51, 72, 74-76, 86, 94, 117, 150, 179, 197, 210, 213, 215, 219, 226, 228, 240, 251, 336, 238, 314, 316, 340, 342, 349, 351, 354, 356, 358, 387, 397, 399, 403, 409, 410, 413, 425, 441, 448, 449
guerrilla............ 6, 117, 244, 260, 331
gymnasium. 352
haggadoth.................................... 208
halachot....................................... 208
Halley's 232, 382
Hanukkah 5-7, 40, 59, 75, 78, 102, 146, 168, 181, 204, 210, 211, 219, 222, 229, 231-234, 244, 245, 261, 267, 277, 282, 285, 286, 290, 293, 297, 298, 356, 358, 361, 365, 372, 375, 383, 389, 392, 394, 395, 397, 401, 403, 407, 409, 411, 413, 416, 426-430, 432, 435, 439, 440, 443, 447, 450, 451, 453, 456
Hasid 210, 225, 432, 433, 434, 435
Hasmonean........40, 72, 75, 76, 108, 162, 173, 195, 200, 204, 208, 210, 215, 219, 225, 226, 229, 231, 234, 261, 351, 358, 362, 374, 376, 379-384, 388, 391, 397, 401, 403, 408, 419, 425, 426, 430-432, 434, 435,
440, 442, 445, 446, 448, 449, 450, 451
Hebrew............2, 21, 25, 38, 108, 164, 186, 192, 237, 278, 293, 296, 297, 353, 402, 413, 438
Hellenism 86, 342, 345, 365, 389
Hellenistic............6, 79, 108, 341, 346, 349, 352, 355
Hellenization 317
Hellenize.................278, 329, 392, 295, 332, 333
Hellenizer....... 297, 326, 343, 345, 348, 350, 359, 391, 445, 450
holy... 14
Homiletic 1
homily... 10
inclusion 9, 105, 311
intertextual 19
intifada... 30
Iranian.. 189
Isaianic....................................... 243
Islam 70
Israel 266
Israelite......204, 280, 362, 396, 409, 454
Jubilee.........3, 38, 56, 283, 285, 286, 292, 296, 300, 362, 372, 393, 395, 397, 408, 430, 441
judge...........1, 175, 178, 202, 203, 215, 271, 272, 274, 304, 382, 346, 406, 432
judgment..........1, 42, 83, 98, 165, 187, 193, 195, 223, 228, 229, 230, 233, 237, 271-273, 305, 376, 382, 384, 386, 391, 394, 408, 411, 431, 436
kingdom......36, 40, 52, 58, 61, 64, 66, 72, 73, 76, 77, 97, 107, 109, 111, 116, 119, 122-124, 130, 136, 137, 141, 144, 149, 153, 161, 162, 167, 179, 181, 182, 184, 186, 187, 197, 201, 203, 206, 208, 211-213, 215, 217, 219, 224, 226-228, 237, 251, 259, 276, 300, 305, 307, 312, 315-317, 321, 323, 328, 341, 365, 374, 383, 384, 397, 401-403, 406,

409, 413, 414, 417, 418, 423, 425, 426, 428, 430, 441, 444, 446, 447, 451
Kittim... 197, 336, 337, 340, 419, 454
Latin 9, 10
lawyers 1
legal 1
leopards 167
Levites 174
Leviticus 2, 12
Libyans 363
lion 167, 168, 171
liturgies 42
Lugal-girra 125
Maccabean 94, 192, 204, 209, 210, 212, 223, 228, 242-244, 265, 267, 278, 285, 286, 291, 294, 295, 326, 332, 338, 342, 350, 352, 360, 376, 383, 392, 398, 400, 402, 408, 420, 426, 430, 432, 435, 440, 453
Maccabee 69, 77, 152, 173-175, 186, 189, 194, 196, 200, 203, 205, 208, 209, 222, 224, 225, 245, 260, 344, 345, 349, 355, 357, 366, 375, 378, 379, 403, 406-408, 411, 415, 416, 428, 431, 440, 441, 456
Macedonian 241
magician 45, 54, 112
magicians 32, 42, 109, 111, 137
Magnificat 129
martyr 435, 452
Masoretic 12, 13, 14, 43, 83
Mazdean 187
Mede 44, 67, 144, 149, 150, 152, 154, 156, 256, 257, 311, 313, 336, 372, 387, 405, 417
Median 76, 224, 226, 425
Mekilta 2
Meslamta-ea 125
messiah 7, 8, 58, 62, 93, 112, 127, 187, 192, 196, 201, 203, 204, 210, 211, 225, 233, 285, 290, 291, 293, 353, 427, 437, 441, 444, 450, 453
Midianite 278, 454
midrash 1, 2, 9, 37, 200, 208, 259
midrashic 72, 394

militarily 67, 418
militaristic 61
military 223, 239, 245, 261, 294, 305, 314, 327, 330, 333, 337, 351, 353, 370, 374, 381, 391, 420, 421, 432, 433, 453-456
miracles 96, 274
mishnah 208
Moabite 18
Monze 302
music 88
Muslim 107, 155, 179, 438, 456
mystery 49, 52, 54, 57, 79, 107, 112
myth 5, 78, 87, 185, 211, 212, 227, 228, 300, 401-403, 412, 415, 441
mythical 179, 215
mythologist 64, 220, 398, 423
mythologize 66, 78, 401
mythology 400, 426
nationalistic 61
Nazorean 450
oaths 388
Olympian 64, 349
pagan 14, 61
Palestinian 30, 179, 207, 241, 314, 317, 324, 342, 355, 358, 432
Parthian 68, 450
penalty 175
persecution 426
Persian 21, 44, 49, 76, 80, 86, 116, 120, 121, 125, 134, 144, 145, 154, 156, 183, 202, 213, 224, 226, 240, 252, 305, 306, 309, 313, 316, 336, 346, 355, 359, 368, 405, 425
pestilence 165
pharaoh 18, 36, 37, 41, 44, 45, 47, 51, 54, 57, 80, 109, 111, 139, 140, 144, 145, 201, 214, 317
Pharisee 122, 450
Philistine 433
plaintiff 8, 173, 174, 195, 206, 207, 215, 229, 230, 260, 268, 280, 307, 406, 429

political 64, 76, 129, 205, 212, 330, 345, 379, 391, 404, 441, 447, 452-454
politics 24, 25, 71
pork 27
prayer 256
precedents 1
predicted 67
prison 25, 47
prisoner 75
promised   7-9, 32, 38, 51, 52, 56, 58, 72, 76, 85, 93, 107, 110, 116, 129, 145, 150, 168, 171, 181, 216, 221, 226, 232, 248, 256, 259, 261, 272, 288, 292, 302, 305, 306, 308, 354, 376, 377, 379, 380, 393, 394, 396, 408, 430, 440, 441, 444, 447, 451, 455
prophecy 22, 56, 58, 72, 93, 175, 187, 196, 220, 222, 224, 226, 237, 248, 256, 283, 285, 291, 292, 297, 391, 393, 403, 410, 412, 426, 442
prophesy 40, 55, 134, 281
prophet 7, 8, 48, 67, 78, 85, 126, 166, 259, 262, 270, 271, 273, 284, 340, 373, 396, 397, 399, 410, 428, 447
prostitutes 174
prostrate 32, 87
Ptolemies 74
punish 248, 253
punishment 116, 145, 157, 276, 284, 286, 380
Purim 54, 431
rabbinic 1, 2
rabbi 41, 48, 62, 150, 180, 187, 229, 245, 382, 401
redeemed 23, 124
redemption   8, 9, 33, 58, 107, 129, 286, 379, 436-439, 449, 454
refugees 434
religion 219, 228
resurrection 376, 379, 380
revelation 9, 106
reversal 33

rhetoric 42
rhetorical 8
Roman 85, 197, 208, 213, 221, 224, 242, 294, 325, 328, 329, 336, 337, 340, 341, 344, 350, 351, 358, 369, 388, 389, 397, 419, 421, 442, 446
Sabbath 3, 14, 38, 98, 129, 221, 222, 225, 286, 296, 317, 324, 352, 354, 372, 393, 395, 397, 409, 430, 434, 441, 447
sackcloth 259
Sadducee 450
saint 174, 221, 253
salvation 357, 359
Samaritans   1, 69, 204, 210, 231, 242, 276, 283, 324, 342, 344, 353, 447
savior 92
Scots 30
scribes 48
Scythian 66
sea 167, 216
sealed 284
segregationist 23
senate 344, 419
Septuagint 13, 14
sermon 1, 2, 7
shame 98
shepherd 168
Sibyl 69
sicarius 381
Sifrá 2
signs 107
soldiers 6, 89
sophist 350
sorcerers 109
sovereignty 61
statue 60, 62, 75, 77, 85, 89, 162
Stoicism 338
Sukkoth 290
sword 165, 266, 284, 350, 353, 386, 419, 435
synagogue 447
Syrian 18, 51, 75, 102, 117, 173, 179, 181, 197, 210, 213, 219,

221, 226, 228, 238, 244, 345, 265-267, 294, 298, 324, 329, 336, 339, 340, 343, 346, 348, 349, 351, 355, 356, 360, 362, 364, 376, 380, 387, 397, 399, 408, 411, 441, 448, 449
tabernacles 446
talmud 24
tartans 30, 456
tax 122
taxation 50, 379, 429, 442, 448, 452
temple 4-7, 13, 19, 22, 23, 31, 39, 40, 72, 75, 78, 85, 98, 124, 133, 141, 145, 151, 175, 181, 186, 189, 192, 193, 207, 208, 222, 229-232, 245, 247, 248, 259, 264-266, 275, 279, 286, 287, 290, 292, 294, 308, 319, 333, 342, 348-350, 353, 360, 361, 365, 369, 372, 373, 384, 387, 388, 389, 392, 393, 397, 398, 405-409, 415, 416, 418, 419, 423, 427, 429, 430, 434, 437, 441, 445, 446, 449
terrorist.................................... 183
Tetragrammaton 11, 18
Torah............................. 2, 28, 399

treaty............. 6, 31, 52, 108, 167, 224, 231, 268, 288, 290, 291, 295, 318, 320, 330, 331, 341, 342, 343, 344, 346, 349, 359, 364, 388, 409, 416, 417, 419, 422, 455
truth 3
turban... 91
types 454
typological................... 72, 200
typologies................................. 324
typology 7, 37, 107, 204, 259, 286, 297, 448
vegetable......................... 27, 29, 31
vengeance 101, 353, 431, 434
verdict... 32
vessels...... 6, 17, 19, 20, 22, 135, 405
villain.................................... 45, 60
vision   116, 119, 166, 170, 171, 197, 236, 237, 246, 247, 257, 250, 282, 284, 297, 300, 301, 302, 304, 401, 407, 414, 445
Watergate.................................. 250
wilderness....................... 7, 38, 454
Yom Kippur 59
Zionistic 75
Zodiac 240

ANCIENT PERSONALITIES

Aaron 433
Abednego...... 23, 79, 87, 89, 92, 94, 95, 98, 148, 404, 432
Abraham ... 98, 231, 245, 288, 409, 433, 451, 455
Abram 21
Abu Issa,..................................... 453
Achan 160
Aeacis.. 241
Aesop 117, 230
Ahab.. 89
Ahasuerus...................... 96, 98, 256
Ahaz.. 326
Ahikar 149
Ahura Mazda................. 24, 117, 185
Akiba 192, 392, 403, 442

Ahikar 399
Alcimus............................... 433, 434
Alexander 1, 68, 72, 73, 79, 86, 172, 182, 183, 201, 213, 218, 224, 226, 227, 239-241, 246, 252, 273, 294, 302, 306, 309, 312, 315, 316, 318, 332, 336, 342, 346, 348, 351, 354, 372, 410, 412, 414, 415, 421, 423, 448, 451
Alexander Janneus 160, 201
Alroy................................... 444, 453
Amalek 192
Amiziah..................................... 134
Amos 50, 51, 78, 134, 166, 171, 271, 440
Amraphel 21

Andromachus 342
Andronicus 330
Anthony 314
Antigonus 73, 173, 241, 312, 316, 348
Antiochus 6, 14, 77-79, 85, 89, 90, 97, 127, 135, 172-175, 177, 181, 194, 195, 197, 207-210, 216, 220, 221, 224, 225, 229, 232, 233, 242-246, 253, 254, 279, 282, 294, 298, 306, 318, 320-322, 324, 326, 327-331, 333-335, 337-340, 343, 344, 346, 348, 349, 351, 353, 355, 356, 358, 360, 363, 364, 367, 369, 372, 374, 378, 380, 381, 385, 387-394, 402, 405, 406, 411, 413, 415-420, 422, 425, 427, 429, 432, 439, 441, 449
Antipater 351
Apaturius 329
Apollonius 222, 244
Appian 68
Aquila 399
Archelaus 6, 229
Arioch 53
Aristeas 162
Aristobulus 408, 416, 446
Aristotle 229, 273
Arrian 239, 241
Artaxerxes 22, 314
Artaxias 220
Artemis 182, 207
Ashpenaz 21, 22, 31
Assurbanipal 117
Assyria 264
Astyges 44, 63, 145
Athena 85
Attalus 329
Augustine 204
Azariah 20, 23, 31, 42, 46, 48, 98, 402, 433
Baal 188
Baal Shamem 117, 185, 189
Baal shamem-Melcarth 188
Balaam 42

Bar Cochba 4, 13, 192, 208, 242, 392, 444, 450-453
Baruch 140, 180
Bath Sheba 36, 79
Bel 13, 121, 125, 369, 400, 427, 430
Belit 127
Belshazzar ... 10, 105, 126, 133, 135-137, 139-144, 165, 166, 206, 216, 236, 237, 405
Belteshazzar 23, 26, 48, 53, 109, 111, 112, 119, 300, 312
Beltis 120
Ben Cozebah 243
Ben Sira 24, 126
Berenice 318, 319
Berosus 140
Caleb 433
Caligula 349
Callandrus 73, 241
Cambyses 150, 314, 319, 369
Cassander 316, 320
Cestius 449
Chamor 288
Charybdis 120
Cleopatra 318, 320, 325, 326, 335, 361, 402, 451
Constantine ... 13, 71, 161, 183, 204, 452, 455, 456
Crassus 6, 397, 446, 452
Croesus 65, 399
Cyaxares 67
Cyrus 6, 22, 29, 31, 62-66, 70, 72, 87, 111, 114, 117, 122, 127, 134, 144, 149, 150, 152, 154, 156, 166, 171, 224, 238, 239, 251, 256, 257, 283, 287, 291-293, 300, 302, 305, 313, 314, 346, 351, 354, 372, 384, 399, 420, 438, 448, 455
Daniel 1, 4, 7-11, 17, 20, 22, 23, 26, 27, 30, 31, 37-39, 42, 45, 46, 48, 51-59, 61, 65, 68, 72, 75, 78, 79, 85, 96, 97, 101, 104-109, 117, 119, 120-122, 126, 128, 137-141, 143-145, 149-151, 153, 154, 156, 157, 160, 161, 164, 165, 174,

180, 183, 185, 188, 192, 194, 197, 200, 203, 204, 209-212, 214, 215, 218, 219, 223-225, 227, 229, 232, 233, 244, 246, 249, 250, 253, 254, 256, 259-261, 271, 272, 280, 281, 283, 285, 292, 296, 297, 300, 302-309, 311, 312, 323, 334, 346, 351, 352, 357, 362, 365, 366, 372, 383-385, 387, 392-394, 396-400, 402, 405, 407, 409, 410, 412-414, 416, 417, 420, 426, 429, 431, 433, 435-438, 440, 443

Darius 32, 67, 149-151, 154, 161, 177, 197, 216, 238, 239, 256, 257, 283, 311, 336, 372, 417

David 5, 7, 28, 39, 43, 44, 52, 56, 80, 107, 112, 117, 120, 125, 126, 150, 159, 187, 188, 204, 210, 211, 220, 243, 264, 273, 281, 289, 292, 302, 379, 428, 433, 445, 447, 454

Deborah.................................. 117
Deioces..................................... 66
Demetrius....................220, 320, 348
Diana...................................... 65
Dio 312, 366
Dositheus 451
Ea-Oannes............................. 189
Eleazar 192, 350, 381, 383, 454
Elijah...................... 12, 27, 176, 433
Elisha 27, 41
Enun Elish............................. 189
Ephraim Syrus 72
Ephraim............................ 379, 453
Epicurus 305
Esau 122, 124, 287
Esther...... 2, 27, 96, 98, 114, 137, 138, 149, 161, 234, 430, 431
Euergetes.............................. 319
Eulaeus................................. 334
Eumenes............................... 329
Euripides 162
Eusebius............................... 452
Evil-merodach.............28, 134, 140
Ezekiel   9, 27, 58, 59, 78, 113, 126, 167, 168, 170, 180, 189, 190, 192-194, 230, 237, 249, 250, 258, 271, 302-304, 307, 332, 378, 386, 387, 404, 406, 407, 410, 437, 440, 455

Ezra 24, 29, 32, 33, 40, 72, 77, 85, 201, 206, 210, 258-260, 264, 277, 292, 332, 397, 412, 418, 428, 442, 449

Flamininus............................... 327
Gabriel 188, 246, 281, 284, 289, 387, 414, 417, 430
Gaius..................................... 85
Gamaliel............................... 208
Gamata................................. 314
Gaumata 54
Gayomart 189
Gog....................................... 59
Goliath............................28, 159
Gorgias 244
Guburu 149
Habakkuk 180, 197, 248, 249, 336-339, 359, 371, 372, 392, 394, 402
Hadrian................................. 286
Hagar 288
Haggai 72, 293, 440
Haman....................96, 114, 431
Hammurabi........................... 48
Hananiah 20, 23, 31, 42, 46, 48, 402, 403
Hannah................................. 129
Hannibal............. 327, 338, 339, 421
Harpagus........................44, 145
Heliodorus 173, 220, 329
Hera 85
Hercules 342
Herod.......44, 138, 162, 213, 229, 288, 351, 356, 381, 452
Herodia................................ 138
Herodotus.67, 70, 140, 170, 182, 313
Herod's................................ 397
Hesiod.....................29, 61, 162
Hezekiah......21, 22, 41, 89, 90, 92, 94, 95, 98, 159, 260, 264, 266, 279, 296, 411
Homer 162

Horus 117, 185, 201
Hosea 28, 78, 171, 258, 271, 332, 376, 440
Hyrcanus 342, 446, 451
Hystaspes 152, 238, 257
Isaac 98, 122, 451
Isaiah ... 3, 8, 13, 21, 22, 24, 57, 66, 70, 78, 80, 93, 126, 144, 151, 166, 170, 193, 194, 223, 224, 226, 243, 257, 258, 264, 271, 281, 287, 313, 321, 326, 367, 376, 383, 384, 387, 394, 410, 413, 434, 437, 440
Ishmael 122
Israel 98
Jacob 66, 122, 124, 287, 373, 451
Jael 185
Jannaeus 446, 451
Jason 224, 330, 342, 343, 344, 418
Jeconiah 22
Jehoiakim 19, 20, 22, 25, 40, 56, 64, 65, 75, 209, 410
Jehoiakin 5, 19, 25, 56, 75, 209, 410
Jehoshaphat 12
Jeremiah 7-9, 13, 18, 19, 33, 78, 108, 169, 191, 219, 222, 231, 242, 256, 258, 271, 276, 283, 290, 292, 296, 313, 346, 374, 397, 407, 409, 410, 416, 440, 447, 452
Jerome 319, 329, 366, 381, 388, 392, 449
Jesus 7, 8, 42, 58, 122, 124, 129, 155, 178, 185, 203, 211, 230, 303, 407, 451, 455
Joab 281
Job 174
Jochanan 12
John 7, 8, 138
Jonathan 12, 201, 288, 349
Joseph 5, 22, 27, 37, 40, 41, 43, 47, 52, 54, 55, 66, 94, 96, 109, 118, 129, 137-140, 146, 149, 161, 296, 401, 433
Josephus 4, 22, 29, 40, 66, 68, 78, 138, 140, 141, 160, 162, 181, 232, 306, 312, 342, 344, 353, 366, 377, 380, 381, 396, 410, 420, 429, 431, 446, 451
Joshua 93, 220, 226, 283, 289, 292, 308, 332, 433
Josiah 17, 18, 185, 289
Judah 89
Judas 6, 77, 117, 152, 173, 174, 186, 187, 189, 192, 194, 196, 200, 203, 205, 208, 209, 211, 212, 222, 223-226, 228, 230, 232, 244, 248, 260, 279, 290, 294, 326, 345, 350, 351, 355, 357, 358, 361, 366, 378, 381, 384, 403, 406-409, 411, 415, 416, 420, 428, 429, 431, 432, 434, 435, 440, 441, 448, 449, 453, 456
Judith 161, 399
Jupiter Lapsis 388
Kahana 2
Laban 320
Laborosoardochus 140
Labynetus 140
Lenaeus 334
Leviathan 167
Linus 162
Livy 312, 340
Lysias 244, 411
Lysimachus ... 73, 173, 241, 316, 415
Magog 59
Maimonides 380
Mandane 67
Marduk 28, 33, 113, 121, 125, 334
Mattathias 185, 225, 351, 379, 380
Matthew 396
Matthias 353
Megasthenes 121
Melchizedek 94, 285
Menahem 350, 381
Menelaus ... 89, 224, 248, 330, 343, 344
Meshach   23, 79, 87, 89, 92, 94, 95, 98, 148, 404, 432
Messiah 259
Methuselah 32
Micah 57, 78, 271, 440

Michael 174, 188, 305, 306, 309, 374
Minos 241
Miriam 41, 397
Mishael...20, 23, 31, 42, 46, 48, 98, 402, 433
Mithridates 213
Mordecai . 80, 98, 114, 149, 259, 260
Moses 7, 26, 41, 88, 161, 165, 178, 187, 194, 262, 271, 273, 274, 303, 308, 343, 428
Nabonidus............29, 71, 110, 111, 113, 117, 118, 122, 127, 129, 134, 137, 140-142, 144, 166, 209, 216, 237, 405
Nabopolassar 125, 334
Nabu.. 334
Nanna... 122
Nebo.. 113
Nebuchadnezzar.....4-6, 17, 18, 20, 22, 25, 28, 30-32, 36, 43-45, 47, 48, 51, 53, 54, 57, 59, 63, 65, 69, 71, 75, 79, 80, 84-87, 89, 92, 94, 95, 97, 101, 105, 106, 109, 110, 119-123, 125-128, 130, 133, 134, 137, 140-142, 145, 148, 149, 169, 177, 186, 197, 206, 209, 213, 214, 216, 220, 230, 237, 300, 302, 372, 391, 400-403, 405, 410, 416, 423, 430, 447
Neco... 18
Nehemiah 6, 22, 24, 29, 32, 33, 40, 50, 72, 77, 118, 161, 210, 258, 260, 264, 268, 277, 292, 293, 296. 332, 397, 411, 416, 418, 428, 442
Nicanor 181, 244, 260, 329
Nicotris 67, 71, 151, 387
Nusku.. 41
Obadiah 453
Onias.......................293, 330, 451
Othello... 308
Oxyartes 241
Paul................... 204, 215, 272, 303
Persian... 127
Peter... 203
Phaedyma 54
Phanuel 188
Phillip........................... 336, 345, 346
Philometer 325, 335, 343, 415, 451
Phineas............... 225, 278, 433, 454
Physcon.............................335, 344
Pilate... 7
Plotinus 366
Polybius .68, 333, 339, 340, 367, 419
Polychronius................................. 72
Pompey...6, 68, 213, 288, 397, 446, 448, 452
Popilius 337, 340, 346, 419, 434
Porphyry..........72, 229, 319, 357, 366, 379, 381, 389, 392
Potiphar 22
Ptolemy............73, 74, 135, 173, 220, 241, 312, 316, 317-319, 322, 324, 326, 334, 335, 341, 343, 348, 362, 402, 414, 421
Quintillian 273
Quirinius................. 6, 397, 448, 452
Rabshakeh 89, 90, 159, 264, 265
Radamanthus 241
Raphael 188
Re 117, 185
Rezin.. 326
Rhea.. 85
Roxane 241
Ruth 2, 81
Saadia... 437
Sahlin... 188
Samuel 428
Saul 44, 112, 120, 129, 150, 187, 220, 303, 374
Scipio...........315, 326, 336, 368, 369
Scopus.................................325, 420
Seleucid 62, 73, 79, 173, 181, 182, 187, 200, 213, 219, 238, 252, 300, 312, 318, 324, 326, 333, 334, 338, 340, 348, 355, 358, 359, 365, 368, 369, 374, 391, 402, 411, 415, 418, 421, 423, 428, 431, 434, 435, 452
Seleucus............73, 127, 172, 220, 241, 312, 316, 318, 327, 328, 329, 333, 397, 414, 421, 423

Senacherib 266
Serenus 453
Seron 244
Seth 201
Shadrach 23, 79, 87, 89, 92, 94, 95, 98, 148, 432
Shamash 42, 48
Shaoshyant 189
Shimon ben Yohai 107, 437
Shishak 274
Simon ... 6, 75, 219, 224, 233, 285, 289, 408, 413, 444, 445, 448, 455
Sin 113, 127
Sira 323, 325, 326, 330, 334, 336, 337, 350, 354, 359, 361, 371, 381, 386, 390, 394, 413, 445
Sisera 185
Smerdis 54
Solomon 5, 7, 31, 39, 43, 52, 56, 75, 155, 162, 186, 189, 243, 259, 264, 265, 273, 275, 279, 287, 289, 296, 397, 302, 372, 416, 427, 428, 447
Spitamenes 241
Strabo 182, 366
Sura 68
Suzanna 27, 400, 427, 430
Symmachus 399
Tammuz 362
Tanhuma 377
Theodotion 62, 399
Tiglath-Pileser 33, 69, 322, 367
Timothy 411
Titus 135, 449
Tobiad 341, 343
Tobias 27, 351
Tobit 67, 399
Tryphon 289
Uzziah 165
Vespasian 449
Xenophon 70, 127, 182
Xerxes 114, 313, 314
Zacchaeus 124
Zadok 445
Zechariah 9, 12, 29, 166, 239, 248, 249, 259, 292, 293, 308, 385, 412, 436, 437, 440
Zedekiah 22, 89, 410
Zeno 338
Zerubbabel 107, 283, 292, 379, 410 437
Zeus 64, 85, 117, 185, 201, 297, 349
Zimri 454

MODERN SCHOLARS

Aalen 202
Anderson 205
Arnold 153
Atkins 54
Barton 29
Baumgartner 172
Beasley-Murray 175
Beckwith 450
Begin 152
Betz 9
Bevan 44, 63, 80, 87, 121, 152, 196, 241, 248, 261, 300, 314, 316, 319, 322, 330, 332, 344, 348, 355, 362, 367-369, 382, 400, 411, 414, 415, 429, 452
Bickerman 62, 74, 225, 333, 342, 350, 358, 359
Bleek 145
Bowden 316, 415
Breckelmanns 174
Brewer 140
Buchanan 2, 9, 13, 18, 26, 28, 32, 37, 48, 55, 94, 106, 107, 117, 150, 151, 187, 189, 190, 197, 201, 202, 204, 207, 233, 246, 250, 258, 268, 269, 278, 279, 287, 338, 340, 351, 353, 378, 381, 383, 388, 393, 410, 436, 437, 442, 444, 450, 455
Bultmann 39, 55, 202, 360
Burkitt 62, 101, 222, 403, 430
Burrows 339

Butler 10
Caird 211
Caquot 204
Caragounis 173, 332
Carlos 58
Casey ...208, 210, 229, 365, 369, 379
Charles 43, 55, 83, 84, 104-106,
   111, 113, 134, 140, 151-53, 176,
   194, 205, 216, 230, 243, 292, 295,
   297, 300, 331, 353, 358, 361, 366,
   400, 432, 434
Clermont-Ganneau 144
Colless 150, 257
Collins....19, 43, 62, 149, 173, 175,
   189, 193, 202, 204, 205, 210, 211,
   219, 221, 224, 226, 234, 243, 245,
   253, 265, 297, 302, 352, 357, 367,
   369, 381, 393, 407, 428, 432, 433
Cook 85
Coppens 210, 212, 365
Cowley 67
Coxon 45, 91, 438
Cumont 187
Dahl 55
Daise 341
Daniel 62
Daremberg 187
Davies 441, 443
Day 377, 378
De Jonge 395
de Sola Pool 378
Delcor 312, 369
Delitzsch 196, 220
Denkler 55
Dequeker 210, 212, 257, 365
Dickens 78
DiLella 25, 54, 86, 209, 211,
   432, 441
Donahue 194, 229
Doran 411
Doughtery 29
Doukhan...... 237, 258, 284, 291, 294
Driver 28, 55, 85, 121,
   181, 194, 220, 225, 297, 306, 356
Dunker 127
Dupont-Sommer 339

Easton 277, 375
Eisenman 351
Eliade 37
Emerton 187, 230, 377
Evans 455
Fenton 10
Ferguson 402
Feuillet 185
Filson 38
Fishbein 57
Fitzmyer 194, 197, 198, 202, 203
Fletcher-Louis 185
Flusser 68
Fox 323
Frankfort 201
Freedman 121, 405
Frerichs 55, 57
Frölich 61, 196, 224
Frost 38, 55
Fulbright 24
Gammie 189, 443
Gardner 376
Gaster 55, 205
Ginsberg 80, 172, 220, 382, 435
Girard 188
Glasson 177
Goldingay 11, 155, 205, 216,
   220, 249, 355, 357, 368
Good 438
Grabbe 150
Grayson 316
Greenberg 55
Grelot 86, 117
Gressmann 187
Gunkel 187, 393
Gurney 412
Haag 405
Haller 233
Hallo 121
Handel 413, 427
Hanhart 205, 211
Hanson 8
Hardy 283
Hartman 4, 54, 77, 86, 172, 179,
   205, 209-211, 216, 412, 432
Hasel 126, 175, 282

Hawthorne 78
Heaton ... 62, 76, 261, 356, 357, 425, 427, 428, 432, 443, 451
Helholm 59
Hengel 316, 415
Herodotus 202
Hill 9
Hitzig 358
Hoelscher 233
Hugo 78
Hurvitz 118, 121
Ibn Shemuel 9, 437
Jansen 189
Jellinek 107
Judas 175
Kaufman 55, 410
Keil 28, 51, 76, 78, 88, 97, 127, 145, 160, 162, 173, 187, 194, 227, 243, 249, 277, 282, 288, 292, 293, 366, 374, 402, 412
Kelso 61
Kirschner 380
Klausner 76
Knibb 9
Koch 110, 117, 443
Kvanvig 443
Laato 291, 293, 296
LaCocque 140, 185, 205, 286, 356, 405, 415, 420, 426, 432, 433
Lambert 316
Lantero 202
Lawson 49, 80
Lebram 369
Leiman 442
Lenglet 105, 439
Liebermann 323
Lindsey 57
Lucas 167, 168, 180
Maier 397
Malter 29
Mandell 356
Mattila 198, 223
Mauet 173
Maurice 26
Mazzaferri 9
Meadowcroft 119

Mendenhall 117, 185
Mercer 19
Milik 286
Millard 67, 146
Miller 164, 187
Montgomery 19, 25, 55, 61, 80, 138, 195, 196, 212, 225, 249, 335, 356, 358, 433, 437
Morgenstern 188
Mosca 188
Mowinckel 179, 188, 203
Mueller 407
Muilenburg 38, 203
Müller 27
Murphy 37
Nader 173
Neubauer 444
Newton 398, 436
Nicol 166, 257
North 338
Noth 205, 211, 218
Noth, ... 234
Oppenheim 42, 113, 127, 136
Oppert 85, 127
Pace 400
Parker 118, 401
Paton, ... 399
Patterson 26, 412
Paul 23
Pellauer 185, 405
Peters 213, 316, 415
Pfandl 72
Porteous ... 211, 226, 302, 309, 317, 356, 365, 403, 415, 417, 420
Prinsloo 51
Pritchard 20, 70, 136, 181, 309, 411
Proudman 205
Pusey 401
Reid 110, 182, 214, 237, 302, 370
Rhodes 24
Ringgren 59
Rissi 187
Robertson 58
Robinson 57
Rowley 9, 338, 435, 440

Russell 55
Sachs 181
Saglio 187
Sahlin 188, 210, 228, 365, 403, 405
Satran 341
Schechter 323
Schnutenhaus 187
Schweitzer 406
Shakespeare 87, 308
Shea 86, 105, 137, 146, 149, 284
Sheriffs 75, 125, 334
Shiloh 58
Shrader 121
Shvilly 58, 59
Singer 14, 381
Smith 192, 202, 221, 333, 342, 436
Smith-Christopher 27, 250, 258, 292, 350, 435
Soesilo 28
Sokoloff 178
Speiser 20
Stahl 220
Stefanovic 33
Stegner 455
Stephenson 232
Stone 341
Struckenbruck 206
Swain 68, 168
Taylor 323
Tcherikover 341, 448

Tedesche 408
Teeple 204
Torrey 323
Towner 207, 211, 358, 417, 432
Trompf 38
Ungnad 444
Van der Woude 62, 395
VanderKam 187
Vermes 194, 339
Wacholder ... 162, 285, 296, 416, 429
Waldbaum 87
Walker 443
Walters 181, 426
Webster 340, 419
Welch 432
Wellhausen 366
Wenham 211
Wertheimer 107
White 57, 58, 398
Wills 29, 65, 399
Wilson 261, 438
Wise 351
Wiseman 150, 181
Witstruck 167
Wolters 136, 144, 232
Woodard 412
Wright 121
Yamauchi 412
Yau 232
Zunz 453
Zusman 4, 286

BIBLICAL REFERENCES

1Bar 1.11 140
1Chron 17:9 221
1Chron 23:30 155
1Chron 28:6-7 .... 161, 162
1Chron 29:20 49
1Chron 3:1 28
1Cor 6:2 .... 215, 227
1Kgs 1:31 80
1Kgs 10:8; 12:8 22
1Kgs 15:12 174
1Kgs 17:17 306

1Kgs 21:5-14 304
1Kgs 22:19 .... 93, 116, 171, 176, 179
1Kgs 8:15 .... 262, 278
1Kgs 8:21 262
1Kgs 8:23-24 .... 262, 267
1Kgs 8:26-28 .... 45, 262
1Kgs 8:28-29 278
1Kgs 8:30-34 .... 262, 277
1Kgs 8:38, 48-50 155
1Kgs 8:44-45 154
1Kgs 8:46-47 .... 262, 267

1Kgs 8:50	26
1Kgs 8:56	393
1Kgs 8:63	85
1Kgs 8:65-66	361, 427
1Mac 1:29-40	245
1Macc 1:1; 8:5	336, 337
1Macc 1:11-16	295, 333, 341, 343
1Macc 1:15	108
1Macc 1:19	335
1Macc 1:20, 29	222, 249
1Macc 1:20-24	348
1Macc 1:20-53	434
1Macc 1:24, 30	415
1Macc 1:29	345
1Macc 1:29-40	253
1Macc 1:41-42	415
1Macc 1:41-63; 4:26-55	209
1Macc 1:42	434
1Macc 1:44-49	221
1Macc 1:45-47	434
1Macc 1:47	245, 297
1Macc 1:50, 57; 2:15-18	434
1Macc 1:52	342, 349
1Macc 1:53	434
1Macc 1:54	249, 349, 392, 434
1Macc 1:54; 4:42-47	348
1Macc 1:54-55	221
1Macc 1:63	26
1Macc 10:20	145
1Macc 10:51-58	320
1Macc 11:17-19	320
1Macc 11:57	289
1Macc 11:9-12	320
1Macc 13:34-35, 41-43;	289
1Macc 13:35-14:15	233
1Macc 13:39-42	444
1Macc 13:42	455
1Macc 13:43-52	365
1Macc 14:14	445
1Macc 14:27	152
1Macc 2:14	353
1Macc 2:23-28	455
1Macc 2:42-48	433
1Macc 2:51-60	433
1Macc 2:54; 3:8	225
1Macc 2:57-63	434
1Macc 2:64	361
1Macc 3.7	352
1Macc 3:10-12	244
1Macc 3:13-26	244
1Macc 3:19, 21	433
1Macc 3:38-41	244
1Macc 3:8	246, 361
1Macc 3:8-9	244
1Macc 4:1-25	244
1Macc 4:26-36	245
1Macc 4:34-61	181
1Macc 4:36-58	6
1Macc 4:52-54	248
1Macc 4:54	392, 429
1Macc 4:58	361
1Macc 4:6-36	354, 361
1Macc 4:8-10, 30-33; 7:36-38	433
1Macc 5:5-10	343
1Macc 6	254
1Macc 6:1-13	182
1Macc 7:15-24	434
1Macc 7:4-14	434
1Macc 8:1-11	356
1Macc 8:17	356
1Macc 9:27	373
1Pet 1:12	8
1Peter 2:17	51
1Sam 10:1	292
1Sam 10:1, 6, 10; 16:13-14	290
1Sam 16:13	293
1Sam 2:1-10	129
1Sam 2:4	347
1Sam 28:20	303
1Sam 4:4	98
2 Macc 2:17	391
2 Sam 7:11	393
2Chron 12:7	274
2Chron 28:5	162
2Chron 32:21	94
2Chron 35:3	174
2Chron 36:21	256
2Chron 36:5-7	17, 19
2Chron 36:6-7	17, 22
2Chron 36:7, 10, 18	20
2Chron 6:36	266, 270
2Kgs 10:18	12

2Kgs 10:4	237	2Macc 6:14	253
2Kgs 18:33-35; 19:12-13	89	2Macc 6:2	349
2Kgs 19:15-19	264	2Macc 6:5	297
2Kgs 19:4, 16	159, 161	2Macc 7:14	378
2Kgs 2:11	176	2Macc 7:9	91
2Kgs 20:18	22	2Macc 8.33	389
2Kgs 23:34	18, 26	2Macc 8:29	248, 391
2Kgs 23:7	174	2Macc 9:1-7	181
2Kgs 24:11-12	17, 19	2Macc 9:8, 10	243
2Kgs 24:14-17	71	2Macc 9:8-10	361
2Kgs 24:15	75	2Sam 1:14	120, 293
2Kgs 24:1-7	19, 21	2Sam 1:17-27	120
2Kgs 24-25	19	2Sam 11:2	125
2Kgs 25:27-29	25	2Sam 12:28	281
2Kgs 25:27-30	28	2Sam 15:1-4	81
2Kgs 9:32-33	21	2Sam 23:27	21
2Macc 12:39-43	378	2Sam 6:2	98
2Macc 8:29	391	2Sam 7:11	393
2Macc 1:10-2:18	416, 429	2Sam 7:14	201, 243
2Macc 10:1	186	Acts 13:36	126, 212, 230
2Macc 10:14-38	181	Acts 8:4-9	303
2Macc 10:3-5	392, 429	Amos 3:7	46
2Macc 10:37	181, 411	Amos 5:19	168
2Macc 11:1-13	181	Amos 5:8	49
2Macc 12:2	181, 411	Amos 7:1-2	166
2Macc 12:39-43	378	Amos 7:12, 15	134
2Macc 13:4-7	89	Amos 7:3-7	166
2Macc 14:6	433	Amos 8:12	259, 384
2Macc 2:13-15	442	Amos 9:11	97, 379
2Macc 2:17	391	Col 1:12-14	204
2Macc 2:13-17	182	Dan 1:1-2	19, 40
2Macc 2:14	210, 357, 448	Dan 1:17	48
2Macc 2:22	442	Dan 1:21	254
2Macc 2:54	278	Dan 1:4	43
2Macc 2:8-25	427	Dan 10:1	300, 312
2Macc 3:3-40	329	Dan 10:1, 13, 20; 11:1	170
2Macc 4:13-15	343	Dan 10:18	308
2Macc 4:13-17	333	Dan 10:2	110, 305
2Macc 4:13-20	342	Dan 10:8-16	43
2Macc 4:18-20	342	Dan 10:20-21	312, 433
2Macc 4:21-22	332	Dan 10:9-12	304
2Macc 4:7-12	332	Dan 11: 24	348
2Macc 4:7-9	330	Dan 11:11	197
2Macc 4:7-9, 23-38	293	Dan 11:1-2	312
2Macc 5:22-23	342	Dan 11:14-19	300, 364, 373, 422
2Macc 5:27	29, 117	Dan 11:15, 22	348

Dan 11:16-12:13 324
Dan 11:17 371
Dan 11:17-12:13 .... 324, 394
Dan 11:17-39 371
Dan 11:18 .... 328, 421
Dan 11:20-21 329
Dan 11:21-12[:13], ... 229
Dan 11:2-31 417
Dan 11:24, 27, 29, 35, 36 359
Dan 11:24-29 372
Dan 11:27, 35 323
Dan 11:27, 35, 40 .... 336, 354
Dan 11:27-36 298
Dan 11:3, 16 360
Dan 11:30 .... 218, 337, 419
Dan 11:30-31 .... 348, 434
Dan 11:32 .... 218, 434
Dan 11:32-34 417
Dan 11:33 .... 353, 434
Dan 11:33-35 .... 383, 435
Dan 11:33-36 43
Dan 11:34 418
Dan 11:34-35 358
Dan 11:35 385
Dan 11:35, 45 250
Dan 11:35-39 372
Dan 11:36-39 364
Dan 11:39 .... 362, 372, 420
Dan 11:40 .... 58, 357, 367, 420
Dan 11:40-45 ... 131, 300, 364, 365, 369, 371, 420, 422
Dan 11:41 420
Dan 11:44 421
Dan 11:45 .... 294, 364, 373, 374, 422
Dan 11:6 318
Dan 12:1 .... 374, 454
Dan 12:11 .... 222, 294, 429
Dan 12:11-12 429
Dan 12:12 222
Dan 12:1-2 385
Dan 12:1-3 .... 364, 376, 377
Dan 12:2 379
Dan 12:2, 13 380
Dan 12:3 ...... 382, 383, 385, 434, 435
Dan 12:4, 6, 9, 13 336
Dan 12:6 390

Dan 12:7 .... 118, 381, 392
Dan 12:7-8 390
Dan 2, 8, 10, 11, and 12 220
Dan 2:1; 3:1; 4:1 32
Dan 2:1-11 41
Dan 2:18, 19; 4:6 49
Dan 2:20-23 162
Dan 2:2-3 43
Dan 2:26 159
Dan 2:2-6 43
Dan 2:28 .... 77, 197
Dan 2:31-35 .... 401, 455
Dan 2:36-45 401
Dan 2:40 259
Dan 2:41-45 58
Dan 2:42-43 418
Dan 2:43 74
Dan 2:44 .... 73, 98, 162, 197
Dan 2:44-45 .... 77, 456
Dan 2:45 .... 402, 403
Dan 2:46 197
Dan 2:46-49 402
Dan 2:48 96
Dan 2:5-13 111
Dan 3:10 197
Dan 3:15 90
Dan 3:25 95
Dan 3:29 432
Dan 3:30 96
Dan 3:33 162
Dan 3:53-54 101
Dan 3:88-90 102
Dan 3:9 197
Dan 4:1 .... 110, 197, 214, 237
Dan 4:1-24 108
Dan 4:17, 21 118
Dan 4:24 323
Dan 4:25-30 108
Dan 4:31-34 .... 108, 162
Dan 4:32 52
Dan 4:34 197
Dan 4:4-25 404
Dan 4:5-6, 15 159
Dan 5:1; 7:1; 8:1 32
Dan 5:10 197
Dan 5:1-16 146

Dan 5:1-3	135
Dan 5:2-3, 5	135
Dan 5:26-28	405
Dan 5:6, 16	137
Dan 6:1; 9:1	32
Dan 6:2	152
Dan 6:24	432
Dan 6:26	197, 426
Dan 6:27	197
Dan 6:29; 10:1	32
Dan 6:5	159
Dan 6:7	197
Dan 6:9, 13, 16	170
Dan 7:1	227
Dan 7:10	180
Dan 7:11	229, 433
Dan 7:12	181, 197, 206
Dan 7:13	193, 197, 230, 307, 308
Dan 7:13-14	407
Dan 7:14	195, 202, 208, 416
Dan 7:17	172
Dan 7:17-18	228
Dan 7:17-27	175
Dan 7:18	253
Dan 7:19	173
Dan 7:21	218, 253
Dan 7:22	208, 224
Dan 7:22, 25, and 27	218
Dan 7:23-27	217, 416
Dan 7:25	118, 218, 245, 429
Dan 7:25; 8:14; 12:6, 11; 13	354
Dan 7:25;12:7	429
Dan 7:26	197, 223
Dan 7:27	197, 407
Dan 7:2-7	182
Dan 7:28	188, 197
Dan 7:7	237
Dan 7:7, 24	74
Dan 7:8, 20-21	173
Dan 7:9-14	177
Dan 8:10	243, 253
Dan 8:1-14	414
Dan 8:1-2, 15-17	387
Dan 8:13	248
Dan 8:14	429
Dan 8:15	193
Dan 8:15-17	414
Dan 8:17	407
Dan 8:17, 19	354
Dan 8:18-19	280
Dan 8:19	323
Dan 8:19-26	415
Dan 8:20	170
Dan 8:20-21	43
Dan 8:2-14	415
Dan 8:24	197, 218
Dan 8:25	76, 250, 298
Dan 8:26	387
Dan 8:3	251
Dan 8:4	170, 222
Dan 8:5	237
Dan 8:7	237, 246
Dan 8:8; 11:4	167
Dan 8:9	415
Dan 9:1	150
Dan 9:10, 11, 14	274
Dan 9:1-2, 24; 12:11-13	429
Dan 9:16	280
Dan 9:17	323
Dan 9:17, 19	280
Dan 9:24	56, 259, 416, 449
Dan 9:24-26	293
Dan 9:24-27	416
Dan 9:25	72, 418
Dan 9:9	280
Dan 5:6, 16	137
Dan 7,13	206
Dan iii 5, 7, 10, 15	86
Dan	268
Deut 1:1	165, 166
Deut 1:16-17	271
Deut 1:38	22
Deut 1:7	302
Deut 10:17	79
Deut 11:13-14	267
Deut 13:6-9	334
Deut 13:7	331
Deut 15:1-12	129
Deut 15:12-13	259
Deut 15:18	285
Deut 15:18	409
Deut 17:15	126

Deut 17:20	126
Deut 18:10	42
Deut 18:21-22	428, 440
Deut 18:22	403
Deut 19:16-19	160
Deut 20:1	304
Deut 20:1-21:14	350
Deut 24:1	12, 231, 276, 281, 288
Deut 24:16	160
Deut 27:11-26	226
Deut 28:15	278
Deut 29:11	274
Deut 29:11, 13	276
Deut 29:20	274
Deut 29:26	243
Deut 3:20; 12:10; 25:19	393
Deut 3:24	161
Deut 30:1	270, 276
Deut 30:15-20	377
Deut 30:3-4, 6	377
Deut 31:6	304
Deut 31:6, 7, 23	306
Deut 32:35-36	347, 353
Deut 32:40	386
Deut 32:40-41	388
Deut 33:2	175, 178, 179
Deut 33:3	174
Deut 4:20	89
Deut 4:24	176
Deut 4:28	133, 142
Deut 4:30	273
Deut 4:34	161
Deut 5:26	159
Deut 5:4	178
Deut 6:1	2
Deut 6:2	267
Deut 6:22	109
Deut 6:4-11:19	10
Deut 6:4-9//11:18-22	2
Deut 7:6; 14:2	381
Deut 7:9	267
Deut 8:14	142
Eccles 1:4	3
Eccles 1:9	3
Eccles 12:13	166, 219
Esth 9:6, 10, 16	96
Esth 1:18-19	145
Esth 4:1	259
Esth 5:1-5	138
Esth 6:3-13	80
Esth 8:15	137, 143, 145
Esth 9:5	96
Esther 3:2	81
Exod 12:40	430, 449
Exod 12:41	39, 55
Exod 13:21	178
Exod 14:19	94, 186
Exod 14:24	92, 185
Exod 15:26	274
Exod 15:3-9	266
Exod 17:9	192
Exod 19:18-20	187
Exod 19:6	243
Exod 20:2-5	94
Exod 22:1	280
Exod 23:23-33	52, 160
Exod 29:36	282
Exod 29:36; 30:26-29; 40:9-11	290
Exod 32:32	88
Exod 33:14	393
Exod 33:7-11	187
Exod 34:14	94
Exod 7:3	109
Exod 7:4; 12:41	243
Exod 9:18	274, 373, 374
Exod 9:27	270
Exod. 24:16-17	185
Ezek 1:1	165, 171, 190, 236, 300, 301, 303
Ezek 1:10	168, 190
Ezek 1:13	190
Ezek 1:1-4	386
Ezek 1:1-7:27	167
Ezek 1:22	191
Ezek 1:24	301, 303
Ezek 1:26	84, 190, 246, 301, 306, 307
Ezek 1:26	190
Ezek 1:28	246, 303, 306
Ezek 1:3	236
Ezek 1:4	176, 184
Ezek 1:5	165, 184, 192, 193

Ezek 1:5-7	168, 171	Ezra 4:5-7	314
Ezek 1:7	190, 301	Ezra 6:16	85
Ezek 14:14; 28:3	27	Ezra 7:1; 8:2	20
Ezek 14:14-20; 28:3	28	Ezra 7:12	63
Ezek 14:21	165	Ezra 8:2	27, 28
Ezek 17:11-21	404	Ezra 9:11	273
Ezek 17:20	262	Ezra 9:7	270
Ezek 2:1	304, 406	Gen 1:1	165, 166
Ezek 2:1-6	304	Gen 10:10	21
Ezek 2:2; 3:24	304	Gen 11:1-9	116, 118
Ezek 2:3	406	Gen 11:2	21
Ezek 2:6	304, 306	Gen 11:5	115
Ezek 20:6	238, 242	Gen 14:1, 9	21
Ezek 22:26	14	Gen 14:20	94
Ezek 26:7	63	Gen 15:13	39, 55, 430, 439
Ezek 28:2	243	Gen 15:16	253
Ezek 28:2-3	126	Gen 15:1-6	455
Ezek 28:3	126, 129	Gen 15:18	302
Ezek 3:14	306	Gen 21:14	288
Ezek 3:24	246	Gen 22:17	98
Ezek 31:10-11	142	Gen 24:3	46, 129
Ezek 31:6	115	Gen 3:19	375, 376
Ezek 34:11-14	168	Gen 3:22	375
Ezek 37:1-12	379	Gen 31:30-35	320
Ezek 37:12-14	378	Gen 32:21	287
Ezek 38:17	151	Gen 32:22-28	26
Ezek 39:17	236	Gen 32-33	287
Ezek 39:18	238	Gen 33:11-19	287
Ezek 39:6	58	Gen 38:24	89
Ezek 4:14	26	Gen 39:6-20	22
Ezek 40:2	236	Gen 41:1	36
Ezek 44:23	14, 28	Gen 41:1,8,14,38,17	109
Ezek 47:12	190	Gen 41:10	111
Ezek 8:2	184	Gen 41:12-28	53
Ezek 8:3	236	Gen 41:12b	137
Ezek 8:4	362	Gen 41:14	139
Ezek 8:5	236	Gen 41:1-8	41
Ezek 9:11	386	Gen 41:25	49
Ezek 9:2	301	Gen 41:32	79, 143
Ezek 9:4	379	Gen 41:33-34	79
Ezek 9:7	380	Gen 41:38	137, 139
Ezra 1:1-8	72	Gen 41:41	79
Ezra 1:2-4	72	Gen 41:42	137, 143, 145
Ezra 1:7-11	20	Gen 41:8	45, 137, 214
Ezra 10:1	259	Gen 41:9-10	46
Ezra 4:5-6	256	Gen 42:42, 43	143

Gen 6:2	93
Gen 7:11; 8:2	167
Gen 8:21-22	3
Hab 1:2	246
Hab 1:6, 8	168, 171
Hab 1:8-9	339
Hab 2:2	347, 359, 362
Hab 2:20	179
Hab 2:2-3	393, 394
Hab 2:3	246, 384, 390
Hab 2:4	391, 392
Heb 1:1-3	10
Heb 1:14	10
Heb 1:5, 13	10
Heb 12:22	381
Heb 4:16	11
Heb 8:6-13; 10:16; 12:24	13
Hos 13:7	168, 171
Hos 13:7-8	168
Hos 4:5; 5:5	377
Hos 4:8	377
Hos 5:13	377
Hos 6:1-2	377, 378
Hos 6:2	375, 376
Hos 9:3	28
Isa 10:23	290
Isa 10:25	246
Isa 10:5	246
Isa 11:1	115, 117
Isa 11:11	21
Isa 13:1	151
Isa 13:17-18	170
Isa 13:17-22	66, 151, 313
Isa 14:12	242
Isa 14:12-13	238
Isa 14:12-15	126, 243
Isa 14:13-14	415
Isa 14:9	240
Isa 17:12-14	230
Isa 19:1	184
Isa 2:2	55, 403
Isa 2:2 //Micah 4:1	53
Isa 2:2-4	61
Isa 21:2, 9	66
Isa 21:5	134
Isa 22:2-9	151
Isa 26:19	375, 376, 377, 378
Isa 26:20	246
Isa 29:1-24	387
Isa 29:14	386
Isa 29:1-8	230
Isa 3:8	347
Isa 30:29	403
Isa 35:9-10	447
Isa 36:11	36
Isa 36:18	88
Isa 36:19-20; 37:11-12	89
Isa 37:16-20	264, 265
Isa 37:17	159, 266, 278
Isa 37:36	92, 93, 279
Isa 39:7	21
Isa 4:3	373
Isa 4:3-5	377
Isa 40:17	123
Isa 40:19; 41:7	85
Isa 41:21-24	3
Isa 41:3	239
Isa 42:1	159
Isa 43:2	92, 93
Isa 43:25	282, 287
Isa 43:3	89
Isa 44:14	79
Isa 44:26	158
Isa 44:26-28	70
Isa 44:28	292
Isa 45:1	70, 71
Isa 45:1, 2-4, 13	305
Isa 45:1-3	71
Isa 45:17	161
Isa 45:7	49
Isa 46:6	133
Isa 47:10	52
Isa 49:19-20	226
Isa 49:23	79, 224
Isa 49:23; 60:14	402
Isa 50:1	13
Isa 51:22-23	223
Isa 52:13	159, 375, 377, 434
Isa 52:14	159
Isa 52:7	292, 334
Isa 52:7a	285
Isa 53:11	375, 382, 434

Isa 53:8 378
Isa 53:8-9 384
Isa 6:1 .... 165, 168, 171, 179,
   189, 256, 257, 308
Isa 6:11 290
Isa 6:5 259
Isa 6:6 281
Isa 6:7 306
Isa 6:9 281
Isa 60:10 224
Isa 66:15 176
Isa 66:19 379
Isa 66:2, 5 379
Isa 66:24 .... 375, 380
Isa 7:7 .... 323, 326
Isa 8:7 .... 321, 362
Isa 9:2 197
Jer 1:12 274
Jer 10:10; 23:36 159
Jer 10:3-5 85
Jer 10:9 301
Jer 11:4 274
Jer 16:14; 23:3, 8; 32:37 270
Jer 17:9 190
Jer 20:4 17
Jer 22:13-19; 25; 36 18
Jer 23:18 .... 116, 118
Jer 23:20//30:24 277
Jer 25:11, 29:10 416
Jer 25:12 .... 256, 290
Jer 25:9-11, 18-26; 46:25-26 21
Jer 26:4 270
Jer 27:4, 6 63
Jer 27:9 42
Jer 29:10 256
Jer 29:22 89
Jer 3:19 242
Jer 3:8 13
Jer 3:9 108
Jer 30:7 .... 373, 374
Jer 30:7-11 374
Jer 31:28 274
Jer 32:1; 52:29 84
Jer 32:20, 21 274
Jer 32:9-44 283
Jer 35:17 274

Jer 39:1 17
Jer 4:4 262
Jer 42:18 277
Jer 44:21 .... 262, 270
Jer 44:27 274
Jer 46:2 .... 17, 18
Jer 49:19, 22 169
Jer 50:1-3, 8-10 313
Jer 50:17 170
Jer 50:2, 8-10, 39-42; 51:11 67
Jer 51:1 151
Jer 51:39 134
Jer 51:64 .... 166, 219
Jer 51:8-14, 28 151
Jer 52:17 .... 165, 191
Jer 52:17-23 20
Jer 52:25 22
Jer 7:20 274
Jer 7:25 262
Job 1:6 93
Job 1:6, 12; 2:1, 6 118
Job 12:10 143
Job 12:16 49
Job 12:22 49
Job 12:23 .... 49, 117
Job 14:11 .... 375, 376
Job 14:7 115
Job 33:4 143
Job 34:16-30 144
Job 34:20 .... 143, 254
Job 34:30 144
Job 5:1 174
Job 5:1; 15:15 116
Job 9:13; 25:12-13 167
Job 9:7 286
Joel 2:2 .... 373, 374
Joel 2:5 376
Joel 3:5 373
Josh 1:4 302
Josh 1:6, 9, 18 306
Josh 7:24-25 160
Josh 7:25 207
Josh 8:30-35 226
Judges 2:14 237
Judges 5:31 .... 117, 185
Judges 8:32 21

Judith 1:1, 4; 2:19; 3:1, 8; 4:1	67	Matt 26:64	90
Judith 12:1-2	29	Matt 4:5	297
Lev 10:10	216, 332	Matt 6:19-20	10
Lev 10:10,	381	Matt 7:16-20	10
Lev 10:10; 11:47;	28	Matt 7:6	11
Lev 11:44, 45	174	Matt 8:22	377
Lev 19:2; 20:7, 26	174	Mic 6:6-7	98
Lev 20:14	89	Micah 4:2	403
Lev 20:14; 21:9	207	Neh 1:4	46
Lev 21:17-20	22	Neh 1:5	267
Lev 21:9	89	Neh 1:5-11	259, 268
Lev 22:18-25	23	Neh 1:6	259, 270, 278
Lev 22:24	22	Neh 1:7-8	273
Lev 25:25-28	362	Neh 1:8	270, 274
Lev 26:17-28	416	Neh 10:30	274
Lev 26:18	259	Neh 10:6	28
Lev 26:18, 21, 24, 28	416	Neh 2:1	22
Lev 26:18-28	285	Neh 2:1-20	71
Lev 26:21	165	Neh 2; Hag 2:1-5	293
Lev 26:27-45	276	Neh 3:33-4:23	293
Lev 26:33	290	Neh 4:10-23, 27	72
Lev 26:37	347	Neh 6:11	22
Luke 1:47-55	129	Neh 8:4; 10:2, 6, 23	20
Luke 1:76	94	Neh 9:1	259
Luke 19:5-8	124	Neh 9:10	262
Luke 2:14	454	Neh 9:17	273
Luke 4:9	297	Neh 9:2	277
Luke 9:34-35	187	Neh 9:32	267
Luke 9:59-60	134	Neh 9:33	262
Luke 9:60	377	Neh 9:33-34	270
Mal 3:16	373, 384	Neh 9:34	262
Mal 3:5	42	Neh 9:5	49
Matt 10:28; 12:49-50	11	Neh 9:6	265
Matt 10:6-15	28	Num 11:25	185
Matt 11:13	8	Num 12:6	396
Matt 12:38-39	134	Num 15:40	174
Matt 17:1-7	194	Num 16:3	174
Matt 17:4	178	Num 21:14	3
Matt 17:5	185, 212, 230	Num 24:17	242, 243
Matt 18:19-20	48	Num 24:17/Sir 36:10	362
Matt 19:28	215	Num 24:23	337
Matt 19:30	11	Num 24:23-24	336
Matt 2:1	42	Num 24:24	337
Matt 21:18-22	190	Num 25:1-9	454
Matt 21:31; 15:30	109	Num 25:4	277
Matt 24:15	396, 443	Num 5:11-31	160

Num 6:24-26	2	Ps 79:4	277
Num 6:25	277	Ps 79:5	246
OG Dan 5:9	138	Ps 8:2; 99:1	98
OG Ps 50:17	98	Ps 8:5, 7	168
OG Dan 2:40	73	Ps 8:7-8	63
OG Ps 140:2	98	Ps 80:4	277
Prov 16:6	124	Ps 80:5	246
Prov 18:15	168	Ps 82:1, 6	126
Prov 25:6-7	32	Ps 82:1; 94:2; 96:13	195
Ps 1:3	190	Ps 84:2	159
Ps 106:30-31	454	Ps 85:11-12	289
Ps 106:31	225	Ps 89:6, 8	116, 118
Ps 107:2	89	Ps 89:7	116
Ps 108:3	242	Ps 9:8-9	176
Ps 110	2	Ps 90:13	246
Ps 113:2	49	Ps 90:2	49
Ps 113:5-9	129	Ps 93:2	176
Ps 115:4	142	Ps 95:6	94
Ps 12:4	171	Ps 95; 100, 145, 148, 150	101
Ps 121:3-8	276	Ps 97:1-2	184
Ps 139:12	49	Ps 97:2-3	176
Ps 139:16	309	Ps 97:3	178
Ps 145:13	97, 109, 123, 161	Rev 1:1	9
Ps 145:5	96	Rev 11:2; 13:5	222
Ps 15:1	278	Rev 16:12	58
Ps 16:3	174, 218	Rev 2:10	30
Ps 2:11	274	Rev 21:27	14
Ps 2:2; 20:6; 84:9, 38; 132:10	293	Rev 4:1-22:5	438
Ps 29:11	176	Rev 4:4-8	190
Ps 34:10	218	Rev 4:6	191
Ps 34:7	160	Rom 1:3-4	201
Ps 36:10	49	Rom 13:1	51
Ps 41:14	49, 277	Rom 5:17, 21	377
Ps 45:9	123, 126	Rom 8:33-34	272
Ps 50:3-4	176	Ruth 4:1	81
Ps 52:5-8	377	Sir 3:30	323
Ps 55:17, 18	155	Sir 36:10	323
Ps 55:20	171, 176, 186	Sir 36:1-17	324, 371
Ps 57:3-6	157	Sir 36:13	381
Ps 66:12	92	Sir 36:14	328, 360
Ps 68:18	175	Sir 36:17	323, 347, 360, 384, 390
Ps 69:28	377	Sir 36:3	331, 360
Ps 69:29	373, 384	Sir 36:6/OG	323
Ps 74:13-14	167	Sir 36:8	123, 359, 384, 394
Ps 74:4	338	Sir 36:8(Heb)	347
Ps 74:9	222	Sir 39:1-4	24

Sir 36:3, 5, 17	392
Sir 36:4	360
Sir 36:5	347, 360, 384
Sir 36:6	325, 328, 346, 362
Sir 36:8	324, 331, 336, 347, 362, 386, 390
Tob 1:10-11	28, 29
Tob 1:10-11	28
Zech 1:12	246, 256, 292
Zech 1:7-6:15	166
Zech 1:8	60
Zech 1:9; 4:4, 5; 13; 6:4	308
Zech 10:3	239
Zech 12:1	290
Zech 12:10-14	293
Zech 12:2-3	58
Zech 12:4	403
Zech 12-14	230
Zech 13:1	282, 286
Zech 13:2-5	289
Zech 13:4	282
Zech 14:1-15	381
Zech 2:1; 5:1; 6:1	60
Zech 2:10(M)	165, 167
Zech 4:1, 5	248
Zech 4:10	384
Zech 4:14	292
Zech 5:8-11	21

NON-BIBLICAL REFERENCES

1 Enoch 62.9	197
1QM 1.2	197
1QM 1.4	312
1QM 1.6; 11.11	197
11QMelch 3.II, 15-16	334
11QMelch 4, 6, 7	285
11QMelch	395
1Enoch 14.1-25	177
1Enoch 2.2	3
1Enoch 46.1-9	178
1Enoch 48.1-10; 62:7-12	213
1Enoch 52.4-6	429
1Enoch 62.13	201
1Enoch 62.14	197
1Enoch 63.8-12; 69.27-29	429
1Enoch 89.31	351
1Enoch 90.9	172
1Enoch 90.6-12	434
1Enoch 93.4	196
1Qdana	43
1QH 7.14-15	377
1QM 1.11-12	453
1QM 1.12; 15:1	453
1QM 1.9	204
1QM 10.10	204
1QM 11.1-12	433
1QM 17.7; 1.9	223
1QS 1.8-10	51
1QS 1.8-9	52
1QS 2:1-18	226
2Bar 24.1	180
2Bar 24.3-4	180
2Bar 39.3	449
4Ezra 11.38-39; 12.10	449
4Ezra 13.1-38	206
4Ezra 13.31	197
4Ezra 7.28	201
4Macc 5.3, 14	29
4Q 174.2, 3	413
4Q246	94
4Q246.2, 1	232
4Q448.B2, C.8	446
4Q448.B.8	446
4Q521.1	201
4Qflor 2.3	443
4Qflor 2.4	396
4QLXX Lev	12
4QM 12.8	186
4QOrNab	110, 405
Ant 1.128	337, 338
Ant 10.10, 3	40
Ant 10.11.1	29
Ant 10.186	22
Ant 10.221-28	64

Ant 10.231, 237 140
Ant 10.241 141
Ant 10.260-62 160
Ant 10.267-68 .... 78, 396
Ant 10.268-69 410
Ant 10.275-76 410
Ant 11.338-39 354
Ant 11:33 402
Ant 12.129-55 420
Ant 12.131-54 420
Ant 12.29-31 320
Ant 12.54 325
Ant 12.242-44 337
Ant 12.253 392
Ant 12.271 225
Ant 12.282 380
Ant 12.285-312 .... 215, 231
Ant 12.3, 3 325
Ant 12.300 260
Ant 12.312 181
Ant 12.315 181
Ant 12.317-18 279
Ant 12.320 392
Ant 12.325 232
Ant 12.354-59 207
Ant 12.357-59 182
Ant 12.3-7 317
Ant 12.414-19 355
Ant 12.8 306
Ant 12.9, 1 254
Ant 13.145 289
Ant 13.215 289
Ant 13.237-38 451
Ant 13.301-309 445
Ant 13.311-313; 20.97, 169 449
Ant 13.372-73 446
Ant 14.105-109 446
Ant 14.110-114 446
Ant 14.58-76 446
Ant 14.74-79 446
Ant 19.270 239
Apion 2.277 450
Apion 2.49 451
Apion. 1.21 .... 66, 84
Appian, *Roman History* 11.10, 61
.... 202, 241
Appian, *Roman History* 11.11, 70
.... 213
Appian, *Roman History* 11.7, 46.. 346
Appian, *Roman History* 11.8, 46.. 419
Appian, *Roman History* 11.8, 50.. 448
Appian, *Roman History*, preface 9 . 69
Arrian, *Anabasis* 4.19, 5 241
Arrian, *Anabasis*, 5.13, 1; 7.22, 5. 241
Arrian, *Anabasis*, 5.29, 1 239
Arrian, *Anabasis*, 7.15, 5 241
Arrian, *Anabasis*, 7.15, 5 241
Arrian, *Anabasis*, 7.2, 3 182
Arrian, *Anabasis* 7.22, 5......317, 423
Arrian, *Anabasis* 7.27, 3 239
Arrian, *Anabasis*, 7.29, 3 241
bBer 34b 155
bBer 55b 42
bBer 70b 62
bBer 8a 48
Ber 6a 202
bKet 111b 380, 381
bMegilla 17b 286
bSan 38b; 94a 118
bSan 93b 22
bSan 98b 454
bSan 99a 454
bYoma 77a 396
CDC 20B.1, 5, 7 226
CDC 20B.4-5 226
CDC 20B.4-8 225
CDC 20B.4-8 226
Clement of Alexandria (Paed ii.10)
.... 176
Contra Apion 1.20 140
Contra Apion 1.180 342
Dio 19, *Zonaras* 9, 18-19 ....330, 421
Dio 19, *Zonaras* 9,18 ....327, 330 421
Dio 19, *Zonaras* 9,20, 21 329
Dio 19, *Zonaras* 9,21 329
Dio 19.62 339
Dio 19, *Zonaras* 9.18-20 420
Dio 19.62, *Zoneras* 9, 18-20 421
Dio, *RomHist* 49.25-44...........68, 314
Diodorus 1.4 43
Diodorus 2.9 85
Diodorus 29.15 328

Eusebius, *PraepEvang.* 9.4 .. 118, 121
Eusebius, *PraepEvang* 9.41, 6...... 127
Eusebius, *PrepEvang* 9.41.6......... 29
ExodR 15.6 185
Hamlet, Act 2, sc 2, line 622......... 64
HE 10.46 456
HE 6.19, 2-4 78
HE 8.4 452
Herodotus 54
Herodotus 1.119 45
Herodotus, 1.127 313
Herodotus 1.132 111
Herodotus 1.132, 139 42
Herodotus 1.171 43
Herodotus 1.178-82 86
Herodotus 1.188 140
Herodotus 1.189-91 72
Herodotus, 1.74 73
Herodotus 1.83 85
Herodotus 15.2, 13 241
Herodotus 2.92 21
Herodotus 3.31 .... 157, 202
Herodotus 3.89-90 152
Herodotus 5.18 138
Herodotus 7.19 114
Herodotus 7.20-99 314
Hesiod 64
Hesiod, *The Works and Days* 1.236-50 276
Jerome 25.709, p. 563 325
Jerome 25.716-17, pp. 569 449
Jerome 25.717, p. 569 357
Jerome 25.717-18, p. 570 450
Jerome 25.724, p. 575 381
Jerome 25.725, p. 576 379
Jerome 25.727, p. 577 379
Jerome 25.728, p. 578 389
Jerome 25.729, p. 578 389
Jerome 25.730, pp. 579-80 392
Jerome, *on Daniel* 11:30-31 (PL 25:569 = CCSL 75A, 922, 11 ... 338
Jerome, *on Daniel* 11:10, 20 329
Jub 22.16 28
Jub 24.28-29; 37:10 337
Justin 12.16 315
Justin, Apol. 1.31 179

LevR 36.2 401
Livy 34.58, 5 316
Livy 34.60, 1-6 327
Livy 36.20, 2-3 ....85, 327
Livy 37.39-45 421
Livy 37.45 328
Livy 38.12, 3-6 329
Livy 38.8, 7; 34.60, 1-6 327
Livy 41.20.5-10 361
Livy 44.19 ....336, 344
Livy 44.19, 6-14 337
Livy 45.11 336
Livy 45.12 340
Livy 45.12, 1-6 338
mAboth 2.1 180
mAboth 3.2 48
mAboth 5.18 382
mAboth 5.4 30
Macrobius 7.1 138
Mek, *Vayassa* 5.71-73 454
Mek, *Amalek* 1.96-98 ....192, 334
Mek, *Vayassa* 5.76 453
mErubin 447
mGittin 1-9 13
Mid Ps 82 202
MPG 25.617A 366
mSan 3.4 173
mSan 4.1 229
mTaan 4.6 349
mYoma 8.9 287
mYoma 8.9 409
NeoTarg Exod 12.41-42 97
NeoTarg Exod 12.41-42 379
NumR 13 62
Ovid, *Metam* 1.89 ff 29
pHab 3.13-14 339
Philo, *De Fuga* 78, 97 377
Philo, *Som* 2.250 381
PirkeEliezer on Isa 39:7; 56:4-5 ... 22
PirkeEliezer chapter 2 62
Plutarch, *de Iside et Osiride* 13, 356 C; 19, 366 F 378
Plutarch, *Symp* 1.1 138
Polybius 16.39, 3-5 ....322, 325
Polybius 18.51, 3-4 ....316, 415
Polybius 18.51, 4-6 418

Polybius 19.1, 2-4 340
Polybius 19.27, 11-13 341
Polybius 19.27, 2-10 341
Polybius 21.14 328
Polybius 21.17,1-9 418
Polybius 21.42 336
Polybius 21.42,1-27 .... 339, 418
Polybius 26.1, 10-11 .... 333, 361
Polybius 28.20, 5, 9; 23, 2.... 320, 326
Polybius 28.20, 7 316
Polybius 28.20, 8-9 402
Polybius 28.20-23 336
Polybius 29.26-27,13 419
Polybius 29.27, 2-13 340
Polybius 29.27, 4-5 419
Polybius 3.25, 6-9 388
Polybius 30.26, 9 .... 333, 361, 415
Polybius 31.9 .... 182, 207
Polybius 5.67, 8 316
Polybius 5.68, 1 367
Polybius 5.68, 1-73, 16 368
Polybius 5.86, 10-11 322
Polybius 5.86, 5-6 322
Polybius 68.1-78.6 322
Polybius, *Frag* 29.2, 1-4 337
Polybius, *Hist* 18.49, 1-51, 10; 20.8, 1-5; 21.6, 1-43, 3 420
Ps Sol 3.16 376
RhShen 16b 187
Sifre Deut 33.3, Piska 344. 143b. 208

Strabo 11.13.1-2 314
Strabo 15.1, 6 43
Strabo 16.1 #6 25
Sutonian, *The Lives of the Caesars*. 44
T12Pat, ... 30
Tanhuma 31.4, 34 62
Targ Isa 53:8 378
TSol 16.6-7 287
Vellius. Paterculus. 1.6.6 68
War 1.117 408
War 1.19 429
War 1.53 408
War 1.656 207
War 1.97 160
War 2.117-118 .... 6, 350
War 2.184-203 .... 85, 349
War 2.398 450
War 2.433 381
War 2.433-45 350
War 6.250 4
War 6.285-86 449
War 7.329 381
War 7.340-50 382
Xenophon, *Anabasis* 1.5, 8; 8. 29. 137
Xenophon, *Cyrop* 7.5 43
Xenophon, *Cyrop* 7.28-30 122
Xenophon, *Cyrop* 7.35 112
Xenophon, *Cyrop* 8.6, 22 238
yBer 2.4, 4d-5a 286
yTa'an 68d 192, 244

GEOGRAPHICAL REFERENCES

Adasa 248
Aegean 412
Aetolia 327
Afghanistan 239
Africa 213, 339
Akkad 21, 122
Akko 74
Alexandria 240, 320, 335-337, 341
Amazon 302
Amman 322, 368
Anathoth 283, 410
Anatolia 316

Antioch 73, 181, 242, 244, 279, 319, 320, 338
Appollonia 74
Aqaba 224
Arabia 113, 128, 218, 446
Arbela, ... 183
Armenia 68, 220
Ascalon 74
Asham 369
Asia 87, 446
Asia Minor 69, 74, 128, 213, 238, 315, 316, 321, 327, 338, 339, 355, 364, 368, 369, 397, 418, 421

Asia..................................312
Assyria.........28, 63, 68, 72, 88, 89,
    120, 125, 150, 168, 170, 197, 231,
    251, 257, 266, 272, 313, 321, 340,
    362, 447, 448
Atropatian 313
Babel.. 21
Babylon......4, 7, 10, 17, 19, 20-22,
    28, 31-33, 37-40, 42, 46, 51, 53,
    56, 62, 63, 65, 66, 69-72, 79, 84-
    87, 109, 110, 113, 114, 116, 118,
    119, 121, 122, 125-127, 130, 136,
    139, 140, 144, 145, 148, 149-153,
    157, 160, 165, 168, 170, 171, 182,
    183, 191, 222, 227, 230, 237, 242,
    249, 251, 252, 257, 262, 272, 281,
    283, 284, 287, 291-293, 297, 300,
    305, 312, 313, 316, 317, 319, 334,
    354, 372, 384, 391, 400-404, 410,
    414-416, 420, 431, 438, 447-449,
    451, 455
Babylon   17, 63, 85, 136, 230,
    317, 238, 438, 447
Bashan....................................... 236
Beitar 4, 286
Belshazzar 254
Belus 85
Beruth.. 322
Bethel 134
Beth-horon 6, 59, 62, 75, 78,
    101, 151, 162, 181-183, 185, 186,
    193, 195, 210, 212, 213, 215, 219,
    222, 223, 225, 231-234, 244, 247,
    248, 252, 253, 265, 278, 279, 288,
    296, 297, 354, 356, 361, 372, 374,
    376, 383, 384, 387, 389, 391, 393,
    406, 408, 409, 411, 413, 416, 426-
    429, 431, 432, 435, 438, 440, 442,
    449, 453
Bethlehem 42
Beth-zur........59, 78, 101, 151, 162,
    181-183, 185, 186, 193, 195, 210,
    212, 215, 233, 244, 252, 261, 265,
    279, 354, 356, 372, 374, 376, 394,
    411, 413, 416, 427-429, 431, 440,
    444, 453

Bosphorus.................................. 338
Canaan 5, 40, 56, 188, 227, 362,
    397, 409, 442, 454
Carchemish 5, 17, 18
Carthage...68, 76, 327, 338, 345, 421
Caspian...............................67, 313
Celica,...448
Chebar 300, 302, 386
China 58
Choaspes.................................... 238
Coprates 238
Coronea..............................85, 327
Cyprus........68, 197, 327, 337, 338,
    340, 341, 346
Cyrene..............................316, 414
Damascus.........................225, 303
Danube...................................... 240
Dead Sea 8, 49, 51, 55, 94,
    197, 200, 202, 216, 285, 334, 400,
    402, 413, 446
Dora,.. 452
Dura.................................... 84, 85
Ebal... 226
Ecbatana.................................... 348
Edom................................362, 420
Egypt ...4, 7, 18, 22, 28, 37-39, 43,
    48, 51, 55-57, 62, 66, 69, 72, 74,
    76, 79, 93, 94, 96, 97, 109, 110,
    125, 135, 140, 142, 149, 161, 183,
    184, 197, 198, 200, 218, 221, 231,
    239, 240, 242, 244, 252, 253, 262,
    272, 274, 276, 278, 294, 301, 309,
    312, 315, 316, 319, 320, 324, 326,
    327, 333-335, 337-345, 356, 358,
    362-364, 368, 373, 379, 387, 397,
    402, 404, 410, 414, 418, 419, 421,
    422, 446, 448
Elam................................151, 236
Eleusis....................................... 337
Elymais   181, 182, 207, 327,
    333, 364, 369, 416
Erech... 21
Erythraeun 240
Ethiopia..........64, 69, 84, 240, 363,
    364, 368, 422
Eulaeus..................................... 238

Euphrates.......17, 58, 64, 68, 71, 86, 97, 125, 183, 302, 387, 404, 415, 448
Europe...... 87, 213, 242, 364, 415, 418, 446
Fertile Crescent 216, 313, 407
Galilee.............................6, 350, 381
Gaza............ 322, 325, 354, 368, 452
Gazara.. 444
Geniza....................................... 323
Gerizim...........226, 231, 276, 317, 342, 409
Golan 58, 59, 323, 420
Goldingay..................................... 17
Gomorah.................................... 151
Gomorrah.................................... 66
Great Britain.............................. 213
Greece...70, 85, 150, 152, 168, 227, 242, 257, 313, 321, 327, 338, 339, 355, 364, 406, 414, 421, 438, 448, 449
Hades... 102
Harran 110, 113
Hebron............................... 124, 287
Hellespont 183, 239
India 62, 63, 72, 84, 183, 218, 224, 240, 309, 321, 421
Indus 183
Ipsus.. 241
Iran.. 241
Israel........21, 22, 26, 33, 44, 58, 62, 69, 78, 92, 165, 174, 187, 205, 211, 228, 230, 232, 249, 250, 262, 269, 270, 272, 274-276, 278, 290, 297, 326, 352, 359, 361, 373, 375, 377, 381, 383, 403-407, 414, 426, 428, 435, 436, 437, 438, 440, 444, 445, 447
Italy............................327, 338, 421
Jamestown................................. 358
Jericho... 41
Jerusalem 5-7, 17, 19, 20, 28, 32, 40, 65, 70, 72, 75, 85, 89, 93, 98, 107, 126, 133, 135, 141, 145, 154, 162, 165, 171, 175, 182, 183, 186, 189, 191, 202, 213, 220, 221, 230, 231, 236, 241, 244, 252, 253, 256, 261, 262, 265, 268, 272, 274, 276, 277, 279, 281, 283, 284, 286-293, 306, 317, 320, 322, 324, 332, 333, 338, 340-343, 345, 348, 349, 353, 354, 361, 368, 369, 373, 374, 381, 384, 387, 391, 392, 400, 403, 404, 407, 409-411, 414, 415, 417, 418-420, 423, 427, 429, 430, 434, 446-449, 451, 456
Joppa.. 74
Jordan............... 74, 93, 302, 341, 368
Judah 5, 6, 9, 17, 19, 22-24, 40, 59, 64, 70, 91, 119, 127, 134, 139, 140, 150, 159, 168, 193, 218, 224, 226, 229, 233, 246, 262, 264, 270, 271, 274, 275, 284, 289, 300, 317, 320, 321, 325, 326, 332, 341, 344, 345, 356, 362, 373, 381, 385, 388, 391, 394, 402, 406, 411, 413, 420, 428, 440, 447-449
Kebar 236
Khorsabad 117
Kidron....................................... 455
Kissel Dagh 319
Lebanon 113, 302, 368, 404
Libya............. 73, 363, 364, 368, 422
Lydia... 421
Lysimachia................................ 421
Macedonia 72, 183, 218, 224, 239, 309, 312, 315, 316, 336, 355, 419, 448
Magnesia..........241, 327, 329, 339, 359, 368, 369, 421
Marah... 41
Mari 23
Marisa... 74
Masada..................................... 350
Meander 421
Media............63, 66-68, 72, 145, 150-152, 154, 168, 170, 182, 227, 230, 238, 240, 242, 246, 251, 312, 314, 354, 402, 406, 410, 414, 415, 438, 447, 448
Media-Persia 70

Mediterranean......63, 68, 86, 150, 167, 315, 319, 321, 327, 336, 338, 339, 368, 369, 418, 419, 421, 431, 448
Megiddo.................. 18
Memphis.................. 337
Middle East.............. 372, 405
Mississippi.............. 302
Moab..................... 362, 368, 420
Modein................... 357
Modi'im.................. 192, 454
Nanaea................... 182, 416
Near East................ 412
Nile..................... 58, 335
Nineveh.................. 66, 69, 183, 261, 313
Olives................... 264, 455
Olympian................. 297
Orontes.................. 242, 319
Pakistan................. 239, 240
Palestine........14, 18, 23, 33, 43, 59, 72-75, 77, 101, 127, 128, 144, 167, 182, 183, 192, 205, 213, 219, 221, 223, 225, 226, 230, 238, 239, 242, 244, 246, 272, 283, 293, 295, 309, 316, 317, 320, 322, 325, 327, 329, 331-333, 336, 340, 342-344, 351, 363, 364, 367, 369, 374, 377, 384, 389, 397, 400, 401, 403, 411, 412, 414, 415, 420-422, 425, 427, 444, 447, 448
Palestine............. 317, 364, 412, 448
Pamphylia................ 68
Panias........73, 323, 325, 329, 338, 363, 367, 420-422
Parthia.................. 446
Pelusium................. 335, 337
Peniel................... 26, 287
Pergamos................. 330
Persia........6, 22, 54, 66, 68, 71, 86, 111, 114, 117, 122, 127, 144, 149, 150, 154, 168, 181-183, 191, 207, 227, 230, 238-240, 242, 246, 251, 252, 256, 257, 259, 294, 300, 305, 309, 313, 314, 319, 327, 351, 354, 369, 402, 405, 406, 414-416, 420, 433, 438, 444, 447, 448, 449, 451

Persia................... 406, 449, 451
Philistine............... 74
Phoenicia............. 320, 325, 420, 448
Phrygia.................. 329
Pontus................... 213
Qoussier................. 399
Qumran 110, 189, 198, 202, 396, 429
Raphia................... 322, 367
Rome......68, 70, 76, 79, 135, 173, 183, 196, 208, 213, 241, 314, 316, 320, 326, 327, 329, 336, 339, 340, 343, 344, 353-356, 358, 381, 397, 418-420, 440, 446, 448, 449, 452
Russia................... 58
Samaria 150, 313, 317, 320, 322, 325, 341, 342, 368, 420, 428
Sardis................... 70, 300
Scopus................... 264, 322
Scythopolis.............. 322
Seleucia................. 319
Shechem.................. 124, 288
Shinar................... 21
Sidon.................... 325, 367
Sinai.................... 7, 175, 178, 187
Sodom.................... 66, 151
Soviet................... 58
Spain.................... 58, 339
Strato's Tower........... 452
Susa..................... 96, 183, 236, 237
Syria......3, 6, 68, 73, 74, 76, 197, 198, 200, 213, 221, 230, 241, 244, 252, 253, 289, 301, 302, 314, 316-320, 322, 325-327, 331, 334, 336, 341, 345, 363, 364, 369, 387, 391, 399, 402, 411, 414, 415, 418, 419, 421, 422, 446, 448, 451, 452
Syria. 3, 301, 363, 411, 419, 422
Tazania.................. 173
Taurus......240-242, 328, 336, 355, 59, 418
Teima.................... 10, 114, 122
Thermopile............... 327, 339, 369
Thrace..315, 316, 321, 327, 355, 415
Tigris..........68, 86, 97, 125, 170, 241, 301, 302, 415
Transfiguration.......... 185, 187

Transjordan 322, 368
Tyre 126, 183, 243
Ugarit 189
Ulai 236, 387, 414
Uphaz 301
Usha 208
Waterloo 250
Zambia 110, 214, 237, 302
Ziggurat 126
Zion 55, 61, 76, 292, 328, 329, 360, 373, 449

www.ingramcontent.com/pod-product-compliance
Lightning Source LLC
Chambersburg PA
CBHW081143290426
44108CB00018B/2421